Pro LINQ

Language Integrated Query in C# 2010

Adam Freeman and Joseph C. Rattz, Jr.

Apress®

Pro LINQ: Language Integrated Query in C# 2010

ISBN-13 (pbk): 978-1-4302-2653-6

ISBN-13 (electronic): 978-1-4302-2654-3

Printed and bound in the United States of America 9 8 7 6 5 4 3 2 1

President and Publisher: Paul Manning
Lead Editor: Ewan Buckingham
Technical Reviewer: Fabio Claudio Ferracchiati
Editorial Board: Clay Andres, Steve Anglin, Mark Beckner, Ewan Buckingham, Gary Cornell, Jonathan Gennick, Jonathan Hassell, Michelle Lowman, Matthew Moodie, Duncan Parkes, Jeffrey Pepper, Frank Pohlmann, Douglas Pundick, Ben Renow-Clarke, Dominic Shakeshaft, Matt Wade, Tom Welsh
Coordinating Editor: Mary Tobin
Copy Editor: Kim Wimpsett
Compositor: Bronkella Publishing LLC
Indexer: BIM Indexing & Proofreading Services
Artist: April Milne
Cover Designer: Anna Ishchenko

Distributed to the book trade worldwide by Springer Science+Business Media, LLC., 233 Spring Street, 6th Floor, New York, NY 10013. Phone 1-800-SPRINGER, fax (201) 348-4505, e-mail orders-ny@springer-sbm.com, or visit www.springeronline.com.

For information on translations, please e-mail rights@apress.com, or visit www.apress.com.

Apress and friends of ED books may be purchased in bulk for academic, corporate, or promotional use. eBook versions and licenses are also available for most titles. For more information, reference our Special Bulk Sales–eBook Licensing web page at www.apress.com/info/bulksales.

The source code for this book is available to readers at www.apress.com. You will need to answer questions pertaining to this book in order to successfully download the code.

Dedicated to my wife, Jacqui Griffyth

—Adam Freeman

For my parents, Joe and Josie Rattz, that believed I could do anything and encouraged me to believe the same. Thank you.

—Joseph C. Rattz, Jr.

Contents at a Glance

Contents

About the Authors

 **Adam Freeman** is an experienced IT professional who has held senior positions in a range of companies, most recently as Chief Technology Officer and Chief Operating Officer of a global bank. He has written several books on Java and .NET and has had a long-term interest in all things parallel.

Joseph C. Rattz, Jr., unknowingly began his career in software development in 1990 when a friend asked him for assistance writing an ANSI text editor named ANSI Master for the Commodore Amiga. A hangman game (The Gallows) soon followed. From these compiled Basic programs, he moved on to programming in C for more speed and power. Joe then developed applications that were sold to JumpDisk, an Amiga disk magazine, as well as Amiga World magazine. Due to developing in a small town on a fairly isolated platform, Joe learned all the wrong ways to write code. It was while trying to upgrade his poorly written applications that he gained respect for the importance of easily maintainable code. It was love at first sight when Joe spotted a source-level debugger in use for the first time.

Two years later, Joe obtained his first software development opportunity at Policy Management Systems Corporation as an entry-level programmer developing a client/server insurance application for OS/2 and Presentation Manager. Through the years, he added C++, Unix, Java, ASP, ASP.NET, C#, HTML, DHTML, and XML to his skill set while developing applications for SCT, DocuCorp, IBM and the Atlanta Committee for the Olympic Games, CheckFree, NCR, EDS, Delta Technology, Radiant Systems, and the Genuine Parts Company. Joe enjoys the creative aspects of user interface design, and he appreciates the discipline necessary for server-side development. But, given his druthers, his favorite development pastime is debugging code.

Joe can be found working for the Genuine Parts Company—the parent company of NAPA—in the Automotive Parts Group Information Systems department, where he works on his baby, the Storefront web site. This site for NAPA stores provides a view into their accounts and data on a network of AS/400s. Joe can be reached at his web site, `www.linqdev.com`.

About the Technical Reviewer

■ Fabio Claudio Ferracchiati is a senior consultant and a senior analyst/developer using Microsoft technologies. He works for Brain Force (`www.brainforce.com`) in its Italian branch (`www.brainforce.it`). He is a Microsoft Certified Solution Developer for .NET, a Microsoft Certified Application Developer for .NET, a Microsoft Certified Professional, and a prolific author and technical reviewer. Over the past ten years, he's written articles for Italian and international magazines and coauthored more than ten books on a variety of computer topics.

Acknowledgments

We would like to thank Jon Skeet and Judson White, and everyone at Apress for working so hard to bring this book to print. In particular, we would like to thank Mary Tobin for keeping things on track and Ewan Buckingham for commissioning and editing the book. We would also like to thank Kim Wimpsett and Fabio Ferracchiati whose respective efforts as copy editor and technical reviewer made this book far better than it would have been without them.

Adam Freeman and Joseph C. Rattz, Jr.

■ ■ ■

PART 1

Pro LINQ: Language Integrated Query in C# 2010

CHAPTER 1

■ ■ ■

Hello LINQ

Listing 1-1. *Hello LINQ*

```
using System;
using System.Linq;

string[] greetings = {"hello world", "hello LINQ", "hello Apress"};

var items =
  from s in greetings
  where s.EndsWith("LINQ")
  select s;

foreach (var item in items)
  Console.WriteLine(item);
```

■ **Note** The code in Listing 1-1 was added to a project created with the Console Application template in Visual Studio 2010. If one is not already present, you should add a `using` directive for the `System.Linq` namespace.

Running the previous code by pressing Ctrl+F5 outputs the following data to the console window:

```
hello LINQ
```

A Paradigm Shift

Did you just feel *your* world shift? As a .NET developer, you should have. With the trivial programming example in Listing 1-1, you just ran what somewhat appears to be a Structured Query Language (SQL) query on an array of strings.[1] Check out that `where` clause. If it looks like we used the `EndsWith` method of a `string` object, it's because we did. You may be wondering, what is with that variable type `var`? Is C# still performing static type checking? The answer is yes; it still statically checks types at compile time. What feature of C# is allowing all of this? The answer is Microsoft's Language Integrated Query, otherwise known as LINQ.

Query XML

Although the example in Listing 1-1 is trivial, the example in Listing 1-2 may begin to indicate the potential power that LINQ puts into the hands of the .NET developer. It displays the ease with which one can interact with and query Extensible Markup Language (XML) data utilizing the LINQ to XML API. You should pay particular attention to how we construct the XML data into an object named `books` that we can programmatically interact with.

Listing 1-2. A Simple XML Query Using LINQ to XML

```
using System;
using System.Linq;
using System.Xml.Linq;

XElement books = XElement.Parse(
  @"<books>
     <book>
        <title>Pro LINQ: Language Integrated Query in C# 2010</title>
        <author>Joe Rattz</author>
     </book>
     <book>
        <title>Pro .NET 4.0 Parallel Programming in C#</title>
        <author>Adam Freeman</author>
     </book>
     <book>
        <title>Pro VB 2010 and the .NET 4.0 Platform</title>
        <author>Andrew Troelsen</author>
     </book>
   </books>");

var titles =
  from book in books.Elements("book")
  where (string) book.Element("author") == "Joe Rattz"
  select book.Element("title");

foreach(var title in titles)
  Console.WriteLine(title.Value);
```

---

[1] Most noticeably, the order is inverted from typical SQL. Additionally, there is the added s in portion of the query that provides a reference to the set of elements contained in the source, which in this case is the array of strings "hello world", "hello LINQ", and "hello Apress".

■ **Note** The code in Listing 1-2 requires adding the `System.Xml.Linq.dll` assembly to the project references if it is not already added. Also notice that we added a `using` directive for the `System.Xml.Linq` namespace.

Running the previous code by pressing Ctrl+F5 outputs the following data to the console window:

```
Pro LINQ: Language Integrated Query in C# 2010
```

Did you notice how we parsed the XML data into an object of type `XElement`? Nowhere did we create an `XmlDocument`. Among the benefits of LINQ to XML are the extensions made to the XML API. Now instead of being `XmlDocument`-centric as the W3C Document Object Model (DOM) XML API requires, LINQ to XML allows the developer to interact at the element level using the `XElement` class.

■ **Note** In addition to query features, LINQ to XML provides a more powerful and easier-to-use interface for working with XML data.

Again, notice that we used the same SQL-like syntax to query the XML data as though it were a database.

Query a SQL Server Database

Our next example shows how to use LINQ to SQL to query database tables. In Listing 1-3, we query the standard Microsoft Northwind sample database.

Listing 1-3. *A Simple Database Query Using LINQ to SQL*

```
using System;
using System.Linq;
using System.Data.Linq;

using nwind;

Northwind db = new Northwind(@"Data Source=.\SQLEXPRESS;Initial
Catalog=Northwind");

var custs =
  from c in db.Customers
  where c.City == "Rio de Janeiro"
  select c;
```

```
foreach (var cust in custs)
  Console.WriteLine("{0}", cust.CompanyName);
```

■ **Note** The code in Listing 1-3 requires adding the `System.Data.Linq.dll` assembly to the project references if it is not already added. Also notice that we added a `using` directive for the `System.Data.Linq` namespace.

You can see that we added a `using` directive for the `nwind` namespace. For this example to work, you must use the SQLMetal command-line utility or the Object Relational Designer to generate entity classes for the targeted database, which in this example is the Microsoft Northwind sample database. See Chapter 12 to read how this is done with SQLMetal. The generated entity classes are created in the `nwind` namespace, which we specified when generating them. We then added the SQLMetal-generated source module to our project and the `using` directive for the `nwind` namespace.

■ **Note** You may need to change the connection string that is passed to the Northwind constructor in Listing 1-3 for the connection to be properly made. Read the section on `DataContext()` and `[Your]DataContext()` in Chapter 16 to see different ways to connect to the database.

Running the previous code by pressing Ctrl+F5 outputs the following data to the console window:

```
Hanari Carnes
Que Delícia
Ricardo Adocicados
```

This simple example demonstrates querying the Customers table of the Northwind database for customers in Rio de Janeiro. Although it may appear that there is nothing new or special going on here that we wouldn't already have with existing means, there are some significant differences. Most noticeably, this query is integrated into the language, and this means we get language-level support that includes syntax checking and IntelliSense. Gone are the days of writing a SQL query into a string and not detecting a syntax error until runtime. Want to make your `where` clause dependent on a field in the Customers table but cannot remember the name of the field? IntelliSense will show the table's fields to you. Once you type in `c.` in the previous example, IntelliSense will display all the fields of the Customers table to you.

All the previous queries use the *query expression* syntax. You will learn in Chapter 2 that two syntaxes are available for LINQ queries, of which the query expression syntax is one. Of course, you can always use the *standard dot notation* syntax that you are accustomed to seeing in C# instead. This syntax is the normal `object.method()` invocation pattern you have always been using.

Introduction

As the Microsoft .NET platform and its supporting languages C# and VB have matured, it has become apparent that one of the more troublesome areas still remaining for developers is that of accessing data from different data sources. In particular, database access and XML manipulation are often cumbersome at best and problematic at worst.

The database problems are numerous. First, there is the issue that we cannot programmatically interact with a database at the native language level. This means syntax errors often go undetected until runtime. Incorrectly referenced database fields are not detected either. This can be disastrous, especially if this occurs during the execution of error-handling code. Nothing is more frustrating than having an entire error-handling mechanism fail because of syntactically invalid code that has never been tested. Sometimes this is unavoidable because of unanticipated error behavior. Having database code that is not validated at compile time can certainly lead to this problem.

A second problem is the nuisance caused by the differing data types utilized by a particular data domain, such as database or XML data types versus the native language in which the program is written. In particular, dates and times can be quite a hassle.

XML parsing, iterating, and manipulation can be quite tedious. Often an XML fragment is all that is desired, but because of the W3C DOM XML API, an `XmlDocument` must be created just to perform various operations on the XML fragment.

Rather than just add more classes and methods to address these deficiencies in a piecemeal fashion, the development team at Microsoft decided to go one step further by abstracting the fundamentals of data query from these particular data domains. The result was LINQ. LINQ is Microsoft's technology to provide a language-level support mechanism for querying data of all types. These types include in-memory arrays and collections, databases, XML documents, and more.

LINQ Is About Data Queries

For the most part, LINQ is all about queries, whether they are queries returning a set of matching objects, a single object, or a subset of fields from an object or set of objects. In LINQ, this returned set of objects is called a *sequence*. Most LINQ sequences are of type `IEnumerable<T>`, where `T` is the data type of the objects stored in the sequence. For example, if you have a sequence of integers, they would be stored in a variable of type `IEnumerable<int>`. You will see that `IEnumerable<T>` runs rampant in LINQ. Many of the LINQ methods return an `IEnumerable<T>`.

In the previous examples, all the queries actually return an `IEnumerable<T>` or a type that inherits from `IEnumerable<T>`. However, we use the `var` keyword for the sake of simplicity at this point, which is a new shorthand technique that we cover in Chapter 2. You will see that the examples will begin demonstrating that sequences are truly stored in variables implementing the `IEnumerable<T>` interface.

LINQ to Objects

LINQ to Objects is the name given to the `IEnumerable<T>` API for the Standard Query Operators. It is LINQ to Objects that allows you to perform queries against arrays and in-memory data collections. Standard Query Operators are the static methods of the static `System.Linq.Enumerable` class that you use to create LINQ to Objects queries.

LINQ to XML

LINQ to XML is the name given to the LINQ API dedicated to working with XML. Not only has Microsoft added the necessary XML libraries to work with LINQ, it has addressed other deficiencies in the standard XML DOM, thereby making it easier to work with XML. Gone are the days of having to create an XmlDocument just to work with a small piece of XML. To take advantage of LINQ to XML, you must have a reference to the System.Xml.Linq.dll assembly in your project and have a using directive such as the following:

```
using System.Xml.Linq;
```

LINQ to DataSet

LINQ to DataSet is the name given to the LINQ API for DataSets. Many developers have a lot of existing code relying on DataSets. Those who do will not be left behind, nor will they need to rewrite their code to take advantage of the power of LINQ.

LINQ to SQL

LINQ to SQL is the name given to the IQueryable<T> API that allows LINQ queries to work with Microsoft's SQL Server database. To take advantage of LINQ to SQL, you must have a reference to the System.Data.Linq.dll assembly in your project and have a using directive such as the following:

```
using System.Data.Linq;
```

LINQ to Entities

LINQ to Entities is an alternative LINQ API that is used to interface with a database. It decouples the entity object model from the physical database by injecting a logical mapping between the two. With this decoupling comes increased power and flexibility, as well as complexity. Because LINQ to Entities appears to be outside the core LINQ framework, it is not covered in this book. However, if you find that you need more flexibility than LINQ to SQL permits, it would be worth considering as an alternative. Specifically, if you need looser coupling between your entity object model and database, entity objects comprised of data coming from multiple tables, or more flexibility in modeling your entity objects, LINQ to Entities may be your answer.

How to Obtain LINQ

Technically, there is no LINQ product to obtain. LINQ has been fully integrated in the .NET Framework since version 3.5 and Visual Studio 2008. And .NET 4 and Visual Studio 2010 added support for the Parallel LINQ features that we cover in Chapters 22 to 24.

LINQ Is Not Just for Queries

You might think that LINQ is just for queries because it stands for *Language Integrated Query*. But please don't think of it only in that context. Its power transcends mere data queries. We prefer to think of LINQ as a data iteration engine—but perhaps Microsoft didn't want a technology named DIE.

Have you ever called a method and it returned data in some data structure that you then needed to convert to yet another data structure before you could pass it to another method? Let's say, for example, you call method A, and method A returns an array of type string that contains numeric values stored as strings. You then need to call method B, but method B requires an array of integers. You normally end up writing a loop to iterate through the array of strings and populate a newly constructed array of integers. What a nuisance. Allow us to give a quick example of the power of LINQ.

Let's pretend we have an array of strings that we received from some method A, as shown in Listing 1-4.

Listing 1-4. *Converting an Array of Strings to Integers*

```
string[] numbers = { "0042", "010", "9", "27" };
```

For this example, we'll just statically declare an array of strings. Now before we call method B, we need to convert the array of strings to an array of integers:

```
int[] nums = numbers.Select(s => Int32.Parse(s)).ToArray();
```

That's it. How much easier could it get? Even just saying "abracadabra" only saves you 48 characters. Here is some code to display the resulting array of integers:

```
foreach(int num in nums)
  Console.WriteLine(num);
```

Here is the output showing the integers:

```
42
10
9
27
```

We know what you are thinking: maybe we just trimmed off the leading zeros. If we sort it, will you then be convinced? If they were still strings, 9 would be at the end, and 10 would be first. Listing 1-5 contains some code to do the conversion and sort the output.

Listing 1-5. *Converting an Array of Strings to Integers and Sorting It*

```
string[] numbers = { "0042", "010", "9", "27" };

int[] nums = numbers.Select(s => Int32.Parse(s)).OrderBy(s => s).ToArray();

foreach(int num in nums)
  Console.WriteLine(num);
```

Here are the results:

```
9
10
27
42
```

How slick is that? OK, you say, that is nice, but it sure is a simple example. Now we'll give you a more complex example.

Let's say you have some common code that contains an `Employee` class. In that `Employee` class is a method to return all the employees. Also assume you have another code base of common code that contains a `Contact` class, and in that class is a method to publish contacts. Let's assume you have the assignment to publish all employees as contacts.

The task seems simple enough, but there is a catch. The common `Employee` method that retrieves the employees returns the employees in an `ArrayList` of `Employee` objects, and the `Contact` method that publishes contacts requires an array of type `Contact`. Here is that common code:

```
namespace LINQDev.HR
{
  public class Employee
  {
    public int id;
    public string firstName;
    public string lastName;

    public static ArrayList GetEmployees()
    {
      //  Of course the real code would probably be making a database query
      //  right about here.
      ArrayList al = new ArrayList();

      //  Man, do the C# object initialization features make this a snap.
      al.Add(new Employee { id = 1, firstName = "Joe", lastName = "Rattz"} );
      al.Add(new Employee { id = 2, firstName = "William", lastName = "Gates"} );
      al.Add(new Employee { id = 3, firstName = "Anders", lastName = "Hejlsberg"}
);
      return(al);
    }
  }
}

namespace LINQDev.Common
{
  public class Contact
  {
    public int Id;
```

```
    public string Name;

    public static void PublishContacts(Contact[] contacts)
    {
      //  This publish method just writes them to the console window.
      foreach(Contact c in contacts)
        Console.WriteLine("Contact Id:  {0}  Contact:  {1}", c.Id, c.Name);
    }
  }
}
```

As you can see, the Employee class and GetEmployees method are in one namespace, LINQDev.HR, and the GetEmployees method returns an ArrayList. The PublishContacts method is in another namespace, LINQDev.Common, and requires an array of Contact objects to be passed.

Previously, this always meant iterating through the ArrayList returned by the GetEmployees method and creating a new array of type Contact to be passed to the PublishContacts method. LINQ makes it easy, as shown in Listing 1-6.

Listing 1-6. *Calling the Common Code*

```
ArrayList alEmployees = LINQDev.HR.Employee.GetEmployees();

LINQDev.Common.Contact[] contacts = alEmployees
  .Cast<LINQDev.HR.Employee>()
  .Select(e => new LINQDev.Common.Contact {
              Id = e.id,
              Name = string.Format("{0} {1}", e.firstName, e.lastName)
            })
  .ToArray<LINQDev.Common.Contact>();

LINQDev.Common.Contact.PublishContacts(contacts);
```

To convert the ArrayList of Employee objects to an array of Contact objects, we first cast the ArrayList of Employee objects to an IEnumerable<Employee> sequence using the Cast Standard Query Operator. This is necessary because the legacy ArrayList collection class was used. Syntactically speaking, objects of the System.Object class type are stored in an ArrayList, not objects of the Employee class type. So, we must cast them to Employee objects. Had the GetEmployees method returned a generic List collection, this would not have been necessary. However, that collection type was not available when this legacy code was written.

Next, we call the Select operator on the returned sequence of Employee objects, and in the *lambda expression*, the code passed inside the call to the Select method, we instantiate and initialize a Contact object using the C# object initialization features to assign the values from the input Employee element into a newly constructed output Contact element. A lambda expression is a C# feature that allows a shorthand for specifying anonymous methods that we explain in Chapter 2. Lastly, we convert the sequence of newly constructed Contact objects to an array of Contact objects using the ToArray operator because that is what the PublishContacts method requires. Isn't that slick? Here are the results:

```
Contact Id:  1  Contact:  Joe Rattz
Contact Id:  2  Contact:  William Gates
Contact Id:  3  Contact:  Anders Hejlsberg
```

As you can see, LINQ can do a lot besides just querying data. As you read through the chapters of this book, try to think of additional uses for the features LINQ provides.

Tips to Get You Started

While working with LINQ to write this book, we often found ourselves confused, befuddled, and stuck. Although many very useful resources are available to the developer wanting to learn to use LINQ to its fullest potential, we want to offer a few tips to get you started. In some ways, these tips feel like they should come at the end of the book. After all, we haven't even explained what some of these concepts are at this point. But it would seem a bit sadistic to make you read the full text of the book first, only to offer the tips at the end. So with that said, this section contains some tips we think you might find useful, even if you do not fully understand them or the context.

Use the var Keyword When Confused

Although it is necessary to use the var keyword when capturing a sequence of anonymous classes to a variable, sometimes it is a convenient way to get code to compile if you are confused. We are very much in favor of developers knowing exactly what type of data is contained in a sequence—meaning that for IEnumerable<T> you should know what data type T is—but sometimes, especially when just starting with LINQ, it can get confusing. If you find yourself stuck, where code will not compile because of a data type mismatch, consider changing explicitly stated types so that they use the var keyword instead.

For example, let's say you have the following code:

```
//  This code will not compile.
Northwind db = new Northwind(@"Data Source=.\SQLEXPRESS;Initial
Catalog=Northwind");

IEnumerable<?> orders = db.Customers
  .Where(c => c.Country == "USA" && c.Region == "WA")
  .SelectMany(c => c.Orders);
```

It may be a little unclear what data type you have an IEnumerable sequence of. You know it is an IEnumerable of some type T, but what is T? A handy trick would be to assign the query results to a variable whose type is specified with the var keyword and then to get the type of the current value of that variable so you know what type T is. Listing 1-7 shows what the code would look like.

Listing 1-7. *Code Sample Using the var Keyword*

```
Northwind db = new Northwind(@"Data Source=.\SQLEXPRESS;Initial
Catalog=Northwind");

var orders = db.Customers
  .Where(c => c.Country == "USA" && c.Region == "WA")
  .SelectMany(c => c.Orders);

Console.WriteLine(orders.GetType());
```

In this example, notice that the orders variable type is now specified using the var keyword. Running this code produces the following:

```
System.Data.Linq.DataQuery`1[nwind.Order]
```

There is a lot of compiler gobbledygook there, but the important part is the nwind.Order portion. You now know that the data type you are getting a sequence of is nwind.Order.

If the gobbledygook is throwing you, running the example in the debugger and examining the orders variable in the Locals window reveals that the data type of orders is this:

```
System.Linq.IQueryable<nwind.Order> {System.Data.Linq.DataQuery<nwind.Order>}
```

This makes it clearer that you have a sequence of nwind.Order. Technically, you have an IQueryable<nwind.Order> here, but that can be assigned to an IEnumerable<nwind.Order> if you like, since IQueryable<T> inherits from IEnumerable<T>.

So, you could rewrite the previous code, plus enumerate through the results, as shown in Listing 1-8.

Listing 1-8. *Sample Code from Listing 1-7 Except with Explicit Types*

```
Northwind db = new Northwind(@"Data Source=.\SQLEXPRESS;Initial
Catalog=Northwind");

IEnumerable<Order> orders = db.Customers
  .Where(c => c.Country == "USA" && c.Region == "WA")
  .SelectMany(c => c.Orders);

foreach(Order item in orders)
  Console.WriteLine("{0} - {1} - {2}", item.OrderDate, item.OrderID,
item.ShipName);
```

■ **Note** For the previous code to work, you will need to have a using directive for the System.Collections.Generic namespace, in addition to the System.Linq namespace you should always expect to have when LINQ code is present.

This code would produce the following abbreviated results:

```
3/21/1997 12:00:00 AM - 10482 - Lazy K Kountry Store
5/22/1997 12:00:00 AM - 10545 - Lazy K Kountry Store
...
4/17/1998 12:00:00 AM - 11032 - White Clover Markets
5/1/1998 12:00:00 AM - 11066 - White Clover Markets
```

Use the Cast or OfType Operators for Legacy Collections

You will find that the majority of LINQ's Standard Query Operators can be called only on collections implementing the IEnumerable<T> interface. None of the legacy C# collections—those in the System.Collections namespace—implement IEnumerable<T>. So, the question becomes, how do you use LINQ with legacy collections?

There are two Standard Query Operators specifically for this purpose, Cast and OfType. Both of these operators can be used to convert legacy collections to IEnumerable<T> sequences. Listing 1-9 shows an example.

Listing 1-9. Converting a Legacy Collection to an IEnumerable<T> Using the Cast Operator

```
//  We'll build a legacy collection.
ArrayList arrayList = new ArrayList();
arrayList.Add("Adams");
arrayList.Add("Arthur");
arrayList.Add("Buchanan");

IEnumerable<string> names = arrayList.Cast<string>().Where(n => n.Length < 7);
foreach(string name in names)
  Console.WriteLine(name);
```

Listing 1-10 shows the same example using the OfType operator.

Listing 1-10. Using the OfType Operator

```
//  We'll build a legacy collection.
ArrayList arrayList = new ArrayList();
arrayList.Add("Adams");
arrayList.Add("Arthur");
arrayList.Add("Buchanan");

IEnumerable<string> names = arrayList.OfType<string>().Where(n => n.Length < 7);
foreach(string name in names)
  Console.WriteLine(name);
```

Both examples provide the same results. Here they are:

```
Adams
Arthur
```

The difference between the two operators is that the `Cast` operator will attempt to cast every element in the collection to the specified type to be put into the output sequence. If there is a type in the collection that cannot be cast to the specified type, an exception will be thrown. The `OfType` operator will only attempt to put those elements that can be cast to the type specified into the output sequence.

The OfType Operator versus the Cast Operator

One of the most important reasons why generics were added to C# was to give the language the ability to have data collections with static type checking. Prior to generics—barring creating your own specific collection type for every type of data for which you wanted a collection—there was no way to ensure that every element in a legacy collection, such as an `ArrayList`, `Hashtable`, and so on, was of the same and correct type. Nothing in the language prevented code from adding a `Textbox` object to an `ArrayList` meant to contain only `Label` objects.

Since the introduction of generics in version 2.0, C# developers have had a way to explicitly state that a collection can contain only those elements of a specified type. Although either the `OfType` or `Cast` operator may work for a legacy collection, `Cast` requires that every object in the collection be of the correct type, which is the fundamental original flaw in the legacy collections for which generics were created. When using the `Cast` operator, if any object is unable to be cast to the specified data type, an exception is thrown. By contrast, with the `OfType` operator only objects of the specified type will be stored in the output `IEnumerable<T>` sequence, and no exception will be thrown. The best-case scenario is that every object will be of the correct type and be in the output sequence. The worst case is that some elements will get skipped, but they would have thrown an exception had the `Cast` operator been used instead.

Don't Assume a Query Is Bug-Free

In Chapter 3, we explain that LINQ queries are often deferred and not executed when it *appears* you are calling them. For example, consider this code fragment from Listing 1-1:

```
var items =
  from s in greetings
  where s.EndsWith("LINQ")
  select s;

foreach (var item in items)
  Console.WriteLine(item);
```

Although it might appear that the query is occurring when the `items` variable is being initialized, that is not the case. Because the `Where` and `Select` operators are deferred, the query is not actually being performed at that point. The query is merely being called, declared, or defined, but not performed. The query will actually take place the first time a result from it is needed. This is typically when the query results variable is enumerated. In this example, a result from the query is not needed until the `foreach` statement is executed. In this way, we say that the query is *deferred*.

It is easy to forget that many of the query operators are deferred and will not execute until a result is enumerated. This means you could have an improperly written query that will throw an exception when the resulting sequence is enumerated. That enumeration could take place far enough downstream that it is easily forgotten that a query may be the culprit.

Let's examine the code in Listing 1-11.

Listing 1-11. Query with Intentional Exception Deferred Until Enumeration

```
string[] strings = { "one", "two", null, "three" };

Console.WriteLine("Before Where() is called.");
IEnumerable<string> ieStrings = strings.Where(s => s.Length == 3);
Console.WriteLine("After Where() is called.");

foreach(string s in ieStrings)
{
  Console.WriteLine("Processing " + s);
}
```

We know that the third element in the array of strings is a null, and we cannot call null.Length without throwing an exception. The execution steps over the line of code calling the query just fine. It is not until we enumerate the sequence ieStrings, and specifically the third element, that the exception occurs. Here are the results of this code:

```
Before Where() is called.
After Where() is called.
Processing one
Processing two

Unhandled Exception: System.NullReferenceException: Object reference not set to an
instance of an object.
…
```

As you can see, we called the Where operator without exception. It's not until we try to enumerate the third element of the sequence that an exception is thrown. Now imagine if that sequence, ieStrings, is passed to a function that downstream enumerates the sequence, perhaps to populate a drop-down list or some other control. It would be easy to think the exception is caused by a fault in that function, not the LINQ query itself.

Take Advantage of Deferred Queries

In Chapter 3, we go into deferred queries in more depth. However, we want to point out that a deferred query that ultimately returns an IEnumerable<T> can be enumerated over, time and time again, obtaining the latest data from the data source. You don't need to actually call or, as we earlier pointed out, declare the query again.

In most of the code samples in this book, you will see a query called and an IEnumerable<T> for some type T being returned and stored in a variable. Then we typically call foreach on the IEnumerable<T> sequence. This is for demonstration purposes. If that code is executed multiple times, calling the actual query each time is needless work. It might make more sense to have a query initialization method that gets called once for the lifetime of the scope and to construct all the queries there. Then you could enumerate over a particular sequence to get the latest version of the query results at will.

Use the DataContext Log

When working with LINQ to SQL, don't forget that the database class that is generated by SQLMetal inherits from System.Data.Linq.DataContext. This means that your generated DataContext class has some useful built-in functionality, such as a TextWriter property named Log.

One of the niceties of the Log object is that it will output the equivalent SQL statement of an IQueryable<T> query prior to the parameter substitution. Have you ever had code break in production that you think might be data related? Wouldn't it be nice if there was a way to get the query executed against the database so that you could enter it in SQL Server Enterprise Manager or Query Analyzer and see the exact data coming back? The DataContext's Log object will output the SQL query for you. Listing 1-12 shows an example.

Listing 1-12. An Example Using the DataContext.Log Object

```
Northwind db = new Northwind(@"Data Source=.\SQLEXPRESS;Initial
Catalog=Northwind");

db.Log = Console.Out;

IQueryable<Order> orders = from c in db.Customers
                           from o in c.Orders
                           where c.Country == "USA" && c.Region == "WA"
                           select o;

foreach(Order item in orders)
  Console.WriteLine("{0} - {1} - {2}", item.OrderDate, item.OrderID,
item.ShipName);
```

This code produces the following output:

```
SELECT [t1].[OrderID], [t1].[CustomerID], [t1].[EmployeeID], [t1].[OrderDate],
 [t1].[RequiredDate], [t1].[ShippedDate], [t1].[ShipVia], [t1].[Freight],
 [t1].[ShipName], [t1].[ShipAddress], [t1].[ShipCity], [t1].[ShipRegion],
 [t1].[ShipPostalCode], [t1].[ShipCountry]
FROM [dbo].[Customers] AS [t0], [dbo].[Orders] AS [t1]
WHERE ([t0].[Country] = @p0) AND ([t0].[Region] = @p1) AND ([t1].[CustomerID] =
[t0].[CustomerID])
-- @p0: Input String (Size = 3; Prec = 0; Scale = 0) [USA]
```

```
-- @p1: Input String (Size = 2; Prec = 0; Scale = 0) [WA]
-- Context: SqlProvider(Sql2005) Model: AttributedMetaModel Build: 3.5.20706.1

3/21/1997 12:00:00 AM - 10482 - Lazy K Kountry Store
5/22/1997 12:00:00 AM - 10545 - Lazy K Kountry Store
6/19/1997 12:00:00 AM - 10574 - Trail's Head Gourmet Provisioners
6/23/1997 12:00:00 AM - 10577 - Trail's Head Gourmet Provisioners
1/8/1998 12:00:00 AM - 10822 - Trail's Head Gourmet Provisioners
7/31/1996 12:00:00 AM - 10269 - White Clover Markets
11/1/1996 12:00:00 AM - 10344 - White Clover Markets
3/10/1997 12:00:00 AM - 10469 - White Clover Markets
3/24/1997 12:00:00 AM - 10483 - White Clover Markets
4/11/1997 12:00:00 AM - 10504 - White Clover Markets
7/11/1997 12:00:00 AM - 10596 - White Clover Markets
10/6/1997 12:00:00 AM - 10693 - White Clover Markets
10/8/1997 12:00:00 AM - 10696 - White Clover Markets
10/30/1997 12:00:00 AM - 10723 - White Clover Markets
11/13/1997 12:00:00 AM - 10740 - White Clover Markets
1/30/1998 12:00:00 AM - 10861 - White Clover Markets
2/24/1998 12:00:00 AM - 10904 - White Clover Markets
4/17/1998 12:00:00 AM - 11032 - White Clover Markets
5/1/1998 12:00:00 AM - 11066 - White Clover Markets
```

Use the LINQ Forum

Despite providing the best tips we can think of, there will more than likely be times when you get stuck. Don't forget that there is a forum dedicated to LINQ at MSDN.com (`http://www.linqdev.com`). This forum is monitored by Microsoft developers, and you will find a wealth of knowledgeable resources there.

Summary

We sense that by now you are chomping at the bit to move on to the next chapter, but before you do, we want to remind you of a few things.

First, LINQ changes the way .NET developers can query data. Bear in mind that LINQ is not just a library to be added to your project. It is a total approach to querying data that comprises several components depending on the data store being queried. Currently, you can use LINQ to query the following data sources: in-memory data collections using LINQ to Objects, XML using LINQ to XML, DataSets using LINQ to DataSet, and SQL Server databases using LINQ to SQL.

Also, please remember what we said about LINQ not being just for queries. We have found LINQ very useful not only for querying data but for formatting, validating, and even getting data into the necessary format for use in WinForm and WPF controls.

Last but not least, we hope you didn't skip over the tips we provided in this chapter. If you don't understand some of them, that is no problem. They will make more sense as you progress through the book. Just keep them in mind if you find yourself stalled.

No doubt that after seeing some of the LINQ examples and tips in this chapter, you may find yourself puzzled by some of the syntax shown. If so, don't worry because in the next chapter, we cover the enhancements Microsoft has made to C# that make all of this possible.

CHAPTER 2

■ ■ ■

C# Language Enhancements for LINQ

In the previous chapter, we introduced you to LINQ. We provided some examples to whet your appetite and shared some premature tips. You may be perplexed, though, by some of the syntax. If so, it is probably because C# has been enhanced with new features that are specific to LINQ. These features were added in C# 3.0 and further supplemented in .NET 4.0. In this chapter, we introduce you to the powerful C# additions.

C# Language Additions

To make LINQ seamlessly integrate with C#, significant enhancements were needed for the C# language. Although all these features have merit on their own, it is really the sum of the parts contributing to LINQ that makes the C# enhancements so noteworthy.

To truly understand much of the syntax of LINQ, it is necessary for us to cover some of the relevant C# language features before proceeding with the workings of the components of LINQ. This chapter will cover the following language additions:

- Lambda expressions

- Expression trees

- The keyword `var`, object and collection initialization, and anonymous types

- Extension methods

- Partial methods

- Query expressions

In the examples in this chapter, we do not explicitly show which assemblies should be added and which namespaces you should specify in your `using` directives for the assemblies and namespaces we cover in Chapter 1. We do point out any new ones, though, but only in the first example introducing them.

Lambda Expressions

Since version 3, C# has supported *lambda expressions*. Lambda expressions have been used in computer languages as far back as LISP; they were conceptualized in 1936 by Alonzo Church, an American mathematician. These expressions provide shorthand syntax for specifying an algorithm.

But before jumping immediately into lambda expressions, let's take a look at the evolution of specifying an algorithm as an argument to a method since that is the primary purpose of lambda expressions.

Using Named Methods

Previously, when a method or variable was typed to require a `delegate`, a developer would have to create a named method and pass that name where the `delegate` was required.

As an example, consider the following situation. Let's pretend we have two developers; one is a common-code developer, and the other is an application developer. It isn't necessary that there be two different developers; we just need labels to delineate the two different roles. The common-code developer wants to create general-purpose code that can be reused throughout the project. The application developer will consume that general-purpose code to create an application. In this example scenario, the common-code developer wants to create a generic method for filtering arrays of integers, but with the ability to specify the algorithm used to filter the array. First, he must declare the `delegate`. It will be prototyped to receive an `int` and return `true` if the `int` should be *included* in the filtered array.

So, he creates a utility class and adds the delegate and filtering method. Here is the common code:

```
public class Common
{
  public delegate bool IntFilter(int i);

  public static int[] FilterArrayOfInts(int[] ints, IntFilter filter)
  {
    ArrayList aList = new ArrayList();
    foreach (int i in ints)
    {
      if (filter(i))
      {
        aList.Add(i);
      }
    }
    return ((int[])aList.ToArray(typeof(int)));
  }
}
```

The common-code developer will put both the `delegate` declaration and the `FilterArrayOfInts` into a common library assembly, a dynamic link library (DLL), so that it can be used in multiple applications.

The `FilterArrayOfInts` method listed previously allows the application developer to pass in an array of integers and a `delegate` to the filter method and get back a filtered array.

Now let's assume the application developer wants to filter (in) just the odd integers. Here is his filter method, which is declared in his application code:

The application developer's filter method

```
public class Application
{
  public static bool IsOdd(int i)
  {
    return ((i & 1) == 1);
  }
}
```

Based on the code in the `FilterArrayOfInts` method, this method will get called for every `int` in the array that gets passed in. This filter will return `true` only if the `int` passed in is odd. Listing 2-1 shows an example using the `FilterArrayOfInts` method, followed by the results.

Listing 2-1. *Calling the Common Library Filter Method*

```
using System.Collections;

int[] nums = { 1, 2, 3, 4, 5, 6, 7, 8, 9, 10 };

int[] oddNums = Common.FilterArrayOfInts(nums, Application.IsOdd);

foreach (int i in oddNums)
  Console.WriteLine(i);
```

Here are the results:

```
1
3
5
7
9
```

Notice that to pass the `delegate` as the second parameter of `FilterArrayOfInts`, the application developer just passes the name of the method. By simply creating another filter, he can filter differently. He could have a filter for even numbers, prime numbers, or whatever criteria he wants. Delegates lend themselves to highly reusable code.

Using Anonymous Methods

That's all well and good, but it can get tedious writing all these filter methods and whatever other `delegate` methods you may need. Many of these methods will get used in a single call only, and it's a bother to create named methods for them all. Since C# 2.0, developers have had the ability to create `delegate` instances by providing inline-code as anonymous methods. Anonymous methods allow the developer to specify the code right where the delegate would normally get passed. Instead of creating the

IsOdd method, he may specify the filtering code right where the delegate would normally be passed. Listing 2-2 shows the same code from Listing 2-1 but uses an anonymous method instead.

Listing 2-2. Calling the Filter Method with an Anonymous Method

```
int[] nums = { 1, 2, 3, 4, 5, 6, 7, 8, 9, 10 };

int[] oddNums =
  Common.FilterArrayOfInts(nums, delegate(int i) { return ((i & 1) == 1); });

foreach (int i in oddNums)
  Console.WriteLine(i);
```

This is pretty cool. The application developer no longer has to declare a method anywhere. This is great for filtering logic code that isn't likely to get reused. As required, the output is the same as the previous example:

```
1
3
5
7
9
```

Using anonymous methods does have one drawback. They're kind of verbose and hard to read. If only there was a more concise way to write the method |code.

Using Lambda Expressions

Lambda expressions are specified as a comma-delimited list of parameters followed by the lambda operator, followed by an expression or statement block. If there is more than one input parameter, enclose the input parameters in parentheses. In C#, the lambda operator is =>. Therefore, a lambda expression in C# looks like this:

```
(param1, param2, ...paramN) => expr
```

Or when needing more complexity, a statement block can be used:

```
(param1, param2, ...paramN) =>
{
  statement1;
  statement2;
  ...
  statementN;
  return(lambda_expression_return_type);
}
```

In this example, the data type returned at the end of the statement block must match the return type specified by the `delegate`. Here is an example lambda expression:

```
x => x
```

This lambda expression could be read as "x goes to x," or perhaps "input x returns x." It means that for input variable x, return x. This expression merely returns what is passed in. Since there is only a single input parameter, x, it does not need to be enclosed in parentheses. It is important to know that it is the `delegate` that is dictating what the type of x being input is and what type must be returned. For example, if the `delegate` is defined as passing a `string` in but returning a `bool`, then `x => x` could not be used because if x going in is a `string`, then x being returned would be a `string` as well, but the `delegate` specified it must be `bool`. So with a `delegate` defined like that, the portion of the expression to the right of the lambda operator (`=>`) must evaluate to or return a `bool`, such as this:

```
x => x.Length > 0
```

This lambda expression could be read as "x goes to `x.Length > 0`" or "input x returns `x.Length > 0`." Since the right-hand portion of this expression does evaluate to a `bool`, the `delegate` had better specify that the method returns a `bool`; otherwise, a compiler error will result.

The following lambda expression will attempt to return the length of the input argument. So, the `delegate` had better specify a return type of `int`:

```
s => s.Length
```

If multiple parameters are passed into the lambda expression, separate them with commas, and enclose them in parentheses like this:

```
(x, y) => x == y
```

Complex lambda expressions may even be specified with a statement block like this:

```
(x, y) =>
{
  if (x > y)
    return (x);
  else
    return (y);
}
```

What is important to remember is that the `delegate` is defining what the input types are and what the return type must be. So, make sure your lambda expression matches the delegate definition.

■ **Caution** Make sure your lambda expressions are written to accept the input types specified by the delegate definition and return the type the delegate defines to be returned.

To refresh your memory, here is the delegate declaration that the common code developer defined:

```
delegate bool IntFilter(int i);
```

The application developer's lambda expression must support an `int` passed in and a `bool` being returned. This can be inferred from the method he is calling and the purpose of the filter method, but it is important to remember the `delegate` is dictating this.

So, the previous example shown using a lambda expression this time would look like Listing 2-3.

Listing 2-3. Calling the Filter Method with a Lambda Expression

```
int[] nums = { 1, 2, 3, 4, 5, 6, 7, 8, 9, 10 };

int[] oddNums = Common.FilterArrayOfInts(nums, i => ((i & 1) == 1));

foreach (int i in oddNums)
  Console.WriteLine(i);
```

Wow, that's concise code. We know it may look a little funny because it is so new, but once you get used to it, it sure is readable and maintainable. As is required, the results are the same as the previous examples:

```
1
3
5
7
9
```

For a recap, here are the significant lines from the sample code for each approach:

```
int[] oddNums =   //  using named method
  Common.FilterArrayOfInts(nums, Application.IsOdd);

int[] oddNums =   //  using anonymous method
  Common.FilterArrayOfInts(nums, delegate(int i){return((i & 1) == 1);});

int[] oddNums =   // using lambda expression
  Common.FilterArrayOfInts(nums, i => ((i & 1) == 1));
```

We know that first line is actually shorter, but don't forget that there is a named method declared somewhere else defining what the method does. Of course, if that filtering logic is going to be reused in several places or perhaps if the algorithm is complex and should be trusted only to a specialized developer, it may make more sense to create a named method to be consumed by other developers.

■ **Tip** Complex or reused algorithms may be better served by named methods so they can be reused by any developer without that developer necessarily understanding the algorithm.

Whether named methods, anonymous methods, or lambda expressions are used is up to the developer. Use whatever makes the most sense for the situation at hand.

You will often take advantage of lambda expressions by passing them as arguments to your LINQ query operator calls. Since every LINQ query is likely to have unique or scarcely reused operator lambda expressions, this provides the flexibility of specifying your operator logic without having to create named methods for virtually every query.

Expression Trees

An *expression tree* is an efficient data representation, in tree form, of a query operator's lambda expression. These expression tree data representations can be evaluated, all simultaneously, so that a single query can be built and executed against a data source, such as a database.

In the majority of the examples we have discussed so far, the query's operators have been performed in a linear fashion. Let's examine the following code:

```
int[] nums = new int[] { 6, 2, 7, 1, 9, 3 };
IEnumerable<int> numsLessThanFour = nums
  .Where(i => i < 4)
  .OrderBy(i => i);
```

This query contains two operators, `Where` and `OrderBy`, that are expecting delegates as their arguments. When this code is compiled, .NET intermediate language (IL) code is emitted that is identical to an anonymous method for each of the query operator's lambda expressions.

When this query is executed, the `Where` operator is called first, followed by the `OrderBy` operator.

This linear execution of the operators seems reasonable for this example, but you should consider a query against a very large data source, such as a database. Would it make sense for a SQL query to first call the database with the `Where` statement only to turn around and order it in a subsequent call? Of course, this just isn't feasible for database queries, as well as potentially other types of queries. This is where expression trees become necessary. Since an expression tree allows the simultaneous evaluation and execution of all operators in a query, a single query can be made instead of a separate query for each operator.

So, there now are two different things the compiler can generate for an operator's lambda expression: IL code or an expression tree. What determines whether an operator's lambda expression gets compiled into IL code or an expression tree? The operator's prototype will define which of these actions the compiler will take. If the operator is declared to accept a delegate, IL code will be emitted. If the operator is declared to accept an *expression* of a delegate, an expression tree is emitted.

As an example, let's look at two different implementations of the `Where` operator. The first is the Standard Query Operator that exists in the LINQ to Objects API, which is defined in the `System.Linq.Enumerable` class:

```
public static IEnumerable<T> Where<T>(
  this IEnumerable<T> source,
  Func<T, bool> predicate);
```

The second `Where` operator implementation exists in the LINQ to SQL API and is in the `System.Linq.Queryable` class:

```
public static IQueryable<T> Where<T>(
  this IQueryable<T> source,
  System.Linq.Expressions.Expression<Func<int, bool>> predicate);
```

As you can see, the first `Where` operator is declared to accept a delegate, as specified by the `Func` delegate, and the compiler will generate IL code for this operator's lambda expression. We will cover the `Func` delegate in Chapter 3. For now just be aware that it is defining the signature of the `delegate` passed as the predicate argument. The second `Where` operator is declared to accept an expression tree (`Expression`), so the compiler will generate an expression tree data representation of the lambda expression.

The operators that accept an `IEnumerable<T>` sequence as their first argument are declared to accept a delegate for their lambda expressions. The operators that accept an `IQueryable<T>` sequence as their first argument are declared to accept an expression tree.

■ **Note** Extension methods on `IEnumerable<T>` sequences have IL code emitted by the compiler. Extension methods on `IQueryable<T>` sequences have expression trees emitted by the compiler.

Merely being a consumer of LINQ does not require the developer to be very cognizant of expression trees. It is the vendor's developer who adds LINQ capability to a data storage product who needs to fully understand expression trees. Because of this, we don't cover them in any detail in this book.

Keyword var, Object Initialization, and Anonymous Types

Be forewarned: it is nearly impossible to discuss the `var` keyword and implicit type inference without demonstrating object initialization or anonymous types. Likewise, it is nearly impossible to discuss object initialization or anonymous types without discussing the `var` keyword. All three of these C# language enhancements are tightly coupled.

Before describing each of these three language features in detail—because each will describe itself in terms of the other—allow us to introduce all three simultaneously. Let's examine the following statement:

```
var¹ mySpouse = new {² FirstName = "Vickey"³, LastName = "Rattz"³ };
```

In this example, we declare a variable named `mySpouse` using the `var` keyword. It is assigned the value of an anonymous type that is initialized using the new object initialization features. That one line of code is taking advantage of the `var` keyword, anonymous types, and object initialization.

[1]You can detect the line of code is using the `var` keyword because it is explicitly stated. [2]You are able to detect there is an anonymous type because we use the `new` operator without specifying a named class. [3]And you can see the anonymous object is being explicitly initialized using the new object initialization feature.

In a nutshell, the `var` keyword allows the data type of a local variable to be inferred based on the data type with which it has been initialized. Anonymous types allow new class data types to be created at compile time. True to the word *anonymous*, these new data types have no name. You can't very well create an anonymous data type if you don't know what member variables it contains, and you can't know what members it contains unless you know what types those members are. Lastly, you won't know what data type those new members are unless they are initialized. The object initialization feature handles all that.

From that line of code, the compiler will create a new anonymous class type containing two public `string` members; the first is named `FirstName`, and the second is named `LastName`.

The Implicitly Typed Local Variable Keyword var

With anonymous types in C#, a new problem becomes apparent. If a variable is being instantiated that is an unnamed type, as in an anonymous type, what type of variable would you assign it to? Consider the following code as an example:

```
//  This code will not compile.
??? unnamedTypeVar = new {firstArg = 1, secondArg = "Joe" };
```

What variable type would you declare `unnamedTypeVar` to be? This is a problem. The folks at Microsoft chose to remedy this by creating a keyword, `var`. This keyword informs the compiler that it should implicitly infer the variable type from the variable's initializer. This means that a variable declared with the `var` keyword *must* have an initializer.

If you leave off an initializer, you will get a compiler error. Listing 2-4 shows some code that declares a variable with the keyword `var` but fails to initialize it.

Listing 2-4. *An Invalid Variable Declaration Using the var Keyword*

```
var name;
```

And here is the compiler error it produces:

```
Implicitly-typed local variables must be initialized
```

Because these variables are statically type checked at compile time, an initializer is required so the compiler can implicitly infer the type from it. Attempting to assign a value of a different data type elsewhere in the code will result in a compiler error. For example, let's examine the code in Listing 2-5.

Listing 2-5. *An Invalid Assignment to a Variable Declared Using the var Keyword*

```
var name = "Joe";     //  So far so good.
name = 1;             //  Uh oh.
Console.WriteLine(name);
```

This code is going to fail to compile because the `name` variable is going to be implicitly inferred to be of type `string`; yet we attempt to assign an integer value of 1 to the variable. Here is the compiler error this code generates:

```
Cannot implicitly convert type 'int' to 'string'
```

As you can see, the compiler is enforcing the variable's type. Back to that original code example of an anonymous type assignment, using the var keyword, my code with an additional line to display the variable would look like Listing 2-6.

Listing 2-6. *An Anonymous Type Assigned to a Variable Declared with the var Keyword*

```
var unnamedTypeVar = new {firstArg = 1, secondArg = "Joe" };
Console.WriteLine(unnamedTypeVar.firstArg + ". " + unnamedTypeVar.secondArg);
```

Here are the results of this code:

```
1. Joe
```

As you can see, using the var keyword, you get static type checking plus the flexibility to support anonymous types. This will become very important when we discuss projection type operators in the remainder of this book.

In these examples so far, usage of the var keyword has been mandatory because there is no alternative. If you are assigning an object of an anonymous class type to a variable, you have no choice but to assign it to a variable declared with the var keyword. However, it is possible to use var any time you declare a variable, as long as it is getting initialized properly. We recommend refraining from that indulgence, though, for the sake of maintainability. We feel like developers should always know the type of data they are working with, and, although the actual data type may be known to you now, will it be when you revisit this code in six months? What about when another developer is responsible once you leave?

■ **Tip** For the sake of maintainable code, refrain from using the var keyword just because it is convenient. Use it when necessary, such as when assigning an object of anonymous type to a variable.

Object and Collection Initialization Expressions

Because of the need for the dynamic data types that anonymous types allow, there needed to be a change in the way objects and collections could be initialized. Since expressions are provided in a lambda expression or an expression tree, object and collection initialization was simplified for initialization.

Object Initialization

Object initialization allows you to specify the initialization values for publicly accessible fields and properties of a class during instantiation. As an example, consider this class:

```
public class Address
{
  public string address;
  public string city;
  public string state;
  public string postalCode;
}
```

Prior to the object initialization feature added to C#, without a specialized constructor you would have to initialize an object of type `Address`, as shown in Listing 2-7.

Listing 2-7. Instantiating and Initializing the Class the Old Way

```
Address address = new Address();
address.address = "105 Elm Street";
address.city = "Atlanta";
address.state = "GA";
address.postalCode = "30339";
```

This will become very cumbersome in a lambda expression. Imagine you have queried the values from a data source and are projecting specific members into an `Address` object with the `Select` operator:

```
//  This code will not compile.
IEnumerable<Address> addresses = somedatasource
  .Where(a => a.State = "GA")
  .Select(a => new Address(???)???);
```

You just won't have a convenient way to get the members initialized in the newly constructed `Address` object. Have no fear: object initialization to the rescue. Now you may be saying that you could create a constructor that would allow you to pass all those initialization values in when the object is instantiated. Yes, you could, some of the time. But what a hassle that would be, wouldn't it? And how are you going to do that with an anonymous type? Wouldn't it be much easier to just instantiate the object as shown in Listing 2-8?

Listing 2-8. Instantiating and Initializing the Class the New Fancy-Pants Way

```
Address address = new Address {
                    address = "105 Elm Street",
                    city = "Atlanta",
                    state = "GA",
                    postalCode = "30339"
                  };
```

You *can* get away with that in a lambda expression. Also, remember these object initialization capabilities can be used anywhere, not just with LINQ queries.

When using object initialization, the compiler instantiates the object using the class's parameterless constructor, and then it initializes the named members with the specified values. Any members that are not specified will have the default value for their data type.

Collection Initialization

As if the object initialization enhancements were not enough, someone at Microsoft must have said, "What about collections?" *Collection initialization* allows you to specify the initialization values for a collection, just like you would for an object. As an example of collection initialization, consider the code in Listing 2-9.

Listing 2-9. An Example of Collection Initialization

```
using System.Collections.Generic;

List<string> presidents = new List<string> { "Adams", "Arthur", "Buchanan" };
foreach(string president in presidents)
{
  Console.WriteLine(president);
}
```

When running the example by pressing Ctrl+F5, you get the following results:

```
Adams
Arthur
Buchanan
```

In addition to using collection initialization with LINQ, it can be very handy for creating initialized collections in code where LINQ queries are not even present.

Anonymous Types

Creating a language-level API for generic data query is made more difficult by the C# language's lack of ability to dynamically create new data types at compile time. If we want data queries to retrieve first-class language-level elements, the language must have the ability to create first-class language-level data elements, which for C# are classes. So, the C# language specification now includes the ability to dynamically create new unnamed classes and objects from those classes. This type of class is known as an *anonymous type*.

An anonymous type has no name and is generated by the compiler based on the initialization of the object being instantiated. Since the class has no type name, any variable assigned to an object of an anonymous type must have some way to declare it. This is the purpose of the C# var keyword.

The anonymous type is invaluable when projecting new data types using the Select or SelectMany operators. Without anonymous types, predefined named classes would always have to exist for the purpose of projecting data into the predefined named classes when calling the Select or SelectMany operators. It would be very inconvenient to have to create named classes for every query.

In the "Object Initialization" section of this chapter, we discussed the following object instantiation and initialization code:

```
Address address = new Address {
                    address = "105 Elm Street",
                    city = "Atlanta",
                    state = "GA",
                    postalCode = "30339"
                };
```

If instead of using the named `Address` class we want to use an anonymous type, we would just omit the class name. However, you can't store the newly instantiated object in a variable of `Address` type because it is no longer a variable of type `Address`. It now has a generated type name known only to the compiler. So, we have to change the data type of the `address` variable too. This again is what the `var` keyword is for, as demonstrated by Listing 2-10.

Listing 2-10. Instantiating and Initializing an Anonymous Type Using Object Initialization

```
var address = new {
                address = "105 Elm Street",
                city = "Atlanta",
                state = "GA",
                postalCode = "30339"
            };

Console.WriteLine("address = {0} : city = {1} : state = {2} : zip = {3}",
   address.address, address.city, address.state, address.postalCode);

Console.WriteLine("{0}", address.GetType().ToString());
```

We added that last call to the `Console.WriteLine` method just so you can see the internal compiler-generated name for the anonymous class. Here are the results:

```
address = 105 Elm Street : city = Atlanta : state = GA : zip = 30339
<>f__AnonymousType5`4[System.String,System.String,System.String,System.String]
```

That anonymous class type certainly looks compiler-generated to us. Of course, your compiler-generated anonymous class name could be different.

Extension Methods

An *extension method* is a static method of a static class that you can call as though it were an instance method of a different class. For example, you could create an extension method named `ToDouble` that is a static method in a static class you create named `StringConversions`, but that is called as though it were a method of an object of type `string`.

Before we explain extension methods in detail, let's first review the problem that led to their creation by discussing static (class) versus instance (object) methods. Instance methods can be called only on *instances* of a class, otherwise known as *objects*. You cannot call an instance method on the class itself. Likewise, static methods must be called on the class, as opposed to an instance of a class.

Instance (Object) vs. Static (Class) Methods Recap

The string class ToUpper method is an example of an instance-level method. You cannot call ToUpper on the string class itself; you must call it on a string object.

In the code in Listing 2-11, we demonstrate this by calling the ToUpper method on the object named name.

Listing 2-11. Calling an Instance Method on an Object

```
//  This code will compile.
string name = "Joe";
Console.WriteLine(name.ToUpper());
```

The previous code compiles and, when run, produces the following output:

```
JOE
```

However, if we try to call the ToUpper method on the string class itself, we will get a compiler error because the ToUpper method is an instance-level method, and we are attempting to call it on the class, rather than the object. Listing 2-12 shows an example of an attempt to do this and the compiler error generated by it.

Listing 2-12. Trying to Call an Instance Method on a Class

```
//  This code will not even compile.
string.ToUpper();
```

Just trying to compile this code produces the following compiler error:

```
An object reference is required for the nonstatic field, method, or property
'string.ToUpper()'
```

This example seems a little hokey, though, since it couldn't possibly work because we never gave it any string value to convert to uppercase. Any attempt to do so, though, would result in trying to call some variation of the ToUpper method that does not exist because there is no prototype for the ToUpper method whose signature includes a string.

Contrast the ToUpper method with the string class Format method. This method is defined to be static. This requires the Format method to be called on the string class itself, rather than on an object of type string. First we will try to call it on an object with the code in Listing 2-13.

Listing 2-13. Trying to Call a Class Method on an Object

```
string firstName = "Joe";
string lastName = "Rattz";
```

```
string name = firstName.Format("{0} {1}", firstName, lastName);
Console.WriteLine(name);
```

This code produces the following compiler error:

```
Member 'string.Format(string, object, object)' cannot be accessed with an instance
reference; qualify it with a type name instead
```

However, if instead we call the Format method on the string class itself, it compiles and works as desired, as demonstrated in Listing 2-14.

Listing 2-14. Calling a Class Method on a Class

```
string firstName = "Joe";
string lastName = "Rattz";
string name = string.Format("{0} {1}", firstName, lastName);
Console.WriteLine(name);
```

The code produces the following results:

```
Joe Rattz
```

It is sometimes obvious from parts of the signature other than the static keyword itself that the method must be an instance-level method. For example, consider the ToUpper method. It doesn't have any arguments other than one overloaded version taking a CultureInfo object reference. So if it isn't relying on a string instance's internal data, what string would it convert to uppercase?

The Problem Solved by Extension Methods

So, what is the problem, you ask? For this discussion, assume you are the developer responsible for designing a new way to query multitudes of objects. Let's say you decide to create a Where method to help with the where clauses. How would you do it?

Would you make the Where operator an instance method? If so, to what class would you add that Where method? You want the Where method to work for querying any collection of objects. There just isn't a logical class to add the Where method to. Taking this approach, you would have to modify a zillion different classes if you want universal data querying capability.

So, now that you realize the method must be static, what is the problem? Think of your typical (SQL) query and how many where clauses you often have. Also consider the joins, grouping, and ordering.

Let's imagine that you have created the concept of a new data type, a sequence of generic data objects that we will call an Enumerable. It makes sense that the Where method would need to operate on an Enumerable (of data) and return another filtered Enumerable. In addition, the Where method will need to accept an argument allowing the developer to specify the exact logic used to filter data records from or into the Enumerable. This argument, which we will call the *predicate*, could be specified as a named method, an anonymous method, or a lambda expression.

■ **Caution** The following three code examples in this section are hypothetical and will not compile.

Since the `Where` method requires an input `Enumerable` to filter and the method is `static`, that input `Enumerable` must be specified as an argument to the `Where` method. It would appear something like the following:

```
static Enumerable Enumerable.Where(Enumerable input, LambdaExpression predicate) {
...
}
```

Ignoring for the moment the semantics of a lambda expression, calling the `Where` method would look something like the following:

```
Enumerable enumerable = {"one", "two", "three"};
Enumerable filteredEnumerable = Enumerable.Where(enumerable, lambdaExpression);
```

That doesn't look too ornery. But what happens when we need several `where` clauses? Since the `Enumerable` that the `Where` method is operating on must be an argument to the method, the result is that chaining methods together requires embedding them inside each other. Three `where` clauses suddenly change the code to the following:

```
Enumerable enumerable = {"one", "two", "three"};
Enumerable finalEnumerable =
  Enumerable.Where(Enumerable.Where(Enumerable.Where(enumerable, lX1), lX2), lX3);
```

You have to read the statement from the inside out. That gets hard to read in a hurry. Can you imagine what a complex query would look like? If only there was a better way.

The Solution

A nice solution would be if you could call the `static` `Where` method on each `Enumerable` object, rather than on the class. Then it would no longer be necessary to pass each `Enumerable` into the `Where` method because the `Enumerable` object would have access to its own internal `Enumerable`. That would change the syntax of the query proposed previously to something more like this:

```
Enumerable enumerable = {"one", "two", "three"};
Enumerable finalEnumerable = enumerable.Where(lX1).Where(lX2).Where(lX3);
```

■ **Caution** The previous code and the following code example are hypothetical and will not compile.

This could even be rewritten as the following:

```
Enumerable enumerable = {"one", "two", "three"};
Enumerable finalEnumerable = enumerable
  .Where(lX1)
  .Where(lX2)
  .Where(lX3);
```

Wow, that's much easier to read. You can now read the statement from left to right, top to bottom. As you can see, this syntax is very easy to follow once you understand what it is doing. Because of this, you will often see LINQ queries written in this format in much of the LINQ documentation and in this book.

Ultimately what you need is the ability to have a static method that you can call on a class instance. This is exactly what extension methods are and what they allow. They were added to C# to provide a syntactically elegant way to call a static method without having to pass the method's first argument. This allows the extension method to be called as though it were a method of the first argument, which makes chaining extension method calls far more readable than if the first argument was passed. Extension methods assist LINQ by allowing the Standard Query Operators to be called on the IEnumerable<T> interface.

■ **Note** Extension methods are methods that, although static, can be called on an instance (object) of a class rather than on the class itself.

Extension Method Declarations and Invocations

Specifying a method's first argument with the this keyword modifier will make that method an extension method.

The extension method will appear as an instance method of any object with the same type as the extension method's first argument's data type. For example, if the extension method's first argument is of type string, the extension method will appear as a string instance method and can be called on any string object.

Also keep in mind that extension methods can be declared only in static classes.

Here are two examples of an extension method:

```
namespace Netsplore.Utilities
{
  public static class StringConversions
  {
    public static double ToDouble(this string s) {
      return Double.Parse(s);
    }

    public static bool ToBool(this string s) {
      return Boolean.Parse(s);
    }
```

```
    }
}
```

Notice that both the class and every method it contains are static. Now you can take advantage of those extension methods by calling the static methods on the object instances, as shown in Listing 2-15. Because the ToDouble method is static and its first argument specifies the this keyword, ToDouble is an extension method.

Listing 2-15. Calling an Extension Method

```
using Netsplore.Utilities;

double pi = "3.1415926535".ToDouble();
Console.WriteLine(pi);
```

This produces the following results:

```
3.1415926535
```

It is important that you specify the using directive for the Netsplore.Utilities namespace; otherwise, the compiler will not find the extension methods, and you will get compiler errors such as the following:

```
'string' does not contain a definition for 'ToDouble' and no extension method
'ToDouble' accepting a first argument of type 'string' could be found (are you
missing a using directive or an assembly reference?)
```

As mentioned previously, attempting to declare an extension method inside a nonstatic class is not allowed. If you do so, you will see a compiler error like the following:

```
Extension methods must be defined in a non-generic static class
```

Extension Method Precedence

Normal object instance methods take precedence over extension methods when their signature matches the calling signature.

Extension methods seem like a really useful concept, especially when you want to be able to extend a class you cannot, such as a sealed class or one for which you do not have source code. The previous extension method examples all effectively add methods to the string class. Without extension methods, you couldn't do that because the string class is s is sealed.

Partial Methods

Included since C# version 3.0, *partial methods* add a lightweight event-handling mechanism to C#. Forget the conclusions you are more than likely drawing about partial methods based on their name. About the only thing partial methods have in common with partial classes is that a partial method can exist only in a partial class. In fact, that is rule 1 for partial methods.

Before we get to all the rules concerning partial methods, we'll tell you what they are. Partial methods are methods where the prototype or definition of the method is specified in the declaration of a partial class, but an implementation for the method is not provided in that same declaration of the partial class. In fact, there may not be *any* implementation for the method in *any* declaration of that same partial class. And if there is no implementation of the method in any other declaration for the same partial class, no IL code is emitted by the compiler for the declaration of the method, the call to the method, or the evaluation of the arguments passed to the method. It's as if the method never existed.

Some people do not like the term *partial methods* because it is somewhat of a misnomer due to their behavior when compared to that of a partial class. Perhaps the method modifier should have been ghost instead of partial.

A Partial Method Example

Let's take a look at a partial class containing the definition of a partial method in the following class file named MyWidget.cs:

The MyWidget Class File

```
public partial class MyWidget
{
  partial void MyWidgetStart(int count);
  partial void MyWidgetEnd(int count);

  public MyWidget()
  {
    int count = 0;
    MyWidgetStart(++count);
    Console.WriteLine("In the constructor of MyWidget.");
    MyWidgetEnd(++count);
    Console.WriteLine("count = " + count);
  }
}
```

In the MyWidget class declaration, we have a partial class named MyWidget. The first two lines of code are partial method definitions. We have defined partial methods named MyWidgetStart and MyWidgetEnd that each accept an int input parameter and return void. It is another rule that partial methods must return void.

The next piece of code in the MyWidget class is the constructor. As you can see, we declare an int named count and initialize it to 0. We then call the MyWidgetStart method, write a message to the console, call the MyWidgetEnd method, and finally output the value of count to the console. Notice we are incrementing the value of count each time it is passed into a partial method. We are doing this to prove that if no implementation of a partial method exists, even its arguments are not evaluated.

In Listing 2-16 we instantiate a MyWidget object.

Listing 2-16. Instantiating a MyWidget

```
MyWidget myWidget = new MyWidget();
```

Let's take a look at the output of this example by pressing Ctrl+F5:

```
In the constructor of MyWidget.
count = 0
```

As you can see, even after the `MyWidget` constructor has incremented its `count` variable twice, when it displays the value of `count` at the end of the constructor, it is still 0. This is because the code for the evaluation of the arguments to the unimplemented partial methods is never emitted by the compiler. No IL code was emitted for either of those two partial method calls.

Now let's add an implementation for the two partial methods:

Another Declaration for MyWidget but Containing Implementations for the Partial Methods

```
public partial class MyWidget
{
  partial void MyWidgetStart(int count)
  {
    Console.WriteLine("In MyWidgetStart(count is {0})", count);
  }

  partial void MyWidgetEnd(int count)
  {
    Console.WriteLine("In MyWidgetEnd(count is {0})", count);
  }
}
```

Now that you have added this declaration, run Listing 2-16 again and look at the results:

```
In MyWidgetStart(count is 1)
In the constructor of MyWidget.
In MyWidgetEnd(count is 2)
count = 2
```

As you can see, not only are the partial method implementations getting called, but the arguments passed are evaluated as well. You can see this because of the value of the `count` variable at the end of the output.

What Is the Point of Partial Methods?

So, you may be wondering, what is the point? Others have said, "This is similar to using inheritance and virtual methods. Why corrupt the language with something similar?" To them we say, "Take a chill-pill, Jill." Partial methods are more efficient if you plan on allowing many potentially unimplemented hooks in the code. They allow code to be written with the intention of someone else extending it via the partial class paradigm but without the degradation in performance if they choose not to do so.

The case in point for which partial methods were probably added is the code generated for LINQ to SQL entity classes by the entity class generator tools. To make the generated entity classes more usable, partial methods have been added to them. For example, each mapped property of a generated entity class has a partial method that is called before the property is changed and another partial method that is called after the property is changed. This allows you to add another module that declares the same entity class, implement these partial methods, and be notified every time a property is about to be changed and after it is changed. How cool is that? And if you don't do it, the code is no bigger and no slower. Who wouldn't want that?

The Rules

It has been all fun and games up to here, but unfortunately, there are some rules that apply to partial methods:

- Partial methods must be defined and implemented only in partial classes.

- Partial methods must specify the `partial` modifier.

- Partial methods are private but must not specify the `private` modifier, or a compiler error will result.

- Partial methods must return `void`.

- Partial methods may be unimplemented.

- Partial methods may be `static`.

- Partial methods may have arguments.

These rules are not too bad. For what we gain in terms of flexibility in the generated entity classes plus what we can do with them ourselves, we think C# has gained a nice feature.

Query Expressions

One of the conveniences that the C# language provides is the `foreach` statement. When you use `foreach`, the compiler translates it into a loop with calls to methods such as `GetEnumerator` and `MoveNext`. The simplicity the `foreach` statement provides for enumerating through arrays and collections has made it very popular and often used.

One of the features of LINQ that seems to attract developers is the SQL-like syntax available for LINQ queries. The first few LINQ examples in the first chapter of this book use this syntax. This syntax is provided via the C# language enhancement known as *query expressions*. Query expressions allow LINQ queries to be expressed in nearly SQL form, with just a few minor deviations.

To perform a LINQ query, it is not required to use query expressions. The alternative is to use standard C# dot notation, calling methods on objects and classes. In many cases, we find using the standard dot notation favorable for instructional purposes because we think it is more demonstrative of what is actually happening and when. There is no compiler translating what we write into the standard dot notation equivalent. Therefore, many examples in this book do not use query expression syntax but instead opt for the standard dot notation syntax. However, there is no disputing the allure of query expression syntax. The familiarity it provides in formulating your first queries can be very enticing indeed.

To get an idea of what the two different syntaxes look like, Listing 2-17 shows a query using the standard dot notation syntax.

Listing 2-17. *A Query Using the Standard Dot Notation Syntax*

```
string[] names = {
  "Adams", "Arthur", "Buchanan", "Bush", "Carter", "Cleveland",
  "Clinton", "Coolidge", "Eisenhower", "Fillmore", "Ford", "Garfield",
  "Grant", "Harding", "Harrison", "Hayes", "Hoover", "Jackson",
  "Jefferson", "Johnson", "Kennedy", "Lincoln", "Madison", "McKinley",
  "Monroe", "Nixon", "Obama", "Pierce", "Polk", "Reagan", "Roosevelt", "Taft",
  "Taylor", "Truman", "Tyler", "Van Buren", "Washington", "Wilson"};

IEnumerable<string> sequence = names
  .Where(n => n.Length < 6)
  .Select(n => n);

foreach (string name in sequence)
{
  Console.WriteLine("{0}", name);
}
```

Listing 2-18 is the equivalent query using the query expression syntax.

Listing 2-18. *The Equivalent Query Using the Query Expression Syntax*

```
string[] names = {
  "Adams", "Arthur", "Buchanan", "Bush", "Carter", "Cleveland",
  "Clinton", "Coolidge", "Eisenhower", "Fillmore", "Ford", "Garfield",
  "Grant", "Harding", "Harrison", "Hayes", "Hoover", "Jackson",
  "Jefferson", "Johnson", "Kennedy", "Lincoln", "Madison", "McKinley",
  "Monroe", "Nixon", "Obama", "Pierce", "Polk", "Reagan", "Roosevelt",
  "Taft", "Taylor", "Truman", "Tyler", "Van Buren", "Washington", "Wilson"};

IEnumerable<string> sequence = from n in names
                               where n.Length < 6
                               select n;

foreach (string name in sequence)
{
  Console.WriteLine("{0}", name);
}
```

The first thing you may notice about the query expression example is that unlike SQL, the `from` statement precedes the `select` statement. One of the compelling reasons for this change is to narrow the scope for IntelliSense. Without this inversion of the statements, if in the Visual Studio text editor you typed `select` followed by a space, IntelliSense would have no idea what variables to display in its drop-down list. The scope of possible variables at this point is not restricted in any way. By specifying where the data is coming from first, IntelliSense has the scope of what variables to offer you for selection. Both of these examples provide the same results:

```
Adams
Bush
Ford
Grant
Hayes
Nixon
Obama
Polk
Taft
Tyler
```

It is important to note that the query expression syntax translates only the most common query operators: `Where`, `Select`, `SelectMany`, `Join`, `GroupJoin`, `GroupBy`, `OrderBy`, `ThenBy`, `OrderByDescending`, and `ThenByDescending`.

Query Expression Grammar

Your query expressions *must* adhere to the following rules:

1. A query expression must begin with a `from` clause.

2. The remainder of the query expression may then contain zero or more `from`, `let`, or `where` clauses. A `from` clause is a generator that declares one or more range variables enumerating over a sequence or a `join` of multiple sequences. A `let` clause introduces a range variable and assigns a value to it. A `where` clause filters elements from an input sequence or join of multiple input sequences *into* the output sequence.

3. The remainder of the query expression may then be followed by an `orderby` clause that contains one or more ordering fields with optional ordering direction. Direction is either `ascending` or `descending`.

4. The remainder of the query expression must then be followed by a `select` or `group` clause.

5. The remainder of the query expression may then be followed by an optional continuation clause. A continuation clause is either the `into` clause, zero or more `join` clauses, or another repeating sequence of these numbered elements beginning with the clauses in #2. An `into` clause directs the query results into an imaginary output sequence, which functions as a `from` clause for a subsequent query expression beginning with the clauses in #2.

Query Expression Translation

Now assuming you have created a syntactically correct query expression, the next issue becomes how the compiler translates the query expression into C# code. It must translate your query expression into the standard C# dot notation that we discuss in the query expression section. But how does it do this?

To translate a query expression, the compiler is looking for code patterns in the query expression that need to be translated. The compiler will perform several translation steps in a specific order to translate the query expression into standard C# dot notation. Each translation step is looking for one or more related code patterns. The compiler must repeatedly translate all occurrences of the code patterns for that translation step in the query expression before moving on to the next translation step. Likewise, each step operates on the assumption that the query has had the code patterns for all previous translation steps translated.

Transparent Identifiers

Some translations insert enumeration variables with transparent identifiers. In the translation step descriptions in the next section, a transparent identifier is identified with an asterisk (*). This should not be confused with the SQL-selected field wildcard character, *. When translating query expressions, sometimes additional enumerations are generated by the compiler, and transparent identifiers are used to enumerate through them. The transparent identifiers exist only during the translation process, and once the query expression is fully translated, no transparent identifiers will remain in the query.

Translation Steps

Next we discuss the translation steps. In doing so, we use the variable letters shown in Table 2-1 to represent specific portions of the query.

Table 2-1. *Translation Step Variables*

Variable	Description	Example
c	A compiler-generated temporary variable	N/A
e	A range variable	from **e** in s
f	Selected field element or new anonymous type	from e in s select **f**
g	A grouped element	from e in s group **g** by k
i	An imaginary **into** sequence	from e in s select f into **i**
k	Grouped or joined key element	from e in s group g by **k**
l	A variable introduced by **let**	from e in s let **l** = v
o	An ordering element	from e in s orderby **o**

s	Input sequence	`from e in s`
v	A value assigned to a `let` variable	`from e in s let l = v`
w	A `where` clause	`from e in s where w`

Allow us to provide a word of warning. The soon to be described translation steps are quite complicated. Do not allow this to discourage you. You no more need to fully understand the translation steps to write LINQ queries than you need to know how the compiler translates the `foreach` statement to use it. They are here to provide additional translation information should you need it, which should be rarely, or never.

The translation steps are documented as `code pattern` ➤ `translation`. Oddly, even though we present the translation steps in the order the compiler performs them, we think the translation process is simpler to understand if you learn them in the reverse order. The reason is that when you look at the first translation step, it handles only the first code pattern translation, and you are left with a lot of untranslated code patterns that you have yet to be introduced to. To our minds, this leaves a lot of unaccounted for gobbledygook. Since each translation step requires the previous translation step's code patterns to already be translated, by the time you get to the final translation step, there is no gobbledygook left. We think this makes the final translation step easier to understand than the first. And in our opinion, traversing backward through the translation steps is the easiest way to understand what is going on.

That said, here are the translation steps presented in the order in which the compiler performs them.

Select and Group Clauses with an into Continuation Clause

If your query expression contains an `into` continuation clause, the following translation is made:

```
from ...₁ into i ...₂
```
➤
```
from i in
  from ...₁
  ...₂
```

Here is an example:

```
from c in customers
group c by c.Country into g
select new
  { Country = g.Key,
    CustCount = g.Count() }
```
➤
```
from g in
from c in customers
group c by c.Country
select new
  { Country = g.Key,
    CustCount = g.Count() }
```

Using subsequent translation steps this is eventually translated to:

```
customers.GroupBy(c => c.Country)
  .Select(g => new { Country = g.Key, CustCount = g.Count() })
```

Explicit Enumeration Variable Types

If your query expression contains a `from` clause that explicitly specifies an enumeration variable type, the following translation will be made:

```
from T e in s                    ➤   from e in s.Cast<T>()
```

Here is an example:

```
from Customer c in customers     ➤   from c in customers.Cast<Customer>()
select c
```

Using subsequent translation steps this is eventually translated to:

```
customers.Cast<Customer>()
```

If your query expression contains a `join` clause that explicitly specifies an enumeration variable type, the following translation will be made:

```
join T e in s                    ➤   join e in s.Cast<T>()
on k₁ equals k₂                      on k₁ equals k₂
```

Here is an example:

```
from c in customers                  from c in customers
join Order o in orders               join o in orders.Cast<Order>()
on c.CustomerID equals o.CustomerID  on c.CustomerID equals o.CustomerID
select new { c.Name,          ➤      select new
            o.OrderDate,               { c.Name, o.OrderDate, o.Total }
            o.Total }
```

Using subsequent translation steps this is eventually translated to:

```
customers
.Join(orders.Cast<Order>(),
      c => c.CustomerID,
      o => o.CustomerID,
      (c, o) => new { c.Name, o.OrderDate, o.Total })
```

■ **Tip** Explicitly typing enumeration variables is necessary when the enumerated data collection is one of the C# legacy data collections, such as `ArrayList`. The casting that is done when explicitly typing the enumeration variable converts the legacy collection into a sequence implementing `IEnumerable<T>` so that other query operators can be performed.

Join Clauses

If the query expression contains a `from` clause followed by a `join` clause *without* an `into` continuation clause followed by a select clause, the following translation takes place (t is a temporary compiler-generated variable):

```
from e₁ in s₁                        from t in s₁
join e₂ in s₂                        .Join(s₂,
on k₁ equals k₂            ➤               e₁ => k₁,
select f                                   e₂ => k₂,
                                           (e₁, e₂) => f)
                                     select t
```

Here is an example:

```
from c in customers                  from t in customers
join o in orders                     .Join(orders,
on c.CustomerID equals o.CustomerID        c => c.CustomerID,
select new { c.Name,                       o => o.CustomerID,
            o.OrderDate,     ➤             (c, o) => new
            o.Total }                                  { c.Name,
                                                        o.OrderDate,
                                                        o.Total })
                                     select t
```

Using subsequent translation steps this is eventually translated to:

```
customers
.Join(orders,
      c => c.CustomerID,
      o => o.CustomerID,
      (c, o) => new { c.Name, o.OrderDate, o.Total })
```

If the query expression contains a `from` clause followed by a join clause *with* an into continuation clause followed by a `select` clause, the following translation takes place (t is a temporary compiler-generated variable):

```
from e₁ in s₁                        from t in s₁
join e₂ in s₂                        .GroupJoin(s₂,
on k₁ equals k₂                            e₁ => k₁,
into i                     ➤               e₂ => k₂,
select f                                   (e₁, i) => f)
                                     select t
```

Here is an example:

```
from c in customers                        from t in customers
join o in orders                             .GroupJoin(orders,
on c.CustomerID equals o.CustomerID                    c => c.CustomerID,
into co                                                o => o.CustomerID,
select new                          ➤                  (c, co) => new
  { c.Name, Sum = co.Sum(o => o.Total) }                 { c.Name,
                                                             Sum = co.Sum(
                                                               o =>co.Total) })
                                           Select t
```

Using subsequent translation steps this is eventually translated to:

```
Customers
.GroupJoin(orders,
          c => c.CustomerID,
          o => o.CustomerID,
          (c, co) => new { c.Name, Sum = co.Sum(o = o.Total) })
```

If the query expression contains a `from` clause followed by a `join` clause without an `into` continuation clause followed by something other than a `select` clause, the following translation takes place (* is a transparent identifier):

```
from e₁ in s₁                       from * in
join e₂ in s₂                         from e₁ in s₁
on k₁ equals k₂               ➤        join e₂ in s₂
...                                    on k₁ equals k₂
                                       select new { e₁, e₂ }
```

Notice that you now have a code pattern that matches the first code pattern in this translation step. Specifically, you have a query expression that contains a `from` clause followed by a `join` clause without an `into` continuation clause followed by a `select` clause. So, the compiler will repeat this translation step.

If the query expression contains a `from` clause followed by a `join` clause with an `into` continuation clause followed by something other than a `select` clause, the following translation takes place (* is a transparent identifier):

```
from e₁ in s₁                       from * in
join e₂ in s₂                         from e₁ in s₁
on k₁ equals k₂               ➤        join e₂ in s₂
into i                                 on k₁ equals k₂
...                                    into i
                                       select new { e₁, i }
```

This time notice that there is now a code pattern that matches the second code pattern in this translation step. Specifically, there is a query expression that contains a `from` clause followed by a `join` clause with an `into` continuation clause followed by a `select` clause. So, the compiler will repeat this translation step.

Let and Where Clauses

If the query expression contains a `from` clause followed immediately by a `let` clause, the following translation takes place (* is a transparent identifier):

```
from e in s                          from * in
let l = v               ➤            from e₁ in s₁
                                     select new { e, l = v }
```

Here is an example (`t` is a compiler-generated identifier that is invisible and inaccessible to any code you write):

```
from c in customers                  from * in
let cityStateZip =                   from c in customers
  c.City + ", " + c.State + " " + c.Zip    select new {
select new { c.Name, cityStateZip }    c,
                        ➤                cityStateZip =
                                           c.City + ", " + c.State + " " +
                                             c.Zip }
                                     select new { c.Name, cityStateZip }
```

Using subsequent translation steps this is eventually translated to:

```
customers
.Select(c => new { c, cityStateZip = c.City + ", " + c.State + " " + c.Zip })
.Select(t => new { t.c.Name, t.cityStateZip })
```

If the query expression contains a `from` clause followed immediately by a `where` clause, the following translation takes place:

```
from e in s             ➤            from e in s
where w                              .Where(e => w)
```

Here is an example:

```
from c in customers                  from c in customers
where c.Country == "USA"    ➤        .Where(c => c.Country == "USA")
select new { c.Name, c.Country }     select new { c.Name, c.Country }
```

Using subsequent translation steps this is eventually translated to:

```
customers
.Where(c => c.Country == "USA")
.Select(c => new { c.Name, c.Country })
```

Multiple Generator (From) Clauses

If the query expression contains two `from` clauses followed by a `select` clause, the following translation takes place:

```
from e₁ in s₁                    from c in s₁
from e₂ in s₂          ➤          .SelectMany(e₁ => from e₂ in s₂
select f                                          select f)
                                 select c
```

Here is an example (t is a temporary compiler-generated variable):

```
from c in customers              from t in customers
from o in c.Orders               .SelectMany(c => from o in c.Orders
select new                                         select new {
  { c.Name, o.OrderID, o.OrderDate }                     c.Name,
                     ➤                                    o.OrderID,
                                                          o.OrderDate
                                                   })
                                 Select t
```

Using subsequent translation steps this is eventually translated to:

```
customers
.SelectMany(c => c.Orders.Select(o => new { c.Name, o.OrderID, o.OrderDate }))
```

If the query expression contains two from clauses followed by something other than a select clause, the following translation takes place (* is a transparent identifier):

```
from e₁ in s₁                    from * in
from e₂ in s₂                     from e₁ in s₁
...                  ➤            from e₂ in s₂
                                 select new { e₁, e₂ }
                                 ...
```

Here is an example (* is a transparent identifier):

```
from c in customers              from * in
from o in c.Orders               from c in customers
orderby o.OrderDate descending   from o in c.Orders
select new            ➤          select new { c, o }
  { c.Name, o.OrderID, o.OrderDate }  orderby o.OrderDate descending
                                 select new
                                   { c.Name, o.OrderID, o.OrderDate }
```

Using subsequent translation steps this is eventually translated to:

In addition to the subsequent translation steps, the previous translated code must call this translation step again because after the previous first step, you now have a from clause followed by a from clause followed by a select clause, which is the first code pattern this translation step looks to translate. This is an example of translation steps sometimes needing to be called multiple times to fully translate all the code patterns any particular step is looking for.

```
customers
.SelectMany(c => c.Orders.Select(o => new { c, o }))
.OrderByDescending(t => t.o.OrderDate)
.Select(t => new { t.c.Name, t.o.OrderID, t.o.OrderDate})
```

Orderby Clauses

If the direction of the ordering is ascending, the following translations take place:

```
from e in s                          from e in s
orderby o₁, o₂                   ➤   .OrderBy(e => o₁).ThenBy(e => o₂)
```

Here is an example:

```
from c in customers                  from c in customers
orderby c.Country, c.Name            .OrderBy(c => c.Country)
select new { c.Country, c.Name } ➤   .ThenBy(c.Name)
                                     select new { c.Country, c.Name }
```

Using subsequent translation steps this is eventually translated to:

```
customers
.OrderBy(c => c.Country)
.ThenBy(c.Name)
.Select(c => new { c.Country, c.Name }
```

If the direction of any of the orderings is descending, the translations will be to the OrderByDescending or ThenByDescending operators. Here is the same example as the previous, except this time the names are requested in descending order:

```
from c in customers                  from c in customers
orderby c.Country, c.Name descending .OrderBy(c => c.Country)
select new { c.Country, c.Name }  ➤  .ThenByDescending(c.Name)
                                     select new { c.Country, c.Name }
```

Using subsequent translation steps this is eventually translated to:

```
customers
.OrderBy(c => c.Country)
.ThenByDescending(c.Name)
.Select(c => new { c.Country, c.Name }
```

Select Clauses

In the query expression, if the selected element is the same identifier as the sequence enumerator variable, meaning you are selecting the entire element that is stored in the sequence, the following translation takes place:

```
from e in s                      ➤   s
select f
```

Here is an example:

```
from c in customers              ➤   customers
select c
```

If the selected element is not the same identifier as the sequence enumerator variable, meaning you are selecting something other than the entire element stored in the sequence such as a member of the element or an anonymous type constructed of several members of the element, the following translation takes place:

```
from e in s                              s.Select(e => f)
select f
```

Here is an example:

```
from c in customers                      customers.Select(c => c.Name)
select c.Name
```

Group Clauses

In the query expression, if the grouped element is the same identifier as the sequence enumerator, meaning you are grouping the entire element stored in the sequence, the following translation takes place:

```
from e in s                              s.GroupBy(e => k)
group g by k
```

Here is an example:

```
from c in customers                      customers.GroupBy(c => c.Country)
group c by c.Country
```

If the grouped element is not the same identifier as the sequence enumerator, meaning you are grouping something other than the entire element stored in the sequence, the following translation takes place:

```
from e in s                              s.GroupBy(e => k, e => g)
group g by k
```

Here is an example:

```
from c in customers                      customers
group new { c.Country, c.Name }          .GroupBy(c => c.Country,
by c.Country                                         c => new {
                                                         c.Country,
                                                         c.Name
                                                     })
```

At this point, all translation steps are completed, and the query expression should be fully translated to standard dot notation syntax.

Summary

As you can see, Microsoft's C# team has added many enhancements to C#. All of the C# enhancements discussed in this chapter have been made specifically for LINQ. But even without LINQ, there is a lot to be gained from the new C# features.

The new object and collection initialization expressions are a godsend. Stubbing in static, sample, or test data is much easier than before, significantly reducing the lines of code needed to create the data. This feature, combined with the new var keyword and anonymous types, makes it much easier to create data and data types on the fly.

Extension methods now make it possible to add functionality to objects, such as sealed classes or perhaps classes for which you don't even have the source code, which just wasn't possible before.

Lambda expressions allow for concise specification of functionality. While not eliminating the need for anonymous methods, they add to the arsenal of ways to specify simple functionality, and we like the brevity of the syntax. Although you may initially be put off by them, we think with time and experience you will grow to appreciate them, too.

Expression trees provide third-party vendors wanting to make their proprietary data stores support LINQ with the ability to provide first-class performance.

Partial methods offer a very lightweight event-handling mechanism. Microsoft leverage this in its LINQ to SQL entity class generation tools so that you can hook into the entity classes at key points in time.

Finally, query expressions provide that warm fuzzy feeling when first seeing a LINQ query that makes you want to get on board with LINQ. Nothing makes a developer analyzing a new technology feel comfortable quicker than technology resembling a familiar and proven technology. By giving LINQ queries the ability to resemble SQL queries, Microsoft has made LINQ compelling to learn.

Although all these language enhancements by themselves are nice features, together they form the foundation for LINQ. Now that we have covered what LINQ is and what C# features and syntax it requires, it's time to get to the nitty-gritty. Please don't let our technical jargon—*nitty-gritty*—intimidate you. The next stop is learning about performing LINQ queries on in-memory data collections such as `arrays`, `ArrayLists`, and all of the .NET generic collection classes. In Part 2 you will find a bevy of functions to supplement your queries. This portion of LINQ is known as LINQ to Object

LINQ to Objects

CHAPTER 3

■ ■ ■

LINQ to Objects Introduction

Listing 3-1. *A Simple LINQ to Objects Query*

```
string[] presidents = {
  "Adams", "Arthur", "Buchanan", "Bush", "Carter", "Cleveland",
  "Clinton", "Coolidge", "Eisenhower", "Fillmore", "Ford", "Garfield",
  "Grant", "Harding", "Harrison", "Hayes", "Hoover", "Jackson",
  "Jefferson", "Johnson", "Kennedy", "Lincoln", "Madison", "McKinley",
  "Monroe", "Nixon", "Obama", "Pierce", "Polk", "Reagan", "Roosevelt",
  "Taft", "Taylor", "Truman", "Tyler", "Van Buren", "Washington", "Wilson"};

string president = presidents.Where(p => p.StartsWith("Lin")).First();

Console.WriteLine(president);
```

■ **Note** This code has been added to a Visual Studio 2010 console application.

Listing 3-1 shows what LINQ to Objects is all about—performing SQL-like queries on in-memory data collections and arrays. We will run the example by pressing Ctrl+F5. Here are the results:

```
Lincoln
```

LINQ to Objects Overview

Part of what makes LINQ so cool and easy to use is the way it seamlessly integrates with the C# language. Instead of having an entirely new cast of characters in the form of classes that must be used to get the benefits of LINQ, you can use all of the same collections[1] and arrays that you are accustomed to with your existing classes. This means you can gain the advantages of LINQ queries with little or no modification to existing code. The functionality of LINQ to Objects is accomplished with the `IEnumerable<T>` interface, sequences, and the Standard Query Operators.

For example, if you have an array of integers and need it to be sorted, you can perform a LINQ query to order the results, much as if it were a SQL query. Maybe you have an `ArrayList` of `Customer` objects and need to find a specific `Customer` object. If so, LINQ to Objects is your answer.

We know there will be a tendency by many to use the LINQ to Objects chapters as a reference. Although we have made significant effort to make them useful for this purpose, you will gain more by reading them from beginning to end. Many of the concepts that apply to one operator apply to another operator. Although we have tried to make each operator's section independently stand on its own merit, there is a context created when reading from beginning to end that will be missed when just reading about a single operator or skipping around.

IEnumerable<T>, Sequences, and the Standard Query Operators

`IEnumerable<T>`, pronounced "I enumerable of T," is an interface that all the C# generic collection classes implement, as do arrays. This interface permits the enumeration of a collection's elements.

A *sequence* is a term for a collection implementing the `IEnumerable<T>` interface. If you have a variable of type `IEnumerable<T>`, then you might say you have a sequence of *T*s. For example, if you have an `IEnumerable` of `string`, written as `IEnumerable<string>`, you could say you have a sequence of strings.

■ **Note** Any variable declared as `IEnumerable<T>` for type `T` is considered a sequence of type `T`.

Most of the Standard Query Operators are extension methods in the `System.Linq.Enumerable` static class and are prototyped with an `IEnumerable<T>` as their first argument. Because they are extension methods, it is preferable to call them on a variable of type `IEnumerable<T>` as the extension method syntax permits instead of passing a variable of type `IEnumerable<T>` as the first argument.

The Standard Query Operator methods of the `System.Linq.Enumerable` class that are not extension methods are static methods and must be called on the `System.Linq.Enumerable` class. The combination of these Standard Query Operator methods gives you the ability to perform complex data queries on an `IEnumerable<T>` sequence.

The legacy collections, those nongeneric collections existing prior to C# 2.0, support the `IEnumerable` interface, not the `IEnumerable<T>` interface. This means you cannot *directly* call those extension methods whose first argument is an `IEnumerable<T>` on a legacy collection. However, you can still perform LINQ queries on legacy collections by calling the `Cast` or `OfType` Standard Query Operator on the legacy collection to produce a sequence that implements `IEnumerable<T>`, thereby allowing you access to the full arsenal of the Standard Query Operators.

---

[1] A collection must implement IEnumerable<T> or IEnumerable to be queryable with the Standard Query Operators.

■ **Note** Use the `Cast` or `OfType` operators to perform LINQ queries on legacy, nongeneric C# collections.

To gain access to the Standard Query Operators, add a `using System.Linq;` directive to your code, if one is not already present. You do not need to add an assembly reference because the code is contained in the `System.Core.dll` assembly, which is automatically added to your project by Visual Studio 2010.

Returning IEnumerable<T>, Yielding, and Deferred Queries

It is important to remember that, although many of the Standard Query Operators are prototyped to return an `IEnumerable<T>` and we think of `IEnumerable<T>` as a sequence, the operators are not actually returning the sequence at the time the operators are called. Instead, the operators return an object that when enumerated will *yield* an element from the sequence. It is during enumeration of the returned object that the query is actually performed and an element is yielded to the output sequence. In this way, the query is deferred.

In case you are unaware, when we use the term *yield*, we are referring to the `yield` keyword that was added to the C# language to make writing enumerators easier.

For example, examine the code in Listing 3-2.

Listing 3-2. *A Trivial Sample Query*

```
string[] presidents = {
   "Adams", "Arthur", "Buchanan", "Bush", "Carter", "Cleveland",
   "Clinton", "Coolidge", "Eisenhower", "Fillmore", "Ford", "Garfield",
   "Grant", "Harding", "Harrison", "Hayes", "Hoover", "Jackson",
   "Jefferson", "Johnson", "Kennedy", "Lincoln", "Madison", "McKinley",
   "Monroe", "Nixon", "Obama", "Pierce", "Polk", "Reagan", "Roosevelt",
   "Taft", "Taylor", "Truman", "Tyler", "Van Buren", "Washington", "Wilson"};
IEnumerable<string> items = presidents.Where(p => p.StartsWith("A"));

foreach(string item in items)
   Console.WriteLine(item);
```

The query using the `Where` operator is not actually performed when the line containing the query is executed. Instead, an object is returned. It is during the enumeration of the returned object that the `Where` query is actually performed. This means it is possible that an error that occurs in the query itself may not get detected until the time the enumeration takes place.

■ **Note** Query errors may not be detected until the output sequence is enumerated.

The results of the previous query are the following:

```
Adams
Arthur
```

That query performed as expected. However, we'll intentionally introduce an error. The following code will attempt to index into the fifth character of each president's name. When the enumeration reaches an element whose length is less than five characters, an exception will occur. Remember, though, that the exception will not happen until the output sequence is enumerated. Listing 3-3 shows the sample code.

Listing 3-3. *A Trivial Sample Query with an Intentionally Introduced Exception*

```
string[] presidents = {
  "Adams", "Arthur", "Buchanan", "Bush", "Carter", "Cleveland",
  "Clinton", "Coolidge", "Eisenhower", "Fillmore", "Ford", "Garfield",
  "Grant", "Harding", "Harrison", "Hayes", "Hoover", "Jackson",
  "Jefferson", "Johnson", "Kennedy", "Lincoln", "Madison", "McKinley",
  "Monroe", "Nixon", "Pierce", "Polk", "Reagan", "Roosevelt", "Taft",
  "Taylor", "Truman", "Tyler", "Van Buren", "Washington", "Wilson"};

IEnumerable<string> items = presidents.Where(s => Char.IsLower(s[4]));

Console.WriteLine("After the query.");

foreach (string item in items)
  Console.WriteLine(item);
```

This code compiles just fine, but when run, here are the results:

```
After the query.
Adams
Arthur
Buchanan

Unhandled Exception: System.IndexOutOfRangeException: Index was outside the bounds
of the array.
…
```

Notice the output of `After the query`. It isn't until the fourth element, `Bush`, was enumerated that the exception occurred. The lesson to be learned is that just because a query compiles and seems to have no problem executing, don't assume the query is bug-free.

Additionally, because these types of queries, those returning `IEnumerable<T>`, are deferred, you can call the code to define the query once but use it multiple times by enumerating it multiple times. If you do this, each time you enumerate the results, you will get different results if the data changes. Listing 3-4 shows an example of a deferred query where the query results are not cached and can change from one enumeration to the next.

Listing 3-4. *An Example Demonstrating the Query Results Changing Between Enumerations*

```
// Create an array of ints.
int[] intArray = new int[] { 1,2,3 };

IEnumerable<int> ints = intArray.Select(i => i);

// Display the results.
foreach(int i in ints)
  Console.WriteLine(i);

// Change an element in the source data.
intArray[0] = 5;

Console.WriteLine("---------");

// Display the results again.
foreach(int i in ints)
  Console.WriteLine(i);
```

To make what is happening crystal clear, we will get more technical in our description. When we call the Select operator, an object is returned that is stored in the variable named ints of a type that implements IEnumerable<int>. At this point, the query has not actually taken place yet, but the query is stored in the object named ints. Technically speaking, since the query has not been performed, a sequence of integers doesn't exist yet, but the object named ints knows how to obtain the sequence by performing the query that was assigned to it, which in this case is the Select operator.

When we call the foreach statement on ints the first time, ints performs the query and obtains the sequence one element at a time.

Next we change an element in the original array of integers. Then we call the foreach statement again. This causes ints to perform the query again. Since we changed an element in the original array and the query is being performed again because ints is being enumerated again, the changed element is returned.

Technically speaking, the query we called returned an object that implemented IEnumerable<int>. However, in most LINQ discussions in this book, as well as other discussions outside of this book, it would be said that the query returned a sequence of integers. Logically speaking, this is true and ultimately what we are after. But it is important for you to understand what is really happening.

Here are the results of this code:

```
1
2
3
---------
5
2
3
```

Notice that even though we called the query only once, the results of the enumeration are different for each of the enumerations. This is further evidence that the query is deferred. If it were not, the results of both enumerations would be the same. This could be a benefit or detriment. If you do not want this to happen, use one of the conversion operators that do not return an IEnumerable<T> so that the query is not deferred, such as ToArray, ToList, ToDictionary, or ToLookup, to create a different data structure with cached results that will not change if the data source changes.

Listing 3-5 is the same as the previous code example except instead of having the query return an IEnumerable<int>, it will return a List<int> by calling the ToList operator.

Listing 3-5. *Returning a List So the Query Is Executed Immediately and the Results Are Cached*

```
// Create an array of ints.
int[] intArray = new int[] { 1, 2, 3 };

List<int> ints = intArray.Select(i => i).ToList();

// Display the results.
foreach(int i in ints)
  Console.WriteLine(i);

// Change an element in the source data.
intArray[0] = 5;

Console.WriteLine("---------");

// Display the results again.
foreach(int i in ints)
  Console.WriteLine(i);
```

Here are the results:

```
1
2
3
---------
1
2
3
```

Notice the results do not change from one enumeration to the next. This is because the ToList method is not deferred, and the query is actually performed at the time the query is called.

To return to a technical discussion of what is different between this example and Listing 3-4, while the Select operator is still deferred in Listing 3-5, the ToList operator is not. When the ToList operator is called in the query statement, it enumerates the object returned from the Select operator immediately, making the entire query not deferred.

CHAPTER 3 ■ LINQ TO OBJECTS INTRODUCTION

Func Delegates

Several of the Standard Query Operators are prototyped to take a Func delegate as an argument. This prevents you from having to explicitly declare delegate types. Here are the Func delegate declarations:

```
public delegate TR Func<TR>();
public delegate TR Func<T0, TR>(T0 a0);
public delegate TR Func<T0, T1, TR>(T0 a0, T1 a1);
public delegate TR Func<T0, T1, T2, TR>(T0 a0, T1 a1, T2 a2);
public delegate TR Func<T0, T1, T2, T3, TR>(T0 a0, T1 a1, T2 a2, T3 a3);
```

In each declaration, TR refers to the data type returned. Notice that the return type argument, TR, is at the end of the parameter type template for every overload of the Func delegate. The other type parameters, T0, T1, T2, and T3, refer to the input parameters passed to the method. The multiple declarations exist because some Standard Query Operators have delegate arguments that require more parameters than others. By looking at the declarations, you can see that no Standard Query Operator has a delegate argument that will require more than four input parameters.

Let's take a look at one of the prototypes of the Where operator:

```
public static IEnumerable<T> Where<T>(
  this IEnumerable<T> source,
  Func<T, bool> predicate);
```

The predicate argument is specified as a Func<T, bool>. From this, you can see the predicate method or lambda expression had better accept a single argument, the T parameter, and return a bool. You know this because you know the return type is specified at the end of the parameter template list.

Of course, you can use the Func declaration, as shown in Listing 3-6.

Listing 3-6. *An Example Using One of the Func Delegate Declarations*

```
// Create an array of ints.
int[] ints = new int[] { 1,2,3,4,5,6 };

// Declare our delegate.
Func<int, bool> GreaterThanTwo = i => i > 2;

// Perform the query ... not really.  Don't forget about deferred queries!!!
IEnumerable<int> intsGreaterThanTwo = ints.Where(GreaterThanTwo);

// Display the results.
foreach(int i in intsGreaterThanTwo)
  Console.WriteLine(i);
```

This code provides the following results:

```
3
4
5
6
```

The Standard Query Operators Alphabetical Cross-Reference

Table 3-1 shows the Standard Query Operators listed alphabetically. Since these operators will be separated into chapters based upon whether they are deferred, this table will help you locate each operator in the remaining LINQ to Objects chapters.

Table 3-1. *Standard Query Operators Alphabetical Cross-Reference*

Operator	Purpose	Deferred?
Aggregate	Aggregate	
All	Quantifiers	
Any	Quantifiers	
AsEnumerable	Conversion	✓
Average	Aggregate	
Cast	Conversion	✓
Concat	Concatenation	✓
Contains	Quantifiers	
Count	Aggregate	
DefaultIfEmpty	Element	✓
Distinct	Set	✓
ElementAt	Element	
ElementAtOrDefault	Element	

`Empty`	Generation	✓
`Except`	Set	✓
`First`	Element	
`FirstOrDefault`	Element	
`GroupBy`	Grouping	✓
`GroupJoin`	Join	✓
`Intersect`	Set	✓
`Join`	Join	✓
`Last`	Element	
`LastOrDefault`	Element	
`LongCount`	Aggregate	
`Max`	Aggregate	
`Min`	Aggregate	
`OfType`	Conversion	✓
`OrderBy`	Ordering	✓
`OrderByDescending`	Ordering	✓
`Range`	Generation	✓
`Repeat`	Generation	✓
`Reverse`	Ordering	✓
`Select`	Projection	✓
`SelectMany`	Projection	✓
`SequenceEqual`	Equality	

Single	Element	
SingleOrDefault	Element	
Skip	Partitioning	✓
SkipWhile	Partitioning	✓
Sum	Aggregate	
Take	Partitioning	✓
TakeWhile	Partitioning	✓
ThenBy	Ordering	✓
ThenByDescending	Ordering	✓
ToArray	Conversion	
ToDictionary	Conversion	
ToList	Conversion	
ToLookup	Conversion	
Union	Set	✓
Where	Restriction	✓

A Tale of Two Syntaxes

Since you may write LINQ queries using either query expression syntax or standard dot notation syntax, you may wonder which syntax you should use. In many cases, this is largely a matter of preference as long as the standard query operators you are using in your query are supported by query expression syntax. Not all of the operators are supported by query expression syntax, so when using any of the unsupported operators, you must defer to standard dot notation syntax.

However, you should be aware that you can use a mixture of both syntaxes by enclosing a query expression inside parentheses and appending a call to an unsupported operator like this:

```
IEnumerable<int> oddNumbers = (from n in nums
                               where n % 2 == 1
                               select n).Reverse();
```

Summary

In this chapter, we introduced you to the term *sequence* and its technical data type, `IEnumerable<T>`. If you feel uncomfortable with some of this terminology, we are sure that with time it will become second nature for you. Just think of `IEnumerable<T>` as a sequence of objects you are going to call methods on to do things with those objects.

However, if there is one thing we want you to take with you from this chapter, it is the importance of deferred query execution. It can work for you or against you. Understanding it is key, and being conscious of it is important. It is so important that we have divided the Standard Query Operators into separate chapters based upon this characteristic. The deferred operators are covered in Chapter 4, and the nondeferred operators are covered in Chapter 5.

Since we have deferred queries in your thoughts right now, we will begin an in-depth examination of the deferred operators in the next chapter.

CHAPTER 4

∎∎∎

Deferred Operators

In the previous chapter, we covered what sequences are, the data type that represents them, and the impact of deferred query execution. Because of the importance of deferred query operator awareness, we have separated deferred and nondeferred operators into separate chapters to highlight whether a Standard Query Operator's action is deferred.

In this chapter, we will be covering the deferred query operators. A deferred operator is easy to spot because it has a return type of `IEnumerable<T>` or `IOrderedEnumerable<T>`. Each of these deferred operators will be categorized by its purpose.

To code and execute the examples in this chapter, you will need to make sure you have `using` directives for all the necessary namespaces, references for all the necessary assemblies, and the common code that the examples will share.

Referenced Namespaces

The examples in this chapter will use the `System.Linq`, `System.Collections`, `System.Collections.Generic`, and `System.Data.Linq` namespaces. Therefore, you should add the following `using` directives to your code if they are not present:

```
using System.Linq;
using System.Collections;
using System.Collections.Generic;
using System.Data.Linq;
```

In addition to these namespaces, if you download the companion code, you will see that we have also added a `using` directive for the `System.Diagnostics` namespace. This will not be necessary if you are typing in the examples from this chapter. It is necessary in the companion code because of some housekeeping code we have added.

Referenced Assemblies

In addition to the typical assemblies, you will need references for the `System.Data.Linq.dll` assembly.

Common Classes

Several of the examples in this chapter will require classes to fully demonstrate an operator's behavior. A list of classes that will be shared by more than one example follows.

The Employee class is meant to represent an employee. For convenience, it contains static methods to return an ArrayList or array of employees.

The Shared Employee Class

```
public class Employee
{
  public int id;
  public string firstName;
  public string lastName;

  public static ArrayList GetEmployeesArrayList()
  {
    ArrayList al = new ArrayList();

    al.Add(new Employee { id = 1, firstName = "Joe", lastName = "Rattz" });
    al.Add(new Employee { id = 2, firstName = "William", lastName = "Gates" });
    al.Add(new Employee { id = 3, firstName = "Anders", lastName = "Hejlsberg" });
    al.Add(new Employee { id = 4, firstName = "David", lastName = "Lightman" });
    al.Add(new Employee { id = 101, firstName = "Kevin", lastName = "Flynn" });
    return (al);
  }

  public static Employee[] GetEmployeesArray()
  {
    return ((Employee[])GetEmployeesArrayList().ToArray());
  }
}
```

The EmployeeOptionEntry class represents an award of stock options to a specific employee. For convenience, it contains a static method to return an array of awarded option entries.

The Shared EmployeeOptionEntry Class

```
public class EmployeeOptionEntry
{
  public int id;
  public long optionsCount;
  public DateTime dateAwarded;

  public static EmployeeOptionEntry[] GetEmployeeOptionEntries()
  {
    EmployeeOptionEntry[] empOptions = new EmployeeOptionEntry[] {
```

```
      new EmployeeOptionEntry {
        id = 1,
        optionsCount = 2,
        dateAwarded = DateTime.Parse("1999/12/31") },
      new EmployeeOptionEntry {
        id = 2,
        optionsCount = 10000,
        dateAwarded = DateTime.Parse("1992/06/30")  },
      new EmployeeOptionEntry {
        id = 2,
        optionsCount = 10000,
        dateAwarded = DateTime.Parse("1994/01/01")  },
      new EmployeeOptionEntry {
        id = 3,
        optionsCount = 5000,
        dateAwarded = DateTime.Parse("1997/09/30") },
      new EmployeeOptionEntry {
        id = 2,
        optionsCount = 10000,
        dateAwarded = DateTime.Parse("2003/04/01")  },
      new EmployeeOptionEntry {
        id = 3,
        optionsCount = 7500,
        dateAwarded = DateTime.Parse("1998/09/30") },
      new EmployeeOptionEntry {
        id = 3,
        optionsCount = 7500,
        dateAwarded = DateTime.Parse("1998/09/30") },
      new EmployeeOptionEntry {
        id = 4,
        optionsCount = 1500,
        dateAwarded = DateTime.Parse("1997/12/31") },
      new EmployeeOptionEntry {
        id = 101,
        optionsCount = 2,
        dateAwarded = DateTime.Parse("1998/12/31") }
    };

    return (empOptions);
  }
}
```

The Deferred Operators by Purpose

The deferred Standard Query Operators are organized by their purpose in this section.

Restriction

Restriction operators are used for including or excluding elements of an input sequence.

Where

The Where operator is used to filter elements *into* a sequence.

Prototypes

The Where operator has two prototypes we will cover.

The First Where Prototype

```
public static IEnumerable<T> Where<T>(
  this IEnumerable<T> source,
  Func<T, bool> predicate);
```

This prototype of Where takes an input source sequence and a predicate method delegate and returns an object that, when enumerated, enumerates through the input source sequence yielding elements for which the predicate method delegate returns true.

Because this is an extension method, we do not actually pass the input sequence, as long as we call the Where operator using the instance method syntax.

■ **Note** Thanks to extension methods, it is not necessary to pass the first argument to the Standard Query Operators whose first argument has the this keyword modifier, as long as we call the operator on an object of the same type as the first argument.

When calling Where, you pass a delegate to a predicate method. Your predicate method must accept a type T as input, where T is the type of elements contained in the input sequence, and return a bool. The Where operator will call your predicate method for each element in the input sequence and pass it the element. If your predicate method returns true, Where will yield that element into Where's output sequence. If your predicate method returns false, it will not.

The Second Where Prototype

```
public static IEnumerable<T> Where<T>(
  this IEnumerable<T> source,
  Func<T, int, bool> predicate);
```

The second `Where` prototype is identical to the first one, except it specifies that your predicate method delegate receives an additional integer input argument. That argument will be the index number for the element from the input sequence.

The index is zero-based, so the index passed for the first element will be zero. The last element will be passed the total number of elements in the sequence minus one.

■ **Note** Remember, the index that gets passed will be zero-based.

Exceptions

`ArgumentNullException` is thrown if any of the arguments are `null`.

Examples

Listing 4-1 is an example of calling the first prototype.

Listing 4-1. *An Example of the First Where Prototype*

```
string[] presidents = {
  "Adams", "Arthur", "Buchanan", "Bush", "Carter", "Cleveland",
  "Clinton", "Coolidge", "Eisenhower", "Fillmore", "Ford", "Garfield",
  "Grant", "Harding", "Harrison", "Hayes", "Hoover", "Jackson",
  "Jefferson", "Johnson", "Kennedy", "Lincoln", "Madison", "McKinley",
  "Monroe", "Nixon", "Obama", "Pierce", "Polk", "Reagan", "Roosevelt",
  "Taft", "Taylor", "Truman", "Tyler", "Van Buren", "Washington", "Wilson"};

IEnumerable<string> sequence = presidents.Where(p => p.StartsWith("J"));

foreach (string s in sequence)
  Console.WriteLine("{0}", s);
```

In the preceding example, restricting a sequence using the first prototype of the `Where` operator is as simple as calling the `Where` method on the sequence and passing a lambda expression that returns a `bool` indicating whether an element should be included in the output sequence. In this example, we are returning only those elements that start with the `string` `"J"`. This code will produce the following results when Ctrl+F5 is pressed:

```
Jackson
Jefferson
Johnson
```

Notice we are passing our predicate method using a lambda expression.

Listing 4-2 shows code calling the second prototype of the Where operator. Notice that this version doesn't even use the actual element itself, p; it uses only the index, i. This code will cause every other element, the ones with an odd index number, to be yielded into the output sequence.

Listing 4-2. *An Example of the Second Where Prototype*

```
string[] presidents = {
  "Adams", "Arthur", "Buchanan", "Bush", "Carter", "Cleveland",
  "Clinton", "Coolidge", "Eisenhower", "Fillmore", "Ford", "Garfield",
  "Grant", "Harding", "Harrison", "Hayes", "Hoover", "Jackson",
  "Jefferson", "Johnson", "Kennedy", "Lincoln", "Madison", "McKinley",
  "Monroe", "Nixon", "Obama", "Pierce", "Polk", "Reagan", "Roosevelt",
  "Taft", "Taylor", "Truman", "Tyler", "Van Buren", "Washington", "Wilson"};

IEnumerable<string> sequence = presidents.Where((p, i) => (i & 1) == 1);

foreach (string s in sequence)
  Console.WriteLine("{0}", s);
```

Pressing Ctrl+F5 produces the following results:

```
Arthur
Bush
Cleveland
Coolidge
Fillmore
Garfield
Harding
Hayes
Jackson
Johnson
Lincoln
McKinley
Nixon
Pierce
Reagan
Taft
Truman
Van Buren
Wilson
```

Projection

Projection operators return an output sequence of elements that are generated by selecting elements or instantiating altogether new elements containing portions of elements from an input sequence. The data type of elements in the output sequence may be different from the type of elements in the input sequence.

Select

The Select operator is used to create an output sequence of one type of element from an input sequence of another type of element. It is not necessary that the input element type and the output element type be the same.

Prototypes

There are two prototypes for this operator we will cover.

The First Select Prototype

```
public static IEnumerable<S> Select<T, S>(
  this IEnumerable<T> source,
  Func<T, S> selector);
```

This prototype of Select takes an input source sequence and a selector method delegate as input arguments, and it returns an object that, when enumerated, enumerates the input source sequence yielding a sequence of elements of type S. As mentioned earlier, T and S could be the same type or different types.

When calling Select, you pass a delegate to a selector method via the selector argument. Your selector method must accept a type T as input, where T is the type of elements contained in the input sequence, and it returns a type S element. Select will call your selector method for each element in the input sequence, passing it the element. Your selector method will select the portions of the input element it is interested in, creating a new, possibly different typed element, which may be of an anonymous type, and return it.

The Second Select Prototype

```
public static IEnumerable<S> Select<T, S>(
  this IEnumerable<T> source,
  Func<T, int, S> selector);
```

In this prototype of the Select operator, an additional integer is passed to the selector method delegate. This will be the zero-based index of the input element in the input sequence.

Exceptions

ArgumentNullException is thrown if any of the arguments are null.

Examples

Listing 4-3 shows an example calling the first prototype.

Listing 4-3. An Example of the First Select Prototype

```
string[] presidents = {
  "Adams", "Arthur", "Buchanan", "Bush", "Carter", "Cleveland",
  "Clinton", "Coolidge", "Eisenhower", "Fillmore", "Ford", "Garfield",
  "Grant", "Harding", "Harrison", "Hayes", "Hoover", "Jackson",
  "Jefferson", "Johnson", "Kennedy", "Lincoln", "Madison", "McKinley",
  "Monroe", "Nixon", "Obama", "Pierce", "Polk", "Reagan", "Roosevelt",
  "Taft", "Taylor", "Truman", "Tyler", "Van Buren", "Washington", "Wilson"};

IEnumerable<int> nameLengths = presidents.Select(p => p.Length);

foreach (int item in nameLengths)
  Console.WriteLine(item);
```

Notice we are passing our selector method using a lambda expression. In this case, our lambda expression will return the length of each element in the input sequence. Also notice that, although our input types are strings, our output types are ints.

This code will produce the following results when you press Ctrl+F5:

```
5
6
8
4
6
9
7
8
10
8
4
8
5
7
8
5
6
7
9
7
7
7
7
8
6
5
```

```
5
6
4
6
9
4
6
6
5
9
10
6
```

This is a simple example because we are not generating any classes. To provide an even better demonstration of the first prototype, consider the code in Listing 4-4.

Listing 4-4. *Another Example of the First Select Prototype*

```
string[] presidents = {
   "Adams", "Arthur", "Buchanan", "Bush", "Carter", "Cleveland",
   "Clinton", "Coolidge", "Eisenhower", "Fillmore", "Ford", "Garfield",
   "Grant", "Harding", "Harrison", "Hayes", "Hoover", "Jackson",
   "Jefferson", "Johnson", "Kennedy", "Lincoln", "Madison", "McKinley",
   "Monroe", "Nixon", "Obama", "Pierce", "Polk", "Reagan", "Roosevelt",
   "Taft", "Taylor", "Truman", "Tyler", "Van Buren", "Washington", "Wilson"};

var nameObjs = presidents.Select(p => new { p, p.Length });

foreach (var item in nameObjs)
   Console.WriteLine(item);
```

Notice that our lambda expression is instantiating a new, anonymous type. The compiler will dynamically generate an anonymous type for us that will contain a `string p` and an `int Length`, and our selector method will return that newly instantiated object. Because the type of the returned element is anonymous, we have no type name to reference it by. So, we cannot assign the output sequence from `Select` to an `IEnumerable` of some known type, as we did in the first example where we assigned a variable of type `IEnumerable<int>` to the output sequence. Therefore, we assign the output sequence to a variable specified with the `var` keyword.

■ **Note** Projection operators whose selector methods instantiate anonymous types to return must have their output sequence assigned to a variable whose type is specified with the `var` keyword.

When run by pressing Ctrl+F5, this code produces the following output:

```
{ p = Adams, Length = 5 }
{ p = Arthur, Length = 6 }
{ p = Buchanan, Length = 8 }
{ p = Bush, Length = 4 }
{ p = Carter, Length = 6 }
{ p = Cleveland, Length = 9 }
{ p = Clinton, Length = 7 }
{ p = Coolidge, Length = 8 }
{ p = Eisenhower, Length = 10 }
{ p = Fillmore, Length = 8 }
{ p = Ford, Length = 4 }
{ p = Garfield, Length = 8 }
{ p = Grant, Length = 5 }
{ p = Harding, Length = 7 }
{ p = Harrison, Length = 8 }
{ p = Hayes, Length = 5 }
{ p = Hoover, Length = 6 }
{ p = Jackson, Length = 7 }
{ p = Jefferson, Length = 9 }
{ p = Johnson, Length = 7 }
{ p = Kennedy, Length = 7 }
{ p = Lincoln, Length = 7 }
{ p = Madison, Length = 7 }
{ p = McKinley, Length = 8 }
{ p = Monroe, Length = 6 }
{ p = Nixon, Length = 5 }
{ p = Obama, Length = 5 }
{ p = Pierce, Length = 6 }
{ p = Polk, Length = 4 }
{ p = Reagan, Length = 6 }
{ p = Roosevelt, Length = 9 }
{ p = Taft, Length = 4 }
{ p = Taylor, Length = 6 }
{ p = Truman, Length = 6 }
{ p = Tyler, Length = 5 }
{ p = Van Buren, Length = 9 }
{ p = Washington, Length = 10 }
{ p = Wilson, Length = 6 }
```

There is one problem with this code as it is; we can't control the names of the members of the dynamically generated anonymous class. However, thanks to the *object initialization* features of C# , we could write the lambda expression and specify the anonymous class member names as shown in Listing 4-5.

Listing 4-5. *A Third Example of the First Select Prototype*

```
string[] presidents = {
  "Adams", "Arthur", "Buchanan", "Bush", "Carter", "Cleveland",
  "Clinton", "Coolidge", "Eisenhower", "Fillmore", "Ford", "Garfield",
  "Grant", "Harding", "Harrison", "Hayes", "Hoover", "Jackson",
  "Jefferson", "Johnson", "Kennedy", "Lincoln", "Madison", "McKinley",
  "Monroe", "Nixon", "Obama", "Pierce", "Polk", "Reagan", "Roosevelt",
  "Taft", "Taylor", "Truman", "Tyler", "Van Buren", "Washington", "Wilson"};

var nameObjs = presidents.Select(p => new { LastName = p, Length = p.Length });

foreach (var item in nameObjs)
  Console.WriteLine("{0} is {1} characters long.", item.LastName, item.Length);
```

Notice that we specified a name for each member in the lambda expression and then accessed each member by name in the Console.WriteLine method call. Here are the results of this code:

```
Adams is 5 characters long.
Arthur is 6 characters long.
Buchanan is 8 characters long.
Bush is 4 characters long.
Carter is 6 characters long.
Cleveland is 9 characters long.
Clinton is 7 characters long.
Coolidge is 8 characters long.
Eisenhower is 10 characters long.
Fillmore is 8 characters long.
Ford is 4 characters long.
Garfield is 8 characters long.
Grant is 5 characters long.
Harding is 7 characters long.
Harrison is 8 characters long.
Hayes is 5 characters long.
Hoover is 6 characters long.
Jackson is 7 characters long.
Jefferson is 9 characters long.
Johnson is 7 characters long.
Kennedy is 7 characters long.
Lincoln is 7 characters long.
Madison is 7 characters long.
McKinley is 8 characters long.
Monroe is 6 characters long.
Nixon is 5 characters long.
Obama is 5 characters long.
Pierce is 6 characters long.
```

```
Polk is 4 characters long.
Reagan is 6 characters long.
Roosevelt is 9 characters long.
Taft is 4 characters long.
Taylor is 6 characters long.
Truman is 6 characters long.
Tyler is 5 characters long.
Van Buren is 9 characters long.
Washington is 10 characters long.
Wilson is 6 characters long.
```

For the second Select prototype's example, we will embed the index that is passed to our selector method into our output sequence's element type, as shown in Listing 4-6.

Listing 4-6. An Example of the Second Select Prototype

```
string[] presidents = {
   "Adams", "Arthur", "Buchanan", "Bush", "Carter", "Cleveland",
   "Clinton", "Coolidge", "Eisenhower", "Fillmore", "Ford", "Garfield",
   "Grant", "Harding", "Harrison", "Hayes", "Hoover", "Jackson",
   "Jefferson", "Johnson", "Kennedy", "Lincoln", "Madison", "McKinley",
   "Monroe", "Nixon", "Obama", "Pierce", "Polk", "Reagan", "Roosevelt",
   "Taft", "Taylor", "Truman", "Tyler", "Van Buren", "Washington", "Wilson"};

var nameObjs = presidents.Select((p, i) => new { Index = i, LastName = p });

foreach (var item in nameObjs)
   Console.WriteLine("{0}. {1}", item.Index + 1, item.LastName);
```

This example will output the index number plus one, followed by the name. This code produces the following abbreviated results:

```
1.   Adams
2.   Arthur
3.   Buchanan
4.   Bush
5.   Carter
...
35.  Tyler
36.  Van Buren
37.  Washington
38.  Wilson
```

SelectMany

The `SelectMany` operator is used to create a one-to-many output projection sequence over an input sequence. Although the `Select` operator will return one output element for every input element, `SelectMany` will return zero or more output elements for every input element.

Prototypes

This operator has two prototypes we will cover.

The First SelectMany Prototype

```
public static IEnumerable<S> SelectMany<T, S>(
  this IEnumerable<T> source,
  Func<T, IEnumerable<S>> selector);
```

This prototype of the operator is passed an input source sequence of elements of type T and a selector method delegate, and it returns an object that, when enumerated, enumerates the input source sequence, passing each element individually from the input sequence to the selector method. The selector method then returns an object that, when enumerated, yields zero or more elements of type S in an intermediate output sequence. The `SelectMany` operator will return the concatenated output sequences from each call to your selector method.

The Second SelectMany Prototype

```
public static IEnumerable<S> SelectMany<T, S>(
  this IEnumerable<T> source,
  Func<T, int, IEnumerable<S>> selector);
```

This prototype behaves just like the first prototype, except a zero-based index of the element in the input sequence is passed to your selector method.

Exceptions

`ArgumentNullException` is thrown if any of the arguments are `null`.

Examples

Listing 4-7 shows an example calling the first prototype.

Listing 4-7. *An Example of the First SelectMany Prototype*

```
string[] presidents = {
  "Adams", "Arthur", "Buchanan", "Bush", "Carter", "Cleveland",
  "Clinton", "Coolidge", "Eisenhower", "Fillmore", "Ford", "Garfield",
  "Grant", "Harding", "Harrison", "Hayes", "Hoover", "Jackson",
```

```
   "Jefferson", "Johnson", "Kennedy", "Lincoln", "Madison", "McKinley",
   "Monroe", "Nixon", "Obama", "Pierce", "Polk", "Reagan", "Roosevelt",
   "Taft", "Taylor", "Truman", "Tyler", "Van Buren", "Washington", "Wilson"};

IEnumerable<char> chars = presidents.SelectMany(p => p.ToArray());

foreach (char ch in chars)
  Console.WriteLine(ch);
```

In the preceding example, our selector method receives a string as input, and by calling the ToArray method on that string, it returns an array of chars, which becomes an output sequence of type char.

So, for a single input sequence element, which in this case is a string, our selector method returns a sequence of characters. For each input string, a sequence of characters is output. The SelectMany operator concatenates each of those character sequences into a single character sequence that is returned.

The output of the previous code is as follows:

```
A
d
a
m
s
A
r
t
h
u
r
B
u
c
h
a
n
a
n
B
u
s
h
...
W
a
s
h
i
n
```

g
t
o
n
W
i
l
s
o
n

That was a pretty simple query but not very demonstrative of a more typical usage. For the next example, we will use the Employee and EmployeeOptionEntry common classes.

We will call the SelectMany operator on the array of Employee elements, and for each Employee element in the array, our selector method delegate will return zero or more elements of the anonymous class we create containing the id and the optionsCount from the array of EmployeeOptionEntry elements for that Employee object. Let's take a look at the code to accomplish this in Listing 4-8.

Listing 4-8. *A More Complex Example of the First SelectMany Prototype*

```
Employee[] employees = Employee.GetEmployeesArray();
EmployeeOptionEntry[] empOptions = EmployeeOptionEntry.GetEmployeeOptionEntries();

var employeeOptions = employees
  .SelectMany(e => empOptions
                    .Where(eo => eo.id == e.id)
                    .Select(eo => new {
                                   id = eo.id,
                                   optionsCount = eo.optionsCount }));

foreach (var item in employeeOptions)
  Console.WriteLine(item);
```

In this example, every employee in the Employee array is passed into the lambda expression that is passed into the SelectMany operator. That lambda expression will then retrieve every EmployeeOptionEntry element whose id matches the id of the current employee passed into it by using the Where operator. This is effectively joining the Employee array and the EmployeeOptionEntry array on their id members. The lambda expression's Select operator then creates an anonymous object containing the id and optionsCount members for each matching record in the EmployeeOptionEntry array. This means a sequence of zero or more anonymous objects for each passed employee is returned by the lambda expression. This results in a sequence of sequences that the SelectMany operator then concatenates together.

The previous code produces the following output:

```
{ id = 1, optionsCount = 2 }
{ id = 2, optionsCount = 10000 }
{ id = 2, optionsCount = 10000 }
{ id = 2, optionsCount = 10000 }
{ id = 3, optionsCount = 5000 }
{ id = 3, optionsCount = 7500 }
{ id = 3, optionsCount = 7500 }
{ id = 4, optionsCount = 1500 }
{ id = 101, optionsCount = 2 }
```

Although a bit contrived, the example in Listing 4-9 shows the second SelectMany prototype being called.

Listing 4-9. An Example of the Second SelectMany Prototype

```
string[] presidents = {
  "Adams", "Arthur", "Buchanan", "Bush", "Carter", "Cleveland",
  "Clinton", "Coolidge", "Eisenhower", "Fillmore", "Ford", "Garfield",
  "Grant", "Harding", "Harrison", "Hayes", "Hoover", "Jackson",
  "Jefferson", "Johnson", "Kennedy", "Lincoln", "Madison", "McKinley",
  "Monroe", "Nixon", "Pierce", "Polk", "Reagan", "Roosevelt", "Taft",
  "Taylor", "Truman", "Tyler", "Van Buren", "Washington", "Wilson"};

IEnumerable<char> chars = presidents
  .SelectMany((p, i) => i < 5 ? p.ToArray() : new char[] { });

foreach (char ch in chars)
  Console.WriteLine(ch);
```

The lambda expression we provided checks the incoming index and outputs the array of characters from the input string only if the index is less than five. This means we will get the characters for the first five input strings only, as evidenced by the output results:

```
A
d
a
m
s
A
r
t
h
u
r
B
```

```
u
c
h
a
n
a
n
B
u
s
h
C
a
r
t
e
r
```

Keep in mind that this lambda expression is not all that efficient, particularly if there are a lot of input elements. The lambda expression is getting called for *every* input element. We are merely returning an empty array after the first five input elements. For better performance, we prefer the Take operator that we cover in the next section for this purpose.

The SelectMany operator is also useful for concatenating multiple sequences together. Read our section on the Concat operator later in this chapter for an example.

Partitioning

The partitioning operators allow you to return an output sequence that is a subset of an input sequence.

Take

The Take operator returns a specified number of elements from the input sequence, starting from the beginning of the sequence.

Prototypes

The Take operator has one prototype we will cover.

The Take Prototype

```
public static IEnumerable<T> Take<T>(
  this IEnumerable<T> source,
  int count);
```

This prototype specifies that Take will receive an input source sequence and an integer named count that specifies how many input elements to return, and it will return an object that, when enumerated, will yield the first count number of elements from the input sequence.

If the count value is greater than the number of elements in the input sequence, then every element of the input sequence will be yielded into the output sequence.

Exceptions

ArgumentNullException is thrown if the input source sequence is null.

Examples

Listing 4-10 is an example calling Take.

Listing 4-10. *An Example of the Only Take Prototype*

```
string[] presidents = {
  "Adams", "Arthur", "Buchanan", "Bush", "Carter", "Cleveland",
  "Clinton", "Coolidge", "Eisenhower", "Fillmore", "Ford", "Garfield",
  "Grant", "Harding", "Harrison", "Hayes", "Hoover", "Jackson",
  "Jefferson", "Johnson", "Kennedy", "Lincoln", "Madison", "McKinley",
  "Monroe", "Nixon", "Obama", "Pierce", "Polk", "Reagan", "Roosevelt",
  "Taft", "Taylor", "Truman", "Tyler", "Van Buren", "Washington", "Wilson"};

IEnumerable<string> items = presidents.Take(5);

foreach (string item in items)
  Console.WriteLine(item);
```

This code will return the first five input elements from the presidents array. The results are as follows:

```
Adams
Arthur
Buchanan
Bush
Carter
```

In Listing 4-9, we showed some code that we stated would be more efficient if the Take operator were used instead of relying on the index being passed into the lambda expression. Listing 4-11 provides the equivalent code using the Take operator. We will have the exact same results that we had with our code in Listing 4-9, but this code is much more efficient.

Listing 4-11. *Another Example of the Take Prototype*

```
string[] presidents = {
  "Adams", "Arthur", "Buchanan", "Bush", "Carter", "Cleveland",
  "Clinton", "Coolidge", "Eisenhower", "Fillmore", "Ford", "Garfield",
  "Grant", "Harding", "Harrison", "Hayes", "Hoover", "Jackson",
  "Jefferson", "Johnson", "Kennedy", "Lincoln", "Madison", "McKinley",
  "Monroe", "Nixon", "Obama", "Pierce", "Polk", "Reagan", "Roosevelt",
  "Taft", "Taylor", "Truman", "Tyler", "Van Buren", "Washington", "Wilson"};

IEnumerable<char> chars = presidents.Take(5).SelectMany(s => s.ToArray());

foreach (char ch in chars)
  Console.WriteLine(ch);
```

Just like in the `SelectMany` example using the second prototype, Listing 4-9, the preceding code returns the following results:

```
A
d
a
m
s
A
r
t
h
u
r
B
u
c
h
a
n
a
n
B
u
s
h
C
a
r
t
e
r
```

The differences between this code example and Listing 4-9 are that this one takes only the first five elements from the input sequence and then only they are passed as the input sequence into `SelectMany`. The other code example, Listing 4-9, passes all elements into `SelectMany`; it will just return an empty array for all except the first five.

TakeWhile

The `TakeWhile` operator yields elements from an input sequence while some condition is true, starting from the beginning of the sequence. The remaining input elements will be skipped.

Prototypes

There are two prototypes for the `TakeWhile` operator we will cover.

The First TakeWhile Prototype

```
public static IEnumerable<T> TakeWhile<T>(
  this IEnumerable<T> source,
  Func<T, bool> predicate);
```

The `TakeWhile` operator accepts an input source sequence and a predicate method delegate and returns an object that, when enumerated, yields elements until the predicate method returns `false`. The predicate method receives one element at a time from the input sequence and returns whether the element should be included in the output sequence. If so, it continues processing input elements. Once the predicate method returns `false`, no other input elements will be processed.

The Second TakeWhile Prototype

```
public static IEnumerable<T> TakeWhile<T>(
  this IEnumerable<T> source,
  Func<T, int, bool> predicate);
```

This prototype is just like the first except that the predicate method will also be passed a zero-based index of the element in the input source sequence.

Exceptions

`ArgumentNullException` is thrown if any arguments are `null`.

Examples

Listing 4-12 shows an example calling the first `TakeWhile` prototype.

Listing 4-12. An Example of Calling the First TakeWhile Prototype

```
string[] presidents = {
  "Adams", "Arthur", "Buchanan", "Bush", "Carter", "Cleveland",
```

```
    "Clinton", "Coolidge", "Eisenhower", "Fillmore", "Ford", "Garfield",
    "Grant", "Harding", "Harrison", "Hayes", "Hoover", "Jackson",
    "Jefferson", "Johnson", "Kennedy", "Lincoln", "Madison", "McKinley",
    "Monroe", "Nixon", "Obama", "Pierce", "Polk", "Reagan", "Roosevelt",
    "Taft", "Taylor", "Truman", "Tyler", "Van Buren", "Washington", "Wilson"};

IEnumerable<string> items = presidents.TakeWhile(s => s.Length < 10);

foreach (string item in items)
  Console.WriteLine(item);
```

In the preceding code, we wanted to retrieve input elements until we hit one ten or more characters long. Here are the results:

```
Adams
Arthur
Buchanan
Bush
Carter
Cleveland
Clinton
Coolidge
```

Eisenhower is the name that caused the TakeWhile operator to stop processing input elements. Now, we will provide an example of the second prototype for the TakeWhile operator in Listing 4-13.

Listing 4-13. An Example of Calling the Second TakeWhile Prototype

```
string[] presidents = {
    "Adams", "Arthur", "Buchanan", "Bush", "Carter", "Cleveland",
    "Clinton", "Coolidge", "Eisenhower", "Fillmore", "Ford", "Garfield",
    "Grant", "Harding", "Harrison", "Hayes", "Hoover", "Jackson",
    "Jefferson", "Johnson", "Kennedy", "Lincoln", "Madison", "McKinley",
    "Monroe", "Nixon", "Obama", "Pierce", "Polk", "Reagan", "Roosevelt",
    "Taft", "Taylor", "Truman", "Tyler", "Van Buren", "Washington", "Wilson"};

IEnumerable<string> items = presidents
    .TakeWhile((s, i) => s.Length < 10 && i < 5);

foreach (string item in items)
  Console.WriteLine(item);
```

This example will stop when an input element exceeds nine characters in length or when the sixth element is reached, whichever comes first. Here are the results:

```
Adams
Arthur
Buchanan
Bush
Carter
```

In this case, it stopped because the sixth element was reached.

Skip

The Skip operator skips a specified number of elements from the input sequence starting from the beginning of the sequence and yields the rest.

Prototypes

The Skip operator has one prototype we will cover.

The Skip Prototype

```
public static IEnumerable<T> Skip<T>(
  this IEnumerable<T> source,
  int count);
```

The Skip operator is passed an input source sequence and an integer named count that specifies how many input elements should be skipped and returns an object that, when enumerated, will skip the first count elements and yield all subsequent elements.

If the value of count is greater than the number of elements in the input sequence, the input sequence will not even be enumerated, and the output sequence will be empty.

Exceptions

ArgumentNullException is thrown if the input source sequence is null.

Examples

Listing 4-14 shows a simple example calling the Skip operator.

Listing 4-14. An Example of the Only Skip Prototype

```
string[] presidents = {
  "Adams", "Arthur", "Buchanan", "Bush", "Carter", "Cleveland",
  "Clinton", "Coolidge", "Eisenhower", "Fillmore", "Ford", "Garfield",
  "Grant", "Harding", "Harrison", "Hayes", "Hoover", "Jackson",
  "Jefferson", "Johnson", "Kennedy", "Lincoln", "Madison", "McKinley",
  "Monroe", "Nixon", "Obama", "Pierce", "Polk", "Reagan", "Roosevelt",
```

```
  "Taft", "Taylor", "Truman", "Tyler", "Van Buren", "Washington", "Wilson"};

IEnumerable<string> items = presidents.Skip(1);

foreach (string item in items)
  Console.WriteLine(item);
```

In this example, we wanted to skip the first element. Notice in the following output that we did indeed skip the first input element, "Adams":

```
Arthur
Buchanan
Bush
...
Van Buren
Washington
Wilson
```

SkipWhile

The SkipWhile operator will process an input sequence, skipping elements while a condition is true, and then yield the remaining elements into an output sequence.

Prototypes

There are two prototypes for the SkipWhile operator we will cover.

The First SkipWhile Prototype

```
public static IEnumerable<T> SkipWhile<T>(
  this IEnumerable<T> source,
  Func<T, bool> predicate);
```

The SkipWhile operator accepts an input source sequence and a predicate method delegate and returns an object that, when enumerated, skips elements while the predicate method returns true. Once the predicate method returns false, the SkipWhile operator yields all subsequent elements. The predicate method receives one element at a time from the input sequence and returns whether the element should be skipped in the output sequence.

SkipWhile has a second prototype that looks like this:

The Second SkipWhile Prototype

```
public static IEnumerable<T> SkipWhile<T>(
  this IEnumerable<T> source,
  Func<T, int, bool> predicate);
```

This prototype is just like the first except that our predicate method will also be passed a zero-based index of the element in the input source sequence.

Exceptions

ArgumentNullException is thrown if any arguments are null.

Examples

Listing 4-15 shows an example of the first SkipWhile prototype.

Listing 4-15. An Example Calling the First SkipWhile Prototype

```
string[] presidents = {
  "Adams", "Arthur", "Buchanan", "Bush", "Carter", "Cleveland",
  "Clinton", "Coolidge", "Eisenhower", "Fillmore", "Ford", "Garfield",
  "Grant", "Harding", "Harrison", "Hayes", "Hoover", "Jackson",
  "Jefferson", "Johnson", "Kennedy", "Lincoln", "Madison", "McKinley",
  "Monroe", "Nixon", "Obama", "Pierce", "Polk", "Reagan", "Roosevelt",
  "Taft", "Taylor", "Truman", "Tyler", "Van Buren", "Washington", "Wilson"};

IEnumerable<string> items = presidents.SkipWhile(s => s.StartsWith("A"));

foreach (string item in items)
  Console.WriteLine(item);
```

In this example, we told the SkipWhile method to skip elements as long as they started with the string "A". All the remaining elements will be yielded to the output sequence. Here are the results of the previous query:

```
Buchanan
Bush
Carter
...
Van Buren
Washington
Wilson
```

Now, we will try the second SkipWhile prototype, which is shown in Listing 4-16.

Listing 4-16. An Example of Calling the Second SkipWhile Prototype

```
string[] presidents = {
  "Adams", "Arthur", "Buchanan", "Bush", "Carter", "Cleveland",
```

```
    "Clinton", "Coolidge", "Eisenhower", "Fillmore", "Ford", "Garfield",
    "Grant", "Harding", "Harrison", "Hayes", "Hoover", "Jackson",
    "Jefferson", "Johnson", "Kennedy", "Lincoln", "Madison", "McKinley",
    "Monroe", "Nixon", "Obama", "Pierce", "Polk", "Reagan", "Roosevelt",
    "Taft", "Taylor", "Truman", "Tyler", "Van Buren", "Washington", "Wilson"};

IEnumerable<string> items = presidents
    .SkipWhile((s, i) => s.Length > 4 && i < 10);

foreach (string item in items)
    Console.WriteLine(item);
```

In this example, we are going to skip input elements until the length is no longer greater than four characters or until the tenth element is reached. We will then yield the remaining elements. Here are the results:

```
Bush
Carter
Cleveland
...
Van Buren
Washington
Wilson
```

In this case, we stopped skipping elements once we hit "Bush", since it was not greater than four characters long, even though its index is only 3.

Concatenation

The concatenation operators allow multiple input sequences of the same type to be concatenated into a single output sequence.

Concat

The Concat operator concatenates two input sequences and yields a single output sequence.

Prototypes

There is one prototype for the Concat operator we will cover.

The Concat Prototype

```
public static IEnumerable<T> Concat<T>(
    this IEnumerable<T> first,
    IEnumerable<T> second);
```

In this prototype, two sequences of the same type T of elements are input, as first and second. An object is returned that, when enumerated, enumerates the first input sequence, yielding each element to the output sequence, followed by enumerating the second input sequence, yielding each element to the output sequence.

Exceptions

ArgumentNullException is thrown if any arguments are null.

Examples

Listing 4-17 is an example using the Concat operator, as well as the Take and Skip operators.

Listing 4-17. An Example Calling the Only Concat Prototype

```
string[] presidents = {
  "Adams", "Arthur", "Buchanan", "Bush", "Carter", "Cleveland",
  "Clinton", "Coolidge", "Eisenhower", "Fillmore", "Ford", "Garfield",
  "Grant", "Harding", "Harrison", "Hayes", "Hoover", "Jackson",
  "Jefferson", "Johnson", "Kennedy", "Lincoln", "Madison", "McKinley",
  "Monroe", "Nixon", "Obama", "Pierce", "Polk", "Reagan", "Roosevelt",
  "Taft", "Taylor", "Truman", "Tyler", "Van Buren", "Washington", "Wilson"};

IEnumerable<string> items = presidents.Take(5).Concat(presidents.Skip(5));

foreach (string item in items)
  Console.WriteLine(item);
```

This code takes the first five elements from the input sequence, presidents, and concatenates all *but* the first five input elements from the presidents sequence. The results should be a sequence with the identical contents of the presidents sequence, and they are as follows:

```
Adams
Arthur
Buchanan
Bush
Carter
Cleveland
Clinton
Coolidge
Eisenhower
Fillmore
Ford
Garfield
Grant
Harding
```

```
Harrison
Hayes
Hoover
Jackson
Jefferson
Johnson
Kennedy
Lincoln
Madison
McKinley
Monroe
Nixon
Obama
Pierce
Polk
Reagan
Roosevelt
Taft
Taylor
Truman
Tyler
Van Buren
Washington
Wilson
```

An alternative technique for concatenating is to call the SelectMany operator on an array of sequences, as shown in Listing 4-18.

Listing 4-18. An Example Performing Concatenation with an Alternative to Using the Concat Operator

```
string[] presidents = {
    "Adams", "Arthur", "Buchanan", "Bush", "Carter", "Cleveland",
    "Clinton", "Coolidge", "Eisenhower", "Fillmore", "Ford", "Garfield",
    "Grant", "Harding", "Harrison", "Hayes", "Hoover", "Jackson",
    "Jefferson", "Johnson", "Kennedy", "Lincoln", "Madison", "McKinley",
    "Monroe", "Nixon", "Obama", "Pierce", "Polk", "Reagan", "Roosevelt",
    "Taft", "Taylor", "Truman", "Tyler", "Van Buren", "Washington", "Wilson"};


IEnumerable<string> items = new[] {
                                presidents.Take(5),
                                presidents.Skip(5)
                            }
                            .SelectMany(s => s);


foreach (string item in items)
```

```
Console.WriteLine(item);
```

In this example, we instantiated an array consisting of two sequences: one created by calling the Take operator on the input sequence and another created by calling the Skip operator on the input sequence. Notice that this is similar to the previous example except that we are calling the SelectMany operator on the array of sequences. Also, although the Concat operator allows only two sequences to be concatenated together, since this technique allows an array of sequences, it may be more useful when needing to concatenate more than two sequences together.

■ **Tip** When needing to concatenate more than two sequences together, consider using the SelectMany approach.

Of course, none of this would matter if you did not get the same results as calling the Concat operator. Of course, this isn't a problem, since the results are the same:

```
Adams
Arthur
Buchanan
Bush
Carter
Cleveland
Clinton
Coolidge
Eisenhower
Fillmore
Ford
Garfield
Grant
Harding
Harrison
Hayes
Hoover
Jackson
Jefferson
Johnson
Kennedy
Lincoln
Madison
McKinley
Monroe
Nixon
Obama
Pierce
Polk
```

```
Reagan
Roosevelt
Taft
Taylor
Truman
Tyler
Van Buren
Washington
Wilson
```

Ordering

The ordering operators allow input sequences to be ordered. It is important to notice that both the OrderBy and OrderByDescending operators require an input sequence of type IEnumerable<T> and return a sequence of type IOrderedEnumerable<T>. You cannot pass an IOrderedEnumerable<T> as the input sequence into the OrderBy or OrderByDescending operator. You should not pass an IOrderedEnumerable<T> as the input sequence into the OrderBy or OrderByDescending operators because subsequent calls to the OrderBy or OrderByDescending operators will not honor the order created by previous calls to the OrderBy or OrderByDescending operators. This means that you should not pass the returned sequence from either the OrderBy or OrderByDescending operators into a subsequent OrderBy or OrderByDescending operator call.

If you need more ordering than is possible with a single call to the OrderBy or OrderByDescending operators, you should subsequently call the ThenBy or ThenByDescending operators. You may chain calls to the ThenBy and ThenByDescending operators to subsequent calls to the ThenBy and ThenByDescending operators, because they accept an IOrderedEnumerable<T> as their input sequence and return an IOrderedEnumerable<T> as their output sequence.

For example, this calling sequence is not allowed:

```
inputSequence.OrderBy(s => s.LastName).OrderBy(s => s.FirstName)…
```

Instead, you would use this calling sequence:

```
inputSequence.OrderBy(s => s.LastName).ThenBy(s => s.FirstName)…
```

OrderBy

The OrderBy operator allows an input sequence to be ordered based on a keySelector method that will return a key value for each input element, and an ordered output sequence, IOrderedEnumerable<T>, will be yielded in ascending order based on the values of the returned keys.

The sort performed by the OrderBy operator is specified to be *unstable*. This means it will not preserve the input order of the elements. If two input elements come into the OrderBy operator in a particular order and the key value for both elements is the same, the order of the output elements could be reversed or maintained; there is no guarantee of either. Even though it appears to be stable, since it is specified as unstable, you must always assume it to be unstable. This means you can never depend on the order of the elements coming out of the call to the OrderBy or OrderByDescending operators for any field except the field specified in the method call. Any order that exists in the sequence passed to either of those operators cannot be assumed to be maintained.

Prototypes

The `OrderBy` operator has two prototypes we will cover.

The First OrderBy Prototype

```
public static IOrderedEnumerable<T> OrderBy<T, K>(
  this IEnumerable<T> source,
  Func<T, K> keySelector)
where
  K : IComparable<K>;
```

In this prototype of `OrderBy`, an input `source` sequence is passed into the `OrderBy` operator along with a `keySelector` method delegate, and an object is returned that, when enumerated, enumerates the source input sequence collecting all the elements, passes each element to the `keySelector` method thereby retrieving each key, and orders the sequence using the keys.

The `keySelector` method is passed an input element of type `T` and will return the field within the element that is to be used as the key value, of type `K`, for the input element. Types `T` and `K` may be the same or different types. The type of the value returned by the `keySelector` method must implement the `IComparable` interface.

`OrderBy` has a second prototype that looks like the following:

The Second OrderBy Prototype

```
public static IOrderedEnumerable<T> OrderBy<T, K>(
  this IEnumerable<T> source,
  Func<T, K> keySelector,
  IComparer<K> comparer);
```

This prototype is the same as the first except it allows for a comparer object to be passed. If this version of the `OrderBy` operator is used, then it is not necessary that type `K` implement the `IComparable` interface.

Exceptions

`ArgumentNullException` is thrown if any arguments are `null`.

Examples

Listing 4-19 shows an example of the first prototype.

Listing 4-19. *An Example Calling the First OrderBy Prototype*

```
string[] presidents = {
    "Adams", "Arthur", "Buchanan", "Bush", "Carter", "Cleveland",
    "Clinton", "Coolidge", "Eisenhower", "Fillmore", "Ford", "Garfield",
    "Grant", "Harding", "Harrison", "Hayes", "Hoover", "Jackson",
    "Jefferson", "Johnson", "Kennedy", "Lincoln", "Madison", "McKinley",
    "Monroe", "Nixon", "Obama", "Pierce", "Polk", "Reagan", "Roosevelt",
    "Taft", "Taylor", "Truman", "Tyler", "Van Buren", "Washington", "Wilson"};

IEnumerable<string> items = presidents.OrderBy(s => s.Length);

foreach (string item in items)
    Console.WriteLine(item);
```

This example orders the presidents by the length of their names. Here are the results:

```
Bush
Ford
Polk
Taft
Adams
Grant
Hayes
Nixon
Obama
Tyler
Arthur
Carter
Hoover
Monroe
Pierce
Reagan
Taylor
Truman
Wilson
Clinton
Harding
Jackson
Johnson
Kennedy
Lincoln
Madison
Buchanan
Coolidge
Fillmore
Garfield
Harrison
McKinley
Cleveland
```

```
Jefferson
Roosevelt
Van Buren
Eisenhower
Washington
```

Now, we will try an example of the second prototype by using our own comparer. Before we explain the code, it might be helpful to examine the IComparer interface.

The IComparer<T> Interface

```
interface IComparer<T> {
  int Compare(T x, T y);
}
```

The IComparer interface requires us to implement a single method named Compare. This method will receive two arguments of the same type T and will return an int that is less than zero if the first argument is less than the second, zero if the two arguments are equal, and greater than zero if the second argument is greater than the first. Notice how the C# generics support comes to our aid in this interface and prototype.

For this example, to make it clear we are not using any default comparer, we have created a class that implements the IComparer interface, which will order the elements based on their vowel-to-consonant ratios.

My Implementation of the IComparer Interface for an Example Calling the Second OrderBy Prototype

```
public class MyVowelToConsonantRatioComparer : IComparer<string>
{
  public int Compare(string s1, string s2)
  {
    int vCount1 = 0;
    int cCount1 = 0;
    int vCount2 = 0;
    int cCount2 = 0;

    GetVowelConsonantCount(s1, ref vCount1, ref cCount1);
    GetVowelConsonantCount(s2, ref vCount2, ref cCount2);

    double dRatio1 = (double)vCount1/(double)cCount1;
    double dRatio2 = (double)vCount2/(double)cCount2;

    if(dRatio1 < dRatio2)
      return(-1);
    else if (dRatio1 > dRatio2)
      return(1);
    else
```

```
      return(0);
  }

  //  This method is public so our code using this comparer can get the values
  //  if it wants.
  public void GetVowelConsonantCount(string s,
                                     ref int vowelCount,
                                     ref int consonantCount)
  {
    //  DISCLAIMER:  This code is for demonstration purposes only.
    //  This code treats the letter 'y' or 'Y' as a vowel always,
    //  which linguistically speaking, is probably invalid.

    string vowels = "AEIOUY";

    //  Initialize the counts.
    vowelCount = 0;
    consonantCount = 0;

    //  Convert to uppercase so we are case insensitive.
    string sUpper = s.ToUpper();

    foreach(char ch in sUpper)
    {
      if(vowels.IndexOf(ch) < 0)
        consonantCount++;
      else
        vowelCount++;
    }

    return;
  }
}
```

That class contains two methods, `Compare` and `GetVowelConsonantCount`. The `Compare` method is required by the `IComparer` interface. The `GetVowelConsonantCount` method exists because we needed it internally in the `Compare` method so that the number of vowels and consonants for a given input string could be obtained. We also wanted the ability to call that same logic from outside the `Compare` method so that we could obtain the values for display when we looped through our ordered sequence.

The logic of what our comparer is doing isn't that significant. It is highly unlikely that you will ever need to determine the vowel-to-consonant ratio for a string, much less compare two strings based on that ratio. What is important is how we created a class implementing the `IComparer` interface by implementing a `Compare` method. You can see the nitty-gritty implementation of the `Compare` method by examining the if/else block at the bottom of the `Compare` method. As you can see, in that block of code, we return -1, 1, or 0, thereby adhering to the contract of the `IComparer` interface.

Now, we will call the code, which is shown in Listing 4-20.

Listing 4-20. *An Example Calling the Second OrderBy Prototype*

```
string[] presidents = {
  "Adams", "Arthur", "Buchanan", "Bush", "Carter", "Cleveland",
  "Clinton", "Coolidge", "Eisenhower", "Fillmore", "Ford", "Garfield",
  "Grant", "Harding", "Harrison", "Hayes", "Hoover", "Jackson",
  "Jefferson", "Johnson", "Kennedy", "Lincoln", "Madison", "McKinley",
  "Monroe", "Nixon", "Obama", "Pierce", "Polk", "Reagan", "Roosevelt",
  "Taft", "Taylor", "Truman", "Tyler", "Van Buren", "Washington", "Wilson"};

MyVowelToConsonantRatioComparer myComp = new MyVowelToConsonantRatioComparer();

IEnumerable<string> namesByVToCRatio = presidents
  .OrderBy((s => s), myComp);

foreach (string item in namesByVToCRatio)
{
  int vCount = 0;
  int cCount = 0;

  myComp.GetVowelConsonantCount(item, ref vCount, ref cCount);
  double dRatio = (double)vCount / (double)cCount;

  Console.WriteLine(item + " - " + dRatio + " - " + vCount + ":" + cCount);
}
```

In the preceding example, you can see that we instantiate our comparer before calling the OrderBy operator. We could instantiate it in the OrderBy method call, but then we would not have a reference to it when we want to call it in the foreach loop. Here are the results of this code:

```
Grant - 0.25 - 1:4
Bush - 0.333333333333333 - 1:3
Ford - 0.333333333333333 - 1:3
Polk - 0.333333333333333 - 1:3
Taft - 0.333333333333333 - 1:3
Clinton - 0.4 - 2:5
Harding - 0.4 - 2:5
Jackson - 0.4 - 2:5
Johnson - 0.4 - 2:5
Lincoln - 0.4 - 2:5
Washington - 0.428571428571429 - 3:7
Arthur - 0.5 - 2:4
Carter - 0.5 - 2:4
Cleveland - 0.5 - 3:6
Jefferson - 0.5 - 3:6
Truman - 0.5 - 2:4
Van Buren - 0.5 - 3:6
```

```
Wilson - 0.5 - 2:4
Buchanan - 0.6 - 3:5
Fillmore - 0.6 - 3:5
Garfield - 0.6 - 3:5
Harrison - 0.6 - 3:5
McKinley - 0.6 - 3:5
Adams - 0.666666666666667 - 2:3
Nixon - 0.666666666666667 - 2:3
Tyler - 0.666666666666667 - 2:3
Kennedy - 0.75 - 3:4
Madison - 0.75 - 3:4
Roosevelt - 0.8 - 4:5
Coolidge - 1 - 4:4
Eisenhower - 1 - 5:5
Hoover - 1 - 3:3
Monroe - 1 - 3:3
Pierce - 1 - 3:3
Reagan - 1 - 3:3
Taylor - 1 - 3:3
Hayes - 1.5 - 3:2
Obama - 1.5 - 3:2
```

As you can see, the presidents with the lower vowel-to-consonant ratios come first.

OrderByDescending

This operator is prototyped and behaves just like the OrderBy operator, except that it orders in descending order.

Prototypes

This operator has two prototypes we will cover.

The First OrderByDescending Prototype

```
public static IOrderedEnumerable<T> OrderByDescending<T, K>(
  this IEnumerable<T> source,
  Func<T, K> keySelector)
where
  K : IComparable<K>;
```

This prototype of the OrderByDescending operator behaves just like its equivalent OrderBy prototype except the order will be descending.

■ **Caution** The sorting performed by OrderBy and OrderByDescending is unstable.

OrderByDescending has a second prototype that looks like the following:

The Second OrderByDescending Prototype

```
public static IOrderedEnumerable<T> OrderByDescending<T, K>(
  this IEnumerable<T> source,
  Func<T, K> keySelector,
  IComparer<K> comparer);
```

This prototype is the same as the first except it allows for a comparer object to be passed. If this version of the OrderByDescending operator is used, then it is not necessary that type K implement the IComparable interface.

Exceptions

ArgumentNullException is thrown if any arguments are null.

Examples

In the example of the first prototype shown in Listing 4-21, we will order the presidents in descending order by their names.

Listing 4-21. An Example Calling the First OrderByDescending Prototype

```
string[] presidents = {
  "Adams", "Arthur", "Buchanan", "Bush", "Carter", "Cleveland",
  "Clinton", "Coolidge", "Eisenhower", "Fillmore", "Ford", "Garfield",
  "Grant", "Harding", "Harrison", "Hayes", "Hoover", "Jackson",
  "Jefferson", "Johnson", "Kennedy", "Lincoln", "Madison", "McKinley",
  "Monroe", "Nixon", "Obama", "Pierce", "Polk", "Reagan", "Roosevelt",
  "Taft", "Taylor", "Truman", "Tyler", "Van Buren", "Washington", "Wilson"};

IEnumerable<string> items = presidents.OrderByDescending(s => s);

foreach (string item in items)
  Console.WriteLine(item);
```

As you can see, the president names are in descending order:

```
Wilson
Washington
Van Buren
```

```
Tyler
Truman
Taylor
Taft
Roosevelt
Reagan
Polk
Pierce
Obama
Nixon
Monroe
McKinley
Madison
Lincoln
Kennedy
Johnson
Jefferson
Jackson
Hoover
Hayes
Harrison
Harding
Grant
Garfield
Ford
Fillmore
Eisenhower
Coolidge
Clinton
Cleveland
Carter
Bush
Buchanan
Arthur
Adams
```

Now, we will try an example of the second OrderByDescending prototype. We will use the same example that we used for the second prototype of the OrderBy operator, except instead of calling the OrderBy operator, we will call the OrderByDescending operator. We will be using the same comparer, MyVowelToConsonantRatioComparer, that we used in that example. Listing 4-22 shows the code.

Listing 4-22. *An Example Calling the Second OrderByDescending Prototype*

```
string[] presidents = {
  "Adams", "Arthur", "Buchanan", "Bush", "Carter", "Cleveland",
  "Clinton", "Coolidge", "Eisenhower", "Fillmore", "Ford", "Garfield",
```

```
   "Grant", "Harding", "Harrison", "Hayes", "Hoover", "Jackson",
   "Jefferson", "Johnson", "Kennedy", "Lincoln", "Madison", "McKinley",
   "Monroe", "Nixon", "Obama", "Pierce", "Polk", "Reagan", "Roosevelt",
   "Taft", "Taylor", "Truman", "Tyler", "Van Buren", "Washington", "Wilson"};

MyVowelToConsonantRatioComparer myComp = new MyVowelToConsonantRatioComparer();

IEnumerable<string> namesByVToCRatio = presidents
  .OrderByDescending((s => s), myComp);

foreach (string item in namesByVToCRatio)
{
  int vCount = 0;
  int cCount = 0;

  myComp.GetVowelConsonantCount(item, ref vCount, ref cCount);
  double dRatio = (double)vCount / (double)cCount;

  Console.WriteLine(item + " - " + dRatio + " - " + vCount + ":" + cCount);
}
```

This example works just like the equivalent OrderBy example. Here are the results:

```
Hayes - 1.5 - 3:2
Obama - 1.5 - 3:2
Coolidge - 1 - 4:4
Eisenhower - 1 - 5:5
Hoover - 1 - 3:3
Monroe - 1 - 3:3
Pierce - 1 - 3:3
Reagan - 1 - 3:3
Taylor - 1 - 3:3
Roosevelt - 0.8 - 4:5
Kennedy - 0.75 - 3:4
Madison - 0.75 - 3:4
Adams - 0.666666666666667 - 2:3
Nixon - 0.666666666666667 - 2:3
Tyler - 0.666666666666667 - 2:3
Buchanan - 0.6 - 3:5
Fillmore - 0.6 - 3:5
Garfield - 0.6 - 3:5
Harrison - 0.6 - 3:5
McKinley - 0.6 - 3:5
Arthur - 0.5 - 2:4
Carter - 0.5 - 2:4
Cleveland - 0.5 - 3:6
```

```
Jefferson - 0.5 - 3:6
Truman - 0.5 - 2:4
Van Buren - 0.5 - 3:6
Wilson - 0.5 - 2:4
Washington - 0.428571428571429 - 3:7
Clinton - 0.4 - 2:5
Harding - 0.4 - 2:5
Jackson - 0.4 - 2:5
Johnson - 0.4 - 2:5
Lincoln - 0.4 - 2:5
Bush - 0.333333333333333 - 1:3
Ford - 0.333333333333333 - 1:3
Polk - 0.333333333333333 - 1:3
Taft - 0.333333333333333 - 1:3
Grant - 0.25 - 1:4
```

These results are the same as the equivalent OrderBy example, except the order is reversed. Now, the presidents are listed by their vowel-to-consonant ratio in descending order.

ThenBy

The ThenBy operator allows an input ordered sequence of type IOrderedEnumerable<T> to be ordered based on a keySelector method that will return a key value, and an ordered output sequence of type IOrderedEnumerable<T> will be yielded.

■ **Note** Both the ThenBy and ThenByDescending operators accept a different type of input sequence than most LINQ to Objects deferred query operators. They take an IOrderedEnumerable<T> as the input sequence. This means either the OrderBy or OrderByDescending operator must be called first to create an IOrderedEnumerable, on which you can then call the ThenBy or ThenByDescending operators.

The sort performed by the ThenBy operator is *stable*. This means it will preserve the input order of the elements for equal keys. So, if two input elements come into the ThenBy operator in a particular order and the key value for both elements is the same, the order of the output elements is guaranteed to be maintained.

■ **Note** Unlike OrderBy and OrderByDescending, ThenBy and ThenByDescending are stable sorts.

Prototypes

The ThenBy operator has two prototypes we will cover.

The First ThenBy Prototype

```
public static IOrderedEnumerable<T> ThenBy<T, K>(
  this IOrderedEnumerable<T> source,
  Func<T, K> keySelector)
where
  K : IComparable<K>;
```

In this prototype of the ThenBy operator, an ordered input sequence of type
IOrderedEnumerable<T> is passed into the ThenBy operator along with a keySelector method
delegate. The keySelector method is passed an input element of type T and will return the field within
the element that is to be used as the key value, of type K, for the input element. Types T and K may be the
same or different types. The value returned by the keySelector method must implement the
IComparable interface. The ThenBy operator will order the input sequence in ascending order based on
those returned keys.

There is a second prototype like this:

The Second ThenBy Prototype

```
public static IOrderedEnumerable<T> ThenBy<T, K>(
  this IOrderedEnumerable<T> source,
  Func<T, K> keySelector,
  IComparer<K> comparer);
```

This prototype is the same as the first except it allows for a comparer object to be passed. If this
version of the ThenBy operator is used, then it is not necessary that type K implement the IComparable
interface.

Exceptions

ArgumentNullException is thrown if any arguments are null.

Examples

Listing 4-23 shows an example of the first prototype.

Listing 4-23. An Example Calling the First ThenBy Prototype

```
string[] presidents = {
  "Adams", "Arthur", "Buchanan", "Bush", "Carter", "Cleveland",
  "Clinton", "Coolidge", "Eisenhower", "Fillmore", "Ford", "Garfield",
  "Grant", "Harding", "Harrison", "Hayes", "Hoover", "Jackson",
  "Jefferson", "Johnson", "Kennedy", "Lincoln", "Madison", "McKinley",
  "Monroe", "Nixon", "Obama", "Pierce", "Polk", "Reagan", "Roosevelt",
```

```
    "Taft", "Taylor", "Truman", "Tyler", "Van Buren", "Washington", "Wilson"};

IEnumerable<string> items = presidents.OrderBy(s => s.Length).ThenBy(s => s);

foreach (string item in items)
    Console.WriteLine(item);
```

This example first orders by the input element length, which in this case is the length of the president's name. It then orders by the element itself. The result is that the names are presented in length order, smallest to largest (ascending), and then alphabetically by name, ascending. Here is the proof:

```
Bush
Ford
Polk
Taft
Adams
Grant
Hayes
Nixon
Obama
Tyler
Arthur
Carter
Hoover
Monroe
Pierce
Reagan
Taylor
Truman
Wilson
Clinton
Harding
Jackson
Johnson
Kennedy
Lincoln
Madison
Buchanan
Coolidge
Fillmore
Garfield
Harrison
McKinley
Cleveland
Jefferson
Roosevelt
```

```
Van Buren
Eisenhower
Washington
```

For an example of the second ThenBy operator prototype, we will again use our MyVowelToConsonantRatioComparer comparer object that we introduced in the example of the second OrderBy prototype. However, to call ThenBy, we first must call either OrderBy or OrderByDescending. For this example, we will call OrderBy and order by the number of characters in the name. This way, the names will be ordered ascending by the number of characters, and then within each grouping of names by length, they will be ordered by their vowel to consonant ratio. Listing 4-24 shows the example.

Listing 4-24. An Example of the Second ThenBy Prototype

```
string[] presidents = {
  "Adams", "Arthur", "Buchanan", "Bush", "Carter", "Cleveland",
  "Clinton", "Coolidge", "Eisenhower", "Fillmore", "Ford", "Garfield",
  "Grant", "Harding", "Harrison", "Hayes", "Hoover", "Jackson",
  "Jefferson", "Johnson", "Kennedy", "Lincoln", "Madison", "McKinley",
  "Monroe", "Nixon", "Obama", "Pierce", "Polk", "Reagan", "Roosevelt",
  "Taft", "Taylor", "Truman", "Tyler", "Van Buren", "Washington", "Wilson"};

MyVowelToConsonantRatioComparer myComp = new MyVowelToConsonantRatioComparer();

IEnumerable<string> namesByVToCRatio = presidents
  .OrderBy(n => n.Length)
  .ThenBy((s => s), myComp);

foreach (string item in namesByVToCRatio)
{
  int vCount = 0;
  int cCount = 0;

  myComp.GetVowelConsonantCount(item, ref vCount, ref cCount);
  double dRatio = (double)vCount / (double)cCount;

  Console.WriteLine(item + " - " + dRatio + " - " + vCount + ":" + cCount);
}
```

This code gives the following results:

```
Bush - 0.333333333333333 - 1:3
Ford - 0.333333333333333 - 1:3
Polk - 0.333333333333333 - 1:3
Taft - 0.333333333333333 - 1:3
Grant - 0.25 - 1:4
Adams - 0.666666666666667 - 2:3
```

```
Nixon - 0.666666666666667 - 2:3
Tyler - 0.666666666666667 - 2:3
Hayes - 1.5 - 3:2
Obama - 1.5 - 3:2
Arthur - 0.5 - 2:4
Carter - 0.5 - 2:4
Truman - 0.5 - 2:4
Wilson - 0.5 - 2:4
Hoover - 1 - 3:3
Monroe - 1 - 3:3
Pierce - 1 - 3:3
Reagan - 1 - 3:3
Taylor - 1 - 3:3
Clinton - 0.4 - 2:5
Harding - 0.4 - 2:5
Jackson - 0.4 - 2:5
Johnson - 0.4 - 2:5
Lincoln - 0.4 - 2:5
Kennedy - 0.75 - 3:4
Madison - 0.75 - 3:4
Buchanan - 0.6 - 3:5
Fillmore - 0.6 - 3:5
Garfield - 0.6 - 3:5
Harrison - 0.6 - 3:5
McKinley - 0.6 - 3:5
Coolidge - 1 - 4:4
Cleveland - 0.5 - 3:6
Jefferson - 0.5 - 3:6
Van Buren - 0.5 - 3:6
Roosevelt - 0.8 - 4:5
Washington - 0.428571428571429 - 3:7
Eisenhower - 1 - 5:5
```

As we intended, the names are first ordered by their length, then by their vowel to consonant ratio.

ThenByDescending

This operator is prototyped and behaves just like the ThenBy operator, except that it orders in descending order.

Prototypes

This operator has two prototypes we will cover.

The First ThenByDescending Prototype

```
public static IOrderedEnumerable<T> ThenByDescending<T, K>(
  this IOrderedEnumerable<T> source,
  Func<T, K> keySelector)
where
  K : IComparable<K>;
```

This prototype of the operator behaves the same as the first prototype of the ThenBy operator, except it orders in descending order.

ThenByDescending has a second prototype that looks like the following:

The Second ThenByDescending Prototype

```
public static IOrderedEnumerable<T> ThenByDescending<T, K>(
  this IOrderedEnumerable<T> source,
  Func<T, K> keySelector,
  IComparer<K> comparer);
```

This prototype is the same as the first except it allows for a comparer object to be passed. If this version of the ThenByDescending operator is used, then it is not necessary that K implement the IComparable interface.

Exceptions

ArgumentNullException is thrown if any arguments are null.

Examples

For our example of the first prototype for the ThenByDescending operator, we will use the same basic example we used in the example of the first prototype of the ThenBy operator, except we will call ThenByDescending instead of ThenBy. Listing 4-25 shows this example.

Listing 4-25. An Example Calling the First ThenByDescending Prototype

```
string[] presidents = {
  "Adams", "Arthur", "Buchanan", "Bush", "Carter", "Cleveland",
  "Clinton", "Coolidge", "Eisenhower", "Fillmore", "Ford", "Garfield",
  "Grant", "Harding", "Harrison", "Hayes", "Hoover", "Jackson",
  "Jefferson", "Johnson", "Kennedy", "Lincoln", "Madison", "McKinley",
  "Monroe", "Nixon", "Obama", "Pierce", "Polk", "Reagan", "Roosevelt",
  "Taft", "Taylor", "Truman", "Tyler", "Van Buren", "Washington", "Wilson"};

IEnumerable<string> items =
  presidents.OrderBy(s => s.Length).ThenByDescending(s => s);

foreach (string item in items)
```

```
Console.WriteLine(item);
```

This produces output where the names within each name length are sorted alphabetically in descending order, which is the reverse order that the ThenBy operator provided:

```
Taft
Polk
Ford
Bush
Tyler
Obama
Nixon
Hayes
Grant
Adams
Wilson
Truman
Taylor
Reagan
Pierce
Monroe
Hoover
Carter
Arthur
Madison
Lincoln
Kennedy
Johnson
Jackson
Harding
Clinton
McKinley
Harrison
Garfield
Fillmore
Coolidge
Buchanan
Van Buren
Roosevelt
Jefferson
Cleveland
Washington
Eisenhower
```

For our example of the second prototype of the ThenByDescending operator, which is shown in Listing 4-26, we will use the same example that we did for the second prototype of the ThenBy operator, except we will call ThenByDescending instead of ThenBy.

Listing 4-26. *An Example of the Second ThenByDescending Prototype*

```
string[] presidents = {
  "Adams", "Arthur", "Buchanan", "Bush", "Carter", "Cleveland",
  "Clinton", "Coolidge", "Eisenhower", "Fillmore", "Ford", "Garfield",
  "Grant", "Harding", "Harrison", "Hayes", "Hoover", "Jackson",
  "Jefferson", "Johnson", "Kennedy", "Lincoln", "Madison", "McKinley",
  "Monroe", "Nixon", "Obama", "Pierce", "Polk", "Reagan", "Roosevelt",
  "Taft", "Taylor", "Truman", "Tyler", "Van Buren", "Washington", "Wilson"};

MyVowelToConsonantRatioComparer myComp = new MyVowelToConsonantRatioComparer();

IEnumerable<string> namesByVToCRatio = presidents
  .OrderBy(n => n.Length)
  .ThenByDescending((s => s), myComp);

foreach (string item in namesByVToCRatio)
{
  int vCount = 0;
  int cCount = 0;

  myComp.GetVowelConsonantCount(item, ref vCount, ref cCount);
  double dRatio = (double)vCount / (double)cCount;

  Console.WriteLine(item + " - " + dRatio + " - " + vCount + ":" + cCount);
}
```

This code provides the following results:

```
Bush - 0.333333333333333 - 1:3
Ford - 0.333333333333333 - 1:3
Polk - 0.333333333333333 - 1:3
Taft - 0.333333333333333 - 1:3
Hayes - 1.5 - 3:2
Obama - 1.5 - 3:2
Adams - 0.666666666666667 - 2:3
Nixon - 0.666666666666667 - 2:3
Tyler - 0.666666666666667 - 2:3
Grant - 0.25 - 1:4
Hoover - 1 - 3:3
Monroe - 1 - 3:3
Pierce - 1 - 3:3
Reagan - 1 - 3:3
Taylor - 1 - 3:3
Arthur - 0.5 - 2:4
Carter - 0.5 - 2:4
```

```
Truman - 0.5 - 2:4
Wilson - 0.5 - 2:4
Kennedy - 0.75 - 3:4
Madison - 0.75 - 3:4
Clinton - 0.4 - 2:5
Harding - 0.4 - 2:5
Jackson - 0.4 - 2:5
Johnson - 0.4 - 2:5
Lincoln - 0.4 - 2:5
Coolidge - 1 - 4:4
Buchanan - 0.6 - 3:5
Fillmore - 0.6 - 3:5
Garfield - 0.6 - 3:5
Harrison - 0.6 - 3:5
McKinley - 0.6 - 3:5
Roosevelt - 0.8 - 4:5
Cleveland - 0.5 - 3:6
Jefferson - 0.5 - 3:6
Van Buren - 0.5 - 3:6
Eisenhower - 1 - 5:5
Washington - 0.428571428571429 - 3:7
```

Just as we anticipated, the names are ordered first by ascending length and then by the ratio of their vowels to consonants, descending.

Reverse

The reverse operator outputs a sequence of the same type as the input sequence but in the reverse order.

Prototypes

There is one prototype for this operator we will cover.

The Reverse Prototype

```
public static IEnumerable<T> Reverse<T>(
  this IEnumerable<T> source);
```

This operator returns an object that, when enumerated, enumerates the elements of the input sequence named source and yields elements for the output sequence in reverse order.

Exceptions

ArgumentNullException is thrown if the source argument is null.

Examples

Listing 4-27 is an example of the prototype of the Reverse operator.

Listing 4-27. An Example Calling the Reverse Operator

```
string[] presidents = {
   "Adams", "Arthur", "Buchanan", "Bush", "Carter", "Cleveland",
   "Clinton", "Coolidge", "Eisenhower", "Fillmore", "Ford", "Garfield",
   "Grant", "Harding", "Harrison", "Hayes", "Hoover", "Jackson",
   "Jefferson", "Johnson", "Kennedy", "Lincoln", "Madison", "McKinley",
   "Monroe", "Nixon", "Obama", "Pierce", "Polk", "Reagan", "Roosevelt",
   "Taft", "Taylor", "Truman", "Tyler", "Van Buren", "Washington", "Wilson"};

IEnumerable<string> items = presidents.Reverse();

foreach (string item in items)
   Console.WriteLine(item);
```

If this works properly, we should see the presidents in the reverse order of the order in the presidents array. Here are the results of the previous code:

```
Wilson
Washington
Van Buren
...
Bush
Buchanan
Arthur
Adams
```

Join

The join operators perform joins across multiple sequences.

Join

The Join operator performs an inner equijoin on two sequences based on keys extracted from each element in the sequences.

Prototypes

The Join operator has one prototype we will cover.

The Join Prototype

```
public static IEnumerable<V> Join<T, U, K, V>(
  this IEnumerable<T> outer,
  IEnumerable<U> inner,
  Func<T, K> outerKeySelector,
  Func<U, K> innerKeySelector,
  Func<T, U, V> resultSelector);
```

Notice that the first argument of the method is named outer. Since this is an extension method, the sequence we call the Join operator on will be referred to as the outer sequence.

The Join operator will return an object that, when enumerated, will first enumerate the inner sequence of type U elements, calling the innerKeySelector method once for each element and storing the element, referenced by its key, in a hash table. Next, the returned object will enumerate the outer sequence of type T elements. As the returned object enumerates each outer sequence element, it will call the outerKeySelector method to obtain its key and retrieve the matching inner sequence elements from the hash table using that key. For each outer sequence element and matching inner sequence element pair, the returned object will call the resultSelector method passing both the outer element and the matching inner element. The resultSelector method will return an instantiated object of type V, which the returned object will place in the output sequence of type V.

The order of the outer sequence elements will be preserved, as will the order of the inner elements within each outer element.

Exceptions

ArgumentNullException is thrown if any arguments are null.

Examples

For this operator's example, instead of using the presidents array that most examples use, we will use the two common classes defined at the beginning of this chapter, Employee and EmployeeOptionEntry.

Here is an example calling the Join operator using those classes. We have formatted the code in Listing 4-28 a little differently than is typical to make each Join argument more easily readable.

Listing 4-28. *Example Code Calling the Join Operator*

```
Employee[] employees = Employee.GetEmployeesArray();
EmployeeOptionEntry[] empOptions = EmployeeOptionEntry.GetEmployeeOptionEntries();

var employeeOptions = employees
  .Join(
    empOptions,       //  inner sequence
    e => e.id,        //  outerKeySelector
    o => o.id,        //  innerKeySelector
    (e, o) => new     //  resultSelector
              {
```

```
                    id = e.id,
                    name = string.Format("{0} {1}", e.firstName, e.lastName),
                    options = o.optionsCount
                });

foreach (var item in employeeOptions)
  Console.WriteLine(item);
```

In the preceding code, we first obtain a couple arrays of data to join using the two common classes. Because we are calling the `Join` operator on the `employees` array, it becomes the outer sequence, and `empOptions` becomes the inner sequence. Here are the results of the `Join` operator:

```
{ id = 1, name = Joe Rattz, options = 2 }
{ id = 2, name = William Gates, options = 10000 }
{ id = 2, name = William Gates, options = 10000 }
{ id = 2, name = William Gates, options = 10000 }
{ id = 3, name = Anders Hejlsberg, options = 5000 }
{ id = 3, name = Anders Hejlsberg, options = 7500 }
{ id = 3, name = Anders Hejlsberg, options = 7500 }
{ id = 4, name = David Lightman, options = 1500 }
{ id = 101, name = Kevin Flynn, options = 2 }
```

Notice that `resultSelector` is creating an anonymous class as the element type for the resulting output sequence. You can detect it is an anonymous class because there is no class name specified in the call to new. Because the type is anonymous, it is a necessity that the resulting output sequence be stored in a variable whose type is specified using the `var` keyword. You cannot specify it is an `IEnumerable<>` of some type, because there is no named type of which to declare it as an `IEnumerable`.

■ **Tip** When the last operator called is returning a sequence of an anonymous type, you must use the `var` keyword to store the sequence.

GroupJoin

The `GroupJoin` operator performs a grouped join on two sequences based on keys extracted from each element in the sequences.

The `GroupJoin` operator works very similarly to the `Join` operator with the exception that the `Join` operator passes a single outer sequence element with a single matching inner sequence element to the `resultSelector` method. This means that multiple matching inner sequence elements for a single outer sequence element result in multiple calls to `resultSelector` for the outer sequence element. With the `GroupJoin` operator, all matching inner sequence elements for a specific outer sequence element are passed to `resultSelector` as a *sequence* of that type of element, resulting in the `resultSelector` method being called only once for each outer sequence element.

Prototypes

This operator has one prototype we will cover.

The GroupJoin Prototype

```
public static IEnumerable<V> GroupJoin<T, U, K, V>(
  this IEnumerable<T> outer,
  IEnumerable<U> inner,
  Func<T, K> outerKeySelector,
  Func<U, K> innerKeySelector,
  Func<T, IEnumerable<U>, V> resultSelector);
```

Notice that the first argument of the method is named `outer`. Since this is an extension method, the sequence the `GroupJoin` operator is called on will be referred to as the *outer sequence*.

The `GroupJoin` operator will return an object that, when enumerated, will first enumerate the `inner` sequence of type `U` elements, calling the `innerKeySelector` method once for each element and storing the element, referenced by its key, in a hash table. Next, the returned object will enumerate the `outer` sequence of type `T` elements. As the returned object enumerates each `outer` sequence element, it will call the `outerKeySelector` method to obtain its key and retrieve the matching `inner` sequence elements from the hash table using that key. For each outer sequence element, the returned object will call the `resultSelector` method, passing both the `outer` element and a *sequence* of the matching `inner` elements so that `resultSelector` can return an instantiated object of type `V`, which the returned object will place in the output sequence of type `V`.

The order of the outer sequence elements will be preserved, as will the order of the inner elements within each `outer` element.

Exceptions

`ArgumentNullException` is thrown if any arguments are `null`.

Examples

For the `GroupJoin` example, we will use the same `Employee` and `EmployeeOptionEntry` classes that we used in the `Join` example. Our sample code, which appears in Listing 4-29, will join the employees to the options and calculate a sum of the options for each employee using the `GroupJoin` operator.

Listing 4-29. An Example of the GroupJoin Operator

```
Employee[] employees = Employee.GetEmployeesArray();
EmployeeOptionEntry[] empOptions = EmployeeOptionEntry.GetEmployeeOptionEntries();

var employeeOptions = employees
  .GroupJoin(
    empOptions,
    e => e.id,
```

```
    o => o.id,
    (e, os) => new
                {
                    id = e.id,
                    name = string.Format("{0} {1}", e.firstName, e.lastName),
                    options = os.Sum(o => o.optionsCount)
                });
```

```
foreach (var item in employeeOptions)
  Console.WriteLine(item);
```

The preceding code is almost identical to the example for the Join operator. However, if you examine the second input argument of the lambda expression passed as the resultSelector method, you will notice that we called the input argument o in the Join example, but we are calling it os in this example. This is because, in the Join example, a single employee option object, o, is passed in this argument, but in the GroupJoin example, a *sequence* of employee option objects, os, is being passed. Then, the last member of our instantiated anonymous object is being set to the sum of the sequence of employee option objects' optionsCount members using the Sum operator that we will be covering in the next chapter (since it is not a deferred query operator). For now, you just need to understand that the Sum operator has the ability to calculate the sum of each element or a member of each element in an input sequence.

This code will provide the following results:

```
{ id = 1, name = Joe Rattz, options = 2 }
{ id = 2, name = William Gates, options = 30000 }
{ id = 3, name = Anders Hejlsberg, options = 20000 }
{ id = 4, name = David Lightman, options = 1500 }
{ id = 101, name = Kevin Flynn, options = 2 }
```

Notice that, in these results, there is one record for each employee containing the sum of all of that employee's option records. Contrast this with the Join operator's example where there was a separate record for each of the employee's option records.

Grouping

The grouping operators assist with grouping elements of a sequence together by a common key.

GroupBy

The GroupBy operator is used to group elements of an input sequence.

Prototypes

All prototypes of the GroupBy operator return a sequence of IGrouping<K, T> elements. IGrouping<K, T> is an interface defined as follows:

The IGrouping<K, T> Interface

```
public interface IGrouping<K, T> : IEnumerable<T>
{
  K Key { get; }
}
```

So, an IGrouping is a sequence of type T with a key of type K.
There are four prototypes we will cover.

The First GroupBy Prototype

```
public static IEnumerable<IGrouping<K, T>> GroupBy<T, K>(
  this IEnumerable<T> source,
  Func<T, K> keySelector);
```

This prototype of the GroupBy operator returns an object that when enumerated, enumerates the input source sequence, calls the keySelector method, collects each element with its key, and yields a sequence of IGrouping<K, E> instances, where each IGrouping<K, E> element is a sequence of elements with the same key value. Key values are compared using the default equality comparer, EqualityComparerDefault. Said another way, the return value of the GroupBy method is a sequence of IGrouping objects, each containing a key and a sequence of the elements from the input sequence having that same key.

The order of the IGrouping instances will be in the same order that the keys occurred in the source sequence, and each element in the IGrouping sequence will be in the order that element was found in the source sequence.

The Second GroupBy Prototype

```
public static IEnumerable<IGrouping<K, T>> GroupBy<T, K>(
  this IEnumerable<T> source,
  Func<T, K> keySelector,
  IEqualityComparer<K> comparer);
```

This prototype of the GroupBy operator is just like the first except instead of using the default equality comparer, EqualityComparerDefault, you provide one.

The Third GroupBy Prototype

```
public static IEnumerable<IGrouping<K, E>> GroupBy<T, K, E>(
  this IEnumerable<T> source,
```

```
  Func<T, K> keySelector,
  Func<T, E> elementSelector);
```

This prototype of the GroupBy operator is just like the first except instead of the entire source element being the element in the output IGrouping sequence for its key, you may specify which part of the input element is output with the elementSelector.

The Fourth GroupBy Prototype

```
public static IEnumerable<IGrouping<K, E>> GroupBy<T, K, E>(
  this IEnumerable<T> source,
  Func<T, K> keySelector,
  Func<T, E> elementSelector,
  IEqualityComparer<K> comparer);
```

This prototype of the GroupBy operator is a combination of the second and third so that you may specify a comparer with the comparer argument, and you may output elements of a different type than the input element type using the elementSelector argument.

Exceptions

ArgumentNullException is thrown if any argument other than the comparer argument is null.

Examples

For our example of the first GroupBy prototype, we will use the common EmployeeOptionEntry class. In this example, in Listing 4-30, we are going to group our EmployeeOptionEntry records by id and display them.

Listing 4-30. An Example of the First GroupBy Prototype

```
EmployeeOptionEntry[] empOptions = EmployeeOptionEntry.GetEmployeeOptionEntries();
IEnumerable<IGrouping<int, EmployeeOptionEntry>> outerSequence =
  empOptions.GroupBy(o => o.id);

// First enumerate through the outer sequence of IGroupings.
foreach (IGrouping<int, EmployeeOptionEntry> keyGroupSequence in outerSequence)
{
  Console.WriteLine("Option records for employee: " + keyGroupSequence.Key);

  // Now enumerate through the grouping's sequence of EmployeeOptionEntry
elements.
  foreach (EmployeeOptionEntry element in keyGroupSequence)
    Console.WriteLine("id={0} : optionsCount={1} : dateAwarded={2:d}",
      element.id, element.optionsCount, element.dateAwarded);
}
```

In the preceding code, notice we are enumerating through an outer sequence named outerSequence, where each element is an object implementing IGrouping containing the key and a sequence of EmployeeOptionEntry elements having that same key.

Here are the results:

```
Option records for employee: 1
id=1 : optionsCount=2 : dateAwarded=12/31/1999
Option records for employee: 2
id=2 : optionsCount=10000 : dateAwarded=6/30/1992
id=2 : optionsCount=10000 : dateAwarded=1/1/1994
id=2 : optionsCount=10000 : dateAwarded=4/1/2003
Option records for employee: 3
id=3 : optionsCount=5000 : dateAwarded=9/30/1997
id=3 : optionsCount=7500 : dateAwarded=9/30/1998
id=3 : optionsCount=7500 : dateAwarded=9/30/1998
Option records for employee: 4
id=4 : optionsCount=1500 : dateAwarded=12/31/1997
Option records for employee: 101
id=101 : optionsCount=2 : dateAwarded=12/31/1998
```

For an example of the second GroupBy prototype, let's assume we know that any employee whose id is less than 100 is considered a founder of the company. Those with an id of 100 or greater are not considered founders. Our task is to list all option records grouped by the option record's employee founder status. All founders' option records will be grouped together, and all nonfounders' option records will be grouped together.

Now, we need an equality comparer that can handle this key comparison for us. Our equality comparer must implement the IEqualityComparer interface. Before examining our comparer, let's take a look at the interface.

The iIEqualityComparer<T> Interface

```
interface IEqualityComparer<T> {
  bool Equals(T x, T y);
  int GetHashCode(T x);
}
```

This interface requires us to implement two methods, Equals and GetHashCode. The Equals method is passed two objects of the same type T and returns true if the two objects are considered to be equal or false otherwise. The GetHashCode method is passed a single object and returns a hash code of type int for that object.

A hash code is a numerical value, typically mathematically calculated based on some portion of the data in an object, known as the *key*, for the purpose of uniquely identifying the object. That calculated hash code functions as the index into some data structure to store that object and find it at a later time. Since it is typical for multiple keys to produce the same hash code, thereby making the hash code truly less than unique, it is also necessary to be able to determine whether two keys are equal. This is the purpose of the Equals method.

Here is our class implementing the IEqualityComparer interface.

A Class Implementing the IEqualityComparer Interface for My Second GroupBy Example

```
public class MyFounderNumberComparer : IEqualityComparer<int>
{
  public bool Equals(int x, int y)
  {
    return(isFounder(x) == isFounder(y));
  }

  public int GetHashCode(int i)
  {
    int f = 1;
    int nf = 100;
    return (isFounder(i) ? f.GetHashCode() : nf.GetHashCode());
  }

  public bool isFounder(int id)
  {
    return(id < 100);
  }
}
```

In addition to the methods required by the interface, we have added a method, isFounder, to determine whether an employee is a founder based on our definition. This just makes the code a little easier to understand. We have made that method public so that we can call it from outside the interface, which you will see us do in our example.

Our equality comparer is going to consider any integer less than 100 as representing a founder, and if two integers signify either both founders or both nonfounders, they are considered equal. For the purposes of producing a hash code, we return a hash code of 1 for a founder and 100 for a nonfounder so that all founders end up in the same group and all nonfounders end up in another group.

Our GroupBy example code is in Listing 4-31.

Listing 4-31. *An Example of the Second GroupBy Prototype*

```
MyFounderNumberComparer comp = new MyFounderNumberComparer();

EmployeeOptionEntry[] empOptions = EmployeeOptionEntry.GetEmployeeOptionEntries();
IEnumerable<IGrouping<int, EmployeeOptionEntry>> opts = empOptions
  .GroupBy(o => o.id, comp);

// First enumerate through the sequence of IGroupings.
foreach (IGrouping<int, EmployeeOptionEntry> keyGroup in opts)
{
  Console.WriteLine("Option records for: " +
    (comp.isFounder(keyGroup.Key) ? "founder" : "non-founder"));
```

```
  // Now enumerate through the grouping's sequence of EmployeeOptionEntry
elements.
  foreach (EmployeeOptionEntry element in keyGroup)
    Console.WriteLine("id={0} : optionsCount={1} : dateAwarded={2:d}",
      element.id, element.optionsCount, element.dateAwarded);
}
```

In the example, we instantiate our equality comparer object ahead of time, as opposed to doing it in the call to the GroupBy method, so that we can use it to call the isFounder method in the foreach loop. Here are the results from this code:

```
Option records for: founder
id=1 : optionsCount=2 : dateAwarded=12/31/1999
id=2 : optionsCount=10000 : dateAwarded=6/30/1992
id=2 : optionsCount=10000 : dateAwarded=1/1/1994
id=3 : optionsCount=5000 : dateAwarded=9/30/1997
id=2 : optionsCount=10000 : dateAwarded=4/1/2003
id=3 : optionsCount=7500 : dateAwarded=9/30/1998
id=3 : optionsCount=7500 : dateAwarded=9/30/1998
id=4 : optionsCount=1500 : dateAwarded=12/31/1997
Option records for: non-founder
id=101 : optionsCount=2 : dateAwarded=12/31/1998
```

As you can see, all employee options records for an employee whose id is less than 100 are grouped with the founders. Otherwise, they are grouped with the nonfounders.

For an example of the third GroupBy prototype, we'll assume we are interested only in getting the dates that the options were awarded for each employee. This code will be very similar to the example for the first prototype.

So in Listing 4-32, instead of returning a sequence of groupings of EmployeeOptionEntry objects, we will have groupings of dates.

Listing 4-32. *An Example of the Third GroupBy Prototype*

```
EmployeeOptionEntry[] empOptions = EmployeeOptionEntry.GetEmployeeOptionEntries();
IEnumerable<IGrouping<int, DateTime>> opts = empOptions
  .GroupBy(o => o.id, e => e.dateAwarded);

// First enumerate through the sequence of IGroupings.
foreach (IGrouping<int, DateTime> keyGroup in opts)
{
  Console.WriteLine("Option records for employee: " + keyGroup.Key);

  // Now enumerate through the grouping's sequence of DateTime elements.
  foreach (DateTime date in keyGroup)
    Console.WriteLine(date.ToShortDateString());
}
```

Notice that in the call to the `GroupBy` operator, `elementSelector`, the second argument, is just returning the `dateAwarded` member. Because we are returning a `DateTime`, our `IGrouping` is now for a type of `DateTime`, instead of `EmployeeOptionEntry`.

Just as you would expect, we now have the award dates of the options grouped by employee:

```
Option records for employee: 1
12/31/1999
Option records for employee: 2
6/30/1992
1/1/1994
4/1/2003
Option records for employee: 3
9/30/1997
9/30/1998
9/30/1998
Option records for employee: 4
12/31/1997
Option records for employee: 101
12/31/1998
```

For the fourth and final prototype, we need to use an `elementSelector` method and a `comparer` object, so we will use a combination of the examples for prototypes two and three. We want to group the dates of awarded options by whether they were awarded to a founding employee, where a founding employee is one whose `id` is less than 100. That code is in Listing 4-33.

Listing 4-33. An Example of the Fourth GroupBy Prototype

```
MyFounderNumberComparer comp = new MyFounderNumberComparer();
EmployeeOptionEntry[] empOptions = EmployeeOptionEntry.GetEmployeeOptionEntries();
IEnumerable<IGrouping<int, DateTime>> opts = empOptions
  .GroupBy(o => o.id, o => o.dateAwarded, comp);

// First enumerate through the sequence of IGroupings.
foreach (IGrouping<int, DateTime> keyGroup in opts)
{
  Console.WriteLine("Option records for: " +
    (comp.isFounder(keyGroup.Key) ? "founder" : "non-founder"));

  // Now enumerate through the grouping's sequence of EmployeeOptionEntry
elements.
  foreach (DateTime date in keyGroup)
    Console.WriteLine(date.ToShortDateString());
}
```

In the output, we should see just dates grouped by founders and nonfounders:

```
Option records for: founder
12/31/1999
6/30/1992
1/1/1994
9/30/1997
4/1/2003
9/30/1998
9/30/1998
12/31/1997
Option records for: non-founder
12/31/1998
```

Set

The set operators are used to perform mathematical set-type operations on sequences.

■ **Tip** The prototypes of the set operators that are covered in this chapter do not work properly for DataSets. For use with DataSets, use the prototypes that are covered in Chapter 10.

Distinct

The Distinct operator removes duplicate elements from an input sequence.

Prototypes

The Distinct operator has one prototype we will cover.

The Distinct Prototype

```
public static IEnumerable<T> Distinct<T>(
  this IEnumerable<T> source);
```

This operator returns an object that, when enumerated, enumerates the elements of the input sequence named source and yields any element that is not equal to a previously yielded element. An element is determined to be equal to another element using their GetHashCode and Equals methods.

Isn't it fortuitous that we just covered how and why the GetHashCode and Equals methods are used?

Exceptions

ArgumentNullException is thrown if the source argument is null.

Examples

For this example, we are going to first display the count of the presidents array, and next we will concatenate the presidents array with itself, display the count of the resulting concatenated sequence, then call the Distinct operator on that concatenated sequence, and finally display the count of the distinct sequence, which should be the same as the initial presidents array.

To determine the count of the two generated sequences, we will use the Count Standard Query Operator. Since it is a nondeferred operator, we will not cover it in this chapter. We will cover it in the next chapter, though. For now, just be aware that it returns the count of the sequence on which it is called.

The code is in Listing 4-34.

Listing 4-34. *An Example of the Distinct Operator*

```
string[] presidents = {
  "Adams", "Arthur", "Buchanan", "Bush", "Carter", "Cleveland",
  "Clinton", "Coolidge", "Eisenhower", "Fillmore", "Ford", "Garfield",
  "Grant", "Harding", "Harrison", "Hayes", "Hoover", "Jackson",
  "Jefferson", "Johnson", "Kennedy", "Lincoln", "Madison", "McKinley",
  "Monroe", "Nixon", "Obama", "Pierce", "Polk", "Reagan", "Roosevelt",
  "Taft", "Taylor", "Truman", "Tyler", "Van Buren", "Washington", "Wilson"};

// Display the count of the presidents array.
Console.WriteLine("presidents count:  " + presidents.Count());

// Concatenate presidents with itself.  Now each element should
// be in the sequence twice.
IEnumerable<string> presidentsWithDupes = presidents.Concat(presidents);
// Display the count of the concatenated sequence.
Console.WriteLine("presidentsWithDupes count:  " + presidentsWithDupes.Count());

// Eliminate the duplicates and display the count.
IEnumerable<string> presidentsDistinct = presidentsWithDupes.Distinct();
Console.WriteLine("presidentsDistinct count:  " + presidentsDistinct.Count());
```

If this works as we expect, the count of the elements in the presidentsDistinct sequence should equal the count of the elements in the presidents sequence. Will our results indicate success?

```
presidents count:  38
presidentsWithDupes count:  76
presidentsDistinct count:  38
```

Yes, they do!

Union

The Union operator returns a sequence of the set union of two source sequences.

Prototypes

This operator has one prototype we will cover.

The Union Prototype

```
public static IEnumerable<T> Union<T>(
  this IEnumerable<T> first,
  IEnumerable<T> second);
```

This operator returns an object that, when enumerated, first enumerates the elements of the input sequence named first, yielding any element that is not equal to a previously yielded element, and then enumerates the second input sequence, again yielding any element that is not equal to a previously yielded element. An element is determined to be equal to another element using their GetHashCode and Equals methods.

Exceptions

ArgumentNullException is thrown if any arguments are null.

Examples

To demonstrate the difference between the Union operator and the Concat operator we covered previously, in the example in Listing 4-35, we will create a first and second sequence from our presidents array that results in the fifth element being duplicated in both sequences. We will then display the count of the presidents array and the first and second sequences, as well as the count of a concatenated and union sequence.

Listing 4-35. *An Example of the Union Operator*

```
string[] presidents = {
  "Adams", "Arthur", "Buchanan", "Bush", "Carter", "Cleveland",
  "Clinton", "Coolidge", "Eisenhower", "Fillmore", "Ford", "Garfield",
  "Grant", "Harding", "Harrison", "Hayes", "Hoover", "Jackson",
  "Jefferson", "Johnson", "Kennedy", "Lincoln", "Madison", "McKinley",
  "Monroe", "Nixon", "Obama", "Pierce", "Polk", "Reagan", "Roosevelt",
  "Taft", "Taylor", "Truman", "Tyler", "Van Buren", "Washington", "Wilson"};

IEnumerable<string> first = presidents.Take(5);
IEnumerable<string> second = presidents.Skip(4);
```

```
//  Since we only skipped 4 elements, the fifth element
//  should be in both sequences.

IEnumerable<string> concat = first.Concat<string>(second);
IEnumerable<string> union = first.Union<string>(second);

Console.WriteLine("The count of the presidents array is: " + presidents.Count());
Console.WriteLine("The count of the first sequence is: " + first.Count());
Console.WriteLine("The count of the second sequence is: " + second.Count());
Console.WriteLine("The count of the concat sequence is: " + concat.Count());
Console.WriteLine("The count of the union sequence is: " + union.Count());
```

If this works properly, the concat sequence should have one more element than the presidents array. The union sequence should contain the same number of elements as the presidents array. The proof, however, is in the pudding:

```
The count of the presidents array is: 38
The count of the first sequence is: 5
The count of the second sequence is: 34
The count of the concat sequence is: 39
The count of the union sequence is: 38
```

Success!

Intersect

The Intersect operator returns the set intersection of two source sequences.

Prototypes

The Intersect operator has one prototype we will cover.

The Intersect Prototype

```
public static IEnumerable<T> Intersect<T>(
  this IEnumerable<T> first,
  IEnumerable<T> second);
```

This operator returns an object that, when enumerated, first enumerates the elements of the input sequence named second, collecting any element that is not equal to a previously collected element. It then enumerates the first input sequence, yielding any element also existing in the collection of elements from the second sequence. An element is determined to be equal to another element using their GetHashCode and Equals methods.

Exceptions

ArgumentNullException is thrown if any arguments are null.

Examples

For our example of the Intersect operator in Listing 4-36, we will use the Take and Skip operators to generate two sequences and get some overlap, just like we did in the Union operator example, where we intentionally duplicated the fifth element. When we call the Intersect operator on those two generated sequences, only the duplicated fifth element should be in the returned intersect sequence. We will display the counts of the presidents array and all the sequences. Lastly, we will enumerate through the intersect sequence displaying each element, which should only be the fifth element of the presidents array.

Listing 4-36. An Example of the Intersect Operator

```
string[] presidents = {
  "Adams", "Arthur", "Buchanan", "Bush", "Carter", "Cleveland",
  "Clinton", "Coolidge", "Eisenhower", "Fillmore", "Ford", "Garfield",
  "Grant", "Harding", "Harrison", "Hayes", "Hoover", "Jackson",
  "Jefferson", "Johnson", "Kennedy", "Lincoln", "Madison", "McKinley",
  "Monroe", "Nixon", "Obama", "Pierce", "Polk", "Reagan", "Roosevelt",
  "Taft", "Taylor", "Truman", "Tyler", "Van Buren", "Washington", "Wilson"};

IEnumerable<string> first = presidents.Take(5);
IEnumerable<string> second = presidents.Skip(4);
//  Since we only skipped 4 elements, the fifth element
//  should be in both sequences.

IEnumerable<string> intersect = first.Intersect(second);

Console.WriteLine("The count of the presidents array is: " + presidents.Count());
Console.WriteLine("The count of the first sequence is: " + first.Count());
Console.WriteLine("The count of the second sequence is: " + second.Count());
Console.WriteLine("The count of the intersect sequence is: " + intersect.Count());

//  Just for kicks, we will display the intersection sequence,
//  which should be just the fifth element.
foreach (string name in intersect)
  Console.WriteLine(name);
```

If this works the way it should, we should have an Intersect sequence with just one element containing the duplicated fifth element of the presidents array, "Carter":

```
The count of the presidents array is: 38
The count of the first sequence is: 5
```

```
The count of the second sequence is: 34
The count of the intersect sequence is: 1
Carter
```

LINQ rocks! How many times have you needed to perform set-type operations on two collections? Wasn't it a pain? Thanks to LINQ, those days are gone.

Except

The `Except` operator returns a sequence that contains all the elements of a first sequence that do not exist in a second sequence.

Prototypes

This operator has one prototype we will cover.

The Except Prototype

```
public static IEnumerable<T> Except<T>(
  this IEnumerable<T> first,
  IEnumerable<T> second);
```

This operator returns an object that, when enumerated, enumerates the elements of the input sequence named `second`, collecting any element that is not equal to a previously collected element. It then enumerates the `first` input sequence, yielding any element from the first sequence not existing in the collection of elements from the second sequence. An element is determined to be equal to another element using their `GetHashCode` and `Equals` methods.

Exceptions

`ArgumentNullException` is thrown if any arguments are `null`.

Examples

For this example, we will use the `presidents` array that we use in most of the examples. Imagine a scenario where you have a primary data source, the `presidents` array, with entries that you need to perform some processing on. As you complete the processing of each entry, you want to add it to a collection of processed entries so that if you need to start processing again, you can use the `Except` operator to produce an exception sequence consisting of the primary data source elements, minus the entries from the processed entry collection. You can then process this exception sequence again without the concern of reprocessing an entry.

For this example in Listing 4-37, we will pretend that we have already processed the first four entries. To obtain a sequence containing the first four elements of the `presidents` array, we will just call the `Take` operator on it.

Listing 4-37. *An Example of the Except Prototype*

```
string[] presidents = {
  "Adams", "Arthur", "Buchanan", "Bush", "Carter", "Cleveland",
  "Clinton", "Coolidge", "Eisenhower", "Fillmore", "Ford", "Garfield",
  "Grant", "Harding", "Harrison", "Hayes", "Hoover", "Jackson",
  "Jefferson", "Johnson", "Kennedy", "Lincoln", "Madison", "McKinley",
  "Monroe", "Nixon", "Obama", "Pierce", "Polk", "Reagan", "Roosevelt",
  "Taft", "Taylor", "Truman", "Tyler", "Van Buren", "Washington", "Wilson"};

//  First generate a processed sequence.
IEnumerable<string> processed = presidents.Take(4);

IEnumerable<string> exceptions = presidents.Except(processed);
foreach (string name in exceptions)
  Console.WriteLine(name);
```

In this example, our results should contain the names of the `presidents` array after the fourth element, `"Bush"`:

```
Carter
Cleveland
Clinton
Coolidge
Eisenhower
Fillmore
Ford
Garfield
Grant
Harding
Harrison
Hayes
Hoover
Jackson
Jefferson
Johnson
Kennedy
Lincoln
Madison
McKinley
Monroe
Nixon
Obama
Pierce
Polk
Reagan
```

```
Roosevelt
Taft
Taylor
Truman
Tyler
Van Buren
Washington
Wilson
```

That worked just as we would have expected.

Conversion

The conversion operators provide a simple and convenient way of converting sequences to other collection types.

Cast

The Cast operator is used to cast every element of an input sequence to an output sequence of the specified type.

Prototypes

The Cast operator has one prototype we will cover.

The Cast Prototype

```
public static IEnumerable<T> Cast<T>(
  this IEnumerable source);
```

The first thing you should notice about the Cast operator is that its first argument, named source, is of type IEnumerable, not IEnumerable<T>, while most of the deferred Standard Query Operators' first arguments are of type IEnumerable<T>. This is because the Cast operator is designed to be called on classes that implement the IEnumerable interface, as opposed to the IEnumerable<T> interface. In particular, we are talking about all the legacy collections prior to C# 2.0 and generics.

You can call the Cast operator on a legacy collection as long as it implements IEnumerable, and an IEnumerable<T> output sequence will be created. Since most of the Standard Query Operators only work on IEnumerable<T> type sequences, you must call some method like this one, or perhaps the OfType operator that we will cover next, to get a legacy collection converted to a sequence the Standard Query Operators can be called on. This is important when trying to use the Standard Query Operators on legacy collections.

This operator will return an object that, when enumerated, enumerates the source data collection, yielding each element cast to type T. If the element cannot be cast to type T, an exception will be thrown. Because of this, this operator should be called only when it is known that every element in the sequence can be cast to type T.

■ **Tip** When trying to perform LINQ queries on legacy collections, don't forget to call `Cast` or `OfType` on the legacy collection to create an `IEnumerable<T>` sequence that the Standard Query Operators can be called on.

Exceptions

`ArgumentNullException` is thrown if the source argument is null, and `InvalidCastException` is thrown if an element in the input source collection cannot be cast to type T.

Examples

For this example, we will use our common `Employee` class's `GetEmployeesArrayList` method to return a legacy, nongeneric `ArrayList`.

In Listing 4-38 is some code illustrating how the data type of the elements of an `ArrayList` get cast to elements in a sequence, `IEnumerable<T>`.

Listing 4-38. *Code Converting an ArrayList to an IEnumerable<T> That Can Be Used with the Typical Standard Query Operators*

```
ArrayList employees = Employee.GetEmployeesArrayList();
Console.WriteLine("The data type of employees is " + employees.GetType());

var seq = employees.Cast<Employee>();
Console.WriteLine("The data type of seq is " + seq.GetType());

var emps = seq.OrderBy(e => e.lastName);
foreach (Employee emp in emps)
  Console.WriteLine("{0} {1}", emp.firstName, emp.lastName);
```

First we call the `GetEmployeesArrayList` method to return an `ArrayList` of `Employee` objects, and then we display the data type of the employees variable. Next we convert that `ArrayList` to an `IEnumerable<T>` sequence by calling the `Cast` operator, and then we display the data type of the returned sequence. Lastly, we enumerate through that returned sequence to prove that the ordering did indeed work.

Here is the output from the code:

```
The data type of employees is System.Collections.ArrayList
The data type of seq is
System.Linq.Enumerable+<CastIterator>d__b0`1[LINQChapter4.Employee]
Kevin Flynn
William Gates
Anders Hejlsberg
David Lightman
Joe Rattz
```

You can see the data type of the employees variable is an ArrayList. It is a little more difficult determining what the data type of seq is. We can definitely see it is different, and it looks like a sequence. We can also see the word CastIterator in its type. Have you noticed that when we discuss the deferred operators that they don't actually return the output sequence but really return an object that, when enumerated, would yield the elements to the output sequence? The seq variable's data type displayed in the previous example is just this kind of object. However, this is an implementation detail and could change.

■ **Caution** The Cast operator will attempt to cast each element in the input sequence to the specified type. If any of those elements cannot be cast to the specified type, an InvalidCastException exception will be thrown. If it is at all possible that there may be elements of differing types, use the OfType operator instead.

OfType

The OfType operator is used to build an output sequence containing only the elements that can be successfully cast to a specified type.

Prototypes

This operator has one prototype we will cover.

The OfType Prototype

```
public static IEnumerable<T> OfType<T>(
  this IEnumerable source);
```

The first thing you should notice about the OfType operator is that, just like the Cast operator, its first argument, named source, is of type IEnumerable, not IEnumerable<T>. Most of the deferred Standard Query Operators' first arguments are of type IEnumerable<T>. This is because the OfType operator is designed to be called on classes that implement the IEnumerable interface, as opposed to the IEnumerable<T> interface. In particular, we are talking about all the legacy collections prior to C# 2.0 and generics.

So, you can call the OfType operator on a legacy collection as long as it implements IEnumerable, and an IEnumerable<T> output sequence will be created. Since most of the Standard Query Operators work on IEnumerable<T> type sequences only, you must call some method like this one, or perhaps the Cast operator, to get the legacy collection converted to a sequence the Standard Query Operators can be called on. This is important when trying to use the Standard Query Operators on legacy collections.

The OfType operator will return an object that, when enumerated, will enumerate the source sequence, yielding only those elements whose type matches the type specified, T.

The OfType operator differs from the Cast operator in that the Cast operator will attempt to cast every element of the input sequence to type T and yield it to the output sequence. If the cast fails, an exception is thrown. The OfType operator will attempt to yield the input element only if it *can* be cast to type T. Technically, the element must return true for element e is T for the element to be yielded to the output sequence.

Exceptions

ArgumentNullException is thrown if the source argument is null.

Examples

For the example in Listing 4-39, we are going to create an ArrayList containing objects of our two common classes, Employee and EmployeeOptionEntry. Once we have the ArrayList populated with objects of both classes, we will first call the Cast operator to show how it fails in this circumstance. We will follow that call with a call to the OfType operator showing its prowess in the same situation.

Listing 4-39. *Sample Code Calling the Cast and OfType Operator*

```
ArrayList al = new ArrayList();
al.Add(new Employee { id = 1, firstName = "Joe", lastName = "Rattz" });
al.Add(new Employee { id = 2, firstName = "William", lastName = "Gates" });
al.Add(new EmployeeOptionEntry { id = 1, optionsCount = 0 });
al.Add(new EmployeeOptionEntry { id = 2, optionsCount = 99999999999 });
al.Add(new Employee { id = 3, firstName = "Anders", lastName = "Hejlsberg" });
al.Add(new EmployeeOptionEntry { id = 3, optionsCount = 848475745 });

var items = al.Cast<Employee>();

Console.WriteLine("Attempting to use the Cast operator ...");
try
{
  foreach (Employee item in items)
    Console.WriteLine("{0} {1} {2}", item.id, item.firstName, item.lastName);
}
catch (Exception ex)
{
  Console.WriteLine("{0}{1}", ex.Message, System.Environment.NewLine);
}

Console.WriteLine("Attempting to use the OfType operator ...");
var items2 = al.OfType<Employee>();
foreach (Employee item in items2)
  Console.WriteLine("{0} {1} {2}", item.id, item.firstName, item.lastName);
```

Once we have the ArrayList created and populated, we call the Cast operator. The next step is to try to enumerate it. This is a necessary step because the Cast operator is deferred. If we never enumerate the results of that query, it will never be performed, and we would not detect a problem. Notice that we wrapped the foreach loop that enumerates the query results with a try/catch block. This is necessary in this case, because we know an exception will be thrown since there are objects of two completely different types. Next, we call the OfType operator and enumerate and display its results. Notice our pluck as we brazenly choose not to wrap our foreach loop in a try/catch block. Of course, in your real production code, you may not want to ignore the protection a try/catch block offers.

Here are the results of this query:

```
Attempting to use the Cast operator ...
1 Joe Rattz
2 William Gates
Unable to cast object of type 'LINQChapter4.EmployeeOptionEntry' to type
'LINQChapter4.Employee'.

Attempting to use the OfType operator ...
1 Joe Rattz
2 William Gates
3 Anders Hejlsberg
```

Notice that we were not able to completely enumerate the query results of the Cast operator without an exception being thrown. But, we were able to enumerate the query results of the OfType operator, and only elements of type Employee were included in the output sequence.

The moral of this story is that if it is feasible that the input sequence contains elements of more than one data type, prefer the OfType operator to the Cast operator.

■ **Tip** If you are trying to convert a nongeneric collection, such as the legacy collection classes, to an IEnumerable<T> type that can be used with the Standard Query Operators operating on that type, use the OfType operator instead of the Cast operator if it is possible that the input collection could contain objects of differing types.

AsEnumerable

The AsEnumerable operator simply causes its input sequence of type IEnumerable<T> to be returned as type IEnumerable<T>.

Prototypes

The AsEnumerable operator has one prototype we will cover.

The AsEnumerable Prototype

```
public static IEnumerable<T> AsEnumerable<T>(
  this IEnumerable<T> source);
```

The preceding prototype declares that the AsEnumerable operator operates on an IEnumerable<T> named source and returns that same sequence typed as IEnumerable<T>. It serves no other purpose than changing the output sequence type at compile time.

This may seem odd since it must be called on an IEnumerable<T>. You may ask, "Why would you possibly need to convert a sequence of type IEnumerable<T> to a sequence of type IEnumerable<T>?" That would be a good question.

The Standard Query Operators are declared to operate on normal LINQ to Objects sequences, those collections implementing the IEnumerable<T> interface. However, other domains' collections, such as those for accessing a database, could choose to implement their own sequence type and operators. Ordinarily, when calling a query operator on a collection of one of those types, a collection-specific operator would be called. The AsEnumerable operator allows the input sequence to be cast as a normal IEnumerable<T> sequence, allowing a Standard Query Operator method to be called.

For example, when we cover LINQ to SQL in a later part of this book, you will see that LINQ to SQL actually uses its own type of sequence, IQueryable<T>, and implements its own operators. The LINQ to SQL operators will be called on sequences of type IQueryable<T>. When you call the Where method on a sequence of type IQueryable<T>, it is the LINQ to SQL Where method that will get called, not the LINQ to Objects Standard Query Operator Where method. In fact, without the AsEnumerable method, you cannot call a Standard Query Operator on a sequence of type IQueryable<T>. If you try to call one of the Standard Query Operators, you will get an exception unless a LINQ to SQL operator exists with the same name, and the LINQ to SQL operator will be called. With the AsEnumerable operator, you can call it to cast the IQueryable<T> sequence to an IEnumerable<T> sequence, thereby allowing Standard Query Operators to be called. This becomes very handy when you need to control in which API an operator is called.

Exceptions

There are no exceptions.

Examples

To better understand this operator, we need a situation where a domain-specific operator is implemented. For that, we need a LINQ to SQL example. We will start with the first LINQ to SQL example in this book from Chapter 1. For your perusal, here is that example.

Reprinted Here for Convenience Is Listing 1-3

```
using System;
using System.Linq;
using System.Data.Linq;

using nwind;

Northwind db = new Northwind(@"Data Source=.\SQLEXPRESS;Initial
Catalog=Northwind");

var custs =
  from c in db.Customers
  where c.City == "Rio de Janeiro"
  select c;

foreach (var cust in custs)
  Console.WriteLine("{0}", cust.CompanyName);
```

Here are the results of that example:

```
Hanari Carnes
Que Delícia
Ricardo Adocicados
```

For that example to work, you must add the System.Data.Linq.dll assembly to your project, add a using directive for the nwind namespace, and add the generated entity classes that we will cover in the LINQ to SQL chapters to your project. Additionally, you may need to tweak the connection string.

Let's assume that we need to reverse the order of the records coming from the database for some reason. We are not concerned because we know there is a Reverse operator that we covered earlier in this chapter. Listing 4-40 shows the previous example modified to call the Reverse operator.

Listing 4-40. *Calling the Reverse Operator*

```
Northwind db = new Northwind(@"Data Source=.\SQLEXPRESS;Initial
Catalog=Northwind");

var custs =
  (from c in db.Customers
   where c.City == "Rio de Janeiro"
   select c)
  .Reverse();

foreach (var cust in custs)
  Console.WriteLine("{0}", cust.CompanyName);
```

It seems simple enough. As you can see, our only change is to add the call to the Reverse method. The code compiles just fine. Here are the results of the example:

```
Unhandled Exception: System.NotSupportedException: The query operator 'Reverse' is
not supported.
...
```

Boy, that seemed like it should have been so simple; what happened? What happened is that there is no Reverse method for the IQueryable<T> interface, so the exception was thrown. We need to use the AsEnumerable method to convert the sequence of type IQueryable<T> to a sequence of type IEnumerable<T> so that when we call the Reverse method, the IEnumerable<T> Reverse method gets called. The code modified to do this is in Listing 4-41.

Listing 4-41. *Calling the AsEnumerable Operator Before Calling the Reverse Operator*

```
Northwind db = new Northwind(@"Data Source=.\SQLEXPRESS;Initial
Catalog=Northwind");

var custs =
  (from c in db.Customers
   where c.City == "Rio de Janeiro"
```

```
  select c)
  .AsEnumerable()
  .Reverse();

foreach (var cust in custs)
  Console.WriteLine("{0}", cust.CompanyName);
```

Now, we are calling the AsEnumerable method first, followed by the Reverse operator, so the LINQ to Objects Reverse operator will be called. Here are the results:

```
Ricardo Adocicados
Que Delícia
Hanari Carnes
```

Those results are in the reverse order of the initial example, so it worked.

Element

The element operators allow you to retrieve single elements from an input sequence.

DefaultIfEmpty

The DefaultIfEmpty operator returns a sequence containing a default element if the input source sequence is empty.

Prototypes

There are two prototypes for the DefaultIfEmpty operator we will cover.

The First DefaultIfEmpty Prototype

```
public static IEnumerable<T> DefaultIfEmpty<T>(
  this IEnumerable<T> source);
```

This prototype of the DefaultIfEmpty operator returns an object that, when enumerated, enumerates the input source sequence, yielding each element unless the source sequence is empty, in which case it returns a sequence yielding a single element of default(T). For reference and nullable types, the default value is null.

Unlike all the other element type operators, notice that DefaultIfEmpty returns a sequence of type IEnumerable<T> instead of a type T. There are additional element type operators, but they are not included in this chapter, because they are not deferred operators.

The second prototype allows the default value to be specified.

The Second DefaultIfEmpty Prototype

```
public static IEnumerable<T> DefaultIfEmpty<T>(
```

```
this IEnumerable<T> source,
T defaultValue);
```

This operator is useful for all the other operators that throw exceptions if the input source sequence is empty. Additionally, this operator is useful in conjunction with the GroupJoin operator for producing left outer joins.

Exceptions

ArgumentNullException is thrown if the source argument is null.

Examples

Listing 4-42 shows the example of the first DefaultIfEmpty prototype with an empty sequence. In this example, we will not use the DefaultIfEmpty operator to see what happens. We will search our presidents array for "Jones", return the first element, and, if it's not null, output a message.

Listing 4-42. *The First Example for the First DefaultIfEmpty Prototype, Without Using DefaultIfEmpty*

```
string[] presidents = {
  "Adams", "Arthur", "Buchanan", "Bush", "Carter", "Cleveland",
  "Clinton", "Coolidge", "Eisenhower", "Fillmore", "Ford", "Garfield",
  "Grant", "Harding", "Harrison", "Hayes", "Hoover", "Jackson",
  "Jefferson", "Johnson", "Kennedy", "Lincoln", "Madison", "McKinley",
  "Monroe", "Nixon", "Obama", "Pierce", "Polk", "Reagan", "Roosevelt",
  "Taft", "Taylor", "Truman", "Tyler", "Van Buren", "Washington", "Wilson"};

string jones = presidents.Where(n => n.Equals("Jones")).First();
if (jones != null)
  Console.WriteLine("Jones was found");
else
  Console.WriteLine("Jones was not found");
```

Here are the results:

```
Unhandled Exception: System.InvalidOperationException: Sequence contains no
elements
...
```

In the preceding code, the query didn't find any elements equal to "Jones", so an empty sequence was passed to the First operator. The First operator doesn't like empty sequences, so an exception is thrown.

Now, in Listing 4-43, we will call the same code, except we will insert a call to the DefaultIfEmpty operator between the Where operator and the First operator. This way, instead of an empty sequence, a sequence containing a null element will be passed to First.

Listing 4-43. The Second Example for the First DefaultIfEmpty Prototype, Using DefaultIfEmpty

```
string[] presidents = {
  "Adams", "Arthur", "Buchanan", "Bush", "Carter", "Cleveland",
  "Clinton", "Coolidge", "Eisenhower", "Fillmore", "Ford", "Garfield",
  "Grant", "Harding", "Harrison", "Hayes", "Hoover", "Jackson",
  "Jefferson", "Johnson", "Kennedy", "Lincoln", "Madison", "McKinley",
  "Monroe", "Nixon", "Obama", "Pierce", "Polk", "Reagan", "Roosevelt",
  "Taft", "Taylor", "Truman", "Tyler", "Van Buren", "Washington", "Wilson"};

string jones = presidents.Where(n => n.Equals("Jones")).DefaultIfEmpty().First();
if (jones != null)
  Console.WriteLine("Jones was found.");
else
  Console.WriteLine("Jones was not found.");
```

The results now are as follows:

```
Jones was not found.
```

For an example of the second prototype, we are allowed to specify the default value for an empty sequence, as shown in Listing 4-44.

Listing 4-44. An Example for the Second DefaultIfEmpty Prototype

```
string[] presidents = {
  "Adams", "Arthur", "Buchanan", "Bush", "Carter", "Cleveland",
  "Clinton", "Coolidge", "Eisenhower", "Fillmore", "Ford", "Garfield",
  "Grant", "Harding", "Harrison", "Hayes", "Hoover", "Jackson",
  "Jefferson", "Johnson", "Kennedy", "Lincoln", "Madison", "McKinley",
  "Monroe", "Nixon", "Obama", "Pierce", "Polk", "Reagan", "Roosevelt",
  "Taft", "Taylor", "Truman", "Tyler", "Van Buren", "Washington", "Wilson"};

string name =
  presidents.Where(n => n.Equals("Jones")).DefaultIfEmpty("Missing").First();
Console.WriteLine(name);
```

The results are as follows:

```
Missing
```

Next, for one last set of examples, we will perform a left outer join using both the GroupJoin and DefaultIfEmpty operators. We will use our two common classes, Employee and EmployeeOptionEntry. In Listing 4-45 is an example *without* using the DefaultIfEmpty operator.

Listing 4-45. *An Example Without the DefaultIfEmpty Operator*

```
ArrayList employeesAL = Employee.GetEmployeesArrayList();
//  Add a new employee so one employee will have no EmployeeOptionEntry records.
employeesAL.Add(new Employee {
                    id = 102,
                    firstName = "Michael",
                    lastName = "Bolton" });
Employee[] employees = employeesAL.Cast<Employee>().ToArray();
EmployeeOptionEntry[] empOptions = EmployeeOptionEntry.GetEmployeeOptionEntries();

var employeeOptions = employees
  .GroupJoin(
    empOptions,
    e => e.id,
    o => o.id,
    (e, os) => os
      .Select(o => new
                      {
                        id = e.id,
                        name = string.Format("{0} {1}", e.firstName, e.lastName),
                        options = o != null ? o.optionsCount : 0
                      }))
  .SelectMany(r => r);

foreach (var item in employeeOptions)
  Console.WriteLine(item);
```

There are three things we want to point out about this example. First, it is very similar to the example we presented for the GroupJoin operator example when we discussed it. Second, since our common EmployeeOptionEntry class already has a matching object for every employee in the common Employee class, we are getting the ArrayList of employees and adding a new employee, Michael Bolton, to it so that we will have one employee with no matching EmployeeOptionEntry objects. Third, we are not making a call to the DefaultIfEmpty operator in that example.

The results of this query are as follows:

```
{ id = 1, name = Joe Rattz, options = 2 }
{ id = 2, name = William Gates, options = 10000 }
{ id = 2, name = William Gates, options = 10000 }
{ id = 2, name = William Gates, options = 10000 }
{ id = 3, name = Anders Hejlsberg, options = 5000 }
{ id = 3, name = Anders Hejlsberg, options = 7500 }
{ id = 3, name = Anders Hejlsberg, options = 7500 }
{ id = 4, name = David Lightman, options = 1500 }
{ id = 101, name = Kevin Flynn, options = 2 }
```

Please notice that, since there were no matching objects in the EmployeeOptionEntry array for employee Michael Bolton, we got no record for that employee in the output sequence. By using the DefaultIfEmpty operator, we can provide a matching default record, as shown in Listing 4-46.

Listing 4-46. *An Example with the DefaultIfEmpty Operator*

```
ArrayList employeesAL = Employee.GetEmployeesArrayList();
// Add a new employee so one employee will have no EmployeeOptionEntry records.
employeesAL.Add(new Employee {
                  id = 102,
                  firstName = "Michael",
                  lastName = "Bolton" });
Employee[] employees = employeesAL.Cast<Employee>().ToArray();
EmployeeOptionEntry[] empOptions = EmployeeOptionEntry.GetEmployeeOptionEntries();

var employeeOptions = employees
  .GroupJoin(
    empOptions,
    e => e.id,
    o => o.id,
    (e, os) => os
      .DefaultIfEmpty()
      .Select(o => new
                   {
                     id = e.id,
                     name = string.Format("{0} {1}", e.firstName, e.lastName),
                     options = o != null ? o.optionsCount : 0
                   }))
  .SelectMany(r => r);

foreach (var item in employeeOptions)
  Console.WriteLine(item);
```

In the preceding example, we are still adding an employee object for Michael Bolton with no matching EmployeeOptionEntry objects. We am now calling the DefaultIfEmpty operator. Here are the results of our resulting left outer join:

```
{ id = 1, name = Joe Rattz, options = 2 }
{ id = 2, name = William Gates, options = 10000 }
{ id = 2, name = William Gates, options = 10000 }
{ id = 2, name = William Gates, options = 10000 }
{ id = 3, name = Anders Hejlsberg, options = 5000 }
{ id = 3, name = Anders Hejlsberg, options = 7500 }
{ id = 3, name = Anders Hejlsberg, options = 7500 }
{ id = 4, name = David Lightman, options = 1500 }
{ id = 101, name = Kevin Flynn, options = 2 }
```

```
{ id = 102, name = Michael Bolton, options = 0 }
```

As you can see, we now have a record for Michael Bolton even though there are no matching EmployeeOptionEntry objects. From the results, you can see Michael Bolton has received no employee options.

Generation

The generation operators assist with generating sequences.

Range

The Range operator generates a sequence of integers.

Prototypes

There is one prototype for the Range operator we will cover.

The Range Prototype

```
public static IEnumerable<int> Range(
  int start,
  int count);
```

A sequence of integers will be generated starting with the value passed as start and continuing for the number of count.

Notice that this is not an extension method and one of the few Standard Query Operators that does not extend IEnumerable<T>.

■ **Note** Range is not an extension method. It is a static method called on System.Linq.Enumerable.

Exceptions

ArgumentOutOfRangeException is thrown if the count is less than zero or if start plus count minus one is greater than int.MaxValue.

Examples

Listing 4-47. An Example Calling the Range Operator

```
IEnumerable<int> ints = Enumerable.Range(1, 10);
foreach(int i in ints)
```

```
Console.WriteLine(i);
```

Again, we want to stress that we am not calling the Range operator on a sequence. It is a static method of the System.Linq.Enumerable class. There are no surprises here, as the results prove:

```
1
2
3
4
5
6
7
8
9
10
```

Repeat

The Repeat operator generates a sequence by repeating a specified element a specified number of times.

Prototypes

The Repeat operator has one prototype we will cover.

The Repeat Prototype

```
public static IEnumerable<T> Repeat<T>(
  T element,
  int count);
```

This prototype returns an object that, when enumerated, will yield count number of T elements.
Notice that this is not an extension method and one of the few Standard Query Operators that does not extend IEnumerable<T>.

■ **Note** Repeat is not an extension method. It is a static method called on System.Linq.Enumerable.

Exceptions

ArgumentOutOfRangeException is thrown if the count is less than zero.

Examples

In Listing 4-48 we will generate a sequence containing ten elements where each element is the number 2.

Listing 4-48. *Returning a Sequence of Ten Integers All with the Value 2*

```
IEnumerable<int> ints = Enumerable.Repeat(2, 10);
foreach(int i in ints)
  Console.WriteLine(i);
```

Here are the results of this example:

```
2
2
2
2
2
2
2
2
2
2
```

Empty

The `Empty` operator generates an empty sequence of a specified type.

Prototypes

The `Empty` operator has one prototype we will cover.

The Empty Prototype

```
public static IEnumerable<T> Empty<T>();
```

This prototype returns an object that, when enumerated, will return a sequence containing zero elements of type T.

Notice that this is not an extension method and one of the few Standard Query Operators that does not extend IEnumerable<T>.

___

■ **Note** Empty is not an extension method. It is a static method called on System.Linq.Enumerable.

___

Exceptions

There are no exceptions.

Examples

In Listing 4-49 we generate an empty sequence of type `string` using the `Empty` operator and display the `Count` of the generated sequence, which should be zero since the sequence is empty.

Listing 4-49. *An Example to Return an Empty Sequence of Strings*

```
IEnumerable<string> strings = Enumerable.Empty<string>();
foreach(string s in strings)
  Console.WriteLine(s);
Console.WriteLine(strings.Count());
```

Here is the output of the preceding code:

0

Since the sequence is empty, there are no elements to display in the `foreach` loop, so we added the display of the count of the number of elements in the sequence.

Summary

We know this has been a whirlwind tour of the deferred Standard Query Operators. We have attempted to provide examples for virtually every prototype of each deferred operator, instead of just the simplest prototype. We always dislike it when books show the simplest form of calling a method but leave it to you to figure out the more complex versions. Ideally, we will have made calling the more complex prototypes simple for you.

Additionally, we hope that by breaking up the Standard Query Operators into those that are deferred and those that are not, we have properly emphasized the significance this can have on your queries.

While this chapter covered the bulk of the Standard Query Operators, in the next chapter we will conclude our coverage of LINQ to Objects with an examination of the nondeferred Standard Query Operators.

CHAPTER 5

Nondeferred Operators

In the previous chapter, we covered the deferred Standard Query Operators. These are easy to spot because they return either `IEnumerable<T>` or `OrderedSequence<T>`. But the deferred operators are only half the Standard Query Operator story. For the full story, we must also cover the nondeferred query operators. A nondeferred operator is easy to spot because it has a return data type other than `IEnumerable<T>` or `OrderedSequence<T>`. These nondeferred operators are categorized in this chapter by their purpose.

To code and execute the examples in this chapter, you will need to make sure you have `using` directives for all the necessary namespaces. You must also have some common code that the examples share.

Referenced Namespaces

The examples in this chapter will use the `System.Linq`, `System.Collections`, and `System.Collections.Generic` namespaces. Therefore, you should add the following `using` directives to your code if they are not present:

```
using System.Linq;
using System.Collections;
using System.Collections.Generic;
```

In addition to these namespaces, if you download the companion code, you will see that we have also added a `using` directive for the `System.Diagnostics` namespace. This will not be necessary if you are typing in the examples from this chapter. It is necessary in the companion code because of some housekeeping code.

Common Classes

Several of the examples in this chapter require classes to fully demonstrate an operator's behavior. This section describes four classes that will be shared by more than one example, beginning with the `Employee` class.

The `Employee` class is meant to represent an employee. For convenience, it contains static methods to return an `ArrayList` or array of employees.

The Shared Employee Class

```
public class Employee
{
  public int id;
  public string firstName;
  public string lastName;

  public static ArrayList GetEmployeesArrayList()
  {
    ArrayList al = new ArrayList();

    al.Add(new Employee { id = 1, firstName = "Joe", lastName = "Rattz" });
    al.Add(new Employee { id = 2, firstName = "William", lastName = "Gates" });
    al.Add(new Employee { id = 3, firstName = "Anders", lastName = "Hejlsberg" });
    al.Add(new Employee { id = 4, firstName = "David", lastName = "Lightman" });
    al.Add(new Employee { id = 101, firstName = "Kevin", lastName = "Flynn" });
    return (al);
  }

  public static Employee[] GetEmployeesArray()
  {
    return ((Employee[])GetEmployeesArrayList().ToArray());
  }
}
```

The EmployeeOptionEntry class represents an award of stock options to a specific employee. For convenience, it contains a static method to return an array of awarded option entries.

The Shared EmployeeOptionEntry Class

```
public class EmployeeOptionEntry
{
  public int id;
  public long optionsCount;
  public DateTime dateAwarded;

  public static EmployeeOptionEntry[] GetEmployeeOptionEntries()
  {
    EmployeeOptionEntry[] empOptions = new EmployeeOptionEntry[] {
      new EmployeeOptionEntry {
        id = 1,
        optionsCount = 2,
        dateAwarded = DateTime.Parse("1999/12/31") },
      new EmployeeOptionEntry {
        id = 2,
        optionsCount = 10000,
```

```
          dateAwarded = DateTime.Parse("1992/06/30")  },
      new EmployeeOptionEntry {
        id = 2,
        optionsCount = 10000,
        dateAwarded = DateTime.Parse("1994/01/01")  },
      new EmployeeOptionEntry {
        id = 3,
        optionsCount = 5000,
        dateAwarded = DateTime.Parse("1997/09/30") },
      new EmployeeOptionEntry {
        id = 2,
        optionsCount = 10000,
        dateAwarded = DateTime.Parse("2003/04/01")  },
      new EmployeeOptionEntry {
        id = 3,
        optionsCount = 7500,
        dateAwarded = DateTime.Parse("1998/09/30") },
      new EmployeeOptionEntry {
        id = 3,
        optionsCount = 7500,
        dateAwarded = DateTime.Parse("1998/09/30") },
      new EmployeeOptionEntry {
        id = 4,
        optionsCount = 1500,
        dateAwarded = DateTime.Parse("1997/12/31") },
      new EmployeeOptionEntry {
        id = 101,
        optionsCount = 2,
        dateAwarded = DateTime.Parse("1998/12/31") }
    };

    return (empOptions);
  }
}
```

Several of the operators will accept classes that implement the IEqualityComparer<T> interface for the purpose of comparing elements to determine whether they are equal. This is useful for those times when two values may not exactly be equal but you want them to be deemed equal. For example, you may want to be able to ignore case when comparing two strings. However, for this situation, an equality comparison class already exists in the .NET Framework.

Since we covered the IEqualityComparer<T> interface in detail in the previous chapter, we will not explain it here.

For our examples, we want an equality comparison class that will know how to check for the equality of numbers in string format. So for example, the strings "17" and "00017" would be considered equal. Here is our MyStringifiedNumberComparer class that does just that:

The Shared MyStringifiedNumberComparer Class

```
public class MyStringifiedNumberComparer : IEqualityComparer<string>
{
  public bool Equals(string x, string y)
  {
    return(Int32.Parse(x) == Int32.Parse(y));
  }

  public int GetHashCode(string obj)
  {
    return Int32.Parse(obj).ToString().GetHashCode();
  }
}
```

Notice that this implementation of the IEqualityComparer interface will work only for variables of type string, but that will suffice for this example. Basically, for all comparisons, we just convert all the values from string to Int32. This way, "002" gets converted to an integer with a value of 2, so leading zeros do not affect the key value.

For some of the examples in this chapter, we need a class that could have records with nonunique keys. For this purpose, we have created the Actor class here. We will use the birthYear member as the key specifically for this purpose.

The Shared Actor Class

```
public class Actor
{
  public int birthYear;
  public string firstName;
  public string lastName;

  public static Actor[] GetActors()
  {
    Actor[] actors = new Actor[] {
      new Actor { birthYear = 1964, firstName = "Keanu", lastName = "Reeves" },
      new Actor { birthYear = 1968, firstName = "Owen", lastName = "Wilson" },
      new Actor { birthYear = 1960, firstName = "James", lastName = "Spader" },
      new Actor { birthYear = 1964, firstName = "Sandra", lastName = "Bullock" },
    };

    return (actors);
  }
}
```

The Nondeferred Operators by Purpose

The nondeferred Standard Query Operators are organized by their purposes in this section.

Conversion

The following conversion operators provide a simple and convenient way of converting sequences to other collection types.

ToArray

The `ToArray` operator creates an array of type T from an input sequence of type T.

Prototypes

There is one prototype we will cover.

The ToArray Prototype

```
public static T[] ToArray<T>(
  this IEnumerable<T> source);
```

This operator takes an input sequence named `source`, of type T elements, and returns an array of type T elements.

Exceptions

`ArgumentNullException` is thrown if the source argument is `null`.

Examples

For an example demonstrating the `ToArray` operator, we need a sequence of type `IEnumerable<T>`. We will create a sequence of that type by calling the `OfType` operator, which we covered in the previous chapter, on an array. Once we have that sequence, we can call the `ToArray` operator to create an array, as shown in Listing 5-1.

Listing 5-1. A Code Sample Calling the ToArray Operator

```
string[] presidents = {
  "Adams", "Arthur", "Buchanan", "Bush", "Carter", "Cleveland",
  "Clinton", "Coolidge", "Eisenhower", "Fillmore", "Ford", "Garfield",
  "Grant", "Harding", "Harrison", "Hayes", "Hoover", "Jackson",
  "Jefferson", "Johnson", "Kennedy", "Lincoln", "Madison", "McKinley",
  "Monroe", "Nixon", "Obama", "Pierce", "Polk", "Reagan", "Roosevelt",
  "Taft", "Taylor", "Truman", "Tyler", "Van Buren", "Washington", "Wilson"};
```

```
string[] names = presidents.OfType<string>().ToArray();

foreach (string name in names)
  Console.WriteLine(name);
```

First we convert the `presidents` array to a sequence of type `IEnumerable<string>` using the `OfType` operator. Then we convert that sequence to an array using the `ToArray` operator. Since the `ToArray` is a nondeferred operator, the query is performed immediately, even prior to enumerating it.

Here is the output when running the previous code:

```
Adams
Arthur
Buchanan
Bush
Carter
Cleveland
Clinton
Coolidge
Eisenhower
Fillmore
Ford
Garfield
Grant
Harding
Harrison
Hayes
Hoover
Jackson
Jefferson
Johnson
Kennedy
Lincoln
Madison
McKinley
Monroe
Nixon
Obama
Pierce
Polk
Reagan
Roosevelt
Taft
Taylor
Truman
Tyler
```

```
Van Buren
Washington
Wilson
```

Now, technically, the code in this example is a little redundant. The `presidents` array is already a sequence, because in C#, arrays implement the `IEnumerable<T>` interface. So, we could have omitted the call to the `OfType` operator and merely called the `ToArray` operator on the `presidents` array. However, we didn't think it would be very impressive to convert an array to an array.

This operator is often useful for caching a sequence so that it cannot change before you can enumerate it. Also, because this operator is not deferred and is executed immediately, multiple enumerations on the array created will always see the same data.

ToList

The `ToList` operator creates a `List` of type T from an input sequence of type T.

Prototypes

There is one prototype we will cover.

The ToList Prototype

```
public static List<T> ToList<T>(
  this IEnumerable<T> source);
```

This operator takes an input sequence named `source`, of type T elements, and returns a `List` of type T elements.

Exceptions

`ArgumentNullException` is thrown if the source argument is null.

Examples

Listing 5-2 demonstrates the `ToList` operator.

Listing 5-2. A Code Sample Calling the ToList Operator

```
string[] presidents = {
  "Adams", "Arthur", "Buchanan", "Bush", "Carter", "Cleveland",
  "Clinton", "Coolidge", "Eisenhower", "Fillmore", "Ford", "Garfield",
  "Grant", "Harding", "Harrison", "Hayes", "Hoover", "Jackson",
  "Jefferson", "Johnson", "Kennedy", "Lincoln", "Madison", "McKinley",
  "Monroe", "Nixon", "Obama", "Pierce", "Polk", "Reagan", "Roosevelt",
```

157

```
    "Taft", "Taylor", "Truman", "Tyler", "Van Buren", "Washington", "Wilson"};

List<string> names = presidents.ToList();

foreach (string name in names)
    Console.WriteLine(name);
```

In the previous code, we use the array from the previous example. Unlike the previous example, we do not call the OfType operator to create an intermediate sequence of IEnumerable<T> because it seems sufficient to convert the presidents array to a List<string>.

Here are the results:

```
Adams
Arthur
Buchanan
Bush
Carter
Cleveland
Clinton
Coolidge
Eisenhower
Fillmore
Ford
Garfield
Grant
Harding
Harrison
Hayes
Hoover
Jackson
Jefferson
Johnson
Kennedy
Lincoln
Madison
McKinley
Monroe
Nixon
Obama
Pierce
Polk
Reagan
Roosevelt
Taft
Taylor
Truman
Tyler
```

```
Van Buren
Washington
Wilson
```

This operator is often useful for caching a sequence so that it cannot change before you can enumerate it. Also, because this operator is not deferred and is executed immediately, multiple enumerations on the List<T> created will always see the same data.

ToDictionary

The ToDictionary operator creates a Dictionary of type <K, T>, or perhaps <K, E> if the prototype has the elementSelector argument, from an input sequence of type T, where K is the type of the key and T is the type of the stored values. Or if the Dictionary is of type <K, E>, the type of stored values are of type E, which is different from the type of elements in the sequence, which is type T.

■ **Note** If you are unfamiliar with the C# Dictionary collection class, it allows elements to be stored that can be retrieved with a key. Each key must be unique, and only one element can be stored for a single key. You index into the Dictionary using the key to retrieve the stored element for that key.

Prototypes

There are four prototypes we cover.

The First Prototype for the ToDictionary Operator

```
public static Dictionary<K, T> ToDictionary<T, K>(
  this IEnumerable<T> source,
  Func<T, K> keySelector);
```

In this prototype, a Dictionary of type <K, T> is created and returned by enumerating the input sequence named source. The keySelector method delegate is called to extract the key value from each input element, and that key is the element's key into the Dictionary. This version of the operator results in elements in the Dictionary being the same type as the elements in the input sequence.

Since this prototype prevents the specification of an IEqualityComparer<K> object, this version of ToDictionary defaults to the EqualityComparer<K>.Default equality comparison object.

The second ToDictionary prototype is similar to the first, except it provides the ability to specify an IEqualityComparer<K> equality comparison object. Here is the second prototype:

The Second Prototype for the ToDictionary Operator

```
public static Dictionary<K, T> ToDictionary<T, K>(
  this IEnumerable<T> source,
```

```
Func<T, K> keySelector,
IEqualityComparer<K> comparer);
```

This prototype provides the ability to specify an IEqualityComparer<K> equality comparison object. This object is used to make comparisons on the key value. So if you add or access an element in the Dictionary, it will use this comparer to compare the key you specify to the keys already in the Dictionary to determine whether it has a match.

A default implementation of the IEqualityComparer<K> interface is provided by EqualityComparer.Default. However, if you are going to use the default equality comparison class, there is no reason to specify the comparer, because the previous prototype where the comparer is not specified defaults to this one anyway. The StringComparer class implements several equality comparison classes, such as one that ignores case. This way, using the keys "Joe" and "joe" evaluates to being the same key.

The third ToDictionary prototype is just like the first except it allows you to specify an element selector so that the data type of the value stored in the Dictionary can be of a different type than the input sequence element.

The Third Prototype for the ToDictionary Operator

```
public static Dictionary<K, E> ToDictionary<T, K, E>(
  this IEnumerable<T> source,
  Func<T, K> keySelector,
  Func<T, E> elementSelector);
```

Through the elementSelector argument, you can specify a method delegate that returns a portion of the input element—or a newly created object of an altogether different data type—that you want to be stored in the Dictionary.

The fourth prototype for the ToDictionary operator gives you the best of all worlds. It is a combination of the second and third prototypes, which means you can specify an elementSelector and a comparer object.

The Fourth Prototype for the ToDictionary Operator

```
public static Dictionary<K, E> ToDictionary<T, K, E>(
  this IEnumerable<T> source,
  Func<T, K> keySelector,
  Func<T, E> elementSelector,
  IEqualityComparer<K> comparer);
```

This prototype allows you to specify the elementSelector and comparer object.

Exceptions

ArgumentNullException is thrown if the source, keySelector, or elementSelector argument is null or if a key returned by keySelector is null.

ArgumentException is thrown if a keySelector returns the same key for two elements.

Examples

In this example, instead of using the typical `presidents` array we have been using, we use our common `Employee` class. We are going to create a dictionary of type `Dictionary<int, Employee>` where the key of type `int` is the `id` member of the `Employee` class and the `Employee` object itself is the element stored.

Listing 5-3 is an example calling the `ToDictionary` operator using the `Employee` class.

***Listing 5-3.** Sample Code Calling the First ToDictionary Prototype*

```
Dictionary<int, Employee> eDictionary =
  Employee.GetEmployeesArray().ToDictionary(k => k.id);

Employee e = eDictionary[2];
Console.WriteLine("Employee whose id == 2 is {0} {1}", e.firstName, e.lastName);
```

We declare our `Dictionary` to have a key type of integer because we will be using the `Employee.id` field as the key. Since this `ToDictionary` operator prototype only allows us to store the entire input element, which is an `Employee` object, as the element in the `Dictionary`, the `Dictionary` element type is `Employee` as well. The `Dictionary<int, Employee>` then allows me to look up employees by their employee `id` providing the performance efficiencies and retrieval convenience of a `Dictionary`. Here are the results of the previous code:

```
Employee whose id == 2 is William Gates
```

For an example demonstrating the second prototype, since the purpose of the second prototype is to allow me to specify an equality comparison object of type `IEqualityComparer<T>`, we need a situation where an equality comparison class would be useful. This is a situation where keys that may not literally be equal will be considered equal by our equality comparison class. We will use a numeric value in string format as the key for this purpose, such as `"1"`. Since sometimes numeric values in string format end up with leading zeros, it is quite feasible that a key for the same data could end up being `"1"`, or `"01"`, or even `"00001"`. Since those string values are not equal, we need an equality comparison class that would know how to determine that they should be considered equal.

First, though, we need a class with a key of type `string`. For this, we will make a slight modification to the common `Employee` class that we have been using on occasion. We will create the following `Employee2` class that is identical to the `Employee` class, except that the `id` member type is now `string` instead of `int`.

A Class for the Second Prototype Code Sample of the ToDictionary Operator

```
public class Employee2
{
  public string id;
  public string firstName;
  public string lastName;
```

```
public static ArrayList GetEmployeesArrayList()
{
  ArrayList al = new ArrayList();

  al.Add(new Employee2 { id = "1", firstName = "Joe", lastName = "Rattz" });
  al.Add(new Employee2 { id = "2", firstName = "William", lastName = "Gates" });
  al.Add(new Employee2 { id = "3", firstName = "Anders",
          lastName = "Hejlsberg" });
  al.Add(new Employee2 { id = "4", firstName = "David", lastName = "Lightman" });
  al.Add(new Employee2 { id = "101", firstName = "Kevin", lastName = "Flynn" });
  return (al);
}

public static Employee2[] GetEmployeesArray()
{
  return ((Employee2[])GetEmployeesArrayList().ToArray(typeof(Employee2)));
}
}
```

We have changed the key type to string to demonstrate how an equality comparison class can be used to determine whether two keys are equal, even though they may not literally be equal. In this example, because our keys are now string, we will use our common MyStringifiedNumberComparer class that will know that the key "02" is equal to the key "2".

Now let's look at some code using the Employee2 class and our implementation of IEqualityComparer, shown in Listing 5-4.

Listing 5-4. *Sample Code Calling the Second ToDictionary Prototype*

```
Dictionary<string, Employee2> eDictionary = Employee2.GetEmployeesArray()
  .ToDictionary(k => k.id, new MyStringifiedNumberComparer());

Employee2 e = eDictionary["2"];
Console.WriteLine("Employee whose id == \"2\" : {0} {1}",
  e.firstName, e.lastName);

e = eDictionary["000002"];
Console.WriteLine("Employee whose id == \"000002\" : {0} {1}",
  e.firstName, e.lastName);
```

In this example, we try to access elements in the Dictionary with key values of "2" and "000002". If our equality comparison class works properly, we should get the same element from the Dictionary both times. Here are the results:

```
Employee whose id == "2" : William Gates
Employee whose id == "000002" : William Gates
```

As you can see, we did get the same element from the `Dictionary` regardless of our `string` key used for access, as long as each string value parsed to the same integer value.

The third prototype allows us to store an element in the `Dictionary` that is a different type from the input sequence element type. For the third prototype example, we use the same `Employee` class that we use in the first prototype sample code for `ToDictionary`. Listing 5-5 is the sample code calling the third `ToDictionary` prototype.

Listing 5-5. *Sample Code Calling the Third ToDictionary Prototype*

```
Dictionary<int, string> eDictionary = Employee.GetEmployeesArray()
  .ToDictionary(k => k.id,
                i => string.Format("{0} {1}",    //  elementSelector
                  i.firstName, i.lastName));

string name = eDictionary[2];
Console.WriteLine("Employee whose id == 2 is {0}", name);
```

In this code, we provide a lambda expression that concatenates the `firstName` and `lastName` into a `string`. That concatenated `string` becomes the value stored in the `Dictionary`. So, although our input sequence element type is `Employee`, our element data type stored in the dictionary is `string`. Here are the results of this query:

```
Employee whose id == 2 is William Gates
```

To demonstrate the fourth `ToDictionary` prototype, we will use our `Employee2` class and our common `MyStringifiedNumberComparer` class. Listing 5-6 is our sample code.

Listing 5-6. *Sample Code Calling the Fourth ToDictionary Prototype*

```
Dictionary<string, string> eDictionary = Employee2.GetEmployeesArray()
  .ToDictionary(k => k.id,                            //  keySelector
                i => string.Format("{0} {1}",         //  elementSelector
                  i.firstName, i.lastName),
                new MyStringifiedNumberComparer());   //  comparer

string name = eDictionary["2"];
Console.WriteLine("Employee whose id == \"2\" : {0}", name);

name = eDictionary["000002"];
Console.WriteLine("Employee whose id == \"000002\" : {0}", name);
```

In the previous code, we provide an `elementSelector` that specifies a single `string` as the value to store in the `Dictionary`, and we provide a custom equality comparison object. The result is that we can use `"2"` or `"000002"` to retrieve the element from the `Dictionary` because of our equality comparison class, and what we get out of the Dictionary is now just a string, which happens to be the employee's lastName appended to the firstName. Here are the results:

```
Employee whose id == "2" : William Gates
Employee whose id == "000002" : William Gates
```

As you can see, indexing into the Dictionary with the key values of "2" and "000002" retrieve the same element.

ToLookup

The ToLookup operator creates a Lookup of type <K, T>, or perhaps <K, E>, from an input sequence of type T, where K is the type of the key and T is the type of the stored values. Or if the Lookup is of type <K, E>, the type of stored values are of type E, which is different from the type of elements in the sequence, which is type T.

Although all prototypes of the ToLookup operator create a Lookup, they return an object that implements the ILookup interface. In this section, we will commonly refer to the object implementing the ILookup interface that is returned as a Lookup.

■ **Note** If you are unfamiliar with the C# Lookup collection class, it allows elements to be stored that can be retrieved with a key. Each key need not be unique, and *multiple* elements can be stored for a single key. You index into the Lookup using the key to retrieve a *sequence* of the stored elements for that key.

Prototypes

There are four prototypes we cover.

The First Prototype for the ToLookup Operator

```
public static ILookup<K, T> ToLookup<T, K>(
  this IEnumerable<T> source,
  Func<T, K> keySelector);
```

In this prototype, a Lookup of type <K, T> is created and returned by enumerating the input sequence, named source. The keySelector method delegate is called to extract the key value from each input element, and that key is the element's key into the Lookup. This version of the operator results in stored values in the Lookup being the same type as the elements in the input sequence.

Since this prototype prevents the specification of an IEqualityComparer<K> equality comparison object, this version of ToLookup defaults to the EqualityComparer<K>.Default equality comparison class.

The second `ToLookup` prototype is similar to the first, except it provides the ability to specify an `IEqualityComparer<K>` equality comparison object. Here is the second prototype:

The Second Prototype for the ToLookup Operator

```
public static ILookup<K, T> ToLookup<T, K>(
  this IEnumerable<T> source,
  Func<T, K> keySelector,
  IEqualityComparer<K> comparer);
```

This prototype provides the ability to specify an `IEqualityComparer comparer` object. This object is used to make comparisons on the key value. So if you add or access an element in the `Lookup`, it will use this `comparer` object to compare the key you specify to the keys already in the `Lookup` to determine whether there is a match.

A default implementation of the `IEqualityComparer<K>` interface is provided by `EqualityComparer.Default`. However, if you are going to use the default equality comparison class, there is no reason to specify the equality comparison object because the previous prototype where the equality comparison object is not specified defaults to this one anyway. The `StringComparer` class implements several equality comparison classes, such as one that ignores case. This way, using the keys `"Joe"` and `"joe"` evaluates to being the same key.

The third `ToLookup` prototype is just like the first one except it allows you to specify an element selector so that the data type of the value stored in the `Lookup` can be of a different type than the input sequence element. Here is the third prototype:

The Third Prototype for the ToLookup Operator

```
public static ILookup<K, E> ToLookup<T, K, E>(
  this IEnumerable<T> source,
  Func<T, K> keySelector,
  Func<T, E> elementSelector);
```

Through the `elementSelector` argument, you can specify a method delegate that returns the portion of the input element—or a newly created object of an altogether different data type—that you want to be stored in the `Lookup`.

The fourth prototype for the `ToLookup` operator gives you the best of all worlds. It is a combination of the second and third prototypes, which means you can specify an `elementSelector` and a `comparer` equality comparison object. Here is the fourth prototype:

The Fourth Prototype for the ToLookup Operator

```
public static ILookup<K, E> ToLookup<T, K, E>(
  this IEnumerable<T> source,
  Func<T, K> keySelector,
  Func<T, E> elementSelector,
  IEqualityComparer<K> comparer);
```

This prototype allows you to specify the elementSelector and comparer.

Exceptions

ArgumentNullException is thrown if the source, keySelector, or elementSelector argument is null or if a key returned by keySelector is null.

Examples

In this example of the first ToLookup prototype, instead of using the typical presidents array we have been using, we need a class with elements containing members that can be used as keys but are not unique. For this purpose, we will use our common Actor class.

Listing 5-7 is an example calling the ToLookup operator using the Actor class.

Listing 5-7. Sample Code Calling the First ToLookup Prototype

```
ILookup<int, Actor> lookup = Actor.GetActors().ToLookup(k => k.birthYear);

// Let's see if we can find the 'one' born in 1964.
IEnumerable<Actor> actors = lookup[1964];
foreach (var actor in actors)
  Console.WriteLine("{0} {1}", actor.firstName, actor.lastName);
```

First we create the Lookup using the Actor.birthYear member as the key into the Lookup. Next we index into the Lookup using our key, 1964. Then we enumerate through the returned values. Here are the results:

```
Keanu Reeves
Sandra Bullock
```

Uh-oh, it looks like we got multiple results. We guess he isn't "the one" after all. It's a good thing we converted this input sequence to a Lookup instead of a Dictionary, because there were multiple elements with the same key.

For an example demonstrating the second ToLookup prototype, we will make a slight modification to our common Actor class. We will create an Actor2 class that is identical to the Actor class except that the birthYear member type is now string instead of int.

A Class for the Second Prototype Code Sample of the ToLookup Operator

```
public class Actor2
{
  public string birthYear;
  public string firstName;
  public string lastName;
```

```
public static Actor2[] GetActors()
{
  Actor2[] actors = new Actor2[] {
    new Actor2 { birthYear = "1964", firstName = "Keanu", lastName = "Reeves" },
    new Actor2 { birthYear = "1968", firstName = "Owen", lastName = "Wilson" },
    new Actor2 { birthYear = "1960", firstName = "James", lastName = "Spader" },
    // The world's first Y10K-compliant date!
    new Actor2 { birthYear = "01964", firstName = "Sandra",
      lastName = "Bullock" },
  };

  return(actors);
}
}
```

Notice we changed the `birthYear` member to be a `string` for the class. Now we will call the `ToLookup` operator, as shown in Listing 5-8.

Listing 5-8. *Sample Code Calling the Second ToLookup Prototype*

```
ILookup<string, Actor2> lookup = Actor2.GetActors()
  .ToLookup(k => k.birthYear, new MyStringifiedNumberComparer());

// Let's see if we can find the 'one' born in 1964.
IEnumerable<Actor2> actors = lookup["0001964"];
foreach (var actor in actors)
  Console.WriteLine("{0} {1}", actor.firstName, actor.lastName);
```

We are using the same equality comparison object we use in the `Dictionary` examples. In this case, we convert the input sequence to a `Lookup`, and we provide an equality comparison object because we know that the key, which is stored as a `string`, may sometimes contain leading zeros. Our equality comparison object knows how to handle that. Here are the results:

```
Keanu Reeves
Sandra Bullock
```

Notice that when we try to retrieve all elements whose key is `"0001964"`, we get back elements whose keys are `"1964"` and `"01964"`. So we know our equality comparison object works.

For the third prototype for the `ToLookup` operator, we will use the same `Actor` class that we use in the first prototype sample code for `ToLookup`. Listing 5-9 is our sample code calling the third `ToLookup` prototype.

Listing 5-9. *Sample Code Calling the Third ToLookup Prototype*

```
ILookup<int, string> lookup = Actor.GetActors()
  .ToLookup(k => k.birthYear,
```

```
            a => string.Format("{0} {1}", a.firstName, a.lastName));

// Let's see if we can find the 'one' born in 1964.
IEnumerable<string> actors = lookup[1964];
foreach (var actor in actors)
  Console.WriteLine("{0}", actor);
```

For our elementSelector, we just concatenate the firstName and lastName members. Here are the results:

```
Keanu Reeves
Sandra Bullock
```

Using the elementSelector variation of the ToLookup operator allows me to store a different data type in the Lookup than the input sequence element's data type.

For an example of the fourth ToLookup prototype, we will use our Actor2 class and our common MyStringifiedNumberComparer class. Listing 5-10 is our sample code.

***Listing 5-10.** Sample Code Calling the Fourth ToLookup Prototype*

```
ILookup<string, string> lookup = Actor2.GetActors()
  .ToLookup(k => k.birthYear,
           a => string.Format("{0} {1}", a.firstName, a.lastName),
           new MyStringifiedNumberComparer());

// Let's see if we can find the 'one' born in 1964.
IEnumerable<string> actors = lookup["0001964"];
foreach (var actor in actors)
  Console.WriteLine("{0}", actor);
```

Here is the output:

```
Keanu Reeves
Sandra Bullock
```

You can see that we index into the Lookup using a key value different from either of the values retrieved using that key, so we can tell our equality comparison object is working. And instead of storing the entire Actor2 object, we merely store the string we are interested in.

Equality

The following equality operators are used for testing the equality of sequences.

SequenceEqual

The `SequenceEqual` operator determines whether two input sequences are equal.

Prototypes

There are two prototypes we cover.

The First SequenceEqual Prototype

```
public static bool SequenceEqual<T>(
  this IEnumerable<T> first,
  IEnumerable<T> second);
```

This operator enumerates each input sequence in parallel, comparing the elements of each using the `System.Object.Equals` method. If the elements are all equal and the sequences have the same number of elements, the operator returns `true`. Otherwise, it returns `false`.

The second prototype of the operator works just as the first, except an `IEqualityComparer<T>` comparer object can be used to determine element equality.

The Second SequenceEqual Prototype

```
public static bool SequenceEqual<T>(
  this IEnumerable<T> first,
  IEnumerable<T> second,
  IEqualityComparer<T> comparer);
```

Exceptions

`ArgumentNullException` is thrown if either argument is `null`.

Examples

Listing 5-11 is an example.

Listing 5-11. *An Example of the First SequenceEqual Operator Prototype*

```
string[] presidents = {
  "Adams", "Arthur", "Buchanan", "Bush", "Carter", "Cleveland",
  "Clinton", "Coolidge", "Eisenhower", "Fillmore", "Ford", "Garfield",
  "Grant", "Harding", "Harrison", "Hayes", "Hoover", "Jackson",
  "Jefferson", "Johnson", "Kennedy", "Lincoln", "Madison", "McKinley",
  "Monroe", "Nixon", "Obama", "Pierce", "Polk", "Reagan", "Roosevelt",
  "Taft", "Taylor", "Truman", "Tyler", "Van Buren", "Washington", "Wilson"};

bool eq = presidents.SequenceEqual(presidents);
```

```
Console.WriteLine(eq);
```

And here are the results:

```
True
```

That seems a little cheap, doesn't it? OK, we will make it a little more difficult, as shown in Listing 5-12.

Listing 5-12. Another Example of the First SequenceEqual Operator Prototype

```
string[] presidents = {
  "Adams", "Arthur", "Buchanan", "Bush", "Carter", "Cleveland",
  "Clinton", "Coolidge", "Eisenhower", "Fillmore", "Ford", "Garfield",
  "Grant", "Harding", "Harrison", "Hayes", "Hoover", "Jackson",
  "Jefferson", "Johnson", "Kennedy", "Lincoln", "Madison", "McKinley",
  "Monroe", "Nixon", "Obama", "Pierce", "Polk", "Reagan", "Roosevelt",
  "Taft", "Taylor", "Truman", "Tyler", "Van Buren", "Washington", "Wilson"};
```

```
bool eq = presidents.SequenceEqual(presidents.Take(presidents.Count()));
Console.WriteLine(eq);
```

In the previous code, we use the Take operator to take only the first N number of elements of the presidents array and then compare that output sequence to the original presidents sequence. So in the previous code, if we take all the elements of the presidents array by taking the number of the presidents.Count(), we should get the entire sequence output. Sure enough, here are the results:

```
True
```

OK, that worked as expected. Now we will take all the elements except the last one by subtracting one from the presidents.Count(), as shown in Listing 5-13.

Listing 5-13. Yet Another Example of the First SequenceEqual Operator Prototype

```
string[] presidents = {
  "Adams", "Arthur", "Buchanan", "Bush", "Carter", "Cleveland",
  "Clinton", "Coolidge", "Eisenhower", "Fillmore", "Ford", "Garfield",
  "Grant", "Harding", "Harrison", "Hayes", "Hoover", "Jackson",
  "Jefferson", "Johnson", "Kennedy", "Lincoln", "Madison", "McKinley",
  "Monroe", "Nixon", "Obama", "Pierce", "Polk", "Reagan", "Roosevelt",
  "Taft", "Taylor", "Truman", "Tyler", "Van Buren", "Washington", "Wilson"};
```

```
bool eq = presidents.SequenceEqual(presidents.Take(presidents.Count() - 1));
Console.WriteLine(eq);
```

Now the results should be `false`, because the two sequences should not even have the same number of elements. The second sequence, the one we passed, should be missing the very last element:

```
False
```

This is going well. Just out of curiosity, let's try one more. We recall that in our discussion of the `Take` and `Skip` operators in the previous chapter, we said that when concatenated together properly, they should output the original sequence. We will now give that a try. We will get to use the `Take`, `Skip`, `Concat`, and `SequenceEqual` operators to prove this statement, as shown in Listing 5-14.

Listing 5-14. *A More Complex Example of the First SequenceEqual Operator Prototype*

```
string[] presidents = {
  "Adams", "Arthur", "Buchanan", "Bush", "Carter", "Cleveland",
  "Clinton", "Coolidge", "Eisenhower", "Fillmore", "Ford", "Garfield",
  "Grant", "Harding", "Harrison", "Hayes", "Hoover", "Jackson",
  "Jefferson", "Johnson", "Kennedy", "Lincoln", "Madison", "McKinley",
  "Monroe", "Nixon", "Obama", "Pierce", "Polk", "Reagan", "Roosevelt",
  "Taft", "Taylor", "Truman", "Tyler", "Van Buren", "Washington", "Wilson"};

bool eq =
  presidents.SequenceEqual(presidents.Take(5).Concat(presidents.Skip(5)));
Console.WriteLine(eq);
```

In this example, we get the first five elements of the original input sequence by calling the `Take` operator. We then concatenate on the input sequence starting with the sixth element using the `Skip` and `Concat` operators. Finally, we determine whether that concatenated sequence is equal to the original sequence calling the `SequenceEqual` operator. What do you think? Let's see:

```
True
```

Cool, it worked! For an example of the second prototype, we create two arrays of type `string` where each element is a number in `string` form. The elements of the two arrays will be such that when parsed into integers, they will be equal. We use our common `MyStringifiedNumberComparer` class for this example, shown in Listing 5-15.

Listing 5-15. *An Example of the Second SequenceEqual Operator Prototype*

```
string[] stringifiedNums1 = {
  "001", "49", "017", "0080", "00027", "2" };

string[] stringifiedNums2 = {
  "1", "0049", "17", "080", "27", "02" };
```

```
bool eq = stringifiedNums1.SequenceEqual(stringifiedNums2,
                                   new MyStringifiedNumberComparer());
```

```
Console.WriteLine(eq);
```

In this example, if you examine the two arrays, you can see that if you parse each element from each array into an integer and then compare the corresponding integers, the two arrays would be considered equal. Let's see whether the results indicate that the two sequences are equal:

```
True
```

Element

The following element operators allow you to retrieve single elements from an input sequence.

First

The First operator returns the first element of a sequence or the first element of a sequence matching a predicate, depending on the prototype used.

Prototypes

There are two prototypes we cover.

The First First Prototype

```
public static T First<T>(
  this IEnumerable<T> source);
```

Using this prototype of the First operator enumerates the input sequence named source and returns the first element of the sequence.

The second prototype of the First operator allows a predicate to be passed.

The Second First Prototype

```
public static T First<T>(
  this IEnumerable<T> source,
  Func<T, bool> predicate);
```

This version of the First operator returns the first element it finds for which the predicate returns true. If no elements cause the predicate to return true, the First operator throws an InvalidOperationException.

Exceptions

`ArgumentNullException` is thrown if any arguments are `null`.

`InvalidOperationException` is thrown if the `source` sequence is empty or if the `predicate` never returns `true`.

Examples

Listing 5-16 is an example of the first `First` prototype.

Listing 5-16. *Sample Code Calling the First First Prototype*

```
string[] presidents = {
    "Adams", "Arthur", "Buchanan", "Bush", "Carter", "Cleveland",
    "Clinton", "Coolidge", "Eisenhower", "Fillmore", "Ford", "Garfield",
    "Grant", "Harding", "Harrison", "Hayes", "Hoover", "Jackson",
    "Jefferson", "Johnson", "Kennedy", "Lincoln", "Madison", "McKinley",
    "Monroe", "Nixon", "Obama", "Pierce", "Polk", "Reagan", "Roosevelt",
    "Taft", "Taylor", "Truman", "Tyler", "Van Buren", "Washington", "Wilson"};

string name = presidents.First();
Console.WriteLine(name);
```

Here are the results:

Adams

You may be asking yourself how this operator differs from calling the `Take` operator and passing it a 1. The difference is the `Take` operator returns a *sequence* of elements, even if that sequence contains only a single element. The `First` operator always returns exactly one *element*, or it throws an exception if there is no first element to return.

Listing 5-17 is some sample code using the second prototype of the `First` operator.

Listing 5-17. *Code Calling the Second First Prototype*

```
string[] presidents = {
    "Adams", "Arthur", "Buchanan", "Bush", "Carter", "Cleveland",
    "Clinton", "Coolidge", "Eisenhower", "Fillmore", "Ford", "Garfield",
    "Grant", "Harding", "Harrison", "Hayes", "Hoover", "Jackson",
    "Jefferson", "Johnson", "Kennedy", "Lincoln", "Madison", "McKinley",
    "Monroe", "Nixon", "Obama", "Pierce", "Polk", "Reagan", "Roosevelt",
    "Taft", "Taylor", "Truman", "Tyler", "Van Buren", "Washington", "Wilson"};

string name = presidents.First(p => p.StartsWith("H"));
Console.WriteLine(name);
```

This should return the first element in the input sequence that begins with the string "H". Here are the results:

```
Harding
```

Remember, if either prototype of the First operator ends up with no element to return, an InvalidOperationException is thrown. To avoid this, use the FirstOrDefault operator.

FirstOrDefault

The FirstOrDefault operator is similar to the First operator except for how it behaves when an element is not found.

Prototypes

There are two prototypes we cover.

The First FirstOrDefault Prototype

```
public static T FirstOrDefault<T>(
  this IEnumerable<T> source);
```

This version of the FirstOrDefault prototype returns the first element found in the input sequence. If the sequence is empty, default(T) is returned. For reference and nullable types, the default value is null.

The second prototype of the FirstOrDefault operator allows you to pass a predicate to determine which element should be returned.

The Second FirstOrDefault Prototype

```
public static T FirstOrDefault<T>(
  this IEnumerable<T> source,
  Func<T, bool> predicate);
```

Exceptions

ArgumentNullException is thrown if any arguments are null.

Examples

Listing 5-18 is an example of the first FirstOrDefault prototype where no element is found. We have to get an empty sequence to do this. We'll call Take(0) for this purpose.

Listing 5-18. *Calling the First FirstOrDefault Prototype Where an Element Is Not Found*

```
string[] presidents = {
  "Adams", "Arthur", "Buchanan", "Bush", "Carter", "Cleveland",
  "Clinton", "Coolidge", "Eisenhower", "Fillmore", "Ford", "Garfield",
  "Grant", "Harding", "Harrison", "Hayes", "Hoover", "Jackson",
  "Jefferson", "Johnson", "Kennedy", "Lincoln", "Madison", "McKinley",
  "Monroe", "Nixon", "Obama", "Pierce", "Polk", "Reagan", "Roosevelt",
  "Taft", "Taylor", "Truman", "Tyler", "Van Buren", "Washington", "Wilson"};

string name = presidents.Take(0).FirstOrDefault();
Console.WriteLine(name == null ? "NULL" : name);
```

Here are the results:

```
NULL
```

Listing 5-19 is the same example without the Take(0) call, so an element is found.

Listing 5-19. *Calling the First FirstOrDefault Prototype Where an Element Is Found*

```
string[] presidents = {
  "Adams", "Arthur", "Buchanan", "Bush", "Carter", "Cleveland",
  "Clinton", "Coolidge", "Eisenhower", "Fillmore", "Ford", "Garfield",
  "Grant", "Harding", "Harrison", "Hayes", "Hoover", "Jackson",
  "Jefferson", "Johnson", "Kennedy", "Lincoln", "Madison", "McKinley",
  "Monroe", "Nixon", "Obama", "Pierce", "Polk", "Reagan", "Roosevelt",
  "Taft", "Taylor", "Truman", "Tyler", "Van Buren", "Washington", "Wilson"};

string name = presidents.FirstOrDefault();
Console.WriteLine(name == null ? "NULL" : name);
```

And finally, here are the results for the code when we find an element:

```
Adams
```

For the second FirstOrDefault prototype, we specify that we want the first element that starts with the string "B", as shown in Listing 5-20.

Listing 5-20. *Calling the Second FirstOrDefault Prototype Where an Element Is Found*

```
string[] presidents = {
  "Adams", "Arthur", "Buchanan", "Bush", "Carter", "Cleveland",
  "Clinton", "Coolidge", "Eisenhower", "Fillmore", "Ford", "Garfield",
```

```
  "Grant", "Harding", "Harrison", "Hayes", "Hoover", "Jackson",
  "Jefferson", "Johnson", "Kennedy", "Lincoln", "Madison", "McKinley",
  "Monroe", "Nixon", "Obama", "Pierce", "Polk", "Reagan", "Roosevelt",
  "Taft", "Taylor", "Truman", "Tyler", "Van Buren", "Washington", "Wilson"};

string name = presidents.FirstOrDefault(p => p.StartsWith("B"));
Console.WriteLine(name == null ? "NULL" : name);
```

Here are the results:

```
Buchanan
```

Now we will try that with a predicate that will not find a match, as shown in Listing 5-21.

Listing 5-21. Calling the Second FirstOrDefault Prototype Where an Element Is Not Found

```
string[] presidents = {
  "Adams", "Arthur", "Buchanan", "Bush", "Carter", "Cleveland",
  "Clinton", "Coolidge", "Eisenhower", "Fillmore", "Ford", "Garfield",
  "Grant", "Harding", "Harrison", "Hayes", "Hoover", "Jackson",
  "Jefferson", "Johnson", "Kennedy", "Lincoln", "Madison", "McKinley",
  "Monroe", "Nixon", "Obama", "Pierce", "Polk", "Reagan", "Roosevelt",
  "Taft", "Taylor", "Truman", "Tyler", "Van Buren", "Washington", "Wilson"};

string name = presidents.FirstOrDefault(p => p.StartsWith("Z"));
Console.WriteLine(name == null ? "NULL" : name);
```

Since there is no name in the presidents array beginning with a "Z", here are the results:

```
NULL
```

Last

The Last operator returns the last element of a sequence or the last element of a sequence matching a predicate, depending on the prototype used.

Prototypes

There are two prototypes we cover.

The First Last Prototype

```
public static T Last<T>(
```

```
this IEnumerable<T> source);
```

Using this prototype, the `Last` operator enumerates the input sequence named `source` and returns the last element of the sequence.

The second prototype of `Last` allows a `predicate` to be passed and looks like this:

The Second Last Prototype

```
public static T Last<T>(
  this IEnumerable<T> source,
  Func<T, bool> predicate);
```

This version of the `Last` operator returns the last element it finds for which the predicate returns true.

Exceptions

`ArgumentNullException` is thrown if any arguments are `null`.

`InvalidOperationException` is thrown if the `source` sequence is empty or if the `predicate` never returns true.

Examples

Listing 5-22 is an example of the first `Last` prototype.

Listing 5-22. *Sample Code Calling the First Last Prototype*

```
string[] presidents = {
  "Adams", "Arthur", "Buchanan", "Bush", "Carter", "Cleveland",
  "Clinton", "Coolidge", "Eisenhower", "Fillmore", "Ford", "Garfield",
  "Grant", "Harding", "Harrison", "Hayes", "Hoover", "Jackson",
  "Jefferson", "Johnson", "Kennedy", "Lincoln", "Madison", "McKinley",
  "Monroe", "Nixon", "Obama", "Pierce", "Polk", "Reagan", "Roosevelt",
  "Taft", "Taylor", "Truman", "Tyler", "Van Buren", "Washington", "Wilson"};

string name = presidents.Last();
Console.WriteLine(name);
```

Here are the results:

```
Wilson
```

The `Last` operator always returns exactly one *element*, or it throws an exception if there is no last element to return.

Listing 5-23 is some sample code using the second prototype of the Last operator.

Listing 5-23. *Calling the Second Last Prototype*

```
string[] presidents = {
  "Adams", "Arthur", "Buchanan", "Bush", "Carter", "Cleveland",
  "Clinton", "Coolidge", "Eisenhower", "Fillmore", "Ford", "Garfield",
  "Grant", "Harding", "Harrison", "Hayes", "Hoover", "Jackson",
  "Jefferson", "Johnson", "Kennedy", "Lincoln", "Madison", "McKinley",
  "Monroe", "Nixon", "Obama", "Pierce", "Polk", "Reagan", "Roosevelt",
  "Taft", "Taylor", "Truman", "Tyler", "Van Buren", "Washington", "Wilson"};

string name = presidents.Last(p => p.StartsWith("H"));
Console.WriteLine(name);
```

This should return the last element in the input sequence that begins with the string "H". Here are the results:

Hoover

Remember, if either prototype of the Last operator ends up with no element to return, an InvalidOperationException is thrown. To avoid this, use the LastOrDefault operator.

LastOrDefault

The LastOrDefault operator is similar to the Last operator except for how it behaves when an element is not found.

Prototypes

There are two prototypes we cover.

The First LastOrDefault Prototype

```
public static T LastOrDefault<T>(
  this IEnumerable<T> source);
```

This version of the LastOrDefault prototype returns the last element found in the input sequence. If the sequence is empty, default(T) is returned. For reference and nullable types, the default value is null.

The second prototype of the LastOrDefault operator allows you to pass a predicate to determine which element should be returned.

The Second LastOrDefault Prototype

```
public static T LastOrDefault<T>(
  this IEnumerable<T> source,
  Func<T, bool> predicate);
```

Exceptions

ArgumentNullException is thrown if any arguments are null.

Examples

Listing 5-24 is an example of the first LastOrDefault operator where no element is found. We have to get an empty sequence to do this. We'll call Take(0) for this purpose.

Listing 5-24. *Calling the First LastOrDefault Prototype Where an Element Is Not Found*

```
string[] presidents = {
  "Adams", "Arthur", "Buchanan", "Bush", "Carter", "Cleveland",
  "Clinton", "Coolidge", "Eisenhower", "Fillmore", "Ford", "Garfield",
  "Grant", "Harding", "Harrison", "Hayes", "Hoover", "Jackson",
  "Jefferson", "Johnson", "Kennedy", "Lincoln", "Madison", "McKinley",
  "Monroe", "Nixon", "Obama", "Pierce", "Polk", "Reagan", "Roosevelt",
  "Taft", "Taylor", "Truman", "Tyler", "Van Buren", "Washington", "Wilson"};

string name = presidents.Take(0).LastOrDefault();
Console.WriteLine(name == null ? "NULL" : name);
```

Here are the results:

```
NULL
```

Listing 5-25 is the same example without the Take(0), so an element is found.

Listing 5-25. *Calling the First LastOrDefault Prototype Where an Element Is Found*

```
string[] presidents = {
  "Adams", "Arthur", "Buchanan", "Bush", "Carter", "Cleveland",
  "Clinton", "Coolidge", "Eisenhower", "Fillmore", "Ford", "Garfield",
  "Grant", "Harding", "Harrison", "Hayes", "Hoover", "Jackson",
  "Jefferson", "Johnson", "Kennedy", "Lincoln", "Madison", "McKinley",
  "Monroe", "Nixon", "Obama", "Pierce", "Polk", "Reagan", "Roosevelt",
  "Taft", "Taylor", "Truman", "Tyler", "Van Buren", "Washington", "Wilson"};

string name = presidents.LastOrDefault();
Console.WriteLine(name == null ? "NULL" : name);
```

And finally, here are the results for the code when we find an element:

```
Wilson
```

For the second prototype of the `LastOrDefault` operator, shown in Listing 5-26, we specify that we want the last element to start with the string "B".

Listing 5-26. *Calling the Second LastOrDefault Prototype Where an Element Is Found*

```
string[] presidents = {
  "Adams", "Arthur", "Buchanan", "Bush", "Carter", "Cleveland",
  "Clinton", "Coolidge", "Eisenhower", "Fillmore", "Ford", "Garfield",
  "Grant", "Harding", "Harrison", "Hayes", "Hoover", "Jackson",
  "Jefferson", "Johnson", "Kennedy", "Lincoln", "Madison", "McKinley",
  "Monroe", "Nixon", "Obama", "Pierce", "Polk", "Reagan", "Roosevelt",
  "Taft", "Taylor", "Truman", "Tyler", "Van Buren", "Washington", "Wilson"};

string name = presidents.LastOrDefault(p => p.StartsWith("B"));
Console.WriteLine(name == null ? "NULL" : name);
```

Here are the results:

```
Bush
```

Now we will try that with a `predicate` that will not find a match, as shown in Listing 5-27.

Listing 5-27. *Calling the Second LastOrDefault Prototype Where an Element Is Not Found*

```
string[] presidents = {
  "Adams", "Arthur", "Buchanan", "Bush", "Carter", "Cleveland",
  "Clinton", "Coolidge", "Eisenhower", "Fillmore", "Ford", "Garfield",
  "Grant", "Harding", "Harrison", "Hayes", "Hoover", "Jackson",
  "Jefferson", "Johnson", "Kennedy", "Lincoln", "Madison", "McKinley",
  "Monroe", "Nixon", "Obama", "Pierce", "Polk", "Reagan", "Roosevelt",
  "Taft", "Taylor", "Truman", "Tyler", "Van Buren", "Washington", "Wilson"};

string name = presidents.LastOrDefault(p => p.StartsWith("Z"));
Console.WriteLine(name == null ? "NULL" : name);
```

Since there is no name in the `presidents` array beginning with a "Z", here are the results:

```
NULL
```

Single

The Single operator returns the only element of a single element sequence or the only element of a sequence matching a predicate, depending on the prototype used.

Prototypes

There are two prototypes we cover.

The First Single Prototype

```
public static T Single<T>(
  this IEnumerable<T> source);
```

Using this prototype, the Single operator enumerates the input sequence named source and returns the only element of the sequence.

The second prototype of Single allows a predicate to be passed and looks like this:

The Second Single Prototype

```
public static T Single<T>(
  this IEnumerable<T> source,
  Func<T, bool> predicate);
```

This version of the Single operator returns the only element it finds for which the predicate returns true. If no elements cause the predicate to return true or multiple elements cause the predicate to return true, the Single operator throws an InvalidOperationException.

Exceptions

ArgumentNullException is thrown if any arguments are null.

InvalidOperationException is thrown if the source sequence is empty or if the predicate never returns true or finds more than one element for which it returns true.

Examples

Listing 5-28 is an example of the first Single prototype using the common Employee class.

Listing 5-28. *Sample Code Calling the First Single Prototype*

```
Employee emp = Employee.GetEmployeesArray()
  .Where(e => e.id == 3).Single();

Console.WriteLine("{0} {1}", emp.firstName, emp.lastName);
```

In this example, instead of wanting the query to produce a sequence, we just want a reference to a particular employee. The `Single` operator is very useful for this as long as you can ensure there will be only a single element in the sequence passed to it. In this case, since we called the `Where` operator and specified a unique key, we are safe. Here are the results:

Anders Hejlsberg

Listing 5-29 is some sample code using the second prototype of the `Single` operator.

Listing 5-29. *Code Calling the Second Single Prototype*

```
Employee emp = Employee.GetEmployeesArray()
    .Single(e => e.id == 3);

Console.WriteLine("{0} {1}", emp.firstName, emp.lastName);
```

This code is functionally equivalent to the previous example. Instead of calling the `Where` operator to ensure a single element *is* in the sequence, we can provide the same sequence filtering operation in the `Single` operator. This should return the only element in the input sequence whose `id` is 3. Here are the results:

Anders Hejlsberg

Remember, if either prototype of the `Single` operator ends up with no element to return, an `InvalidOperationException` is thrown. To avoid this, use the `SingleOrDefault` operator.

SingleOrDefault

The `SingleOrDefault` operator is similar to the `Single` operator except for how it behaves when an element is not found.

Prototypes

There are two prototypes we cover.

The First SingleOrDefault Prototype

```
public static T SingleOrDefault<T>(
  this IEnumerable<T> source);
```

This version of the prototype returns the only element found in the input sequence. If the sequence is empty, `default(T)` is returned. For reference and nullable types, the default value is `null`. If more than one element is found, an `InvalidOperationException` is thrown.

The second prototype of the `SingleOrDefault` operator allows you to pass a `predicate` to determine which element should be returned.

The Second SingleOrDefault Prototype

```
public static T SingleOrDefault<T>(
  this IEnumerable<T> source,
  Func<T, bool> predicate);
```

Exceptions

`ArgumentNullException` is thrown if any arguments are `null`.

`InvalidOperationException` is thrown if the operator finds more than one element for which the predicate returns true.

Examples

Listing 5-30 is an example of the first `SingleOrDefault` prototype where no element is found. We have to get an empty sequence to do this. I'll use the `Where` operator and provide a key comparison for a key that doesn't exist for this purpose.

Listing 5-30. *Calling the First SingleOrDefault Prototype Where an Element Is Not Found*

```
Employee emp = Employee.GetEmployeesArray()
  .Where(e => e.id == 5).SingleOrDefault();

Console.WriteLine(emp == null ? "NULL" :
  string.Format("{0} {1}", emp.firstName, emp.lastName));
```

We queried for the employee whose `id` is 5 since we know none exists, so an empty sequence will be returned. Unlike the `Single` operator, the `SingleOrDefault` operator handles empty sequences just fine. Here are the results:

```
NULL
```

Listing 5-31 is the same example where a single element is found. We use the `Where` operator to provide a sequence with just one element.

Listing 5-31. *Calling the First SingleOrDefault Prototype Where an Element Is Found*

```
Employee emp = Employee.GetEmployeesArray()
  .Where(e => e.id == 4).SingleOrDefault();

Console.WriteLine(emp == null ? "NULL" :
  string.Format("{0} {1}", emp.firstName, emp.lastName));
```

This time we specify an id we know exists. Here are the results for the code when an element is found:

David Lightman

As you can see, the employee has been found. For the second SingleOrDefault prototype, shown in Listing 5-32, we specify an id that we know exists. Instead of using the Where operator, we embed the filter into the SingleOrDefault operator call.

Listing 5-32. *Calling the Second SingleOrDefault Prototype Where an Element Is Found*

```
Employee emp = Employee.GetEmployeesArray()
  .SingleOrDefault(e => e.id == 4);

Console.WriteLine(emp == null ? "NULL" :
  string.Format("{0} {1}", emp.firstName, emp.lastName));
```

This example is functionally equivalent to the previous example except instead of filtering the elements using the Where operator, we filter them by passing a predicate to the SingleOrDefault operator. Here are the results:

David Lightman

Now we will try that with a predicate that will not find a match, as shown in Listing 5-33.

Listing 5-33. *Calling the Second SingleOrDefault Prototype Where an Element Is Not Found*

```
Employee emp = Employee.GetEmployeesArray()
  .SingleOrDefault(e => e.id == 5);

Console.WriteLine(emp == null ? "NULL" :
  string.Format("{0} {1}", emp.firstName, emp.lastName));
```

Since there is no element whose id is 5, no elements are found. Here are the results:

NULL

Although no elements were found in the sequence, the SingleOrDefault operator handled the situation gracefully instead of throwing an exception.

ElementAt

The `ElementAt` operator returns the element from the source sequence at the specified index.

Prototypes

There is one prototype we cover.

The ElementAt Prototype

```
public static T ElementAt<T>(
  this IEnumerable<T> source,
  int index);
```

If the sequence implements `IList<T>`, the `IList` interface is used to retrieve the indexed element directly. If the sequence does not implement `IList<T>`, the sequence is enumerated until the indexed element is reached. An `ArgumentOutOfRangeException` is thrown if the index is less than zero or greater than or equal to the number of elements in the sequence.

■ **Note** In C#, indexes are zero-based. This means the first element's index is zero. The last element's index is the sequence's count minus one.

Exceptions

`ArgumentNullException` is thrown if the source argument is `null`.

`ArgumentOutOfRangeException` is thrown if the index is less than zero or greater than or equal to the number of elements in the sequence.

Examples

Listing 5-34 is an example calling the only prototype of the `ElementAt` operator.

Listing 5-34. *Calling the ElementAt Operator*

```
Employee emp = Employee.GetEmployeesArray()
  .ElementAt(3);

Console.WriteLine("{0} {1}", emp.firstName, emp.lastName);
```

We specified that we want the element whose index is 3, which is the fourth element. Here are the results of the query:

```
David Lightman
```

ElementAtOrDefault

The `ElementAtOrDefault` operator returns the element from the source sequence at the specified index.

Prototypes

There is one prototype we cover.

The ElementAtOrDefault Prototype

```
public static T ElementAtOrDefault<T>(
  this IEnumerable<T> source,
  int index);
```

If the sequence implements `IList<T>`, the `IList` interface is used to retrieve the indexed element directly. If the sequence does not implement `IList<T>`, the sequence will be enumerated until the indexed element is reached.

If the index is less than zero or greater than or equal to the number of elements in the sequence, `default(T)` is returned. For reference and nullable types, the default value is `null`. This is the behavior that distinguishes it from the `ElementAt` operator.

Exceptions

`ArgumentNullException` is thrown if the source argument is `null`.

Examples

Listing 5-35 is an example calling the `ElementAtOrDefault` operator when the index is valid.

Listing 5-35. *Calling the ElementAtOrDefault Operator with a Valid Index*

```
Employee emp = Employee.GetEmployeesArray()
  .ElementAtOrDefault(3);

Console.WriteLine(emp == null ? "NULL" :
  string.Format("{0} {1}", emp.firstName, emp.lastName));
```

Here are the results of the query:

```
David Lightman
```

Just as expected, the element at index 3 is retrieved. Now we will try a query with an invalid index using the code in Listing 5-36.

Listing 5-36. *Calling the ElementAtOrDefault Operator with an Invalid Index*

```
Employee emp = Employee.GetEmployeesArray()
  .ElementAtOrDefault(5);

Console.WriteLine(emp == null ? "NULL" :
  string.Format("{0} {1}", emp.firstName, emp.lastName));
```

There is no element whose index is 5. Here are the results of the query:

```
NULL
```

Quantifiers

The following quantifier operators allow you to perform quantification type operations on input sequences.

Any

The Any operator returns true if any element of an input sequence matches a condition.

Prototypes

There are two prototypes we cover.

The First Any Prototype

```
public static bool Any<T>(
  this IEnumerable<T> source);
```

This prototype of the Any operator will return true if the source input sequence contains any elements. The second prototype of the Any operator enumerates the source input sequence and returns true if at least one element in the input sequence causes the predicate method delegate to return true. The source input sequence enumeration halts once the predicate returns true.

The Second Any Prototype

```
public static bool Any<T>(
  this IEnumerable<T> source,
  Func<T, bool> predicate);
```

Exceptions

ArgumentNullException is thrown if any of the arguments are null.

Examples

First we will try the case of an empty sequence, as shown in Listing 5-37. We will use the `Empty` operator we covered in the previous chapter.

Listing 5-37. *First Any Prototype Where No Elements Are in the Source Input Sequence*

```
bool any = Enumerable.Empty<string>().Any();
Console.WriteLine(any);
```

Here are the results of this code:

```
False
```

Next we will try the same prototype but, this time, with elements in the input sequence, as shown in Listing 5-38.

Listing 5-38. *First Any Prototype Where Elements Are in the Source Input Sequence*

```
string[] presidents = {
  "Adams", "Arthur", "Buchanan", "Bush", "Carter", "Cleveland",
  "Clinton", "Coolidge", "Eisenhower", "Fillmore", "Ford", "Garfield",
  "Grant", "Harding", "Harrison", "Hayes", "Hoover", "Jackson",
  "Jefferson", "Johnson", "Kennedy", "Lincoln", "Madison", "McKinley",
  "Monroe", "Nixon", "Obama", "Pierce", "Polk", "Reagan", "Roosevelt",
  "Taft", "Taylor", "Truman", "Tyler", "Van Buren", "Washington", "Wilson"};

bool any = presidents.Any();
Console.WriteLine(any);
```

Here are the results of this code:

```
True
```

For the next example, we use the second prototype, first with no elements matching the predicate, as shown in Listing 5-39.

Listing 5-39. *Second Any Prototype Where No Elements Cause the Predicate to Return True*

```
string[] presidents = {
  "Adams", "Arthur", "Buchanan", "Bush", "Carter", "Cleveland",
  "Clinton", "Coolidge", "Eisenhower", "Fillmore", "Ford", "Garfield",
  "Grant", "Harding", "Harrison", "Hayes", "Hoover", "Jackson",
  "Jefferson", "Johnson", "Kennedy", "Lincoln", "Madison", "McKinley",
  "Monroe", "Nixon", "Obama", "Pierce", "Polk", "Reagan", "Roosevelt",
```

```
  "Taft", "Taylor", "Truman", "Tyler", "Van Buren", "Washington", "Wilson"};

bool any = presidents.Any(s => s.StartsWith("Z"));
Console.WriteLine(any);
```

We specify that we want the `presidents` that start with the string `"Z"`. Since there are none, an empty sequence will be returned causing the Any operator to return `false`. The results are as one would expect:

False

Finally, we try an example of the second prototype with a `predicate` that should return `true` for at least one element, as shown in Listing 5-40.

Listing 5-40. *Second Any Prototype Where at Least One Element Causes the Predicate to Return True*

```
string[] presidents = {
  "Adams", "Arthur", "Buchanan", "Bush", "Carter", "Cleveland",
  "Clinton", "Coolidge", "Eisenhower", "Fillmore", "Ford", "Garfield",
  "Grant", "Harding", "Harrison", "Hayes", "Hoover", "Jackson",
  "Jefferson", "Johnson", "Kennedy", "Lincoln", "Madison", "McKinley",
  "Monroe", "Nixon", "Obama", "Pierce", "Polk", "Reagan", "Roosevelt",
  "Taft", "Taylor", "Truman", "Tyler", "Van Buren", "Washington", "Wilson"};

bool any = presidents.Any(s => s.StartsWith("A"));
Console.WriteLine(any);
```

And finally, here are the results:

True

All

The `All` operator returns `true` if every element in the input sequence matches a condition.

Prototypes

There is one prototype we cover.

The All Prototype

```
public static bool All<T>(
  this IEnumerable<T> source,
```

```
Func<T, bool> predicate);
```

The All operator enumerates the source input sequence and returns true only if the predicate returns true for every element in the sequence. Once the predicate returns false, the enumeration will cease.

Exceptions

ArgumentNullException is thrown if any of the arguments are null.

Examples

In Listing 5-41 we begin with a predicate with which we know at least some of the elements will return false.

Listing 5-41. *All Prototype Where Not Every Element Causes the Predicate to Return True*

```
string[] presidents = {
  "Adams", "Arthur", "Buchanan", "Bush", "Carter", "Cleveland",
  "Clinton", "Coolidge", "Eisenhower", "Fillmore", "Ford", "Garfield",
  "Grant", "Harding", "Harrison", "Hayes", "Hoover", "Jackson",
  "Jefferson", "Johnson", "Kennedy", "Lincoln", "Madison", "McKinley",
  "Monroe", "Nixon", "Obama", "Pierce", "Polk", "Reagan", "Roosevelt",
  "Taft", "Taylor", "Truman", "Tyler", "Van Buren", "Washington", "Wilson"};

bool all = presidents.All(s => s.Length > 5);
Console.WriteLine(all);
```

Since we know not every president in the array has a length of more than five characters, we know that predicate will return false for some elements. Here is the output:

```
False
```

Now we will try a case where we know every element will cause the predicate to return true, as shown in Listing 5-42.

Listing 5-42. *All Prototype Where Every Element Causes the Predicate to Return True*

```
string[] presidents = {
  "Adams", "Arthur", "Buchanan", "Bush", "Carter", "Cleveland",
  "Clinton", "Coolidge", "Eisenhower", "Fillmore", "Ford", "Garfield",
  "Grant", "Harding", "Harrison", "Hayes", "Hoover", "Jackson",
  "Jefferson", "Johnson", "Kennedy", "Lincoln", "Madison", "McKinley",
  "Monroe", "Nixon", "Obama", "Pierce", "Polk", "Reagan", "Roosevelt",
  "Taft", "Taylor", "Truman", "Tyler", "Van Buren", "Washington", "Wilson"};
```

```
bool all = presidents.All(s => s.Length > 3);
Console.WriteLine(all);
```

Since we know every president's name has at least four characters, the All operator should return true. Here is the output:

```
True
```

Contains

The Contains operator returns true if any element in the input sequence matches the specified value.

Prototypes

There are two prototypes we cover.

The First Contains Prototype

```
public static bool Contains<T>(
  this IEnumerable<T> source,
  T value);
```

This prototype of the Contains operator first checks the source input sequence to see whether it implements the ICollection<T> interface, and if it does, it calls the Contains method of the sequence's implementation. If the sequence does not implement the ICollection<T> interface, it enumerates the source input sequence to see whether any element matches the specified value. Once it finds an element that does match, the enumeration halts.

The specified value is compared to each element using the EqualityComparer<K>.Default default equality comparison class.

The second prototype is like the previous except an IEqualityComparer<T> object can be specified. If this prototype is used, each element in the sequence is compared to the passed value using the passed equality comparison object.

The Second Contains Prototype

```
public static bool Contains<T>(
  this IEnumerable<T> source,
  T value,
  IEqualityComparer<T> comparer);
```

Exceptions

ArgumentNullException is thrown if the source input sequence is null.

Examples

For an example of the first prototype, we begin with a value that we know is not in our input sequence, as shown in Listing 5-43.

Listing 5-43. First Contains Prototype Where No Element Matches the Specified Value

```
string[] presidents = {
  "Adams", "Arthur", "Buchanan", "Bush", "Carter", "Cleveland",
  "Clinton", "Coolidge", "Eisenhower", "Fillmore", "Ford", "Garfield",
  "Grant", "Harding", "Harrison", "Hayes", "Hoover", "Jackson",
  "Jefferson", "Johnson", "Kennedy", "Lincoln", "Madison", "McKinley",
  "Monroe", "Nixon", "Obama", "Pierce", "Polk", "Reagan", "Roosevelt",
  "Taft", "Taylor", "Truman", "Tyler", "Van Buren", "Washington", "Wilson"};

bool contains = presidents.Contains("Rattz");
Console.WriteLine(contains);
```

Since there is no element whose value is `"Rattz"` in the array, the `contains` variable should be `false`. Here is the output:

```
False
```

In Listing 5-44, we know an element will match our specified value.

Listing 5-44. First Contains Prototype Where an Element Matches the Specified Value

```
string[] presidents = {
  "Adams", "Arthur", "Buchanan", "Bush", "Carter", "Cleveland",
  "Clinton", "Coolidge", "Eisenhower", "Fillmore", "Ford", "Garfield",
  "Grant", "Harding", "Harrison", "Hayes", "Hoover", "Jackson",
  "Jefferson", "Johnson", "Kennedy", "Lincoln", "Madison", "McKinley",
  "Monroe", "Nixon", "Obama", "Pierce", "Polk", "Reagan", "Roosevelt",
  "Taft", "Taylor", "Truman", "Tyler", "Van Buren", "Washington", "Wilson"};

bool contains = presidents.Contains("Hayes");
Console.WriteLine(contains);
```

Since there is an element with the value of `"Hayes"`, the `contains` variable should be `true`. Here is the output:

```
True
```

For an example of the second `Contains` operator prototype, we will use our common `MyStringifiedNumberComparer` class. We will check an array of numbers in string format for a number in string format that is technically unequal to any element in the array, but because we use our equality comparison class, the appropriate element will be found. Listing 5-45 shows the example.

Listing 5-45. Second Contains Prototype Where an Element Matches the Specified Value

```
string[] stringifiedNums = {
  "001", "49", "017", "0080", "00027", "2" };

bool contains = stringifiedNums.Contains("0000002",
                                new MyStringifiedNumberComparer());

Console.WriteLine(contains);
```

We are looking for an element with a value of "0000002". Our equality comparison object will be used, which will convert that string value as well as all the sequence elements to an integer before making the comparison. Since our sequence contains the element "2", the contains variable should be true. Let's take a look at the results:

```
True
```

Now we will try the same example except this time we will query for an element that we know doesn't exist. Listing 5-46 shows the code.

Listing 5-46. Second Contains Prototype Where an Element Does Not Match the Specified Value

```
string[] stringifiedNums = {
  "001", "49", "017", "0080", "00027", "2" };

bool contains = stringifiedNums.Contains("000271",
                                new MyStringifiedNumberComparer());

Console.WriteLine(contains);
```

Since we know that none of the elements when converted to an integer equals 271, we search the array for "000271". Here are the results:

```
False
```

Aggregate

The following aggregate operators allow you to perform aggregate operations on the elements of an input sequence.

Count

The Count operator returns the number of elements in the input sequence.

Prototypes

There are two prototypes we cover.

The First Count Prototype

```
public static int Count<T>(
  this IEnumerable<T> source);
```

This prototype of the Count operator returns the total number of elements in the source input sequence by first checking the input sequence to see whether it implements the ICollection<T> interface, and if so, it obtains the sequence's count using the implementation of that interface. If the source input sequence does not implement the ICollection<T> interface, it enumerates the entire input sequence counting the number of elements.

The second prototype of the Count operator enumerates the source input sequence and counts every element that causes the predicate method delegate to return true.

The Second Count Prototype

```
public static int Count<T>(
  this IEnumerable<T> source,
  Func<T, bool> predicate);
```

Exceptions

ArgumentNullException is thrown if any argument is null.

OverflowException is thrown if the count exceeds the capacity of int.MaxValue.

Examples

Listing 5-47 begins with the first prototype. How many elements are there in the presidents sequence?

Listing 5-47. The First Count Prototype

```
string[] presidents = {
  "Adams", "Arthur", "Buchanan", "Bush", "Carter", "Cleveland",
  "Clinton", "Coolidge", "Eisenhower", "Fillmore", "Ford", "Garfield",
  "Grant", "Harding", "Harrison", "Hayes", "Hoover", "Jackson",
  "Jefferson", "Johnson", "Kennedy", "Lincoln", "Madison", "McKinley",
  "Monroe", "Nixon", "Obama", "Pierce", "Polk", "Reagan", "Roosevelt",
  "Taft", "Taylor", "Truman", "Tyler", "Van Buren", "Washington", "Wilson"};
```

```
int count = presidents.Count();
Console.WriteLine(count);
```

Here are the results:

```
38
```

Now we will try an example of the second prototype, shown in Listing 5-48. We will count the number of presidents beginning with the letter "J".

Listing 5-48. The Second Count Prototype

```
string[] presidents = {
  "Adams", "Arthur", "Buchanan", "Bush", "Carter", "Cleveland",
  "Clinton", "Coolidge", "Eisenhower", "Fillmore", "Ford", "Garfield",
  "Grant", "Harding", "Harrison", "Hayes", "Hoover", "Jackson",
  "Jefferson", "Johnson", "Kennedy", "Lincoln", "Madison", "McKinley",
  "Monroe", "Nixon", "Obama", "Pierce", "Polk", "Reagan", "Roosevelt",
  "Taft", "Taylor", "Truman", "Tyler", "Van Buren", "Washington", "Wilson"};

int count = presidents.Count(s => s.StartsWith("J"));
Console.WriteLine(count);
```

The results from this code are the following:

```
3
```

So what happens if the count exceeds the capacity of Int32.MaxValue? That's what the LongCount operator is for.

LongCount

The LongCount operator returns the number of elements in the input sequence as a long.

Prototypes

There are two prototypes we cover.

The First LongCount Prototype

```
public static long LongCount<T>(
  this IEnumerable<T> source);
```

The first prototype of the `LongCount` operator returns the total number of elements in the `source` input sequence by enumerating the entire input sequence and counting the number of elements.

The second prototype of the `LongCount` operator enumerates the `source` input sequence and counts every element that causes the `predicate` method delegate to return `true`.

The Second LongCount Prototype

```
public static long LongCount<T>(
  this IEnumerable<T> source,
  Func<T, bool> predicate);
```

Exceptions

`ArgumentNullException` is thrown if any argument is `null`.

Examples

We will begin with an example of the first prototype, shown in Listing 5-49. We could just reiterate the same two examples we use for the `Count` operator, changing the relevant parts to type `long`, but that wouldn't be very demonstrative of the operator. Since it isn't feasible for me to have a sequence long enough to require the `LongCount` operator, we use a standard query operator to generate one. Unfortunately, the generation operators we covered in the previous chapter only allow you to specify the number of elements to generate using an `int`. We have to concatenate a couple of those generated sequences together to get enough elements to require the `LongCount` operator.

Listing 5-49. The First LongCount Prototype

```
long count = Enumerable.Range(0, int.MaxValue).
  Concat(Enumerable.Range(0, int.MaxValue)).LongCount();

Console.WriteLine(count);
```

As you can see, we generated two sequences using the `Range` operator we cover in the previous chapter and concatenated them together using the `Concat` operator also covered in the previous chapter.

■ **Caution** This example takes a while to run. On our four-core machine with 4GB of memory, it took approximately one minute.

Before you run that example, let us warn you that it takes a long time to run. Don't be surprised if it takes several minutes. After all, it has to generate two sequences, each with 2,147,483,647 elements. Here are the results:

4294967294

If you try to run that same example using the Count operator, you will get an exception. Now we will try an example of the second prototype. For this example, we use the same basic example as the previous, except we specify a predicate that only returns true for integers greater than 1 and less than 4. This essentially means 2 and 3. Since we have two sequences with the same values, we should get a count of 4, as shown in Listing 5-50.

Listing 5-50. *An Example of the Second LongCount Prototype*

```
long count = Enumerable.Range(0, int.MaxValue).
  Concat(Enumerable.Range(0, int.MaxValue)).LongCount(n => n > 1 && n < 4);

Console.WriteLine(count);
```

This code is much the same as the previous example except we have specified a predicate. This example takes even longer to run than the previous example.

The results from this code are the following:

4

Sum

The Sum operator returns the sum of numeric values contained in the elements of the input sequence.

Prototypes

There are two prototypes we cover.

The First Sum Prototype

```
public static Numeric Sum(
  this IEnumerable<Numeric> source);
```

The *Numeric* type must be one of int, long, double, or decimal or one of their nullable equivalents, int?, long?, double?, or decimal?.

The first prototype of the Sum operator returns the sum of each element in the source input sequence.

An empty sequence will return the sum of zero. The Sum operator will not include null values in the result for *Numeric* types that are nullable.

The second prototype of the Sum operator behaves like the previous, except it will sum the value selected from each element by the selector method delegate.

The Second Sum Prototype

```
public static Numeric Sum<T>(
  this IEnumerable<T> source,
  Func<T, Numeric> selector);
```

Exceptions

ArgumentNullException is thrown if any argument is null.

OverflowException is thrown if the sum is too large to be stored in the Numeric type if the Numeric type is other than decimal or decimal?. If the *Numeric* type is decimal or decimal?, a positive or negative infinity value is returned.

Examples

We will begin with an example of the first prototype, shown in Listing 5-51. First we generate a sequence of integers using the Range operator, and then we use the Sum operator to sum them.

Listing 5-51. An Example of the First Sum Prototype

```
IEnumerable<int> ints = Enumerable.Range(1, 10);

foreach (int i in ints)
  Console.WriteLine(i);

Console.WriteLine("--");

int sum = ints.Sum();
Console.WriteLine(sum);
```

Here are the results:

```
1
2
3
4
5
6
7
8
9
10
--
55
```

Now we will try an example of the second prototype, shown in Listing 5-52. For this example, we use the common `EmployeeOptionEntry` class and sum the count of the options for all employees.

Listing 5-52. *An Example of the Second Sum Prototype*

```
IEnumerable<EmployeeOptionEntry> options =
  EmployeeOptionEntry.GetEmployeeOptionEntries();

long optionsSum = options.Sum(o => o.optionsCount);
Console.WriteLine("The sum of the employee options is: {0}", optionsSum);
```

Instead of trying to sum the entire element, which makes no sense in this example because it is an `employee` object, we can use the second prototype's element `selector` to retrieve just the member we am interested in summing, which in this case is the `optionsCount` member. The results of this code are the following:

```
The sum of the employee options is: 51504
```

Min

The `Min` operator returns the minimum value of an input sequence.

Prototypes

There are four prototypes we cover.

The First Min Prototype

```
public static Numeric Min(
  this IEnumerable<Numeric> source);
```

The *Numeric* type must be one of `int`, `long`, `double`, or `decimal` or one of their nullable equivalents, `int?`, `long?`, `double?`, or `decimal?`.

The first prototype of the `Min` operator returns the element with the minimum numeric value in the `source` input sequence. If the element type implements the `IComparable<T>` interface, that interface will be used to compare the elements. If the elements do not implement the `IComparable<T>` interface, the nongeneric `IComparable` interface will be used.

An empty sequence, or one that contains only `null` values, will return the value of `null`.

The second prototype of the `Min` operator behaves like the previous, except it is for non-*Numeric* types.

The Second Min Prototype

```
public static T Min<T>(
  this IEnumerable<T> source);
```

The third prototype is for *Numeric* types and is like the first, except now a selector method delegate can be provided, allowing a member of each element in the input sequence to be compared while searching for the minimum value in the input sequence and returning that minimum value.

The Third Min Prototype

```
public static Numeric Min<T>(
    this IEnumerable<T> source,
    Func<T, Numeric> selector);
```

The fourth prototype is for non-*Numeric* types and is like the second, except now a `selector` method delegate can be provided, allowing a member of each element in the input sequence to be compared while searching for the minimum value in the input sequence and returning that minimum value.

The Fourth Min Prototype

```
public static S Min<T, S>(
    this IEnumerable<T> source,
    Func<T, S> selector);
```

Exceptions

`ArgumentNullException` is thrown if any argument is `null`.

`InvalidOperationException` is thrown if the `source` sequence is empty for the *Numeric* versions of the prototypes if the type T is non-nullable, such as `int`, `long`, `double`, or `decimal`. If the types are nullable, that is, `int?`, `long?`, `double?`, or `decimal?`, a `null` is returned from the operator instead.

Examples

In the example of the first `Min` prototype, shown in Listing 5-53, we declare an array of integers and return the minimum from it.

Listing 5-53. An Example of the First Min Prototype

```
int[] myInts = new int[] { 974, 2, 7, 1374, 27, 54 };
int minInt = myInts.Min();
Console.WriteLine(minInt);
```

That is a pretty trivial example. The following is the result:

2

For our example of the second prototype, shown in Listing 5-54, we will just call the `Min` operator on our standard `presidents` array. This should return the element with the lowest value, alphabetically speaking.

Listing 5-54. An Example of the Second Min Prototype

```
string[] presidents = {
  "Adams", "Arthur", "Buchanan", "Bush", "Carter", "Cleveland",
  "Clinton", "Coolidge", "Eisenhower", "Fillmore", "Ford", "Garfield",
  "Grant", "Harding", "Harrison", "Hayes", "Hoover", "Jackson",
  "Jefferson", "Johnson", "Kennedy", "Lincoln", "Madison", "McKinley",
  "Monroe", "Nixon", "Obama", "Pierce", "Polk", "Reagan", "Roosevelt",
  "Taft", "Taylor", "Truman", "Tyler", "Van Buren", "Washington", "Wilson"};

string minName = presidents.Min();
Console.WriteLine(minName);
```

This example provides the following results:

```
Adams
```

Although this may be the same output that calling the `First` operator would provide, this is only because the `presidents` array is already sequenced alphabetically. Had the array been in some other order, or disordered, the results would have still been `Adams`.

For the example of the third prototype of the `Min` operator, we use our common `Actor` class to find the earliest actor birth year by calling the `Min` operator on the birth year.

Listing 5-55 is the code calling the `Min` operator.

Listing 5-55. An Example of the Third Min Prototype

```
int oldestActorAge = Actor.GetActors().Min(a => a.birthYear);
Console.WriteLine(oldestActorAge);
```

And the birth year of the actor with the most plastic surgery, we mean, the earliest birth year is the following:

```
1960
```

For an example of the fourth `Min` prototype, shown in Listing 5-56, we obtain the last name of the actor that would come first alphabetically using our common `Actor` class.

Listing 5-56. An Example of the Fourth Min Prototype

```
string firstAlphabetically = Actor.GetActors().Min(a => a.lastName);
```

```
Console.WriteLine(firstAlphabetically);
```

And the Oscar goes to...

Bullock

Max

The Max operator returns the maximum value of an input sequence.

Prototypes

There are four prototypes we cover.

The First Max Prototype

```
public static Numeric Max(
  this IEnumerable<Numeric> source);
```

The *Numeric* type must be one of int, long, double, or decimal or one of their nullable equivalents, int?, long?, double?, or decimal?.

The first prototype of the Max operator returns the element with the maximum numeric value in the source input sequence. If the element type implements the IComparable<T> interface, that interface will be used to compare the elements. If the elements do not implement the IComparable<T> interface, the nongeneric IComparable interface will be used.

An empty sequence, or one that contains only null values, will return the value of null.

The second prototype of the Max operator behaves like the previous, except it is for non-*Numeric* types.

The Second Max Prototype

```
public static T Max<T>(
  this IEnumerable<T> source);
```

The third prototype is for *Numeric* types and like the first, except now a selector method delegate can be provided, allowing a member of each element in the input sequence to be compared while searching for the maximum value in the input sequence and returning that maximum value.

The Third Max Prototype

```
public static Numeric Max<T>(
  this IEnumerable<T> source,
  Func<T, Numeric> selector);
```

The fourth prototype is for non-*Numeric* types and is like the second, except now a `selector` method delegate can be provided, allowing a member of each element in the input sequence to be compared while searching for the maximum value in the input sequence and returning that maximum value.

The Fourth Max Prototype

```
public static S Max<T, S>(
  this IEnumerable<T> source,
  Func<T, S> selector);
```

Exceptions

`ArgumentNullException` is thrown if any argument is `null`.

`InvalidOperationException` is thrown if the source sequence is empty for the *Numeric* versions of the prototypes if the type T is non-nullable, such as `int`, `long`, `double`, or `decimal`. If the types are nullable, such as `int?`, `long?`, `double?`, or `decimal?`, a `null` is returned from the operator instead.

Examples

As an example of the first `Max` prototype, shown in Listing 5-57, we declare an array of integers and return the maximum from it.

Listing 5-57. *An Example of the First Max Prototype*

```
int[] myInts = new int[] { 974, 2, 7, 1374, 27, 54 };
int maxInt = myInts.Max();
Console.WriteLine(maxInt);
```

The results are the following:

```
1374
```

For an example of the second prototype, shown in Listing 5-58, we just call the `Max` operator on our standard `presidents` array.

Listing 5-58. *An Example of the Second Max Prototype*

```
string[] presidents = {
  "Adams", "Arthur", "Buchanan", "Bush", "Carter", "Cleveland",
  "Clinton", "Coolidge", "Eisenhower", "Fillmore", "Ford", "Garfield",
  "Grant", "Harding", "Harrison", "Hayes", "Hoover", "Jackson",
  "Jefferson", "Johnson", "Kennedy", "Lincoln", "Madison", "McKinley",
  "Monroe", "Nixon", "Obama", "Pierce", "Polk", "Reagan", "Roosevelt",
  "Taft", "Taylor", "Truman", "Tyler", "Van Buren", "Washington", "Wilson"};
```

```
string maxName = presidents.Max();
Console.WriteLine(maxName);
```

This provides the following results:

```
Wilson
```

Again, like we mentioned in the equivalent example for the Min operator, although this example provides the same result that the Last operator would, this is only because the presidents array is already ordered alphabetically.

For the example of the third prototype of the Max operator, we use our common Actor class to find the latest actor birth year by calling the Max operator on the birth year.

Listing 5-59 is the code calling the Max operator.

Listing 5-59. *An Example of the Third Max Prototype*

```
int youngestActorAge = Actor.GetActors().Max(a => a.birthYear);
Console.WriteLine(youngestActorAge);
```

And the latest actor birth year in our Actor class is the following:

```
1968
```

For an example of the fourth Max prototype, shown in Listing 5-60, we will obtain the last name of the actor who would come last alphabetically using the same Actor class as previously.

Listing 5-60. *An Example of the Fourth Max Prototype*

```
string lastAlphabetically = Actor.GetActors().Max(a => a.lastName);
Console.WriteLine(lastAlphabetically);
```

The results are the following:

```
Wilson
```

Average

The Average operator returns the average of numeric values contained in the elements of the input sequence.

Prototypes

There are two prototypes we cover.

The First Average Prototype

```
public static Result Average(
  this IEnumerable<Numeric> source);
```

The *Numeric* type must be one of int, long, double, or decimal or one of their nullable equivalents, int?, long?, double?, or decimal?. If the *Numeric* type is int or long, the *Result* type will be double. If the *Numeric* type is int? or long?, the *Result* type will be double?. Otherwise, the *Result* type will be the same as the *Numeric* type.

The first prototype of the Average operator enumerates the input source sequence of *Numeric* type elements, creating an average of the elements themselves.

The second prototype of the Average operator enumerates the source input sequence and determines the average for the member returned by the selector for every element in the input source sequence.

The Second Average Prototype

```
public static Result Average<T>(
  this IEnumerable<T> source,
  Func<T, Numeric> selector);
```

Exceptions

ArgumentNullException is thrown if any argument is null.

OverflowException is thrown if the sum of the averaged values exceeds the capacity of a long for *Numeric* types int, int?, long, and long?.

Examples

We will begin with an example of the first prototype, shown in Listing 5-61. For this example, we use the Range operator to create a sequence of integers, and then we will average them.

Listing 5-61. An Example of the First Average Prototype

```
IEnumerable<int> intSequence = Enumerable.Range(1, 10);
Console.WriteLine("Here is our sequence of integers:");
foreach (int i in intSequence)
  Console.WriteLine(i);

double average = intSequence.Average();
Console.WriteLine("Here is the average:  {0}", average);
```

Here are the results:

```
Here is our sequence of integers:
1
2
3
4
5
6
7
8
9
10
Here is the average:  5.5
```

Now we will try an example of the second prototype, which will access a member of the element. For this example, shown in Listing 5-62, we use our common `EmployeeOptionEntry` class.

Listing 5-62. *An Example of the Second Average Prototype*

```
IEnumerable<EmployeeOptionEntry> options =
  EmployeeOptionEntry.GetEmployeeOptionEntries();

Console.WriteLine("Here are the employee ids and their options:");
foreach (EmployeeOptionEntry eo in options)
  Console.WriteLine("Employee id: {0},  Options:  {1}", eo.id, eo.optionsCount);

// Now I'll get the average of the options.
double optionAverage = options.Average(o => o.optionsCount);
Console.WriteLine("The average of the employee options is: {0}", optionAverage);
```

First we retrieve the `EmployeeOptionEntry` objects. Then we enumerate through the sequence of objects and display each. At the end, we calculate the average and display it. The results of this code are the following:

```
Here are the employee ids and their options:
Employee id:  1,  Options:  2
Employee id:  2,  Options:  10000
Employee id:  2,  Options:  10000
Employee id:  3,  Options:  5000
Employee id:  2,  Options:  10000
Employee id:  3,  Options:  7500
Employee id:  3,  Options:  7500
Employee id:  4,  Options:  1500
Employee id:  101,  Options:  2
The average of the employee options is: 5722.66666666667
```

Aggregate

The Aggregate operator performs a user-specified function on each element of an input sequence, passing in the function's return value from the previous element and returning the return value of the last element.

Prototypes

There are two prototypes we cover.

The First Aggregate Prototype

```
public static T Aggregate<T>(
  this IEnumerable<T> source,
  Func<T, T, T> func);
```

In this version of the prototype, the Aggregate operator enumerates through each element of the input source sequence, calling the func method delegate on each, passing the return value from the previous element as the first argument and the element itself as the second argument, and finally storing the value returned by func into an internal accumulator, which will then be passed to the next element. The first element will be passed itself as the input value to the func method delegate.

The second prototype of the Aggregate operator behaves like the first version, except a seed value is provided that will be the input value for the first invocation of the func method delegate instead of the first element.

The Second Aggregate Prototype

```
public static U Aggregate<T, U>(
  this IEnumerable<T> source,
  U seed,
  Func<U, T, U> func);
```

Exceptions

ArgumentNullException is thrown if the source or func argument is null.

InvalidOperationException is thrown if the input source sequence is empty, only for the first Aggregate prototype, where no seed value is provided.

Examples

We will begin with an example of the first prototype, shown in Listing 5-63. In the example, we calculate the factorial for the number 5. A *factorial* is the product of all positive integers less than or equal to some number. The factorial of 5 is the product of all positive integers less than or equal to 5. So, 5!, pronounced *5 factorial*, will be equal to 1 * 2 * 3 * 4 * 5. It looks like we could use the Range operator and the Aggregate operator to calculate this.

Listing 5-63. An Example of the First Aggregate Prototype

```
int N = 5;
IEnumerable<int> intSequence = Enumerable.Range(1, N);

// we will just output the sequence so all can see it.
foreach (int item in intSequence)
  Console.WriteLine(item);

// Now calculate the factorial and display it.
// av == aggregated value, e == element
int agg = intSequence.Aggregate((av, e) => av * e);
Console.WriteLine("{0}! = {1}", N, agg);
```

In the previous code, we generate a sequence containing the integers from 1 to 5 using the Range operator. After displaying each element in the generated sequence, we call the Aggregate operator passing a lambda expression that multiplies the passed aggregated value with the passed element itself. The following are the results:

```
1
2
3
4
5
5! = 120
```

■ **Caution** You should be careful when using this version of the Aggregate operator that the first element doesn't get operated on twice, since it is passed in as the input value and the element for the first element. In the previous example, our first call to our func lambda expression would have passed in 1 and 1. Since we just multiplied these two values and they are both ones, there is no bad side effect. But if we had added the two values, we would have a sum that included the first element twice.

For the second prototype's example, shown in Listing 5-64, we roll our own version of the Sum operator.

Listing 5-64. *An Example of the Second Aggregate Prototype*

```
IEnumerable<int> intSequence = Enumerable.Range(1, 10);

//  I'll just output the sequence so all can see it.
foreach (int item in intSequence)
  Console.WriteLine(item);
Console.WriteLine("--");

//  Now calculate the sum and display it.
int sum = intSequence.Aggregate(0, (s, i) => s + i);
Console.WriteLine(sum);
```

Notice that we passed 0 as the seed for this call to the `Aggregate` operator. And the envelope, please...

```
1
2
3
4
5
6
7
8
9
10
--
55
```

As you can see, we got the same results that we did when calling the `Sum` operator in Listing 5-51.

Summary

Wow, our head is spinning. We hope we didn't lose too many of you. We know a lot of this chapter and the previous chapter was a little dry, but these two chapters are packed with the essentials of LINQ. We hope that as we covered each query operator you tried to visualize when you might use it. A large part of making LINQ effective for you is having a feel for the operators and what they do. Even if you can't remember every variation of each operator, just knowing they exist and what they can do for you is essential.

From our coverage of LINQ to Objects and the Standard Query Operators, we hope you can see just how powerful and convenient LINQ is for querying data of all types of in-memory data collections.

With nearly 50 operators to choose from, LINQ to Objects is sure to make your data-querying code more consistent, more reliable, and more expedient to write.

We can't emphasize enough that most of the Standard Query Operators work on collections that implement the `IEnumerable<T>` interface, and this excludes the legacy C# collections. We know that some readers are going to miss this fact and get frustrated because they have legacy code with an

`ArrayList` and cannot seem to find a way to query data from it. If this is you, please read about the `Cast` and `OfType` operators.

Now that you have a sound understanding of LINQ to Objects and just what LINQ can do for you, it's time to learn about using LINQ to query and generate XML. This functionality is called LINQ to XML and, not so coincidentally, that is the name of the next part of this book.

PART 3

LINQ to XML

CHAPTER 6

LINQ to XML Introduction

So you want to be an XML hero? Are you willing to suffer the slings and arrows? Listing 6-1 shows some code that creates a trivial XML hierarchy using Microsoft's original XML Document Object Model (DOM) API, which is based on the W3C DOM XML API, demonstrating just how painful that model can be.

Listing 6-1. *A Simple XML Example*

```
using System.Xml;

// I'll declare some variables we will reuse.
XmlElement xmlBookParticipant;
XmlAttribute xmlParticipantType;
XmlElement xmlFirstName;
XmlElement xmlLastName;

// First, we must build an XML document.
XmlDocument xmlDoc = new XmlDocument();

// I'll create the root element and add it to the document.
XmlElement xmlBookParticipants = xmlDoc.CreateElement("BookParticipants");
xmlDoc.AppendChild(xmlBookParticipants);

// I'll create a participant and add it to the book participants list.
xmlBookParticipant = xmlDoc.CreateElement("BookParticipant");

xmlParticipantType = xmlDoc.CreateAttribute("type");
xmlParticipantType.InnerText = "Author";
xmlBookParticipant.Attributes.Append(xmlParticipantType);

xmlFirstName = xmlDoc.CreateElement("FirstName");
xmlFirstName.InnerText = "Joe";
xmlBookParticipant.AppendChild(xmlFirstName);

xmlLastName = xmlDoc.CreateElement("LastName");
xmlLastName.InnerText = "Rattz";
xmlBookParticipant.AppendChild(xmlLastName);
```

```
xmlBookParticipants.AppendChild(xmlBookParticipant);

// I'll create another participant and add it to the book participants list.
xmlBookParticipant = xmlDoc.CreateElement("BookParticipant");

xmlParticipantType = xmlDoc.CreateAttribute("type");
xmlParticipantType.InnerText = "Editor";
xmlBookParticipant.Attributes.Append(xmlParticipantType);

xmlFirstName = xmlDoc.CreateElement("FirstName");
xmlFirstName.InnerText = "Ewan";
xmlBookParticipant.AppendChild(xmlFirstName);

xmlLastName = xmlDoc.CreateElement("LastName");
xmlLastName.InnerText = "Buckingham";
xmlBookParticipant.AppendChild(xmlLastName);

xmlBookParticipants.AppendChild(xmlBookParticipant);

// Now, I'll search for authors and display their first and last name.
XmlNodeList authorsList =
  xmlDoc.SelectNodes("BookParticipants/BookParticipant[@type=\"Author\"]");

foreach (XmlNode node in authorsList)
{
  XmlNode firstName = node.SelectSingleNode("FirstName");
  XmlNode lastName = node.SelectSingleNode("LastName");
  Console.WriteLine("{0} {1}", firstName, lastName);
}
```

That last line of code, the call to the WriteLine method, is in bold because we will be changing it momentarily. All that code does is build the following XML hierarchy and attempt to display the name of each book participant:

The Desired Xml Structure

```
<BookParticipants>
  <BookParticipant type="Author">
    <FirstName>Joe</FirstName>
    <LastName>Rattz</LastName>
  </BookParticipant>
  <BookParticipant type="Editor">
    <FirstName>Ewan</FirstName>
    <LastName>Buckingham</LastName>
  </BookParticipant>
</BookParticipants>
```

That code is a nightmare to write, understand, and maintain. It is very verbose. Looking at it gives you no idea what the XML structure should look like. Part of what makes it so cumbersome is that you cannot create an element, initialize it, and attach it to the hierarchy in a single statement. Instead, each element must first be created, then have its `InnerText` member set to the desired value, and finally appended to some node already existing in the XML document. This must be done for every element and attribute. This leads to a lot of code. Additionally, an XML document must first be created because without it, you cannot even create an element. It is common to not want an actual XML document because sometimes just a fragment like the previous is all that is needed. Finally, look at how many lines of code it takes to generate such a small amount of XML.

Now let's take a look at the glorious output; just press Ctrl+F5:

```
System.Xml.XmlElement System.Xml.XmlElement
```

Oops! It looks like we didn't get the actual text out of the `FirstName` and `LastName` nodes in that `foreach` loop. We'll modify that `Console.WriteLine` method call to get the data:

```
Console.WriteLine("{0} {1}", firstName.ToString(), lastName.ToString());
```

Now prepare to be impressed! Abracadabra, Ctrl+F5:

```
System.Xml.XmlElement System.Xml.XmlElement
```

Heavy sigh.

If chicks really do dig scars as Keanu Reeves's character suggests in the movie *The Replacements*, they ought to love Extensible Markup Language (XML) developers. If you have had any experience using XML, then you will have stories to tell that involve frustration, confusion, and different "industry-standard" schemas produced by each and every company in each and every industry.

Regardless of the battle scars we may have, there is no doubt that XML has become *the* standard for data exchange. And as one of our friends says when struggling for a compliment for XML, it compresses well.

So the next time you want to turn that young lady's head, let her hear you whisper a sweet something about namespaces, nodes, or attributes. She will be putty in your hands:

```
<PuttyInYourHands>True</PuttyInYourHands>
```

Introduction

Microsoft could have given us a new LINQ XML API that only added the ability to perform LINQ queries and been done with it. Fortunately for XML developers, Microsoft went the extra mile. In addition to making XML support LINQ queries, Microsoft addressed many of the deficiencies of the standard DOM XML API. After years of suffering with the W3C DOM XML API, most developers were aware that many tasks did not seem as simple as they should. When dealing with small fragments of XML, using the W3C DOM required creating an XML document just to create a few elements. Have you ever just built a string so that it looks like XML, rather than using the DOM API because it was such a hassle? We sure have.

Several key deficiencies were addressed. A new object model was created. And the result is a far simpler and more elegant method for creating XML trees. Bloated code like that in Listing 6-1 will be an artifact of an API past its prime and left in the wake of LINQ. Creating a full XML tree in a single statement is now a reality thanks to *functional construction*. Functional construction is the term used to describe the ability to construct an entire XML hierarchy in a single statement. That alone makes LINQ to XML worth its weight in gold.

Of course, it wouldn't be part of LINQ if the new XML API didn't support LINQ queries. In that vein, several new XML-specific query operators, implemented as extension methods, were added. Combining these new XML-specific operators with the LINQ to Objects Standard Query Operators we discuss in Part 2 of this book creates a powerfully elegant solution for finding whatever data you are searching for in an XML tree.

Not only does LINQ support all this, but combine a query with functional construction, and you get an XML transformation. LINQ to XML is very flexible.

Cheating the W3C DOM XML API

OK, you are working on your project, and you know some particular data should be stored as XML. In one case, one of us was developing a general logging class that tracked everything a user does within an ASP.NET web application. The logging class was developed for two reasons. First, it was developed to prove someone was abusing the system should that ever happen. Second, and most important, when the web application would signal via e-mail that an exception had occurred, the users who triggered the exceptions could never remember what they were doing at the time they happened. They could never recall the details that led them to the error.

So, we wanted something tracking their every move, at least on the server side. Every different type of action a user would make, such as an invoice query or an order submission, would be considered an *event*. In the database, there were fields that captured the user, the date, the time, the *event* type, and all the common fields you would want. However, it wasn't enough to know they were perhaps querying for an invoice; we also had to know what the search parameters were. If they were submitting an order, we needed to know what the part ID was and how many they ordered. Basically, we needed all the data so that we could perform the same operation they attempted in order to reproduce the exception condition. Each type of event had different parameter data. We didn't want a different table for each event type, and we didn't want the Event Viewer code to have to hit a zillion different tables to reconstruct the user's actions. We wanted one table to capture it all so that when viewing the table we could see every action (event) the user performed. So there we were, confronted with the notion that what we needed was a string of XML data stored in the database that contained the event's parameter data.

There would be no schema defining what the XML looked like, because it was whatever data a particular event needed it to be. If the event was an invoice inquiry across a date range, it might look like this:

```
<StartDate>10/2/2006</StartDate>
<EndDate>10/9/2006</EndDate>
<IncludePaid>False</IncludePaid>
```
If it was an order submission, it might look like this:
```
<PartId>4754611903</PartId>
<Quantity>12</Quantity>
<DistributionCenter>Atlanta<DistributionCenter>
<ShippingCode>USPS First Class<ShippingCode>
```

We captured whatever fields would be necessary to manually reproduce the event. Since the data varied with the event type, this ruled out validating the XML, so there went one benefit of using the XML DOM API.

This event tracker became a first-class support tool, as well as making it much easier to identify and resolve bugs. As a side note, it is quite entertaining to call a user the next day and tell them that the error they saw when they tried to pull up invoice number 3847329 the previous day is now fixed. The paranoia that results when users know you know exactly what they did is often reward enough for the tracking code.

Those of you who are already familiar with XML may be looking at those schemas and saying, "Hey, that's not well-formed. There's no root node." OK, that's true and is a problem if you use the W3C DOM API. However, we didn't use the W3C DOM API to produce that XML; we used a different XML API. You have probably used it too. It's called the `String.Format` XML API, and using it looks a little like this:

```
string xmlData =
  string.Format(
    "<StartDate>{0}</StartDate><EndDate>{1}</EndDate><IncPaid>{2}</IncPaid>",
    Date.ToShortDateString(),
    endDate.ToShortDateString(),
    includePaid.ToString());
```

Yes, we are aware this is a poor way to create XML data. And, yes, it is prone to bugs. It's certainly easy to misspell, or set the case of (`EndDate` vs. `endDate`, for example), a closing tag this way. We even went so far as to create a method to pass a parameter list of element names and their data. So, the code actually looks a little more like this:

```
string xmlData =
  XMLHelper(
    "StartDate", startDate.ToShortDateString(),
    "EndDate", endDate.ToShortDateString(),
    "IncPaid", includePaid.ToString());
```

That `XMLHelper` method will create a root node, too. Yet again, this isn't much better. You can see that there is nothing to encode the data in that call. So, it was an error down the road before we realized we had better be encoding those data values that get passed.

Although using the `String.Format` method, or any technique other than the XML DOM API, is a poor substitute for the DOM, the existing API is often too much trouble when dealing with just an XML fragment, as in this case.

If you think this is a unique approach to creating XML, we were at a Microsoft seminar recently, and the presenter demonstrated code that built a string of XML using string concatenation. If only there was a better way. If only LINQ had been available!

Summary

Whenever someone utters the word *LINQ*, the first image that most developers seem to conjure is that of performing a data query. More specifically than that, they seem to want to exclude data sources other than databases. LINQ to XML is here to tell you that LINQ is about XML too—and not just about querying XML.

In this chapter, we demonstrated some of the pain of dealing with XML when using the existing W3C DOM XML API and some of the traditional cheats to avoid that pain. In the next chapter, we cover the LINQ to XML API. Using this API, we demonstrate how to create XML hierarchies in a fraction of the code possible with the W3C DOM XML API. Just to tease you, we will tell you now that in the next chapter we create the same XML hierarchy that is created in Listing 6-1 using LINQ to XML, and instead of the 29 lines of code that Listing 6-1 requires to create the hierarchy, LINQ to XML allows us to create that same hierarchy with only 10 lines of code.

By the time you are finished reading the next two chapters, you will agree that LINQ is as revolutionary for XML manipulation as it is for database queries.

CHAPTER 7

The LINQ to XML API

In the previous chapter, we demonstrated creating an XML document using the W3C DOM XML API and just how cumbersome that API can be. We also showed you some of the techniques we have seen used to circumvent the pain it causes.

We also let you in on a seemingly little-known secret about LINQ: LINQ is not just about data queries—it is also about XML. We told you there was a new XML API on the horizon and that API is the LINQ to XML API.

Now, there is a better, or at least simpler, way to construct, traverse, manipulate, and query XML, and it's called LINQ to XML. In this chapter, we show you how to create, manipulate, and traverse XML documents using the LINQ to XML API, as well as how to perform searches on an XML object.

For the examples in this chapter, we created a console application. However, before you can leverage this new API, you need to add a reference to your project for the `System.Xml.Linq` assembly if it is not already present.

Referenced Namespaces

The examples in this chapter use the `System.Linq`, `System.Xml.Linq`, and `System.Collections.Generic` namespaces. Therefore, you should add `using` directives for these namespaces to your code if they are not already present:

```
using System.Linq;
using System.Xml.Linq;
using System.Collections.Generic;
```

In addition to these namespaces, if you download the companion code, you will see that we also added a `using` directive for the `System.Diagnostics` namespace. This will not be necessary if you are typing in the examples from this chapter. It is necessary in the downloadable companion code because of some housekeeping code.

Significant API Design Enhancements

After a few years of experience with Microsoft's W3C XML DOM API, several key areas have been identified by Microsoft as inconveniences, annoyances, or weaknesses in the original API. To combat these issues, the following points have been addressed:

- XML tree construction

- Document centricity

- Namespaces and prefixes

- Node value extraction

Each of these problem domains has been a stumbling block to working with XML. Not only have these issues made XML code bloated and unintentionally obfuscated, they needed to be addressed for XML to really work seamlessly with LINQ queries. For example, if you want to use projection to return XML from a LINQ query, it's a bit of a problem if you can't instantiate an element with a new statement. This limitation of the existing XML API had to be addressed in order for LINQ to be practical with XML. Let's take a look at each of these problem areas and how they have been addressed in the new LINQ to XML API.

XML Tree Construction Simplified with Functional Construction

When reading the first sample code of the previous chapter, Listing 6-1, it becomes clear that it is very difficult to determine the XML schema by looking at the code that creates the XML tree. The code is also verbose. After creating the XML document, we must create some type of XML node such as an element, set its value, and append it to its parent element. However, each of those three steps must be performed individually using the W3C DOM API. This leads to an obfuscated schema and a lot of code. The API just doesn't support creating an element, or any other type of node, in place in the XML tree with respect to its parent and then initializing it, all in a single operation.

The LINQ to XML API not only provides the same ability to create the XML tree as the W3C DOM does, but it also provides a new technique known as *functional construction* to create an XML tree. Functional construction allows the schema to be dictated as the XML objects are constructed and the values are initialized all at the same time in a single statement. The API accomplishes this by providing constructors for the new API's XML objects that accept either a single object or multiple objects that specify its value. The type of object, or objects, being added determines where in the schema the added object belongs. The pattern looks like this:

```
XMLOBJECT o =
    new XMLOBJECT(OBJECTNAME,
                  XMLOBJECT1,
                  XMLOBJECT2,
                  ...
                  XMLOBJECTN);
```

■ **Note** The preceding code is merely pseudocode meant to illustrate a pattern. None of the classes referenced in the pseudocode actually exists; they just represent conceptually abstract XML classes.

If you add an XML attribute, which is implemented with the LINQ to XML XAttribute class, to an element, implemented with the XElement class, the attribute becomes an attribute of the element. For example, if XMLOBJECT1 in the previous pseudocode is added to the newly created XMLOBJECT named o, where o is an XElement and XMLOBJECT1 is an XAttribute, then XMLOBJECT1 becomes an attribute of XElement named o.

If you add an XElement to an XElement, the added XElement becomes a child element of the element to which it is added. So for example, if XMLOBJECT1 is an element and o is an element, XMLOBJECT1 becomes a child element of o.

When we instantiate an XMLOBJECT, as indicated in the previous pseudocode, we can specify its contents by specifying 1 to N XMLOBJECTs. As you will learn later in the section titled "Creating Text with XText," you can even specify its contents to include a string, because that string will be automatically converted to an XMLOBJECT for you.

This makes complete sense and is at the heart of functional construction. Listing 7-1 shows an example.

Listing 7-1. Using Functional Construction to Create an XML Schema

```
XElement xBookParticipant =
  new XElement("BookParticipant",
    new XElement("FirstName", "Joe"),
    new XElement("LastName", "Rattz"));

Console.WriteLine(xBookParticipant.ToString());
```

Notice that when we constructed the element named BookParticipant, we passed two XElement objects as its value, and each of which becomes a child element. Also notice that when we constructed the FirstName and LastName elements, instead of specifying multiple child objects, as we did when constructing the BookParticipant element, we provided the element's text value. Here are the results of that code:

```
<BookParticipant>
  <FirstName>Joe</FirstName>
  <LastName>Rattz</LastName>
</BookParticipant>
```

Notice how much easier it is now to visualize the XML schema from the code. Also notice how much less verbose that code is than the first code sample of the previous chapter (Listing 6-1). The LINQ to XML API code necessary to replace the code in Listing 6-1 that actually creates the XML tree is significantly shorter, as shown in Listing 7-2.

Listing 7-2. Creates the Same XML Tree as Listing 6-1 but with Far Less Code

```
XElement xBookParticipants =
  new XElement("BookParticipants",
    new XElement("BookParticipant",
      new XAttribute("type", "Author"),
      new XElement("FirstName", "Joe"),
      new XElement("LastName", "Rattz")),
    new XElement("BookParticipant",
```

```
        new XAttribute("type", "Editor"),
        new XElement("FirstName", "Ewan"),
        new XElement("LastName", "Buckingham")));

Console.WriteLine(xBookParticipants.ToString());
```

That is far less code to create and maintain. Also, the schema is fairly ascertainable by just reading the code. Here is the output:

```
<BookParticipants>
  <BookParticipant type="Author">
    <FirstName>Joe</FirstName>
    <LastName>Rattz</LastName>
  </BookParticipant>
  <BookParticipant type="Editor">
    <FirstName>Ewan</FirstName>
    <LastName>Buckingham</LastName>
  </BookParticipant>
</BookParticipants>
```

There is one more additional benefit to the new API that is apparent in the example's results. Please notice that the output is formatted to look like a *tree* of XML. If we output the XML tree created in Listing 6-1, it actually looks like this:

```
<BookParticipants><BookParticipant type="Author"><FirstName>Joe</FirstName>…
```

Which would you rather read? In the next chapter, when we get to the section on performing LINQ queries that produce XML output, you will see the necessity of functional construction.

Document Centricity Eliminated in Favor of Element Centricity

With the original W3C DOM API, you could not simply create an XML element, XmlElement; you must have an XML document, XmlDocument, from which to create it. If you try to instantiate an XmlElement like this:

```
XmlElement xmlBookParticipant = new XmlElement("BookParticipant");
```

you will be greeted with the following compiler error:

```
'System.Xml.XmlElement.XmlElement(string, string, string, System.Xml.XmlDocument)'
is inaccessible due to its protection level
```

With the W3C DOM API, you can create an XmlElement only by calling an XmlDocument object's CreateElement method like this:

```
XmlDocument xmlDoc = new XmlDocument();
XmlElement xmlBookParticipant = xmlDoc.CreateElement("BookParticipant");
```

This code compiles just fine. But it is often inconvenient to be forced to create an XML document when you just want to create an XML element. The new LINQ-enabled XML API allows you to instantiate an element itself without creating an XML document:

```
XElement xeBookParticipant = new XElement("BookParticipant");
```

XML elements are not the only XML type of node impacted by this W3C DOM restriction. Attributes, comments, CData sections, processing instructions, and entity references all must be created from an XML document. Thankfully, the LINQ to XML API has made it possible to directly instantiate each of these on the fly.

Of course, nothing prevents you from creating an XML document with the new API. For example, you could create an XML document and add the BookParticipants element and one BookParticipant to it, as shown in Listing 7-3.

Listing 7-3. *Using the LINQ to XML API to Create an XML Document and Adding Some Structure to It*

```
XDocument xDocument =
  new XDocument(
    new XElement("BookParticipants",
      new XElement("BookParticipant",
        new XAttribute("type", "Author"),
        new XElement("FirstName", "Joe"),
        new XElement("LastName", "Rattz"))));

Console.WriteLine(xDocument.ToString());
```

Pressing Ctrl+F5 yields the following results:

```
<BookParticipants>
  <BookParticipant type="Author">
    <FirstName>Joe</FirstName>
    <LastName>Rattz</LastName>
  </BookParticipant>
</BookParticipants>
```

The XML produced by the previous code is very similar to the XML we created in Listing 6-1, with the exception that we added only one BookParticipant instead of two. This code is much more readable, though, than Listing 6-1, thanks to our new functional construction capabilities. And it is feasible to determine the schema from looking at the code. However, now that XML documents are no longer necessary, we could just leave the XML document out and obtain the same results, as shown in Listing 7-4.

Listing 7-4. Same Example as the Previous but Without the XML Document

```
XElement xElement =
  new XElement("BookParticipants",
    new XElement("BookParticipant",
      new XAttribute("type", "Author"),
      new XElement("FirstName", "Joe"),
      new XElement("LastName", "Rattz")));

Console.WriteLine(xElement.ToString());
```

Running the code produces the same results as the previous example:

```
<BookParticipants>
  <BookParticipant type="Author">
    <FirstName>Joe</FirstName>
    <LastName>Rattz</LastName>
  </BookParticipant>
</BookParticipants>
```

In addition to creating XML trees without an XML document, you can do most of the other things that a document requires, such as reading XML from a file and saving it to a file.

Names, Namespaces, and Prefixes

To eliminate some of the confusion stemming from names, namespaces, and namespace prefixes, namespace prefixes are out—out of the API, that is. With the LINQ to XML API, namespace prefixes get expanded on input and honored on output. On the inside, they no longer exist.

A namespace is used in XML to uniquely identify the XML schema for some portion of the XML tree. A URI is used for XML namespaces because they are already unique to any organization. In several of our code samples, we have created an XML tree that looks like this:

```
<BookParticipants>
  <BookParticipant type="Author">
    <FirstName>Joe</FirstName>
    <LastName>Rattz</LastName>
  </BookParticipant>
</BookParticipants>
```

Any code that is processing that XML data will be written to expect the BookParticipants node to contain multiple BookParticipant nodes, each of which have a type attribute and a FirstName and LastName node. But what if this code also needs to be able to process XML from another source, and it too has a BookParticipants node but the schema within that node is different from the previous? A namespace will alert the code as to what the schema should look like, thereby allowing the code to handle the XML appropriately.

With XML, every element needs a name. When an element gets created, if its name is specified in the constructor, that name is implicitly converted from a string to an XName object. An XName object consists of a namespace (XNamespace), object, and its local name, which is the name you provided. So, for example, you can create the BookParticipants element like this:

```
XElement xBookParticipants = new XElement("BookParticipants");
```

When you create the element, an XName object gets created with an empty namespace and a local name of BookParticipants. If you debug that line of code and examine the xBookParticipants variable in the watch window, you will see that its Name member is set to {BookParticipants}. If you expand the Name member, it contains a member named LocalName that will be set to BookParticipants, and a member named Namespace that is empty, {}. In this case, there is no namespace.

To specify a namespace, you need merely create an XNamespace object and prepend it to the local name you specify like this:

```
XNamespace nameSpace = "http://www.linqdev.com";
XElement xBookParticipants = new XElement(nameSpace + "BookParticipants");
```

Now when you examine the xBookParticipants element in the debugger watch window, the Name is set to http://www.linqdev.com/BookParticipants. Expanding the Name member reveals that the LocalName member is still BookParticipants, but now the Namespace member is set to http://www.linqdev.com.

It is not necessary to actually use an XNamespace object to specify the namespace. We could have specified it as a hard-coded string literal like this:

```
XElement xBookParticipants = new XElement("{http://www.linqdev.com}" +
  "BookParticipants");
```

Notice that we enclose the namespace in braces. This clues the XElement constructor into the fact that this portion is the namespace. If you examine the BookParticipants's Name member in the watch window again, you will see that the Name member and its embedded LocalName and Namespace members are all set identically to the same values as the previous example where we used an XNamespace object to create the element.

Keep in mind that when setting the namespace, merely specifying the URI to your company or organization domain may not be enough to guarantee its uniqueness. It only guarantees you won't have any collisions with any other organization that also plays by the namespace naming convention rules. However, once inside your organization, any other department could have a collision if you provide nothing more than the organization URI. This is where your knowledge of your organization's divisions, departments, and so on, can be quite useful. It would be best if your namespace could extend all the way to some level you have control over. For example, if you work at LINQDev.com and you are creating a schema for the human resources department that will contain information for the pension plan, your namespace might be the following:

```
XNamespace nameSpace = "http://www.linqdev.com/humanresources/pension";
```

So for a final example showing how namespaces are used, we will modify the code from Listing 7-2 to use a namespace, as shown in Listing 7-5.

Listing 7-5. *Modified Version Listing 7-2 with a Namespace Specified*

```
XNamespace nameSpace = "http://www.linqdev.com";

XElement xBookParticipants =
  new XElement(nameSpace + "BookParticipants",
    new XElement(nameSpace + "BookParticipant",
      new XAttribute("type", "Author"),
      new XElement(nameSpace + "FirstName", "Joe"),
      new XElement(nameSpace + "LastName", "Rattz")),
    new XElement(nameSpace + "BookParticipant",
      new XAttribute("type", "Editor"),
      new XElement(nameSpace + "FirstName", "Ewan"),
      new XElement(nameSpace + "LastName", "Buckingham"))));

Console.WriteLine(xBookParticipants.ToString());
```

Pressing Ctrl+F5 reveals the following results:

```
<BookParticipants xmlns="http://www.linqdev.com">
  <BookParticipant type="Author">
    <FirstName>Joe</FirstName>
    <LastName>Rattz</LastName>
  </BookParticipant>
  <BookParticipant type="Editor">
    <FirstName>Ewan</FirstName>
    <LastName>Buckingham</LastName>
  </BookParticipant>
</BookParticipants>
```

Now any code could read that and know that the schema should match the schema provided by LINQDev.com.

To have control over the namespace prefixes going out, use the XAttribute object to create a prefix as in Listing 7-6.

Listing 7-6. *Specifying a Namespace Prefix*

```
XNamespace nameSpace = "http://www.linqdev.com";

XElement xBookParticipants =
  new XElement(nameSpace + "BookParticipants",
    new XAttribute(XNamespace.Xmlns + "linqdev", nameSpace),
    new XElement(nameSpace + "BookParticipant"));

Console.WriteLine(xBookParticipants.ToString());
```

In the previous code, we specify `linqdev` as the namespace prefix, and we use the `XAttribute` object to get the prefix specification into the schema. Here is the output from this code:

```
<linqdev:BookParticipants xmlns:linqdev="http://www.linqdev.com">
  <linqdev:BookParticipant />
</linqdev:BookParticipants>
```

Node Value Extraction

If you read the first code sample of the previous chapter, Listing 6-1, and laughed at our results, you no doubt have experienced the same issue that prevented us from getting the results we were after—getting the actual value from a node is a bit of a nuisance. We find that if we haven't been working with XML DOM code for a while, we inevitably end up with an error like the one in Listing 6-1. We always forget we have to take the extra step to get the value of the node.

The LINQ to XML API fixes that problem very nicely. First, calling the `ToString` method of an element outputs the XML string itself, not the object type as it does with the W3C DOM API. This is very handy when you want an XML fragment from a certain point in the tree and makes far more sense than outputting the object type. Listing 7-7 shows an example.

Listing 7-7. *Calling the ToString Method on an Element Produces the XML Tree*

```
XElement name = new XElement("Name", "Joe");
Console.WriteLine(name.ToString());
```

Pressing Ctrl+F5 gives us the following:

```
<Name>Joe</Name>
```

Wow, that's a nice change. But wait, it gets better. Of course, child nodes are included in the output, and since the `WriteLine` method doesn't have an explicit overload accepting an `XElement`, it calls the `ToString` method for you, as shown in Listing 7-8.

Listing 7-8. *Console.WriteLine Implicitly Calling the ToString Method on an Element to Produce an XML Tree*

```
XElement name = new XElement("Person",
  new XElement("FirstName", "Joe"),
  new XElement("LastName", "Rattz"));
Console.WriteLine(name);
```

And the following is the output:

```
<Person>

  <FirstName>Joe</FirstName>
  <LastName>Rattz</LastName>
```

```
</Person>
```

Even more important, if you cast a node to a data type that its value can be converted to, the value itself will be output. Listing 7-9 shows another example, but we will also print out the node cast to a string.

Listing 7-9. Casting an Element to Its Value's Data Type Outputs the Value

```
XElement name = new XElement("Name", "Joe");
Console.WriteLine(name);
Console.WriteLine((string)name);
```

Here are the results of this code:

```
<Name>Joe</Name>
Joe
```

How slick is that? Now how much would you pay? And there are cast operators provided for string, int, int?, uint, uint?, long, long?, ulong, ulong?, bool, bool?, float, float?, double, double?, decimal, decimal?, TimeSpan, TimeSpan?, DateTime, DateTime?, GUID, and GUID?.

Listing 7-10 shows an example of a few different node value types.

Listing 7-10. Different Node Value Types Retrieved via Casting to the Node Value's Type

```
XElement count = new XElement("Count", 12);
Console.WriteLine(count);
Console.WriteLine((int)count);

XElement smoker = new XElement("Smoker", false);
Console.WriteLine(smoker);
Console.WriteLine((bool)smoker);

XElement pi = new XElement("Pi", 3.1415926535);
Console.WriteLine(pi);
Console.WriteLine((double)pi);
```

And the envelope, please!

```
<Count>12</Count>
12
<Smoker>false</Smoker>
False
<Pi>3.1415926535</Pi>
3.1415926535
```

That seems very simple and intuitive. If we use the LINQ to XML API instead of the W3C DOM API, errors like the one in Listing 6-1 of the previous chapter will be a thing of the past.

Although all of those examples make obtaining an element's value simple, they are all cases of casting the element to the same data type that its value initially was. This is not necessary. All that is necessary is for the element's value to be able to be converted to the specified data type. Listing 7-11 shows an example where the initial data type is string, but we will obtain its value as a bool.

Listing 7-11. Casting a Node to a Different Data Type Than Its Value's Original Data Type

```
XElement smoker = new XElement("Smoker", "true");
Console.WriteLine(smoker);
Console.WriteLine((bool)smoker);
```

Since we have specified the value of the element to be "true" and since the string "true" can be successfully converted to a bool, the code works:

```
<Smoker>true</Smoker>
True
```

Unfortunately, exactly how the values get converted is not specified, but it appears that the conversion methods in the System.Xml.XmlConvert class are used for this purpose. Listing 7-12 demonstrates that this is the case when casting as a bool.

Listing 7-12. Casting to a Bool Calls the System.Xml.XmlConvert.ToBoolean Method

```
try
{
  XElement smoker = new XElement("Smoker", "Tue");
  Console.WriteLine(smoker);
  Console.WriteLine((bool)smoker);
}
catch (Exception ex)
{
  Console.WriteLine(ex);
}
```

Notice that we intentionally misspell "True" in the previous code to force an exception in the conversion hoping for a clue to be revealed in the exception that is thrown. Will we be so lucky? Let's press Ctrl+F5 to find out.

```
<Smoker>Tue</Smoker>
System.FormatException: The string 'tue' is not a valid Boolean value.
   at System.Xml.XmlConvert.ToBoolean(String s)
...
```

As you can see, the exception occurred in the call to the `System.Xml.XmlConvert.ToBoolean` method.

The LINQ to XML Object Model

With the new LINQ to XML API comes a new object model containing many new classes that exist in the `System.Xml.Linq` namespace. One is the static class where the LINQ to XML extension methods live, Extensions; two are comparer classes, `XNodeDocumentOrderComparer` and `XNodeEqualityComparer`, and the remaining are used to build your XML trees. Those remaining classes are displayed in Figure 7-1.

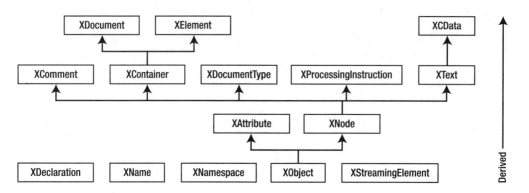

Figure 7-1. *LINQ to XML API object model*

There are some interesting things to note:

* Of those remaining classes, three are abstract—`XObject`, `XContainer`, and `XNode`—so you will never construct them.

* An attribute, `XAttribute`, is not derived from a node, `XNode`. In fact, it is not a node at all but instead is a totally different type of class that is basically a name-value pair.

* Streaming elements, `XStreamingElement`, have no inheritance relationship with elements, `XElement`.

* The `XDocument` and `XElement` classes are the only classes that have child nodes derived from `XNode`.

These are the classes you will use to build your XML trees. Most notably, you will use the `XElement` class, because as we have already discussed, the LINQ to XML API is very element-centric, as opposed to document-centric like the W3C XML DOM.

Deferred Query Execution, Node Removal, and the Halloween Problem

This section serves as a warning that there are some goblins out there to be leery of. First up is *deferred query execution*. Never forget that many of the LINQ operators defer query execution until absolutely necessary, and this can cause potential side effects.

Another problem to be on the lookout for is the *Halloween problem*. The Halloween problem earned its name because it was first openly discussed among a small group of experts on Halloween. The problem is basically any problem that occurs by changing data that is being iterated over that affects the iteration. It was first detected by database engineers while working on the database optimizer. Their run-in with the problem occurred when their test query was changing the value of a database column that the optimizer they were developing was using as an index. Their test query would retrieve a record based on an index created over one of the table's columns, and the query would change the value in that column. Since that column affected the indexing of the record, the record appeared again further down in the list of records, causing it to be retrieved again in the same query and reprocessed. This caused an endless loop, because every time it was retrieved from the record set, it was updated and moved further down the record set where it would only be picked up again and processed the same way indefinitely.

You may have seen the Halloween problem yourself even though you may have not known the name for it. Have you ever worked with some sort of collection, iterated through it, and deleted an item, and this caused the iteration to break or misbehave? We have seen this recently working with a major suite of ASP.NET server controls. The suite has a `DataGrid` server control, and we needed to remove selected records from it. We iterated through the records from start to finish, deleting the ones we needed to, but in doing so, it messed up the pointers being used for the iteration. The result was some records that should not have been deleted were, and some that should have been deleted were not. We called the vendor for support, and its solution was to iterate through the records backward. This resolved the problem.

With LINQ to XML, you will most likely run into this problem when removing nodes from an XML tree, although it can occur at other times, so you want to keep this in your mind when you are coding. Let's examine the example in Listing 7-13.

Listing 7-13. Intentionally Exposing the Halloween Problem

```
XDocument xDocument = new XDocument(
  new XElement("BookParticipants",
    new XElement("BookParticipant",
      new XAttribute("type", "Author"),
      new XElement("FirstName", "Joe"),
      new XElement("LastName", "Rattz")),
    new XElement("BookParticipant",
      new XAttribute("type", "Editor"),
      new XElement("FirstName", "Ewan"),
      new XElement("LastName", "Buckingham")))));

IEnumerable<XElement> elements =
  xDocument.Element("BookParticipants").Elements("BookParticipant");

foreach (XElement element in elements)
{
  Console.WriteLine("Source element: {0} : value = {1}",
```

```
      element.Name, element.Value);
}

foreach (XElement element in elements)
{
  Console.WriteLine("Removing {0} = {1} ...", element.Name, element.Value);
  element.Remove();
}

Console.WriteLine(xDocument);
```

In the previous code, we first build our XML document. Next, we build a sequence of the BookParticipant elements. This is the sequence we will enumerate through, removing elements. Next, we display each element in our sequence so you can see that we do indeed have two BookParticipant elements. We then enumerate through the sequence again, displaying a message that we are removing the element, and we remove the BookParticipant element. We then display the resulting XML document.

If the Halloween problem does not manifest itself, you should see the "Removing …" message twice; when the XML document is displayed at the end, you should have an empty BookParticipants element. Here are the results:

```
Source element: BookParticipant : value = JoeRattz
Source element: BookParticipant : value = EwanBuckingham
Removing BookParticipant = JoeRattz ...
<BookParticipants>
  <BookParticipant type="Editor">
    <FirstName>Ewan</FirstName>
    <LastName>Buckingham</LastName>
  </BookParticipant>
</BookParticipants>
```

Just as we anticipated, there are two source BookParticipant elements in the sequence to remove. You can see the first one, Joe Rattz, gets removed. However, we never see the second one get removed, and when we display the resulting XML document, the last BookParticipant element is still there. The enumeration misbehaved; the Halloween problem got us. Keep in mind that the Halloween problem does not always manifest itself in the same way. Sometimes enumerations may terminate sooner than they should; sometimes they throw exceptions. Their behavior varies depending on exactly what is happening.

I know that you are wondering, what is the solution? The solution for this case is to cache the elements and to enumerate through the cache instead of through the normal enumeration technique, which relies on internal pointers that are getting corrupted by the removal or modification of elements. For this example, we will cache the sequence of elements using one of the Standard Query Operators that is designed for the purpose of caching to prevent deferred query execution problems. We will use the ToArray operator. Listing 7-14 shows the same code as before, except we call the ToArray operator and enumerate on it.

Listing 7-14. *Preventing the Halloween Problem*

```
XDocument xDocument = new XDocument(
  new XElement("BookParticipants",
    new XElement("BookParticipant",
      new XAttribute("type", "Author"),
      new XElement("FirstName", "Joe"),
      new XElement("LastName", "Rattz")),
    new XElement("BookParticipant",
      new XAttribute("type", "Editor"),
      new XElement("FirstName", "Ewan"),
      new XElement("LastName", "Buckingham")))));

IEnumerable<XElement> elements =
  xDocument.Element("BookParticipants").Elements("BookParticipant");

foreach (XElement element in elements)
{
  Console.WriteLine("Source element: {0} : value = {1}",
    element.Name, element.Value);
}

foreach (XElement element in elements.ToArray())
{
  Console.WriteLine("Removing {0} = {1} ...", element.Name, element.Value);
  element.Remove();
}

Console.WriteLine(xDocument);
```

This code is identical to the previous example except we call the ToArray operator in the final enumeration where we remove the elements. Here are the results:

```
Source element: BookParticipant : value = JoeRattz
Source element: BookParticipant : value = EwanBuckingham
Removing BookParticipant = JoeRattz ...
Removing BookParticipant = EwanBuckingham ...
<BookParticipants />
```

Notice that this time we got two messages informing us that a BookParticipant element was being removed. Also, when we display the XML document after the removal, we do have an empty BookParticipants element because all the child elements have been removed. The Halloween problem has been foiled!

XML Creation

As we have already discussed, functional construction provided by the LINQ to XML API makes creating an XML tree a breeze compared to the W3C DOM API. We will now take a look at creating each of the major XML classes in the LINQ to XML API.

Because the new API is centered on elements and that is what you will be creating the majority of the time, we cover creating elements with the XElement class first. We then cover the rest of the XML classes in alphabetical order.

Creating Elements with XElement

First, you should keep in mind that with the new API, the XElement class is the one you will use most. That said, let's take a look at instantiating an XElement object. XElement has several constructors, but we are going to examine two of them:

```
XElement.XElement(XName name, object content);
XElement.XElement(XName name, params object[] content);
```

The first constructor is the simplest case where an element has a text value and no child nodes. It's as simple as Listing 7-15.

Listing 7-15. Creating an Element Using the First Prototype

```
XElement firstName = new XElement("FirstName", "Joe");
Console.WriteLine((string)firstName);
```

The first argument of the constructor is an XName object. As previously mentioned, an XName object will be created by implicitly converting the input string to an XName. The second argument is a single object representing the element's content. In this case, the content is a string with the value of "Joe". The API will convert that string literal of "Joe" to an XText object for us on the fly. Notice that we are taking advantage of the new node value extraction capabilities to get the value from the firstName element variable. That is, we are casting the element to the type of its value, which in this case is a string. So, the value of the firstName element variable will be extracted. Here are the results:

Joe

The data type of the single content object is very flexible. It is the data type of the content object that controls its relationship to the element to which it is added. Table 7-1 shows all of the allowed content object data types and how they are handled.

Remember that even though the element's value may be stored as a string, as it would be for *any remaining type*[1] such as an integer, you can get it out as the original type thanks to the new node value extraction facilities. So for example, if when you create the XElement object you specify an integer (int) as the content object, by casting the node to an integer (int), you get the value converted to an integer for you. As long as you are casting to one of the data types a cast operator is provided for, and as long as

---

[1]   This term is explained in Table 7-1.

the element's value can be converted to the type you are casting to, casting provides a simple way of obtaining the element's value.

The second XElement constructor listed previously is just like the first one, except you can provide multiple objects for the content. This is what makes functional construction so powerful. You need only examine Listing 7-1 or Listing 7-2 to see an example using the second constructor where multiple content objects are provided to the XElement constructor.

Table 7-1. *LINQ to XML Object to Parent Insertion Behavior Table*

Content Object Data Type	Manner Handled
string	A string object or string literal is automatically converted to an XText object and handled as XText from there.
XText	This object can have either a string or an XText value. It is added as a child node of the element but treated as the element's text content.
XCData	This object can have either a string or an XCData value. It is added as a child node of the element but treated as the element's CData content.
XElement	This object is added as a child element.
XAttribute	This object is added as an attribute.
XProcessingInstruction	This object is added as child content.
XComment	This object is added as child content.
IEnumerable	This object is enumerated, and the handling of the object types is applied recursively.
null	This object is ignored. You may be wondering why you would ever want to pass null into the constructor of an element, but it turns out that this can be quite handy for XML transformations.
Any remaining type	The ToString method is called, and the resulting value is treated as string content.

Earlier, we mentioned that functional construction is going to be very useful for LINQ queries that produce XML. As an example, we will create the standard BookParticipants XML tree that we have been using, but instead of hard-coding the element values with string literals, we will retrieve the data from a LINQ-queryable data source. In this case, the data source will be an array.

First, we need a class that the data can be stored in. Also, since we have types of BookParticipants, we will create an enum for the different types, as follows:

An enum and Class for the Next Example

```
enum ParticipantTypes
{
    Author = 0,
    Editor
}

class BookParticipant
{
    public string FirstName;
    public string LastName;
    public ParticipantTypes ParticipantType;
}
```

Now we will build an array of the BookParticipant type and generate an XML tree using a LINQ query to retrieve the data from the array, as shown in Listing 7-16.

Listing 7-16. *Generating an XML Tree with a LINQ Query*

```
BookParticipant[] bookParticipants = new[] {
  new BookParticipant {FirstName = "Joe", LastName = "Rattz",
                       ParticipantType = ParticipantTypes.Author},
  new BookParticipant {FirstName = "Ewan", LastName = "Buckingham",
                       ParticipantType = ParticipantTypes.Editor}
};

XElement xBookParticipants =
   new XElement("BookParticipants",
                bookParticipants.Select(p =>
                   new XElement("BookParticipant",
                     new XAttribute("type", p.ParticipantType),
                     new XElement("FirstName", p.FirstName),
                     new XElement("LastName", p.LastName))));

Console.WriteLine(xBookParticipants);
```

In the previous code, we create an array of BookParticipant objects named bookParticipants. Next, the code queries the values from the bookParticipants array using the Select operator and generates a BookParticipant element for each, using the members of the element of the array. Here is the XML tree generated by the previous code:

```
<BookParticipants>
  <BookParticipant type="Author">
    <FirstName>Joe</FirstName>
    <LastName>Rattz</LastName>
  </BookParticipant>
```

```
  <BookParticipant type="Editor">
    <FirstName>Ewan</FirstName>
    <LastName>Buckingham</LastName>
  </BookParticipant>
</BookParticipants>
```

Imagine trying to do that with the W3C XML DOM API. Actually, you don't have to imagine it; you can just look at Listing 6-1 because that code creates the same XML tree.

Creating Attributes with XAttribute

Unlike the W3C DOM API, attributes do not inherit from nodes. An attribute, implemented in LINQ to XML with the XAttribute class, is a name-value pair that is stored in a collection of XAttribute objects belonging to an XElement object.

We can create an attribute and add it to its element on the fly using functional construction, as shown in Listing 7-17.

Listing 7-17. *Creating an Attribute with Functional Construction*

```
XElement xBookParticipant = new XElement("BookParticipant",
                                      new XAttribute("type", "Author"));

Console.WriteLine(xBookParticipant);
```

Running this code provides the following results:

```
<BookParticipant type="Author" />
```

Sometimes, however, you can't create the attribute at the same time its element is being constructed. For that, you must instantiate one and then add it to its element as in Listing 7-18.

Listing 7-18. *Creating an Attribute and Adding It to Its Element*

```
XElement xBookParticipant = new XElement("BookParticipant");
XAttribute xAttribute = new XAttribute("type", "Author");
xBookParticipant.Add(xAttribute);

Console.WriteLine(xBookParticipant);
```

The results are identical:

```
<BookParticipant type="Author" />
```

Notice again how flexible the XElement.Add method is. It accepts any object, applying the same rules for the element's content that are followed when instantiating an XElement. Sweet!

Creating Comments with XComment

Creating comments with LINQ to XML is trivial. XML comments are implemented in LINQ to XML with the XComment class. You can create a comment and add it to its element on the fly using functional construction, as in Listing 7-19.

Listing 7-19. Creating a Comment with Functional Construction

```
XElement xBookParticipant = new XElement("BookParticipant",
                                         new XComment("This person is retired."));

Console.WriteLine(xBookParticipant);
```

Running this code provides the following results:

```
<BookParticipant>
  <!--This person is retired.-->
</BookParticipant>
```

Sometimes, however, you can't create the comment at the same time its element is being constructed. For that, you must instantiate one and then add it to its element, as in Listing 7-20.

Listing 7-20. Creating a Comment and Adding It to Its Element

```
XElement xBookParticipant = new XElement("BookParticipant");
XComment xComment = new XComment("This person is retired.");
xBookParticipant.Add(xComment);

Console.WriteLine(xBookParticipant);
```

The results are identical:

```
<BookParticipant>
  <!--This person is retired.-->
</BookParticipant>
```

Creating Containers with XContainer

Because XContainer is an abstract class, you cannot instantiate it. Instead, you must instantiate one of its subclasses, XDocument or XElement. Conceptually, an XContainer is a class that inherits from the XNode class that can contain other classes inheriting from XNode.

Creating Declarations with XDeclaration

With the LINQ to XML API, creating declarations is a simple matter. XML declarations are implemented in LINQ to XML with the XDeclaration class.

Unlike most of the other classes in the LINQ to XML API, declarations are meant to be added to an XML document, not an element. Do you recall, though, how flexible the constructor was for the XElement class? Any class it wasn't specifically designed to handle would have its ToString method called, and that text would be added to the element as text content. So, you can inadvertently add a declaration using the XDeclaration class to an element. But it will not give you the results you are looking for.

■ **Caution** Although XML declarations apply to an XML document as a whole and should be added to an XML document, an XElement object will gladly accept an XDeclaration object being added to it. However, this will not be the result you want.

We can create a declaration and add it to an XML document on the fly using functional construction, as in Listing 7-21.

Listing 7-21. Creating a Declaration with Functional Construction

```
XDocument xDocument = new XDocument(new XDeclaration("1.0", "UTF-8", "yes"),
                                    new XElement("BookParticipant"));

Console.WriteLine(xDocument);
```

This code produces the following results:

```
<BookParticipant />
```

Did you notice that the declaration is missing from the output? That's right; the ToString method will omit the declaration. However, if you debug the code and put a watch on the document, you will see that the declaration is there.

Sometimes, however, you can't create the declaration at the same time the document is being constructed. For that, you must instantiate one and then set the document's Declaration property to the instantiated declaration, as in Listing 7-22.

Listing 7-22. Creating a Declaration and Setting the Document's Declaration Property to It

```
XDocument xDocument = new XDocument(new XElement("BookParticipant"));

XDeclaration xDeclaration = new XDeclaration("1.0", "UTF-8", "yes");
xDocument.Declaration = xDeclaration;
```

```
Console.WriteLine(xDocument);
```

This code produces the following results:

```
<BookParticipant />
```

Again, notice that the declaration does not get output when a document's ToString method is called. But just as with the previous example, if you debug the code and examine the document, the declaration is indeed there.

Creating Document Types with XDocumentType

The LINQ to XML API makes creating document types a fairly painless operation. XML document types are implemented in LINQ to XML with the XDocumentType class.

Unlike most of the other classes in the LINQ to XML API, document types are meant to be added to an XML document, not an element. Do you recall, though, how flexible the constructor was for the XElement class? Any class it wasn't specifically designed to handle would have its ToString method called, and that text would be added to the element as text content. So, you can inadvertently add a document type using the XDocumentType class to an element. But it will not give you the results you want.

■ **Caution** Although XML document types apply to an XML document as a whole and should be added to an XML document, an XElement object will gladly accept an XDocumentType object being added to it. However, this will not be the result you want.

You can create a document type and add it to an XML document on the fly using functional construction, as in Listing 7-23.

Listing 7-23. Creating a Document Type with Functional Construction

```
XDocument xDocument = new XDocument(new XDocumentType("BookParticipants",
                                                      null,
                                                      "BookParticipants.dtd",
                                                      null),
                                    new XElement("BookParticipant"));

Console.WriteLine(xDocument);
```

This code produces the following results:

```
<!DOCTYPE BookParticipants SYSTEM "BookParticipants.dtd">
<BookParticipant />
```

Sometimes, however, you can't create the document type at the same time the document is being constructed. For that, you must instantiate one and then add it to the document as in Listing 7-24.

Listing 7-24. *Creating a Document Type and Adding It to a Document*

```
XDocument xDocument = new XDocument();

XDocumentType documentType =
  new XDocumentType("BookParticipants", null, "BookParticipants.dtd", null);

xDocument.Add(documentType, new XElement("BookParticipants"));

Console.WriteLine(xDocument);
```

The following is the result of this code:

```
<!DOCTYPE BookParticipants SYSTEM "BookParticipants.dtd">
<BookParticipants />
```

Notice in the previous code that we did not add any elements prior to adding the document type. If you do add a document type after adding any elements, you will receive the following exception:

```
Unhandled Exception: System.InvalidOperationException: This operation would create
an incorrectly structured document.
...
```

So if you are going to specify a document type after the document's instantiation, make sure you do not specify any elements during the document's instantiation using functional construction or add any elements prior to adding the document type.

Creating Documents with XDocument

We have probably stated this so many times by now that you are sick of hearing it, but with LINQ to XML, it isn't necessary to create an XML document just to create an XML tree or fragment. However, should the need arise, creating an XML document with LINQ to XML is trivial too. XML documents are implemented in LINQ to XML with the XDocument class. Listing 7-25 is an example.

Listing 7-25. A Simple Example of Creating an XML Document with XDocument

```
XDocument xDocument = new XDocument();
Console.WriteLine(xDocument);
```

This code produces no output, though, because the XML document is empty. The previous example may be a little too trivial, so we will create a document with all the LINQ to XML classes that are specifically designed to be added to an XDocument object, as shown in Listing 7-26.

Listing 7-26. A Slightly More Complex Example of Creating an XML Document with XDocument

```
XDocument xDocument = new XDocument(
  new XDeclaration("1.0", "UTF-8", "yes"),
  new XDocumentType("BookParticipants", null, "BookParticipants.dtd", null),
  new XProcessingInstruction("BookCataloger", "out-of-print"),
  new XElement("BookParticipants"));

Console.WriteLine(xDocument);
```

Both the processing instruction and element can be added to elements as well, but we wanted to create an XML document with some meat, so here it is. And we wanted to include a processing instruction so you could see one in action.

The results of this code are the following:

```
<!DOCTYPE BookParticipants SYSTEM "BookParticipants.dtd">
<?BookCataloger out-of-print?>
<BookParticipants />
```

You may have noticed that the declaration is missing. Just as was mentioned with the examples of creating declarations, the document's ToString method omits the declaration from its output. However, if you debug the code and examine the document, you will see that the declaration is there.

Creating Names with XName

As we discussed earlier in this chapter, with LINQ to XML, you have no need to directly create names via the XName object. In fact, the XName class has no public constructors, so there is no way for you to instantiate one. An XName object will get created for you from a string, and optionally a namespace, automatically when an XName object is required.

An XName object consists of a LocalName—which is a string—and a namespace—which is an XNamespace.

Listing 7-27 is some code calling the XElement constructor requiring an XName as its only argument.

Listing 7-27. Sample Code Where an XName Object Is Created for You

```
XElement xBookParticipant = new XElement("BookParticipant");
```

```
Console.WriteLine(xBookParticipant);
```

In the previous example, we instantiate an XElement object by passing the element's name as a string, so an XName object is created for us with a LocalName of BookParticipant and is assigned to the XElement object's Name property. In this case, no namespace is provided, so the XName object has no namespace.

Pressing Ctrl+F5 reveals the following results:

```
<BookParticipant />
```

We could have specified a namespace with the code in Listing 7-28.

Listing 7-28. *Sample Code Where an XName Object Is Created for You and a Namespace Is Specified*

```
XNamespace ns = "http://www.linqdev.com/Books";
XElement xBookParticipant = new XElement(ns + "BookParticipant");
Console.WriteLine(xBookParticipant);
```

This code will output this XML:

```
<BookParticipant xmlns="http://www.linqdev.com/Books" />
```

For more information about creating names using the LINQ to XML API, see the section titled "Names, Namespaces, and Prefixes" earlier in this chapter.

Creating Namespaces with XNamespace

In the LINQ to XML API, namespaces are implemented with the XNamespace class. For an example of creating and using a namespace, see the previous example, Listing 7-28. It demonstrates creating a namespace with the XNamespace class.

For more information about creating namespaces using the LINQ to XML API, see the section titled "Names, Namespaces, and Prefixes" earlier in this chapter.

Creating Nodes with XNode

Because XNode is an abstract class, you cannot instantiate it. Instead, you must instantiate one of its subclasses: XComment, XContainer, XDocumentType, XProcessingInstruction, or XText. Conceptually, an XNode is any class that functions as a node in the XML tree.

Creating Processing Instructions with XProcessingInstruction

Processing instructions have never been easier to create than with the LINQ to XML API. With the LINQ to XML API, processing instructions are implemented with the XProcessingInstruction class.

You can create processing instructions at the document or element level. Listing 7-29 shows an example of doing both on the fly using functional construction.

Listing 7-29. *Creating a Processing Instruction at Both the Document and Element Levels*

```
XDocument xDocument = new XDocument(
  new XProcessingInstruction("BookCataloger", "out-of-print"),
  new XElement("BookParticipants",
    new XElement("BookParticipant",
      new XProcessingInstruction("ParticipantDeleter", "delete"),
      new XElement("FirstName", "Joe"),
      new XElement("LastName", "Rattz"))));

Console.WriteLine(xDocument);
```

In the previous code, we added a processing instruction to both the document and the BookParticipant element. Before displaying the results, we want to take a second to point out just how well this functional construction flows. It is a very simple matter to create this XML tree with two processing instructions. Comparing this to our very first sample program in the previous chapter, Listing 6-1, again proves how much the new LINQ to XML API is going to simplify your code. And, lastly, here are the results:

```
<?BookCataloger out-of-print?>
<BookParticipants>
  <BookParticipant>
    <?ParticipantDeleter delete?>
    <FirstName>Joe</FirstName>
    <LastName>Rattz</LastName>
  </BookParticipant>
</BookParticipants>
```

By now we would presume you can already imagine the code for adding a processing instruction after construction, since it would be just like adding any of the other nodes we have already covered. So instead of boring you with the mundane, Listing 7-30 shows a significantly more complex example of creating and adding a processing instruction after the fact.

Listing 7-30. *A More Complex Example of Adding Processing Instructions After the Document and Element Have Been Constructed*

```
XDocument xDocument =
  new XDocument(new XElement("BookParticipants",
                   new XElement("BookParticipant",
                      new XElement("FirstName", "Joe"),
                      new XElement("LastName", "Rattz"))));
```

```
XProcessingInstruction xPI1 = new XProcessingInstruction("BookCataloger",
                                                         "out-of-print");
xDocument.AddFirst(xPI1);

XProcessingInstruction xPI2 = new XProcessingInstruction("ParticipantDeleter",
                                                         "delete");
XElement outOfPrintParticipant = xDocument
  .Element("BookParticipants")
  .Elements("BookParticipant")
  .Where(e => ((string)((XElement)e).Element("FirstName")) == "Joe"
          && ((string)((XElement)e).Element("LastName")) == "Rattz")
  .Single<XElement>();

outOfPrintParticipant.AddFirst(xPI2);

Console.WriteLine(xDocument);
```

There are several items worth mentioning in this sample. First, we created the document and its XML tree using functional construction. Then, after the construction of the document and tree, we added a processing instruction to the document. However, here we are using the XElement.AddFirst method to make it the first child node of the document, as opposed to the XElement.Add method, which would just append it to the end of the document's child nodes, which may be too late for any processing instruction to be honored.

In addition, to add a processing instruction to one of the elements, we had to have a reference to it. We could have just constructed an XElement object and kept the reference to it, but we thought it might be time to start giving a hint about some of the query capabilities coming. You can see we perform a rather complex query where we get the BookParticipants element from the document using the Element method that we cover later in the section titled "XML Traversal" and then get the sequence of XElement objects named BookParticipant where the BookParticipant element's FirstName element equals "Joe" and the LastName element equals "Rattz". Notice that we use the new node value extraction features of the LINQ to XML API that we previously discussed to get the values of the FirstName and LastName node by casting them as a string.

Finally, the Where operator returns an IEnumerable<T>, but we want a XElement object directly. So, in our coverage of the LINQ to Objects deferred Standard Query Operators in Chapter 5, we recall that there is an operator that will return the actual element from a sequence, provided there is only one, and that operator is the Single operator. Once we have the reference to the proper XElement object with that query, it is trivial to add the processing instruction to it and display the results. And, speaking of results, here they are:

```
<?BookCataloger out-of-print?>
<BookParticipants>
  <BookParticipant>
    <?ParticipantDeleter delete?>
    <FirstName>Joe</FirstName>
    <LastName>Rattz</LastName>
  </BookParticipant>
</BookParticipants>
```

Creating Streaming Elements with XStreamingElement

Do you recall in Part 2 of this book, "LINQ to Objects," that many of the Standard Query Operators actually defer their work until the time the returned data is enumerated? If we call some operators that do in fact defer their operation and we want to project our query's output as XML, we would have a dilemma. On the one hand, we want to take advantage of the deferred nature of the operator since there is no need to do work until it needs to be done. But on the other hand, our LINQ to XML API call will cause the query to execute immediately.

Notice in Listing 7-31 that even though we change the fourth element of the names array when we output our XElement object's value, the XML tree contains the original value. This is because the xNames element was fully created before we changed the names array element.

Listing 7-31. *Immediate Execution of the XML Tree Construction*

```
string[] names = { "John", "Paul", "George", "Pete" };

XElement xNames = new XElement("Beatles",
                              from n in names
                              select new XElement("Name", n));

names[3] = "Ringo";

Console.WriteLine(xNames);
```

Before discussing the results of this code, we want to point out just how cool this example is. Notice that we are creating an element whose name is Beatles and whose content is a sequence of XElement objects whose element is named Name. This code produces the following XML tree:

```
<Beatles>
  <Name>John</Name>
  <Name>Paul</Name>
  <Name>George</Name>
  <Name>Pete</Name>
</Beatles>
```

That is pretty awesome. Each XElement object from the sequence becomes a child element. How cool is that? As we mentioned, notice that even though we changed names[3] to "Ringo" prior to outputting the XML, the last element still contains Pete, the original value. This is because the names sequence has to be enumerated in order to construct the XElement object, thereby immediately executing the query.

If we do indeed want the XML tree construction deferred, we need another way to do this, and that is exactly what streaming elements are for. With LINQ to XML, a streaming element is implemented with the XStreamingElement class.

So, Listing 7-32 shows the same example, except this time we will use XStreamingElement objects instead of XElement objects.

Listing 7-32. *Demonstrating the Deferred Execution of the XML Tree Construction by Using the XStreamingElement Class*

```
string[] names = { "John", "Paul", "George", "Pete" };

XStreamingElement xNames =
  new XStreamingElement("Beatles",
                          from n in names
                          select new XStreamingElement("Name", n));

names[3] = "Ringo";

Console.WriteLine(xNames);
```

If this works as we have explained, the last Name node's value will now be Ringo and not Pete. But the proof is in the pudding:

```
<Beatles>
  <Name>John</Name>
  <Name>Paul</Name>
  <Name>George</Name>
  <Name>Ringo</Name>
</Beatles>
```

Sorry, Pete, it looks like you have been replaced yet again.

Creating Text with XText

Creating an element with a text value is a pretty simple task. Listing 7-33 is some code doing just that.

Listing 7-33. *Creating an Element and Assigning a String As Its Value*

```
XElement xFirstName = new XElement("FirstName", "Joe");
Console.WriteLine(xFirstName);
```

This is straightforward, and there are no surprises. Running the code by pressing Ctrl+F5 produces the following results:

```
<FirstName>Joe</FirstName>
```

What is hidden, though, is the fact that the string "Joe" is converted into an XText object, and it is that object that is added to the XElement object. In fact, examining the xFirstName object in the debugger reveals that it contains a single node, an XText object whose value is "Joe". Since this is all done automatically for you, in most circumstances you will not need to directly construct a text object.

However, should the need arise, you can create a text object by instantiating an XText object, as shown in Listing 7-34.

Listing 7-34. Creating a Text Node and Passing It As the Value of a Created Element

```
XText xName = new XText("Joe");
XElement xFirstName = new XElement("FirstName", xName);
Console.WriteLine(xFirstName);
```

This code produces the same output as the previous example, and if we examine the internal state of the xFirstName object, it too is identical to the one created in the previous example:

```
<FirstName>Joe</FirstName>
```

Creating CData with XCData

Creating an element with a CData value is also pretty simple. Listing 7-35 is an example.

Listing 7-35. Creating an XCData Node and Passing It As the Value of a Created Element

```
XElement xErrorMessage = new XElement("HTMLMessage",
                        new XCData("<H1>Invalid user id or password.</H1>"));

Console.WriteLine(xErrorMessage);
```

This code produces the following output:

```
<HTMLMessage><![CDATA[<H1>Invalid user id or password.</H1>]]></HTMLMessage>
```

As you can see, the LINQ to XML API makes handling CData simple.

XML Output

Of course, creating, modifying, and deleting XML data does no good if you cannot persist the changes. This section contains a few ways to output your XML.

Saving with XDocument.Save()

You can save your XML document using any of several XDocument.Save methods. Here is a list of prototypes:

```
void XDocument.Save(string filename);
void XDocument.Save(TextWriter textWriter);
```

```
void XDocument.Save(XmlWriter writer);
void XDocument.Save(string filename, SaveOptions options);
void XDocument.Save(TextWriter textWriter, SaveOptions options);
```

Listing 7-36 is an example where we save the XML document to a file in our project's folder.

Listing 7-36. *Saving a Document with the XDocument.Save Method*

```
XDocument xDocument = new XDocument(
  new XElement("BookParticipants",
    new XElement("BookParticipant",
      new XAttribute("type", "Author"),
      new XAttribute("experience", "first-time"),
      new XAttribute("language", "English"),
      new XElement("FirstName", "Joe"),
      new XElement("LastName", "Rattz"))));

xDocument.Save("bookparticipants.xml");
```

Notice that we called the Save method on an *object* of type XDocument. This is because the Save methods are instance methods. The Load methods you will read about later in the "XML Input" section are static methods and must be called on the XDocument or XElement *class*.

Here are the contents of the generated bookparticipants.xml file when viewing them in a text editor such as Notepad:

```
<?xml version="1.0" encoding="utf-8"?>
<BookParticipants>
  <BookParticipant type="Author" experience="first-time" language="English">
    <FirstName>Joe</FirstName>
    <LastName>Rattz</LastName>
  </BookParticipant>
</BookParticipants>
```

That XML document output is easy to read because the version of the Save method that we called is formatting the output. That is, if we call the version of the Save method that accepts a string file name and a SaveOptions argument, passing a value of SaveOptions.None would give the same results as the previous. Had we called the Save method like this:

```
xDocument.Save("bookparticipants.xml", SaveOptions.DisableFormatting);
```

the results in the file would look like this:

```
<?xml version="1.0" encoding="utf-8"?><BookParticipants><BookParticipant type=
"Author" experience="first-time" language="English"><FirstName>Joe</FirstName>
<LastName>Rattz</LastName></BookParticipant></BookParticipants>
```

This is one single continuous line of text. However, you would have to examine the file in a text editor to see the difference because a browser will format it nicely for you.

Of course, you can use any of the other methods available to output your document as well; it's up to you.

Saving with XElement.Save()

We have said many times that with the LINQ to XML API, creating an XML document is not necessary. And to save your XML to a file, it still isn't. The XElement class has several Save methods for this purpose:

```
void XElement.Save(string filename);
void XElement.Save(TextWriter textWriter);
void XElement.Save(XmlWriter writer);
void XElement.Save(string filename, SaveOptions options);
void XElement.Save(TextWriter textWriter, SaveOptions options);
```

Listing 7-37 is an example very similar to the previous, except we never even create an XML document.

Listing 7-37. *Saving an Element with the XElement.Save Method*

```
XElement bookParticipants =
  new XElement("BookParticipants",
    new XElement("BookParticipant",
      new XAttribute("type", "Author"),
      new XAttribute("experience", "first-time"),
      new XAttribute("language", "English"),
      new XElement("FirstName", "Joe"),
      new XElement("LastName", "Rattz")));

bookParticipants.Save("bookparticipants.xml");
```

And the saved XML looks identical to the previous example where we actually have an XML document:

```
<?xml version="1.0" encoding="utf-8"?>
<BookParticipants>
  <BookParticipant type="Author" experience="first-time" language="English">
    <FirstName>Joe</FirstName>
    <LastName>Rattz</LastName>
  </BookParticipant>
</BookParticipants>
```

XML Input

Creating and persisting XML to a file does no good if you can't load it back into an XML tree. Here are some techniques to read XML back in.

Loading with XDocument.Load()

Now that you know how to save your XML documents and fragments, you would probably like to know how to load them. You can load your XML document using any of several methods. Here is a list:

```
static XDocument XDocument.Load(string uri);
static XDocument XDocument.Load(TextReader textReader);
static XDocument XDocument.Load(XmlReader reader);
static XDocument XDocument.Load(string uri, LoadOptions options);
static XDocument XDocument.Load(TextReader textReader, LoadOptions options);
static XDocument XDocument.Load(XmlReader reader, LoadOptions options);
```

You may notice how symmetrical these methods are to the XDocument.Save methods. However, there are a couple differences worth pointing out. First, in the Save methods, you must call the Save method on an *object* of XDocument or XElement type because the Save method is an instance method. But the Load method is static, so you must call it on the XDocument *class* itself. Second, the Save methods that accept a string are requiring file names to be passed, whereas the Load methods that accept a string are allowing a URI to be passed.

Additionally, the Load method allows a parameter of type LoadOptions to be specified while loading the XML document. The LoadOptions enum has the options shown in Table 7-2.

Table 7-2. The LoadOptions Enumeration

Option	Description
LoadOptions.None	Use this option to specify that no load options are to be used.
LoadOptions.PreserveWhitespace	Use this option to preserve the whitespace in the XML source, such as blank lines.
LoadOptions.SetLineInfo	Use this option so that you may obtain the line and position of any object inheriting from XObject by using the IXmlLineInfo interface.
LoadOptions.SetBaseUri	Use this option so that you may obtain the base URI of any object inheriting from XObject.

These options can be combined with a bitwise OR (|) operation. However, some options will not work in some contexts. For example, when creating an element or a document by parsing a string, there is no line information available, nor is there a base URI. Or, when creating a document with an XmlReader, there is no base URI.

Listing 7-38 shows an example where we load our XML document created in the previous example, Listing 7-37.

Listing 7-38. *Loading a Document with the XDocument.Load Method*

```
XDocument xDocument = XDocument.Load("bookparticipants.xml",
  LoadOptions.SetBaseUri | LoadOptions.SetLineInfo);

Console.WriteLine(xDocument);

XElement firstName = xDocument.Descendants("FirstName").First();

Console.WriteLine("FirstName Line:{0} - Position:{1}",
  ((IXmlLineInfo)firstName).LineNumber,
  ((IXmlLineInfo)firstName).LinePosition);

Console.WriteLine("FirstName Base URI:{0}", firstName.BaseUri);
```

■ **Note** You must either add a `using` directive for `System.Xml`, if one is not present, or specify the namespace when referencing the `IXmlLineInfo` interface in your code; otherwise, the `IXmlLineInfo` type will not be found.

This code is loading the same XML file we created in the previous example. After we load and display the document, we obtain a reference for the `FirstName` element and display the line and position of the element in the source XML document. Then we display the base URI for the element.

Here are the results:

```
<BookParticipants>
  <BookParticipant type="Author" experience="first-time" language="English">
    <FirstName>Joe</FirstName>
    <LastName>Rattz</LastName>
  </BookParticipant>
</BookParticipants>
FirstName Line:4 - Position:6
FirstName Base URI:file:///C:/Documents and Settings/…/Projects/LINQChapter7/
LINQChapter7/bin/Debug/bookparticipants.xml
```

This output looks just as we would expect, with one possible exception. First, the actual XML document looks fine. We see the line and position of the `FirstName` element, but the line number is causing us concern. It is shown as four, but in the displayed XML document, the `FirstName` element is on the third line. What is that about? If you examine the XML document we loaded, you will see that it begins with the document declaration, which is omitted from the output:

```
<?xml version="1.0" encoding="utf-8"?>
```

This is why the FirstName element is being reported as being on line 4.

Loading with XElement.Load()

Just as you could save from either an XDocument or an XElement, we can load from either as well. Loading into an element is virtually identical to loading into a document. Here are the methods available:

```
static XElement XElement.Load(string uri);
static XElement XElement.LoadTextReader textReader);
static XElement XElement.Load(XmlReader reader);
static XElement XElement.Load(string uri, LoadOptions options);
static XElement XElement.Load(TextReader textReader, LoadOptions options);
static XElement XElement.Load(XmlReader reader, LoadOptions options);
```

These methods are static just like the XDocument.Save methods, so they must be called from the XElement class directly. Listing 7-39 contains an example loading the same XML file we saved with the XElement.Save method in Listing 7-37.

Listing 7-39. *Loading an Element with the XElement.Load Method*

```
XElement xElement = XElement.Load("bookparticipants.xml");
Console.WriteLine(xElement);
```

Just as you already expect, the output looks like the following:

```
<BookParticipants>
  <BookParticipant type="Author" experience="first-time" language="English">
    <FirstName>Joe</FirstName>
    <LastName>Rattz</LastName>
  </BookParticipant>
</BookParticipants>
```

Just as the XDocument.Load method does, the XElement.Load method has overloads that accept a LoadOptions parameter. Please see the description of these in the "Loading with XDocument.Load()" section previously in the chapter.

Parsing with XDocument.Parse() or XElement.Parse()

How many times have you passed XML around in your programs as a string, only to suddenly need to do some serious XML work? Getting the data from a string variable to an XML document type variable always seems like such a hassle. Well, worry yourself no longer. One of our personal favorite features of the LINQ to XML API is the parse method.

Both the XDocument and XElement classes have a static method named `Parse` for parsing XML strings. We think by now you probably feel comfortable accepting that if you can parse with the XDocument class, you can probably parse with the XElement class, and vice versa. And since the LINQ to XML API is all about the elements, baby, we are going to only give you an element example this time.

In the "Saving with XDocument.Save()" section earlier in this chapter, we show the output of the Save method if the LoadOptions parameter is specified as DisableFormatting. The result is a single string of XML. For the example in Listing 7-40, we start with that XML string (after escaping the inner quotes), parse it into an element, and output the XML element to the screen.

Listing 7-40. *Parsing an XML String into an Element*

```
string xml = "<?xml version=\"1.0\" encoding=\"utf-8\"?><BookParticipants>" +
  "<BookParticipant type=\"Author\" experience=\"first-time\" language=" +
  "\"English\"><FirstName>Joe</FirstName><LastName>Rattz</LastName>" +
  "</BookParticipant></BookParticipants>";

XElement xElement = XElement.Parse(xml);
Console.WriteLine(xElement);
```

The results are the following:

```
<BookParticipants>
  <BookParticipant type="Author" experience="first-time" language="English">
    <FirstName>Joe</FirstName>
    <LastName>Rattz</LastName>
  </BookParticipant>
</BookParticipants>
```

How cool is that? Remember the old days when you had to create a document using the W3C XML DOM XmlDocument class? Thanks to the elimination of document centricity, you can turn XML strings into real XML trees in the blink of an eye with one method call.

XML Traversal

XML traversal is primarily accomplished with 4 properties and 11 methods. In this section, we try to mostly use the same code example for each property or method, except we change a single argument on one line when possible. The example in Listing 7-41 builds a full XML document.

Listing 7-41. *A Base Example Subsequent Examples May Be Derived From*

```
// we will use this to store a reference to one of the elements in the XML tree.
XElement firstParticipant;

XDocument xDocument = new XDocument(
```

```
new XDeclaration("1.0", "UTF-8", "yes"),
new XDocumentType("BookParticipants", null, "BookParticipants.dtd", null),
new XProcessingInstruction("BookCataloger", "out-of-print"),
// Notice on the next line that we are saving off a reference to the first
// BookParticipant element.
new XElement("BookParticipants", firstParticipant =
  new XElement("BookParticipant",
    new XAttribute("type", "Author"),
    new XElement("FirstName", "Joe"),
    new XElement("LastName", "Rattz")),
  new XElement("BookParticipant",
    new XAttribute("type", "Editor"),
    new XElement("FirstName", "Ewan"),
    new XElement("LastName", "Buckingham")))));

Console.WriteLine(xDocument);
```

First, notice that we are saving a reference to the first `BookParticipant` element we construct. We do this so that we can have a base element from which to do all the traversal. Although we will not be using the `firstParticipant` variable in this example, we will in the subsequent traversal examples. The next thing to notice is the argument for the `Console.WriteLine` method. In this case, we output the document itself. As we progress through these traversal examples, we change that argument to demonstrate how to traverse the XML tree. So, here is the output showing the document from the previous example:

```
<!DOCTYPE BookParticipants SYSTEM "BookParticipants.dtd">
<?BookCataloger out-of-print?>
<BookParticipants>
  <BookParticipant type="Author">
    <FirstName>Joe</FirstName>
    <LastName>Rattz</LastName>
  </BookParticipant>
  <BookParticipant type="Editor">
    <FirstName>Ewan</FirstName>
    <LastName>Buckingham</LastName>
  </BookParticipant>
</BookParticipants>
```

Traversal Properties

We will begin our discussion with the primary traversal properties. When directions (up, down, and so on) are specified, they are relative to the element the method is called on. In the subsequent examples, we save a reference to the first `BookParticipant` element, and it is the base element used for the traversal.

Forward with XNode.NextNode

Traversing forward through the XML tree is accomplished with the NextNode property. Listing 7-42 is an example.

Listing 7-42. Traversing Forward from an XElement Object via the NextNode Property

```
XElement firstParticipant;

//  A full document with all the bells and whistles.
XDocument xDocument = new XDocument(
  new XDeclaration("1.0", "UTF-8", "yes"),
  new XDocumentType("BookParticipants", null, "BookParticipants.dtd", null),
  new XProcessingInstruction("BookCataloger", "out-of-print"),
  //  Notice on the next line that we are saving off a reference to the first
  //  BookParticipant element.
  new XElement("BookParticipants", firstParticipant =
    new XElement("BookParticipant",
      new XAttribute("type", "Author"),
      new XElement("FirstName", "Joe"),
      new XElement("LastName", "Rattz")),
    new XElement("BookParticipant",
      new XAttribute("type", "Editor"),
      new XElement("FirstName", "Ewan"),
      new XElement("LastName", "Buckingham"))));

Console.WriteLine(firstParticipant.NextNode);
```

Since the base element is the first BookParticipant element, firstParticipant, traversing forward should provide us with the second BookParticipant element. Here are the results:

```
<BookParticipant type="Editor">
  <FirstName>Ewan</FirstName>
  <LastName>Buckingham</LastName>
</BookParticipant>
```

Based on these results, we would say we are right on the money. Would you believe us if we told you that if we had accessed the PreviousNode property of the element, it would have been null since it is the first node in its parent's node list? It's true, but we'll leave you the task of proving it to yourself.

Backward with XNode.PreviousNode

If you want to traverse the XML tree backward, use the PreviousNode property. Since there is no previous node for the first participant node, we'll get tricky and access the NextNode property first, obtaining the second participant node, as we did in the previous example, from which we will obtain the

PreviousNode. If you got lost in that, we will end up back at the first participant node. That is, we will go forward with NextNode to then go backward with PreviousNode, leaving us where we started. If you have ever heard the expression "taking one step forward and two steps back," with just one more access of the PreviousNode property, you could actually do that. LINQ makes it possible. Listing 7-43 is the example.

Listing 7-43. Traversing Backward from an XElement Object via the PreviousNode Property

```
XElement firstParticipant;

//  A full document with all the bells and whistles.
XDocument xDocument = new XDocument(
  new XDeclaration("1.0", "UTF-8", "yes"),
  new XDocumentType("BookParticipants", null, "BookParticipants.dtd", null),
  new XProcessingInstruction("BookCataloger", "out-of-print"),
  //  Notice on the next line that we are saving off a reference to the first
  //  BookParticipant element.
  new XElement("BookParticipants", firstParticipant =
    new XElement("BookParticipant",
      new XAttribute("type", "Author"),
      new XElement("FirstName", "Joe"),
      new XElement("LastName", "Rattz")),
    new XElement("BookParticipant",
      new XAttribute("type", "Editor"),
      new XElement("FirstName", "Ewan"),
      new XElement("LastName", "Buckingham")))));

Console.WriteLine(firstParticipant.NextNode.PreviousNode);
```

If this works as we expect, we should have the first BookParticipant element's XML:

```
<BookParticipant type="Author">
  <FirstName>Joe</FirstName>
  <LastName>Rattz</LastName>
</BookParticipant>
```

LINQ to XML actually makes traversing an XML tree fun. Well, sort of. For us, anyway.

Up to Document with XObject.Document

Obtaining the XML document from an XElement object is as simple as accessing the Document property of the element. So, please notice our change to the Console.WriteLine method call, shown in Listing 7-44.

Listing 7-44. Accessing the XML Document from an XElement Object via the Document Property

```
XElement firstParticipant;

//  A full document with all the bells and whistles.
XDocument xDocument = new XDocument(
  new XDeclaration("1.0", "UTF-8", "yes"),
  new XDocumentType("BookParticipants", null, "BookParticipants.dtd", null),
  new XProcessingInstruction("BookCataloger", "out-of-print"),
  //  Notice on the next line that we are saving off a reference to the first
  //  BookParticipant element.
  new XElement("BookParticipants", firstParticipant =
    new XElement("BookParticipant",
      new XAttribute("type", "Author"),
      new XElement("FirstName", "Joe"),
      new XElement("LastName", "Rattz")),
    new XElement("BookParticipant",
      new XAttribute("type", "Editor"),
      new XElement("FirstName", "Ewan"),
      new XElement("LastName", "Buckingham")))));

Console.WriteLine(firstParticipant.Document);
```

This will output the document, which is the same output as Listing 7-41, and here is the output to prove it:

```
<!DOCTYPE BookParticipants SYSTEM "BookParticipants.dtd">
<?BookCataloger out-of-print?>
<BookParticipants>
  <BookParticipant type="Author">
    <FirstName>Joe</FirstName>
    <LastName>Rattz</LastName>
  </BookParticipant>
  <BookParticipant type="Editor">
    <FirstName>Ewan</FirstName>
    <LastName>Buckingham</LastName>
  </BookParticipant>
</BookParticipants>
```

Up with XObject.Parent

If you need to go up one level in the tree, it will probably be no surprise that the Parent property will do the job. Changing the node passed to the WriteLine method to what's shown in Listing 7-45 changes the output (as you will see).

Listing 7-45. Traversing Up from an XElement Object via the Parent Property

```
XElement firstParticipant;

//  A full document with all the bells and whistles.
XDocument xDocument = new XDocument(
  new XDeclaration("1.0", "UTF-8", "yes"),
  new XDocumentType("BookParticipants", null, "BookParticipants.dtd", null),
  new XProcessingInstruction("BookCataloger", "out-of-print"),
  //  Notice on the next line that we are saving off a reference to the first
  //  BookParticipant element.
  new XElement("BookParticipants", firstParticipant =
    new XElement("BookParticipant",
      new XAttribute("type", "Author"),
      new XElement("FirstName", "Joe"),
      new XElement("LastName", "Rattz")),
    new XElement("BookParticipant",
      new XAttribute("type", "Editor"),
      new XElement("FirstName", "Ewan"),
      new XElement("LastName", "Buckingham"))));

Console.WriteLine(firstParticipant.Parent);
```

The output is changed to this:

```
<BookParticipants>
  <BookParticipant type="Author">
    <FirstName>Joe</FirstName>
    <LastName>Rattz</LastName>
  </BookParticipant>
  <BookParticipant type="Editor">
    <FirstName>Ewan</FirstName>
    <LastName>Buckingham</LastName>
  </BookParticipant>
</BookParticipants>
```

Don't let that fool you either. This is not the entire document. Notice it is missing the document type and processing instruction.

Traversal Methods

To demonstrate the traversal methods, since they return sequences of multiple nodes, we must now change that single `Console.WriteLine` method call to a `foreach` loop to output the potential multiple nodes. This will result in the former call to the `Console.WriteLine` method looking basically like this:

```
foreach(XNode node in firstParticipant.Nodes())
{
    Console.WriteLine(node);
}
```

From example to example, the only thing changing will be the method called on the firstParticipant node in the foreach statement.

Down with XContainer.Nodes()

No, we are not expressing our disdain for nodes. Nor are we stating we are all in favor of nodes, as in being "down for" rock climbing—meaning being excited about the prospect of going rock climbing. We are merely describing the direction of traversal we are about to discuss.

Traversing down an XML tree is easily accomplished with a call to the Nodes method. It will return a sequence of an object's child XNode objects. In case you snoozed through some of the earlier chapters, a sequence is an IEnumerable<T>, meaning an IEnumerable of some type T. Listing 7-46 is the example.

Listing 7-46. Traversing Down from an XElement Object via the Nodes Method

```
XElement firstParticipant;

// A full document with all the bells and whistles.
XDocument xDocument = new XDocument(
  new XDeclaration("1.0", "UTF-8", "yes"),
  new XDocumentType("BookParticipants", null, "BookParticipants.dtd", null),
  new XProcessingInstruction("BookCataloger", "out-of-print"),
  // Notice on the next line that we are saving off a reference to the first
  // BookParticipant element.
  new XElement("BookParticipants", firstParticipant =
    new XElement("BookParticipant",
      new XAttribute("type", "Author"),
      new XElement("FirstName", "Joe"),
      new XElement("LastName", "Rattz")),
    new XElement("BookParticipant",
      new XAttribute("type", "Editor"),
      new XElement("FirstName", "Ewan"),
      new XElement("LastName", "Buckingham"))));

foreach (XNode node in firstParticipant.Nodes())
{
  Console.WriteLine(node);
}
```

Here is the output:

```
<FirstName>Joe</FirstName>
<LastName>Rattz</LastName>
```

Don't forget, that method is returning all child nodes, not just elements. So, any other nodes in the first participant's list of child nodes will be included. This could include comments (XComment), text (XText), processing instructions (XProcessingInstruction), document type (XDocumentType), or elements (XElement). Also notice that it does not include the attribute because an attribute is not a node.

To provide a better example of the Nodes method, let's look at the code in Listing 7-47. It is similar to the base example with some extra nodes thrown in.

Listing 7-47. *Traversing Down from an XElement Object via the Nodes Method with Additional Node Types*

```
XElement firstParticipant;

// A full document with all the bells and whistles.
XDocument xDocument = new XDocument(
  new XDeclaration("1.0", "UTF-8", "yes"),
  new XDocumentType("BookParticipants", null, "BookParticipants.dtd", null),
  new XProcessingInstruction("BookCataloger", "out-of-print"),
  // Notice on the next line that we are saving off a reference to the first
  // BookParticipant element.
  new XElement("BookParticipants", firstParticipant =
    new XElement("BookParticipant",
      new XComment("This is a new author."),
      new XProcessingInstruction("AuthorHandler", "new"),
      new XAttribute("type", "Author"),
      new XElement("FirstName", "Joe"),
      new XElement("LastName", "Rattz")),
    new XElement("BookParticipant",
      new XAttribute("type", "Editor"),
      new XElement("FirstName", "Ewan"),
      new XElement("LastName", "Buckingham")))));

foreach (XNode node in firstParticipant.Nodes())
{
  Console.WriteLine(node);
}
```

This example is different from the previous one in that there is now a comment and processing instruction added to the first BookParticipant element. Pressing Ctrl+F5 displays the following:

```
<!--This is a new author.-->
<?AuthorHandler new?>
<FirstName>Joe</FirstName>
<LastName>Rattz</LastName>
```

We can now see the comment and the processing instruction. What if you want only a certain type of node, though, such as just the elements? Do you recall from Chapter 4 the OfType operator? We can use that operator to return only the nodes that are of a specific type, such as XElement. Using the same basic code as Listing 7-47, to return just the elements, we will merely change the foreach line, as shown in Listing 7-48.

Listing 7-48. Using the OfType Operator to Return Just the Elements

```
XElement firstParticipant;

// A full document with all the bells and whistles.
XDocument xDocument = new XDocument(
  new XDeclaration("1.0", "UTF-8", "yes"),
  new XDocumentType("BookParticipants", null, "BookParticipants.dtd", null),
  new XProcessingInstruction("BookCataloger", "out-of-print"),
  // Notice on the next line that we are saving off a reference to the first
  // BookParticipant element.
  new XElement("BookParticipants", firstParticipant =
    new XElement("BookParticipant",
      new XComment("This is a new author."),
      new XProcessingInstruction("AuthorHandler", "new"),
      new XAttribute("type", "Author"),
      new XElement("FirstName", "Joe"),
      new XElement("LastName", "Rattz")),
    new XElement("BookParticipant",
      new XAttribute("type", "Editor"),
      new XElement("FirstName", "Ewan"),
      new XElement("LastName", "Buckingham"))));

foreach (XNode node in firstParticipant.Nodes().OfType<XElement>())
{
  Console.WriteLine(node);
}
```

As you can see, the XComment and XProcessingInstruction objects are still being created. But since we are now calling the OfType operator, the code produces these results:

```
<FirstName>Joe</FirstName>
<LastName>Rattz</LastName>
```

Are you starting to see how cleverly all the C# language features and LINQ are coming together? Isn't it cool that we can use that Standard Query Operator to restrict the sequence of XML nodes this way? So if you want to get just the comments from the first BookParticipant element, could you use the OfType operator to do so? Of course you could, and the code would look like Listing 7-49.

Listing 7-49. Using the OfType Operator to Return Just the Comments

```
XElement firstParticipant;

//  A full document with all the bells and whistles.
XDocument xDocument = new XDocument(
  new XDeclaration("1.0", "UTF-8", "yes"),
  new XDocumentType("BookParticipants", null, "BookParticipants.dtd", null),
  new XProcessingInstruction("BookCataloger", "out-of-print"),
  //  Notice on the next line that we are saving off a reference to the first
  //  BookParticipant element.
  new XElement("BookParticipants", firstParticipant =
    new XElement("BookParticipant",
      new XComment("This is a new author."),
      new XProcessingInstruction("AuthorHandler", "new"),
      new XAttribute("type", "Author"),
      new XElement("FirstName", "Joe"),
      new XElement("LastName", "Rattz")),
    new XElement("BookParticipant",
      new XAttribute("type", "Editor"),
      new XElement("FirstName", "Ewan"),
      new XElement("LastName", "Buckingham"))));

foreach (XNode node in firstParticipant.Nodes().OfType<XComment>())
{
  Console.WriteLine(node);
}
```

Here is the output:

```
<!--This is a new author.-->
```

Just to be anticlimactic, can you use the OfType operator to get just the attributes? No, you cannot. This is a trick question. Remember that unlike the W3C XML DOM API, with the LINQ to XML API, attributes are not nodes in the XML tree. They are a sequence of name-value pairs hanging off the element. To get to the attributes of the first BookParticipant node, we would change the code to that in Listing 7-50.

Listing 7-50. Accessing an Element's Attributes Using the Attributes Method

```
XElement firstParticipant;

//  A full document with all the bells and whistles.
XDocument xDocument = new XDocument(
  new XDeclaration("1.0", "UTF-8", "yes"),
```

```
    new XDocumentType("BookParticipants", null, "BookParticipants.dtd", null),
    new XProcessingInstruction("BookCataloger", "out-of-print"),
    //  Notice on the next line that we are saving off a reference to the first
    //  BookParticipant element.
    new XElement("BookParticipants", firstParticipant =
      new XElement("BookParticipant",
        new XComment("This is a new author."),
        new XProcessingInstruction("AuthorHandler", "new"),
        new XAttribute("type", "Author"),
        new XElement("FirstName", "Joe"),
        new XElement("LastName", "Rattz")),
      new XElement("BookParticipant",
        new XAttribute("type", "Editor"),
        new XElement("FirstName", "Ewan"),
        new XElement("LastName", "Buckingham"))));

foreach (XAttribute attr in firstParticipant.Attributes())
{
  Console.WriteLine(attr);
}
```

Notice we had to change more than just the property or method of the first BookParticipant element that we were accessing. We also had to change the enumeration variable type to XAttribute, because XAttribute doesn't inherit from XNode. Here are the results:

```
type="Author"
```

Down with XContainer.Elements()

Because the LINQ to XML API is so focused on elements and that is what we are working with most, Microsoft provides a quick way to get just the elements of an element's child nodes using the Elements method. It is the equivalent of calling the OfType<XElement> method on the sequence returned by the Nodes method.

Listing 7-51 is an example that is logically the same as Listing 7-48.

Listing 7-51. Accessing an Element's Child Elements Using the Elements Method

```
XElement firstParticipant;

//  A full document with all the bells and whistles.
XDocument xDocument = new XDocument(
  new XDeclaration("1.0", "UTF-8", "yes"),
  new XDocumentType("BookParticipants", null, "BookParticipants.dtd", null),
  new XProcessingInstruction("BookCataloger", "out-of-print"),
  //  Notice on the next line that we are saving off a reference to the first
```

```
  //  BookParticipant element.
  new XElement("BookParticipants", firstParticipant =
    new XElement("BookParticipant",
      new XComment("This is a new author."),
      new XProcessingInstruction("AuthorHandler", "new"),
      new XAttribute("type", "Author"),
      new XElement("FirstName", "Joe"),
      new XElement("LastName", "Rattz")),
    new XElement("BookParticipant",
      new XAttribute("type", "Editor"),
      new XElement("FirstName", "Ewan"),
      new XElement("LastName", "Buckingham")))));

foreach (XNode node in firstParticipant.Elements())
{
  Console.WriteLine(node);
}
```

This code produces the same results as Listing 7-48:

```
<FirstName>Joe</FirstName>
<LastName>Rattz</LastName>
```

The Elements method also has an overloaded version that allows you to pass the name of the element you are looking for, as in Listing 7-52.

Listing 7-52. *Accessing Named Child Elements Using the Elements Method*

```
XElement firstParticipant;

//  A full document with all the bells and whistles.
XDocument xDocument = new XDocument(
  new XDeclaration("1.0", "UTF-8", "yes"),
  new XDocumentType("BookParticipants", null, "BookParticipants.dtd", null),
  new XProcessingInstruction("BookCataloger", "out-of-print"),
  //  Notice on the next line that we aresaving off a reference to the first
  //  BookParticipant element.
  new XElement("BookParticipants", firstParticipant =
    new XElement("BookParticipant",
      new XComment("This is a new author."),
      new XProcessingInstruction("AuthorHandler", "new"),
      new XAttribute("type", "Author"),
      new XElement("FirstName", "Joe"),
      new XElement("LastName", "Rattz")),
    new XElement("BookParticipant",
      new XAttribute("type", "Editor"),
```

```
      new XElement("FirstName", "Ewan"),
      new XElement("LastName", "Buckingham")))));

foreach (XNode node in firstParticipant.Elements("FirstName"))
{
  Console.WriteLine(node);
}
```

This code produces the following:

```
<FirstName>Joe</FirstName>
```

Down with XContainer.Element()

You may obtain the first child element matching a specified name using the Element method. Instead of a sequence being returned requiring a foreach loop, we will have a single element returned, as shown in Listing 7-53.

Listing 7-53. Accessing the First Child Element with a Specified Name

```
XElement firstParticipant;

//  A full document with all the bells and whistles.
XDocument xDocument = new XDocument(
  new XDeclaration("1.0", "UTF-8", "yes"),
  new XDocumentType("BookParticipants", null, "BookParticipants.dtd", null),
  new XProcessingInstruction("BookCataloger", "out-of-print"),
  //  Notice on the next line that we are saving off a reference to the first
  //  BookParticipant element.
  new XElement("BookParticipants", firstParticipant =
    new XElement("BookParticipant",
      new XComment("This is a new author."),
      new XProcessingInstruction("AuthorHandler", "new"),
      new XAttribute("type", "Author"),
      new XElement("FirstName", "Joe"),
      new XElement("LastName", "Rattz")),
    new XElement("BookParticipant",
      new XAttribute("type", "Editor"),
      new XElement("FirstName", "Ewan"),
      new XElement("LastName", "Buckingham")))));

Console.WriteLine(firstParticipant.Element("FirstName"));
```

This code outputs the following:

```
<FirstName>Joe</FirstName>
```

Up Recursively with XNode.Ancestors()

Although you can obtain the single parent element using a node's `Parent` property, you can get a sequence of the ancestor elements using the `Ancestors` method. This is different in that it recursively traverses up the XML tree instead of stopping one level up, and it returns only elements, as opposed to nodes.

To make this demonstration clearer, we will add some child nodes to the first book participant's `FirstName` element. Also, instead of enumerating through the ancestors of the first `BookParticipant` element, we use the `Element` method to reach down two levels to the newly added `NickName` element. This provides more ancestors to provide greater clarity. Listing 7-54 shows the code.

Listing 7-54. *Traversing Up from an XElement Object via the Ancestors Method*

```
XElement firstParticipant;

//  A full document with all the bells and whistles.
XDocument xDocument = new XDocument(
  new XDeclaration("1.0", "UTF-8", "yes"),
  new XDocumentType("BookParticipants", null, "BookParticipants.dtd", null),
  new XProcessingInstruction("BookCataloger", "out-of-print"),
  //  Notice on the next line that we are saving off a reference to the first
  //  BookParticipant element.
  new XElement("BookParticipants", firstParticipant =
    new XElement("BookParticipant",
      new XComment("This is a new author."),
      new XProcessingInstruction("AuthorHandler", "new"),
      new XAttribute("type", "Author"),
      new XElement("FirstName",
        new XText("Joe"),
        new XElement("NickName", "Joey")),
      new XElement("LastName", "Rattz")),
    new XElement("BookParticipant",
      new XAttribute("type", "Editor"),
      new XElement("FirstName", "Ewan"),
      new XElement("LastName", "Buckingham"))));

foreach (XElement element in firstParticipant.
  Element("FirstName").Element("NickName").Ancestors())
{
  Console.WriteLine(element.Name);
}
```

Again, please notice we add some child nodes to the first book participant's `FirstName` element. This causes the first book participant's `FirstName` element to have contents that include an `XText` object equal to the string `"Joe"` and to have a child element, `NickName`. We retrieve the first book participant's `FirstName` element's `NickName` element for which to retrieve the ancestors. In addition, notice we used a `XElement` type variable instead of an `XNode` type for enumerating through the sequence returned from the `Ancestors` method. This is so we can access the `Name` property of the element. Instead of displaying the element's XML as we have done in past examples, we are only displaying the name of each element in the ancestor's sequence. We do this because it would be confusing to display each ancestor's XML, because each would include the previous, and it would get very recursive, thereby obscuring the results. That all said, here they are:

```
FirstName
BookParticipant
BookParticipants
```

Just as expected, the code recursively traverses up the XML tree.

Up Recursively with XElement.AncestorsAndSelf()

This method works just like the `Ancestors` method, except it includes itself in the returned sequence of ancestors. Listing 7-55 is the same example as before, except it calls the `AncestorsAndSelf` method.

Listing 7-55. *Traversing Up from an XElement Object via the AncestorsAndSelf Method*

```
XElement firstParticipant;

// A full document with all the bells and whistles.
XDocument xDocument = new XDocument(
  new XDeclaration("1.0", "UTF-8", "yes"),
  new XDocumentType("BookParticipants", null, "BookParticipants.dtd", null),
  new XProcessingInstruction("BookCataloger", "out-of-print"),
  // Notice on the next line that we are saving off a reference to the first
  // BookParticipant element.
  new XElement("BookParticipants", firstParticipant =
    new XElement("BookParticipant",
      new XComment("This is a new author."),
      new XProcessingInstruction("AuthorHandler", "new"),
      new XAttribute("type", "Author"),
      new XElement("FirstName",
        new XText("Joe"),
        new XElement("NickName", "Joey")),
      new XElement("LastName", "Rattz")),
    new XElement("BookParticipant",
      new XAttribute("type", "Editor"),
      new XElement("FirstName", "Ewan"),
```

```
          new XElement("LastName", "Buckingham")))));

foreach (XElement element in firstParticipant.
  Element("FirstName").Element("NickName").AncestorsAndSelf())
{
  Console.WriteLine(element.Name);
}
```

The results should be the same as when calling the Ancestors method, except we should also see the NickName element's name at the beginning of the output:

```
NickName
FirstName
BookParticipant
BookParticipants
```

Down Recursively with XContainer.Descendants()

In addition to recursively traversing up, you can recursively traverse down with the Descendants method. Again, this method only returns elements. There is an equivalent method named DescendantNodes that will return all descendant nodes. Listing 7-56 is the same code as the previous, except we call the Descendants method on the first book participant element.

Listing 7-56. *Traversing Down from an XElement Object via the Descendants Method*

```
XElement firstParticipant;

//  A full document with all the bells and whistles.
XDocument xDocument = new XDocument(
  new XDeclaration("1.0", "UTF-8", "yes"),
  new XDocumentType("BookParticipants", null, "BookParticipants.dtd", null),
  new XProcessingInstruction("BookCataloger", "out-of-print"),
  //  Notice on the next line that we are saving off a reference to the first
  //  BookParticipant element.
  new XElement("BookParticipants", firstParticipant =
    new XElement("BookParticipant",
      new XComment("This is a new author."),
      new XProcessingInstruction("AuthorHandler", "new"),
      new XAttribute("type", "Author"),
      new XElement("FirstName",
        new XText("Joe"),
        new XElement("NickName", "Joey")),
      new XElement("LastName", "Rattz")),
    new XElement("BookParticipant",
```

```
      new XAttribute("type", "Editor"),
      new XElement("FirstName", "Ewan"),
      new XElement("LastName", "Buckingham")))));

foreach (XElement element in firstParticipant.Descendants())
{
  Console.WriteLine(element.Name);
}
```

The results are the following:

```
FirstName
NickName
LastName
```

As you can see, it traverses all the way to the end of every branch in the XML tree.

Down Recursively with XElement.DescendantsAndSelf()

Just as the Ancestors method has an AncestorsAndSelf method variation, so too does the Descendants method. The DescendantsAndSelf method works just like the Descendants method, except it also includes the element itself in the returned sequence. Listing 7-57 is the same example that we used for the Descendants method call, with the exception that now it calls the DescendantsAndSelf method.

Listing 7-57. *Traversing Down from an XElement Object via the DescendantsAndSelf Method*

```
XElement firstParticipant;

//  A full document with all the bells and whistles.
XDocument xDocument = new XDocument(
  new XDeclaration("1.0", "UTF-8", "yes"),
  new XDocumentType("BookParticipants", null, "BookParticipants.dtd", null),
  new XProcessingInstruction("BookCataloger", "out-of-print"),
  //  Notice on the next line that we are saving off a reference to the first
  //  BookParticipant element.
  new XElement("BookParticipants", firstParticipant =
    new XElement("BookParticipant",
      new XComment("This is a new author."),
      new XProcessingInstruction("AuthorHandler", "new"),
      new XAttribute("type", "Author"),
      new XElement("FirstName",
        new XText("Joe"),
        new XElement("NickName", "Joey")),
      new XElement("LastName", "Rattz")),
```

```
      new XElement("BookParticipant",
        new XAttribute("type", "Editor"),
        new XElement("FirstName", "Ewan"),
        new XElement("LastName", "Buckingham")))));
```

```
foreach (XElement element in firstParticipant.DescendantsAndSelf())
{
  Console.WriteLine(element.Name);
}
```

So, does the output also include the firstParticipant element's name?

```
BookParticipant
FirstName
NickName
LastName
```

Of course it does.

Forward with XNode.NodesAfterSelf()

For this example, in addition to changing the foreach call, we add a couple of comments to the BookParticipants element to make the distinction between retrieving nodes and elements more evident, since XComment is a node but not an element. Listing 7-58 is what the code looks like for this example.

Listing 7-58. *Traversing Forward from the Current Node Using the NodesAfterSelf Method*

```
XElement firstParticipant;

// A full document with all the bells and whistles.
XDocument xDocument = new XDocument(
  new XDeclaration("1.0", "UTF-8", "yes"),
  new XDocumentType("BookParticipants", null, "BookParticipants.dtd", null),
  new XProcessingInstruction("BookCataloger", "out-of-print"),
  // Notice on the next line that we are saving off a reference to the first
  // BookParticipant element.
  new XElement("BookParticipants",
    new XComment("Begin Of List"), firstParticipant =
    new XElement("BookParticipant",
      new XAttribute("type", "Author"),
      new XElement("FirstName", "Joe"),
      new XElement("LastName", "Rattz")),
    new XElement("BookParticipant",
      new XAttribute("type", "Editor"),
```

```
      new XElement("FirstName", "Ewan"),
      new XElement("LastName", "Buckingham")),
   new XComment("End Of List")));

foreach (XNode node in firstParticipant.NodesAfterSelf())
{
  Console.WriteLine(node);
}
```

Notice that we added two comments that are siblings of the two BookParticipant elements. This modification to the constructed XML document will be made for the NodesAfterSelf, ElementsAfterSelf, NodesBeforeSelf, and ElementsBeforeSelf examples.

This causes all sibling nodes after the first BookParticipant node to be enumerated. Here are the results:

```
<BookParticipant type="Editor">
  <FirstName>Ewan</FirstName>
  <LastName>Buckingham</LastName>
</BookParticipant>
<!--End Of List-->
```

As you can see, the last comment is included in the output because it is a node. Don't let that output fool you. The NodesAfterSelf method returns only two nodes: the BookParticipant element whose type attribute is Editor and the End Of List comment. Those other nodes, FirstName and LastName, are merely displayed because the ToString method is being called on the BookParticipant node.

Keep in mind that this method returns nodes, not just elements. If you want to limit the type of nodes returned, you could use the TypeOf operator as we have demonstrated in previous examples. But if the type you are interested in is elements, there is a method just for that called ElementsAfterSelf.

Forward with XNode.ElementsAfterSelf()

This example uses the same modifications to the XML document made in Listing 7-58 concerning the addition of two comments.

To get a sequence of just the sibling elements after the referenced node, you call the ElementsAfterSelf method, as shown in Listing 7-59.

Listing 7-59. *Traversing Forward from the Current Node Using the ElementsAfterSelf Method*

```
XElement firstParticipant;

//  A full document with all the bells and whistles.
XDocument xDocument = new XDocument(
  new XDeclaration("1.0", "UTF-8", "yes"),
  new XDocumentType("BookParticipants", null, "BookParticipants.dtd", null),
  new XProcessingInstruction("BookCataloger", "out-of-print"),
```

```
//  Notice on the next line that we are saving off a reference to the first
//  BookParticipant element.
new XElement("BookParticipants",
  new XComment("Begin Of List"), firstParticipant =
  new XElement("BookParticipant",
    new XAttribute("type", "Author"),
    new XElement("FirstName", "Joe"),
    new XElement("LastName", "Rattz")),
  new XElement("BookParticipant",
    new XAttribute("type", "Editor"),
    new XElement("FirstName", "Ewan"),
    new XElement("LastName", "Buckingham")),
  new XComment("End Of List")));

foreach (XNode node in firstParticipant.ElementsAfterSelf())
{
  Console.WriteLine(node);
}
```

The example code with these modifications produces the following results:

```
<BookParticipant type="Editor">
  <FirstName>Ewan</FirstName>
  <LastName>Buckingham</LastName>
</BookParticipant>
```

Notice that the comment is excluded this time because it is not an element. Again, the FirstName and LastName elements are displayed only because they are the content of the BookParticipant element that was retrieved and because the ToString method was called on the element.

Backward with XNode.NodesBeforeSelf()

This example uses the same modifications to the XML document made in Listing 7-58 concerning the addition of two comments.

This method works just like NodesAfterSelf except it retrieves the sibling nodes before the referenced node. In the example code, since the initial reference into the document is the first BookParticipant node, we obtain a reference to the second BookParticipant node using the NextNode property of the first BookParticipant node so that there are more nodes to return, as shown in Listing 7-60.

Listing 7-60. *Traversing Backward from the Current Node*

```
XElement firstParticipant;

//  A full document with all the bells and whistles.
XDocument xDocument = new XDocument(
```

```
  new XDeclaration("1.0", "UTF-8", "yes"),
  new XDocumentType("BookParticipants", null, "BookParticipants.dtd", null),
  new XProcessingInstruction("BookCataloger", "out-of-print"),
  //  Notice on the next line that we are saving off a reference to the first
  //  BookParticipant element.
  new XElement("BookParticipants",
    new XComment("Begin Of List"), firstParticipant =
    new XElement("BookParticipant",
      new XAttribute("type", "Author"),
      new XElement("FirstName", "Joe"),
      new XElement("LastName", "Rattz")),
    new XElement("BookParticipant",
      new XAttribute("type", "Editor"),
      new XElement("FirstName", "Ewan"),
      new XElement("LastName", "Buckingham")),
    new XComment("End Of List")));

foreach (XNode node in firstParticipant.NextNode.NodesBeforeSelf())
{
  Console.WriteLine(node);
}
```

This modification should result in the return of the first BookParticipant node and the first comment. Here are the results:

```
<!--Begin Of List-->
<BookParticipant type="Author">
  <FirstName>Joe</FirstName>
  <LastName>Rattz</LastName>
</BookParticipant>
```

Interesting! We were expecting the two nodes that were returned, the comment and the first BookParticipant, to be in the reverse order. We expected the method to start with the referenced node and build a sequence via the PreviousNode property. Perhaps it did indeed do this but then called the Reverse or InDocumentOrder operator. We cover the InDocumentOrder operator in the next chapter. Again, don't let the FirstName and LastName nodes confuse you. The NodesBeforeSelf method did not return those. It is only because the ToString method was called on the first BookParticipant node, by the Console.WriteLine method, that they are displayed.

Backward with XNode.ElementsBeforeSelf()

This example uses the same modifications to the XML document made in Listing 7-58 concerning the addition of two comments.

Just like the NodesAfterSelf method has a companion method named ElementsAfterSelf to return only the elements, so too does the NodesBeforeSelf method. The ElementsBeforeSelf method returns only the sibling elements before the referenced node, as shown in Listing 7-61.

Listing 7-61. *Traversing Backward from the Current Node*

```
XElement firstParticipant;

//  A full document with all the bells and whistles.
XDocument xDocument = new XDocument(
  new XDeclaration("1.0", "UTF-8", "yes"),
  new XDocumentType("BookParticipants", null, "BookParticipants.dtd", null),
  new XProcessingInstruction("BookCataloger", "out-of-print"),
  //  Notice on the next line that we are saving off a reference to the first
  //  BookParticipant element.
  new XElement("BookParticipants",
    new XComment("Begin Of List"), firstParticipant =
    new XElement("BookParticipant",
      new XAttribute("type", "Author"),
      new XElement("FirstName", "Joe"),
      new XElement("LastName", "Rattz")),
    new XElement("BookParticipant",
      new XAttribute("type", "Editor"),
      new XElement("FirstName", "Ewan"),
      new XElement("LastName", "Buckingham")),
    new XComment("End Of List")));

foreach (XNode node in firstParticipant.NextNode.ElementsBeforeSelf())
{
  Console.WriteLine(node);
}
```

Notice that again we obtain a reference to the second BookParticipant node via the NextNode property. Will the output contain the comment?

```
<BookParticipant type="Author">
  <FirstName>Joe</FirstName>
  <LastName>Rattz</LastName>
</BookParticipant>
```

Of course not, because it is not an element.

XML Modification

Modifying XML data is easier than ever with the LINQ to XML API. With just a handful of methods, you can perform all the modifications you could want. Whether it is adding, changing, or deleting nodes or elements, there is a method to get the job done.

As has been stated time and time again, with the LINQ to XML API, you will be working with XElement objects most of the time. Because of this, the majority of these examples are with elements. The LINQ to XML API classes inheriting from XNode are covered first, followed by a section on attributes.

Adding Nodes

In this section on adding nodes to an XML tree, we start with a base example of the code in Listing 7-62.

Listing 7-62. A Base Example with a Single Book Participant

```
//  A document with one book participant.
XDocument xDocument = new XDocument(
  new XElement("BookParticipants",
    new XElement("BookParticipant",
      new XAttribute("type", "Author"),
      new XElement("FirstName", "Joe"),
      new XElement("LastName", "Rattz"))));

Console.WriteLine(xDocument);
```

This code produces an XML tree with a single book participant. Here is the code's output:

```
<BookParticipants>
  <BookParticipant type="Author">
    <FirstName>Joe</FirstName>
    <LastName>Rattz</LastName>
  </BookParticipant>
</BookParticipants>
```

For the different methods to add nodes, we will start with this basic code.

■ **Note** Although the following examples all add elements, the techniques used to add the elements work for all LINQ to XML classes that inherit from the XNode class.

In addition to the following ways to add nodes, be sure to check out the section "XElement.SetElementValue() on Child XElement Objects" later in this chapter.

XContainer.Add() (AddLast)

The method you will use most to add nodes to an XML tree is the Add method. It appends a node to the end of the specified node's child nodes. Listing 7-63 is an example.

Listing 7-63. Adding a Node to the End of the Specified Node's Child Nodes with Add

```
//  A document with one book participant.
XDocument xDocument = new XDocument(
  new XElement("BookParticipants",
    new XElement("BookParticipant",
      new XAttribute("type", "Author"),
      new XElement("FirstName", "Joe"),
      new XElement("LastName", "Rattz"))));

xDocument.Element("BookParticipants").Add(
  new XElement("BookParticipant",
    new XAttribute("type", "Editor"),
    new XElement("FirstName", "Ewan"),
    new XElement("LastName", "Buckingham")));

Console.WriteLine(xDocument);
```

In the previous code, you can see we start with the base code and then add a BookParticipant element to the document's BookParticipants element. You can see we use the Element method of the document to obtain the BookParticipants element and add the element to its child nodes using the Add method. This causes the newly added element to be appended to the child nodes:

```
<BookParticipants>
  <BookParticipant type="Author">
    <FirstName>Joe</FirstName>
    <LastName>Rattz</LastName>
  </BookParticipant>
  <BookParticipant type="Editor">
    <FirstName>Ewan</FirstName>
    <LastName>Buckingham</LastName>
  </BookParticipant>
</BookParticipants>
```

The Add method adds the newly constructed BookParticipant element to the end of the BookParticipants element's child nodes. As you can see, the Add method is every bit as flexible as the XElement constructor and follows the same rules for its arguments, allowing for functional construction.

XContainer.AddFirst()

To add a node to the beginning of a node's child nodes, use the AddFirst method. Using the same code as before, except calling the AddFirst method, gives you the code in Listing 7-64.

Listing 7-64. *Adding a Node to the Beginning of the Specified Node's Child Nodes with AddFirst*

```
//  A document with one book participant.
XDocument xDocument = new XDocument(
  new XElement("BookParticipants",
    new XElement("BookParticipant",
      new XAttribute("type", "Author"),
      new XElement("FirstName", "Joe"),
      new XElement("LastName", "Rattz"))));

xDocument.Element("BookParticipants").AddFirst(
  new XElement("BookParticipant",
    new XAttribute("type", "Editor"),
    new XElement("FirstName", "Ewan"),
    new XElement("LastName", "Buckingham")));

Console.WriteLine(xDocument);
```

As one would expect, the newly added BookParticipant element will be added to the head of the BookParticipants element's child nodes:

```
<BookParticipants>
  <BookParticipant type="Editor">
    <FirstName>Ewan</FirstName>
    <LastName>Buckingham</LastName>
  </BookParticipant>
  <BookParticipant type="Author">
    <FirstName>Joe</FirstName>
    <LastName>Rattz</LastName>
  </BookParticipant>
</BookParticipants>
```

Can XML manipulation get any easier than this? We submit that it cannot.

XNode.AddBeforeSelf()

To insert a node into a node's list of child nodes in a specific location, obtain a reference to either the node before or the node after where you want to insert, and call either the AddBeforeSelf method or the AddAfterSelf method.

We will use the XML tree produced by the Add method example, Listing 7-63, as a starting point and add a new node between the two already existing BookParticipant elements. To do this, we must get a reference to the second BookParticipant element, as shown in Listing 7-65.

Listing 7-65. *Adding a Node in the Specified Node's Child Nodes with AddBeforeSelf*

```
//  A document with one book participant.
XDocument xDocument = new XDocument(
  new XElement("BookParticipants",
    new XElement("BookParticipant",
      new XAttribute("type", "Author"),
      new XElement("FirstName", "Joe"),
      new XElement("LastName", "Rattz"))));

xDocument.Element("BookParticipants").Add(
  new XElement("BookParticipant",
    new XAttribute("type", "Editor"),
    new XElement("FirstName", "Ewan"),
    new XElement("LastName", "Buckingham")));

xDocument.Element("BookParticipants").
  Elements("BookParticipant").
  Where(e => ((string)e.Element("FirstName")) == "Ewan").
  Single<XElement>().AddBeforeSelf(
    new XElement("BookParticipant",
      new XAttribute("type", "Technical Reviewer"),
      new XElement("FirstName", "Fabio"),
      new XElement("LastName", "Ferracchiati")));

Console.WriteLine(xDocument);
```

As a refresher of the Standard Query Operators in Part 2 of this book, "LINQ to Objects," and to integrate some of what you have learned in this chapter, we have chosen to find the BookParticipant element we want to insert before using a plethora of LINQ operators. Notice that we are using the Element method to reach down into the document to select the BookParticipants element. Then, we select the BookParticipants child elements named BookParticipant where the BookParticipant element has a child element named FirstName whose value is "Ewan". Since we know there will be only a single BookParticipant element matching this search criterion and because we want an XElement type object back that we can call the AddBeforeSelf method on, we call the Single operator to return the XElement BookParticipant object. This gives us a reference to the BookParticipant element in front of which we want to insert the new XElement.

Also notice that in the call to the Where operator, we cast the FirstName element to a string to use the node value extraction feature to obtain the FirstName element's value for the equality comparison to "Ewan".

Once we have a reference to the proper BookParticipant element, we merely call the AddBeforeSelf method, and *voilà*:

```
<BookParticipants>
  <BookParticipant type="Author">
    <FirstName>Joe</FirstName>
    <LastName>Rattz</LastName>
  </BookParticipant>
  <BookParticipant type="Technical Reviewer">
    <FirstName>Fabio</FirstName>
    <LastName>Ferracchiati</LastName>
  </BookParticipant>
  <BookParticipant type="Editor">
    <FirstName>Ewan</FirstName>
    <LastName>Buckingham</LastName>
  </BookParticipant>
</BookParticipants>
```

Just as we wanted, we inserted the new BookParticipant before the BookParticipant element whose FirstName element's value is "Ewan".

XNode.AddAfterSelf()

After all that finagling to get the reference of the second BookParticipant element in the previous example, the example in Listing 7-66 is sure to be anticlimactic. We will just get a reference to the first BookParticipant element using the Element method and add the new BookParticipant element after it using the AddAfterSelf method.

Listing 7-66. *Adding a Node in a Specific Location of the Specified Node's Child Nodes with AddAfterSelf*

```
//  A document with one book participant.
XDocument xDocument = new XDocument(
  new XElement("BookParticipants",
    new XElement("BookParticipant",
      new XAttribute("type", "Author"),
      new XElement("FirstName", "Joe"),
      new XElement("LastName", "Rattz"))));

xDocument.Element("BookParticipants").Add(
  new XElement("BookParticipant",
    new XAttribute("type", "Editor"),
    new XElement("FirstName", "Ewan"),
    new XElement("LastName", "Buckingham")));

xDocument.Element("BookParticipants").
  Element("BookParticipant").AddAfterSelf(
```

```
    new XElement("BookParticipant",
      new XAttribute("type", "Technical Reviewer"),
      new XElement("FirstName", "Fabio"),
      new XElement("LastName", "Ferracchiati")));

Console.WriteLine(xDocument);
```

This example just seems trivial after the previous one:

```
<BookParticipants>
  <BookParticipant type="Author">
    <FirstName>Joe</FirstName>
    <LastName>Rattz</LastName>
  </BookParticipant>
  <BookParticipant type="Technical Reviewer">
    <FirstName>Fabio</FirstName>
    <LastName>Ferracchiati</LastName>
  </BookParticipant>
  <BookParticipant type="Editor">
    <FirstName>Ewan</FirstName>
    <LastName>Buckingham</LastName>
  </BookParticipant>
</BookParticipants>
```

Deleting Nodes

Deleting nodes is accomplished with either of two methods: Remove or RemoveAll.

In addition to reading about the following ways to delete nodes, be sure to check out the section "XElement.SetElementValue() on Child XElement Objects" later in this chapter.

XNode.Remove()

The Remove method removes any node, as well as its child nodes and attributes, from an XML tree. In the first example, we construct an XML tree and save off a reference to the first book participant element as we did in some of the previous examples. We display the XML tree after the construction but before deleting any nodes. We then delete the first book participant element and display the resulting XML tree, as shown in Listing 7-67.

Listing 7-67. Deleting a Specific Node with Remove

```
//  we will use this to store a reference to one of the elements in the XML tree.
XElement firstParticipant;

Console.WriteLine(System.Environment.NewLine + "Before node deletion");
```

```
XDocument xDocument = new XDocument(
  new XElement("BookParticipants", firstParticipant =
    new XElement("BookParticipant",
      new XAttribute("type", "Author"),
      new XElement("FirstName", "Joe"),
      new XElement("LastName", "Rattz")),
    new XElement("BookParticipant",
      new XAttribute("type", "Editor"),
      new XElement("FirstName", "Ewan"),
      new XElement("LastName", "Buckingham")))));

Console.WriteLine(xDocument);

firstParticipant.Remove();
Console.WriteLine(System.Environment.NewLine + "After node deletion");

Console.WriteLine(xDocument);
```

If all goes as planned, we should get the XML tree initially with the first book participant element and subsequently without it:

```
Before node deletion
<BookParticipants>
  <BookParticipant type="Author">
    <FirstName>Joe</FirstName>
    <LastName>Rattz</LastName>
  </BookParticipant>
  <BookParticipant type="Editor">
    <FirstName>Ewan</FirstName>
    <LastName>Buckingham</LastName>
  </BookParticipant>
</BookParticipants>

After node deletion
<BookParticipants>
  <BookParticipant type="Editor">
    <FirstName>Ewan</FirstName>
    <LastName>Buckingham</LastName>
  </BookParticipant>
</BookParticipants>
```

As you can see, the first BookParticipant element is gone after the node deletion.

IEnumerable<T>.Remove()

In the previous case, we call the Remove method on a single XNode object. We can also call Remove on a sequence (IEnumerable<T>). Listing 7-68 is an example where we use the Descendants method of the document to recursively traverse all the way down the XML tree, returning only those elements whose name is FirstName by using the Where operator. We then call the Remove method on the resulting sequence.

Listing 7-68. *Deleting a Sequence of Nodes with Remove*

```
XDocument xDocument = new XDocument(
  new XElement("BookParticipants",
    new XElement("BookParticipant",
      new XAttribute("type", "Author"),
      new XElement("FirstName", "Joe"),
      new XElement("LastName", "Rattz")),
    new XElement("BookParticipant",
      new XAttribute("type", "Editor"),
      new XElement("FirstName", "Ewan"),
      new XElement("LastName", "Buckingham"))));

xDocument.Descendants().Where(e => e.Name == "FirstName").Remove();

Console.WriteLine(xDocument);
```

We like this example because we really start to tie all the elements of LINQ together with it. We are using the XDocument.Descendants method to get all the child nodes returned in a sequence, and then we call the Where Standard Query Operator to filter just the ones matching the search criteria, which in this case are elements named FirstName. This returns a sequence that we then call the Remove method on. Sweet! Here are the results:

```
<BookParticipants>
  <BookParticipant type="Author">
    <LastName>Rattz</LastName>
  </BookParticipant>
  <BookParticipant type="Editor">
    <LastName>Buckingham</LastName>
  </BookParticipant>
</BookParticipants>
```

Notice that we no longer have any FirstName nodes.

XElement.RemoveAll()

Sometimes, you may want to delete the content of an element but not the element itself. This is what the RemoveAll method is for. Listing 7-69 is an example.

Listing 7-69. *Removing a Node's Content with RemoveAll*

```
XDocument xDocument = new XDocument(
  new XElement("BookParticipants",
    new XElement("BookParticipant",
      new XAttribute("type", "Author"),
      new XElement("FirstName", "Joe"),
      new XElement("LastName", "Rattz")),
    new XElement("BookParticipant",
      new XAttribute("type", "Editor"),
      new XElement("FirstName", "Ewan"),
      new XElement("LastName", "Buckingham"))));

Console.WriteLine(System.Environment.NewLine + "Before removing the content.");
Console.WriteLine(xDocument);

xDocument.Element("BookParticipants").RemoveAll();

Console.WriteLine(System.Environment.NewLine + "After removing the content.");
Console.WriteLine(xDocument);
```

Here we display the document first before removing the content of the BookParticipants node. Then, we remove the content of the BookParticipants node and display the document again. Since you could be from Missouri, we had better show you the results:

```
Before removing the content.
<BookParticipants>
  <BookParticipant type="Author">
    <FirstName>Joe</FirstName>
    <LastName>Rattz</LastName>
  </BookParticipant>
  <BookParticipant type="Editor">
    <FirstName>Ewan</FirstName>
    <LastName>Buckingham</LastName>
  </BookParticipant>
</BookParticipants>

After removing the content.
<BookParticipants />
```

Updating Nodes

Several of the subclasses of XNode, such as XElement, XText, and XComment, have a Value property that can be directly updated. Others, such as XDocumentType and XProcessingInstruction, have specific properties that each can be updated. For elements, in addition to modifying the Value property, you can change its value by calling the XElement.SetElementValue or XContainer.ReplaceAll methods covered later in this chapter.

XElement.Value on XElement Objects, XText.Value on XText Objects, and XComment.Value on XComment Objects

Each of these subclasses of XNode has a Value property that can be set to update the node's value. Listing 7-70 demonstrates all of them.

Listing 7-70. Updating a Node's Value

```
//  we will use this to reference to one of the elements in the XML tree.
XElement firstParticipant;

XDocument xDocument = new XDocument(
  new XElement("BookParticipants", firstParticipant =
    new XElement("BookParticipant",
      new XComment("This is a new author."),
      new XAttribute("type", "Author"),
      new XElement("FirstName", "Joe"),
      new XElement("LastName", "Rattz"))));

Console.WriteLine("Before updating nodes:");
Console.WriteLine(xDocument);

//  Now, lets update an element, a comment, and a text node.
firstParticipant.Element("FirstName").Value = "Joey";
firstParticipant.Nodes().OfType<XComment>().Single().Value =
  "Author of Pro LINQ: Language Integrated Query in C# 2008.";
((XElement)firstParticipant.Element("FirstName").NextNode)
  .Nodes().OfType<XText>().Single().Value = "Rattz, Jr.";

Console.WriteLine("After updating nodes:");
Console.WriteLine(xDocument);
```

In this example, we update the FirstName element first, using its Value property, followed by the comment using its Value property, finally followed by updating the LastName element by accessing its value through its child XText object's Value property. Notice the flexibility LINQ to XML provides for getting references to the different objects we want to update. Just remember that it isn't necessary for us to access the LastName element's value by getting the XText object from its child nodes. We did that merely for demonstration purposes. Other than that, we would have directly accessed its Value property. Here are the results:

```
Before updating nodes:
<BookParticipants>
  <BookParticipant type="Author">
    <!--This is a new author.-->
    <FirstName>Joe</FirstName>
    <LastName>Rattz</LastName>
  </BookParticipant>
</BookParticipants>
After updating nodes:
<BookParticipants>
  <BookParticipant type="Author">
    <!--Author of Pro LINQ: Language Integrated Query in C# 2008.-->
    <FirstName>Joey</FirstName>
    <LastName>Rattz, Jr.</LastName>
  </BookParticipant>
</BookParticipants>
```

As you can see, all of the node's values are updated.

XDocumentType.Name, XDocumentType.PublicId, XDocumentType.SystemId, and XDocumentType.InternalSubset on XDocumentType Objects

To update a document type node, the XDocumentType class provides four properties for updating its values. Listing 7-71 is some sample code demonstrating this.

Listing 7-71. Updating the Document Type

```
//  we will use this to store a reference to the DocumentType for later access.
XDocumentType docType;

XDocument xDocument = new XDocument(
  docType = new XDocumentType("BookParticipants", null,
                              "BookParticipants.dtd", null),
  new XElement("BookParticipants"));

Console.WriteLine("Before updating document type:");
Console.WriteLine(xDocument);

docType.Name = "MyBookParticipants";
docType.SystemId = "http://www.somewhere.com/DTDs/MyBookParticipants.DTD";
docType.PublicId = "-//DTDs//TEXT Book Participants//EN";
```

```
Console.WriteLine("After updating document type:");
Console.WriteLine(xDocument);
```

Here are the results of this code:

```
Before updating document type:
<!DOCTYPE BookParticipants SYSTEM "BookParticipants.dtd">
<BookParticipants />
After updating document type:
<!DOCTYPE MyBookParticipants PUBLIC "-//DTDs//TEXT Book Participants//EN"
"http://www.somewhere.com/DTDs/MyBookParticipants.DTD">
<BookParticipants />
```

XProcessingInstruction.Target on XProcessingInstruction Objects and XProcessingInstruction.Data on XProcessingInstruction Objects

To update the value of a processing instruction, simply modify the Target and Data properties of the XProcessingInstruction object. Listing 7-72 is an example.

Listing 7-72. Updating a Processing Instruction

```
//  we will use this to store a reference for later access.
XProcessingInstruction procInst;

XDocument xDocument = new XDocument(
  new XElement("BookParticipants"),
  procInst = new XProcessingInstruction("BookCataloger", "out-of-print"));

Console.WriteLine("Before updating processing instruction:");
Console.WriteLine(xDocument);

procInst.Target = "BookParticipantContactManager";
procInst.Data = "update";

Console.WriteLine("After updating processing instruction:");
Console.WriteLine(xDocument);
```

Now let's take a look at the output:

```
Before updating processing instruction:
<BookParticipants />
```

```
<?BookCataloger out-of-print?>
After updating processing instruction:
<BookParticipants />
<?BookParticipantContactManager update?>
```

XElement.ReplaceAll()

The ReplaceAll method is useful for replacing an element's entire subtree of XML. You can pass a simple value, such as a new string or a numeric type; or because there is an overloaded method that accepts multiple objects via the params keyword, an entire subtree can be changed. The ReplaceAll method also replaces attributes. Listing 7-73 is some sample code.

Listing 7-73. *Using ReplaceAll to Change an Element's Subtree*

```
//  we will use this to store a reference to one of the elements in the XML tree.
XElement firstParticipant;

XDocument xDocument = new XDocument(
  new XElement("BookParticipants", firstParticipant =
    new XElement("BookParticipant",
      new XAttribute("type", "Author"),
      new XElement("FirstName", "Joe"),
      new XElement("LastName", "Rattz"))));

Console.WriteLine(System.Environment.NewLine + "Before updating elements:");
Console.WriteLine(xDocument);

firstParticipant.ReplaceAll(
  new XElement("FirstName", "Ewan"),
  new XElement("LastName", "Buckingham"));

Console.WriteLine(System.Environment.NewLine + "After updating elements:");
Console.WriteLine(xDocument);
```

Notice that, when we replaced the content with the ReplaceAll method, we omitted specifying an attribute. As you would expect, the content is replaced:

```
Before updating elements:
<BookParticipants>
  <BookParticipant type="Author">
    <FirstName>Joe</FirstName>
    <LastName>Rattz</LastName>
  </BookParticipant>
```

```
</BookParticipants>

After updating elements:
<BookParticipants>
  <BookParticipant>
    <FirstName>Ewan</FirstName>
    <LastName>Buckingham</LastName>
  </BookParticipant>
</BookParticipants>
```

Notice that the BookParticipant type attribute is now gone. This is interesting in that attributes are not child nodes of an element. But the ReplaceAll method replaces them as well.

XElement.SetElementValue() on Child XElement Objects

Don't let this simply named method fool you; it's a powerhouse. It has the ability to add, change, and remove elements. Furthermore, it performs these operations on the child elements of the element you call it on. Stated differently, you call the SetElementValue method on a parent element to affect its content, meaning its child elements.

When calling the SetElementValue method, you pass it the name of the child element you want to set and the value you want to set it to. If a child element is found by that name, its value is updated, as long as the passed value is not null. If the passed value is null, that found child element will be removed. If an element by that name is not found, it will be added with the passed value. Wow, what a method!

Also, the SetElementValue method will only affect the first child element it finds with the specified name. Any subsequent elements with the same name will not be affected, either by the value being changed to the one passed in or the element being removed, because that passed value is null.

Listing 7-74 is an example demonstrating all uses: update, add, and delete.

Listing 7-74. *Using SetElementValue to Update, Add, and Delete Child Elements*

```
// we will use this to store a reference to one of the elements in the XML tree.
XElement firstParticipant;

XDocument xDocument = new XDocument(
  new XElement("BookParticipants", firstParticipant =
    new XElement("BookParticipant",
      new XAttribute("type", "Author"),
      new XElement("FirstName", "Joe"),
      new XElement("LastName", "Rattz"))));

Console.WriteLine(System.Environment.NewLine + "Before updating elements:");
Console.WriteLine(xDocument);

// First, we will use XElement.SetElementValue to update the value of an element.
// Since an element named FirstName is there, its value will be updated to Joseph.
```

```
firstParticipant.SetElementValue("FirstName", "Joseph");

//  Second, we will use XElement.SetElementValue to add an element.
//  Since no element named MiddleInitial exists, one will be added.
firstParticipant.SetElementValue("MiddleInitial", "C");

//  Third, we will use XElement.SetElementValue to remove an element.
//  Setting an element's value to null will remove it.
firstParticipant.SetElementValue("LastName", null);

Console.WriteLine(System.Environment.NewLine + "After updating elements:");
Console.WriteLine(xDocument);
```

As you can see, first we call the SetElementValue method on the firstParticipant element's child element named FirstName. Since an element already exists by that name, its value will be updated. Next, we call the SetElementValue method on the firstParticipant element's child element named MiddleInitial. Since no element exists by that name, the element will be added. Lastly, we call the SetElementValue method on the firstParticipant element's child element named LastName and pass a null. Since a null is passed, the LastName element will be removed. Look at the flexibility that the SetElementValue method provides. We know you can't wait to see the results:

```
Before updating elements:
<BookParticipants>
  <BookParticipant type="Author">
    <FirstName>Joe</FirstName>
    <LastName>Rattz</LastName>
  </BookParticipant>
</BookParticipants>

After updating elements:
<BookParticipants>
  <BookParticipant type="Author">
    <FirstName>Joseph</FirstName>
    <MiddleInitial>C</MiddleInitial>
  </BookParticipant>
</BookParticipants>
```

How cool is that? The FirstName element's value was updated; the MiddleInitial element was added, and the LastName element was removed.

■ **Caution** Just because calling the `SetElementValue` method with a value of `null` removes the node, don't make the mistake of thinking that manually setting an element's value to `null` is the same as removing it in the LINQ to XML API. This is merely the behavior of the `SetElementValue` method. If you attempt to set an element's value to `null` using its `Value` property, an exception will be thrown.

XML Attributes

As we previously mentioned, with the LINQ to XML API, attributes are implemented with the `XAttribute` class, and unlike the W3C XML DOM API, they do not inherit from a node. Therefore, they have no inheritance relationship with elements. However, in the LINQ to XML API, they are every bit as easy to work with as elements. Let's take a look.

Attribute Creation

Attributes are created just like elements and most other LINQ to XML classes. This topic is covered in the "Creating Attributes with XAttribute" section previously in this chapter.

Attribute Traversal

Attributes can be traversed using the `XElement.FirstAttribute`, `XElement.LastAttribute`, `XAttribute.NextAttribute`, and `XAttribute.PreviousAttribute` properties and the `XElement.Attribute` and `XElement.Attributes` methods. These are described in the following sections

Forward with XElement.FirstAttribute

You can gain access to an element's attributes by accessing its first attribute using the element's `FirstAttribute` property. Listing 7-75 is an example.

Listing 7-75. Accessing an Element's First Attribute with the FirstAttribute Property

```
// we will use this to store a reference to one of the elements in the XML tree.
XElement firstParticipant;

XDocument xDocument = new XDocument(
  new XElement("BookParticipants", firstParticipant =
    new XElement("BookParticipant",
      new XAttribute("type", "Author"),
      new XAttribute("experience", "first-time"),
      new XAttribute("language", "English"),
      new XElement("FirstName", "Joe"),
      new XElement("LastName", "Rattz")))));
```

```
Console.WriteLine(firstParticipant.FirstAttribute);
```

This code outputs the following:

```
type="Author"
```

Forward with XAttribute.NextAttribute

To traverse forward through an element's attributes, reference the NextAttribute property on an attribute. Listing 7-76 is an example.

Listing 7-76. Accessing the Next Attribute with the NextAttribute Property

```
//  we will use this to store a reference to one of the elements in the XML tree.
XElement firstParticipant;

XDocument xDocument = new XDocument(
  new XElement("BookParticipants", firstParticipant =
    new XElement("BookParticipant",
      new XAttribute("type", "Author"),
      new XAttribute("experience", "first-time"),
      new XAttribute("language", "English"),
      new XElement("FirstName", "Joe"),
      new XElement("LastName", "Rattz"))));

Console.WriteLine(firstParticipant.FirstAttribute.NextAttribute);
```

Notice we use the FirstAttribute property to obtain a reference to the first attribute and then reference the NextAttribute property on it. Here are the results:

```
experience="first-time"
```

If an attribute's NextAttribute property is null, the attribute is the last attribute of the element.

Backward with XAttribute.PreviousAttribute

To traverse backward through an element's attributes, reference the PreviousAttribute property on an attribute. Listing 7-77 is an example.

Listing 7-77. Accessing the Previous Attribute with the PreviousAttribute Property

```
//  we will use this to store a reference to one of the elements in the XML tree.
```

```
XElement firstParticipant;

XDocument xDocument = new XDocument(
  new XElement("BookParticipants", firstParticipant =
    new XElement("BookParticipant",
      new XAttribute("type", "Author"),
      new XAttribute("experience", "first-time"),
      new XAttribute("language", "English"),
      new XElement("FirstName", "Joe"),
      new XElement("LastName", "Rattz")))));

Console.WriteLine(firstParticipant.FirstAttribute.NextAttribute.PreviousAttribute);
```

Notice we chain the FirstAttribute and NextAttribute properties to get a reference to the second attribute from which to go backward. This should take us back to the first attribute. Here are the results:

```
type="Author"
```

And it does! If an attribute's PreviousAttribute property is null, the attribute is the first attribute of the element.

Backward with XElement.LastAttribute

To get access to the very last attribute of an element so that you can traverse backward through the attributes, use the LastAttribute property, as shown in Listing 7-78.

Listing 7-78. *Accessing the Last Attribute with the LastAttribute Property*

```
//  we will use this to store a reference to one of the elements in the XML tree.
XElement firstParticipant;

XDocument xDocument = new XDocument(
  new XElement("BookParticipants", firstParticipant =
    new XElement("BookParticipant",
      new XAttribute("type", "Author"),
      new XAttribute("experience", "first-time"),
      new XAttribute("language", "English"),
      new XElement("FirstName", "Joe"),
      new XElement("LastName", "Rattz")))));

Console.WriteLine(firstParticipant.LastAttribute);
```

This should output the language attribute. Let's see:

```
language="English"
```

Groovy! We have never actually written the word *groovy* before. We had to let the spelling checker spell it for us.

XElement.Attribute()

This method takes the name of an attribute and returns the *first* attribute with the specified name, if one is found. Listing 7-79 is an example.

***Listing 7-79.** Accessing an Attribute with the Attribute Method*

```
// we will use this to store a reference to one of the elements in the XML tree.
XElement firstParticipant;

XDocument xDocument = new XDocument(
  new XElement("BookParticipants", firstParticipant =
    new XElement("BookParticipant",
      new XAttribute("type", "Author"),
      new XElement("FirstName", "Joe"),
      new XElement("LastName", "Rattz")))));

Console.WriteLine(firstParticipant.Attribute("type").Value);
```

Here we use the `Attribute` method to return a reference to the `type` attribute. We then display the attribute's value using its `Value` property. If all goes as expected, the output should be the following:

```
Author
```

Remember, though, instead of obtaining the attribute's value via its `Value` property, we could have just cast the attribute to a `string`.

XElement.Attributes()

We can gain access to all of an element's attributes with its `Attributes` method. This method returns a *sequence* of `XAttribute` objects. Listing 7-80 is an example.

***Listing 7-80.** Accessing All of an Element's Attributes with the Attributes Method*

```
// we will use this to store a reference to one of the elements in the XML tree.
XElement firstParticipant;

XDocument xDocument = new XDocument(
  new XElement("BookParticipants", firstParticipant =
    new XElement("BookParticipant",
```

```
        new XAttribute("type", "Author"),
        new XAttribute("experience", "first-time"),
        new XElement("FirstName", "Joe"),
        new XElement("LastName", "Rattz"))));

foreach(XAttribute attr in firstParticipant.Attributes())
{
    Console.WriteLine(attr);
}
```

The output is this:

```
type="Author"
experience="first-time"
```

Attribute Modification

There are several methods and properties that can be used to modify attributes. We cover them in this section.

Adding Attributes

As we have pointed out, there is a fundamental difference in the way the W3C XML DOM API handles attributes versus the way the LINQ to XML API handles them. With the W3C API, an attribute is a child node of the node it is an attribute for. With the LINQ to XML API, attributes are *not* child nodes of the node for which they are an attribute. Instead, attributes are name-value pairs that can be accessed via an element's Attributes method or its FirstAttribute property. This is important to remember.

However, working with attributes is very similar to working with elements. The methods and properties for attributes are very symmetrical to those for elements.

The following methods can be used to add an attribute to an element:

```
XElement.Add()
XElement.AddFirst()
XElement.AddBeforeThis()
XElement.AddAfterThis()
```

In the examples provided for each of these methods in the "Adding Nodes" section earlier in this chapter, attributes are added as well. Refer to those examples of adding an attribute. In addition, be sure to check out the section on the XElement.SetAttributeValue method later in this chapter.

Deleting Attributes

Deleting attributes can be accomplished using either the XAttribute.Remove method or the IEnumerable<T>.Remove method, depending on whether you are trying to delete a single attribute or a sequence of attributes.

In addition to the following ways to delete attributes, be sure to check out the "XElement.SetAttributeValue()" section later in this chapter.

XAttribute.Remove()

Just like the XNode class has a remove method, so too does the XAttribute class. Listing 7-81 is an example.

Listing 7-81. Removing an Attribute

```
//  we will use this to store a reference to one of the elements in the XML tree.
XElement firstParticipant;

XDocument xDocument = new XDocument(
  new XElement("BookParticipants", firstParticipant =
    new XElement("BookParticipant",
      new XAttribute("type", "Author"),
      new XElement("FirstName", "Joe"),
      new XElement("LastName", "Rattz"))));

Console.WriteLine(System.Environment.NewLine + "Before removing attribute:");
Console.WriteLine(xDocument);

firstParticipant.Attribute("type").Remove();

Console.WriteLine(System.Environment.NewLine + "After removing attribute:");
Console.WriteLine(xDocument);
```

As you can see, we use the Attribute method to obtain a reference to the attribute we want to remove, and then we call the Remove method on it. Just so you don't think we are just making this all up, here are the results:

```
Before removing attribute:
<BookParticipants>
  <BookParticipant type="Author">
    <FirstName>Joe</FirstName>
    <LastName>Rattz</LastName>
  </BookParticipant>
</BookParticipants>

After removing attribute:
<BookParticipants>
  <BookParticipant>
    <FirstName>Joe</FirstName>
    <LastName>Rattz</LastName>
```

```
      </BookParticipant>
</BookParticipants>
```

Notice that the type attribute is now gone.

IEnumerable<T>.Remove()

Just as you are able to remove a sequence of nodes using the `IEnumerable<T>.Remove` method, you can use the same method to remove all attributes of an element, as shown in Listing 7-82.

Listing 7-82. Removing All of an Element's Attributes

```
//  we will use this to store a reference to one of the elements in the XML tree.
XElement firstParticipant;

XDocument xDocument = new XDocument(
  new XElement("BookParticipants", firstParticipant =
    new XElement("BookParticipant",
      new XAttribute("type", "Author"),
      new XAttribute("experience", "first-time"),
      new XElement("FirstName", "Joe"),
      new XElement("LastName", "Rattz"))));

Console.WriteLine(System.Environment.NewLine + "Before removing attributes:");
Console.WriteLine(xDocument);

firstParticipant.Attributes().Remove();

Console.WriteLine(System.Environment.NewLine + "After removing attributes:");
Console.WriteLine(xDocument);
```

In the previous example, we call the `Attributes` method to return the sequence of all attributes of the element the `Attributes` method is called on, and then we call the `Remove` method on that returned sequence to remove them all. This seems so simple and intuitive, we wonder if we are wasting your time just covering it. Here are the results:

```
Before removing attributes:
<BookParticipants>
  <BookParticipant type="Author" experience="first-time">
    <FirstName>Joe</FirstName>
    <LastName>Rattz</LastName>
  </BookParticipant>
</BookParticipants>

After removing attributes:
```

```
<BookParticipants>
  <BookParticipant>
    <FirstName>Joe</FirstName>
    <LastName>Rattz</LastName>
  </BookParticipant>
</BookParticipants>
```

Like magic, the attributes are gone.

Updating Attributes

To update the value of an attribute, use the `XAttribute.Value` property.

■ **Note** In addition to using the `XAttribute.Value` property to update attributes, be sure to check out the "XElement.SetAttributeValue()" section later in the chapter.

Updating the value of an attribute is easily accomplished using its `Value` property. Listing 7-83 is an example.

Listing 7-83. *Changing an Attribute's Value*

```
// we will use this to store a reference to one of the elements in the XML tree.
XElement firstParticipant;

XDocument xDocument = new XDocument(
  new XElement("BookParticipants", firstParticipant =
    new XElement("BookParticipant",
      new XAttribute("type", "Author"),
      new XAttribute("experience", "first-time"),
      new XElement("FirstName", "Joe"),
      new XElement("LastName", "Rattz"))));

Console.WriteLine(System.Environment.NewLine +
  "Before changing attribute's value:");
Console.WriteLine(xDocument);

firstParticipant.Attribute("experience").Value = "beginner";

Console.WriteLine(System.Environment.NewLine + "After changing attribute's
value:");
Console.WriteLine(xDocument);
```

Notice that we used the `Attribute` method to obtain a reference to the experience attribute. The results are the following:

```
Before changing attribute's value:
<BookParticipants>
  <BookParticipant type="Author" experience="first-time">
    <FirstName>Joe</FirstName>
    <LastName>Rattz</LastName>
  </BookParticipant>
</BookParticipants>

After changing attribute's value:
<BookParticipants>
  <BookParticipant type="Author" experience="beginner">
    <FirstName>Joe</FirstName>
    <LastName>Rattz</LastName>
  </BookParticipant>
</BookParticipants>
```

As you can see, the value of the experience attribute has changed from `"first-time"` to `"beginner"`.

XElement.SetAttributeValue()

To be symmetrical with elements, it's only fair that attributes get a `SetAttributeValue` method every bit as powerful as the `SetElementValue` method; and they did. The `XElement.SetAttributeValue` method has the ability to add, delete, and update an attribute.

Passing an attribute name that does *not* exist causes an attribute to be added. Passing a name that exists with a value other than `null` causes the attribute with that name to have its value updated to the value passed. Passing a name that exists with a `null` value causes the attribute to be deleted. Listing 7-84 is an example doing all three.

Listing 7-84. Using SetAttributeValue to Add, Delete, and Update Attributes

```
// we will use this to store a reference to one of the elements in the XML tree.
XElement firstParticipant;

XDocument xDocument = new XDocument(
  new XElement("BookParticipants", firstParticipant =
    new XElement("BookParticipant",
      new XAttribute("type", "Author"),
      new XAttribute("experience", "first-time"),
      new XElement("FirstName", "Joe"),
      new XElement("LastName", "Rattz"))));

Console.WriteLine(System.Environment.NewLine + "Before changing the attributes:");
```

```
Console.WriteLine(xDocument);

// This call will update the type attribute's value because an attribute whose
// name is "type" exists.
firstParticipant.SetAttributeValue("type", "beginner");

// This call will add an attribute because an attribute with the specified name
// does not exist.
firstParticipant.SetAttributeValue("language", "English");

// This call will delete an attribute because an attribute with the specified name
// exists, and the passed value is null.
firstParticipant.SetAttributeValue("experience", null);

Console.WriteLine(System.Environment.NewLine + "After changing the attributes:");
Console.WriteLine(xDocument);
```

As you can see, in this example, first we update an already existing attribute's value, then we add an attribute, and finally we delete an attribute by passing a null value. Here are the results:

```
Before changing the attributes:
<BookParticipants>
  <BookParticipant type="Author" experience="first-time">
    <FirstName>Joe</FirstName>
    <LastName>Rattz</LastName>
  </BookParticipant>
</BookParticipants>

After changing the attributes:
<BookParticipants>
  <BookParticipant type="beginner" language="English">
    <FirstName>Joe</FirstName>
    <LastName>Rattz</LastName>
  </BookParticipant>
</BookParticipants>
```

XML Annotations

The LINQ to XML API provides the ability to associate a user data object with any class inheriting from the XObject class via annotations. This allows application developers to assign whatever data type object they want to an element, document, or any other object whose class is derived from the XObject class. The object could be additional keys for an element's data; it could be an object that will parse the element's contents into itself or whatever you need.

Adding Annotations with XObject.AddAnnotation()

Adding annotations is accomplished using the `XObject.AddAnnotation` method. Here is the prototype:

```
void XObject.AddAnnotation(object annotation);
```

Accessing Annotations with XObject.Annotation() or XObject.Annotations()

Accessing annotations is accomplished using the `XObject.Annotation` or `XObject.Annotations` methods. Here are the prototypes:

```
object XObject.Annotation(Type type);
T XObject.Annotation<T>();
IEnumerable<object> XObject.Annotations(Type type);
IEnumerable<T> XObject.Annotations<T>();
```

■ **Caution** When retrieving annotations, you must pass the object's actual type, not a base class or interface. Otherwise, the annotation will not be found.

Removing Annotations with XObject.RemoveAnnotations()

Removing annotations is accomplished with the `XObject.RemoveAnnotations` method. There are two prototypes:

```
void XObject.RemoveAnnotations(Type type);
void XObject.RemoveAnnotations<T>();
```

Annotations Example

To demonstrate annotations, we will create one example that adds, retrieves, and removes annotations. In this example, we will use our typical `BookParticipants` XML tree. We want a way to associate a handler to each `BookParticipant` based on its type attribute. In this example, the handler will merely display the element in a type attribute–specific format: one format for authors and another for editors.

First, we need a couple of handler classes, one for authors and another for editors:

```
public class AuthorHandler
{
  public void Display(XElement element)
  {
    Console.WriteLine("AUTHOR BIO");
    Console.WriteLine("--------------------------");
```

```
      Console.WriteLine("Name:          {0} {1}",
        (string)element.Element("FirstName"),
        (string)element.Element("LastName"));
      Console.WriteLine("Language:      {0}", (string)element.Attribute("language"));
      Console.WriteLine("Experience:  {0}", (string)element.Attribute("experience"));
      Console.WriteLine("=========================" + System.Environment.NewLine);
    }
}

public class EditorHandler
{
  public void Display(XElement element)
  {
    Console.WriteLine("EDITOR BIO");
    Console.WriteLine("-------------------------");
    Console.WriteLine("Name:          {0}", (string)element.Element("FirstName"));
    Console.WriteLine("               {0}", (string)element.Element("LastName"));
    Console.WriteLine("=========================" + System.Environment.NewLine);
  }
}
```

There is nothing special here. We just need two handlers that behave differently. In this case, they display the element's data in a slightly different format. Of course, it wouldn't have to just display data. It could do anything you want. Or the annotations might not even be handlers. They might just be some associated data. But in this example, they are handlers.

Because this example is more complex than typical, we will separate sections of the code with explanations, as shown in Listing 7-85.

Listing 7-85. Adding, Retrieving, and Removing Annotations

```
//  we will use this to store a reference to one of the elements in the XML tree.
XElement firstParticipant;

XDocument xDocument = new XDocument(
  new XElement("BookParticipants", firstParticipant =
    new XElement("BookParticipant",
      new XAttribute("type", "Author"),
      new XAttribute("experience", "first-time"),
      new XAttribute("language", "English"),
      new XElement("FirstName", "Joe"),
      new XElement("LastName", "Rattz")),
    new XElement("BookParticipant",
      new XAttribute("type", "Editor"),
      new XElement("FirstName", "Ewan"),
      new XElement("LastName", "Buckingham"))));
//  Display the document for reference.
Console.WriteLine(xDocument + System.Environment.NewLine);
```

All we have done at this point is build the typical XML document that we have been using and display it. For the next section of code, we enumerate through the book participants, and for each, we instantiate a handler based on its type attribute and add an annotation to the element for the appropriate handler:

```
// we'll add some annotations based on their type attribute.
foreach(XElement e in xDocument.Element("BookParticipants").Elements())
{
  if((string)e.Attribute("type") == "Author")
  {
    AuthorHandler aHandler = new AuthorHandler();
    e.AddAnnotation(aHandler);
  }
  else if((string)e.Attribute("type") == "Editor")
  {
    EditorHandler eHandler = new EditorHandler();
    e.AddAnnotation(eHandler);
  }
}
```

Now each BookParticipant element has a handler added as an annotation depending on its type attribute. Now that each element has a handler added via an annotation, we will enumerate through the elements calling the handler by retrieving the element's annotation:

```
AuthorHandler aHandler2;
EditorHandler eHandler2;
foreach(XElement e in xDocument.Element("BookParticipants").Elements())
{
    if((string)e.Attribute("type") == "Author")
    {
        aHandler2 = e.Annotation<AuthorHandler>();
        if(aHandler2 != null)
        {
            aHandler2.Display(e);
        }
    }
    else if((string)e.Attribute("type") == "Editor")
    {
        eHandler2 = e.Annotation<EditorHandler>();
        if(eHandler2 != null)
        {
            eHandler2.Display(e);
        }
    }
}
```

At this point, a display handler will have been called for each element. The display handler called is dependent on the type attribute. Next, we just remove the annotations for each element:

```
foreach(XElement e in xDocument.Element("BookParticipants").Elements())
{
    if((string)e.Attribute("type") == "Author")
    {
        e.RemoveAnnotation<AuthorHandler>();
    }
    else if((string)e.Attribute("type") == "Editor")
    {
        e.RemoveAnnotation<EditorHandler>();
    }
}
```

That is a fairly long piece of sample code, but it has only four main sections. In the first section, we build the XML document and display it. You have seen this done many times by now. In the second section, we enumerate through the BookParticipant elements, and based on their type attribute, add a handler. In the third section, we enumerate through the BookParticipant elements, and based on their type attribute, retrieve the handler and call the Display method of the handler object. In the fourth section, we enumerate through the BookParticipant elements, removing the annotations.

Also, notice that when accessing the attributes, we cast them as a string to get the value out of the attributes.

The thing to remember is that these annotations can be any data object you want to associate with the element.

Finally, here are the results:

```
<BookParticipants>
  <BookParticipant type="Author" experience="first-time" language="English">
    <FirstName>Joe</FirstName>
    <LastName>Rattz</LastName>
  </BookParticipant>
  <BookParticipant type="Editor">
    <FirstName>Ewan</FirstName>
    <LastName>Buckingham</LastName>
  </BookParticipant>
</BookParticipants>

AUTHOR BIO
--------------------------
Name:        Joe Rattz
Language:    English
Experience:  first-time
==========================

EDITOR BIO
--------------------------
Name:        Ewan
             Buckingham
==========================
```

What is important to notice in the results is that the different handlers are called based on the element's type attribute, using annotations. Of course, the objects you add as annotations could be for any purpose, not just handlers.

XML Events

The LINQ to XML API makes it possible for you to register for events so that you can be notified any time any object inheriting from XObject is about to be, or has been, modified.

The first thing you should know is that when you register for an event on an object, the event will be raised on the object if that object, or any descendant object, is changed. This means if you register for an event on the document or root element, any change in the tree will cause your registered method to be called. Because of this, don't make any assumptions about the data type of the object causing the event to be raised. When your registered method is called, the object causing the event to be raised will be passed as the sender of the event, and its data type will be object. Be very careful when casting it, accessing properties on it, or calling its methods. It may not be the type of object you are expecting. We will demonstrate this in Listing 7-86 where the object is actually an XText object when we were expecting it to be a XElement object.

Lastly, please be aware that constructing XML will not cause events to get raised. How could it? No events could have been registered prior to the construction. Only modifying or deleting already existing XML can cause an event to be raised and then only if an event has been registered.

XObject.Changing

This event is raised when an object inheriting from XObject is about to be changed but prior to the change. You register for the event by adding an object of type EventHandler to the object's Changing event like this:

```
    myobject.Changing += new
EventHandler<XObjectChangeEventArgs>(MyHandler);
```

where your method delegate must match this signature:

```
void MyHandler(object sender, XObjectChangeEventArgs cea)
```

The sender object is the object that is about to be changed, which is causing the event to be raised. The change event arguments, cea, contain a property named ObjectChange of type XObjectChange indicating the type of change about to take place: XObjectChange.Add, XObjectChange.Name, XObjectChange.Remove, or XObjectChange.Value.

XObject.Changed

This event is raised after an object inheriting from XObject has been changed. You register for the event by adding an object of type EventHandler to the object's Changed event like this:

```
myobject.Changed += new EventHandler<XObjectChangeEventArgs>(MyHandler);
```

where your method delegate must match this signature:

```
void MyHandler(object sender, XObjectChangeEventArgs cea)
```

The sender object is the object that has changed, which caused the event to be raised. The change event arguments, cea, contain a property named ObjectChange of type XObjectChange indicating the type of change that has taken place: XObjectChange.Add, XObjectChange.Name, XObjectChange.Remove, or XObjectChange.Value.

A Couple of Event Examples

To see all the pieces that go together to handle XObject events, an example is necessary. However, before we can show the code to do that, some event handlers are needed, as follows.

This Method Will Be Registered for the Changing Event for an Element

```
public static void MyChangingEventHandler(object sender, XObjectChangeEventArgs
cea)
{
  Console.WriteLine("Type of object changing: {0}, Type of change: {1}",
    sender.GetType().Name, cea.ObjectChange);
}
```

We will register the previous method as the event handler for when an element is about to be changed. Now, we need a handler method for after the object has been changed, as follows.

This Method Will Be Registered for the Changed Event for an Element

```
public static void MyChangedEventHandler(object sender, XObjectChangeEventArgs cea)
{
  Console.WriteLine("Type of object changed: {0}, Type of change: {1}",
    sender.GetType().Name, cea.ObjectChange);
}
```

We will register the previous method as the event handler for when an element has been changed. Earlier, we mentioned that the event will get raised if any descendant object of a registered object is changed. To better demonstrate this, we will also have one additional method that we will register for when the document is changed. Its only purpose is to make it more apparent that the document is also getting a Changed event raised, despite that it is a descendant object several levels down that was changed. That method follows.

This Method Will be Registered for the Changed Event for the XML Document

```
public static void DocumentChangedHandler(object sender, XObjectChangeEventArgs
cea)
{
  Console.WriteLine("Doc: Type of object changed: {0}, Type of change: {1}{2}",
    sender.GetType().Name, cea.ObjectChange, System.Environment.NewLine);
}
```

The only significant change between the `DocumentChangedHandler` method and the `MyChangedEventHandler` method is that the `DocumentChangedHandler` method begins the screen output with the prefix `"Doc:"` to make it clear that it is the handler method being called by the document's `Changed` event, as opposed to the element's `Changed` event handler.

Now, let's take a look at the example code shown in Listing 7-86.

Listing 7-86. XObject Event Handling

```
XElement firstParticipant;

XDocument xDocument = new XDocument(
  new XElement("BookParticipants", firstParticipant =
    new XElement("BookParticipant",
      new XAttribute("type", "Author"),
      new XElement("FirstName", "Joe"),
      new XElement("LastName", "Rattz")),
    new XElement("BookParticipant",
      new XAttribute("type", "Editor"),
      new XElement("FirstName", "Ewan"),
      new XElement("LastName", "Buckingham")))));

Console.WriteLine("{0}{1}", xDocument, System.Environment.NewLine);
```

There is nothing new so far. As we have done many times, we have created an XML document using functional construction and displayed the XML document. Notice that also, like many previous examples, we have saved a reference to the first `BookParticipant` element. This is the element whose events we will register for:

```
firstParticipant.Changing += new
EventHandler<XObjectChangeEventArgs>(MyChangingEventHandler);
firstParticipant.Changed += new
EventHandler<XObjectChangeEventArgs>(MyChangedEventHandler);
xDocument.Changed += new
EventHandler<XObjectChangeEventArgs>(DocumentChangedHandler);
```

Now we have registered with the first `BookParticipant` element to receive the `Changing` and `Changed` events. Additionally, we have registered with the document to receive its `Changed` event. We are registering for the document's `Changed` event to demonstrate that you receive events even when it is a descendant object that is changing or changed. Now, it's time to make a change:

```
firstParticipant.Element("FirstName").Value = "Seph";

Console.WriteLine("{0}{1}", xDocument, System.Environment.NewLine);
```

All we did was change the value of the first `BookParticipant` element's `FirstName` element's value. Then, we displayed the resulting XML document. Let's examine the results:

```
<BookParticipants>
  <BookParticipant type="Author">
    <FirstName>Joe</FirstName>
    <LastName>Rattz</LastName>
  </BookParticipant>
  <BookParticipant type="Editor">
    <FirstName>Ewan</FirstName>
    <LastName>Buckingham</LastName>
  </BookParticipant>
</BookParticipants>

Type of object changing: XText, Type of change: Remove
Type of object changed: XText, Type of change: Remove
Doc: Type of object changed: XText, Type of change: Remove

Type of object changing: XText, Type of change: Add
Type of object changed: XText, Type of change: Add
Doc: Type of object changed: XText, Type of change: Add

<BookParticipants>
  <BookParticipant type="Author">
    <FirstName>Seph</FirstName>
    <LastName>Rattz</LastName>
  </BookParticipant>
  <BookParticipant type="Editor">
    <FirstName>Ewan</FirstName>
    <LastName>Buckingham</LastName>
  </BookParticipant>
</BookParticipants>
```

You can see the document at the beginning and end of the results, and the FirstName element's value has been changed just as you would expect. What you are interested in here is the output caused by events being raised, which is between the two displays of the XML document. Notice that the type of object being changed is XText. Were you anticipating that? We weren't. We were expecting to see the type as XElement. It is easy to forget that when you set an element's value to a string literal that an object of type XText is being created automatically in the background for you.

Looking at the event output, it is a little clearer exactly what is happening when you change the element's value. You can see that first, the element's XText value is about to be changed by being removed, and that it is then removed. Next, you see that the document's Changed event is raised as well. This makes it apparent that the order of the events being raised flows upstream.

Next, you see the same progression of events being raised, except this time an XText object is being added. So now you know that when you change the string value of an element, an XText object is removed and then added back.

In the previous example, we use named methods, but that doesn't mean that is what you have to do. We could have used anonymous methods, or even lambda expressions. Listing 7-87 is the same example as the previous, except instead of registering the already implemented handler methods, we use lambda expressions to define the code the events call on the fly.

Listing 7-87. XObject Event Handling Using Lambda Expressions

```
XElement firstParticipant;

XDocument xDocument = new XDocument(
  new XElement("BookParticipants", firstParticipant =
    new XElement("BookParticipant",
      new XAttribute("type", "Author"),
      new XElement("FirstName", "Joe"),
      new XElement("LastName", "Rattz")),
    new XElement("BookParticipant",
      new XAttribute("type", "Editor"),
      new XElement("FirstName", "Ewan"),
      new XElement("LastName", "Buckingham"))));

Console.WriteLine("{0}{1}", xDocument, System.Environment.NewLine);

firstParticipant.Changing += new EventHandler<XObjectChangeEventArgs>(
  (object sender, XObjectChangeEventArgs cea) =>
    Console.WriteLine("Type of object changing: {0}, Type of change: {1}",
      sender.GetType().Name, cea.ObjectChange));

firstParticipant.Changed += (object sender, XObjectChangeEventArgs cea) =>
  Console.WriteLine("Type of object changed: {0}, Type of change: {1}",
    sender.GetType().Name, cea.ObjectChange);

xDocument.Changed += (object sender, XObjectChangeEventArgs cea) =>
  Console.WriteLine("Doc: Type of object changed: {0}, Type of change: {1}{2}",
    sender.GetType().Name, cea.ObjectChange, System.Environment.NewLine);

xDocument.Changed += new XObjectChangeEventHandler((sender, cea) =>
  Console.WriteLine("Doc: Type of object changed: {0}, Type of change: {1}{2}",
    sender.GetType().Name, cea.ObjectChange, System.Environment.NewLine));

firstParticipant.Element("FirstName").Value = "Seph";

Console.WriteLine("{0}{1}", xDocument, System.Environment.NewLine);
```

Now the code is totally self-contained and is no longer dependent on previously written handler methods. Let's check the results:

```
<BookParticipants>
  <BookParticipant type="Author">
    <FirstName>Joe</FirstName>
    <LastName>Rattz</LastName>
  </BookParticipant>
```

```
  <BookParticipant type="Editor">
    <FirstName>Ewan</FirstName>
    <LastName>Buckingham</LastName>
  </BookParticipant>
</BookParticipants>

Type of object changing: XText, Type of change: Remove
Type of object changed: XText, Type of change: Remove
Doc: Type of object changed: XText, Type of change: Remove

Type of object changing: XText, Type of change: Add
Type of object changed: XText, Type of change: Add
Doc: Type of object changed: XText, Type of change: Add

<BookParticipants>
  <BookParticipant type="Author">
    <FirstName>Seph</FirstName>
    <LastName>Rattz</LastName>
  </BookParticipant>
  <BookParticipant type="Editor">
    <FirstName>Ewan</FirstName>
    <LastName>Buckingham</LastName>
  </BookParticipant>
</BookParticipants>
```

That output looks the same to us. After looking at this example, how can you not like lambda expressions? We have seen many developers post about their first impressions of LINQ. Most like various aspects, but the common factor we see is that many do not like lambda expressions. Perhaps it is because they are so new and different. But when you see an example like that, what is not to like? We hope you agree.

Trick or Treat, or Undefined?

Do you remember the Halloween problem we discussed earlier in this chapter? Please resist the urge to make changes to the area of the XML tree containing the object for which the current event is raised in your event handlers. Doing so will have an undefined effect on your XML tree and the events that are raised.

Summary

In this chapter, we covered how to use LINQ to XML to create, modify, and traverse XML documents, as well as how to perform LINQ queries on a single XML object. In this demonstration, we hope you saw that the new API for creating and modifying XML data is not just a luxury but instead is a necessity for performing LINQ queries. You can't very well project data into an XML structure if you can't create an XML element on the fly, initialize its value, and place it in the XML tree in a single statement. The W3C

DOM XML API is totally incapable of the flexibility needed to perform a LINQ query, which, as it turns out, is lucky for us because we got an entirely new XML API because of it.

Although this chapter was useful for demonstrating how to perform basic LINQ queries on XML data, there was a fairly serious limitation in the LINQ queries that you saw. That is, the queries we performed were always performing the query on a single XML object, such as an element. We were querying the descendants of an element or the ancestors of an element. What do you do if you need to perform a LINQ query on a *sequence* of elements, such as the descendants of a sequence of elements, which are perhaps the descendants of a single element? For this, you need an additional set of XML operators. In the next chapter, we cover the new LINQ to XML operators that were added for just this purpose.

CHAPTER 8

■ ■ ■

LINQ to XML Operators

At this point, we are deep into LINQ to XML, and you are probably starting to wonder, "When are we going to get to the part about queries?" If so, then we say, "Hold on to your null reference there, Shortcake, you have been seeing them." Throughout the previous chapter, we were performing LINQ to XML queries whether they were merely returning all the child elements of an element or obtaining all of the ancestors of a node. Do you remember seeing the XContainer.Elements method? Do you recall any examples where we called the XContainer.Elements method? If so, you saw a LINQ to XML query. As evidence yet again to the seamless integration of LINQ queries into the language, it is sometimes easy to overlook that you are performing a query.

Because many of the class methods we have covered up to this point return a sequence of XML class objects, that is, IEnumerable<T>, where T is one of the LINQ to XML API classes, you can call the Standard Query Operators on the returned sequence, giving you even more power and flexibility.

So, there are ways to get a sequence of XML objects from a single XML object, such as the descendants or ancestors of any given element, but what is missing are ways to perform LINQ to XML operations on each object in those sequences. For example, there is no simple way to get a sequence of elements and perform another XML-specific operation on each element in the sequence, such as returning each sequence element's child elements. In other words, thus far, you *can* obtain a sequence of an element's child elements by calling that element's Elements method, but you *cannot* obtain a sequence of an element's child elements' child elements. This is because the Elements method must be called on an XContainer, such as XElement or XDocument, but cannot be called on a *sequence* of XContainer objects. This is where the LINQ to XML operators come in handy.

Introduction to LINQ to XML Operators

The LINQ to XML API extends the LINQ to Objects Standard Query Operators with XML-specific operators. These XML operators are extension methods that are defined in the System.Xml.Linq.Extensions class, which itself is nothing more than a container class for these extension methods.

Each of these XML operators is called on a *sequence* of some LINQ to XML data type and performs some action on each entry in that sequence, such as returning all the ancestors or descendants of the entry.

Virtually every XML operator in this chapter has an equivalent method we covered in the previous chapter. The difference is that the method covered in the previous chapter is called on a single object, and the operator in this chapter is called on a *sequence* of objects. For example, in the previous chapter, we covered the XContainer.Elements method. Its prototype looks like this:

```
IEnumerable<XElement> XContainer.Elements()
```

In this chapter, we cover the `Extensions.Elements` operator, and its prototype looks like this:

```
IEnumerable<XElement> Elements<T> (this IEnumerable<T> source) where T : XContainer
```

There is a significant difference between the two methods. The first prototype is called on a single object derived from XContainer, while the second prototype is called on a sequence of objects, where each object in the sequence must be derived from XContainer. Please be cognizant of the difference.

In this chapter, to distinguish between the methods covered in the previous chapter and the extension methods covered in this chapter, we typically refer to the extension methods as *operators*.

Now, let's examine each of these operators.

Ancestors

The `Ancestors` operator can be called on a sequence of nodes and returns a sequence containing the ancestor elements of each source node.

Prototypes

The `Ancestors` operator has two prototypes.

The First Ancestors Prototype

```
public static IEnumerable<XElement> Ancestors<T> (
  this IEnumerable<T> source
) where T : XNode
```

This version of the operator can be called on a sequence of nodes, or objects derived from XNode. It returns a sequence of elements containing the ancestor elements of each node in the source sequence.

The Second Ancestors Prototype

```
public static IEnumerable<XElement> Ancestors<T> (
  this IEnumerable<T> source,
  XName name
) where T : XNode
```

This version is like the first, except a name is passed, and only those ancestor elements matching the specified name are returned in the output sequence.

Examples

Listing 8-1 is an example of calling the first `Ancestors` prototype.

Listing 8-1. *An Example of Calling the First Ancestors Prototype*

```
XDocument xDocument = new XDocument(
  new XElement("BookParticipants",
    new XElement("BookParticipant",
      new XAttribute("type", "Author"),
      new XElement("FirstName", "Joe"),
      new XElement("LastName", "Rattz")),
    new XElement("BookParticipant",
      new XAttribute("type", "Editor"),
      new XElement("FirstName", "Ewan"),
      new XElement("LastName", "Buckingham")))));

IEnumerable<XElement> elements =
  xDocument.Element("BookParticipants").Descendants("FirstName");

// First, we will display the source elements.
foreach (XElement element in elements)
{
  Console.WriteLine("Source element: {0} : value = {1}",
    element.Name, element.Value);
}

// Now, we will display the ancestor elements for each source element.
foreach (XElement element in elements.Ancestors())
{
  Console.WriteLine("Ancestor element: {0}", element.Name);
}
```

In the previous example, first we create an XML document. Next, we generate a sequence of FirstName elements. Remember, this Ancestors method is called on a *sequence* of nodes, not on a single node, so we need a sequence on which to call it. Because we want to be able to display the names of the nodes for identification purposes, we actually build a sequence of elements because elements have names but nodes do not. We then enumerate through the sequence displaying the source elements just so we can see the source sequence. Then, we enumerate on the elements returned from the Ancestors method and display them. Here are the results:

```
Source element: FirstName : value = Joe
Source element: FirstName : value = Ewan
Ancestor element: BookParticipant
Ancestor element: BookParticipants
Ancestor element: BookParticipant
Ancestor element: BookParticipants
```

As you can see, it displays the two source sequence elements, the two FirstName elements. It then displays the ancestors for each of those two elements.

So, using the `Ancestors` operator, we are able to retrieve all the ancestor elements for each node in a sequence of nodes. In this case, our sequence is a sequence of elements, but that is OK because an element is derived from a node. Remember, do not confuse the `Ancestors` operator that is called on a sequence of nodes, which we just demonstrated, with the `Ancestors` method we covered in the previous chapter.

Now, this example is not quite as impressive as it could be because we needed to expand the code for demonstration purposes. For example, we wanted to capture the sequence of `FirstName` elements, because we wanted to display them so you could see the source elements in the output. So, the statement containing the call to the `Descendants` method and the subsequent `foreach` block are for this purpose. Then in the second `foreach` loop, we call the `Ancestors` operator and display each ancestor element. In reality, in that second `foreach` loop, we could have called the `Ancestors` method from the previous chapter on each element in the sequence of `FirstName` elements and not even called the `Ancestors` operator we are demonstrating. Listing 8-2 is an example demonstrating what we could have done, which would have accomplished the same result without even using the `Ancestors` operator.

Listing 8-2. *The Same Results as Listing 8-1 but Without Calling the Ancestors Operator*

```
XDocument xDocument = new XDocument(
  new XElement("BookParticipants",
    new XElement("BookParticipant",
      new XAttribute("type", "Author"),
      new XElement("FirstName", "Joe"),
      new XElement("LastName", "Rattz")),
    new XElement("BookParticipant",
      new XAttribute("type", "Editor"),
      new XElement("FirstName", "Ewan"),
      new XElement("LastName", "Buckingham"))));

IEnumerable<XElement> elements =
  xDocument.Element("BookParticipants").Descendants("FirstName");

// First, we will display the source elements.
foreach (XElement element in elements)
{
  Console.WriteLine("Source element: {0} : value = {1}",
    element.Name, element.Value);
}

foreach (XElement element in elements)
{
  // Call the Ancestors method on each element.
  foreach(XElement e in element.Ancestors())
    // Now, we will display the ancestor elements for each source element.
    Console.WriteLine("Ancestor element: {0}", e.Name);
}
```

The difference between this example and the previous is that instead of calling the Ancestors *operator* on the elements sequence in the foreach loop, we just loop on each element in the sequence and call the Ancestors *method* on it. In this example, we never call the Ancestors *operator;* we merely call the Ancestors *method* from the previous chapter. This code produces the same output, though:

```
Source element: FirstName : value = Joe
Source element: FirstName : value = Ewan
Ancestor element: BookParticipant
Ancestor element: BookParticipants
Ancestor element: BookParticipant
Ancestor element: BookParticipants
```

However, thanks to the Ancestors operator and the conciseness of LINQ, this query can be combined into a single, more concise statement, as demonstrated in Listing 8-3.

Listing 8-3. *A More Concise Example of Calling the First Ancestors Prototype*

```
XDocument xDocument = new XDocument(
  new XElement("BookParticipants",
    new XElement("BookParticipant",
      new XAttribute("type", "Author"),
      new XElement("FirstName", "Joe"),
      new XElement("LastName", "Rattz")),
    new XElement("BookParticipant",
      new XAttribute("type", "Editor"),
      new XElement("FirstName", "Ewan"),
      new XElement("LastName", "Buckingham"))));

foreach (XElement element in
  xDocument.Element("BookParticipants").Descendants("FirstName").Ancestors())
{
  Console.WriteLine("Ancestor element: {0}", element.Name);
}
```

In this example, we cut right to the chase and call the Ancestors operator on the sequence of elements returned by the Descendants method. So, the Descendants method returns a sequence of elements, and the Ancestors operator will return a sequence of elements containing all ancestors of every element in the sequence it is called on.

Since this code is meant to be more concise, it does not display the FirstName elements as the two previous examples did. However, the ancestor elements should be the same. Let's verify that they are:

```
Ancestor element: BookParticipant
Ancestor element: BookParticipants
Ancestor element: BookParticipant
Ancestor element: BookParticipants
```

And they are! In your production code, you would probably opt for a more concise query like the one we just presented. However, in this chapter, the examples will be more verbose, like Listing 8-1, for demonstration purposes.

To demonstrate the second `Ancestors` prototype, we will use the same basic code as Listing 8-1, except we will change the call to the `Ancestors` operator so that it includes the parameter `BookParticipant` so that we only get the elements matching that name. That code looks like Listing 8-4.

Listing 8-4. *Calling the Second Ancestors Prototype*

```
XDocument xDocument = new XDocument(
  new XElement("BookParticipants",
    new XElement("BookParticipant",
      new XAttribute("type", "Author"),
      new XElement("FirstName", "Joe"),
      new XElement("LastName", "Rattz")),
    new XElement("BookParticipant",
      new XAttribute("type", "Editor"),
      new XElement("FirstName", "Ewan"),
      new XElement("LastName", "Buckingham")))));

IEnumerable<XElement> elements =
  xDocument.Element("BookParticipants").Descendants("FirstName");

// First, we will display the source elements.
foreach (XElement element in elements)
{
  Console.WriteLine("Source element: {0} : value = {1}",
    element.Name, element.Value);
}

// Now, we will display the ancestor elements for each source element.
foreach (XElement element in elements.Ancestors("BookParticipant"))
{
  Console.WriteLine("Ancestor element: {0}", element.Name);
}
```

The results now should only include the `BookParticipant` elements and of course the source elements, but the two `BookParticipants` elements that are displayed in the first prototype's example should now be gone:

```
Source element: FirstName : value = Joe
Source element: FirstName : value = Ewan
Ancestor element: BookParticipant
Ancestor element: BookParticipant
```

And they are.

AncestorsAndSelf

The AncestorsAndSelf operator can be called on a sequence of elements and returns a sequence containing the ancestor elements of each source element and the source element itself. This operator is just like the Ancestors operator except that it can be called only on elements, as opposed to on nodes, and it also includes each source element in the returned sequence of ancestor elements.

Prototypes

The AncestorsAndSelf operator has two prototypes.

The First AncestorsAndSelf Prototype

```
public static IEnumerable<XElement> AncestorsAndSelf (
  this IEnumerable<XElement> source
)
```

This version of the operator can be called on a sequence of elements and returns a sequence of elements containing each source element itself and its ancestor elements.

The Second AncestorsAndSelf Prototype

```
public static IEnumerable<XElement> AncestorsAndSelf<T> (
  this IEnumerable<XElement> source,
  XName name
)
```

This version is like the first, except a name is passed, and only those source elements and its ancestors matching the specified name are returned in the output sequence.

Examples

For an example of the first AncestorsAndSelf prototype, we will use the same basic example we used for the first Ancestors prototype, except we will call the AncestorsAndSelf operator instead of the Ancestors operator, as shown in Listing 8-5.

Listing 8-5. Calling the First AncestorsAndSelf Prototype

```
XDocument xDocument = new XDocument(
  new XElement("BookParticipants",
    new XElement("BookParticipant",
      new XAttribute("type", "Author"),
      new XElement("FirstName", "Joe"),
      new XElement("LastName", "Rattz")),
    new XElement("BookParticipant",
      new XAttribute("type", "Editor"),
```

```
      new XElement("FirstName", "Ewan"),
      new XElement("LastName", "Buckingham")))));

IEnumerable<XElement> elements =
  xDocument.Element("BookParticipants").Descendants("FirstName");

//  First, we will display the source elements.
foreach (XElement element in elements)
{
  Console.WriteLine("Source element: {0} : value = {1}",
    element.Name, element.Value);
}

//  Now, we will display the ancestor elements for each source element.
foreach (XElement element in elements.AncestorsAndSelf())
{
  Console.WriteLine("Ancestor element: {0}", element.Name);
}
```

Just as with the first Ancestors prototype, first we create an XML document. Next, we generate a sequence of FirstName elements. Remember, this AncestorsAndSelf method is called on a sequence of elements, not on a single element, so we need a sequence on which to call it. We then enumerate through the sequence displaying the source elements just so we can see the source sequence. Then, we enumerate on the elements returned from the AncestorsAndSelf method and display them.

If this works as we expect, the results should be the same as the results from the first Ancestors prototype's example, except now the FirstName elements should be included in the output. Here are the results:

```
Source element: FirstName : value = Joe
Source element: FirstName : value = Ewan
Ancestor element: FirstName
Ancestor element: BookParticipant
Ancestor element: BookParticipants
Ancestor element: FirstName
Ancestor element: BookParticipant
Ancestor element: BookParticipants
```

For an example of the second AncestorsAndSelf prototype, we will use the same basic example that we used in the example for the second Ancestors prototype, except, of course, we will change the call from the Ancestors method to the AncestorsAndSelf method, as shown in Listing 8-6.

Listing 8-6. *Calling the Second AncestorsAndSelf Prototype*

```
XDocument xDocument = new XDocument(
  new XElement("BookParticipants",
    new XElement("BookParticipant",
```

```
          new XAttribute("type", "Author"),
          new XElement("FirstName", "Joe"),
          new XElement("LastName", "Rattz")),
        new XElement("BookParticipant",
          new XAttribute("type", "Editor"),
          new XElement("FirstName", "Ewan"),
          new XElement("LastName", "Buckingham")))));

IEnumerable<XElement> elements =
  xDocument.Element("BookParticipants").Descendants("FirstName");

// First, we will display the source elements.
foreach (XElement element in elements)
{
  Console.WriteLine("Source element: {0} : value = {1}",
    element.Name, element.Value);
}

// Now, we will display the ancestor elements for each source element.
foreach (XElement element in elements.AncestorsAndSelf("BookParticipant"))
{
  Console.WriteLine("Ancestor element: {0}", element.Name);
}
```

Now, we should receive only the elements named BookParticipant. Here are the results:

```
Source element: FirstName : value = Joe
Source element: FirstName : value = Ewan
Ancestor element: BookParticipant
Ancestor element: BookParticipant
```

Notice that the displayed output from the AncestorsAndSelf method is just the BookParticipant elements, because they are the only elements matching the name we passed. We didn't even get the source elements themselves, because they didn't match the name. So, the function worked as defined.

Call us crazy, but this prototype of the operator seems fairly useless to us. How many levels of elements are you going to have in an XML tree with the same name? If you don't answer *at least two*, how will this method ever return the self elements and any ancestor elements? It just doesn't seem likely to us. Yes, we know; we like symmetrical APIs too.

Attributes

The Attributes operator can be called on a sequence of elements and returns a sequence containing the attributes of each source element.

Prototypes

The Attributes operator has two prototypes.

The First Attributes Prototype

```
public static IEnumerable<XAttribute> Attributes (
  this IEnumerable<XElement> source
)
```

This version of the operator can be called on a sequence of elements and returns a sequence of attributes containing all the attributes for each source element.

The Second Attributes Prototype

```
public static IEnumerable<XAttribute> Attributes (
  this IEnumerable<XElement> source,
  XName name
)
```

This version of the operator is like the first, except only those attributes matching the specified name will be returned in the sequence of attributes.

Examples

For an example of the first Attributes prototype, we will build the same XML tree we have been building for the previous examples. However, the sequence of source elements we generate will be a little different because we need a sequence of elements with attributes. So, I'll generate a sequence of the BookParticipant elements and work from there, as shown in Listing 8-7.

Listing 8-7. Calling the First Attributes Prototype

```
XDocument xDocument = new XDocument(
  new XElement("BookParticipants",
    new XElement("BookParticipant",
      new XAttribute("type", "Author"),
      new XElement("FirstName", "Joe"),
      new XElement("LastName", "Rattz")),
    new XElement("BookParticipant",
      new XAttribute("type", "Editor"),
      new XElement("FirstName", "Ewan"),
      new XElement("LastName", "Buckingham"))));

IEnumerable<XElement> elements =
  xDocument.Element("BookParticipants").Elements("BookParticipant");

// First, we will display the source elements.
```

```
foreach (XElement element in elements)
{
  Console.WriteLine("Source element: {0} : value = {1}",
    element.Name, element.Value);
}

// Now, we will display each source element's attributes.
foreach (XAttribute attribute in elements.Attributes())
{
  Console.WriteLine("Attribute: {0} : value = {1}",
    attribute.Name, attribute.Value);
}
```

Once we obtain the sequence of BookParticipant elements, we display the source sequence. Then, we call the Attributes operator on the source sequence and display the attributes in the sequence returned by the Attributes operator. Here are the results:

```
Source element: BookParticipant : value = JoeRattz
Source element: BookParticipant : value = EwanBuckingham
Attribute: type : value = Author
Attribute: type : value = Editor
```

As you can see, the attributes are retrieved. For an example of the second Attributes prototype, we will use the same basic example as the previous, except we will specify a name that the attributes must match to be returned by the Attributes operator, as shown in Listing 8-8.

Listing 8-8. *Calling the Second Attributes Prototype*

```
XDocument xDocument = new XDocument(
  new XElement("BookParticipants",
    new XElement("BookParticipant",
      new XAttribute("type", "Author"),
      new XElement("FirstName", "Joe"),
      new XElement("LastName", "Rattz")),
    new XElement("BookParticipant",
      new XAttribute("type", "Editor"),
      new XElement("FirstName", "Ewan"),
      new XElement("LastName", "Buckingham"))));

IEnumerable<XElement> elements =
  xDocument.Element("BookParticipants").Elements("BookParticipant");

// First, we will display the source elements.
foreach (XElement element in elements)
{
```

```
    Console.WriteLine("Source element: {0} : value = {1}",
      element.Name, element.Value);
}

//  Now, we will display each source element's attributes.
foreach (XAttribute attribute in elements.Attributes("type"))
{
    Console.WriteLine("Attribute: {0} : value = {1}",
      attribute.Name, attribute.Value);
}
```

In the previous code, we specify that the attributes must match the name type. So, this should return the same output as the previous example. Pressing Ctrl+F5 returns the following:

```
Source element: BookParticipant : value = JoeRattz
Source element: BookParticipant : value = EwanBuckingham
Attribute: type : value = Author
Attribute: type : value = Editor
```

We did get the results we expected. Had we specified the name as Type so that the first letter is capitalized, the two attributes would not have been displayed because the Attributes operator would not have returned those attributes from the source sequence. That demonstrates the case of when the name doesn't match, as well as that the name is case-sensitive, which isn't that surprising since XML is case-sensitive.

DescendantNodes

The DescendantNodes operator can be called on a sequence of elements and returns a sequence containing the descendant nodes of each element or document.

Prototypes

The DescendantNodes operator has one prototype.

The Only DescendantNodes Prototype

```
public static IEnumerable<XNode> DescendantNodes<T> (
  this IEnumerable<T> source
) where T : XContainer
```

This version can be called on a sequence of elements or documents and returns a sequence of nodes containing each source element's or document's descendant nodes.

This is different from the XContainer.DescendantNodes method in that this method is called on a sequence of elements or documents, as opposed to a single element or document.

Examples

For this example, we will build the same XML tree we have used for the previous examples, except we will also add a comment to the first `BookParticipant` element. This is to have at least one node get returned that is not an element. When we build our source sequence of elements, we want some elements that have some descendants, so we will build our source sequence with the `BookParticipant` elements since they have some descendants, as shown in Listing 8-9.

Listing 8-9. *Calling the Only DescendantNodes Prototype*

```
XDocument xDocument = new XDocument(
  new XElement("BookParticipants",
    new XElement("BookParticipant",
      new XAttribute("type", "Author"),
      new XComment("This is a new author."),
      new XElement("FirstName", "Joe"),
      new XElement("LastName", "Rattz")),
    new XElement("BookParticipant",
      new XAttribute("type", "Editor"),
      new XElement("FirstName", "Ewan"),
      new XElement("LastName", "Buckingham"))));

IEnumerable<XElement> elements =
  xDocument.Element("BookParticipants").Elements("BookParticipant");

// First, we will display the source elements.
foreach (XElement element in elements)
{
  Console.WriteLine("Source element: {0} : value = {1}",
    element.Name, element.Value);
}

// Now, we will display each source element's descendant nodes.
foreach (XNode node in elements.DescendantNodes())
{
  Console.WriteLine("Descendant node: {0}", node);
}
```

As is typical with the examples in this section, we built our XML tree and a source sequence of elements. In this case, the source sequence contains the `BookParticipant` elements. We then call the `DescendantNodes` operator on the source sequence and display the results:

```
Source element: BookParticipant : value = JoeRattz
Source element: BookParticipant : value = EwanBuckingham
Descendant node: <!--This is a new author.-->
Descendant node: <FirstName>Joe</FirstName>
Descendant node: Joe
```

```
Descendant node: <LastName>Rattz</LastName>
Descendant node: Rattz
Descendant node: <FirstName>Ewan</FirstName>
Descendant node: Ewan
Descendant node: <LastName>Buckingham</LastName>
Descendant node: Buckingham
```

Notice that not only did we get our descendant elements, but we got our comment node as well. Also notice that for each element in the XML document, we ended up with two nodes. For example, there is a node whose value is "<FirstName>Joe</FirstName>" and a node whose value is "Joe". The first node in the pair is the FirstName element. The second node is the XText node for that element. We bet you had forgotten about those automatically created XText objects. We know we did, but there they are.

DescendantNodesAndSelf

The DescendantNodesAndSelf operator can be called on a sequence of elements and returns a sequence containing each source element itself and each source element's descendant nodes.

Prototypes

The DescendantNodesAndSelf operator has one prototype.

The Only DescendantNodesAndSelf Prototype

```
public static IEnumerable<XNode> DescendantNodesAndSelf (
  this IEnumerable<XElement> source
)
```

This version is called on a sequence of elements and returns a sequence of nodes containing each source element itself and each source element's descendant nodes.

Examples

For this example, we will use the same example used for the DescendantNodes operator, except we will call the DescendantNodesAndSelf operator, as shown in Listing 8-10.

Listing 8-10. Calling the Only DescendantNodesAndSelf Prototype

```
XDocument xDocument = new XDocument(
  new XElement("BookParticipants",
    new XElement("BookParticipant",
      new XAttribute("type", "Author"),
      new XComment("This is a new author."),
```

```
      new XElement("FirstName", "Joe"),
      new XElement("LastName", "Rattz")),
    new XElement("BookParticipant",
      new XAttribute("type", "Editor"),
      new XElement("FirstName", "Ewan"),
      new XElement("LastName", "Buckingham")))));

IEnumerable<XElement> elements =
  xDocument.Element("BookParticipants").Elements("BookParticipant");

//  First, we will display the source elements.
foreach (XElement element in elements)
{
  Console.WriteLine("Source element: {0} : value = {1}",
    element.Name, element.Value);
}

//  Now, we will display each source element's descendant nodes.
foreach (XNode node in elements.DescendantNodesAndSelf())
{
  Console.WriteLine("Descendant node: {0}", node);
}
```

The question is, will the output be the same as the output for the DescendantNodes example except that the source elements will be included too? You bet:

```
Source element: BookParticipant : value = JoeRattz
Source element: BookParticipant : value = EwanBuckingham
Descendant node: <BookParticipant type="Author">
  <!--This is a new author.-->
  <FirstName>Joe</FirstName>
  <LastName>Rattz</LastName>
</BookParticipant>
Descendant node: <!--This is a new author.-->
Descendant node: <FirstName>Joe</FirstName>
Descendant node: Joe
Descendant node: <LastName>Rattz</LastName>
Descendant node: Rattz
Descendant node: <BookParticipant type="Editor">
  <FirstName>Ewan</FirstName>
  <LastName>Buckingham</LastName>
</BookParticipant>
Descendant node: <FirstName>Ewan</FirstName>
Descendant node: Ewan
Descendant node: <LastName>Buckingham</LastName>
Descendant node: Buckingham
```

Not only did we get the BookParticipant elements themselves and their descendants, but we got the single node that is not an element, the comment. This is in contrast to the Descendants and DescendantsAndSelf operators we cover next, which will omit the nodes that are not elements.

Descendants

The Descendants operator can be called on a sequence of elements or documents and returns a sequence of elements containing each source element's or document's descendant elements.

Prototypes

The Descendants operator has two prototypes.

The First Descendants Prototype

```
public static IEnumerable<XElement> Descendants<T> (
  this IEnumerable<T> source
) where T : XContainer
```

This version is called on a sequence of elements or documents and returns a sequence of elements containing each source element's or document's descendant elements.

This is different from the XContainer.Descendants method in that this method is called on a sequence of elements or documents, as opposed to a single element or document.

The Second Descendants Prototype

```
public static IEnumerable<XElement> Descendants<T> (
  this IEnumerable<T> source,
  XName name
) where T : XContainer
```

This version is like the first, except only those elements matching the specified name are returned in the output sequence.

Examples

For the example of the first prototype, we will basically use the same example we used for the DescendantNodes operator, except we will call the Descendants operator instead. The output should be the same, except there should not be any nodes that are not elements. This means you should not see the comment in the output. Listing 8-11 shows the code.

Listing 8-11. *Calling the First Descendants Prototype*

```
XDocument xDocument = new XDocument(
  new XElement("BookParticipants",
    new XElement("BookParticipant",
      new XAttribute("type", "Author"),
      new XComment("This is a new author."),
      new XElement("FirstName", "Joe"),
      new XElement("LastName", "Rattz")),
    new XElement("BookParticipant",
      new XAttribute("type", "Editor"),
      new XElement("FirstName", "Ewan"),
      new XElement("LastName", "Buckingham"))));

IEnumerable<XElement> elements =
  xDocument.Element("BookParticipants").Elements("BookParticipant");

// First, we will display the source elements.
foreach (XElement element in elements)
{
  Console.WriteLine("Source element: {0} : value = {1}",
    element.Name, element.Value);
}

// Now, we will display each source element's descendant elements.
foreach (XElement element in elements.Descendants())
{
  Console.WriteLine("Descendant element: {0}", element);
}
```

This example is basically like all of the previous except you should only see the descendant elements of the two BookParticipant elements. The results of this example are the following:

```
Source element: BookParticipant : value = JoeRattz
Source element: BookParticipant : value = EwanBuckingham
Descendant element: <FirstName>Joe</FirstName>
Descendant element: <LastName>Rattz</LastName>
Descendant element: <FirstName>Ewan</FirstName>
Descendant element: <LastName>Buckingham</LastName>
```

Comparing these results to that of the DescendantNodes operator example, we notice some differences we did not initially anticipate. Sure, the descendants are labeled as elements instead of nodes, and the comment is not there, but additionally, the descendant nodes such as Joe and Rattz are missing as well. Oh yeah, those nodes are not elements either; they are XText objects. The LINQ to XML API handles the text nodes so seamlessly that it is easy to forget about them.

For an example of the second prototype, we will use the same code as the first example except specify a name that the descendant elements must match to be returned by the second prototype of the Descendants operator, as shown in Listing 8-12.

Listing 8-12. *Calling the Second Descendants Prototype*

```
XDocument xDocument = new XDocument(
  new XElement("BookParticipants",
    new XElement("BookParticipant",
      new XAttribute("type", "Author"),
      new XComment("This is a new author."),
      new XElement("FirstName", "Joe"),
      new XElement("LastName", "Rattz")),
    new XElement("BookParticipant",
      new XAttribute("type", "Editor"),
      new XElement("FirstName", "Ewan"),
      new XElement("LastName", "Buckingham")))));

IEnumerable<XElement> elements =
  xDocument.Element("BookParticipants").Elements("BookParticipant");

//  First, we will display the source elements.
foreach (XElement element in elements)
{
  Console.WriteLine("Source element: {0} : value = {1}",
    element.Name, element.Value);
}

//  Now, we will display each source element's descendant elements.
foreach (XElement element in elements.Descendants("LastName"))
{
  Console.WriteLine("Descendant element: {0}", element);
}
```

The results of this example are the following:

```
Source element: BookParticipant : value = JoeRattz
Source element: BookParticipant : value = EwanBuckingham
Descendant element: <LastName>Rattz</LastName>
Descendant element: <LastName>Buckingham</LastName>
```

As you would expect, only the LastName elements are returned.

DescendantsAndSelf

The DescendantsAndSelf operator can be called on a sequence of elements and returns a sequence containing each source element and its descendant elements.

Prototypes

The DescendantsAndSelf operator has two prototypes.

The First DescendantsAndSelf Prototype

```
public static IEnumerable<XElement> DescendantsAndSelf (
  this IEnumerable<XElement> source
)
```

This version is called on a sequence of elements and returns a sequence of elements containing each source element and its descendant elements.

The Second DescendantsAndSelf Prototype

```
public static IEnumerable<XElement> DescendantsAndSelf (
  this IEnumerable<XElement> source,
  XName name
)
```

This version is like the first, except only those elements matching the specified name are returned in the output sequence.

Examples

For this example, we will use the same code as the example for the first prototype of the Descendants operator, except we will call the DescendantsAndSelf operator, as shown in Listing 8-13.

Listing 8-13. Calling the First DescendantsAndSelf Prototype

```
XDocument xDocument = new XDocument(
  new XElement("BookParticipants",
    new XElement("BookParticipant",
      new XAttribute("type", "Author"),
      new XComment("This is a new author."),
      new XElement("FirstName", "Joe"),
      new XElement("LastName", "Rattz")),
    new XElement("BookParticipant",
      new XAttribute("type", "Editor"),
      new XElement("FirstName", "Ewan"),
      new XElement("LastName", "Buckingham"))));
```

```
IEnumerable<XElement> elements =
  xDocument.Element("BookParticipants").Elements("BookParticipant");

//  First, we will display the source elements.
foreach (XElement element in elements)
{
  Console.WriteLine("Source element: {0} : value = {1}",
    element.Name, element.Value);
}

//  Now, we will display each source element's descendant elements.
foreach (XElement element in elements.DescendantsAndSelf())
{
  Console.WriteLine("Descendant element: {0}", element);
}
```

Now, you should see all the descendant elements and the source elements themselves. The results of this example are the following:

```
Source element: BookParticipant : value = JoeRattz
Source element: BookParticipant : value = EwanBuckingham
Descendant element: <BookParticipant type="Author">
  <!--This is a new author.-->
  <FirstName>Joe</FirstName>
  <LastName>Rattz</LastName>
</BookParticipant>
Descendant element: <FirstName>Joe</FirstName>
Descendant element: <LastName>Rattz</LastName>
Descendant element: <BookParticipant type="Editor">
  <FirstName>Ewan</FirstName>
  <LastName>Buckingham</LastName>
</BookParticipant>
Descendant element: <FirstName>Ewan</FirstName>
Descendant element: <LastName>Buckingham</LastName>
```

The output is the same as the first prototype for the Descendants operator, except it does include the source elements themselves, the BookParticipant elements. Don't let the existence of the comment in the results fool you. It is not there because the comment was returned by the DescendantsAndSelf operator; it is there because we display the BookParticipant element, which was returned by the operator.

For the second DescendantsAndSelf prototype, we will use the same example as the first prototype, except specify a name the element must match to be returned, as shown in Listing 8-14.

Listing 8-14. Calling the Second DescendantsAndSelf Prototype

```
XDocument xDocument = new XDocument(
  new XElement("BookParticipants",
    new XElement("BookParticipant",
      new XAttribute("type", "Author"),
      new XComment("This is a new author."),
      new XElement("FirstName", "Joe"),
      new XElement("LastName", "Rattz")),
    new XElement("BookParticipant",
      new XAttribute("type", "Editor"),
      new XElement("FirstName", "Ewan"),
      new XElement("LastName", "Buckingham"))));

IEnumerable<XElement> elements =
  xDocument.Element("BookParticipants").Elements("BookParticipant");

//  First, we will display the source elements.
foreach (XElement element in elements)
{
  Console.WriteLine("Source element: {0} : value = {1}",
    element.Name, element.Value);
}

//  Now, we will display each source element's descendant elements.
foreach (XElement element in elements.DescendantsAndSelf("LastName"))
{
  Console.WriteLine("Descendant element: {0}", element);
}
```

The results of this example are the following:

```
Source element: BookParticipant : value = JoeRattz
Source element: BookParticipant : value = EwanBuckingham
Descendant element: <LastName>Rattz</LastName>
Descendant element: <LastName>Buckingham</LastName>
```

The results only include the descendant elements that match the name we specified. There isn't much evidence that we called the DescendantsAndSelf operator, as opposed to the Descendants operator, since the source elements were not returned because of their name not matching the specified name. Again, as with all the operators that return elements from multiple levels of the XML tree, it is unlikely that you will need the AndSelf versions of the operators. You probably won't have that many levels of elements having the same name.

Elements

The `Elements` operator can be called on a sequence of elements or documents and returns a sequence of elements containing each source element's or document's child elements.

This operator is different from the `Descendants` operator, because the `Elements` operator returns only the immediate child elements of each element in the source sequence of elements, whereas the `Descendants` operator recursively returns all child elements until the end of each tree is reached.

Prototypes

The `Elements` operator has two prototypes.

The First Elements Prototype

```
public static IEnumerable<XElement> Elements<T> (
  this IEnumerable<T> source
) where T : XContainer
```

This version is called on a sequence of elements or documents and returns a sequence of elements containing each source element's or document's child elements.

This is different from the `XContainer.Elements` method in that this method is called on a sequence of elements or documents, as opposed to a single element or document.

The Second Elements Prototype

```
public static IEnumerable<XElement> Elements<T> (
  this IEnumerable<T> source,
  XName name
) where T : XContainer
```

This version is like the first, except only those elements matching the specified name are returned in the output sequence.

Examples

By now, you probably know the drill. For an example of the first prototype, we will use the same basic example as the `DescendantsAndSelf` operator used, except we will call the `Elements` operator instead, as shown in Listing 8-15.

Listing 8-15. *Calling the First Elements Prototype*

```
XDocument xDocument = new XDocument(
  new XElement("BookParticipants",
    new XElement("BookParticipant",
      new XAttribute("type", "Author"),
      new XComment("This is a new author."),
```

```
      new XElement("FirstName", "Joe"),
      new XElement("LastName", "Rattz")),
    new XElement("BookParticipant",
      new XAttribute("type", "Editor"),
      new XElement("FirstName", "Ewan"),
      new XElement("LastName", "Buckingham")))));

IEnumerable<XElement> elements =
  xDocument.Element("BookParticipants").Elements("BookParticipant");

// First, we will display the source elements.
foreach (XElement element in elements)
{
  Console.WriteLine("Source element: {0} : value = {1}",
    element.Name, element.Value);
}

// Now, we will display each source element's elements.
foreach (XElement element in elements.Elements())
{
  Console.WriteLine("Child element: {0}", element);
}
```

As in the previous examples, we build our XML tree, obtain a sequence of source elements, display each source element, retrieve a sequence of each source element's child elements, and display the child elements:

```
Source element: BookParticipant : value = JoeRattz
Source element: BookParticipant : value = EwanBuckingham
Child element: <FirstName>Joe</FirstName>
Child element: <LastName>Rattz</LastName>
Child element: <FirstName>Ewan</FirstName>
Child element: <LastName>Buckingham</LastName>
```

That example returns all child elements. To retrieve just those matching a specific name, we use the second prototype of the Elements operator, as shown in Listing 8-16.

Listing 8-16. Calling the Second Elements Prototype

```
XDocument xDocument = new XDocument(
  new XElement("BookParticipants",
    new XElement("BookParticipant",
      new XAttribute("type", "Author"),
      new XComment("This is a new author."),
      new XElement("FirstName", "Joe"),
      new XElement("LastName", "Rattz")),
```

```
        new XElement("BookParticipant",
          new XAttribute("type", "Editor"),
          new XElement("FirstName", "Ewan"),
          new XElement("LastName", "Buckingham")))));

IEnumerable<XElement> elements =
  xDocument.Element("BookParticipants").Elements("BookParticipant");

// First, we will display the source elements.
foreach (XElement element in elements)
{
  Console.WriteLine("Source element: {0} : value = {1}",
    element.Name, element.Value);
}

// Now, we will display each source element's elements.
foreach (XElement element in elements.Elements("LastName"))
{
  Console.WriteLine("Child element: {0}", element);
}
```

Now, we should get only the child elements matching the name LastName:

```
Source element: BookParticipant : value = JoeRattz
Source element: BookParticipant : value = EwanBuckingham
Child element: <LastName>Rattz</LastName>
Child element: <LastName>Buckingham</LastName>
```

That works just as expected.

InDocumentOrder

The InDocumentOrder operator can be called on a sequence of nodes and returns a sequence containing each source node sorted in document order.

Prototypes

The InDocumentOrder operator has one prototype.

The Only InDocumentOrder Prototype

```
public static IEnumerable<T> InDocumentOrder<T> (
  this IEnumerable<T> source
) where T : XNode
```

This version is called on a sequence of a specified type, which must be nodes or some type derived from nodes, and returns a sequence of that same type containing each source node in document order.

Examples

This is a fairly odd operator. For this example, we need a source sequence of nodes. Since we want to see some nodes that are not elements in addition to elements, we will build a sequence of nodes that are the child nodes of the BookParticipant elements. We do this because one of them has a comment, which is a node but not an element. Listing 8-17 shows the source.

Listing 8-17. Calling the Only InDocumentOrder Prototype

```
XDocument xDocument = new XDocument(
  new XElement("BookParticipants",
    new XElement("BookParticipant",
      new XAttribute("type", "Author"),
      new XComment("This is a new author."),
      new XElement("FirstName", "Joe"),
      new XElement("LastName", "Rattz")),
    new XElement("BookParticipant",
      new XAttribute("type", "Editor"),
      new XElement("FirstName", "Ewan"),
      new XElement("LastName", "Buckingham"))));

IEnumerable<XNode> nodes =
  xDocument.Element("BookParticipants").Elements("BookParticipant").
    Nodes().Reverse();

// First, we will display the source nodes.
foreach (XNode node in nodes)
{
  Console.WriteLine("Source node: {0}", node);
}

// Now, we will display each source node's child nodes.
foreach (XNode node in nodes.InDocumentOrder())
{
  Console.WriteLine("Ordered node: {0}", node);
}
```

As you can see in the previous code, we build our XML tree. When we retrieve our source sequence, we get the BookParticipant element's child nodes by calling the Nodes operator, and then we call the Reverse Standard Query Operator. If you recall from Part 2 of this book about LINQ to Objects, the Reverse operator will return a sequence where entries in the input sequence have had their order reversed. So, now we have a sequence of nodes that are not in the original order. We take this additional step of altering the order so that when we call the InDocumentOrder operator, a difference can be detected. Then we display the disordered source nodes, call the `InDocumentOrder` operator, and display the results. Here they are:

```
Source node: <LastName>Buckingham</LastName>
Source node: <FirstName>Ewan</FirstName>
Source node: <LastName>Rattz</LastName>
Source node: <FirstName>Joe</FirstName>
Source node: <!--This is a new author.-->
Ordered node: <!--This is a new author.-->
Ordered node: <FirstName>Joe</FirstName>
Ordered node: <LastName>Rattz</LastName>
Ordered node: <FirstName>Ewan</FirstName>
Ordered node: <LastName>Buckingham</LastName>
```

As you can see, the source nodes are in the reverse order that we built them in, and the ordered nodes are back in the original order. Cool, but odd.

Nodes

The `Nodes` operator can be called on a sequence of elements or documents and returns a sequence of nodes containing each source element's or document's child nodes.

This operator is different from the `DescendantNodes` operator in that the `Nodes` operator returns only the immediate child elements of each element in the source sequence of elements, whereas the `DescendantNodes` operator recursively returns all child nodes until the end of each tree is reached.

Prototypes

The `Nodes` operator has one prototype.

The Only Nodes Prototype

```
public static IEnumerable<XNode> Nodes<T> (
  this IEnumerable<T> source
) where T : XContainer
```

This version is called on a sequence of elements or documents and returns a sequence of nodes containing each source element's or document's child nodes.

This is different from the `XContainer.Nodes` method in that this method is called on a sequence of elements or documents, as opposed to a single element or document.

Examples

For this example, we will build our typical XML tree and build a source sequence of BookParticipant elements. We will display each of them, and then we will return the child nodes of each source element and display them, as shown in Listing 8-18.

Listing 8-18. *Calling the Only Nodes Prototype*

```
XDocument xDocument = new XDocument(
  new XElement("BookParticipants",
    new XElement("BookParticipant",
      new XAttribute("type", "Author"),
      new XComment("This is a new author."),
      new XElement("FirstName", "Joe"),
      new XElement("LastName", "Rattz")),
    new XElement("BookParticipant",
      new XAttribute("type", "Editor"),
      new XElement("FirstName", "Ewan"),
      new XElement("LastName", "Buckingham"))));

IEnumerable<XElement> elements =
  xDocument.Element("BookParticipants").Elements("BookParticipant");

// First, we will display the source elements.
foreach (XElement element in elements)
{
  Console.WriteLine("Source element: {0} : value = {1}",
    element.Name, element.Value);
}

// Now, we will display each source element's child nodes.
foreach (XNode node in elements.Nodes())
{
  Console.WriteLine("Child node: {0}", node);
}
```

Since this operator returns the child nodes, as opposed to elements, the output should have the comment of the first BookParticipant element in the results:

```
Source element: BookParticipant : value = JoeRattz
Source element: BookParticipant : value = EwanBuckingham
Child node: <!--This is a new author.-->
Child node: <FirstName>Joe</FirstName>
Child node: <LastName>Rattz</LastName>
Child node: <FirstName>Ewan</FirstName>
Child node: <LastName>Buckingham</LastName>
```

The results display each source element's child nodes. Notice that because only the immediate child nodes are retrieved, we didn't get the XText nodes that are children of each FirstName and LastName element, as we did in the DescendantNodes operator example.

Remove

The Remove operator can be called on a sequence of nodes or attributes to remove them. This method will cache a copy of the nodes or attributes in a List to eliminate the Halloween problem discussed in the previous chapter.

Prototypes

The Remove operator has two prototypes.

The First Remove Prototype

```
public static void Remove (
  this IEnumerable<XAttribute> source
)
```

This version is called on a sequence of attributes and removes all attributes in the source sequence.

The Second Remove Prototype

```
public static void Remove<T> (
  this IEnumerable<T> source
) where T : XNode
```

This version is called on a sequence of a specified type, which must be nodes or some type derived from nodes, and removes all nodes in the source sequence.

Examples

Since the first prototype is for removing attributes, we need a sequence of attributes. So, we will build our standard XML tree and retrieve a sequence of the BookParticipant element's attributes. We will display each source attribute and then call the Remove operator on the sequence of source attributes. Then, just to prove it worked, we will display the entire XML document, and the attributes will be gone, as shown in Listing 8-19.

Listing 8-19. Calling the First Remove Prototype

```
XDocument xDocument = new XDocument(
  new XElement("BookParticipants",
    new XElement("BookParticipant",
      new XAttribute("type", "Author"),
```

```
      new XComment("This is a new author."),
      new XElement("FirstName", "Joe"),
      new XElement("LastName", "Rattz")),
    new XElement("BookParticipant",
      new XAttribute("type", "Editor"),
      new XElement("FirstName", "Ewan"),
      new XElement("LastName", "Buckingham")))));

IEnumerable<XAttribute> attributes =
  xDocument.Element("BookParticipants").Elements("BookParticipant").Attributes();

// First, we will display the source attributes.
foreach (XAttribute attribute in attributes)
{
  Console.WriteLine("Source attribute: {0} : value = {1}",
    attribute.Name, attribute.Value);
}

attributes.Remove();

// Now, we will display the XML document.
Console.WriteLine(xDocument);
```

Will it work? Let's see:

```
Source attribute: type : value = Author
Source attribute: type : value = Editor
<BookParticipants>
  <BookParticipant>
    <!--This is a new author.-->
    <FirstName>Joe</FirstName>
    <LastName>Rattz</LastName>
  </BookParticipant>
  <BookParticipant>
    <FirstName>Ewan</FirstName>
    <LastName>Buckingham</LastName>
  </BookParticipant>
</BookParticipants>
```

So far, all is good. Now, we'll try the second prototype. For this example, instead of merely obtaining a sequence of nodes and removing them, we'll show something that might be a little more interesting. We'll get a sequence of the comments of some particular elements and remove just them, as shown in Listing 8-20.

Listing 8-20. *Calling the Second Remove Prototype*

```
XDocument xDocument = new XDocument(
  new XElement("BookParticipants",
    new XElement("BookParticipant",
      new XAttribute("type", "Author"),
      new XComment("This is a new author."),
      new XElement("FirstName", "Joe"),
      new XElement("LastName", "Rattz")),
    new XElement("BookParticipant",
      new XAttribute("type", "Editor"),
      new XElement("FirstName", "Ewan"),
      new XElement("LastName", "Buckingham"))));

IEnumerable<XComment> comments =
  xDocument.Element("BookParticipants").Elements("BookParticipant").
    Nodes().OfType<XComment>();

//  First, we will display the source comments.
foreach (XComment comment in comments)
{
  Console.WriteLine("Source comment: {0}", comment);
}

comments.Remove();

//  Now, we will display the XML document.
Console.WriteLine(xDocument);
```

In this example, when building our source sequence, we retrieve the child nodes of each
BookParticipant element. We could just call the Remove operator on that sequence, and then all the
child nodes of each BookParticipant element would be gone. But instead, to spice it up, we call the
OfType Standard Query Operator. If you recall from Part 2 of this book on LINQ to Objects, this operator
will return only the objects in the input sequence matching the type specified. By calling the OfType
operator and specifying a type of XComment, we get a sequence of just the comments. Then, we call the
Remove method on the comments. The results should be that the original document is missing the one
comment that it initially had:

```
Source comment: <!--This is a new author.-->
<BookParticipants>
  <BookParticipant type="Author">
    <FirstName>Joe</FirstName>
    <LastName>Rattz</LastName>
  </BookParticipant>
  <BookParticipant type="Editor">
    <FirstName>Ewan</FirstName>
```

```
    <LastName>Buckingham</LastName>
  </BookParticipant>
</BookParticipants>
```

That worked like a charm. Look how handy the `OfType` operator is and how we can integrate it into the LINQ to XML query. That seems like it could be very useful.

Summary

In the previous chapter, we covered the new LINQ to XML API that allows you to create, modify, save, and load XML trees. Notice we said *trees* as opposed to *documents,* because with LINQ to XML, documents are no longer a requirement. In that chapter, we demonstrated how to query a single node or element for nodes and elements hierarchically related to it. In this chapter, we covered doing the same thing with sequences of nodes or elements using the LINQ to XML operators. We hope we have made it clear how to perform elementary queries on XML trees using LINQ to XML. We believe that this new XML API will prove to be quite useful for querying XML data. In particular, the way the Standard Query Operators can be mingled with LINQ to XML operators lends itself to quite elegant and powerful queries.

At this point, we have covered just about all there is to know about the building blocks needed for performing LINQ to XML queries. In the next chapter, we provide some slightly more complex queries and cover some of the remaining XML necessities such as validation and transformation.

CHAPTER 9

■ ■ ■

Additional XML Capabilities

In the previous two chapters, we demonstrated how to create, modify, and traverse XML data with the LINQ to XML API. We also demonstrated the building blocks for creating powerful XML queries. We hope by now you would agree that LINQ to XML will handle about 90 percent of your XML needs, but what about the remaining 10 percent? Let's see whether we can get that percentage higher. If Microsoft added schema validation, transformations, and XPath query capability, what percentage of your use cases would that achieve?

Although we have covered the LINQ to XML API and how to perform the most basic of queries with it, we have yet to demonstrate slightly more complex, real-world queries. In this chapter, we provide some examples that will make querying XML with the LINQ to XML API seem trivial, including some that use the query expression syntax for those of you who prefer it.

Additionally, the new LINQ to XML API just wouldn't be complete without a few additional capabilities such as transformation and validation. In this chapter, we cover these LINQ to XML leftovers, as well as any other good-to-know information.

Specifically, we cover how to perform transformations with XSLT and without. We demonstrate how to validate an XML document against a schema, and we even present an example performing an XPath-style query.

Referenced Namespaces

Examples in this chapter reference the `System.Xml`, `System.Xml.Schema`, `System.Xml.Xsl`, and `System.Xml.XPath` namespaces, in addition to the typical LINQ and LINQ to XML namespaces, `System.Linq` and `System.Xml.Linq`. Therefore, you will want to add `using` directives for these if they are not already present:

```
using System.Linq;
using System.Xml;
using System.Xml.Linq;
using System.Xml.Schema;
using System.Xml.XPath;
using System.Xml.Xsl;
```

Queries

In the previous LINQ to XML chapters, we demonstrated the core principles needed to perform XML queries using LINQ to XML. However, most of the examples are specifically designed to demonstrate an operator or a property. In this section, we provide some examples that are more solution-oriented.

No Reaching

In the previous chapters, many of the examples would reach down into the XML hierarchy to obtain a reference to a particular element by calling the `Element` or `Elements` operator recursively until the desired element was reached.

For instance, many of the examples contained lines such as this:

```
IEnumerable<XElement> elements =
  xDocument.Element("BookParticipants").Elements("BookParticipant");
```

In this statement, we start at the document level, then obtain its child element named `BookParticipants`, and then obtain its child elements named `BookParticipant`. However, it is not necessary to reach down through each level like that. Instead, we could simply write the code as shown in Listing 9-1.

Listing 9-1. *Obtaining Elements Without Reaching*

```
XDocument xDocument = new XDocument(
  new XElement("BookParticipants",
    new XElement("BookParticipant",
      new XAttribute("type", "Author"),
      new XElement("FirstName", "Joe"),
      new XElement("LastName", "Rattz")),
    new XElement("BookParticipant",
      new XAttribute("type", "Editor"),
      new XElement("FirstName", "Ewan"),
      new XElement("LastName", "Buckingham"))));

IEnumerable<XElement> elements = xDocument.Descendants("BookParticipant");

foreach (XElement element in elements)
{
  Console.WriteLine("Element: {0} : value = {1}",
    element.Name, element.Value);
}
```

In this example, we obtain every descendant element in the document named `BookParticipant`. Since we are not reaching into a specific branch of the XML tree, it is necessary that we know the schema because we could get back elements from a branch we do not want. However, in many cases, including this one, it works just fine. Here are the results:

```
Element: BookParticipant : value = JoeRattz
Element: BookParticipant : value = EwanBuckingham
```

However, we might not want all of the BookParticipant elements; perhaps we need to restrict the returned elements? Listing 9-2 is an example returning just the elements whose FirstName element's value is "Ewan":

Listing 9-2. *Obtaining Restricted Elements Without Reaching*

```
XDocument xDocument = new XDocument(
  new XElement("BookParticipants",
    new XElement("BookParticipant",
      new XAttribute("type", "Author"),
      new XElement("FirstName", "Joe"),
      new XElement("LastName", "Rattz")),
    new XElement("BookParticipant",
      new XAttribute("type", "Editor"),
      new XElement("FirstName", "Ewan"),
      new XElement("LastName", "Buckingham")))));

IEnumerable<XElement> elements = xDocument
  .Descendants("BookParticipant")
  .Where(e => ((string)e.Element("FirstName")) == "Ewan");

foreach (XElement element in elements)
{
  Console.WriteLine("Element: {0} : value = {1}",
    element.Name, element.Value);
}
```

This time we appended a call to the Where operator. Notice that we cast the FirstName element to a string to get its value for the comparison to "Ewan". Here are the results:

```
Element: BookParticipant : value = EwanBuckingham
```

Of course, sometimes you need to control the order. This time, so that we have more than one returned element so the order matters, we will change the Where operator lambda expression so that both elements will be returned. To make it interesting, we will query on the type attribute, and we will try this one in query expression syntax, as shown in Listing 9-3.

Listing 9-3. *Obtaining Restricted Elements Without Reaching While Ordering and Using Query Expression Syntax*

```
XDocument xDocument = new XDocument(
```

```
  new XElement("BookParticipants",
    new XElement("BookParticipant",
      new XAttribute("type", "Author"),
      new XElement("FirstName", "Joe"),
      new XElement("LastName", "Rattz")),
    new XElement("BookParticipant",
      new XAttribute("type", "Editor"),
      new XElement("FirstName", "Ewan"),
      new XElement("LastName", "Buckingham")))));

IEnumerable<XElement> elements =
  from e in xDocument.Descendants("BookParticipant")
  where ((string)e.Attribute("type")) != "Illustrator"
  orderby ((string)e.Element("LastName"))
  select e;

foreach (XElement element in elements)
{
  Console.WriteLine("Element: {0} : value = {1}",
    element.Name, element.Value);
}
```

In this example, we still query for the document's BookParticipant elements but retrieve only the ones whose type attribute is not Illustrator. In this case, that is all of the BookParticipant elements. We then order them by each element's LastName element. Again, notice that we cast both the type attribute and the LastName element to get their values. Here are the results:

```
Element: BookParticipant : value = EwanBuckingham
Element: BookParticipant : value = JoeRattz
```

A Complex Query

So far, all the example queries have been very trivial, so before we leave the topic of queries, we want to provide one complex query. For this example, we will use sample data suggested by the W3C specifically for XML query use case testing.

The example in Listing 9-4 contains data from three different XML documents. In our example code, we create each document by parsing a text representation of each of the W3C's suggested XML documents. Since this is a complex example, we will explain as we go.

The first step is to create the documents from the XML.

Listing 9-4. *A Complex Query Featuring a Three-Document Join with Query Expression Syntax*

```
XDocument users = XDocument.Parse(
  @"<users>
    <user_tuple>
      <userid>U01</userid>
      <name>Tom Jones</name>
```

```
        <rating>B</rating>
      </user_tuple>
      <user_tuple>
        <userid>U02</userid>
        <name>Mary Doe</name>
        <rating>A</rating>
      </user_tuple>
      <user_tuple>
        <userid>U03</userid>
        <name>Dee Linquent</name>
        <rating>D</rating>
      </user_tuple>
      <user_tuple>
        <userid>U04</userid>
        <name>Roger Smith</name>
        <rating>C</rating>
      </user_tuple>
      <user_tuple>
        <userid>U05</userid>
        <name>Jack Sprat</name>
        <rating>B</rating>
      </user_tuple>
      <user_tuple>
        <userid>U06</userid>
        <name>Rip Van Winkle</name>
        <rating>B</rating>
      </user_tuple>
    </users>");

XDocument items = XDocument.Parse(
  @"<items>
      <item_tuple>
        <itemno>1001</itemno>
        <description>Red Bicycle</description>
        <offered_by>U01</offered_by>
        <start_date>1999-01-05</start_date>
        <end_date>1999-01-20</end_date>
        <reserve_price>40</reserve_price>
      </item_tuple>
      <item_tuple>
        <itemno>1002</itemno>
        <description>Motorcycle</description>
        <offered_by>U02</offered_by>
        <start_date>1999-02-11</start_date>
        <end_date>1999-03-15</end_date>
        <reserve_price>500</reserve_price>
      </item_tuple>
```

```xml
<item_tuple>
  <itemno>1003</itemno>
  <description>Old Bicycle</description>
  <offered_by>U02</offered_by>
  <start_date>1999-01-10</start_date>
  <end_date>1999-02-20</end_date>
  <reserve_price>25</reserve_price>
</item_tuple>
<item_tuple>
  <itemno>1004</itemno>
  <description>Tricycle</description>
  <offered_by>U01</offered_by>
  <start_date>1999-02-25</start_date>
  <end_date>1999-03-08</end_date>
  <reserve_price>15</reserve_price>
</item_tuple>
<item_tuple>
  <itemno>1005</itemno>
  <description>Tennis Racket</description>
  <offered_by>U03</offered_by>
  <start_date>1999-03-19</start_date>
  <end_date>1999-04-30</end_date>
  <reserve_price>20</reserve_price>
</item_tuple>
<item_tuple>
  <itemno>1006</itemno>
  <description>Helicopter</description>
  <offered_by>U03</offered_by>
  <start_date>1999-05-05</start_date>
  <end_date>1999-05-25</end_date>
  <reserve_price>50000</reserve_price>
</item_tuple>
<item_tuple>
  <itemno>1007</itemno>
  <description>Racing Bicycle</description>
  <offered_by>U04</offered_by>
  <start_date>1999-01-20</start_date>
  <end_date>1999-02-20</end_date>
  <reserve_price>200</reserve_price>
</item_tuple>
<item_tuple>
  <itemno>1008</itemno>
  <description>Broken Bicycle</description>
  <offered_by>U01</offered_by>
  <start_date>1999-02-05</start_date>
  <end_date>1999-03-06</end_date>
  <reserve_price>25</reserve_price>
```

```
            </item_tuple>
        </items>");

XDocument bids = XDocument.Parse(
    @"<bids>
        <bid_tuple>
          <userid>U02</userid>
          <itemno>1001</itemno>
          <bid>35</bid>
          <bid_date>1999-01-07</bid_date>
        </bid_tuple>
        <bid_tuple>
          <userid>U04</userid>
          <itemno>1001</itemno>
          <bid>40</bid>
          <bid_date>1999-01-08</bid_date>
        </bid_tuple>
        <bid_tuple>
          <userid>U02</userid>
          <itemno>1001</itemno>
          <bid>45</bid>
          <bid_date>1999-01-11</bid_date>
        </bid_tuple>
        <bid_tuple>
          <userid>U04</userid>
          <itemno>1001</itemno>
          <bid>50</bid>
          <bid_date>1999-01-13</bid_date>
        </bid_tuple>
        <bid_tuple>
          <userid>U02</userid>
          <itemno>1001</itemno>
          <bid>55</bid>
          <bid_date>1999-01-15</bid_date>
        </bid_tuple>
        <bid_tuple>
          <userid>U01</userid>
          <itemno>1002</itemno>
          <bid>400</bid>
          <bid_date>1999-02-14</bid_date>
        </bid_tuple>
        <bid_tuple>
          <userid>U02</userid>
          <itemno>1002</itemno>
          <bid>600</bid>
          <bid_date>1999-02-16</bid_date>
        </bid_tuple>
```

```
<bid_tuple>
  <userid>U03</userid>
  <itemno>1002</itemno>
  <bid>800</bid>
  <bid_date>1999-02-17</bid_date>
</bid_tuple>
<bid_tuple>
  <userid>U04</userid>
  <itemno>1002</itemno>
  <bid>1000</bid>
  <bid_date>1999-02-25</bid_date>
</bid_tuple>
<bid_tuple>
  <userid>U02</userid>
  <itemno>1002</itemno>
  <bid>1200</bid>
  <bid_date>1999-03-02</bid_date>
</bid_tuple>
<bid_tuple>
  <userid>U04</userid>
  <itemno>1003</itemno>
  <bid>15</bid>
  <bid_date>1999-01-22</bid_date>
</bid_tuple>
<bid_tuple>
  <userid>U05</userid>
  <itemno>1003</itemno>
  <bid>20</bid>
  <bid_date>1999-02-03</bid_date>
</bid_tuple>
<bid_tuple>
  <userid>U01</userid>
  <itemno>1004</itemno>
  <bid>40</bid>
  <bid_date>1999-03-05</bid_date>
</bid_tuple>
<bid_tuple>
  <userid>U03</userid>
  <itemno>1007</itemno>
  <bid>175</bid>
  <bid_date>1999-01-25</bid_date>
</bid_tuple>
<bid_tuple>
  <userid>U05</userid>
  <itemno>1007</itemno>
  <bid>200</bid>
  <bid_date>1999-02-08</bid_date>
```

```
        </bid_tuple>
        <bid_tuple>
          <userid>U04</userid>
          <itemno>1007</itemno>
          <bid>225</bid>
          <bid_date>1999-02-12</bid_date>
        </bid_tuple>
      </bids>");
```

This sample data is basically meant to represent an Internet auction-type site and the data it would have. We just created three XML documents by calling the XDocument.Parse method on string representations of the XML data. There are documents for users, items, and bids.

For our query, we want to produce a list of each bid greater than $50. In the results, we want to see the date and price of the bid as well as the user placing the bid and the item number and item description. Here is the query:

```
var biddata = from b in bids.Descendants("bid_tuple")
              where ((double)b.Element("bid")) > 50
              join u in users.Descendants("user_tuple")
              on ((string)b.Element("userid")) equals
                ((string)u.Element("userid"))
              join i in items.Descendants("item_tuple")
              on ((string)b.Element("itemno")) equals
                ((string)i.Element("itemno"))
              select new { Item = ((string)b.Element("itemno")),
                      Description = ((string)i.Element("description")),
                      User = ((string)u.Element("name")),
                      Date = ((string)b.Element("bid_date")),
                      Price = ((double)b.Element("bid"))};
```

OK, that is a complex query. The first step is that we query for the descendants named bid_tuple in the bids document using the Descendants method. Next, we perform a where statement for elements that have a child element named bid whose value is greater than 50. This is so we only retrieve the bids that are greater than $50. It may seem a little unusual that we are performing a where statement this soon in the query. We actually could have called the where statement further down in the query, just before the select statement call. However, this means we would have retrieved and performed a join against the users and items XML documents even for bids not greater than $50, which is not necessary. By filtering the results set as soon as possible, we have reduced the workload for the remainder of the query, thereby leading to better performance.

Once we have filtered the results set to just the bids that are greater than $50, we join those bids on the users XML document by the commonly named userid element so that we can obtain the user's name. At this point, we have the bids and users joined for the bids greater than $50.

Next, we join the results on the items XML document by the commonly named itemno element so that we can obtain the item's description. At this point, we have the bids, users, and items joined.

Notice again that we have cast all elements to the data type we are interested in to get the element's value. Especially interesting is that we obtain the bid price by casting the bid element to a double. Even though the actual input bid value is just a string, because the bid value could be successfully converted to a double, we were able to cast it to a double to get its value as a double. How cool is that?

The next step is to simply select an anonymous class containing the joined element's child elements we are interested in.

Our next step is to display a header:

```
Console.WriteLine("{0,-12} {1,-12} {2,-6} {3,-14} {4,10}",
  "Date",
  "User",
  "Item",
  "Description",
  "Price");

Console.WriteLine("==========================================================");
```

There is nothing special about that. All that is left is to enumerate the sequence and display each bid:

```
foreach (var bd in biddata)
{
  Console.WriteLine("{0,-12} {1,-12} {2,-6} {3,-14} {4,10:C}",
    bd.Date,
    bd.User,
    bd.Item,
    bd.Description,
    bd.Price);
}
```

That part is trivial. Actually, all but the query itself is trivial. Are you ready to see the results? We know we are:

Date	User	Item	Description	Price
1999-01-15	Mary Doe	1001	Red Bicycle	$55.00
1999-02-14	Tom Jones	1002	Motorcycle	$400.00
1999-02-16	Mary Doe	1002	Motorcycle	$600.00
1999-02-17	Dee Linquent	1002	Motorcycle	$800.00
1999-02-25	Roger Smith	1002	Motorcycle	$1,000.00
1999-03-02	Mary Doe	1002	Motorcycle	$1,200.00
1999-01-25	Dee Linquent	1007	Racing Bicycle	$175.00
1999-02-08	Jack Sprat	1007	Racing Bicycle	$200.00
1999-02-12	Roger Smith	1007	Racing Bicycle	$225.00

OK, come on, you have to admit that is pretty spectacular, don't you think? We just joined three XML documents in a single query.

Surely you now see the power of LINQ to XML. Are you starting to see why LINQ to XML is our favorite part of LINQ? Now how much would you pay? But wait, there's more!

Transformations

With LINQ to XML, you can perform XML transformations using two completely different approaches. The first approach is to use XSLT via the bridge classes, `XmlReader` and `XmlWriter`. The second approach is to use LINQ to XML to perform the transformation itself by functionally constructing the target XML document and embedding a LINQ to XML query on the source XML document.

Using XSLT provides the benefit that it is a standard XML technology. Tools already exist to assist with writing, debugging, and testing XSLT transformations. Additionally, because it already exists, you may have XSLT documents and can leverage them in new code using LINQ to XML. There is a world full of existing XSLT documents from which to choose. Additionally, using XSLT for your transformations is just more dynamic. Unlike using the LINQ to XML functional construction approach, you do not have to recompile code to change the transformation. Merely changing the XSLT document allows you to modify the transformation at runtime. Lastly, XSLT is a known technology with many developers having expertise that may be able to assist you. At least in the early days of LINQ, this may not be available if you take the functional construction approach.

Using the functional construction approach does not really buy you much. It does allow you to perform XML transformations knowing nothing more than LINQ to XML. So if you do not already know XSLT and your transformation needs are modest, this may be a fine approach for you. Also, although functional construction is less convenient than merely modifying an XSLT document, having to recompile code to modify a transformation could add security. Someone cannot simply muck with an outside document to modify the transformation. So for those times when you think you are pushing the limits by using Sarbanes-Oxley as the excuse for not doing something, blame it on the fact that you cannot simply change the transformation without a code overhaul. Or if you are in the medical field and you don't think you can get away with blaming HIPAA one more time, transformation via functional construction may just be the obstacle you need on which to blame a lack of agility.

Transformations Using XSLT

To perform an XML transformation using XSLT, you will utilize the `XmlWriter` and `XmlReader` bridge classes that you will obtain from the `XDocument` classes' `CreateWriter` and `CreateReader` methods, respectively.

Because the example shown in Listing 9-5 requires a bit of explanation, we will explain it as we go. First, we will specify the transformation style sheet.

Listing 9-5. *Transforming an XML Document with XSLT*

```
string xsl =
  @"<xsl:stylesheet version='1.0' xmlns:xsl='http://www.w3.org/1999/XSL/Transform'>
    <xsl:template match='//BookParticipants'>
        <html>
            <body>
            <h1>Book Participants</h1>
            <table>
                <tr align='left'>
                    <th>Role                     <th>First Name
<th>Last Name           </tr>
                <xsl:apply-templates></xsl:apply-templates>
            </table>
            </body>
```

```
        </html>
    </xsl:template>
    <xsl:template match='BookParticipant'>
        <tr>
            <td><xsl:value-of select='@type'/></td>
            <td><xsl:value-of select='FirstName'/></td>
            <td><xsl:value-of select='LastName'/></td>
        </tr>
    </xsl:template>
</xsl:stylesheet>";
```

There is nothing earth-shattering here. We are just specifying some XSL to create some HTML to display our typical book participant XML as an HTML table. Next, we will create our XML document with the book participants:

```
XDocument xDocument = new XDocument(
  new XElement("BookParticipants",
    new XElement("BookParticipant",
      new XAttribute("type", "Author"),
      new XElement("FirstName", "Joe"),
      new XElement("LastName", "Rattz")),
    new XElement("BookParticipant",
      new XAttribute("type", "Editor"),
      new XElement("FirstName", "Ewan"),
      new XElement("LastName", "Buckingham"))));
```

This is just our typical XML. Now is where the magic happens. We need to create a new XDocument for the transformed version. Then, from that document, we will create an XmlWriter, instantiate an XslCompiledTransform object, load the transform object with the transformation style sheet, and transform our input XML document into the output XmlWriter:

```
XDocument transformedDoc = new XDocument();
using (XmlWriter writer = transformedDoc.CreateWriter())
{
  XslCompiledTransform transform = new XslCompiledTransform();
  transform.Load(XmlReader.Create(new StringReader(xsl)));
  transform.Transform(xDocument.CreateReader(), writer);
}
Console.WriteLine(transformedDoc);
```

Of course, after all that, we display the transformed version of the document. As you can see, we use both bridge classes, XmlWriter and XmlReader, to perform the transformation. Here are the results:

```
<html>
  <body>
    <h1>Book Participants</h1>
```

```
    <table>
      <tr align="left">
        <th>Role          <th>First Name          <th>Last Name          </tr>
      <tr>
        <td>Author</td>
        <td>Joe</td>
        <td>Rattz</td>
      </tr>
      <tr>
        <td>Editor</td>
        <td>Ewan</td>
        <td>Buckingham</td>
      </tr>
    </table>
  </body>
</html>
```

Transformations Using Functional Construction

Although the LINQ to XML API does support XSLT transformations, there are some very effective ways to produce transformations using the LINQ to XML API. Logically speaking, a transformation can be as simple as combining a functionally constructed XML tree with an embedded XML query.

■ **Tip** Combine functional construction with an embedded XML LINQ query to perform a transformation.

We will explain XML transformations via an example. In many of the examples in the LINQ to XML chapters, we have worked with the following XML tree:

```
<BookParticipants>
  <BookParticipant type="Author">
    <FirstName>Joe</FirstName>
    <LastName>Rattz</LastName>
  </BookParticipant>
  <BookParticipant type="Editor">
    <FirstName>Ewan</FirstName>
    <LastName>Buckingham</LastName>
  </BookParticipant>
</BookParticipants>
```

Let's pretend that we need to transform this XML tree to this:

```
<MediaParticipants type="book">
  <Participant Role="Author" Name="Joe Rattz" />
```

```
<Participant Role="Editor" Name="Ewan Buckingham" / >
</MediaParticipants>
```

To accomplish this transformation, we will use functional construction with an embedded query. With this approach, you basically functionally construct a new document matching the desired output XML tree structure while obtaining the needed data from the original source XML document by performing a LINQ to XML query. It is the desired output XML tree structure that drives your functional construction and query logic.

Because this task is slightly more complex than some of the previous LINQ to XML examples, we will explain this one as we go. Listing 9-6 shows the code.

Listing 9-6. *Transforming an XML Document*

```
XDocument xDocument = new XDocument(
  new XElement("BookParticipants",
    new XElement("BookParticipant",
      new XAttribute("type", "Author"),
      new XElement("FirstName", "Joe"),
      new XElement("LastName", "Rattz")),
    new XElement("BookParticipant",
      new XAttribute("type", "Editor"),
      new XElement("FirstName", "Ewan"),
      new XElement("LastName", "Buckingham"))));

Console.WriteLine("Here is the original XML document:");
Console.WriteLine("{0}{1}{1}", xDocument, System.Environment.NewLine);
```

The previous code simply creates the original source XML document that we are going to transform and displays it. Next, we need to build the new document and root element:

```
XDocument xTransDocument = new XDocument(
  new XElement("MediaParticipants",
```

Remember, our desired output XML tree structure is driving our functional construction. At this point, we have the document and root element, `MediaParticipants`. Next, we need to add the `type` attribute to the root element:

```
  new XAttribute("type", "book"),
```

The `type` attribute and its value do not exist in the source XML document. This would be hard-coded, or possibly configured, in our program logic, which is safe because we already know this code is for a book; otherwise, this code would not be getting called.

Now, we have the `MediaParticipants` type attribute handled. Next up, we need to generate a `Participant` element for each `BookParticipant` element in the original XML. To do this, we will query the original XML document for its `BookParticipant` elements:

```
    xDocument.Element("BookParticipants")
      .Elements("BookParticipant")
```

Now, we have a returned sequence of the BookParticipant elements. Next, we need to generate a Participant element for each BookParticipant element and populate its attributes. We will use projection via the Select operator to construct the Participant elements:

```
.Select(e => new XElement("Participant",
```

Next, we construct the two attributes, Role and Name, for the Participant element by getting their values from the BookParticipant element:

```
new XAttribute("Role", (string)e.Attribute("type")),
new XAttribute("Name", (string)e.Element("FirstName") + " " +
  (string)e.Element("LastName"))))));
```

Last, we display the transformed XML document:

```
Console.WriteLine("Here is the transformed XML document:");
Console.WriteLine(xTransDocument);
```

Let's see whether this outputs what we are looking for:

```
Here is the original XML document:
<BookParticipants>
  <BookParticipant type="Author">
    <FirstName>Joe</FirstName>
    <LastName>Rattz</LastName>
  </BookParticipant>
  <BookParticipant type="Editor">
    <FirstName>Ewan</FirstName>
    <LastName>Buckingham</LastName>
  </BookParticipant>
</BookParticipants>


Here is the transformed XML document:
<MediaParticipants type="book">
  <Participant Role="Author" Name="Joe Rattz" />
  <Participant Role="Editor" Name="Ewan Buckingham" />
</MediaParticipants>
```

Wow, that went great! We got the exact output we were looking for. That's not bad for using nothing more than LINQ to XML.

Tips

There are a few tips to pass on when it comes to performing XML transformations with the LINQ to XML API. Although you may not have a need for these, there is no reason not to point them out.

Simplify Complex Tasks with Helper Methods

There is no requirement that every bit of code needed to perform a transformation or query actually exist in the transformation code itself. It is possible to create helper methods that carry out more complex transformation chores.

Here is some code demonstrating how you can create a helper method to break up a more complex task:

A Helper Method to Transform an XML Document

```
static IEnumerable<XElement> Helper()
{
  XElement[] elements = new XElement[] {
    new XElement("Element", "A"),
    new XElement("Element", "B")}};

  return(elements);
}
```

In Listing 9-7, we begin the construction of an XML tree. It creates the root node, named RootElement, in the call to the constructor. To create the child nodes, it calls a helper method named Helper. It isn't important what the helper method is doing specifically; it just matters that it is helping us build some part of our XML tree and that the call to the method can be embedded in the functional construction of the XML tree.

Listing 9-7. Using a Helper Method to Transform an XML Document

```
XElement xElement = new XElement("RootElement", Helper());
Console.WriteLine(xElement);
```

Here are the results of this code:

```
<RootElement>
  <Element>A</Element>
  <Element>B</Element>
</RootElement>
```

Remember, as we discussed in Chapter 7, the XElement constructor knows how to handle IEnumerable<T>, which happens to be the returned data type of our Helper method. How cool is that?

Suppressing Node Construction with null

There may be times when you want to suppress some nodes from being constructed for one reason or another. Perhaps some essential data is missing from the source that causes you to want to omit an element from being created, or perhaps the data is such that you want to skip it.

Back in the "Creating Elements with XElement" section of Chapter 7 when we described the constructor for XElement, we mentioned that you could pass null as an object value for an element's content and that this can be handy when performing transformations. Suppressing node construction is what it is handy for.

As an example, we will first build a sequence of elements. We will then begin constructing a new XML tree based on that sequence. However, if an input element's value is "A", then we don't want to create an output element for that input element. We will pass its value as null to make that happen. The code is in Listing 9-8.

Listing 9-8. *Suppressing Node Construction with null*

```
IEnumerable<XElement> elements =
  new XElement[] {
    new XElement("Element", "A"),
    new XElement("Element", "B")};

XElement xElement = new XElement("RootElement",
  elements.Select(e => (string)e != "A" ? new XElement(e.Name, (string)e) : null));

Console.WriteLine(xElement);
```

As you can see in the previous code, we do build an input source sequence of elements. We then construct the root element and enumerate through the input source sequence. Then, using the Select operator, as long as the input element's value is not equal to "A", we construct an XElement object using the input element. If the input element's value is equal to "A", we return null. The XElement constructor knows how to handle null; it ignores it. The result is that any element whose value is equal to "A" is eliminated from the output XML tree. We can see we are using the new node value extraction feature by casting the element e as a string in the Select operator's lambda expression.

Here are the results:

```
<RootElement>
  <Element>B</Element>
</RootElement>
```

Notice that the element "A" is missing. Of course, there are other ways to implement this same logic without using null. For example, we could have just used the Where operator to filter out the elements whose value is equal to "A". But we wanted to show you the effect of using null in a very simple example.

There are other ways to use this same concept. Perhaps we have some XML to generate that would cause me to have an empty element in some instances that we would prefer not exist. Consider the code in Listing 9-9.

Listing 9-9. *An Example That Generates an Empty Element*

```
IEnumerable<XElement> elements =
  new XElement[] {
    new XElement("BookParticipant",
```

```
      new XElement("Name", "Joe Rattz"),
      new XElement("Book", "Pro LINQ: Language Integrated Query in C# 2008")),
    new XElement("BookParticipant",
      new XElement("Name", "John Q. Public"))};

XElement xElement =
  new XElement("BookParticipants",
    elements.Select(e =>
      new XElement(e.Name,
        new XElement(e.Element("Name").Name, e.Element("Name").Value),
        new XElement("Books", e.Elements("Book")))));

Console.WriteLine(xElement);
```

In the previous code, in the first statement, we generate a sequence of BookParticipant elements, two to be precise. Notice that some of the BookParticipant elements have Book child elements, such as the BookParticipant with the Name child element whose value is "Joe Rattz", and some have no Book elements, such as the BookParticipant whose Name child element is "John Q. Public".

In the second statement, we build an XML tree using the sequence of elements we obtained. In the XML tree, we create an element with the same name as the source sequence, which will be BookParticipant. We then make the participant's name a child element, and then we create a list of Books for each participant. Here is the output from this code:

```
<BookParticipants>
  <BookParticipant>
    <Name>Joe Rattz</Name>
    <Books>
      <Book>Pro LINQ: Language Integrated Query in C# 2008</Book>
    </Books>
  </BookParticipant>
  <BookParticipant>
    <Name>John Q. Public</Name>
    <Books />
  </BookParticipant>
</BookParticipants>
```

The XML is just as we would expect based on the code, but notice that the Books element for the second BookParticipant is empty. What if you didn't want an empty Books element if there were no Book elements? You could use null to suppress the Books element as well, with the correct operator. In Listing 9-10, we make a slight change to the code that produces the XML.

Listing 9-10. *An Example That Prevents an Empty Element*

```
IEnumerable<XElement> elements =
  new XElement[] {
    new XElement("BookParticipant",
```

```
        new XElement("Name", "Joe Rattz"),
        new XElement("Book", "Pro LINQ: Language Integrated Query in C# 2008")),
    new XElement("BookParticipant",
        new XElement("Name", "John Q. Public"))};

XElement xElement =
  new XElement("BookParticipants",
    elements.Select(e =>
      new XElement(e.Name,
        new XElement(e.Element("Name").Name, e.Element("Name").Value),
        e.Elements("Book").Any() ?
          new XElement("Books", e.Elements("Book")) : null)));

Console.WriteLine(xElement);
```

The significant change in the previous code is in bold. Instead of just creating a Books element and specifying all the existing Book elements as its content, we use the Any Standard Query Operator combined with the ternary operator (if ? then : else) to create the Books element only if there are in fact any Book elements. If there are no Book elements, the ternary operator returns null, and the XElement constructor knows to just ignore null, thereby eliminating the creation of the Books element. This can be very handy. Here are the results after the modification:

```
<BookParticipants>
  <BookParticipant>
    <Name>Joe Rattz</Name>
    <Books>
      <Book>Pro LINQ: Language Integrated Query in C# 2008</Book>
    </Books>
  </BookParticipant>
  <BookParticipant>
    <Name>John Q. Public</Name>
  </BookParticipant>
</BookParticipants>
```

As you can see, the second BookParticipant element no longer has an empty Books element, as it did in the previous example.

Handling Multiple Peer Nodes While Remaining Flat

Sometimes when making an XML transformation, you know exactly how many of each type of output element you are going to want. But what happens if there are several known elements as well as a variable number of repeating elements all at the same level in the tree for each entry in the source XML? Let's say we have the following XML:

What We Want Our Source XML to Look Like

```
<BookParticipants>
  <BookParticipant type="Author">
    <FirstName>Joe</FirstName>
    <LastName>Rattz</LastName>
    <Nickname>Joey</Nickname>
    <Nickname>Null Pointer</Nickname>
  </BookParticipant>
  <BookParticipant type="Editor">
    <FirstName>Ewan</FirstName>
    <LastName>Buckingham</LastName>
  </BookParticipant>
</BookParticipants>
```

What if we want to flatten the structure so that the `BookParticipants` root node contains only repeating sets of `FirstName`, `LastName`, and `Nickname` elements, instead of those elements being contained in a child `BookParticipant` element? We would like for the target XML to look like this:

What We Want the XML to Look Like After Transformation

```
<BookParticipants>
  <!- BookParticipant  -->
  <FirstName>Joe</FirstName>
  <LastName>Rattz</LastName>
  <Nickname>Joey</Nickname>
  <Nickname>Null Pointer</Nickname>
  <!- BookParticipant  -->
  <FirstName>Ewan</FirstName>
  <LastName>Buckingham</LastName>
</BookParticipants>
```

The comments are not necessary, but they make it easier for a human to know what they are looking at. Plus, without them, if you looked further down in the list, it might be confusing as to whether the `FirstName` or `LastName` comes first, causing a human to think that there is a `BookParticipant` named Ewan Rattz when there really isn't.

Because this example is more complex, we will explain it as we go. Let's take a look at the example code in Listing 9-11 to make this transformation.

Listing 9-11. Handling Multiple Peer Nodes While Maintaining a Flat Structure

```
XDocument xDocument = new XDocument(
  new XElement("BookParticipants",
    new XElement("BookParticipant",
      new XAttribute("type", "Author"),
      new XElement("FirstName", "Joe"),
      new XElement("LastName", "Rattz"),
```

```
        new XElement("Nickname", "Joey"),
        new XElement("Nickname", "Null Pointer")),
    new XElement("BookParticipant",
        new XAttribute("type", "Editor"),
        new XElement("FirstName", "Ewan"),
        new XElement("LastName", "Buckingham"))));

Console.WriteLine("Here is the original XML document:");
Console.WriteLine("{0}{1}{1}", xDocument, System.Environment.NewLine);
```

At this point, we have built the source XML tree and displayed it. It does indeed match the XML we specified previously as the source. Now we just have to transform the source XML:

```
XDocument xTransDocument = new XDocument(
    new XElement("BookParticipants",
        xDocument.Element("BookParticipants")
            .Elements("BookParticipant")
```

Here is where the challenge occurs. We are about to use projection via the Select operator to create an object in which we will contain the comment, first name, last name, and any nicknames. But what object type should we create? We could create an element and make the comment, first name, and the remainder child elements of it, but that would expand the XML tree by adding a level. So, we must create something that will not add a level to the XML tree. An array of objects will work for this, because in C#, an array implements IEnumerable<T>, thereby making the array of objects work just like a sequence. As you probably recall from Chapter 7, when an IEnumerable is passed into a XElement constructor as its content, the sequence is enumerated, and each object in the sequence is applied to the element being constructed. We will use the C# collection initialization features to populate that array with the comment, first name, last name, and any nicknames:

```
            .Select(e => new object[] {
                new XComment(" BookParticipant "),
                new XElement("FirstName", (string)e.Element("FirstName")),
                new XElement("LastName", (string)e.Element("LastName")),
                e.Elements("Nickname")}})));

Console.WriteLine("Here is the transformed XML document:");
Console.WriteLine(xTransDocument);
```

At this point, we have projected an array containing a comment, a FirstName element, a LastName element, and however many Nickname elements there are in the source XML. Finally, we display the transformed XML document.

This example is actually quite complex. Notice that our array of objects includes an XComment object, two XElement objects, and an IEnumerable<XElement>. By projecting a newly instantiated array as the return value of the Select operator, a sequence of object[], IEnumerable<object[]>, is being returned as the content of the newly constructed BookParticipants element.

In this case, each object in that sequence is an array of objects, where the array contains the comment, the FirstName and LastName elements, and the sequence of Nickname elements. Because, as we just mentioned, an array of objects does not inject a level into the XML tree, the array adds its elements directly into the BookParticipants element.

This may be confusing; let's take a look at the results:

```
Here is the original XML document:
<BookParticipants>
  <BookParticipant type="Author">
    <FirstName>Joe</FirstName>
    <LastName>Rattz</LastName>
    <Nickname>Joey</Nickname>
    <Nickname>Null Pointer</Nickname>
  </BookParticipant>
  <BookParticipant type="Editor">
    <FirstName>Ewan</FirstName>
    <LastName>Buckingham</LastName>
  </BookParticipant>
</BookParticipants>


Here is the transformed XML document:
<BookParticipants>
  <!-- BookParticipant -->
  <FirstName>Joe</FirstName>
  <LastName>Rattz</LastName>
  <Nickname>Joey</Nickname>
  <Nickname>Null Pointer</Nickname>
  <!-- BookParticipant -->
  <FirstName>Ewan</FirstName>
  <LastName>Buckingham</LastName>
</BookParticipants>
```

The transformed XML matches the specification exactly. Bravo! The real nifty part of this example is how we project an array of objects, a non-XML class, to create peer XML elements without inflicting a level of XML to the tree.

Validation

An XML API would just not be complete without the ability to validate XML. So, LINQ to XML has the ability to validate an XML document against an XML schema.

The Extension Methods

LINQ to XML has addressed the need for validation by creating the System.Xml.Schema.Extensions static class, which contains the validation methods. These validation methods are implemented as extension methods.

Prototypes

Here is a list of some of the validation method prototypes available in the
`System.Xml.Schema.Extensions` class:

```
void Extensions.Validate(this XDocument source, XmlSchemaSet schemas,
  ValidationEventHandler validationEventHandler)

void Extensions.Validate(this XDocument source, XmlSchemaSet schemas,
  ValidationEventHandler validationEventHandler, bool addSchemaInfo)


void Extensions.Validate(this XElement source,
  XmlSchemaObject partialValidationType, XmlSchemaSet schemas,
  ValidationEventHandler validationEventHandler)

void Extensions.Validate(this XElement source,
  XmlSchemaObject partialValidationType, XmlSchemaSet schemas,
  ValidationEventHandler validationEventHandler, bool addSchemaInfo)


void Extensions.Validate(this XAttribute source,
  XmlSchemaObject partialValidationType, XmlSchemaSet schemas,
  ValidationEventHandler validationEventHandler)

void Extensions.Validate(this XAttribute source,
  XmlSchemaObject partialValidationType, XmlSchemaSet schemas,
  ValidationEventHandler validationEventHandler, bool addSchemaInfo)
```

There are two prototypes for each object type the method can be called on. These object types are
`XDocument`, `XElement`, and `XAttribute`. The second prototype for each object type merely adds a `bool`
argument specifying whether schema information should be added to the `XElement` and `XAttribute`
objects after validation. The first method for each object type, the ones without the `bool` argument, are
the same as passing `false` for the `addSchemaInfo` argument. In this case, no schema information would
be added to the LINQ to XML objects after validation.

To obtain the schema information for an `XElement` or `XAttribute` object, call the `GetSchemaInfo`
method on the object. If the schema information is not added because either the first prototype is called
or the second prototype is called and `false` is passed for the `addSchemaInfo` argument, the
`GetSchemaInfo` method will return `null`. Otherwise, it will return an object that implements
`IXmlSchemaInfo`. That object will contain properties named `SchemaElement`, which will return an
`XmlSchemaElement` object, and `SchemaAttribute`, which will return an `XmlSchemaAttribute` object,
assuming the element or attribute is valid. These objects can be used to obtain additional information
about the schema.

It is important to note that the schema information is not available *during* validation, only after
validation has completed. This means you cannot obtain the schema information in your validation
event handler. Calling the `GetSchemaInfo` method will return `null` in your validation event handler.
This also means that the validation must complete and that you must not throw an exception in your
validation event handler.

■ **Tip** Schema information is not available during validation, only after. Calling the GetSchemaInfo method in your validation event handling code will return null.

Notice that the Validate method prototypes for elements and attributes require that you pass an XmlSchemaObject as one of the arguments. This means that you must have already validated the document that they are in.

Lastly, if you pass null for the ValidationEventHandler argument, an exception of type XmlSchemaValidationException will be thrown should a validation error occur. This will be the simplest approach to validate an XML document.

Obtaining an XML Schema

Odds are good that if you are interested in validating your XML document, you either have, or know how to produce, an XSD schema file. Just in case you don't, we will demonstrate how to let the .NET Framework do it for you. Let's examine the example in Listing 9-12.

Listing 9-12. Creating an XSD Schema by Inferring It from an XML Document

```
XDocument xDocument = new XDocument(
  new XElement("BookParticipants",
    new XElement("BookParticipant",
      new XAttribute("type", "Author"),
      new XElement("FirstName", "Joe"),
      new XElement("LastName", "Rattz")),
    new XElement("BookParticipant",
      new XAttribute("type", "Editor"),
      new XElement("FirstName", "Ewan"),
      new XElement("LastName", "Buckingham"))));

Console.WriteLine("Here is the source XML document:");
Console.WriteLine("{0}{1}{1}", xDocument, System.Environment.NewLine);

xDocument.Save("bookparticipants.xml");

XmlSchemaInference infer = new XmlSchemaInference();
XmlSchemaSet schemaSet =
  infer.InferSchema(new XmlTextReader("bookparticipants.xml"));

XmlWriter w = XmlWriter.Create("bookparticipants.xsd");
foreach (XmlSchema schema in schemaSet.Schemas())
{
  schema.Write(w);
}
w.Close();
```

```
XDocument newDocument = XDocument.Load("bookparticipants.xsd");
Console.WriteLine("Here is the schema:");
Console.WriteLine("{0}{1}{1}", newDocument, System.Environment.NewLine);
```

In the previous code, we first create our typical XML document that we have been using in many of the examples and display it for inspection. Then, we save the XML document to disk. Next, we instantiate an XmlSchemaInference object and create an XmlSchemaSet by calling the InferSchema method on the XmlSchemaInference object. We create a writer and enumerate through the set of schemas, writing each to the bookparticipants.xsd file. Last, we load in the generated XSD schema file and display it. Here are the results:

```
Here is the source XML document:
<BookParticipants>
  <BookParticipant type="Author">
    <FirstName>Joe</FirstName>
    <LastName>Rattz</LastName>
  </BookParticipant>
  <BookParticipant type="Editor">
    <FirstName>Ewan</FirstName>
    <LastName>Buckingham</LastName>
  </BookParticipant>
</BookParticipants>


Here is the schema:
<xs:schema attributeFormDefault="unqualified" elementFormDefault="qualified"
    xmlns:xs="http://www.w3.org/2001/XMLSchema">
  <xs:element name="BookParticipants">
    <xs:complexType>
      <xs:sequence>
        <xs:element maxOccurs="unbounded" name="BookParticipant">
          <xs:complexType>
            <xs:sequence>
              <xs:element name="FirstName" type="xs:string" />
              <xs:element name="LastName" type="xs:string" />
            </xs:sequence>
            <xs:attribute name="type" type="xs:string" use="required" />
          </xs:complexType>
        </xs:element>
      </xs:sequence>
    </xs:complexType>
  </xs:element>
</xs:schema>
```

Obtaining the schema this way is not too painful. We will use this generated XSD schema file named bookparticipants.xsd in the validation examples. Also, you should notice that we use the XmlSchemaSet class in that example, which is used in the validation examples as well.

Examples

For the first example, we will demonstrate the simplest means of validating an XML document, which will be the approach many developers will take. To do this, we merely specify null as the ValidationEventHandler argument, as shown in Listing 9-13.

Listing 9-13. Validating an XML Document with Default Validation Event Handling

```
XDocument xDocument = new XDocument(
  new XElement("BookParticipants",
    new XElement("BookParticipant",
      new XAttribute("type", "Author"),
      new XElement("FirstName", "Joe"),
      new XElement("MiddleInitial", "C"),
      new XElement("LastName", "Rattz")),
    new XElement("BookParticipant",
      new XAttribute("type", "Editor"),
      new XElement("FirstName", "Ewan"),
      new XElement("LastName", "Buckingham")))));

Console.WriteLine("Here is the source XML document:");
Console.WriteLine("{0}{1}{1}", xDocument, System.Environment.NewLine);

XmlSchemaSet schemaSet = new XmlSchemaSet();
schemaSet.Add(null, "bookparticipants.xsd");

try
{
  xDocument.Validate(schemaSet, null);
  Console.WriteLine("Document validated successfully.");
}
catch (XmlSchemaValidationException ex)
{
  Console.WriteLine("Exception occurred: {0}", ex.Message);
  Console.WriteLine("Document validated unsuccessfully.");
}
```

In this example, we construct our typical XML document, except we add a MiddleInitial element to intentionally make the document invalid. We are using the schema we inferred in the previous example. Notice that for the ValidationEventHandler argument for the Validate method that we passed a null. This means that if a validation error occurs, an exception of type XmlSchemaValidationException will automatically be thrown. Here are the results:

```
Here is the source XML document:
<BookParticipants>
  <BookParticipant type="Author">
    <FirstName>Joe</FirstName>
    <MiddleInitial>C</MiddleInitial>
    <LastName>Rattz</LastName>
  </BookParticipant>
  <BookParticipant type="Editor">
    <FirstName>Ewan</FirstName>
    <LastName>Buckingham</LastName>
  </BookParticipant>
</BookParticipants>
```

```
Exception occurred: The element 'BookParticipant' has invalid child element
'MiddleInitial'. List of possible elements expected: 'LastName'.
Document validated unsuccessfully.
```

That worked like a charm. It was also very simple. Not too bad.

For the next example, we will validate our typical XML document, the one we used to infer the schema, against the schema we obtained by inference. Of course, since the schema was inferred from this very XML document, it should work. However, for this example, we will need a ValidationEventHandler method. Let's take a look at the one we are going to use.

My ValidationEventHandler

```
static void MyValidationEventHandler(object o, ValidationEventArgs vea)
{

  Console.WriteLine("A validation error occurred processing object type {0}.",
    o.GetType().Name);

  Console.WriteLine(vea.Message);
  throw (new Exception(vea.Message));
}
```

In that handler, we really don't do much except display the problem and throw an exception. Of course, the handling is completely up to our handler. It isn't required to throw an exception. We could choose to implement it so that it handles validation errors more gracefully, perhaps choosing to ignore any or specific errors.

Let's examine an example using that handler, as shown in Listing 9-14.

Listing 9-14. *Successfully Validating an XML Document Against an XSD Schema*

```
XDocument xDocument = new XDocument(
  new XElement("BookParticipants",
```

```
      new XElement("BookParticipant",
        new XAttribute("type", "Author"),
        new XElement("FirstName", "Joe"),
        new XElement("LastName", "Rattz")),
      new XElement("BookParticipant",
        new XAttribute("type", "Editor"),
        new XElement("FirstName", "Ewan"),
        new XElement("LastName", "Buckingham"))));

Console.WriteLine("Here is the source XML document:");
Console.WriteLine("{0}{1}{1}", xDocument, System.Environment.NewLine);

XmlSchemaSet schemaSet = new XmlSchemaSet();
schemaSet.Add(null, "bookparticipants.xsd");

try
{
  xDocument.Validate(schemaSet, MyValidationEventHandler);
  Console.WriteLine("Document validated successfully.");
}
catch (Exception ex)
{
  Console.WriteLine("Exception occurred: {0}", ex.Message);
  Console.WriteLine("Document validated unsuccessfully.");
}
```

In the example, we create our typical XML document and display it to the console. Next, we instantiate an XmlSchemaSet object and add the inferred schema file we created using the Add method. Next, we merely call the Validate extension method on the XML document passing it the schema set and our validation event handling method. Notice that we wrap the call to the Validate method in a try/catch block for safety's sake. Let's look at the results:

```
Here is the source XML document:
<BookParticipants>
  <BookParticipant type="Author">
    <FirstName>Joe</FirstName>
    <LastName>Rattz</LastName>
  </BookParticipant>
  <BookParticipant type="Editor">
    <FirstName>Ewan</FirstName>
    <LastName>Buckingham</LastName>
  </BookParticipant>
</BookParticipants>


Document validated successfully.
```

As you can see, the XML document is successfully validated. Now, let's try an example, shown in Listing 9-15, where the document is invalid.

Listing 9-15. *Unsuccessfully Validating an XML Document Against an XSD Schema*

```
XDocument xDocument = new XDocument(
  new XElement("BookParticipants",
    new XElement("BookParticipant",
      new XAttribute("type", "Author"),
      new XAttribute("language", "English"),
      new XElement("FirstName", "Joe"),
      new XElement("LastName", "Rattz")),
    new XElement("BookParticipant",
      new XAttribute("type", "Editor"),
      new XElement("FirstName", "Ewan"),
      new XElement("LastName", "Buckingham")))));

Console.WriteLine("Here is the source XML document:");
Console.WriteLine("{0}{1}{1}", xDocument, System.Environment.NewLine);

XmlSchemaSet schemaSet = new XmlSchemaSet();
schemaSet.Add(null, "bookparticipants.xsd");

try
{
  xDocument.Validate(schemaSet, MyValidationEventHandler);
  Console.WriteLine("Document validated successfully.");
}
catch (Exception ex)
{
  Console.WriteLine("Exception occurred: {0}", ex.Message);
  Console.WriteLine("Document validated unsuccessfully.");
}
```

This code is identical to the previous example, except we added an additional attribute, language. Since the schema doesn't specify this attribute, the XML document is not valid. Here are the results:

```
Here is the source XML document:
<BookParticipants>
  <BookParticipant type="Author" language="English">
    <FirstName>Joe</FirstName>
    <LastName>Rattz</LastName>
  </BookParticipant>
  <BookParticipant type="Editor">
    <FirstName>Ewan</FirstName>
    <LastName>Buckingham</LastName>
```

```
      </BookParticipant>
</BookParticipants>

A validation error occurred processing object type XAttribute.
The 'language' attribute is not declared.
Exception occurred: The 'language' attribute is not declared.
Document validated unsuccessfully.
```

As you can see, the XML document did not validate successfully. In the two previous examples, we create a named method, named MyValidationEventHandler, to handle the validation. Listing 9-16 is the same example as the previous except this time we use a lambda expression for the ValidationEventHandler instead of using the named method.

Listing 9-16. *Unsuccessfully Validating an XML Document Against an XSD Schema Using a Lambda Expression*

```
XDocument xDocument = new XDocument(
  new XElement("BookParticipants",
    new XElement("BookParticipant",
      new XAttribute("type", "Author"),
      new XAttribute("language", "English"),
      new XElement("FirstName", "Joe"),
      new XElement("LastName", "Rattz")),
    new XElement("BookParticipant",
      new XAttribute("type", "Editor"),
      new XElement("FirstName", "Ewan"),
      new XElement("LastName", "Buckingham"))));

Console.WriteLine("Here is the source XML document:");
Console.WriteLine("{0}{1}{1}", xDocument, System.Environment.NewLine);

XmlSchemaSet schemaSet = new XmlSchemaSet();
schemaSet.Add(null, "bookparticipants.xsd");

try
{
  xDocument.Validate(schemaSet, (o, vea) =>
    {
      Console.WriteLine(
        "A validation error occurred processing object type {0}.",
        o.GetType().Name);

      Console.WriteLine(vea.Message);

      throw (new Exception(vea.Message));
```

```
  });

  Console.WriteLine("Document validated successfully.");
}
catch (Exception ex)
{
  Console.WriteLine("Exception occurred: {0}", ex.Message);
  Console.WriteLine("Document validated unsuccessfully.");
}
```

Check that out. An entire method specified as a lambda expression. Do lambda expressions rock or what? Here are the results:

```
Here is the source XML document:
<BookParticipants>
  <BookParticipant type="Author" language="English">
    <FirstName>Joe</FirstName>
    <LastName>Rattz</LastName>
  </BookParticipant>
  <BookParticipant type="Editor">
    <FirstName>Ewan</FirstName>
    <LastName>Buckingham</LastName>
  </BookParticipant>
</BookParticipants>


A validation error occurred processing object type XAttribute.
The 'language' attribute is not declared.
Exception occurred: The 'language' attribute is not declared.
Document validated unsuccessfully.
```

Now, we'll try an example specifying to add the schema information, as shown in Listing 9-17.

Listing 9-17. *Unsuccessfully Validating an XML Document Against an XSD Schema Using a Lambda Expression and Specifying to Add Schema Information*

```
XDocument xDocument = new XDocument(
  new XElement("BookParticipants",
    new XElement("BookParticipant",
      new XAttribute("type", "Author"),
      new XElement("FirstName", "Joe"),
      new XElement("MiddleName", "Carson"),
      new XElement("LastName", "Rattz")),
    new XElement("BookParticipant",
      new XAttribute("type", "Editor"),
```

```
        new XElement("FirstName", "Ewan"),
        new XElement("LastName", "Buckingham")))));

Console.WriteLine("Here is the source XML document:");
Console.WriteLine("{0}{1}{1}", xDocument, System.Environment.NewLine);

XmlSchemaSet schemaSet = new XmlSchemaSet();
schemaSet.Add(null, "bookparticipants.xsd");

xDocument.Validate(schemaSet, (o, vea) =>
  {
    Console.WriteLine("An exception occurred processing object type {0}.",
      o.GetType().Name);

    Console.WriteLine("{0}{1}", vea.Message, System.Environment.NewLine);
  },
  true);

foreach(XElement element in xDocument.Descendants())
{
  Console.WriteLine("Element {0} is {1}", element.Name,
    element.GetSchemaInfo().Validity);

  XmlSchemaElement se = element.GetSchemaInfo().SchemaElement;
  if (se != null)
  {
    Console.WriteLine(
      "Schema element {0} must have MinOccurs = {1} and MaxOccurs = {2}{3}",
      se.Name, se.MinOccurs, se.MaxOccurs, System.Environment.NewLine);
  }
  else
  {
    //  Invalid elements will not have a SchemaElement.
    Console.WriteLine();
  }
}
```

This example starts like the previous. It creates an XML document. This time, though, we added an additional element for the first BookParticipant: MiddleName. This is invalid because it is not specified in the schema we are validating against. Unlike the previous example, we specify for the Validate method to add the schema information. Also, unlike the previous example, we are not throwing an exception in our validation event handling code. As you may recall, we mentioned previously that the validation must complete to have the schema information added, so your handler must not throw an exception. Therefore, we also removed the try/catch block as well.

After the validation completes, we are enumerating all the elements in the document and displaying whether they are valid. Additionally, we obtain the SchemaElement object from the added schema information. Notice that we make sure the SchemaElement property is not null, because if the element is not valid, the SchemaElement property may be null. After all, the element may not be valid because it

is not in the schema, so how could there be schema information? The same applies to the
SchemaAttribute property for invalid attributes. Once we have a SchemaElement object, we display its
Name, MinOccurs, and MaxOccurs properties.

Here are the results:

```
Here is the source XML document:
<BookParticipants>
  <BookParticipant type="Author">
    <FirstName>Joe</FirstName>
    <MiddleName>Carson</MiddleName>
    <LastName>Rattz</LastName>
  </BookParticipant>
  <BookParticipant type="Editor">
    <FirstName>Ewan</FirstName>
    <LastName>Buckingham</LastName>
  </BookParticipant>
</BookParticipants>


An exception occurred processing object type XElement.
The element 'BookParticipant' has invalid child element 'MiddleName'. List of
possible elements expected: 'LastName'.

Element BookParticipants is Invalid
Schema element BookParticipants must have MinOccurs = 1 and MaxOccurs = 1

Element BookParticipant is Invalid
Schema element BookParticipant must have MinOccurs = 1 and MaxOccurs =
79228162514264337593543950335

Element FirstName is Valid
Schema element FirstName must have MinOccurs = 1 and MaxOccurs = 1

Element MiddleName is Invalid

Element LastName is NotKnown

Element BookParticipant is Valid
Schema element BookParticipant must have MinOccurs = 1 and MaxOccurs =
79228162514264337593543950335

Element FirstName is Valid
Schema element FirstName must have MinOccurs = 1 and MaxOccurs = 1

Element LastName is Valid
Schema element LastName must have MinOccurs = 1 and MaxOccurs = 1
```

There are no real surprises in this output. Notice that the MaxOccurs property value for the BookParticipant element is a very large number. This is because in the schema, the *maxOccurs* attribute is specified to be "unbounded".

For the final pair of validation examples, we will use one of the Validate method prototypes that apply to validating elements. The first thing you will notice about it is that it has an argument that requires an XmlSchemaObject to be passed. This means the document must have already been validated. This seems odd. This is for a scenario where we have already validated once and need to revalidate a portion of the XML tree.

For this scenario, imagine we load an XML document and validate it to start. Next, we have allowed a user to update the data for one of the book participants and now need to update the XML document to reflect the user's changes, and we want to validate that portion of the XML tree again, after the updates. This is where the Validate method prototypes of the elements and attributes can come in handy.

Because this example, shown in Listing 9-18, is more complex than some of the previous examples, we will explain it as we go. First, to be a little different, and because we need an expanded schema to facilitate an edit to the XML tree, we will define the schema programmatically instead of loading it from a file, as we have in the previous examples.

Listing 9-18. *Successfully Validating an XML Element*

```
string schema =
  @"<?xml version='1.0' encoding='utf-8'?>
    <xs:schema attributeFormDefault='unqualified' elementFormDefault='qualified'
      xmlns:xs='http://www.w3.org/2001/XMLSchema'>
      <xs:element name='BookParticipants'>
        <xs:complexType>
          <xs:sequence>
            <xs:element maxOccurs='unbounded' name='BookParticipant'>
              <xs:complexType>
                <xs:sequence>
                  <xs:element name='FirstName' type='xs:string' />
                  <xs:element minOccurs='0' name='MiddleInitial'
                    type='xs:string' />
                  <xs:element name='LastName' type='xs:string' />
                </xs:sequence>
                <xs:attribute name='type' type='xs:string' use='required' />
              </xs:complexType>
            </xs:element>
          </xs:sequence>
        </xs:complexType>
      </xs:element>
    </xs:schema>";

XmlSchemaSet schemaSet = new XmlSchemaSet();
schemaSet.Add("", XmlReader.Create(new StringReader(schema)));
```

In the previous code, we merely copied the schema from the file that we have been using. We did a search on the double quotes and replaced them with single quotes. We also added a MiddleInitial element between the FirstName and LastName elements. Notice that we specify the minOccurs attribute as 0, so the element is not required. Next, we create a schema set from the schema. Next, it's time to create an XML document:

```
XDocument xDocument = new XDocument(
  new XElement("BookParticipants",
    new XElement("BookParticipant",
      new XAttribute("type", "Author"),
      new XElement("FirstName", "Joe"),
      new XElement("LastName", "Rattz")),
    new XElement("BookParticipant",
      new XAttribute("type", "Editor"),
      new XElement("FirstName", "Ewan"),
      new XElement("LastName", "Buckingham"))));

Console.WriteLine("Here is the source XML document:");
Console.WriteLine("{0}{1}{1}", xDocument, System.Environment.NewLine);
```

There is nothing new here. We just created the same document we usually do for the examples and displayed it. Now we will validate the document:

```
bool valid = true;
xDocument.Validate(schemaSet, (o, vea) =>
  {
    Console.WriteLine("An exception occurred processing object type {0}.",
      o.GetType().Name);

    Console.WriteLine(vea.Message);

    valid = false;
  }, true);

Console.WriteLine("Document validated {0}.{1}",
  valid ? "successfully" : "unsuccessfully",
  System.Environment.NewLine);
```

Notice that we validate a little differently than we have in previous examples. We initialize a bool to true, representing whether the document is valid. Inside the validation handler, we set it to false. So if a validation error occurs, valid will be set to false. We then check the value of valid after validation to determine whether the document is valid and display its validity. In this example, the document is valid at this point.

Now, it's time to imagine that we are allowing a user to edit any particular book participant. The user has edited the book participant whose first name is "Joe". So, we obtain a reference for that element, update it, and revalidate it after the update:

```
XElement bookParticipant = xDocument.Descendants("BookParticipant").
  Where(e => ((string)e.Element("FirstName")).Equals("Joe")).First();

bookParticipant.Element("FirstName").
```

```
    AddAfterSelf(new XElement("MiddleInitial", "C"));

valid = true;
bookParticipant.Validate(bookParticipant.GetSchemaInfo().SchemaElement, schemaSet,
  (o, vea) =>
  {
    Console.WriteLine("An exception occurred processing object type {0}.",
      o.GetType().Name);

    Console.WriteLine(vea.Message);

    valid = false;
  }, true);

Console.WriteLine("Element validated {0}.{1}",
  valid ? "successfully" : "unsuccessfully",
  System.Environment.NewLine);
```

As you can see, we initialize valid to true and call the Validate method, this time on the bookParticipant element instead of the entire document. Inside the validation event handler, we set valid to false. After validation of the book participant element, we display its validity. Here are the results:

```
Here is the source XML document:
<BookParticipants>
  <BookParticipant type="Author">
    <FirstName>Joe</FirstName>
    <LastName>Rattz</LastName>
  </BookParticipant>
  <BookParticipant type="Editor">
    <FirstName>Ewan</FirstName>
    <LastName>Buckingham</LastName>
  </BookParticipant>
</BookParticipants>


Document validated successfully.

Element validated successfully.
```

As you can see, the validation of the element is successful. For the final example, we have the same code, except this time when we update the BookParticipant element we will create a MiddleName element, as opposed to MiddleInitial, which is not valid. Listing 9-19 is the code.

Listing 9-19. *Unsuccessfully Validating an XML Element*

```
string schema =
  @"<?xml version='1.0' encoding='utf-8'?>
    <xs:schema attributeFormDefault='unqualified' elementFormDefault='qualified'
     xmlns:xs='http://www.w3.org/2001/XMLSchema'>
      <xs:element name='BookParticipants'>
        <xs:complexType>
          <xs:sequence>
            <xs:element maxOccurs='unbounded' name='BookParticipant'>
              <xs:complexType>
                <xs:sequence>
                  <xs:element name='FirstName' type='xs:string' />
                  <xs:element minOccurs='0' name='MiddleInitial' type='xs:string'
/>
                  <xs:element name='LastName' type='xs:string' />
                </xs:sequence>
                <xs:attribute name='type' type='xs:string' use='required' />
              </xs:complexType>
            </xs:element>
          </xs:sequence>
        </xs:complexType>
      </xs:element>
    </xs:schema>";

XmlSchemaSet schemaSet = new XmlSchemaSet();
schemaSet.Add("", XmlReader.Create(new StringReader(schema)));

XDocument xDocument = new XDocument(
  new XElement("BookParticipants",
    new XElement("BookParticipant",
      new XAttribute("type", "Author"),
      new XElement("FirstName", "Joe"),
      new XElement("LastName", "Rattz")),
    new XElement("BookParticipant",
      new XAttribute("type", "Editor"),
      new XElement("FirstName", "Ewan"),
      new XElement("LastName", "Buckingham"))));

Console.WriteLine("Here is the source XML document:");
Console.WriteLine("{0}{1}{1}", xDocument, System.Environment.NewLine);

bool valid = true;
xDocument.Validate(schemaSet, (o, vea) =>
  {
    Console.WriteLine("An exception occurred processing object type {0}.",
      o.GetType().Name);
```

```
    Console.WriteLine(vea.Message);

    valid = false;
  }, true);

Console.WriteLine("Document validated {0}.{1}",
  valid ? "successfully" : "unsuccessfully",
  System.Environment.NewLine);

XElement bookParticipant = xDocument.Descendants("BookParticipant").
  Where(e => ((string)e.Element("FirstName")).Equals("Joe")).First();

bookParticipant.Element("FirstName").
  AddAfterSelf(new XElement("MiddleName", "Carson"));

valid = true;
bookParticipant.Validate(bookParticipant.GetSchemaInfo().SchemaElement, schemaSet,
  (o, vea) =>
  {
    Console.WriteLine("An exception occurred processing object type {0}.",
      o.GetType().Name);

    Console.WriteLine(vea.Message);

    valid = false;
  }, true);

Console.WriteLine("Element validated {0}.{1}",
  valid ? "successfully" : "unsuccessfully",
  System.Environment.NewLine);
```

This code is identical to the previous example except instead of adding a MiddleInitial element, we added a MiddleName element that is invalid. Here are the results:

```
Here is the source XML document:
<BookParticipants>
  <BookParticipant type="Author">
    <FirstName>Joe</FirstName>
    <LastName>Rattz</LastName>
  </BookParticipant>
  <BookParticipant type="Editor">
    <FirstName>Ewan</FirstName>
    <LastName>Buckingham</LastName>
  </BookParticipant>
</BookParticipants>
```

```
Document validated successfully.

An exception occurred processing object type XElement.
The element 'BookParticipant' has invalid child element 'MiddleName'. List of
possible elements expected: 'MiddleInitial, LastName'.

Element validated unsuccessfully.
```

As you can see, the element is no longer valid. Now, this example may seem a little hokey because we said to imagine a user is editing the document. No developer in their right mind would create a user interface that would intentionally allow a user to create edits that would be invalid. But imagine if that user is in reality some other process on the XML document. Perhaps you passed the XML document to someone else's program to make some update and you know they personally have it in for you and are seeking your personal destruction. Now it may make sense to revalidate. You know you can't trust them.

XPath

If you are accustomed to using XPath, you can also gain some XPath query capabilities thanks to the System.Xml.XPath.Extensions class in the System.Xml.XPath namespace. This class adds XPath search capability via extension methods.

Prototypes

Here is a list of some of the method prototypes available in the System.Xml.XPath.Extensions class:

```
XPathNavigator Extensions.CreateNavigator(this XNode node);
XPathNavigator Extensions.CreateNavigator(this XNode node, XmlNameTable nameTable);

object Extensions.XPathEvaluate(this XNode node, string expression);
object Extensions.XPathEvaluate(this XNode node, string expression,
  IXmlNamespaceResolver resolver);

XElement Extensions.XPathSelectElement(this XNode node, string expression);
XElement Extensions.XPathSelectElement(this XNode node, string expression,
  IXmlNamespaceResolver resolver);

IEnumerable<XElement> Extensions.XPathSelectElements(this XNode node,
  string expression);
IEnumerable<XElement> Extensions.XPathSelectElements(this XNode node,
  string expression, IXmlNamespaceResolver resolver);
```

Examples

Using these extension methods, it is possible to query a LINQ to XML document using XPath search expressions. Listing 9-20 is an example.

Listing 9-20. *Querying XML with XPath Syntax*

```
XDocument xDocument = new XDocument(
  new XElement("BookParticipants",
    new XElement("BookParticipant",
      new XAttribute("type", "Author"),
      new XElement("FirstName", "Joe"),
      new XElement("LastName", "Rattz")),
    new XElement("BookParticipant",
      new XAttribute("type", "Editor"),
      new XElement("FirstName", "Ewan"),
      new XElement("LastName", "Buckingham"))));

XElement bookParticipant = xDocument.XPathSelectElement(
  "//BookParticipants/BookParticipant[FirstName='Joe']");

Console.WriteLine(bookParticipant);
```

As you can see, we created our typical XML document. We didn't display the document this time, though. We called the `XPathSelectElement` method on the document and provided an XPath search expression to find the `BookParticipant` element whose `FirstName` element's value is `"Joe"`. Here are the results:

```
<BookParticipant type="Author">
  <FirstName>Joe</FirstName>
  <LastName>Rattz</LastName>
</BookParticipant>
```

Using the XPath extension methods, you can obtain a reference to a `System.Xml.XPath.XPathNavigator` object to navigate your XML document, perform an XPath query to return an element or sequence of elements, or evaluate an XPath query expression.

Summary

At this point, if you came into this chapter without any knowledge of XML, we can only assume you are overwhelmed. If you did have a basic understanding of XML, but not of LINQ to XML, we hope we have made this understandable for you. The power and flexibility of the LINQ to XML API is quite intoxicating.

Having written the many examples in this chapter and the previous LINQ to XML chapters, we can't tell you how useful we find the LINQ to XML API in real production code. The fact is that with LINQ to XML, because XML creation is largely based on elements rather than documents coupled with the capability of functional construction, creating XML is painless. It might even be fun. Combine the easy creation with the intuitive traversal and modification, and it becomes a joy to work with—especially considering the alternatives.

Having all this ease of use working with XML piled on top of a powerfully flexible query language makes LINQ to XML our personal favorite part of LINQ. If you find yourself dreading XML or intimidated to work with it, we think you will find the LINQ to XML API quite pleasant.

PART 4

LINQ to DataSet

CHAPTER 10

■ ■ ■

LINQ to DataSet Operators

Although we haven't covered LINQ to SQL yet, let us mention at this time that to utilize LINQ to SQL for a given database, source code classes must be generated for that database and compiled, or a mapping file must be created. This means that performing LINQ queries with LINQ to SQL on a database that is unknown until runtime is not possible. Additionally, LINQ to SQL works only with Microsoft SQL Server. What is a developer to do?

The LINQ to DataSet operators allow a developer to perform LINQ queries on a `DataSet`, and since a `DataSet` can be obtained using normal ADO.NET SQL queries, LINQ to DataSet allows LINQ queries over *any* database that can be queried with ADO.NET. This provides a far more dynamic database-querying interface than LINQ to SQL.

You may be wondering, under what circumstances would you not know the database until runtime? It is true that for the typical application, the database is known while the application is being developed, and therefore LINQ to DataSet is not as necessary. But what about a database utility type application? For example, consider an application such as SQL Server Enterprise Manager. It doesn't know what databases are going to be installed on the server until runtime. The Enterprise Manager application allows you to examine whatever databases are installed on the server, with whatever tables are in a specified database. There is no way the Enterprise Manager application developer could generate the LINQ to SQL classes at compile time for *your* database. This is when LINQ to DataSet becomes a necessity.

Although this part of the book is named "LINQ to DataSet," you will find that the added operators really pertain to `DataTable`, `DataRow`, and `DataColumn` objects. Don't be surprised that you don't see `DataSet` objects referenced often in this chapter. We understand that in real-life circumstances, your `DataTable` objects will almost always come from `DataSet` objects. However, for the purpose of database independence, brevity, and clarity, we have intentionally created simple `DataTable` objects programmatically, rather than retrieved them from a database, for most of the examples.

The LINQ to DataSet operators consist of several special operators from multiple assemblies and namespaces that allow the developer to do the following:

- Perform set operations on sequences of `DataRow` objects

- Retrieve and set `DataColumn` values

- Obtain a LINQ standard `IEnumerable<T>` sequence from a `DataTable` so Standard Query Operators may be called

- Copy modified sequences of `DataRow` objects to a `DataTable`

In addition to these LINQ to DataSet operators, once you have called the AsEnumerable operator, you can call the LINQ to Objects Standard Query Operators on the returned sequence of DataRow objects, resulting in even more power and flexibility.

Assembly References

For the examples in this chapter, you will need to add references to your project for the System.Data.dll and System.Data.DataSetExtensions.dll assembly DLLs, if they have not already been added.

Referenced Namespaces

To use the LINQ to DataSet operators, add a using directive to the top of your code for the System.Linq and System.Data namespaces if they are not already there:

```
using System.Data;
using System.Linq;
```

This will allow your code to find the LINQ to DataSet operators.

Common Code for the Examples

Virtually every example in this chapter will use a DataTable object on which to perform LINQ to DataSet queries. In production code, you would typically obtain these DataTable objects by querying a database. However, for some of these examples, we present situations where the data conditions in a typical database table will not suffice. For example, we need duplicate records to demonstrate the Distinct method. Rather than jump through hoops trying to manipulate the database to contain the data we may need, we programmatically create a DataTable containing the specific data we need for each example. This also relieves you of the burden of having a database for testing the majority of these examples.

Since we will not actually be querying a database for the DataTable objects (and to make creating the DataTable objects easy), we generate them from an array of objects of a predefined class. For the predefined class, we use the Student class.

A Simple Class with Two Public Members

```
class Student
{
    public int Id;
    public string Name;
}
```

You should just imagine that we are querying a table named Students where each record is a student, and the table contains two columns: Id and Name.

To make creating the `DataTable` simple and to prevent obscuring the relevant details of each example, we use a common method to convert an array of `Student` objects into a `DataTable` object. This allows the data to easily vary from example to example. Here is that common method:

Converting an Array of Student Objects to a DataTable

```
static DataTable GetDataTable(Student[] students)
{
  DataTable table = new DataTable();

  table.Columns.Add("Id", typeof(Int32));
  table.Columns.Add("Name", typeof(string));

  foreach (Student student in students)
  {
    table.Rows.Add(student.Id, student.Name);
  }

  return (table);
}
```

There isn't anything complex in this method. We just instantiate a `DataTable` object, add two columns, and add a row for each element in the passed `students` array.

For many of the examples of the LINQ to DataSet operators, we need to display a `DataTable` for the results of the code to be clear. Although the data in the `DataTable` varies, the code needed to display the `DataTable` object's header will not. Instead of repeating this code throughout all the examples, we create the following method and call it in any example needing to display a `DataTable` header:

The OutputDataTableHeader Method

```
static void OutputDataTableHeader(DataTable dt, int columnWidth)
{
    string format = string.Format("{0}0,-{1}{2}", "{", columnWidth, "}");

    //  Display the column headings.
    foreach(DataColumn column in dt.Columns)
    {
        Console.Write(format, column.ColumnName);
    }
    Console.WriteLine();
    foreach(DataColumn column in dt.Columns)
    {
        for(int i = 0; i < columnWidth; i++)
        {
            Console.Write("=");
        }
    }
```

```
        Console.WriteLine();
}
```

The purpose of the method is to output the header of a DataTable in a tabular form.

DataRow Set Operators

As you may recall, in the LINQ to Objects API, there are a handful of Standard Query Operators that exist for the purpose of making sequence set-type comparisons. We are referring to the Distinct, Except, Intersect, Union, and SequenceEqual operators. Each of these operators performs a set operation on two sequences.

For these set-type operators, determining sequence element equality is necessary to perform the set operation. These operators perform comparisons by calling the GetHashCode and Equals methods on the elements. For a DataRow, this results in a reference comparison, which is not the desired behavior. This will result in the wrong determination of element equality, causing the operators to return unexpected results. Because of this, each of these operators has an additional prototype that we omitted in the LINQ to Objects chapters; this additional prototype allows an IEqualityComparer object to be provided as an argument. Conveniently, a comparer object has been provided for us specifically for these versions of the operators, System.Data.DataRowComparer.Default. This comparer class is in the System.Data namespace in the System.Data.Entity.dll assembly. This comparer determines element equality by comparing the number of columns and the static data type of each column and using the IComparable interface on the column's dynamic data type if that type implements the interface; otherwise, it calls the System.Object's static Equals method.

Each of these additional operator prototypes is defined in the System.Linq.Enumerable static class just as the other prototypes of these operators are.

In this section, we provide some examples to illustrate the incorrect and, more importantly, correct way to make these sequence comparisons when working with DataSet objects.

Distinct

The Distinct operator removes duplicate rows from a sequence of objects. It returns an object that, when enumerated, enumerates a source sequence of objects and returns a sequence of objects with the duplicate rows removed. Typically, this operator determines duplicates by calling each element's data type's GetHashCode and Equals methods. However, for DataRow type objects, this would cause an incorrect result.

Because we are going to call the additional prototype and provide the System.Data.DataRowComparerDefault comparer object, the element equality will be properly determined. With it, a row is deemed to be a duplicate by comparing DataRow objects using the number of columns in a row and the static data type of each column and then using the IComparable interface on each column if its dynamic data type implements the IComparable interface, or calling the static Equals method in System.Object if it does not.

Prototypes

The Distinct operator has one prototype we will cover.

The Distinct Prototype

```
public static IEnumerable<T> Distinct<T> (
  this IEnumerable<T> source,
  IEqualityComparer<T> comparer);
```

Examples

In the first example, we create a DataTable from an array of Student objects using our common GetDataTable method, and the array will have one duplicate in it. The record whose Id is equal to 1 is repeated in the array. We then display the DataTable. This shows that the record is in the DataTable twice. Then we remove any duplicate rows by calling the Distinct operator and display the DataTable again, showing that the duplicate row has been removed. Listing 10-1 shows the code.

Listing 10-1. *The Distinct Operator with an Equality Comparer*

```
Student[] students = {
  new Student { Id = 1, Name = "Joe Rattz" },
  new Student { Id = 6, Name = "Ulyses Hutchens" },
  new Student { Id = 19, Name = "Bob Tanko" },
  new Student { Id = 45, Name = "Erin Doutensal" },
  new Student { Id = 1, Name = "Joe Rattz" },
  new Student { Id = 12, Name = "Bob Mapplethorpe" },
  new Student { Id = 17, Name = "Anthony Adams" },
  new Student { Id = 32, Name = "Dignan Stephens" }
};

DataTable dt = GetDataTable(students);

Console.WriteLine("{0}Before calling Distinct(){0}",
  System.Environment.NewLine);

OutputDataTableHeader(dt, 15);

foreach (DataRow dataRow in dt.Rows)
{
  Console.WriteLine("{0,-15}{1,-15}",
    dataRow.Field<int>(0),
    dataRow.Field<string>(1));
}

IEnumerable<DataRow> distinct =
  dt.AsEnumerable().Distinct(DataRowComparer.Default);

Console.WriteLine("{0}After calling Distinct(){0}",
  System.Environment.NewLine);
```

```
OutputDataTableHeader(dt, 15);

foreach (DataRow dataRow in distinct)
{
  Console.WriteLine("{0,-15}{1,-15}",
    dataRow.Field<int>(0),
    dataRow.Field<string>(1));
}
```

Notice that we use the AsEnumerable method to get a sequence of DataRow objects from the DataTable because that is what we must call the Distinct operator on. Also notice that, in the students array, the record with an Id equal to 1 is repeated.

You no doubt noticed that we call a method named Field on the DataRow object. For now, just understand that this is a convenient helper method that obtains a DataColumn object's value from a DataRow. We cover the Field<T> operator in depth later in the "DataRow Field Operators" section of this chapter.

Here are the results:

```
Before calling Distinct()

Id              Name
==============================
1               Joe Rattz
6               Ulyses Hutchens
19              Bob Tanko
45              Erin Doutensal
1               Joe Rattz
12              Bob Mapplethorpe
17              Anthony Adams
32              Dignan Stephens

After calling Distinct()

Id              Name
==============================
1               Joe Rattz
6               Ulyses Hutchens
19              Bob Tanko
45              Erin Doutensal
12              Bob Mapplethorpe
17              Anthony Adams
32              Dignan Stephens
```

Notice that in the results, before we call the Distinct operator, the record whose Id is 1 is repeated and that after calling the Distinct operator, the second occurrence of that record has been removed.

For a second example, we are going to demonstrate the results if we had called the `Distinct` operator without specifying the comparer object. Listing 10-2 shows the code.

Listing 10-2. The Distinct Operator Without an Equality Comparer

```
Student[] students = {
  new Student { Id = 1, Name = "Joe Rattz" },
  new Student { Id = 6, Name = "Ulyses Hutchens" },
  new Student { Id = 19, Name = "Bob Tanko" },
  new Student { Id = 45, Name = "Erin Doutensal" },
  new Student { Id = 1, Name = "Joe Rattz" },
  new Student { Id = 12, Name = "Bob Mapplethorpe" },
  new Student { Id = 17, Name = "Anthony Adams" },
  new Student { Id = 32, Name = "Dignan Stephens" }
};

DataTable dt = GetDataTable(students);

Console.WriteLine("{0}Before calling Distinct(){0}",
  System.Environment.NewLine);

OutputDataTableHeader(dt, 15);

foreach (DataRow dataRow in dt.Rows)
{
  Console.WriteLine("{0,-15}{1,-15}",
    dataRow.Field<int>(0),
    dataRow.Field<string>(1));
}

IEnumerable<DataRow> distinct = dt.AsEnumerable().Distinct();

Console.WriteLine("{0}After calling Distinct(){0}",
  System.Environment.NewLine);

OutputDataTableHeader(dt, 15);

foreach (DataRow dataRow in distinct)
{
  Console.WriteLine("{0,-15}{1,-15}",
    dataRow.Field<int>(0),
    dataRow.Field<string>(1));
}
```

The difference between this code and the previous example is that the call to the `Distinct` operator does not have an equality comparer provided. Will it remove the duplicate row? Let's take a look:

```
Before calling Distinct()

Id              Name
==============================
1               Joe Rattz
6               Ulyses Hutchens
19              Bob Tanko
45              Erin Doutensal
1               Joe Rattz
12              Bob Mapplethorpe
17              Anthony Adams
32              Dignan Stephens

After calling Distinct()

Id              Name
==============================
1               Joe Rattz
6               Ulyses Hutchens
19              Bob Tanko
45              Erin Doutensal
1               Joe Rattz
12              Bob Mapplethorpe
17              Anthony Adams
32              Dignan Stephens
```

No, it did not remove the duplicate—these two examples are comparing rows differently.

Except

The Except operator produces a sequence of DataRow objects that are in the first sequence of DataRow objects that do not exist in the second sequence of DataRow objects. The operator returns an object that, when enumerated, enumerates the second sequence of DataRow objects collecting the unique elements, followed by enumerating the first sequence of DataRow objects removing those elements from the collection that also occur in the second sequence and returning the results as they are generated.

To determine that elements from the same sequence are unique and that one element in one sequence is or is not equal to an element in the other sequence, the operator must be able to determine whether two elements are equal. Typically, this operator determines element equality by calling each element's data type's GetHashCode and Equals methods. However, for DataRow type objects, this would cause an incorrect result.

Because we are going to call the additional prototype and provide the System.Data.DataRowComparer.Default comparer object, the element equality will be properly determined. With it, a row is deemed to be a duplicate by comparing DataRow objects using the number of columns in a row and the static data type of each column and then using the IComparable interface on each column if its dynamic data type implements the `IComparable` interface, or calling the static `Equals` method in `System.Object` if it does not.

Prototypes

The `Except` operator has one prototype we will cover.

The Except Prototype

```
public static IEnumerable<T> Except<T> (
  this IEnumerable<T> first,
  IEnumerable<T> second,
  IEqualityComparer<T> comparer);
```

Examples

In this example, we call the `Except` operator twice. The first time, we pass the `System.Data.DataRowComparer.Default` comparer object, so the results of the first query with the `Except` operator should be correct. The second time we call the `Except` operator, we will not pass the comparer object. This causes the results of that query to be incorrect. Listing 10-3 shows the code.

Listing 10-3. The Except Operator with and Without the Comparer Object

```
Student[] students = {
  new Student { Id = 1, Name = "Joe Rattz" },
  new Student { Id = 7, Name = "Anthony Adams" },
  new Student { Id = 13, Name = "Stacy Sinclair" },
  new Student { Id = 72, Name = "Dignan Stephens" }
};

Student[] students2 = {
  new Student { Id = 5, Name = "Abe Henry" },
  new Student { Id = 7, Name = "Anthony Adams" },
  new Student { Id = 29, Name = "Future Man" },
  new Student { Id = 72, Name = "Dignan Stephens" }
};

DataTable dt1 = GetDataTable(students);
IEnumerable<DataRow> seq1 = dt1.AsEnumerable();
DataTable dt2 = GetDataTable(students2);
IEnumerable<DataRow> seq2 = dt2.AsEnumerable();

IEnumerable<DataRow> except =
  seq1.Except(seq2, System.Data.DataRowComparer.Default);
```

```
Console.WriteLine("{0}Results of Except() with comparer{0}",
  System.Environment.NewLine);

OutputDataTableHeader(dt1, 15);

foreach (DataRow dataRow in except)
{
  Console.WriteLine("{0,-15}{1,-15}",
    dataRow.Field<int>(0),
    dataRow.Field<string>(1));
}

except = seq1.Except(seq2);

Console.WriteLine("{0}Results of Except() without comparer{0}",
  System.Environment.NewLine);

OutputDataTableHeader(dt1, 15);

foreach (DataRow dataRow in except)
{
  Console.WriteLine("{0,-15}{1,-15}",
    dataRow.Field<int>(0),
    dataRow.Field<string>(1));
}
```

We create two DataTable objects that are populated from the Student arrays. We create sequences from each DataTable object by calling the AsEnumerable method. We then call the Except operator on the two sequences and display the results of each. As you can see, the first time we call the Except operator, we pass the System.Data.DataRowComparer.Default comparer object. The second time we do not.

Let's look at the results of that code by pressing Ctrl+F5:

```
Results of Except() with comparer

Id              Name
===============================
1               Joe Rattz
13              Stacy Sinclair

Results of Except() without comparer

Id              Name
===============================
1               Joe Rattz
```

7	Anthony Adams
13	Stacy Sinclair
72	Dignan Stephens

As you can see, the Except operator called with the System.Data.DataRowComparer.Default comparer object is able to properly determine the element equality for the two sequences, whereas the Except operator without the comparer object does not.

Intersect

The Intersect operator produces a sequence of DataRow objects that is the intersection of two sequences of DataRow objects. It returns an object that when enumerated enumerates the second sequence of DataRow objects collecting the unique elements, followed by enumerating the first sequence of DataRow objects, returning those elements occurring in both sequences as they are generated.

To determine that elements from the same sequence are unique and that one element in one sequence is or is not equal to an element in the other sequence, the operator must be able to determine whether two elements are equal. Typically, this operator determines element equality by calling each element's data type's GetHashCode and Equals methods. However, for DataRow type objects, this would cause an incorrect result.

Because we are going to call the additional prototype and provide the System.Data.DataRowComparer.Default comparer object, the element equality will be properly determined. With it, a row is deemed to be a duplicate by comparing DataRow objects using the number of columns in a row and the static data type of each column and then using the IComparable interface on each column if its dynamic data type implements the IComparable interface, or calling the static Equals method in System.Object if it does not.

Prototypes

The Intersect operator has one prototype we will cover.

The Intersect Prototype

```
public static IEnumerable<T> Intersect<T> (
  this IEnumerable<T> first,
  IEnumerable<T> second,
  IEqualityComparer<T> comparer);
```

Examples

In this example, we use the same basic code we use in the Except example but change the operator calls from Except to Intersect. Listing 10-4 shows that code.

Listing 10-4. The Intersect Operator with and Without the Comparer Object

```
Student[] students = {
  new Student { Id = 1, Name = "Joe Rattz" },
  new Student { Id = 7, Name = "Anthony Adams" },
  new Student { Id = 13, Name = "Stacy Sinclair" },
  new Student { Id = 72, Name = "Dignan Stephens" }
};

Student[] students2 = {
  new Student { Id = 5, Name = "Abe Henry" },
  new Student { Id = 7, Name = "Anthony Adams" },
  new Student { Id = 29, Name = "Future Man" },
  new Student { Id = 72, Name = "Dignan Stephens" }
};

DataTable dt1 = GetDataTable(students);
IEnumerable<DataRow> seq1 = dt1.AsEnumerable();
DataTable dt2 = GetDataTable(students2);
IEnumerable<DataRow> seq2 = dt2.AsEnumerable();

IEnumerable<DataRow> intersect =
  seq1.Intersect(seq2, System.Data.DataRowComparer.Default);

Console.WriteLine("{0}Results of Intersect() with comparer{0}",
  System.Environment.NewLine);

OutputDataTableHeader(dt1, 15);

foreach (DataRow dataRow in intersect)
{
  Console.WriteLine("{0,-15}{1,-15}",
    dataRow.Field<int>(0),
    dataRow.Field<string>(1));
}

intersect = seq1.Intersect(seq2);

Console.WriteLine("{0}Results of Intersect() without comparer{0}",
  System.Environment.NewLine);

OutputDataTableHeader(dt1, 15);

foreach (DataRow dataRow in intersect)
{
  Console.WriteLine("{0,-15}{1,-15}",
    dataRow.Field<int>(0),
```

```
    dataRow.Field<string>(1));
}
```

There is nothing new here. We create a couple of `DataTable` objects from the two `Student` arrays
and obtain sequences from them. We then call the `Intersect` operator first with the comparer object
and then without. We display the results after each `Intersect` call. Let's look at the results of that code
by pressing Ctrl+F5:

```
Results of Intersect() with comparer

Id              Name
==============================
7               Anthony Adams
72              Dignan Stephens

Results of Intersect() without comparer

Id              Name
==============================
```

As you can see, the `Intersect` operator with the comparer is able to properly determine the
element equality from the two sequences, whereas the `Intersect` operator without the comparer is not.

Union

The `Union` operator produces a sequence of `DataRow` objects that is the union of two sequences of
`DataRow` objects. It returns an object that, when enumerated, enumerates the first sequence of `DataRow`
objects, followed by the elements of the second sequence of `DataRow` that were not contained in the first
sequence.

To determine that elements have already been returned, the operator must be able to determine
whether two elements are equal. Typically, this operator determines element equality by calling each
element's data type's `GetHashCode` and `Equals` methods. However, for `DataRow` type objects, this would
cause an incorrect result.

Because we are going to call the additional prototype and provide the
`System.Data.DataRowComparer.Default` comparer object, the element equality will be properly
determined. With it, a row is deemed to be a duplicate by comparing `DataRow` objects using the number
of columns in a row and the static data type of each column and then using the `IComparable` interface
on each column if its dynamic data type implements the `IComparable` interface, or calling the static
`Equals` method in `System.Object` if it does not.

Prototypes

The `Union` operator has one prototype we will cover.

The Union Prototype

```
public static IEnumerable<T> Union<T> (
  this IEnumerable<T> first,
  IEnumerable<T> second,
  IEqualityComparer<T> comparer);
```

Examples

In this example, we use the same basic code we use in the Intersect example, except we will change the operator calls from Intersect to Union. Listing 10-5 shows that code.

Listing 10-5. The Union Operator with and Without the Comparer Object

```
Student[] students = {
  new Student { Id = 1, Name = "Joe Rattz" },
  new Student { Id = 7, Name = "Anthony Adams" },
  new Student { Id = 13, Name = "Stacy Sinclair" },
  new Student { Id = 72, Name = "Dignan Stephens" }
};

Student[] students2 = {
  new Student { Id = 5, Name = "Abe Henry" },
  new Student { Id = 7, Name = "Anthony Adams" },
  new Student { Id = 29, Name = "Future Man" },
  new Student { Id = 72, Name = "Dignan Stephens" }
};

DataTable dt1 = GetDataTable(students);
IEnumerable<DataRow> seq1 = dt1.AsEnumerable();
DataTable dt2 = GetDataTable(students2);
IEnumerable<DataRow> seq2 = dt2.AsEnumerable();

IEnumerable<DataRow> union =
  seq1.Union(seq2, System.Data.DataRowComparer.Default);

Console.WriteLine("{0}Results of Union() with comparer{0}",
  System.Environment.NewLine);

OutputDataTableHeader(dt1, 15);

foreach (DataRow dataRow in union)
{
  Console.WriteLine("{0,-15}{1,-15}",
    dataRow.Field<int>(0),
    dataRow.Field<string>(1));
}
```

```
union = seq1.Union(seq2);

Console.WriteLine("{0}Results of Union() without comparer{0}",
  System.Environment.NewLine);

OutputDataTableHeader(dt1, 15);

foreach (DataRow dataRow in union)
{
  Console.WriteLine("{0,-15}{1,-15}",
    dataRow.Field<int>(0),
    dataRow.Field<string>(1));
}
```

Again, there is nothing new here. We create a couple of DataTable objects from the two Student arrays and obtain sequences from them. We then call the Union operator first with the comparer object and then without. We display the results after each Union call. Here are the results:

```
Results of Union() with comparer

Id              Name
==============================
1               Joe Rattz
7               Anthony Adams
13              Stacy Sinclair
72              Dignan Stephens
5               Abe Henry
29              Future Man

Results of Union() without comparer

Id              Name
==============================
1               Joe Rattz
7               Anthony Adams
13              Stacy Sinclair
72              Dignan Stephens
5               Abe Henry
7               Anthony Adams
29              Future Man
72              Dignan Stephens
```

Notice that the results of the Union operator with the comparer object are correct, but the results of the Union operator without the comparer object are not.

SequenceEqual

The SequenceEqual operator compares two sequences of DataRow objects to determine whether they are equal. It enumerates two source sequences, comparing the corresponding DataRow objects. If the two source sequences have the same number of records, and if all the corresponding DataRow objects are equal, true is returned. Otherwise, false is returned if the two sequences are not equal.

This operator must be able to determine whether two elements are equal. Typically, this operator determines element equality by calling each element's data type's GetHashCode and Equals methods. However, for DataRow type objects, this would cause an incorrect result.

Because we are going to call the additional prototype and provide the System.Data.DataRowComparer.Default comparer object, the element equality will be properly determined. With it, a row is deemed to be a duplicate by comparing DataRow objects using the number of columns in a row and the static data type of each column and then using the IComparable interface on each column if its dynamic data type implements the IComparable interface, or calling the static Equals method in System.Object if it does not.

Prototypes

The SequenceEqual operator has one prototype we will cover.

The SequenceEqual Prototype

```
public static bool SequenceEqual<T> (
  this IEnumerable<T> first,
  IEnumerable<T> second,
  IEqualityComparer<T> comparer);
```

Examples

In this example of the SequenceEqual operator, we build two identical sequences of DataRow objects and compare them first with the SequenceEqual operator with a comparer object followed by a comparison with the SequenceEqual operator without a comparer object. Because of the way equality comparisons are handled by the two different operator calls, the SequenceEqual operator call with the comparer object returns that the two sequences are equal, while the SequenceEqual operator call without the comparer object returns that the two sequences are not equal. Listing 10-6 shows the code.

Listing 10-6. The SequenceEqual Operator with and Without a Comparer Object

```
Student[] students = {
  new Student { Id = 1, Name = "Joe Rattz" },
  new Student { Id = 7, Name = "Anthony Adams" },
  new Student { Id = 13, Name = "Stacy Sinclair" },
  new Student { Id = 72, Name = "Dignan Stephens" }
};

DataTable dt1 = GetDataTable(students);
```

```
IEnumerable<DataRow> seq1 = dt1.AsEnumerable();
DataTable dt2 = GetDataTable(students);
IEnumerable<DataRow> seq2 = dt2.AsEnumerable();

bool equal = seq1.SequenceEqual(seq2, System.Data.DataRowComparer.Default);
Console.WriteLine("SequenceEqual() with comparer : {0}", equal);

equal = seq1.SequenceEqual(seq2);
Console.WriteLine("SequenceEqual() without comparer : {0}", equal);
```

There is not much to discuss here; the first call should indicate that the two sequences are equal, while the second should indicate that they are not. The results are as expected:

```
SequenceEqual() with comparer : True
SequenceEqual() without comparer : False
```

DataRow Field Operators

In addition to the DataRow-specific comparer class for the set-type operators, there is a need for some DataRow-specific operators. These operators are defined in the System.Data.DataSetExtensions.dll assembly, in the static System.Data.DataRowExtensions class.

You have no doubt noticed that in virtually every example thus far, we have used the Field<T> operator to extract a DataColumn object's value from a DataRow. There are two purposes for this operator: correct equality comparisons and null value handling.

With DataRow objects, we have a problem. Their DataColumn values do not get compared properly for equality when they are accessed with the DataRow object's indexer if the column is a value-type. The reason is that because the column's data type could be any type, the indexer returns an object of type System.Object. This allows the indexer to return an integer, a string, or whatever data type is necessary for that column. This means that if a column is of type int, it is a value-type, and it must get *packaged* into an object of type Object. This packaging is known in the Microsoft .NET Framework as *boxing*. Pulling the value-type back out of the object is known as *unboxing*. This boxing is where the problem lies.

Let's take a look at some sample code. First, let's take the example of comparing an integer literal to another integer literal of the same value, as shown in Listing 10-7.

Listing 10-7. Comparing 3 to 3

```
Console.WriteLine("(3 == 3) is {0}.", (3 == 3));
```

The following is the result of this code:

```
(3 == 3) is True.
```

There is absolutely no surprise there. But what happens when an integer gets boxed? Let's examine the code in Listing 10-8 and look at the results.

Listing 10-8. *Comparing 3 Cast to an Object to Another 3 Cast to an Object*

```
Console.WriteLine("((Object)3 == (Object)3) is {0}.", ((Object)3 == (Object)3));
```

And the following are the results:

```
((Object)3 == (Object)3) is False.
```

Uh-oh, what happened? By casting the literal integer 3 to an Object, two objects were created, and the references (addresses) of each object were compared, and those are not equal. When you access DataColumn objects using the DataRow object's indexer, if any of the columns are a value-type, the column values will get boxed and will not compare for equality properly.

To demonstrate this, we'll create a more complex example that uses DataColumn objects. In the example, we have two arrays, each of a different class type. One is the same basic array of students we have been using. The other is an array of class designations with foreign keys into the students array. Here is the StudentClass class.

A Simple Class with Two Public Properties

```
class StudentClass
{
    public int Id;
    public string Class;
}
```

Now that we have a different class type, we are going to need another method to convert this array to an object of type DataTable. Here is that method:

```
static DataTable GetDataTable2(StudentClass[] studentClasses)
{
  DataTable table = new DataTable();

  table.Columns.Add("Id", typeof(Int32));
  table.Columns.Add("Class", typeof(string));

  foreach (StudentClass studentClass in studentClasses)
  {
    table.Rows.Add(studentClass.Id, studentClass.Class);
  }

  return (table);
}
```

This method is nothing more than a copy of the existing common GetTableData method that has been modified to work with arrays of StudentClass objects. Obviously, if you were going to be working from arrays in real production code, you would want something more abstract than creating a method for each class type for which you need a `DataTable` object. Perhaps a generic extension method would be a nice approach. But as we mentioned at the beginning of the examples, you will typically be performing LINQ to DataSet queries on data from databases, not arrays, so we won't worry about that here.

For the example, we'll build a sequence of `DataRow` objects from each array and try to join them using their common `Id` column, which we will retrieve by indexing into the `DataRow` with the column name, which is `Id`. Listing 10-9 shows the code.

Listing 10-9. *Joining Two Value-Type Columns by Indexing into the DataRow*

```
Student[] students = {
  new Student { Id = 1, Name = "Joe Rattz" },
  new Student { Id = 7, Name = "Anthony Adams" },
  new Student { Id = 13, Name = "Stacy Sinclair" },
  new Student { Id = 72, Name = "Dignan Stephens" }
};

StudentClass[] classDesignations = {
  new StudentClass { Id = 1, Class = "Sophmore" },
  new StudentClass { Id = 7, Class = "Freshman" },
  new StudentClass { Id = 13, Class = "Graduate" },
  new StudentClass { Id = 72, Class = "Senior" }
};

DataTable dt1 = GetDataTable(students);
IEnumerable<DataRow> seq1 = dt1.AsEnumerable();
DataTable dt2 = GetDataTable2(classDesignations);
IEnumerable<DataRow> seq2 = dt2.AsEnumerable();

string anthonysClass = (from s in seq1
                        where s.Field<string>("Name") == "Anthony Adams"
                        from c in seq2
                        where c["Id"] == s["Id"]
                        select (string)c["Class"]).
                        SingleOrDefault<string>();

Console.WriteLine("Anthony's Class is: {0}",
  anthonysClass != null ? anthonysClass : "null");
```

There are a couple of things worth pointing out about that query. First notice the line that is bold. There, we are indexing into the `DataRow` object to get the columns' values. Since the column value data types are strings, they will get boxed, which means there will be a problem determining equality. Additionally, you can see that we are using the `Field<T>` operator in this example when we compare the `Name` field to the name `"Anthony Adams"`. Ignore this for now. Just realize that we are calling the `Field<T>` operator to prevent a boxing problem with the `Name` field that we are in the midst of demonstrating with the `Id` field. Also, notice that this query is combining the query expression syntax with the standard dot notation syntax. As you can see, we are performing a join on the two `DataTable` objects too. Let's run the code and see the results:

```
Anthony's Class is: null
```

The `string anthonysClass` is `null`. That is because the join failed to find a record in `seq2` that had an equal value for the `Id` field. This is because of the boxing of the `Id` field when it is retrieved using the `DataRow` indexer. Now, you could handle the unboxing yourself by changing the line:

```
where c["Id"] == s["Id"]
```

to:

```
where (int)c["Id"] == (int)s["Id"]
```

Listing 10-10 is the entire example with that line replaced.

Listing 10-10. *Using Casting to Make the Test for Equality Correct*

```
Student[] students = {
  new Student { Id = 1, Name = "Joe Rattz" },
  new Student { Id = 7, Name = "Anthony Adams" },
  new Student { Id = 13, Name = "Stacy Sinclair" },
  new Student { Id = 72, Name = "Dignan Stephens" }
};

StudentClass[] classDesignations = {
  new StudentClass { Id = 1, Class = "Sophmore" },
  new StudentClass { Id = 7, Class = "Freshman" },
  new StudentClass { Id = 13, Class = "Graduate" },
  new StudentClass { Id = 72, Class = "Senior" }
};

DataTable dt1 = GetDataTable(students);
IEnumerable<DataRow> seq1 = dt1.AsEnumerable();
DataTable dt2 = GetDataTable2(classDesignations);
IEnumerable<DataRow> seq2 = dt2.AsEnumerable();

string anthonysClass = (from s in seq1
                        where s.Field<string>("Name") == "Anthony Adams"
                        from c in seq2
                        where (int)c["Id"] == (int)s["Id"]
                        select (string)c["Class"]).
                        SingleOrDefault<string>();

Console.WriteLine("Anthony's Class is: {0}",
  anthonysClass != null ? anthonysClass : "null");
```

If you run that code, you will get this result:

```
Anthony's Class is: Freshman
```

That solves the boxing problem. However, there is still one other problem. When you attempt to retrieve a column's value using the DataRow object's indexer, remember, the column's value gets returned as an object of type Object. Comparing it to any value or assign it to a variable will require casting it to another data type as we did previously by casting it to an int. Since DataSet objects use DBNull.Value as the value for a column that is null, if that column's value is DBNull.Value, casting it to another data type will throw an exception.

Fortunately, LINQ to DataSet has made both of these problems—boxed value comparisons and null handling—disappear, thanks to the Field<T> and SetField<T> operators. Listing 10-11 shows the previous example using the Field<T> operator.

Listing 10-11. Using the Field Operator

```
Student[] students = {
  new Student { Id = 1, Name = "Joe Rattz" },
  new Student { Id = 7, Name = "Anthony Adams" },
  new Student { Id = 13, Name = "Stacy Sinclair" },
  new Student { Id = 72, Name = "Dignan Stephens" }
};

StudentClass[] classDesignations = {
  new StudentClass { Id = 1, Class = "Sophmore" },
  new StudentClass { Id = 7, Class = "Freshman" },
  new StudentClass { Id = 13, Class = "Graduate" },
  new StudentClass { Id = 72, Class = "Senior" }
};

DataTable dt1 = GetDataTable(students);
IEnumerable<DataRow> seq1 = dt1.AsEnumerable();
DataTable dt2 = GetDataTable2(classDesignations);
IEnumerable<DataRow> seq2 = dt2.AsEnumerable();

string anthonysClass = (from s in seq1
                        where s.Field<string>("Name") == "Anthony Adams"
                        from c in seq2
                        where c.Field<int>("Id") == s.Field<int>("Id")
                        select (string)c["Class"]).
                        SingleOrDefault<string>();

Console.WriteLine("Anthony's Class is: {0}",
  anthonysClass != null ? anthonysClass : "null");
```

This code is the same as the previous example except we call the Field<T> operator instead of casting the field as an int. Here are the results:

```
Anthony's Class is: Freshman
```

Field<T>

As we demonstrated in Listing 10-11, the Field<T> operator allows you to obtain the value of a column from a DataRow object and handles the casting of DBNull.Value and boxed value comparison problems we previously discussed.

Prototypes

The Field operator has six prototypes we cover.

The first prototype returns the column's value for the DataColumn and version specified.

The First Field Prototype

```
public static T Field (
  this DataRow first,
  System.Data.DataColumn column,
  System.Data.DataRowVersion version);
```

The second prototype returns the column's value for the column with the name and version specified.

The Second Field Prototype

```
public static T Field (
  this DataRow first,
  string columnName,
  System.Data.DataRowVersion version);
```

The third prototype returns the column's value for the column with the ordinal and version specified.

The Third Field Prototype

```
public static T Field (
  this DataRow first,
  int ordinal,
  System.Data.DataRowVersion version);
```

The fourth prototype returns the column's current value only for the DataColumn specified.

The Fourth Field Prototype

```
public static T Field (
  this DataRow first,
  System.Data.DataColumn column);
```

The fifth prototype returns the column's current value only for the column with the specified name.

The Fifth Field Prototype

```
public static T Field (
  this DataRow first,
  string columnName);
```

The sixth prototype returns the column's current value only for the column with the specified ordinal.

The Sixth Field Prototype

```
public static T Field (
  this DataRow first,
  int ordinal);
```

As you may have noticed, the first three prototypes allow you to specify which DataRowVersion of the DataColumn object's value you want to retrieve.

Examples

At this point, you have seen the Field<T> operator called many times and in different ways. But just so you can see each prototype in action, Listing 10-12 shows a trivial example of each.

Listing 10-12. An Example of Each Field Operator Prototype

```
Student[] students = {
  new Student { Id = 1, Name = "Joe Rattz" },
  new Student { Id = 7, Name = "Anthony Adams" },
  new Student { Id = 13, Name = "Stacy Sinclair" },
  new Student { Id = 72, Name = "Dignan Stephens" }
};

DataTable dt1 = GetDataTable(students);
IEnumerable<DataRow> seq1 = dt1.AsEnumerable();

int id;

//  Using prototype 1.
```

411

```
id = (from s in seq1
      where s.Field<string>("Name") == "Anthony Adams"
      select s.Field<int>(dt1.Columns[0], DataRowVersion.Current)).
     Single<int>();
Console.WriteLine("Anthony's Id retrieved with prototype 1 is: {0}", id);

// Using prototype 2.
id = (from s in seq1
      where s.Field<string>("Name") == "Anthony Adams"
      select s.Field<int>("Id", DataRowVersion.Current)).
     Single<int>();
Console.WriteLine("Anthony's Id retrieved with prototype 2 is: {0}", id);

// Using prototype 3.
id = (from s in seq1
      where s.Field<string>("Name") == "Anthony Adams"
      select s.Field<int>(0, DataRowVersion.Current)).
     Single<int>();
Console.WriteLine("Anthony's Id retrieved with prototype 3 is: {0}", id);

// Using prototype 4.
id = (from s in seq1
      where s.Field<string>("Name") == "Anthony Adams"
      select s.Field<int>(dt1.Columns[0])).
     Single<int>();
Console.WriteLine("Anthony's Id retrieved with prototype 4 is: {0}", id);

// Using prototype 5.
id = (from s in seq1
      where s.Field<string>("Name") == "Anthony Adams"
      select s.Field<int>("Id")).
     Single<int>();
Console.WriteLine("Anthony's Id retrieved with prototype 5 is: {0}", id);

// Using prototype 6.
id = (from s in seq1
      where s.Field<string>("Name") == "Anthony Adams"
      select s.Field<int>(0)).
     Single<int>();
Console.WriteLine("Anthony's Id retrieved with prototype 6 is: {0}", id);
```

We declare the array of students and create a DataTable object from it just like in most examples in this chapter. We obtain a sequence of DataRow objects and work our way through each Field<T> operator prototype using it to obtain the field named Id. Notice that in each query of the Id field, we are also using the Field<T> operator in the Where operator portion of the query. Here are the results:

```
Anthony's Id retrieved with prototype 1 is: 7
Anthony's Id retrieved with prototype 2 is: 7
Anthony's Id retrieved with prototype 3 is: 7
Anthony's Id retrieved with prototype 4 is: 7
Anthony's Id retrieved with prototype 5 is: 7
Anthony's Id retrieved with prototype 6 is: 7
```

Before moving on to the SetField<T> operator, we want to provide an example demonstrating one of the prototypes that allows you to specify the DataRowVersion of the DataColumn object's value to retrieve. To provide an example, we will have to modify one of the DataColumn object's values using the SetField<T> operator. Although we haven't discussed the SetField<T> operator yet, just ignore it for now. We will be covering it in the next section.

Also, since this chapter is meant to explain the LINQ to DataSet operators and is not meant to be a detailed discussion of how the DataSet class works, we will only briefly cover a couple of additional DataSet methods we are calling in the example. Listing 10-13 is the code.

Listing 10-13. The Field Operator Prototype with a Specified DataRowVersion

```
Student[] students = {
  new Student { Id = 1, Name = "Joe Rattz" },
  new Student { Id = 7, Name = "Anthony Adams" },
  new Student { Id = 13, Name = "Stacy Sinclair" },
  new Student { Id = 72, Name = "Dignan Stephens" }
};

DataTable dt1 = GetDataTable(students);
IEnumerable<DataRow> seq1 = dt1.AsEnumerable();

DataRow row = (from s in seq1
               where s.Field<string>("Name") == "Anthony Adams"
               select s).Single<DataRow>();

row.AcceptChanges();
row.SetField("Name", "George Oscar Bluth");

Console.WriteLine("Original value = {0} : Current value = {1}",
  row.Field<string>("Name", DataRowVersion.Original),
  row.Field<string>("Name", DataRowVersion.Current));

row.AcceptChanges();
Console.WriteLine("Original value = {0} : Current value = {1}",
  row.Field<string>("Name", DataRowVersion.Original),
  row.Field<string>("Name", DataRowVersion.Current));
```

In this example, we obtain a sequence from the array of students as we typically do. We then query for a single DataRow object on which we can make some changes. The first code of interest is the

AcceptChanges method that we call after obtaining the DataRow object. We call this method to make the DataRow object accept the current value for each DataColumn object within it as the original version. Without that, there would be no original version of the DataColumn objects' values, and merely attempting to access the field's original version causes an exception to be thrown. In this way, the DataRow object is ready to begin tracking DataColumn object value changes. We need this to be able to obtain different DataRowVersion versions of the DataRow object's DataColumn values.

Once we call the AcceptChanges method the first time, we set a field using the SetField operator. We then display the original version and current version of the Name DataColumn value to the console. At this point, the original version should be "Anthony Adams", and the current version should be "George Oscar Bluth". This allows you to see the different versions you can obtain from a DataRow object.

Then, just to make it interesting, we call the AcceptChanges method a second time and again display the original and current version of the DataColumn object's value. This time, the original and current version values should both be "George Oscar Bluth", because we have told the DataRow object to accept the changes as the current version. Let's examine the results:

```
Original value = Anthony Adams : Current value = George Oscar Bluth
Original value = George Oscar Bluth : Current value = George Oscar Bluth
```

That works like a charm. Remember, though, without calling the AcceptChanges method the first time, we could have changed the value of the DataColumn object all day long and there would not have been an original version.

We mentioned that one of the additional benefits of using the Field<T> operator is that it handles the situation when fields are null. Let's take a look at the example in Listing 10-14 where a student's name has a null value, but we are not using the Field<T> operator:

Listing 10-14. *An Example Without the Field Operator When There Is a null Present*

```
Student[] students = {
  new Student { Id = 1, Name = "Joe Rattz" },
  new Student { Id = 7, Name = null },
  new Student { Id = 13, Name = "Stacy Sinclair" },
  new Student { Id = 72, Name = "Dignan Stephens" }
};

DataTable dt1 = GetDataTable(students);
IEnumerable<DataRow> seq1 = dt1.AsEnumerable();

string name = seq1.Where(student => student.Field<int>("Id") == 7)
  .Select(student => (string)student["Name"])
  .Single();

Console.WriteLine("Student's name is '{0}'", name);
```

That is a fairly simple example. Notice that we set the Name member of the Student record of the student whose Id is 7 to null. Also notice that instead of using the Field<T> operator, we just index into the DataRow and cast the value to a string. Let's take a look at the results:

```
Unhandled Exception: System.InvalidCastException: Unable to cast object of type
'System.DBNull' to type 'System.String'.
…
```

What happened? What happened is that the DataColumn object's value is DBNull, and you can't cast that to a string. There are some rather verbose solutions we could take to alleviate this complication, but this is what the Field<T> operator is designed to simplify for you. Let's take a look at the same example, except this time we use the Field<T> operator to obtain the DataColumn object's value. Listing 10-15 is the code.

Listing 10-15. *An Example with the Field Operator When There Is a null Present*

```
Student[] students = {
  new Student { Id = 1, Name = "Joe Rattz" },
  new Student { Id = 7, Name = null },
  new Student { Id = 13, Name = "Stacy Sinclair" },
  new Student { Id = 72, Name = "Dignan Stephens" }
};

DataTable dt1 = GetDataTable(students);
IEnumerable<DataRow> seq1 = dt1.AsEnumerable();

string name = seq1.Where(student => student.Field<int>("Id") == 7)
  .Select(student => student.Field<string>("Name"))
  .Single();

Console.WriteLine("Student's name is '{0}'", name);
```

OK, this is the same code except we use the Field<T> operator instead of casting it to a string. Let's look at the results:

```
Student's name is ''
```

This is much easier to deal with.

SetField<T>

Just as with the *retrieval* of DataColumn objects, null affects the *setting* of DataColumn objects. To assist with this issue, the SetField<T> operator was created. It handles the case where a DataColumn object's value is set with a nullable data type whose value is null.

Prototypes

The SetField<T> operator has three prototypes we cover.

The first prototype allows you to set a column's current value for the DataColumn specified.

The First SetField Prototype

```
public static void SetField (
  this DataRow first,
  System.Data.DataColumn column,
  T value);
```

The second prototype allows you to set a column's current value for the column with the specified name.

The Second SetField Prototype

```
public static void SetField (
  this DataRow first,
  string columnName,
  T value);
```

The third prototype allows you to set a column's current value for the column with the specified ordinal.

The Third SetField Prototype

```
public static void SetField (
  this DataRow first,
  int ordinal,
  T value);
```

Examples

As an example of the SetField<T> operator, shown in Listing 10-16, first we display the sequence of DataRow objects that contain the students. Next, we query one of the students by name from the sequence of DataRow objects and change that name using the SetField<T> operator. We then display the sequence of DataRow objects after the change has been made. Rinse and repeat for each prototype.

Listing 10-16. An Example of Each SetField Operator Prototype

```
Student[] students = {
  new Student { Id = 1, Name = "Joe Rattz" },
  new Student { Id = 7, Name = "Anthony Adams" },
  new Student { Id = 13, Name = "Stacy Sinclair" },
  new Student { Id = 72, Name = "Dignan Stephens" }
};

DataTable dt1 = GetDataTable(students);
IEnumerable<DataRow> seq1 = dt1.AsEnumerable();

Console.WriteLine("{0}Results before calling any prototype:",
  System.Environment.NewLine);

foreach (DataRow dataRow in seq1)
{
  Console.WriteLine("Student Id = {0} is {1}", dataRow.Field<int>("Id"),
    dataRow.Field<string>("Name"));
}

//  Using prototype 1.
(from s in seq1
 where s.Field<string>("Name") == "Anthony Adams"
 select s).Single<DataRow>().SetField(dt1.Columns[1], "George Oscar Bluth");

Console.WriteLine("{0}Results after calling prototype 1:",
  System.Environment.NewLine);

foreach (DataRow dataRow in seq1)
{
  Console.WriteLine("Student Id = {0} is {1}", dataRow.Field<int>("Id"),
    dataRow.Field<string>("Name"));
}

//  Using prototype 2.
(from s in seq1
 where s.Field<string>("Name") == "George Oscar Bluth"
 select s).Single<DataRow>().SetField("Name", "Michael Bluth");

Console.WriteLine("{0}Results after calling prototype 2:",
    System.Environment.NewLine);

foreach (DataRow dataRow in seq1)
{
  Console.WriteLine("Student Id = {0} is {1}", dataRow.Field<int>("Id"),
    dataRow.Field<string>("Name"));
```

```
}

// Using prototype 3.
(from s in seq1
 where s.Field<string>("Name") == "Michael Bluth"
 select s).Single<DataRow>().SetField("Name", "Tony Wonder");

Console.WriteLine("{0}Results after calling prototype 3:",
  System.Environment.NewLine);

foreach (DataRow dataRow in seq1)
{
  Console.WriteLine("Student Id = {0} is {1}", dataRow.Field<int>("Id"),
    dataRow.Field<string>("Name"));
}
```

This code is not quite as bad as it looks. After we obtain the sequence of students and display them, there is a block of code that gets repeated three times, once for each prototype. Each block contains a LINQ query that retrieves the field and updates its value, displays a header line to the console, and then displays each row in the sequence to the console to show the change just made to the field.

There are a couple noteworthy things in this example. In each LINQ query where we query the DataRow on its Name field, again, we are mixing query expression syntax and standard dot notation syntax in the query. Also, we are using the Field<T> operator to find the record that we are going to set with the SetField<T> operator. After obtaining the sequence of DataRow objects of students, we work our way through the SetField<T> operator prototypes one by one. Throughout the example, we query the previously changed element by its value and change it again. For example, for the first prototype, we just query the element whose Name field is "Anthony Adams" and set it to "George Oscar Bluth". For the second prototype, we query the element whose Name field is "George Oscar Bluth" and change it to something else, which we will query for on the next prototype. Of course, after each element value update, we display the sequence to the console so you can verify that the element's value did indeed change.

One of the things that we think is neat about this example is that we query the element and update its value in a single statement. This is so powerful one might think it is an illusion, but rest assured, there is no magician present here.

Here are the results:

```
Results before calling any prototype:
Student Id = 1 is Joe Rattz
Student Id = 7 is Anthony Adams
Student Id = 13 is Stacy Sinclair
Student Id = 72 is Dignan Stephens

Results after calling prototype 1:
Student Id = 1 is Joe Rattz
Student Id = 7 is George Oscar Bluth
Student Id = 13 is Stacy Sinclair
Student Id = 72 is Dignan Stephens
```

```
Results after calling prototype 2:
Student Id = 1 is Joe Rattz
Student Id = 7 is Michael Bluth
Student Id = 13 is Stacy Sinclair
Student Id = 72 is Dignan Stephens

Results after calling prototype 3:
Student Id = 1 is Joe Rattz
Student Id = 7 is Tony Wonder
Student Id = 13 is Stacy Sinclair
Student Id = 72 is Dignan Stephens
```

As you can see, the Name field of the appropriate element is updated each time.

DataTable Operators

In addition to the DataRow-specific operators in the DataRowExtensions class, there is a need for some DataTable-specific operators. These operators are defined in the System.Data.Entity.dll assembly, in the static System.Data.DataTableExtensions class.

AsEnumerable

We guess that you are probably surprised to see the AsEnumerable operator here. In fact, you may be surprised to learn that there is an AsEnumerable operator specifically for the DataTable class that returns a sequence of DataRow objects. If so, we are pleased because it means you were not wondering throughout this whole chapter why we hadn't mentioned it yet. After all, we have called it in virtually every example.

Yes, if you look in the System.Data.DataTableExtensions static class, you will see there is an AsEnumerable operator. The purpose of this operator is to return a sequence of type IEnumerable<DataRow> from a DataTable object.

Prototypes

The AsEnumerable operator has one prototype we will cover.

The AsEnumerable Prototype

```
public static IEnumerable<DataRow> AsEnumerable (
  this DataTable source
);
```

This operator when called on a DataTable object returns a sequence of DataRow objects. This is typically the first step of performing a LINQ to DataSet query on a DataSet object's DataTable. By calling this operator, you can obtain a sequence, an IEnumerable<T> where T happens to be a DataRow, thereby allowing you to call the many LINQ operators that may be called on an `IEnumerable<T>` type sequence.

Examples

There is no shortage of examples in this chapter. Since calling the `AsEnumerable` operator is the first step to perform a LINQ to DataSet query, virtually every example in this chapter is calling the `AsEnumerable` operator. Therefore, there is no need to provide one here.

CopyToDataTable<DataRow>

Now that you know how to query and modify the `DataColumn` values of a `DataRow`, you might just be interested in getting that sequence of modified `DataRow` objects into a `DataTable`. The `CopyToDataTable` operator exists for this very purpose.

Prototypes

The `CopyToDataTable` operator has two prototypes we cover.

This first prototype is called on an `IEnumerable<DataRow>` and returns a `DataTable`. This is used to create a new `DataTable` object from a sequence of `DataRow` objects.

The First CopyToDataTable Prototype

```
public static DataTable CopyToDataTable<T> (
  this IEnumerable<T> source
) where T : DataRow;
```

The first prototype establishes original versions for each field for you automatically without you needing to call the `AcceptChanges` method.

The second prototype is called on an `IEnumerable<DataRow>` of the source `DataTable` to update an already existing destination `DataTable` based on the `LoadOption` value specified.

The Second CopyToDataTable Prototype

```
public static void CopyToDataTable<T> (
  this IEnumerable<T> source,
  DataTable table,
  LoadOption options
) where T : DataRow;
```

The value of the `LoadOption` argument passed informs the operator whether the *original* column values only should be changed, the *current* column values only should be changed, or both. This is helpful for managing the `DataTable`'s changes. The following are the available values for `LoadOption`:

- `OverwriteChanges`: Both the current value and original value will be updated for each column.

- • `PreserveChanges`: Only the original value will be updated for each column.

- • `Upsert`: Only the current value will be updated for each column.

This `LoadOption` argument has now created a bit of a problem, though. Notice that the description of each possible value refers to updating the values of a column. This, of course, means updating the columns of a record already in the destination `DataTable`. How would the `CopyToDataTable` operator possibly know which record already in the destination `DataTable` corresponds to a record in the source `DataTable`? In other words, when it tries to copy a record from the source `DataTable` to the destination `DataTable` and has to honor the `LoadOption` parameter, how does it know whether it should just add the record from the source `DataTable` or update an already existing record in the destination `DataTable`? The answer is that it doesn't, unless it is aware of primary key fields in the `DataTable`.

Therefore, for this prototype of the `CopyToDataTable` operator to work properly, the destination `DataTable` object must have the appropriate fields specified as the primary key fields. Without specifying primary keys, this prototype will result in appending all the records from the source `DataTable` to the destination `DataTable`.

There is one additional complication. Since by using this prototype you are possibly interested in original versus current version values of fields, do not forget that with this prototype of the `CopyToDataTable` operator, a field doesn't have an original version unless the `AcceptChanges` method has been called. Attempting to access the original version when one does not exist causes an exception to be thrown. However, you can call the `HasVersion` method on each `DataRow` object before attempting to access the original version to determine if there is an original version to prevent this type of exception.

Examples

As an example of the first `CopyToDataTable` operator prototype, we will simply modify a field in a `DataTable`, create a new `DataTable` from the modified `DataTable` by calling the `CopyToDataTable` operator, and then display the contents of the new `DataTable`. Listing 10-17 is the code.

Listing 10-17. Calling the First Prototype of the CopyToDataTable Operator

```
Student[] students = {
  new Student { Id = 1, Name = "Joe Rattz" },
  new Student { Id = 7, Name = "Anthony Adams" },
  new Student { Id = 13, Name = "Stacy Sinclair" },
  new Student { Id = 72, Name = "Dignan Stephens" }
};

DataTable dt1 = GetDataTable(students);

Console.WriteLine("Original DataTable:");
foreach (DataRow dataRow in dt1.AsEnumerable())
{
  Console.WriteLine("Student Id = {0} is {1}", dataRow.Field<int>("Id"),
    dataRow.Field<string>("Name"));
}
```

```
(from s in dt1.AsEnumerable()
  where s.Field<string>("Name") == "Anthony Adams"
  select s).Single<DataRow>().SetField("Name", "George Oscar Bluth");

DataTable newTable = dt1.AsEnumerable().CopyToDataTable();

Console.WriteLine("{0}New DataTable:", System.Environment.NewLine);
foreach (DataRow dataRow in newTable.AsEnumerable())
{
  Console.WriteLine("Student Id = {0} is {1}", dataRow.Field<int>("Id"),
    dataRow.Field<string>("Name"));
}
```

As we said, first we create a `DataTable` from our array of students as we typically do in the previous examples. We then display the contents of that `DataTable` to the console. Next, we modify the `Name` field in one of the `DataRow` objects. Then we create a new `DataTable` by calling the `CopyToDataTable` operator. Last, we display the contents of the newly created `DataTable`.

Are you ready for the final countdown? Poof!

```
Original DataTable:
Student Id = 1 is Joe Rattz
Student Id = 7 is Anthony Adams
Student Id = 13 is Stacy Sinclair
Student Id = 72 is Dignan Stephens

New DataTable:
Student Id = 1 is Joe Rattz
Student Id = 7 is George Oscar Bluth
Student Id = 13 is Stacy Sinclair
Student Id = 72 is Dignan Stephens
```

As you can see, not only do we have data in the new `DataTable`, but it is the modified version, just as you would expect.

For the next example, we want to demonstrate the second prototype of the `CopyToDataTable` operator. We mentioned that for the `LoadOption` argument to work properly, primary keys must be established on the destination `DataSet`. For this example, we will not establish those so you can see the behavior. Because this example is a little more complex, we describe this one as we go. Listing 10-18 is the code.

Listing 10-18. *Calling the Second Prototype of the CopyToDataTable Operator When Primary Keys Are Not Established*

```
Student[] students = {
  new Student { Id = 1, Name = "Joe Rattz" },
  new Student { Id = 7, Name = "Anthony Adams" },
  new Student { Id = 13, Name = "Stacy Sinclair" },
  new Student { Id = 72, Name = "Dignan Stephens" }
};

DataTable dt1 = GetDataTable(students);
DataTable newTable = dt1.AsEnumerable().CopyToDataTable();
```

There is little new so far. We created what will be our source DataTable from the students array. We created our destination DataTable by calling the CopyToDataTable operator on the source DataTable. Notice that because we called the first prototype of the CopyToDataTable operator, we do not need to call the AcceptChanges method on the destination DataTable. This is important because, in the next segment of code, we reference the original version of the Name field. If it were not for the fact that the first prototype of the CopyToDataTable operator establishes the original versions of fields for you, an exception will be thrown since the original version would not exist.

```
Console.WriteLine("Before upserting DataTable:");
foreach (DataRow dataRow in newTable.AsEnumerable())
{
  Console.WriteLine("Student Id = {0} : original {1} : current {2}",
    dataRow.Field<int>("Id"),
    dataRow.Field<string>("Name", DataRowVersion.Original),
    dataRow.Field<string>("Name", DataRowVersion.Current));
}
```

There is nothing of significance here except that we reference the original version of the Name field in the record, and no exception is thrown when doing so because this prototype of the CopyToDataTable operator established the original version for me.

```
(from s in dt1.AsEnumerable()
 where s.Field<string>("Name") == "Anthony Adams"
 select s).Single<DataRow>().SetField("Name", "George Oscar Bluth");

dt1.AsEnumerable().CopyToDataTable(newTable, LoadOption.Upsert);
```

This is the important segment of this example. Notice that we change the value of the Name field for one of the records in the source DataTable using the SetField<T> operator. Next, we call the CopyToDataTable operator specifying that a LoadOption.Upsert type of copy should occur, meaning update only the current version. This causes a problem, though, in that since we have called the second CopyToDataTable operator prototype, which doesn't establish original versions for records inserted into the database and we haven't called the AcceptChanges method, if we attempt to access the original versions on inserted records, an exception will be thrown. We will have to use the HasVersion method to prevent this from happening if any records are inserted. Since we have not specified any primary keys, we *know* that all the records in the source table will be inserted into the destination table.

```
Console.WriteLine("{0}After upserting DataTable:", System.Environment.NewLine);
foreach (DataRow dataRow in newTable.AsEnumerable())
{
  Console.WriteLine("Student Id = {0} : original {1} : current {2}",
    dataRow.Field<int>("Id"),
    dataRow.HasVersion(DataRowVersion.Original) ?
      dataRow.Field<string>("Name", DataRowVersion.Original) : "-does not exist-",
    dataRow.Field<string>("Name", DataRowVersion.Current));
}
```

In this code segment, we merely display the DataTable content to the console. Now, the interesting thing about this example is that since we do not specify any primary keys for the destination table, when the copy occurs, no records will be deemed the same, so all the copied records from the source DataTable will be appended to the destination DataTable.

Also, notice that we only access the original version of the field's data if the HasVersion method returns true indicating that there is an original version. Here are the results:

```
Before upserting DataTable:
Student Id = 1 : original Joe Rattz : current Joe Rattz
Student Id = 7 : original Anthony Adams : current Anthony Adams
Student Id = 13 : original Stacy Sinclair : current Stacy Sinclair
Student Id = 72 : original Dignan Stephens : current Dignan Stephens

After upserting DataTable:
Student Id = 1 : original Joe Rattz : current Joe Rattz
Student Id = 7 : original Anthony Adams : current Anthony Adams
Student Id = 13 : original Stacy Sinclair : current Stacy Sinclair
Student Id = 72 : original Dignan Stephens : current Dignan Stephens
Student Id = 1 : original -does not exist- : current Joe Rattz
Student Id = 7 : original -does not exist- : current George Oscar Bluth
Student Id = 13 : original -does not exist- : current Stacy Sinclair
Student Id = 72 : original -does not exist- : current Dignan Stephens
```

Notice that several records are now duplicated because we don't specify any primary keys in the destination DataTable. Even the record we actually updated is in the DataTable twice now.

You may be wondering, since we made such a big deal about calling the HasVersion method since the AcceptChanges method was not called, why not just call the AcceptChanges method? You could do that, but if you did, all of the fields' current version values would have become their original version values, and you would not have been able to tell which records had changed. For these examples, we want the original version values and current version values to be distinguishable when a record is changed.

The solution to the problem in the previous example is to specify the primary keys for the destination DataTable. Listing 10-19 is the same example as the previous, except this time we specify the primary keys.

Listing 10-19. *Calling the Second Prototype of the CopyToDataTable Operator When Primary Keys Are Established*

```
Student[] students = {
  new Student { Id = 1, Name = "Joe Rattz" },
  new Student { Id = 7, Name = "Anthony Adams" },
  new Student { Id = 13, Name = "Stacy Sinclair" },
  new Student { Id = 72, Name = "Dignan Stephens" }
};

DataTable dt1 = GetDataTable(students);
DataTable newTable = dt1.AsEnumerable().CopyToDataTable();
newTable.PrimaryKey = new DataColumn[] { newTable.Columns[0] };

Console.WriteLine("Before upserting DataTable:");
foreach (DataRow dataRow in newTable.AsEnumerable())
{
  Console.WriteLine("Student Id = {0} : original {1} : current {2}",
    dataRow.Field<int>("Id"),
    dataRow.Field<string>("Name", DataRowVersion.Original),
    dataRow.Field<string>("Name", DataRowVersion.Current));
}

(from s in dt1.AsEnumerable()
 where s.Field<string>("Name") == "Anthony Adams"
 select s).Single<DataRow>().SetField("Name", "George Oscar Bluth");

dt1.AsEnumerable().CopyToDataTable(newTable, LoadOption.Upsert);

Console.WriteLine("{0}After upserting DataTable:", System.Environment.NewLine);
foreach (DataRow dataRow in newTable.AsEnumerable())
{
  Console.WriteLine("Student Id = {0} : original {1} : current {2}",
    dataRow.Field<int>("Id"),
    dataRow.HasVersion(DataRowVersion.Original) ?
      dataRow.Field<string>("Name", DataRowVersion.Original) : "-does not exist-",
    dataRow.Field<string>("Name", DataRowVersion.Current));
}
```

The only difference between this example and the previous is that we add the line setting the primary key on the new DataTable named newTable. Here are the results:

```
Before upserting DataTable:
Student Id = 1 : original Joe Rattz : current Joe Rattz
Student Id = 7 : original Anthony Adams : current Anthony Adams
Student Id = 13 : original Stacy Sinclair : current Stacy Sinclair
Student Id = 72 : original Dignan Stephens : current Dignan Stephens

After upserting DataTable:
Student Id = 1 : original Joe Rattz : current Joe Rattz
Student Id = 7 : original Anthony Adams : current George Oscar Bluth
Student Id = 13 : original Stacy Sinclair : current Stacy Sinclair
Student Id = 72 : original Dignan Stephens : current Dignan Stephens
```

Now this is more like it. Notice that now, the student whose Id is 7 had the name "Anthony Adams" but now his name is "George Oscar Bluth". This is exactly what we want.

Summary

In this chapter, we showed you how to use all the IEnumerable operators for set-type operations with DataRow objects and how to get and set field values using the Field<T> and SetField<T> operators. We also showed you what can go wrong if you do not use the DataRow specific set-type operator prototypes. Combining the LINQ to Objects Standard Query Operators with these DataSet-specific operators allows one to create powerful LINQ queries for DataSet objects.

In the next chapter, we wrap up the LINQ to DataSet part of this book by covering how to query typed DataSets with LINQ, as well as provide a real database example of a LINQ to DataSet query.

CHAPTER 11

■ ■ ■

Additional DataSet Capabilities

In the previous chapter, we provided numerous examples of querying `DataTable` objects that would naturally come from typical `DataSet`s in a real-world development environment. For the sake of simplicity, we programmatically created the `DataTable` objects using a static array declaration. However, there is more to `DataSet` queries than just creating `DataTable` objects from statically declared arrays.

Also, the examples in the previous chapter were all performed on untyped `DataSet`s. Sometimes, you may find you have a need to query a typed `DataSet`. LINQ to DataSet can do that too.

In this chapter, we address these issues and show you how to make the most of LINQ to DataSet. We begin with a discussion of querying typed `DataSet`s with LINQ to DataSet. Then, since we pointed out that there is more to querying `DataSet`s than programmatically creating `DataTable` objects, we follow up with an example of querying a database with LINQ to DataSet.

Required Namespaces

The examples in this chapter reference classes in the `System.Data`, `System.Data.SqlClient`, and `System.Linq` namespaces. If using directives do not already exist in your code, you should add them like this:

```
using System.Data;
using System.Data.SqlClient;
using System.Linq;
```

Typed DataSets

Typed `DataSet`s can be queried using LINQ, just as untyped `DataSet`s can. However, typed `DataSet`s make your LINQ query code simpler and easier to read. When querying a typed `DataSet`, because there is a class for the `DataSet`, you may access the table and column names using the typed `DataSet` object's class properties instead of indexing into the `Tables` collection or using the `Field<T>` and `SetField<T>` operators.

So, instead of accessing a `DataSet` object's table named `Students` like this:

```
DataTable Students = dataSet.Tables["Students"];
```

you can access it like this:

```
DataTable Students = dataSet.Students;
```

Instead of obtaining a field's value like this:

```
dataRow.Field<string>("Name")
```

you can obtain it like this:

```
dataRow.Name
```

This certainly makes the code more readable and maintainable.

Before showing you an example, we need to create a typed DataSet. Here are the steps to do so:

1. Right-click your project in the Solution Explorer window.

2. Choose the Add/New Item menu option in the context menu.

3. Expand the Categories tree in the Add New Item dialog box that opens. Select the Data node in the tree. Select the DataSet template in the Data Templates list. Edit the name of the DataSet file to StudentsDataSet.xsd, and click the Add button.

4. You should now see the DataSet Designer. Put your mouse pointer over the Toolbox, and drag a DataTable onto the DataSet Designer.

5. Right-click the title bar of the DataTable you just added, and select the Properties menu option from the context menu.

6. Edit the Name of the DataTable to Students in the Properties window.

7. Right-click the DataTable again, and select the Add/Column menu option from the context menu.

8. Edit the newly added DataColumn Name to Id, and change the DataType to System.Int32.

9. Right-click the DataTable again, and select the Add/Column menu option from the context menu.

10. Edit the newly added DataColumn Name to Name.

11. Save the file.

We have now created a typed DataSet named StudentsDataSet. The StudentsDataSet typed DataSet contains a DataTable named Students that contains two data columns of type DataColumn, one named Id of type Int32 and one named Name of type string. We can use this typed DataSet to perform LINQ queries, and because the DataSet is typed, we can access the DataRow fields as first-class object members. Let's take a look at an example.

Now that we have a typed DataSet, we can perform LINQ queries on it, as shown in Listing 11-1.

Listing 11-1. An Example of a Typed DataSet Query

```
StudentsDataSet studentsDataSet = new StudentsDataSet();
studentsDataSet.Students.AddStudentsRow(1, "Joe Rattz");
```

```
studentsDataSet.Students.AddStudentsRow(7, "Anthony Adams");
studentsDataSet.Students.AddStudentsRow(13, "Stacy Sinclair");
studentsDataSet.Students.AddStudentsRow(72, "Dignan Stephens");

string name =
  studentsDataSet.Students.Where(student => student.Id == 7).Single().Name;

Console.WriteLine(name);
```

In this example, we create a `StudentsDataSet` object and add four student records using the student names from the previous chapter. In most production code, you would not be doing this part because more than likely you would be obtaining your data from a database.

Once our typed `DataSet` is populated, we perform a query on it. Notice that we access the `Students DataTable` as a property on the `StudentsDataSet` object. Also, notice in the `Where` operator's lambda expression that we directly access the `Id` property on the element, which happens to be a `DataRow`, as opposed to calling the `Field` property on the `DataRow`. We can do this because the `DataSet` is typed. Also notice that when we obtain the singular `DataRow` object by calling the `Single` operator, we can directly access the `Name` property on it, again because the `DataSet` is typed.

Here are the results:

```
Anthony Adams
```

Isn't that cool? Typed `DataSets` make working with `DataSets` as easy as working with normal class objects and class object properties.

Putting It All Together

We wanted the examples in the previous chapter to be easy for someone trying to learn how to query with the LINQ to DataSet API. We wanted the time you spend working with examples to be focused on LINQ. We didn't want you to have to struggle with getting a database or getting your connection string correct. But, before we leave *this* chapter, we want to provide a more complete example—one that is actually getting a `DataSet` from a database because this is most likely how you will obtain a `DataSet` in your real-life code.

We must admit that creating a reasonable-size example that gets data from a database and uses the LINQ to DataSet API feels contrived. After all, we are going to perform a SQL query on data in a database using ADO.NET to obtain a `DataSet` and then turn right around and query that data again using LINQ to DataSet, all within several lines of code. In real life, some would ask, why not just change the SQL query to get exactly what you need in the first place? To them we say, play along! What we need here is a scenario to explain away the silliness.

In our scenario, we work for a company named Northwind. If ever there was a less than subtle hint at the database we will be using, that was it. Our company has an already existing application that queries our database for orders. This particular application performs various analyses on which employees sold items to which customers, and to what countries the orders were shipped. So, the application is already downloading the employees, customers, and shipping countries for all orders into a `DataSet`. Our task is to perform one more analysis on that already queried data. We are required to produce a unique list of each employee who sold to each company for all orders that were shipped to Germany.

In this example, we instantiate a `SqlDataAdapter` followed by a `DataSet` and call the `SqlDataAdapter` object's `Fill` method to populate the `DataSet`. In this scenario, this would have already been done because this existing application is already doing it. So, the `DataSet` object would be passed into our code. But since we don't have a full-blown application, we will just do it in the example. After we obtain the `DataSet` object with the results of the SQL query, all we have to do for our task is perform a LINQ to DataSet query and display the results. Listing 11-2 is the code.

Listing 11-2. Putting It All Together

```
string connectionString =
  @"Data Source=.\SQLEXPRESS;Initial Catalog=Northwind;Integrated Security=SSPI;";

SqlDataAdapter dataAdapter = new SqlDataAdapter(
  @"SELECT O.EmployeeID, E.FirstName + ' ' + E.LastName as EmployeeName,
    O.CustomerID, C.CompanyName, O.ShipCountry
    FROM Orders O
    JOIN Employees E on O.EmployeeID = E.EmployeeID
    JOIN Customers C on O.CustomerID = C.CustomerID",
  connectionString);

DataSet dataSet = new DataSet();
dataAdapter.Fill(dataSet, "EmpCustShip");

//  All code prior to this comment is legacy code.

var ordersQuery = dataSet.Tables["EmpCustShip"].AsEnumerable()
  .Where(r => r.Field<string>("ShipCountry").Equals("Germany"))
  .Distinct(System.Data.DataRowComparer.Default)
  .OrderBy(r => r.Field<string>("EmployeeName"))
  .ThenBy(r => r.Field<string>("CompanyName"));

foreach(var dataRow in ordersQuery)
{
  Console.WriteLine("{0,-20} {1,-20}", dataRow.Field<string>("EmployeeName"),
    dataRow.Field<string>("CompanyName"));
}
```

As you can see, we are connecting to the Northwind database. You may need to tweak the connection string for your needs.

Notice that in the previous query, we use the `AsEnumerable`, `Distinct`, and `Field<T>` operators we covered in the previous chapter and the `Where`, `OrderBy`, and `ThenBy` operators from the LINQ to Objects API together to create the exact query we want. You really have to admire the way this stuff all plays together so nicely. If the query is doing what we need it to do, we should get a list of each employee who sold an order to each company where that order was shipped to Germany in alphabetical order by employee name and company name, and with no duplicate rows. Here are the results:

Andrew Fuller	Die Wandernde Kuh
Andrew Fuller	Königlich Essen
Andrew Fuller	Lehmanns Marktstand
Andrew Fuller	Morgenstern Gesundkost
Andrew Fuller	Ottilies Käseladen
Andrew Fuller	QUICK-Stop
Andrew Fuller	Toms Spezialitäten
Anne Dodsworth	Blauer See Delikatessen
Anne Dodsworth	Königlich Essen
Anne Dodsworth	Lehmanns Marktstand
Anne Dodsworth	QUICK-Stop
...	
Steven Buchanan	Frankenversand
Steven Buchanan	Morgenstern Gesundkost
Steven Buchanan	QUICK-Stop

Notice that for each employee on the left, no company is repeated on the right. This is important because it is once again demonstrating the necessity of the LINQ to DataSet API set-type operators. As a test, change the call to the `Distinct` operator in the previous code so that the `DataRowComparer.Default` comparer is not specified, and you will see that you get duplicates.

Just so you can see another example using query expression syntax, Listing 11-3 is the same example again, but with the aforementioned syntax.

Listing 11-3. Putting It All Together with Query Expression Syntax

```
string connectionString =
  @"Data Source=.\SQLEXPRESS;Initial Catalog=Northwind;Integrated Security=SSPI;";

SqlDataAdapter dataAdapter = new SqlDataAdapter(
  @"SELECT O.EmployeeID, E.FirstName + ' ' + E.LastName as EmployeeName,
    O.CustomerID, C.CompanyName, O.ShipCountry
    FROM Orders O
    JOIN Employees E on O.EmployeeID = E.EmployeeID
    JOIN Customers C on O.CustomerID = C.CustomerID",
  connectionString);

DataSet dataSet = new DataSet();
dataAdapter.Fill(dataSet, "EmpCustShip");

// All code prior to this comment is legacy code.

var ordersQuery = (from r in dataSet.Tables["EmpCustShip"].AsEnumerable()
                   where r.Field<string>("ShipCountry").Equals("Germany")
                   orderby r.Field<string>("EmployeeName"),
                     r.Field<string>("CompanyName")
                   select r)
```

```
        .Distinct(System.Data.DataRowComparer.Default);

foreach (var dataRow in ordersQuery)
{
  Console.WriteLine("{0,-20} {1,-20}", dataRow.Field<string>("EmployeeName"),
    dataRow.Field<string>("CompanyName"));
}
```

Now the query is using query expression syntax. Although it was our goal to make the query functionally the same as the previous, we were not able to do this. Notice that the Distinct operator is called at the very end of the query now. Remember, the compiler cannot translate all operators from a query specified with query expression syntax, only the most commonly used ones. In this case, it does not know how to translate the Distinct operator. Because of this, we cannot make that call in the query expression syntax portion of the query. As you can see, we did call it at the end of the query. We will end up with the same results from this query.

However, there is a performance difference between the query in Listing 11-3 and the query in Listing 11-2. In Listing 11-2, the Distinct operator is called just after the Where operator, so duplicate records are eliminated from the results set prior to ordering them. In Listing 11-3, the Distinct operator is not called until the end, so the duplicate records are still there during the ordering of the results set. This means records are being sorted that will be eliminated once the Distinct operator is called. This is unnecessary work, but it's unavoidable if you want to use query expression syntax for this query.

Summary

As covered in this chapter, not only can you query normal DataSets with LINQ to DataSet, but you can query typed DataSets. Typed DataSets make your code easier to maintain and more readable, and LINQ to DataSet makes querying those typed DataSets a breeze. We also demonstrated a more real-world LINQ to DataSet query that queried the Northwind database.

The LINQ to DataSet API adds yet another domain to those available for LINQ queries. With all the existing code already utilizing DataSets, LINQ to DataSet promises to be easy to retrofit into your legacy .NET code, thereby making it easier than ever to query data from a DataSet.

One benefit that the LINQ to DataSet API has over the LINQ to SQL API is that no database class code needs to be generated and compiled ahead of time to perform LINQ to DataSet queries. This makes LINQ to DataSet more dynamic and suitable for database-type utilities where the databases will be unknown until runtime.

By providing the AsEnumerable operator to create sequences from DataTable objects, using the LINQ to Objects Standard Query Operators becomes possible, adding even more power to the arsenal of query capabilities.

For the LINQ to DataSet API, operators have been added for the key classes of the DataSet: DataTable, DataRow, and DataColumn. One must not forget the issue that makes the new set-type operator prototypes for the Distinct, Union, Intersect, Except, and SequenceEqual operators necessary: the problem that DataRows have being compared for equality. So when working with DataSets, DataTables, and DataRows, always opt for the LINQ to DataSet set-type operator prototypes for the Distinct, Union, Intersect, Except, and SequenceEqual operators where the equality comparer object is specified instead of the prototype versions without an equality comparer object being specified.

Lastly, when obtaining a column's value, use the Field<T> and SetField<T> operators to eliminate issues with comparisons for equality and null values.

One thing became apparent while working with the LINQ to DataSet API. We had totally underestimated the power and utility of DataSets. They offer so much in the way of a cached, relational data store. And, although they already offer somewhat limited search facilities, with the LINQ to DataSet API, those limitations have been removed. You now have LINQ to query your DataSets with, and that makes coding just that much easier.

PART 5

LINQ to SQL

CHAPTER 12

LINQ to SQL Introduction

Listing 12-1. A Simple Example Updating the ContactName of a Customer in the Northwind Database

```
// Create a DataContext.
Northwind db = new Northwind(@"Data Source=.\SQLEXPRESS;Initial
Catalog=Northwind");

// Retrieve customer LAZYK.
Customer cust = (from c in db.Customers
                 where c.CustomerID == "LAZYK"
                 select c).Single<Customer>();

// Update the contact name.
cust.ContactName = "Ned Plimpton";

try
{
  // Save the changes.
  db.SubmitChanges();
}
// Detect concurrency conflicts.
catch (ChangeConflictException)
{
  // Resolve conflicts.
  db.ChangeConflicts.ResolveAll(RefreshMode.KeepChanges);
}
```

■ **Note** This example requires generation of entity classes, which we will cover later in this chapter.

In Listing 12-1, we used LINQ to SQL to query the record whose CustomerID field is "LAZYK" from the Northwind database's Customers table and to return a Customer object representing that record. We then updated the Customer object's ContactName property and saved the change to the database by calling the SubmitChanges method. That's not much code considering it is also detecting concurrency conflicts and resolving them if they occur.

Run Listing 12-1 by pressing Ctrl+F5. There is no console output, but if you check the database, you should see that the ContactName for customer LAZYK is now "Ned Plimpton".

■ **Note** This example makes a change to the data in the database without changing it back. The original value of the ContactName for customer LAZYK is "John Steel". You should change this back so that no subsequent examples behave improperly. You could change it manually, or you could just change the example code to set it back, and run the example again.

This book uses an extended version of the Northwind database. Please read the section in this chapter titled "Obtaining the Appropriate Version of the Northwind Database" for details.

Introducing LINQ to SQL

At this point, we have discussed using LINQ with in-memory data collections and arrays, XML, and DataSets. Now, we will move on to what many think is the most compelling reason to use LINQ, LINQ to SQL.

LINQ to SQL is an application programming interface (API) for working with SQL Server databases. In the current world of object-oriented programming languages, there is a mismatch between the programming language and the relational database. When writing an application, we model classes to represent real-world objects such as customers, accounts, policies, and flights. We need a way to persist these objects so that when the application is restarted, these objects and their data are not lost. However, most production-caliber databases are still relational and store their data as records in tables, not as objects. A customer class may contain multiple addresses and phone numbers stored in collections that are child properties of that customer class; once persisted, this data will most likely be stored in multiple tables, such as a customer table, an address table, and a phone table.

Additionally, the data types supported by the application language differ from the database data types. Developers are required to write code that loads and saves customer objects from the appropriate tables, handling the data type conversion between the application language and the database. This is a tedious and error-prone process. Because of this object-relational mapping (ORM) problem, often referred to as the *object-relational impedance mismatch*, many prewritten ORM software solutions have been designed through the years. LINQ to SQL is Microsoft's entry-level LINQ-enabled ORM implementation for SQL Server.

Notice that we said "for SQL Server." LINQ to SQL is exclusive to SQL Server. LINQ, however, is not, and third-party LINQ support is available for most mainstream databases, including Oracle, DB2, MySQL, SqlLite, and others.

You may have also noticed that we said LINQ to SQL is an *entry-level* ORM implementation. If you find it is not powerful or flexible enough to meet your requirements, you may want to investigate LINQ to Entities, which we cover in Chapter 19.

Most ORM tools attempt to abstract the physical database into business objects. With that abstraction, we sometimes lose the ability to perform SQL queries, which is a large part of the attraction to relational databases. This is what separates LINQ to SQL from many of its contemporaries. Not only do we get the convenience of business objects that are mapped to the database, we get a full-blown query language, similar to the already familiar SQL, thrown in to boot.

■ **Tip** LINQ to SQL is an entry-level ORM tool that permits powerful SQL queries.

In addition to providing LINQ query capabilities, as long as your query returns LINQ to SQL *entity objects*, as opposed to returning single fields, named nonentity classes, or anonymous classes, LINQ to SQL also provides change tracking and database updates, complete with optimistic concurrency conflict detection and resolution, and transactional integrity.

In Listing 12-1, we first had to instantiate an instance of the Northwind class. That class is derived from the DataContext class, and we will cover this class in-depth in Chapter 16. For now, consider it a supercharged database connection. It also handles updating the database for us, as you can see when we later call the SubmitChanges method on it. Next, we retrieve a single customer from the Northwind database into a Customer object. That Customer object is an instantiation of the Customer class, which is an entity class that had to be either written or generated. In this case, the Customer class was generated by the SQLMetal utility, as was the Northwind class, for that matter. After retrieving the customer, we updated one of the Customer object's properties, ContactName, and called the SubmitChanges method to persist the modified contact name to the database. Notice that we wrapped the call to the SubmitChanges method in a try/catch block and specifically caught the ChangeConflictException exception. This is for handling concurrency conflicts, which we will cover in detail in Chapter 17.

Before you can run this example or any of the others in this chapter, you will need to create entity classes for the Northwind database. Please read the section in this chapter titled "Prerequisites for Running the Examples" to guide you through creating the necessary entity classes.

LINQ to SQL is a complex subject, and providing any example requires involving many LINQ to SQL elements. In the first example at the beginning of this chapter, we are using a derived DataContext class, which is the Northwind class; an entity class, which is the Customer class; concurrency conflict detection and resolution; and database updates via the SubmitChanges method. We can't possibly explain all these concepts simultaneously. So, we need to give you some background on each of these components before we begin so that you will have a basic understanding of the foundation of LINQ to SQL. Rest assured that we will cover each of these concepts in agonizing detail later in the subsequent LINQ to SQL chapters.

The DataContext

The DataContext class establishes a connection to a database. It also provides several services that provide identity tracking, change tracking, and change processing. We'll cover each of these services in more detail in Chapter 16. For now, just know that it is the DataContext class that is connecting us to the database, monitoring what we have changed, and updating the database when we call its SubmitChanges method.

It is typical with LINQ to SQL to use a class derived from the DataContext class. The name of the derived class usually is the same as the database to which it is mapped. We will often refer to that derived class in the LINQ to SQL chapters as [Your]DataContext, because its name is dependent on the database for which it is being created.

In our examples, our derived DataContext class will be named Northwind. We use the SqlMetal tool included with Visual Studio 2010, which automatically generates mapping classes from a SQL Server database. SQLMetal names the generated, derived DataContext class after the database for which it is generated.

This derived DataContext class, [Your]DataContext, will typically have a Table<T> public property for each database table you have mapped in the database, where T is the type of the *entity class* that is instantiated for each retrieved record from that particular database table. The data type Table<T> is a specialized collection. For example, since there is a Customers table in the Northwind database, our Northwind class derived from the DataContext class will have a Table<Customer> named Customers. This means that we can access the records in the Customersdatabase table by directly accessing the Customers property of type Table<Customer> in our Northwind class. You can see an example of this in the first example in this chapter, Listing 12-1, where we coded db.Customers. That code is querying the records in the Customerstable of the Northwind database.

Entity Classes

LINQ to SQL involves using entity classes, where each entity class is typically mapped to a single database table. However, using entity class inheritance mapping, it is possible to map an entire class hierarchy to a single table under special circumstances. You can read more about this in Chapter 18. So, we have entity classes mapping to database tables, and the entity class properties get mapped to table columns. This entity class-to-table and property-to-column mapping is the essence of LINQ to SQL.

■ **Note** The essence of LINQ to SQL is mapping entity classes to database tables and entity class properties to database table columns.

This mapping can occur directly in class source files by decorating classes with the appropriate attributes, or it can be specified with an external XML mapping file. By using an external XML mapping file, the LINQ-to-SQL-specific bits can be kept external to the source code. This could be very handy if you don't have source code or want to keep the code separated from LINQ to SQL. For the majority of examples in the LINQ to SQL chapters, we will be using entity classes that have been generated by the SQLMetal command-line tool. SQLMetal generates the entity classes with the LINQ to SQL mapping bits right in the source module it generates. These mapping bits are in the form of attributes and attribute properties.

You will be able to detect the existence of entity classes in our examples when you see classes or objects that have the singular form of a Northwind database table name. For example, in Listing 12-1, we use a class named Customer. Because *Customer* is the singular form of *Customer*s and the Northwind database has a table named Customers, this is your clue that the Customer class is an entity class for the Northwind database's Customers table.

The SQLMetal command-line tool has an option called /pluralize that causes the entity classes to be named in the singular form of the database table name. Had we not specified the /pluralize option when generating our entity classes, our entity class would be named Customers, as opposed to Customer, because the name of the table is Customers. We mention this in case you get confused reading other writings about LINQ to SQL. Depending on how the author ran the SQLMetal tool and what options were specified, the entity class names may be plural or singular.

Associations

An *association* is the term used to designate a primary key to foreign key relationship between two entity classes. In a one-to-many relationship, the result of an association is that the parent class, the class containing the primary key, contains a collection of the child classes, the classes having the foreign key.

That collection is stored in a private member variable of type EntitySet<T>, where T will be the type of the child entity class.

For example, in the Customer entity class generated by the SQLMetal command-line tool for the Northwind database, there is a private member of type EntitySet<Order> named _Orders that contains all of the Order objects for a specific Customer object:

```
private EntitySet<Order> _Orders;
```

SQLMetal also generated a public property named Orders to be used for accessing the private _Orders collection.

On the other end of the relationship, the child, which is the class containing the foreign key, contains a reference to the parent class, since that is a many-to-one relationship. That reference is stored in a private member variable of type EntityRef<T>, where T is the type of the parent class.

In the generated Northwind entity classes, the Order entity class contains a private member variable of type EntityRef<Customer> named _Customer:

```
private EntityRef<Customer> _Customer;
```

Again, the SQLMetal tool also generated a public property named Customer to provide access to the parent reference.

The association, primary and foreign keys, and the direction of the relationship are all defined by attributes and attribute properties in the generated entity classes' source module.

The benefit gained by the association is the ability to access a parent's child classes, and therefore database records, as easily as accessing a property of the parent class. Likewise, accessing a child's parent class is as easy as accessing a property of the child class.

Concurrency Conflict Detection

One of the services that the DataContext performs is change processing. When you try to update the database by calling the DataContext object's SubmitChanges method, it automatically performs optimistic concurrency conflict detection.

If a conflict is detected, a ChangeConflictException exception is thrown. Any time you call the SubmitChanges method, you should wrap that call in a try/catch block and catch the ChangeConflictException exception. This is the proper way to detect concurrency conflicts.

You can see an example of this in Listing 12-1. We will go into detail about concurrency conflict detection and resolution in Chapter 17. Many of the examples in this and the following LINQ to SQL chapters will not provide concurrency conflict detection or resolution for the sake of brevity and clarity. In real code, you should always do both.

Concurrency Conflict Resolution

Once a concurrency conflict has been detected, the next step will be to resolve the concurrency conflict. This can be done in several ways. In Listing 12-1, we do it the simplest way by calling the ResolveAll method of the ChangeConflicts collection of the derived DataContext class when the ChangeConflictException exception is caught.

Again, in many of the examples in the LINQ to SQL chapters, we will not have code to either detect the concurrency conflicts or to resolve them, but you should always have code handling this in your real production code.

As we mentioned in the previous section, we will cover concurrency conflict resolution in detail in Chapter 17.

Prerequisites for Running the Examples

Since virtually all the examples in this and the following LINQ to SQL chapters use Microsoft's sample *extended* Northwind database, we will need entity classes and mapping files for the Northwind database.

Obtaining the Appropriate Version of the Northwind Database

Unfortunately, the standard Microsoft Northwind database is missing a few things we will need to fully show off LINQ to SQL, such as table-valued and scalar-valued functions. Therefore, instead of using the standard Northwind database, we will use an extended version of it that Microsoft initially distributed to demonstrate LINQ.

We have included the extended version of the Northwind database with the source code for this book, which you can download from the Apress site.

Generating the Northwind Entity Classes

Because we have not yet covered how to generate entity classes, we are going to tell you how to generate them without providing much explanation. However, we cover the details thoroughly in Chapter 13.

To generate the entity classes, you must have the extended version of the Northwind database that we discussed in the previous section.

Open a Visual Studio command prompt. To do so, look in your Microsoft Visual Studio 2010 menu for a submenu named Visual Studio Tools for an item named Visual Studio Command Prompt (2010), and select it. Once the command prompt opens, change your current directory to whatever directory in which you desire to create your entity classes and external mapping file. We are going to change our directory to the root of the C: drive:

```
cd \
```

If you are going to generate your entity classes using the Northwind database files without first attaching the database to them, use the following command:

```
sqlmetal /namespace:nwind /code:Northwind.cs /pluralize /functions /sprocs /views
<path to Northwind MDF file>
```

■ **Caution** Pay particular attention to the MDF file name and its casing, as you specify it on the command line. The name and case of the `DataContext` derived class that is generated will match the file name that is passed on the command line, not the physical file name itself. If you deviate from a `DataContext` derived class name of `Northwind`, none of the examples will work without modification. Therefore, it is critical that you pass the Northwind database file name as `[path]\Northwind.mdf`, not `northwind.mdf`, `NorthWind.mdf`, or any other variation of the name.

So, to create entity classes from a file named `Northwind.mdf`, enter the following command:

```
sqlmetal /namespace:nwind /code:Northwind.cs /pluralize /functions /sprocs /views
"C:\Northwind.mdf"
```

Running this command create an entity class module named `Northwind.cs` in the current directory. If you are going to generate your entity classes from the Northwind database that is already attached to your SQL Server, use the following command:

```
sqlmetal /server:<server> /user:<user> /password:<password> /database:Northwind
/namespace:nwind /code:Northwind.cs /pluralize /functions /sprocs /views
```

So, to create entity classes from an attached database named Northwind, enter the following command:

```
sqlmetal /server:.\SQLExpress /database:Northwind /namespace:nwind
/code:Northwind.cs /pluralize /functions /sprocs /views
```

■ **Note** Depending on your environment, you may need to specify a user with the `/user:[username]` option and a password with the `/password:[password]` option on the command line in the preceding example. Please read the section titled "SQLMetal" in Chapter 13 for more details.

The command entered using either of these approaches tells SQLMetal to generate the source code into a file named `Northwind.cs` in the current directory. We will cover all the program's options in the next chapter. Copy the generated `Northwind.cs` file into your project by adding it as an existing item.

You may now utilize LINQ to SQL on the Northwind database using the entity classes contained in the `Northwind.cs` file.

■ **Tip** Be cautious of making changes to the generated entity class source file. You may find you need to regenerate it at some later point, causing you to lose any changes. You may desire to add business logic by adding methods to the entity classes. Instead of modifying the generated file, consider taking advantage of C# partial classes to keep the added properties and methods in a separate source module.

Generating the Northwind XML Mapping File

We also need to generate a mapping file to use in some of the examples. Again, we will use SQLMetal for this purpose. So, from the same command line and path, execute the following command:

```
sqlmetal /map:northwindmap.xml "C:\Northwind.mdf" /pluralize /functions /sprocs
/views /namespace:nwind /code:Northwind.cs
```

Again, pay close attention to the casing used to specify the MDF file. This will generate a file named `northwindmap.xml` into the current directory.

Using the LINQ to SQL API

To use the LINQ to SQL API, you will need to add the `System.Data.Linq.dll` assembly to your project if it is not already there. Also, if they do not already exist, you will need to add using directives to your source module for the `System.Linq` and `System.Data.Linq` namespaces like this:

```
using System.Data.Linq;
using System.Linq;
```

Additionally, for the examples, you will need to add a using directive for the namespace the entity classes were generated into, `nwind`:

```
using nwind;
```

IQueryable<T>

You will see that in many of the LINQ to SQL examples in this chapter and the subsequent LINQ to SQL chapters, we work with sequences of type `IQueryable<T>`, where T is the type of an entity class. These are the type of sequences that are typically returned by LINQ to SQL queries. They will often appear to work just like an `IEnumerable<T>` sequence, and that is no coincidence. The `IQueryable<T>` interface extends the `IEnumerable<T>` interface. Here is the definition of `IQueryable<T>`:

```
interface IQueryable<T> : IEnumerable<T>, IQueryable
```

Because of this inheritance, you can treat an `IQueryable<T>` sequence like an `IEnumerable<T>` sequence.

Some Common Methods

You will see that the examples in this chapter and the others that deal with LINQ to SQL quickly become complex. Demonstrating a concurrency conflict requires making changes to the database external to LINQ to SQL. To highlight the LINQ to SQL code and to eliminate as many of the trivial details as possible (while at the same time providing useful examples), we have created some common methods. Be sure to add these common methods to your source modules as appropriate when testing the examples in the LINQ to SQL chapters.

GetStringFromDb()

A common method that will come in handy is a method to obtain a simple string from the database using standard ADO.NET. This will allow us to examine what is actually in the database, as opposed to what LINQ to SQL is showing us.

GetStringFromDb: A Method for Retrieving a String Using ADO.NET

```
static private string GetStringFromDb(
  System.Data.SqlClient.SqlConnection sqlConnection, string sqlQuery)
{
  if (sqlConnection.State != System.Data.ConnectionState.Open)
  {
    sqlConnection.Open();
  }

  System.Data.SqlClient.SqlCommand sqlCommand =
    new System.Data.SqlClient.SqlCommand(sqlQuery, sqlConnection);

  System.Data.SqlClient.SqlDataReader sqlDataReader = sqlCommand.ExecuteReader();
  string result = null;

  try
  {
    if (!sqlDataReader.Read())
    {
      throw (new Exception(
        String.Format("Unexpected exception executing query [{0}].", sqlQuery)));
    }
    else
    {
      if (!sqlDataReader.IsDBNull(0))
      {
        result = sqlDataReader.GetString(0);
      }
    }
  }
  finally
  {
    // always call Close when done reading.
    sqlDataReader.Close();
  }

  return (result);
}
```

To call the GetStringFromDb method, a SqlConnection and a string containing a SQL query are passed into the method. The method verifies that the connection is open, and if the connection is not open, the method opens it.

Next, a SqlCommand is created by passing the query and connection into the constructor. Then, a SqlDataReader is obtained by calling the ExecuteReader method on the SqlCommand. The SqlDataReader is read by calling its Read method, and if data was read and the returned first column's value is not null, the returned first column value is retrieved with the GetString method. Finally, the SqlDataReader is closed, and the first column value is returned to the calling method.

ExecuteStatementInDb()

Sometimes, we will need to execute nonquery SQL statements such as insert, update, and delete in ADO.NET to modify the state of the database external to LINQ to SQL. For that purpose, we have created the ExecuteStatementInDb method:

ExecuteStatementInDb: A Method for Executing Insert, Updates, and Deletes in ADO.NET

```
static private void ExecuteStatementInDb(string cmd)
{
  string connection =
    @"Data Source=.\SQLEXPRESS;Initial Catalog=Northwind;Integrated
Security=SSPI;";

  System.Data.SqlClient.SqlConnection sqlConn =
    new System.Data.SqlClient.SqlConnection(connection);

  System.Data.SqlClient.SqlCommand sqlComm =
    new System.Data.SqlClient.SqlCommand(cmd);

  sqlComm.Connection = sqlConn;
  try
  {
    sqlConn.Open();
    Console.WriteLine("Executing SQL statement against database with ADO.NET ...");
    sqlComm.ExecuteNonQuery();
    Console.WriteLine("Database updated.");
  }
  finally
  {
    //  Close the connection.
    sqlComm.Connection.Close();
  }
}
```

To call the ExecuteStatementInDb method, a string is passed containing a SQL command. A SqlConnection is created followed by a SqlCommand. The SqlConnection is assigned to the SqlCommand. The SqlConnection is then opened, and the SQL command is executed by calling the SqlCommand object's ExecuteNonQuery method. Finally, the SqlConnection is closed.

Summary

In this chapter, we have introduced you to LINQ to SQL and some of its most basic terminology, such as `DataContext` objects, entity classes, associations, and concurrency conflict detection and resolution. We showed you how to generate entity classes and external mapping file for the extended Northwind database. These entity classes will be used extensively throughout the LINQ to SQL examples. We also provided a couple of common methods that many of the examples in the subsequent LINQ to SQL chapters will rely on. The next step is to arm you with some tips and show you how to use the necessary tools to leverage LINQ to SQL, and this is exactly what the next chapter is about.

CHAPTER 13

■ ■ ■

LINQ to SQL Tips and Tools

In the previous chapter, we introduced you to LINQ to SQL and most of its terminology. We showed you how to generate the entity classes that most of the examples in the LINQ to SQL chapters will require. We also provided some common methods that many of the examples in these chapters will need.

In this chapter, we will present some tips that we hope you will find useful while working with LINQ to SQL. We will also show you some of the tools that make using LINQ to SQL such a pleasure.

Introduction to LINQ to SQL Tips and Tools

Now would be a good time to remind you that before you can run the examples in this chapter, you must have met the prerequisites. First, you must have the extended Northwind database and already generated the entity classes for it. Please review the section in Chapter 12 titled "Prerequisites for Running the Examples" to ensure that you have the appropriate database and generated entity classes.

In this chapter, because we will be demonstrating code that uses entity classes generated by both SQLMetal and the Object Relational Designer, we will not specify a `using` directive for the `nwind` namespace in the examples. Instead, we will explicitly specify the namespace where it's needed for the `nwind` classes. This is necessary in this chapter to control which `Customer` entity class is referenced in each example. Since, by default, the Object Relational Designer generates a namespace that is the same as your project and since the examples will already exist in your project's namespace, you will not need to specify the namespace for the designer-generated entity classes, but you will for the SQLMetal-generated entity classes.

■ **Note** Unlike most of the LINQ to SQL chapters, do not specify a `using` directive for the `nwind` namespace for the examples in this chapter.

Tips

In keeping with our style, we are going to jump the gun and give you some tips requiring information we have yet to discuss. So if this section makes little sense to you, our work is done! After all, we want you to know about these tips *before* you need them, not after you have learned them the hard way.

Use the DataContext.Log Property

Now is a good time to remind you of some of the LINQ to SQL–specific tips we provided in Chapter 1. One of those tips, titled "The DataContext Log," discussed how you could use the DataContext object's Log property to display what the translated SQL query will be. This can be very useful not only for debugging purposes but also for performance analysis. You may find that LINQ to SQL queries are getting translated into very inefficient SQL queries. Or, you may find that because of the *deferred loading* of associated entity classes, you are making many more SQL queries than necessary. The DataContext.Log property will reveal this type of information to you.

To take advantage of this feature, assign the DataContext.Log property to a System.IO.TextWriter object, such as Console.Out.

Listing 13-1 contains an example.

Listing 13-1. An Example Using the DataContext.Log Property

```
nwind.Northwind db =
  new nwind.Northwind(@"Data Source=.\SQLEXPRESS;Initial Catalog=Northwind");

db.Log = Console.Out;

var custs = from c in db.Customers
            where c.Region == "WA"
            select new { Id = c.CustomerID, Name = c.ContactName };

foreach (var cust in custs)
{
  Console.WriteLine("{0} - {1}", cust.Id, cust.Name);
}
```

Since we will be demonstrating both SQLMetal- and Object Relational Designer–generated entity classes in this chapter, there will be two Customer classes that exist for the examples. As we mentioned earlier, we did not include a using directive for the examples so that the entity classes such as Customer would not be ambiguous. Therefore, we have to specify the namespace nwind for the Northwind class in Listing 13-1, since we are using the SQLMetal-generated entity class code for this example.

As you can see, in Listing 13-1, we simply assign Console.Out to our Northwind DataContext object's Log property. Here are the results of Listing 13-1:

```
SELECT [t0].[CustomerID], [t0].[ContactName]
FROM [dbo].[Customers] AS [t0]
WHERE [t0].[Region] = @p0
-- @p0: Input String (Size = 2; Prec = 0; Scale = 0) [WA]
-- Context: SqlProvider(Sql2005) Model: AttributedMetaModel Build: 3.5.20706.1

LAZYK - John Steel
TRAIH - Helvetius Nagy
WHITC - Karl Jablonski
```

This allows us to see exactly what the generated SQL query looks like. Notice that the generated SQL statement is not just formatting a string; it is using parameters. So by using LINQ to SQL, we automatically get protection from SQL injection attacks.

■ **Caution** If you see in your results that the name associated with customer LAZYK is Ned Plimpton instead of John Steel as we show in the preceding example, you probably ran Listing 13-1 without setting the data back as we recommended.

In later chapters, we will demonstrate how to use this logging feature to detect and resolve potential performance issues.

Use the GetChangeSet() Method

You can use the `DataContext` object's `GetChangeSet` method to obtain all entity objects containing changes that need to be persisted to the database when the `SubmitChanges` method is called. This is useful for logging and debugging purposes. This method is also fully documented in Chapter 16.

Consider Using Partial Classes or Mapping Files

Without a doubt, one of the bigger hassles of using any ORM tool is going to be managing changes to the database. If you keep all your business class logic and LINQ to SQL logic in the same modules, you may be creating a maintenance headache for yourself down the road once the database changes. Consider leveraging partial classes by adding your business logic to a separate module than the generated entity class modules. By using partial classes to keep your LINQ to SQL database attributes separate from your business logic, you will minimize the need to add code back to any generated entity class code.

Alternatively, you could have your business classes and your LINQ to SQL entity mapping decoupled by using an external XML mapping file. This is an XML file that maps business objects to the database without relying on LINQ to SQL attributes. You can read more about mapping files in the "XML External Mapping File Schema" section in Chapter 15 and in the `DataContext` constructor section of Chapter 16.

Consider Using Partial Methods

Partial methods allow you to hook into certain events that occur in entity classes. The beauty of partial methods is that if you do not take advantage of them by implementing the body of a partial method, there is no overhead, and no code is emitted by the compiler to call them.

We discuss how partial methods are used in entity classes in the "Calling the Appropriate Partial Methods" section of Chapter 15.

Tools

Just as there are some tips we want to make you aware of before you actually need them, there are some tools that can make your life easier. Again, we may be bringing these up before they make sense to you, but we want you to be aware of them and how they can facilitate and accelerate your adoption of LINQ to SQL.

SQLMetal

Although we have yet to discuss the different ways to create the entity classes necessary to use LINQ to SQL with a database, you should know that the easiest way to generate all entity classes for an entire database, if you do not already have business classes, is with the SQLMetal program. You can find this tool in your C:\Program Files\Microsoft SDKs\Windows\v7.0A\Bin\NETFX 4.0 Tools directory. SQLMetal is a command-line tool that generates all the necessary and nifty parts of LINQ to SQL entity classes.

To see the options available for the SQLMetal program, open a Visual Studio command prompt. To do so, look in your Microsoft Visual Studio 2010 menu for an item named Visual Studio Command Prompt (2010) in a submenu named Visual Studio Tools , and select it.

Once the command prompt is open, type sqlmetal, and press Enter:

sqlmetal

This command will cause the program's template and options to be displayed:

```
Microsoft (R) Database Mapping Generator 2008 version 4.0.30319.1
for Microsoft (R) .NET Framework version 4.0
Copyright (C) Microsoft Corporation. All rights reserved.

SqlMetal [options] [<input file>]
Generates code and mapping for the LINQ to SQL component of the .NET framework.

SqlMetal can:

  - Generate source code and mapping attributes or a mapping file from a database.
  - Generate an intermediate dbml file for customization from the database.
  - Generate code and mapping attributes or mapping file from a dbml file.

Options:
  /server:<name>             Database server name.
  /database:<name>           Database catalog on server.
  /user:<name>               Login user ID (default: use Windows Authentication).
  /password:<password>       Login password (default: use Windows Authentication).
  /conn:<connection string>  Database connection string. Cannot be used with
/server, /database, /user or /password options.
  /timeout:<seconds>         Timeout value to use when SqlMetal accesses the
database (default: 0 which means infinite).
  /views                     Extract database views.
  /functions                 Extract database functions.
  /sprocs                    Extract stored procedures.
  /dbml[:file]               Output as dbml. Cannot be used with /map option.
```

```
   /code[:file]              Output as source code. Cannot be used with /dbml
option.
   /map[:file]               Generate mapping file, not attributes. Cannot be used
with /dbml option.
   /language:<language>      Language for source code: VB or C# (default: derived
from extension on code file name).
   /namespace:<name>         Namespace of generated code (default: no namespace).
   /context:<type>           Name of data context class (default: derived from
database name).
   /entitybase:<type>        Base class of entity classes in the generated code
(default: entities have no base class).
   /pluralize                Automatically pluralize or singularize class and
member names using English language rules.
   /serialization:<option>   Generate serializable classes: None or Unidirectional
(default: None).
   /provider:<type>          Provider type: SQLCompact, SQL2000, SQL2005, or
SQL2008. (default: provider is determined at run time).
   <input file>              May be a SqlExpress mdf file, a SqlCE sdf file, or a
dbml intermediate file.
Create code from SqlServer:
   SqlMetal /server:myserver /database:northwind /code:nwind.cs /namespace:nwind
Generate intermediate dbml file from SqlServer:
   SqlMetal /server:myserver /database:northwind /dbml:northwind.dbml
/namespace:nwind
Generate code with external mapping from dbml:
   SqlMetal /code:nwind.cs /map:nwind.map northwind.dbml
Generate dbml from a SqlCE sdf file:
   SqlMetal /dbml:northwind.dbml northwind.sdf

Generate dbml from SqlExpress local server:

   SqlMetal /server:.\sqlexpress /database:northwind /dbml:northwind.dbml
Generate dbml by using a connection string in the command line:
   SqlMetal /conn:"server='myserver'; database='northwind'" /dbml:northwind.dbml
```

As you can see, it even provides a few examples too. Table 13-1 summarizes the options.

Table 13-1. *SQLMetal Command-Line Options*

Option / Example	Description
`/server:<name>` `/server:.\SQLExpress`	This option allows you to specify the name of the database server to connect to. If omitted, SQLMetal will default to `localhost/sqlexpress`. To have SQLMetal generate entity classes from an MDF file, omit this option and the `/database` option, and specify the MDF file name at the end of the command.
`/database:<name>` `/database:Northwind`	This is the name of the database on the specified server for which to generate entity classes. To have SQLMetal generate entity classes from an MDF file, omit this option and the `/server` option, and specify the MDF file name at the end of the command.
`/user:<name>` `/user:sa`	This is the user account used to log in to the specified database when connecting to create the entity classes.
`/password:<password>` `/password:1590597893`	This is the password used for the specified user account to log in to the specified database when connecting to create the entity classes.
`/conn:<connection string>` `/conn:"Data Source=.\SQLEXPRESS;Initial Catalog=Northwind;Integrated Security=SSPI;"`	This is a connection string to the database. You may use this instead of specifying the `/server`, `/database`, `/user`, and `/password` options.
`/timeout:<seconds>` `/timeout:120`	This option allows you to specify the time-out value in seconds for SqlMetal to use when generating the entity classes. Omitting this option will cause SqlMetal to default to 0, which means never time out. This option does not control the time-out your generated `DataContext` will use for LINQ to SQL queries. If you want to control the time-out for that, consider setting the `CommandTimeout` property of the `DataContext` class, or for even more granular control, call the `DataContext.GetCommand` method to set the time-out for a specific query. See Chapter 16 for an example doing this.
`/views` `/views`	Specify this option to have SQLMetal generate the necessary `Table<T>` properties and entity classes to support the specified database's views.

`/functions` `/functions`	Specify this option to have SQLMetal generate methods to call the specified database's user-defined functions.
`/sprocs` `/sprocs`	Specify this option to have SQLMetal generate methods to call the specified database's stored procedures.
`/dbml[:file]` `/dbml:Northwind.dbml`	This option specifies the file name for a DBML intermediate file. The purpose of generating this file is so that you control class and property names of the generated entity classes. You would generate the DBML intermediate file with this option, edit the file, and then create a source code module by calling SQLMetal on the intermediate DBML file and specifying the `/code` option. Alternatively, you could load the DBML intermediate file created with this option into the Object Relational Designer, edit the file in the designer using its GUI, and allow the designer to generate the necessary source code. This option cannot be used with the `/map` option.
`/code[:file]` `/code:Northwind.cs`	This is the file for SQLMetal to create and that contains the derived `DataContext` and entity classes in the specified programming language. This option cannot be used with the `/dbml` option. Interestingly, if you specify both the `/code` and `/map` options in the same invocation of SQLMetal, you will get code generated without LINQ to SQL attributes. Of course, you would use the also generated map with the generated code to be able to use LINQ to SQL.
`/map[:file]` `/map:northwindmap.xml`	This option specifies that SQLMetal should generate an XML external mapping file, as opposed to a source code module specified by the `/code` option. This XML external mapping file can then be loaded when instantiating the `DataContext`. This allows LINQ to SQL to be used without any actual LINQ to SQL source code being compiled with your code.
`/language:<language> language:C#`	This option defines for which programming language SQLMetal is to generate the code. The valid options are currently `csharp`, `C#`, and `VB`. Omitting this option will cause SQLMetal to derive the language from the specified code file name's extension.

`/namespace:<name>` `/namespace:nwind`	This dictates the namespace that the generated derived `DataContext` and entity classes will live in.
`/context:<type>` `/context:Northwind`	This specifies the name of the generated class that will be derived from the `DataContext` class.
	If this option is omitted, the class name will be the same as the database for which the code was generated.
`/entitybase:<type>` `/entitybase:MyEntityClassBase`	This specifies the name of a class for SQLMetal to specify as the base class for all generated entity classes.
	If this option is omitted, the generated entity classes will not be derived from any class.
`/pluralize` `/pluralize`	This option causes SQLMetal to retain the plural names for tables but to singularize the entity class names mapped to those tables. So, for a database table named Customers, the entity class generated will be named `Customer` (singular), and a `Table<Customer>` will be generated named `Customers` (plural). In this way, a `Customer` object exists in a `Customers` table. Grammatically speaking, this sounds correct.
	Without specifying this option, the entity class will be named `Customers` (plural), and the `Table<Customers>` will be named `Customers` (plural). This means a `Customers` object will exist in the Customers table. Grammatically speaking, this sounds incorrect.
`/serialization:<option>` `/serialization:None`	This option specifies whether SQLMetal should generate serialization attributes for the classes. The choices are `None` and `Unidirectional`.
	If this option is not specified, SQLMetal will default to `None`.
`/provider:<type>` `/provider:SQL2005`	This option is used to specify the database provider class. The valid values are `SQLCompact`, `SQL2000`, `SQL2005`, and `SQL2008`. SQLMetal will generate a `Provider` attribute that specifies the class you specify with this option.
	Each of these values maps to a provider class in the `System.Data.Linq.SqlClient` namespace. SqlMetal will append `Provider` to the end of the value specified to build the provider class name and generate a `Provider` attribute specifying that provider class name.

Notice that the /dbml, /code, and /map options may be specified without providing a file name. If a file name is not specified, the generated code or XML will be output to the console.

XML Mapping File Vs. DBML Intermediate File

One of the confusing aspects of using SQLMetal is that it allows you to specify two different types of XML files to produce. One is created by specifying the /map option, and the other is created by specifying the /dbml option.

The difference between these two files is that the /map option creates an XML external mapping file intended to be loaded when the DataContext is instantiated. The /map option is an alternative to generating, or writing by hand, a source module containing LINQ to SQL attributes that you compile. With this approach, your source code never has any database-specific LINQ to SQL code compiled with or linked to it. This allows for somewhat dynamic consumption of a database, since you do not need any pregenerated and compiled code. We say it is "somewhat dynamic," because your code has to know the names of tables and fields; otherwise, it wouldn't even know what to query. The XML external mapping file instructs LINQ to SQL as to what tables, columns, and stored procedures exist with which it can interact and to what classes, class properties, and methods they should be mapped.

The /dbml option creates an intermediate DBML (XML) file for the purpose of allowing you to edit class and property names for the soon-to-be-generated entity classes. You would then generate a source code module by running SQLMetal again, this time against the DBML file instead of the database, and specifying the /code option. Or, you can load the DBML intermediate file into the Object Relational Designer, edit it in the designer, and allow the designer to generate the necessary entity class source code.

Another reason that the two XML files that SQLMetal can produce, the XML mapping file and the DBML intermediate file, are confusing is that their schemas are fairly similar. So, don't be surprised when you see just how similar they are. The schema for the XML mapping file will be discussed in Chapter 15.

Working with DBML Intermediate Files

As we said, the purpose of the DBML intermediate file is to allow you the opportunity to insert yourself between the database schema extraction and the entity class generation so that you can control class and property names. Therefore, if you have no need to do that, you have no need to generate a DBML intermediate file. That said, let's continue as though you have the need.

Assuming you have the extended Northwind database attached to your SQL Server database, here is how you would create the intermediate DBML file:

```
sqlmetal /server:.\SQLExpress /database:Northwind /pluralize /sprocs /functions
/views /dbml:Northwind.dbml
```

■ **Note** Specifying the /server and /database options when running SQLMetal requires that the extended Northwind database be attached to SQL Server.

Additionally, you may need to specify the appropriate /user and /password options so that SQLMetal can connect to the database.

Or, if you prefer, you can generate the DBML intermediate file from an MDF file:

```
sqlmetal /pluralize /sprocs /functions /views /dbml:Northwind.dbml
"C:\Northwind.mdf"
```

■ **Note** Generating the DBML intermediate file from an MDF file may cause the MDF database file to be attached to SQL Server with the name C:\NORTHWIND.MDF or something similar. You should rename the database to "Northwind" inside SQL Server Enterprise Manager or SQL Server Management Studio so that the examples work properly.

Either of these two approaches should produce an identical DBML intermediate file. We specified only those options relevant for reading the database and producing the DBML file. Options such as /language and /code are relevant only when creating the source code module.

Once you have edited your intermediate XML file, here is how you would produce the source code module:

```
sqlmetal /namespace:nwind /code:Northwind.cs Northwind.dbml
```

The options we specified in that execution of SQLMetal are relevant when generating the source code.

DBML Intermediate File Schema

If you decide to take the route of creating the DBML intermediate file so that you can edit it and then generate your entity class mappings from that, you will need to know the schema and what the element and attribute names mean.

Because the schema is subject to change, please consult the Microsoft documentation for the DBML intermediate file schema for the most recent schema definition and explanation. Once you understand the schema, you could choose to manually edit the DBML intermediate file to control entity class and property names and then generate the entity class source code with SQLMetal from your edited DBML intermediate file.

Or, even better, you can load the generated DBML intermediate file into Visual Studio's Object Relational Designer and edit it there. This will give you a GUI interface for maintaining your object/relational (O/R) model and free you from the necessity of knowing and understanding the schema. We will describe how to edit your O/R model in the next section.

The Object Relational Designer

In addition to the SQLMetal tool, there is also a graphical user tool for generating entity classes that runs inside Visual Studio. This tool is called the Object Relational Designer, but you will commonly see it referred to as the LINQ to SQL Designer, the O/R Designer, or even DLinq Designer. The Object Relational Designer is a more selective tool than SQLMetal. The designer gives the developer drag-and-drop design-time entity class modeling. You needn't worry; the designer does most of the difficult work for you. You get the easy parts of selecting the database tables you want modeled and, if it suits you, editing entity class and entity class property names. Of course, you still have the option of doing all the modeling manually in the designer if you desire ultimate control.

Creating Your LINQ to SQL Classes File

The first step to use the designer is to create a LINQ to SQL Classes file by right-clicking your project and selecting Add ➤ New Item from the context menu. After doing that, the Add New Item dialog box will open. Select the LINQ to SQL Classes template from the list of installed templates. Edit the name to whatever you choose. The name of the database you will be modeling is typically a good choice for the LINQ to SQL Classes file name. The extension for a LINQ to SQL Classes file is `.dbml`. For this example, we will use `Northwind.dbml` for the name of the file.

■ **Caution** If you create a file named `Northwind.dbml` in a project you have already created for the samples in this book, be careful that you don't end up with a name collision between the designer-generated code and your already existing code.

Click the Add button once you have named the file. You will then be presented with a blank window. This is your designer canvas. Figure 13-1 shows the designer canvas.

If you click the canvas and examine the Properties window, you will see a property named `Name`. The value of the `Name` property will be the name of the generated `DataContext` class. Because we named our LINQ to SQL Classes file `Northwind.dbml`, the `Name` property's value will default to `NorthwindDataContext`, which is just fine. You could change it if you wanted to, but for this discussion, we will leave it as it is.

If you examine the Solution Explorer, you will see that you now have a file nested under `Northwind.dbml` named `Northwind.designer.cs`. If you open this file, you will see that it contains very little code at this point. Basically, it will contain the constructors for the new `DataContext` class it is deriving for that you named `NorthwindDataContext`.

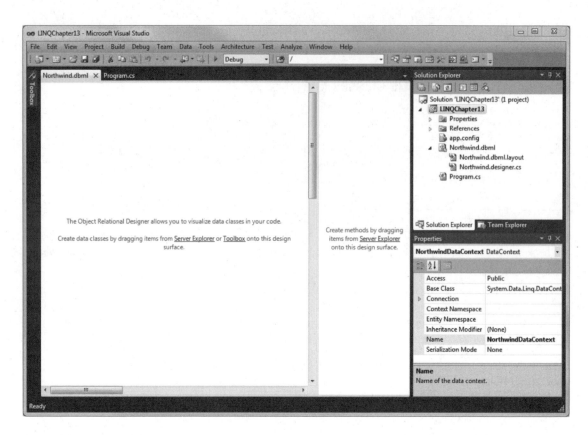

Figure 13-1. *The Object Relational Designer canvas*

Connecting the DataContext to the Database

The next step is to add a connection to the appropriate database server containing the Northwind database in the Server Explorer window if one does not already exist.

■ **Tip** If you do not see the Server Explorer window, select Server Explorer from the Visual Studio View menu.

To add a connection to the database, right-click the Data Connections node in the Server Explorer window, and choose the Add Connection menu item to open the Add Connection dialog box, shown in Figure 13-2. The "Data source" entry field will default to Microsoft SQL Server (SqlClient), which is what we want. Configure the appropriate settings for your Northwind database in the Add Connection dialog box.

Figure 13-2. The Add Connection dialog box

Once you have the connection properly configured, click the OK button. You should now have a node representing your Northwind database connection under the Data Connections node in the Server Explorer. You may now access the Northwind database in the designer.

Before proceeding, make sure you are viewing the `Northwind.dbml` file in the Visual Studio editor.

Adding an Entity Class

Find your Northwind database in the list of Data Connections in the Server Explorer window. Expand the `Tables` node, and you should be presented with a list of tables in the Northwind database. Entity classes are created by dragging tables from the `Table` list in the Server Explorer window to the designer canvas.

From the Server Explorer, drag the Customers table to the designer canvas. You have just instructed the designer to create an entity class for the Customers table named `Customer`. Your canvas should look like Figure 13-3.

You may have to resize some of the panes to be able to see everything clearly. By dragging the Customers table to the designer canvas, the source code for the `Customer` entity class is added to the `Northwind.designer.cs` source file. Once you build your project, which we will do in a few moments, you can begin using the `Customer` entity class to access and update data in the Northwind database. It's just that simple!

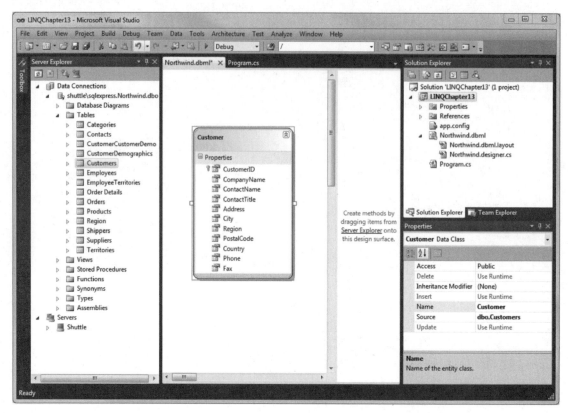

Figure 13-3. The designer after dragging the Customers table to the canvas

However, before we build the project and write code using the generated entity classes, we want to create a few more bits necessary to reap all the benefits of LINQ to SQL. Now, from the Server Explorer, drag the Orders table to the canvas. You may need to move it around the canvas to get it to a desirable location. You have now instructed the designer to create an entity class for the Orders table named `Order`. Your canvas should look something like Figure 13-4.

Looking at the canvas, you will see a dashed line connecting the `Customer` class to the `Order` class. That dashed line represents the relationship, referred to as an *association* in LINQ to SQL, between the Customers and Orders tables, as defined by the `FK_Orders_Customers` foreign key constraint that exists in the Northwind database. That line being there indicates that the designer will also be creating the necessary association in the entity classes to support the relationship between those two entity classes. The existence of that association will allow you to obtain a reference to a collection of a customer's orders by referencing a property on a `Customer` object and to obtain a reference to an order's customer by referencing a property on an `Order` object.

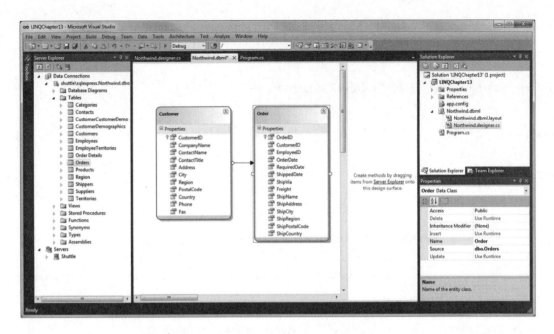

Figure 13-4. *The designer after dragging the Orders table to the canvas*

If you do not want the association to be generated, you can select the dashed line representing the association and delete it by pressing the Delete key or by right-clicking the dashed line and selecting the Delete menu option from the context menu.

Using the Designer-Generated Entity Classes

You are now ready to use the entity classes the designer generated for you. Listing 13-2 contains an example querying the database for the customers whose city is London.

Listing 13-2. *An Example Using the Designer-Generated Entity Classes*

```
NorthwindDataContext db = new NorthwindDataContext();

IQueryable<Customer> custs = from c in db.Customers
                             where c.City == "London"
                             select c;

foreach(Customer c in custs)
{
  Console.WriteLine("{0} has {1} orders.", c.CompanyName, c.Orders.Count);
}
```

This looks like our other examples with one key difference. Notice that we did not specify any connection information when instantiating the `NorthwindDataContext` object. This is because the designer generated our NorthwindDataContext class with a parameterless constructor that gets the connection information from the project's settings file named app.config. It was even kind enough to set the value in the settings file. Here is what the generated parameterless constructor looks like:

The Designer-Generated DataContext Constructor

```
public NorthwindDataContext() :
  base(global::LINQChapter13.Properties.Settings.Default.NorthwindConnectionString,
      mappingSource)
{
  OnCreated();
}
```

■ **Caution** If you download the companion source code for this book, make sure you update the connectionString setting in the app.config file.

Notice in the preceding code that we are able to access the retrieved customer's orders by referencing a Customer object's Orders property. This is because of the association that the designer created automatically for us. How cool is that? Here are the results of Listing 13-2:

```
Around the Horn has 13 orders.
B's Beverages has 10 orders.
Consolidated Holdings has 3 orders.
Eastern Connection has 8 orders.
North/South has 3 orders.
Seven Seas Imports has 9 orders.
```

Editing the Entity Class Model

Naturally, you may want to have some control over entity class names, entity class properties (entity class settings), entity class property (entity class member) names, and entity class property (entity class member) properties (settings). OK, Microsoft, can you make the naming any more confusing? Did you really need to call the members of classes *properties*, knowing that in Visual Studio you call the settings *properties* too?

The flexibility and ease of use for controlling the names of entity classes and their properties are what makes the designer so attractive. It's all drag and drop, point and click, man!

Editing the Entity Class Name

You can edit the entity class name by double-clicking the name on the canvas or by selecting the entity class on the canvas and editing the Name property in the Properties window.

Editing the Entity Class's Properties (Entity Class Settings)

You can edit the properties, as in settings, of the entity class by selecting the entity class on the canvas and editing the appropriate properties in the Properties window, of which the entity class name is one. You have the ability to edit the database table name in which these entities are stored; the insert, update, and delete override methods; and other properties.

Editing an Entity Class Property (Entity Class Member) Name

You can edit the name of an entity class property, as in entity class member, by triple-clicking the property name on the canvas. We weren't aware that there was such a thing as triple-clicking either, but that's what it appears to be responding to. Or, you can select the entity class property on the canvas and edit the `Name` property in the Properties window.

Editing an Entity Class Property's (Entity Class Member's) Properties (Settings)

You can edit an entity class property's properties by selecting the property on the canvas and editing the appropriate property in the Properties window, of which the entity class property name is one. This is where you will find all the properties that correspond to the entity class attribute properties, such as `Name` and `UpdateCheck`, for the `Column` entity class attribute. We will discuss the entity class attributes in detail in Chapter 15.

Adding Objects to the Entity Class Model

Dragging and dropping an entity class on the canvas is simple enough, as long as you have a table in a database in the Server Explorer. There are times when you may not have this luxury. Perhaps you are defining the entity class first and plan to generate the database by calling the `CreateDatabase` method on the `DataContext`. Or, perhaps you are going to be taking advantage of entity class inheritance, and there is no existing table to map to.

Adding New Entity Classes

One way to add new entity classes to your entity class model is to drag them from the tables of a database in your Server Explorer window, as we did in the previous section. Another way you can create a new entity class is by dragging the Object Relational Designer Class object in the Visual Studio Toolbox onto the canvas. Edit the name, and set the entity class's properties as described in the previous section.

Adding New Entity Class Properties (Members)

You can add new entity class properties (members) by right-clicking the entity class in the designer and selecting the Property menu item in the Add context menu. Once the property has been added to the entity class, follow the directions for editing an entity class property's properties in the earlier "Editing an Entity Class Property's (Entity Class Member's) Properties (Settings)" section.

Adding a New Association

Instead of using drag and drop to create an association, like you did when adding a new entity class from the Visual Studio Toolbox, you can create an association by clicking the Association object in the Toolbox followed by clicking the parent entity class (the *one* side of the one-to-many relationship) followed by clicking the child entity class (the *many* side of the one-to-many relationship). Each of the two classes needs to have the appropriate property before you add the association so that you can map the primary key on the *one* side to the foreign key of the *many* side. Once you have selected the second class, the *many* class, of the association by clicking it, the Association Editor dialog box will open allowing you to map the property of the *one* class to its corresponding property of the *many* class.

Once you have mapped the properties and dismissed the Association Editor dialog box, you will see a dotted line connecting the parent to the child entity class.

Select the association by clicking the dotted line, and set the appropriate association properties in the Properties window. Refer to the descriptions of the `Association` attribute and its properties in Chapter 15 for more information about the association properties.

Adding a New Inheritance Relationship

You can use the Object Relational Designer to model inheritance relationships, too. Adding an inheritance relationship works just like adding a new association. Select the Inheritance object in the Visual Studio Toolbox, and click the entity class that will be the derived class, followed by the entity class that will be the base class. Make sure to set all appropriate entity class properties as defined by the `InheritanceMapping` and `Column` entity class attributes, which we cover in Chapter 15.

Adding Stored Procedures and User-Defined Functions

To have the designer generate the code necessary to call stored procedures or user-defined functions, drag the stored procedure or user-defined function from the Server Explorer to the Methods pane of the designer. We will demonstrate this in the next section.

Overriding the Insert, Update, and Delete Methods

In Chapter 14, we will discuss overriding the insert, update, and delete methods used by LINQ to SQL when making changes to an entity class object. You can override the default methods by adding specific methods to an entity class. If you take this approach, be sure to use partial classes so you are not modifying any generated code. We will demonstrate how to do this in Chapter 14.

However, overriding the insert, update, and delete methods is easily accomplished in the designer too. Let's assume you have a stored procedure named `InsertCustomer` that will insert a new customer record into the `Northwind` database's `Customer` table. Here is the stored procedure we will use:

The InsertCustomer Stored Procedure

```
CREATE PROCEDURE dbo.InsertCustomer
  (
  @CustomerID        nchar(5),
  @CompanyName       nvarchar(40),
  @ContactName       nvarchar(30),
  @ContactTitle      nvarchar(30),
  @Address           nvarchar(60),
  @City              nvarchar(15),
  @Region            nvarchar(15),
  @PostalCode        nvarchar(10),
  @Country           nvarchar(15),
  @Phone             nvarchar(24),
```

```
@Fax              nvarchar(24)
)
AS
  INSERT INTO Customers
  (
    CustomerID,
    CompanyName,
    ContactName,
    ContactTitle,
    Address,
    City,
    Region,
    PostalCode,
    Country,
    Phone,
    Fax
  )
  VALUES
  (
    @CustomerID,
    @CompanyName,
    @ContactName,
    @ContactTitle,
    @Address,
    @City,
    @Region,
    @PostalCode,
    @Country,
    @Phone,
    @Fax
  )
```

■ **Note** The `InsertCustomer` stored procedure is not part of the extended Northwind database. We manually added it for this demonstration.

To override the `Customer` entity class's insert method, first make sure the Methods pane is visible. If it is not, right-click the canvas, and select the Show Methods Pane context menu item. Next, open the Server Explorer window in Visual Studio. Find and expand the Stored Procedures node in the appropriate database node in the tree. Your Visual Studio should look very similar to Figure 13-5.

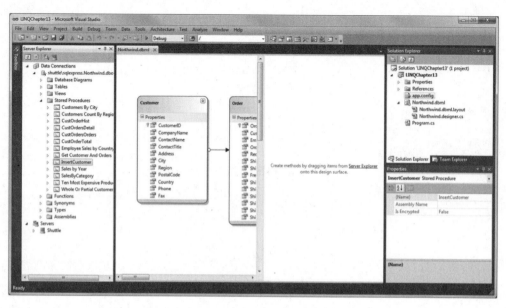

Figure 13-5. Finding the stored procedure

Once you have found your stored procedure, simply drag it to the Methods pane, which is the window to the right of the entity class model. Figure 13-6 shows Visual Studio after we have dragged the `InsertCustomer` stored procedure to the Methods pane.

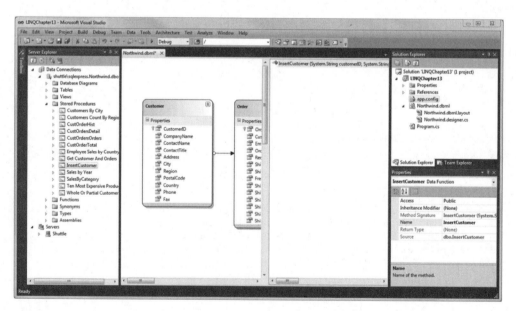

Figure 13-6. Dropping the stored procedure on the Methods pane

Dragging a stored procedure from the Server Explorer window to the Methods pane is the way you instruct the designer to generate the code necessary to call the stored procedure from LINQ to SQL. This is also the same way you instruct the designer to generate the code for a user-defined function too.

Making the stored procedure accessible from LINQ to SQL is the first step to having the insert, update, or delete operation call a stored procedure instead of the default method. The next step is to override one of those operations to call the now accessible stored procedure.

Now that the `InsertCustomer` stored procedure is in the Methods pane, select the `Customer` class in the designer canvas, and examine the Properties window for the `Customer` class. You will now see a list of the Default Methods. Select the Insert method by clicking it. You will now be presented with the ellipses (…) selection button as is displayed in Figure 13-7.

Now, simply click the ellipses selection button to display the Configure Behavior dialog box. Select the Customize radio button, and select the `InsertCustomer` stored procedure from the drop-down list. Map the Method Arguments on the left to the appropriate Customer Class Properties on the right, as illustrated in Figure 13-8.

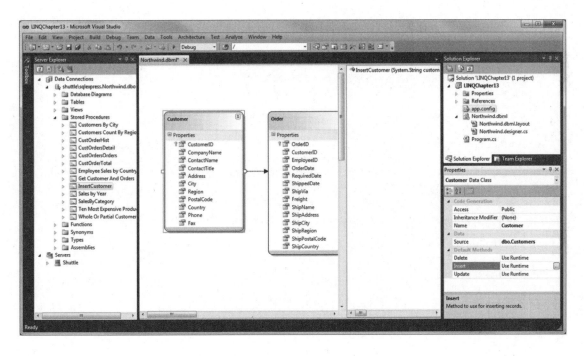

Figure 13-7. Select the Insert method in the Default Methods category of the Properties window.

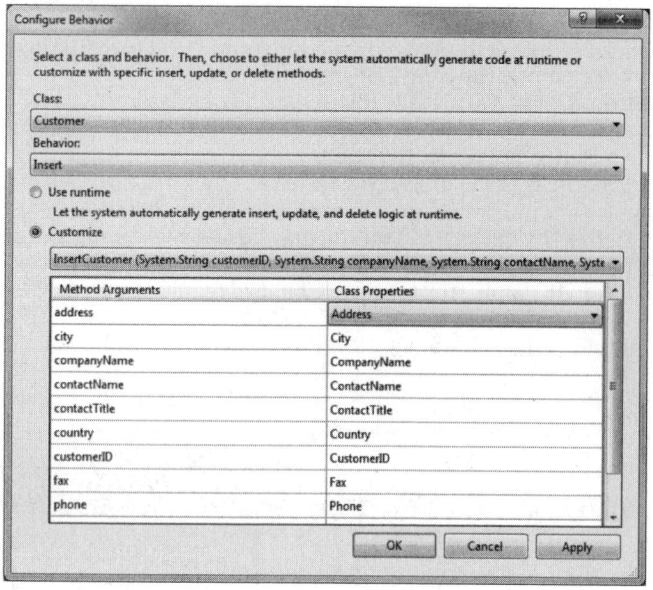

Figure 13-8. Mapping method arguments to class properties

All our method arguments were already mapped by default to the appropriate class properties. Nice!
Once you have mapped all the method arguments, click the OK button. You are now ready to insert
`Customer` records using the `InsertCustomer` stored procedure. In Listing 13-3, we will create a new
customer using the `InsertCustomer` stored procedure.

Listing 13-3. Creating a Customer Record with the Default Insert Method Overridden

```
NorthwindDataContext db = new NorthwindDataContext();

db.Log = Console.Out;

Customer cust =
  new Customer
    {
      CustomerID = "EWICH",
      CompanyName = "Every 'Wich Way",
      ContactName = "Vickey Rattz",
      ContactTitle = "Owner",
      Address = "105 Chip Morrow Dr.",
      City = "Alligator Point",
      Region = "FL",
      PostalCode = "32346",
      Country = "USA",
      Phone = "(800) EAT-WICH",
      Fax = "(800) FAX-WICH"
```

```
    };

db.Customers.InsertOnSubmit(cust);

db.SubmitChanges();

Customer customer = db.Customers.Where(c => c.CustomerID == "EWICH").First();
Console.WriteLine("{0} - {1}", customer.CompanyName, customer.ContactName);

//  Restore the database.
db.Customers.DeleteOnSubmit(cust);
db.SubmitChanges();
```

Notice that we are not specifying any namespace on the `Customer` class that we reference; therefore, we will be using the `Customer` class that exists in the same namespace as the project, which is the designer-generated `Customer` class.

There is nothing special in Listing 13-3. We merely instantiate a `DataContext`, which in this case is the designer-generated `NorthwindDataContext`. We then create a new `Customer` object and insert it into the `Customers` `Table<T>` property. Next, we call the `SubmitChanges` method to persist the new customer to the database. Then, we query for that customer from the database and display it to the console just to prove the record was indeed inserted into the database table. The very last things we do are delete the customer by calling the `DeleteOnSubmit` method and persist to the database by calling the `SubmitChanges` method, so the database is left in the same state it was initially so that subsequent examples will run properly and so that this example can be run multiple times.

Let's examine the output of Listing 13-3:

```
EXEC @RETURN_VALUE = [dbo].[InsertCustomer] @CustomerID = @p0, @CompanyName = @p1,
@ContactName = @p2, @ContactTitle = @p3, @Address = @p4, @City = @p5, @Region =
@p6,
@PostalCode = @p7, @Country = @p8, @Phone = @p9, @Fax = @p10
-- @p0: Input StringFixedLength (Size = 5; Prec = 0; Scale = 0) [EWICH]
-- @p1: Input String (Size = 15; Prec = 0; Scale = 0) [Every 'Wich Way]
-- @p2: Input String (Size = 12; Prec = 0; Scale = 0) [Vickey Rattz]
-- @p3: Input String (Size = 5; Prec = 0; Scale = 0) [Owner]
-- @p4: Input String (Size = 19; Prec = 0; Scale = 0) [105 Chip Morrow Dr.]
-- @p5: Input String (Size = 15; Prec = 0; Scale = 0) [Alligator Point]
-- @p6: Input String (Size = 2; Prec = 0; Scale = 0) [FL]
-- @p7: Input String (Size = 5; Prec = 0; Scale = 0) [32346]
-- @p8: Input String (Size = 3; Prec = 0; Scale = 0) [USA]
-- @p9: Input String (Size = 14; Prec = 0; Scale = 0) [(800) EAT-WICH]
-- @p10: Input String (Size = 14; Prec = 0; Scale = 0) [(800) FAX-WICH]
-- @RETURN_VALUE: Output Int32 (Size = 0; Prec = 0; Scale = 0) []
-- Context: SqlProvider(Sql2005) Model: AttributedMetaModel Build: 3.5.20706.1

SELECT TOP 1 [t0].[CustomerID], [t0].[CompanyName], [t0].[ContactName],
[t0].[ContactTitle], [t0].[Address], [t0].[City], [t0].[Region], [t0].[PostalCode],
[t0].[Country], [t0].[Phone], [t0].[Fax]
```

```
FROM [dbo].[Customers] AS [t0]
WHERE [t0].[CustomerID] = @p0
-- @p0: Input String (Size = 5; Prec = 0; Scale = 0) [EWICH]
-- Context: SqlProvider(Sql2005) Model: AttributedMetaModel Build: 3.5.20706.1

Every 'Wich Way - Vickey Rattz
DELETE FROM [dbo].[Customers] WHERE ([CustomerID] = @p0) AND ([CompanyName] = @p1)
AND ([ContactName] = @p2) AND ([ContactTitle] = @p3) AND ([Address] = @p4) AND
([City] = @p5) AND ([Region] = @p6) AND ([PostalCode] = @p7) AND ([Country] = @p8)
AND ([Phone] = @p9) AND ([Fax] = @p10)
-- @p0: Input StringFixedLength (Size = 5; Prec = 0; Scale = 0) [EWICH]
-- @p1: Input String (Size = 15; Prec = 0; Scale = 0) [Every 'Wich Way]
-- @p2: Input String (Size = 12; Prec = 0; Scale = 0) [Vickey Rattz]
-- @p3: Input String (Size = 5; Prec = 0; Scale = 0) [Owner]
-- @p4: Input String (Size = 19; Prec = 0; Scale = 0) [105 Chip Morrow Dr.]
-- @p5: Input String (Size = 15; Prec = 0; Scale = 0) [Alligator Point]
-- @p6: Input String (Size = 2; Prec = 0; Scale = 0) [FL]

-- @p7: Input String (Size = 5; Prec = 0; Scale = 0) [32346]

-- @p8: Input String (Size = 3; Prec = 0; Scale = 0) [USA]
-- @p9: Input String (Size = 14; Prec = 0; Scale = 0) [(800) EAT-WICH]
-- @p10: Input String (Size = 14; Prec = 0; Scale = 0) [(800) FAX-WICH]
-- Context: SqlProvider(Sql2005) Model: AttributedMetaModel Build: 3.5.20706.1
```

Although it is a little difficult to see with all the output, a SQL insert statement was not created. Instead, the InsertCustomer stored procedure was called. The designer makes it very easy to override the insert, update, and delete methods for an entity class.

Use SQLMetal and the O/R Designer Together

Because SQLMetal's DBML intermediate file format shares the same XML schema as the Object Relational Designer's format, it is possible to use them together.

For example, you could generate a DBML intermediate file for a database using SQLMetal and then load that file into the O/R Designer to tweak any entity class or entity class property names you desire. This approach provides a simple way to generate entity classes for an entire database yet makes it simple to modify what you would like.

Another example where this interchangeability can be useful is for overriding the insert, update, and delete operations that are performed to make changes to the database for an entity class. You can generate the DBML intermediate file for your database with SQLMetal but then load the file into the designer and modify the insert, update, and delete methods, as was described in the section in this chapter about the Object Relational Designer.

Summary

As is typical of our style, much of the information in this chapter may seem premature, since we have yet to actually discuss entity classes or the `DataContext` class. However, we just can't, in good conscience, allow you to continue without you knowing some of these tips and tools that are available for LINQ to SQL development. Refer to these tips once you have the foundation to more fully understand them.

Remember that there are two tools for modeling your entity classes. The first, SQLMetal, is a command-line tool suited to generating entity classes for an entire database. The second tool, the Object Relational Designer, often referred to as the LINQ to SQL Designer, is a GUI drag-and-drop entity class modeling tool that runs in Visual Studio. It is better suited for iterative and new development. But, as we pointed out, these two tools work well together. Your best path may be to start with SQLMetal to generate your entity classes for your entire database and maintain your entity classes with the Object Relational Designer.

Now that we have provided some tips, covered the LINQ to SQL tools, and you have had the opportunity to create your entity classes, in Chapter 14, we will show you how to perform the most common database operations you will use on a regular basis.

LINQ to SQL Database Operations

In this chapter, we will discuss and demonstrate how all of the typical database operations are performed with LINQ to SQL. Specifically, we will cover how to perform the following:

- Inserts
- Queries
- Updates
- Deletes

After we discuss the standard database operations, we will demonstrate how you can override the default insert, update, and delete methods an entity class uses to persist changes to the database.

The last topic we will cover is the automatic translation of LINQ to SQL queries, including what to be mindful of when writing queries.

To discuss the standard database operations, we will have to refer to the `DataContext` and relevant entity classes. We are aware that we have not provided much detail yet as to how entity classes and the `DataContext` class work, but we will cover them in subsequent chapters. We will discuss entity classes in Chapter 15 and the `DataContext` class in Chapter 16. For now, just remember that the `DataContext` manages the connection to the database the entity class objects. An entity class object represents a specific database record in object form.

Prerequisites for Running the Examples

To run the examples in this chapter, you will need to have obtained the extended version of the Northwind database and generated entity classes for it. Please read and follow the instructions in Chapter 12's "Prerequisites for Running the Examples" section.

Some Common Methods

Additionally, to run the examples in this chapter, you will need some common methods that will be utilized by the examples. Please read and follow the instructions in Chapter 12's "Some Common Methods" section.

Using the LINQ to SQL API

To run the examples in this chapter, you may need to add the appropriate references and using directives to your project. Please read and follow the instructions in Chapter 12's "Using the LINQ to SQL API" section.

Standard Database Operations

Although we will be covering the details of performing LINQ to SQL queries in detail in subsequent LINQ to SQL chapters, we want to give you a glimpse of how to perform the rudimentary database operations. These examples are meant to demonstrate the basic concepts. As such, they do not include error checking or exception handling.

For example, since many of the basic operations we discuss make changes to the database, those that make changes should detect and resolve concurrency conflicts. But, for the sake of simplicity, these examples will not demonstrate these principles. However, in Chapter 17, we will discuss concurrency conflict detection and resolution.

Inserts

There are four steps required to perform an insert. The first is to create a DataContext —this is the first step for every LINQ to SQL query, in fact. For the second step, an entity object is instantiated from an entity class (such as the Customer class). Third, that entity object is inserted into the appropriate table collection of type Table<T>, where T is the type of the entity class stored in the table, or is added to an EntitySet<T> on an entity object already being tracked by the DataContext, where T is the type of an entity class.

For the fourth and final step, the SubmitChanges method is called on the DataContext.

Listing 14-1 contains an example of inserting a record into the database.

Listing 14-1. Inserting a Record by Inserting an Entity Object into Table<T>

```
// 1.  Create the DataContext.
Northwind db = new Northwind(@"Data Source=.\SQLEXPRESS;Initial
Catalog=Northwind");

// 2.  Instantiate an entity object.
Customer cust =
  new Customer
    {
      CustomerID = "LAWN",
      CompanyName = "Lawn Wranglers",
      ContactName = "Mr. Abe Henry",
      ContactTitle = "Owner",
      Address = "1017 Maple Leaf Way",
      City = "Ft. Worth",
      Region = "TX",
      PostalCode = "76104",
      Country = "USA",
```

```
      Phone = "(800) MOW-LAWN",
      Fax = "(800) MOW-LAWO"
   };

// 3.  Add the entity object to the Customers table.
db.Customers.InsertOnSubmit(cust);

// 4.  Call the SubmitChanges method.
db.SubmitChanges();

// Query the record.
Customer customer = db.Customers.Where(c => c.CustomerID == "LAWN").First();
Console.WriteLine("{0} - {1}", customer.CompanyName, customer.ContactName);

// This part of the code merely resets the database so the example can be
// run more than once.
Console.WriteLine("Deleting the added customer LAWN.");
db.Customers.DeleteOnSubmit(cust);
db.SubmitChanges();
```

There really isn't much to this example. First, we create a `Northwind` object so that we have a `DataContext` for the Northwind database. Second, we instantiate a `Customer` object and populate it using object initialization. Third, we insert the instantiated `Customer` object into the Customers table, which is of type `Table<Customer>`, in the `Northwind DataContext` class. Fourth, we call the `SubmitChanges` method to persist the newly created `Customer` object to the database. Finally, we query the customer back out of the database just to prove it was inserted.

■ **Note** If you run this example, a new record will be temporarily added to the Northwind Customers table for customer LAWN. Please notice that after the newly added record is queried and displayed, it is then deleted. We do this so that the example can be run more than once and so the newly inserted record does not affect subsequent examples. Any time one of our examples changes the database, the database needs to be returned to its original state so that no examples are impacted. If any example that modifies the database is unable to complete for some reason, you should manually reset the database to its original state.

Here are the results of Listing 14-1:

```
Lawn Wranglers - Mr. Abe Henry
Deleting the added customer LAWN.
```

As you can see from the output, the inserted record was found in the database.

Alternatively, we can add a new instance of an entity class to an already existing entity object being tracked by the DataContext object, as demonstrated in Listing 14-2.

Listing 14-2. *Inserting a Record into the Northwind Database by Adding It to EntitySet<T>*

```
Northwind db = new Northwind(@"Data Source=.\SQLEXPRESS;Initial
Catalog=Northwind");

Customer cust = (from c in db.Customers
                 where c.CustomerID == "LONEP"
                 select c).Single<Customer>();

// Used to query record back out.
DateTime now = DateTime.Now;

Order order = new Order
{
  CustomerID = cust.CustomerID,
  EmployeeID = 4,
  OrderDate = now,
  RequiredDate = DateTime.Now.AddDays(7),
  ShipVia = 3,
  Freight = new Decimal(24.66),
  ShipName = cust.CompanyName,
  ShipAddress = cust.Address,
  ShipCity = cust.City,
  ShipRegion = cust.Region,
  ShipPostalCode = cust.PostalCode,
  ShipCountry = cust.Country
};

cust.Orders.Add(order);

db.SubmitChanges();

IEnumerable<Order> orders =
  db.Orders.Where(o => o.CustomerID == "LONEP" && o.OrderDate.Value == now);

foreach (Order o in orders)
{
  Console.WriteLine("{0} {1}", o.OrderDate, o.ShipName);
}

// This part of the code resets the database
db.Orders.DeleteOnSubmit(order);
db.SubmitChanges();
```

In Listing 14-2, we created a `Northwind DataContext`, retrieved a customer, and added a newly constructed `order` entity object to the `Orders EntitySet<Order>` of the `Customer` entity object. We then queried for the new record and displayed it to the console.

In Listing 14-1, the inserted object, which was a `Customer`, was inserted into a variable of type `Table<Customer>`. In Listing 14-2, the inserted object, which is an `Order`, is added to a variable of type `EntitySet<Order>`.

Here are the results of Listing 14-2:

```
9/2/2007 6:02:16 PM Lonesome Pine Restaurant
```

Inserting Attached Entity Objects

The `DataContext` class detects any associated dependent entity class objects that are attached so that they will be persisted too when the `SubmitChanges` method is called. By dependent, we mean any entity class object containing a foreign key to the inserted entity class object. Listing 14-3 contains an example.

Listing 14-3. Adding Attached Records

```
Northwind db = new Northwind(@"Data Source=.\SQLEXPRESS;Initial
Catalog=Northwind");

Customer cust =
  new Customer {
    CustomerID = "LAWN",
    CompanyName = "Lawn Wranglers",
    ContactName = "Mr. Abe Henry",
    ContactTitle = "Owner",
    Address = "1017 Maple Leaf Way",
    City = "Ft. Worth",
    Region = "TX",
    PostalCode = "76104",
    Country = "USA",
    Phone = "(800) MOW-LAWN",
    Fax = "(800) MOW-LAWO",
    Orders = {
      new Order {
        CustomerID = "LAWN",
        EmployeeID = 4,
        OrderDate = DateTime.Now,
        RequiredDate = DateTime.Now.AddDays(7),
        ShipVia = 3,
        Freight = new Decimal(24.66),
        ShipName = "Lawn Wranglers",
        ShipAddress = "1017 Maple Leaf Way",
        ShipCity = "Ft. Worth",
```

```
            ShipRegion = "TX",
            ShipPostalCode = "76104",
            ShipCountry = "USA"
        }
    }
};

db.Customers.InsertOnSubmit(cust);
db.SubmitChanges();

Customer customer = db.Customers.Where(c => c.CustomerID == "LAWN").First();
Console.WriteLine("{0} - {1}", customer.CompanyName, customer.ContactName);
foreach (Order order in customer.Orders)
{
  Console.WriteLine("{0} - {1}", order.CustomerID, order.OrderDate);
}

//  This part of the code resets the database
db.Orders.DeleteOnSubmit(cust.Orders.First());
db.Customers.DeleteObSubmit(cust);
db.SubmitChanges();
```

In Listing 14-3, we created a new `Customer` object with an assigned `Orders` collection containing one newly instantiated `Order`. Even though we inserted only the `Customer` object `cust` into the Customers table, the new `Order` will be persisted in the database as well when the `SubmitChanges` method is called, because the new `Order` is attached to the new `Customer`.

There is one additional point we would like to make about this example. Notice that, in the cleanup code at the end of Listing 14-3, we call the `DeleteOnSubmit` method for both the new `Order` and the new `Customer`. In this case, we delete only the first `Order`, but since the `Customer` was new, we know this is the only `Order`. We must manually delete the orders, because, although newly attached, associated entity objects are automatically inserted into the database when a parent entity object is inserted, the same is not true when they are deleted. Deleting a parent entity object does not cause attached entity objects to be deleted from the database automatically. Had we not deleted the orders manually, an exception would have been thrown. We will discuss this in more detail in the "Deletes" section of this chapter.

Let's take a look at the output of Listing 14-3 by pressing Ctrl+F5:

```
Lawn Wranglers - Mr. Abe Henry
LAWN - 9/2/2007 6:05:07 PM
```

Queries

Performing LINQ to SQL queries is almost like performing any other LINQ query with a few exceptions. We will cover the exceptions very shortly.

To perform a LINQ to SQL query, we need to first create a `DataContext`. Then we can perform the query on a table in that `DataContext`, as Listing 14-4 demonstrates.

Listing 14-4. Performing a Simple LINQ to SQL Query on the Northwind Database

```
Northwind db = new Northwind(@"Data Source=.\SQLEXPRESS;Initial
Catalog=Northwind");

Customer cust = (from c in db.Customers
                 where c.CustomerID == "LONEP"
                 select c).Single<Customer>();
```

When that code is executed, the customer whose `CustomerID` is `"LONEP"` will be retrieved into the `cust` variable. You should be aware, though, as was mentioned in Chapter 5, that the `Single` standard query operator will throw an exception if the sequence it is called on contains no matching elements. So, using this code, you had better know that customer `"LONEP"` exists. In reality, the `SingleOrDefault` standard query operator provides better protection for the possibility of no record matching the `where` clause.

There are a couple additional points worth mentioning. First, notice that the query is using C# syntax when comparing the `CustomerID` to `"LONEP"`. This is evidenced by the fact that double quotes are used to contain the string `"LONEP"` as opposed to single quotes that SQL syntax requires. Also, the C# equality test operator, `==`, is used instead of the SQL equality test operator, `=`. This demonstrates the fact that the query is indeed integrated into the language, since, after all, this is what LINQ is named for: Language Integrated Query. Second, notice that we are mixing both query expression syntax and standard dot notation syntax in this query. The query expression syntax portion is contained within parentheses, and the `Single` operator is called using standard dot notation syntax.

Now, here is a question for you. We have discussed deferred query execution many times in the book so far. The question is, will just executing the preceding code cause the query to actually be performed? Don't forget to consider deferred query execution when selecting your answer. The answer is yes; the `Single` standard query operator will cause the query to actually execute. Had we left off that operator call and merely returned the query minus the call to the `Single` operator, the query would not have executed.

Listing 14-4 provides no screen output, so just for verification that the code does indeed retrieve the appropriate customer, Listing 14-5 is the same code, plus output to the console has been added to display the customer that is retrieved.

Listing 14-5. Performing the Same Query with Console Output

```
Northwind db = new Northwind(@"Data Source=.\SQLEXPRESS;Initial
Catalog=Northwind");

Customer cust = (from c in db.Customers
                 where c.CustomerID == "LONEP"
                 select c).Single<Customer>();

Console.WriteLine("{0} - {1}", cust.CompanyName, cust.ContactName);
```

Here is the output for Listing 14-5:

```
Lonesome Pine Restaurant - Fran Wilson
```

Exceptions to the Norm

Earlier we mentioned that LINQ to SQL queries are like typical LINQ queries with some exceptions. Now we will discuss the exceptions.

LINQ to SQL Queries Return an IQueryable<T>

Although LINQ queries performed on arrays and collections return sequences of type IEnumerable<T>, a LINQ to SQL query typically returns a sequence of type IQueryable<T>. Listing 14-6 contains an example of a query returning a sequence of type IQueryable<T>.

Listing 14-6. A Simple LINQ to SQL Query Returning an IQueryable<T> Sequence

```
Northwind db = new Northwind(@"Data Source=.\SQLEXPRESS;Initial
Catalog=Northwind");

IQueryable<Customer> custs = from c in db.Customers
                            where c.City == "London"
                            select c;

foreach(Customer cust in custs)
{
    Console.WriteLine("Customer: {0}", cust.CompanyName);
}
```

As you can see, the return type for this query is IQueryable<Customer>. Here are the results of Listing 14-6:

```
Customer: Around the Horn
Customer: B's Beverages
Customer: Consolidated Holdings
Customer: Eastern Connection
Customer: North/South
Customer: Seven Seas Imports
```

As we stated in Chapter 12, since IQueryable<T> implements IEnumerable<T>, you can typically treat a sequence of type IQueryable<T> as though it were a sequence of type IEnumerable<T>. If you are trying to treat an IQueryable<T> sequence like an IEnumerable<T> sequence and you are having trouble, don't forget the AsEnumerable operator.

LINQ to SQL Queries Are Performed on Table<T> Objects

Although most normal LINQ queries are performed on arrays or collections that implement the IEnumerable<T> or IEnumerable interfaces, a LINQ to SQL query is performed on classes that implement the IQueryable<T> interface, such as the Table<T> class.

This means that LINQ to SQL queries have additional query operators available, as well as the standard query operators, since `IQueryable<T>` implements `IEnumerable<T>`.

LINQ to SQL Queries Are Translated to SQL

As we discussed in Chapter 2, because LINQ to SQL queries return sequences of type `IQueryable<T>`, they are not compiled into .NET intermediate language code the way that normal LINQ queries are. Instead, they are converted into expression trees, which allows them to be evaluated as a single unit, and translated to appropriate and optimal SQL statements. Please read the section "SQL Translation" later in this chapter to learn more about the SQL translation that takes place with LINQ to SQL queries.

LINQ to SQL Queries Are Executed in the Database

Unlike normal LINQ queries that are executed in local machine memory, LINQ to SQL queries are translated to SQL calls and actually executed in the database. There are ramifications because of this, such as the way projections are handled, which cannot actually occur in the database since the database knows nothing about your entity classes, or any other classes for that matter.

Also, since the query actually executes in the database and the database doesn't have access to your application code, what you can do in a query must be translated and is therefore limited in some ways based on the translator's capabilities. You can't just embed a call to a method you wrote in a lambda expression and expect SQL Server to know what to do with the call. Because of this, it is good to know what can be translated, what it will be translated to, and what happens when it cannot be translated.

Associations

Querying an associated class in LINQ to SQL is as simple as accessing a member variable of an entity class. This is because an associated class *is* a member variable of the related entity class or stored in a collection of entity classes, where the collection is a member variable of the related entity class. If the associated class is the *many* (child) side of a one-to-many relationship, the *many* class will be stored in a collection of the *many* classes, where the type of the collection is `EntitySet<T>`, and T is the type of the *many* entity class. This collection will be a member variable of the *one* class. If the associated class is the *one* (parent) side of a one-to-many relationship, a reference to the *one* class will be stored in a variable of type `EntityRef<T>`, where T is the type of the *one* class. This reference to the *one* class will be a member variable of the *many* class.

For example, consider the case of the `Customer` and `Order` entity classes that were generated for the Northwind database. A customer may have many orders, but an order can have but one customer. In this example, the `Customer` class is the *one* side of the one-to-many relationship between the `Customer` and `Order` entity classes. The `Order` class is the *many* side of the one-to-many relationship. Therefore, a `Customer` object's orders can be referenced by a member variable, typically named `Orders`, of type `EntitySet<Order>` in the `Customer` class. An `Order` object's customer can be referenced with a member variable, typically named `Customer`, of type `EntityRef<Customer>` in the `Order` class (see Figure 14-1).

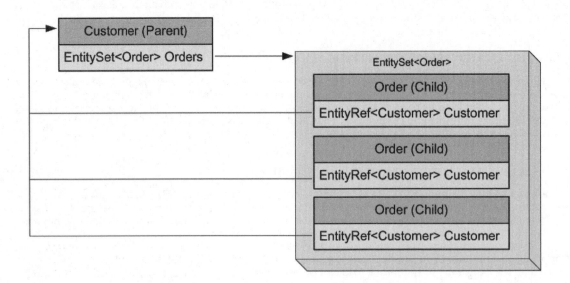

Figure 14-1. *A parent and child entity class association relationship*

Classes are associated by specifying the Association attribute on the class property that contains the reference to the associated class in the entity class definition. Since both the parent and child have a class property referencing the other, the Association attribute is specified in both the parent and child entity classes. We will discuss the Association attribute in depth in Chapter 15.

Listing 14-7 is an example where we query for certain customers and display the retrieved customers and each of their orders.

Listing 14-7. *Using an Association to Access Related Data*

```
Northwind db = new Northwind(@"Data Source=.\SQLEXPRESS;Initial
Catalog=Northwind");

IQueryable<Customer> custs = from c in db.Customers
                            where c.Country == "UK" &&
                              c.City == "London"
                            orderby c.CustomerID
                            select c;

foreach (Customer cust in custs)
{
  Console.WriteLine("{0} - {1}", cust.CompanyName, cust.ContactName);
  foreach (Order order in cust.Orders)
  {
    Console.WriteLine("    {0} {1}", order.OrderID, order.OrderDate);
  }
}
```

As you can see, we enumerate through each customer, display the customer, enumerate through each customer's orders, and display them. We never even specified that we wanted orders in the query. Here are the truncated results for Listing 14-7:

```
Around the Horn - Thomas Hardy
    10355 11/15/1996 12:00:00 AM
    10383 12/16/1996 12:00:00 AM
    10453 2/21/1997 12:00:00 AM
    10558 6/4/1997 12:00:00 AM
    10707 10/16/1997 12:00:00 AM
    10741 11/14/1997 12:00:00 AM
    10743 11/17/1997 12:00:00 AM
    10768 12/8/1997 12:00:00 AM
    10793 12/24/1997 12:00:00 AM
    10864 2/2/1998 12:00:00 AM
    10920 3/3/1998 12:00:00 AM
    10953 3/16/1998 12:00:00 AM
    11016 4/10/1998 12:00:00 AM
...
Consolidated Holdings - Elizabeth Brown
    10435 2/4/1997 12:00:00 AM
    10462 3/3/1997 12:00:00 AM
    10848 1/23/1998 12:00:00 AM
...
```

At this point, you might be thinking, isn't this terribly inefficient if we never access the customer's orders?

The answer is no. The reason is that the orders were not actually retrieved until they were referenced. Had the code not accessed the Orders property of the customer, they would have never been retrieved. This is known as *deferred loading*, which should not be confused with deferred query execution, which we have already discussed.

Deferred Loading

Deferred loading is the type of loading in which records are not actually loaded from the database until absolutely necessary, which is when they are first referenced; hence, the loading of the records is deferred.

In Listing 14-7, had we not referenced the Orders member variable, the orders would never have been retrieved from the database. That's pretty slick. For most situations, deferred loading is a good thing. It prevents needless queries from occurring and unnecessary data from eating up network bandwidth.

However, a problem can occur. Listing 14-8 is the same as Listing 14-7 except we have turned on the logging feature provided by the DataContext.Log object to reveal the problem.

Listing 14-8. An Example Demonstrating Deferred Loading

```
Northwind db = new Northwind(@"Data Source=.\SQLEXPRESS;Initial
Catalog=Northwind");

IQueryable<Customer> custs = from c in db.Customers
                            where c.Country == "UK" &&
                              c.City == "London"
                            orderby c.CustomerID
                            select c;

// Turn on the logging.
db.Log = Console.Out;

foreach (Customer cust in custs)
{
  Console.WriteLine("{0} - {1}", cust.CompanyName, cust.ContactName);
  foreach (Order order in cust.Orders)
  {
    Console.WriteLine("    {0} {1}", order.OrderID, order.OrderDate);
  }
}
```

We will run the example by pressing Ctrl+F5. We are going to severely truncate the output:

```
SELECT [t0].[CustomerID], [t0].[CompanyName], [t0].[ContactName],
[t0].[ContactTitle], [t0].[Address], [t0].[City], [t0].[Region], [t0].[PostalCode],
[t0].[Country], [t0].[Phone], [t0].[Fax]
FROM [dbo].[Customers] AS [t0]
WHERE ([t0].[Country] = @p0) AND ([t0].[City] = @p1)
ORDER BY [t0].[CustomerID]
-- @p0: Input String (Size = 2; Prec = 0; Scale = 0) [UK]
-- @p1: Input String (Size = 6; Prec = 0; Scale = 0) [London]
-- Context: SqlProvider(Sql2005) Model: AttributedMetaModel Build: 3.5.20706.1

Around the Horn - Thomas Hardy
SELECT [t0].[OrderID], [t0].[CustomerID], [t0].[EmployeeID], [t0].[OrderDate],
[t0].[RequiredDate], [t0].[ShippedDate], [t0].[ShipVia], [t0].[Freight],
[t0].[ShipName], [t0].[ShipAddress], [t0].[ShipCity], [t0].[ShipRegion],
[t0].[ShipPostalCode], [t0].[ShipCountry]
FROM [dbo].[Orders] AS [t0]
WHERE [t0].[CustomerID] = @p0
-- @p0: Input String (Size = 5; Prec = 0; Scale = 0) [AROUT]
-- Context: SqlProvider(Sql2005) Model: AttributedMetaModel Build: 3.5.20706.1

    10355 11/15/1996 12:00:00 AM
```

```
    10383 12/16/1996 12:00:00 AM
    10453 2/21/1997 12:00:00 AM
    10558 6/4/1997 12:00:00 AM
    10707 10/16/1997 12:00:00 AM
    10741 11/14/1997 12:00:00 AM
    10743 11/17/1997 12:00:00 AM
    10768 12/8/1997 12:00:00 AM
    10793 12/24/1997 12:00:00 AM
    10864 2/2/1998 12:00:00 AM
    10920 3/3/1998 12:00:00 AM
    10953 3/16/1998 12:00:00 AM
    11016 4/10/1998 12:00:00 AM
B's Beverages - Victoria Ashworth
SELECT [t0].[OrderID], [t0].[CustomerID], [t0].[EmployeeID], [t0].[OrderDate],
[t0].[RequiredDate], [t0].[ShippedDate], [t0].[ShipVia], [t0].[Freight],
[t0].[ShipName], [t0].[ShipAddress], [t0].[ShipCity], [t0].[ShipRegion],
[t0].[ShipPostalCode], [t0].[ShipCountry]
FROM [dbo].[Orders] AS [t0]
WHERE [t0].[CustomerID] = @p0
-- @p0: Input String (Size = 5; Prec = 0; Scale = 0) [BSBEV]
-- Context: SqlProvider(Sql2005) Model: AttributedMetaModel Build: 3.5.20706.1

    10289 8/26/1996 12:00:00 AM
    10471 3/11/1997 12:00:00 AM
    10484 3/24/1997 12:00:00 AM
    10538 5/15/1997 12:00:00 AM
    10539 5/16/1997 12:00:00 AM
    10578 6/24/1997 12:00:00 AM
    10599 7/15/1997 12:00:00 AM
    10943 3/11/1998 12:00:00 AM
    10947 3/13/1998 12:00:00 AM
    11023 4/14/1998 12:00:00 AM
Consolidated Holdings - Elizabeth Brown
...
```

We have marked the SQL queries in bold to make them stand out from the customer and order output data. In the first SQL query, you can see that a query is created to query the customers, and you can see that nothing in the query is querying the orders table. Then you can see that the company name and contact name for the first company are displayed, and then another SQL query is output. In that second SQL query, you can see that the Orders table is queried with a specific customer's CustomerID in the where clause. So, a query is generated and executed just for the specific customer that we just displayed to the console. Next, you will see a list of orders displayed for that previously listed customer, followed by the next customer. Next, another SQL query appears for a specific customer's orders.

As you can see, a separate query is performed to retrieve each customer's orders. The orders are not queried, and therefore not loaded, until the Orders EntityRef<T> variable is referenced in the second foreach loop, which is immediately after the customer information is displayed to the console. Because the orders are not retrieved until they are referenced, their loading is deferred.

Since a separate query is generated and performed for each customer, potentially a lot of SQL queries will be going back and forth to the database. This could be a performance problem. In this case, it may provide better performance if we *could* retrieve the orders when we retrieve the customers. What we need is *immediate loading*.

Immediate Loading with the DataLoadOptions Class

Although deferred loading is the default behavior for associated classes, we can perform immediate loading, which loads associated classes prior to them being referenced. This may provide performance benefits. We can use the DataLoadOptions class's LoadWith<T> operator to instruct the DataContext to immediately load the associated class specified in the LoadWith<T> operator's lambda expression. By using the LoadWith<T> operator, when the query is actually executed, not only will the primary class be retrieved, so will the specified associated class.

In Listing 14-9, we will use the same basic example code as in Listing 14-8 except we will instantiate a DataLoadOptions object; call the LoadWith<T> operator on that DataLoadOptions object, passing the Orders member as a class to immediately load when a Customer object is loaded; and assign the DataLoadOptions object to the Northwind DataContext. Also, to eliminate any doubt that the associated classes, the orders, are being loaded prior to being referenced, we will omit the code that enumerates through the customer's orders, so there will be no reference to them.

Listing 14-9. An Example Demonstrating Immediate Loading Using the DataLoadOptions Class

```
Northwind db = new Northwind(@"Data Source=.\SQLEXPRESS;Initial
Catalog=Northwind");

DataLoadOptions dlo = new DataLoadOptions();
dlo.LoadWith<Customer>(c => c.Orders);
db.LoadOptions = dlo;

IQueryable<Customer> custs = (from c in db.Customers
                              where c.Country == "UK" &&
                                c.City == "London"
                              orderby c.CustomerID
                              select c);
//  Turn on the logging.
db.Log = Console.Out;

foreach (Customer cust in custs)
{
  Console.WriteLine("{0} - {1}", cust.CompanyName, cust.ContactName);
}
```

Again, the only differences between this listing and Listing 14-8 are the instantiation of the DataLoadOptions object, the call to the LoadWith<T> operator, the assignment of the DataLoadOptions object to the Northwind DataContext, and the removal of any reference to each customer's orders. In the call to the LoadWith<T> operator, we instruct the DataLoadOptions to immediately load Orders whenever a Customer object is loaded. Now, let's take a look at the output of Listing 14-9.

```
SELECT [t0].[CustomerID], [t0].[CompanyName], [t0].[ContactName],
[t0].[ContactTitle], [t0].[Address], [t0].[City], [t0].[Region], [t0].[PostalCode],
[t0].[Country], [t0].[Phone], [t0].[Fax], [t1].[OrderID], [t1].[CustomerID] AS
[CustomerID2], [t1].[EmployeeID], [t1].[OrderDate], [t1].[RequiredDate],
[t1].[ShippedDate], [t1].[ShipVia], [t1].[Freight], [t1].[ShipName],
[t1].[ShipAddress], [t1].[ShipCity], [t1].[ShipRegion], [t1].[ShipPostalCode],
[t1].[ShipCountry], (
    SELECT COUNT(*)
    FROM [dbo].[Orders] AS [t2]
    WHERE [t2].[CustomerID] = [t0].[CustomerID]
    ) AS [count]
FROM [dbo].[Customers] AS [t0]
LEFT OUTER JOIN [dbo].[Orders] AS [t1] ON [t1].[CustomerID] = [t0].[CustomerID]
WHERE ([t0].[Country] = @p0) AND ([t0].[City] = @p1)
ORDER BY [t0].[CustomerID], [t1].[OrderID]
-- @p0: Input String (Size = 2; Prec = 0; Scale = 0) [UK]
-- @p1: Input String (Size = 6; Prec = 0; Scale = 0) [London]
-- Context: SqlProvider(Sql2005) Model: AttributedMetaModel Build: 3.5.20706.1

Around the Horn - Thomas Hardy
B's Beverages - Victoria Ashworth
Consolidated Holdings - Elizabeth Brown
Eastern Connection - Ann Devon
North/South - Simon Crowther
Seven Seas Imports - Hari Kumar
```

As you can see, a single SQL query was executed to retrieve all the customers matching our query's where clause. You can also see that, despite that we never even referenced a customer's orders, the single SQL query joined each customer retrieved with that customer's orders. Since the orders were loaded prior to being referenced, their loading was not deferred and therefore is considered to be immediate. Instead of having a number of SQL queries equal to one (for the customers), plus the number of customers (for each customer's orders), there is a single SQL query. If there are a lot of customers, this can make a huge difference.

Using the DataLoadOptions class, you are not limited to the immediate loading of a single associated class or a single hierarchical level of class. However, immediately loading more than one associated class does affect the way immediate loading works.

When Immediate Loading Is Not So Immediate

When classes are not loaded until they are referenced, their loading is said to be *deferred*. If they are loaded prior to being referenced, their loading is said to be *immediate*. However, sometimes, immediate is not as immediate as you might expect.

With the code in Listing 14-9, we saw that, by specifying an associated class as the argument to the DataLoadOptions class's LoadWith<T> method, we could get immediate loading to cause the orders to be loaded along with the customers. If we call the LoadWith<T> method multiple times to have multiple classes loaded immediately, only one of the classes will be joined with the original entity class, and the others will be loaded upon referencing that original entity class. When this happens, since the associated classes not joined with the original entity class are still loaded prior to being referenced, they are still considered immediately loaded, but a separate query is still made for them as you reference each original entity class. In this way, although their loading is still considered to be immediate, it feels less immediate than when they are joined.

The decision as to which associated classes should be joined versus which should just be loaded prior to being referenced is made by LINQ to SQL. It is an optimized decision based on general principles applied to your entity class model, though; it is not an optimization made by the database. It will join the association lowest in the hierarchy of the immediately loaded classes. This will be more easily understood when we get to the section about immediately loading a hierarchy of associated classes.

To better understand this behavior, we will discuss this for each approach where more than one association is immediately loaded. The two approaches are loading multiple associated classes of the original entity class and loading a hierarchy of associated classes.

Immediate Loading of Multiple Associated Classes

The DataLoadOptions class can also be used to immediately load more than one associated classes for a given entity class.

Notice that the generated SQL query in Listing 14-9 made no reference to the customer's associated customer demographics. Had we referenced the customer demographics on the retrieved customers, additional SQL statements would have been executed for each customer whose customer demographics were referenced.

In Listing 14-10, we will instruct the DataLoadOptions to immediately load the customer's customer demographics as well as its orders.

Listing 14-10. Immediately Loading Multiple EntitySets

```
Northwind db = new Northwind(@"Data Source=.\SQLEXPRESS;Initial
Catalog=Northwind");

DataLoadOptions dlo = new DataLoadOptions();
dlo.LoadWith<Customer>(c => c.Orders);
dlo.LoadWith<Customer>(c => c.CustomerCustomerDemos);
db.LoadOptions = dlo;

IQueryable<Customer> custs = (from c in db.Customers
                             where c.Country == "UK" &&
                               c.City == "London"
                             orderby c.CustomerID
                             select c);
// Turn on the logging.
db.Log = Console.Out;

foreach (Customer cust in custs)
{
```

```
Console.WriteLine("{0} - {1}", cust.CompanyName, cust.ContactName);
}
```

In Listing 14-10, we have specified that the customer's orders and demographics are to be loaded immediately. Notice that we do not reference either in the LINQ query. So, any loading of these associated classes is immediate as opposed to deferred. We are really not interested in the returned data so much as the executed SQL statements. Let's examine the output of Listing 14-10.

```
SELECT [t0].[CustomerID], [t0].[CompanyName], [t0].[ContactName],
[t0].[ContactTitle], [t0].[Address], [t0].[City], [t0].[Region], [t0].[PostalCode],
[t0].[Country], [t0].[Phone], [t0].[Fax], [t1].[CustomerID] AS [CustomerID2],
[t1].[CustomerTypeID], (
    SELECT COUNT(*)
    FROM [dbo].[CustomerCustomerDemo] AS [t2]
    WHERE [t2].[CustomerID] = [t0].[CustomerID]
    ) AS [count]
FROM [dbo].[Customers] AS [t0]
LEFT OUTER JOIN [dbo].[CustomerCustomerDemo] AS [t1] ON [t1].[CustomerID] =
[t0].[CustomerID]
WHERE ([t0].[Country] = @p0) AND ([t0].[City] = @p1)
ORDER BY [t0].[CustomerID], [t1].[CustomerTypeID]
-- @p0: Input String (Size = 2; Prec = 0; Scale = 0) [UK]
-- @p1: Input String (Size = 6; Prec = 0; Scale = 0) [London]
-- Context: SqlProvider(Sql2005) Model: AttributedMetaModel Build: 3.5.20706.1

SELECT [t0].[OrderID], [t0].[CustomerID], [t0].[EmployeeID], [t0].[OrderDate],
[t0].[RequiredDate], [t0].[ShippedDate], [t0].[ShipVia], [t0].[Freight],
[t0].[ShipName], [t0].[ShipAddress], [t0].[ShipCity], [t0].[ShipRegion],
[t0].[ShipPostalCode], [t0].[ShipCountry]
FROM [dbo].[Orders] AS [t0]
WHERE [t0].[CustomerID] = @x1
-- @x1: Input StringFixedLength (Size = 5; Prec = 0; Scale = 0) [AROUT]
-- Context: SqlProvider(Sql2005) Model: AttributedMetaModel Build: 3.5.20706.1

Around the Horn - Thomas Hardy
SELECT [t0].[OrderID], [t0].[CustomerID], [t0].[EmployeeID], [t0].[OrderDate],
[t0].[RequiredDate], [t0].[ShippedDate], [t0].[ShipVia], [t0].[Freight],
[t0].[ShipName], [t0].[ShipAddress], [t0].[ShipCity], [t0].[ShipRegion],
[t0].[ShipPostalCode], [t0].[ShipCountry]
FROM [dbo].[Orders] AS [t0]
WHERE [t0].[CustomerID] = @x1
-- @x1: Input StringFixedLength (Size = 5; Prec = 0; Scale = 0) [BSBEV]
-- Context: SqlProvider(Sql2005) Model: AttributedMetaModel Build: 3.5.20706.1

B's Beverages - Victoria Ashworth
...
```

As you can see, the customer demographics were joined with the customers when they were queried, but a separate SQL query was generated to load each customer's orders. That separate query for orders was performed when each customer was actually referenced, which is in the foreach statement. Notice that in the output the query for the orders of a customer is output *before* the customer information is displayed to the console.

Since neither the customer demographics nor the orders are referenced in the code, other than when calling the LoadWith<T> method, the loading is not deferred and is therefore immediate.

Immediate Loading of Hierarchical Associated Classes

In the previous section, we discussed how to cause multiple associated entity classes to be immediately loaded. In this section, we will discuss how to cause a hierarchy of associated entity classes to be loaded immediately. To demonstrate this, in Listing 14-11, we will make the query immediately load not only the orders but also each order's order details.

Listing 14-11. Immediate Loading of a Hierarchy of Entity Classes

```
Northwind db = new Northwind(@"Data Source=.\SQLEXPRESS;Initial
Catalog=Northwind");

DataLoadOptions dlo = new DataLoadOptions();
dlo.LoadWith<Customer>(c => c.Orders);
dlo.LoadWith<Order>(o => o.OrderDetails);
db.LoadOptions = dlo;

IQueryable<Customer> custs = (from c in db.Customers
                              where c.Country == "UK" &&
                                c.City == "London"
                              orderby c.CustomerID
                              select c);
//  Turn on the logging.
db.Log = Console.Out;

foreach (Customer cust in custs)
{
  Console.WriteLine("{0} - {1}", cust.CompanyName, cust.ContactName);
  foreach (Order order in cust.Orders)
  {
    Console.WriteLine("    {0} {1}", order.OrderID, order.OrderDate);
  }
}
```

Notice that we are immediately loading the customer's orders, and for each order, we are immediately loading its order details. Here is the output for Listing 14-11:

```
SELECT [t0].[CustomerID], [t0].[CompanyName], [t0].[ContactName],
[t0].[ContactTitle], [t0].[Address], [t0].[City], [t0].[Region], [t0].[PostalCode],
[t0].[Country], [t0].[Phone], [t0].[Fax]
FROM [dbo].[Customers] AS [t0]
```

```
WHERE ([t0].[Country] = @p0) AND ([t0].[City] = @p1)
ORDER BY [t0].[CustomerID]
-- @p0: Input String (Size = 2; Prec = 0; Scale = 0) [UK]
-- @p1: Input String (Size = 6; Prec = 0; Scale = 0) [London]
-- Context: SqlProvider(Sql2005) Model: AttributedMetaModel Build: 3.5.20706.1

SELECT [t0].[OrderID], [t0].[CustomerID], [t0].[EmployeeID], [t0].[OrderDate],
[t0].[RequiredDate], [t0].[ShippedDate], [t0].[ShipVia], [t0].[Freight],
[t0].[ShipName], [t0].[ShipAddress], [t0].[ShipCity], [t0].[ShipRegion],
[t0].[ShipPostalCode], [t0].[ShipCountry], [t1].[OrderID] AS [OrderID2],
[t1].[ProductID], [t1].[UnitPrice], [t1].[Quantity], [t1].[Discount], (
    SELECT COUNT(*)
    FROM [dbo].[Order Details] AS [t2]
    WHERE [t2].[OrderID] = [t0].[OrderID]
    ) AS [count]
FROM [dbo].[Orders] AS [t0]
LEFT OUTER JOIN [dbo].[Order Details] AS [t1] ON [t1].[OrderID] = [t0].[OrderID]
WHERE [t0].[CustomerID] = @x1
ORDER BY [t0].[OrderID], [t1].[ProductID]
-- @x1: Input StringFixedLength (Size = 5; Prec = 0; Scale = 0) [AROUT]
-- Context: SqlProvider(Sql2005) Model: AttributedMetaModel Build: 3.5.20706.1

Around the Horn - Thomas Hardy
SELECT [t0].[OrderID], [t0].[CustomerID], [t0].[EmployeeID], [t0].[OrderDate],
[t0].[RequiredDate], [t0].[ShippedDate], [t0].[ShipVia], [t0].[Freight],
[t0].[ShipName], [t0].[ShipAddress], [t0].[ShipCity], [t0].[ShipRegion],
[t0].[ShipPostalCode], [t0].[ShipCountry], [t1].[OrderID] AS [OrderID2],
[t1].[ProductID], [t1].[UnitPrice], [t1].[Quantity], [t1].[Discount], (
    SELECT COUNT(*)
    FROM [dbo].[Order Details] AS [t2]
    WHERE [t2].[OrderID] = [t0].[OrderID]
    ) AS [count]
FROM [dbo].[Orders] AS [t0]
LEFT OUTER JOIN [dbo].[Order Details] AS [t1] ON [t1].[OrderID] = [t0].[OrderID]
WHERE [t0].[CustomerID] = @x1
ORDER BY [t0].[OrderID], [t1].[ProductID]
-- @x1: Input StringFixedLength (Size = 5; Prec = 0; Scale = 0) [BSBEV]
-- Context: SqlProvider(Sql2005) Model: AttributedMetaModel Build: 3.5.20706.1

B's Beverages - Victoria Ashworth
...
```

Again, we are not interested in the retrieved data, just the SQL statements. Notice that this time, the query for the customers joined neither the orders nor the order details. Instead, as each customer was referenced, an additional SQL query was made that joined the orders and order details. Since neither was referenced, they were still loaded prior to being referenced and are still considered to be immediately loaded.

From this example, you can see that LINQ to SQL does perform the single join for the association at the lowest level in the hierarchy of the immediately loaded files, as we previously mentioned.

Filtering and Ordering

While we are discussing the DataLoadOptions class, we want you to be aware of its AssociateWith method, which can be used to both filter associated child objects and order them.

In Listing 14-8, we retrieve some customers and enumerate through them displaying the customer and its orders. You can see in the results that the orders' dates are in ascending order. To demonstrate how the AssociateWith method can be used to both filter associated classes and order them, in Listing 14-12 we will do both.

Listing 14-12. Using the DataLoadOptions Class to Filter and Order

```
Northwind db = new Northwind(@"Data Source=.\SQLEXPRESS;Initial
Catalog=Northwind");

DataLoadOptions dlo = new DataLoadOptions();
dlo.AssociateWith<Customer>(c => from o in c.Orders
                                 where o.OrderID < 10700
                                 orderby o.OrderDate descending
                                 select o);
db.LoadOptions = dlo;

IQueryable<Customer> custs = from c in db.Customers
                             where c.Country == "UK" &&
                               c.City == "London"
                             orderby c.CustomerID
                             select c;

foreach (Customer cust in custs)
{
  Console.WriteLine("{0} - {1}", cust.CompanyName, cust.ContactName);
  foreach (Order order in cust.Orders)
  {
    Console.WriteLine("    {0} {1}", order.OrderID, order.OrderDate);
  }
}
```

Notice that in Listing 14-12 we embed a query for the lambda expression passed to the AssociateWith method. In that query, we filter out all records where the OrderID is not less than 10700, and we sort the orders by OrderDate in descending order. Let's examine the results of Listing 14-12:

Around the Horn - Thomas Hardy

```
    10558 6/4/1997 12:00:00 AM
    10453 2/21/1997 12:00:00 AM
    10383 12/16/1996 12:00:00 AM
    10355 11/15/1996 12:00:00 AM
B's Beverages - Victoria Ashworth
    10599 7/15/1997 12:00:00 AM
    10578 6/24/1997 12:00:00 AM
    10539 5/16/1997 12:00:00 AM
    10538 5/15/1997 12:00:00 AM
    10484 3/24/1997 12:00:00 AM
    10471 3/11/1997 12:00:00 AM
    10289 8/26/1996 12:00:00 AM
Consolidated Holdings - Elizabeth Brown
    10462 3/3/1997 12:00:00 AM
    10435 2/4/1997 12:00:00 AM
Eastern Connection - Ann Devon
    10532 5/9/1997 12:00:00 AM
    10400 1/1/1997 12:00:00 AM
    10364 11/26/1996 12:00:00 AM
North/South - Simon Crowther
    10517 4/24/1997 12:00:00 AM
Seven Seas Imports - Hari Kumar
    10547 5/23/1997 12:00:00 AM
    10523 5/1/1997 12:00:00 AM
    10472 3/12/1997 12:00:00 AM
    10388 12/19/1996 12:00:00 AM
    10377 12/9/1996 12:00:00 AM
    10359 11/21/1996 12:00:00 AM
```

As you can see in the preceding results, only the orders whose OrderID is less than 10700 are returned, and they are returned in descending order by date.

Coincidental Joins

One of the benefits of associations is that they are, in effect, performing joins for us automatically. When we query customers from the Northwind database, each customer has a collection of orders that is accessible via the Customer object's Orders property. So, retrieving orders for customers is automatic. Normally, you would have to perform a join to get that type of behavior. The reverse is also true. When we retrieve orders, the Order class has a Customer property that references the appropriate customer.

Although we have this automatic join happening, it is merely a happy little accident. The join happens because when we have an object, say a child object, that has a relationship to another object, say a parent object, we *expect* to be able to access it via a reference in the initial, child object.

For example, when working with XML, when we have a reference to a node, we expect to be able to obtain a reference to its parent by the child node having a member variable that references the parent. We don't expect to have to perform a query on the entire XML structure and provide the child node as a search key. Also, when we have a reference to a node, we expect to be able to access its children with a reference on the node itself as well.

So, although the automatic join is certainly convenient, the implementation has more to do with the nature of object relationships, and our expectations of how they *should* behave, than an intentional effort to make joins happen automatically. In this way, the joins are really coincidental.

Joins

We just discussed that many relationships in the database are specified to be associations and that we can access the associated objects by simply accessing a class member. However, only those relationships that are defined using foreign keys will get mapped this way. Since every type of relationship is not defined using foreign keys, you will sometimes need to explicitly join tables.

Inner Joins

We can perform an inner equijoin by using the `join` operator. As is typical with an inner join, any records in the outer results set will be omitted if a matching record does not exist in the inner results set. Listing 14-13 contains an example.

Listing 14-13. *Performing an Inner Join*

```
Northwind db = new Northwind(@"Data Source=.\SQLEXPRESS;Initial
Catalog=Northwind");

var entities = from s in db.Suppliers
               join c in db.Customers on s.City equals c.City
               select new
               {
                 SupplierName = s.CompanyName,
                 CustomerName = c.CompanyName,
                 City = c.City
               };

foreach (var e in entities)
{
  Console.WriteLine("{0}: {1} - {2}", e.City, e.SupplierName, e.CustomerName);
}
```

In Listing 14-13, we performed an inner join on the suppliers and the customers. If a customer record doesn't exist with the same city as a supplier, the supplier record will be omitted from the results set. Here are the results of Listing 14-13:

```
London: Exotic Liquids - Around the Horn
London: Exotic Liquids - B's Beverages
London: Exotic Liquids - Consolidated Holdings
London: Exotic Liquids - Eastern Connection
London: Exotic Liquids - North/South
London: Exotic Liquids - Seven Seas Imports
Sao Paulo: Refrescos Americanas LTDA - Comércio Mineiro
```

```
Sao Paulo: Refrescos Americanas LTDA - Familia Arquibaldo
Sao Paulo: Refrescos Americanas LTDA - Queen Cozinha
Sao Paulo: Refrescos Americanas LTDA - Tradiçao Hipermercados
Berlin: Heli Süßwaren GmbH & Co. KG - Alfred Futterkiste
Paris: Aux joyeux ecclésiastiques - Paris spécialités
Paris: Aux joyeux ecclésiastiques - Spécialités du monde
Montréal: Ma Maison - Mère Paillarde
```

As you can see, despite that some suppliers are in the output with multiple matching customers, some suppliers are not in the list at all. This is because there were no customers in the same city as the missing suppliers. If we need to still see the supplier regardless of whether there is a matching customer, we need to perform an outer join.

Outer Joins

In Chapter 4, we discussed the DefaultIfEmpty standard query operator and mention that it can be used to perform outer joins. In Listing 14-14, we will use the into clause to direct the matching join results into a temporary sequence that we will subsequently call the DefaultIfEmpty operator on. This way, if the record is missing from the joined results, a default value will be provided. We will use the DataContext logging feature so we can see the generated SQL statement.

Listing 14-14. Performing an Outer Join

```
Northwind db = new Northwind(@"Data Source=.\SQLEXPRESS;Initial
Catalog=Northwind");

db.Log = Console.Out;

var entities =
  from s in db.Suppliers
  join c in db.Customers on s.City equals c.City into temp
  from t in temp.DefaultIfEmpty()
  select new
  {
   SupplierName = s.CompanyName,
   CustomerName = t.CompanyName,
   City = s.City
  };

foreach (var e in entities)
{
  Console.WriteLine("{0}: {1} - {2}", e.City, e.SupplierName, e.CustomerName);
}
```

Notice that in the join statement in Listing 14-14, we direct the join results into the temporary sequence named temp. That temporary sequence name can be whatever you want, as long as it doesn't conflict with any other name or keyword. Then we perform a subsequent query on the results of the temp sequence passed to the DefaultIfEmpty operator. Even though we haven't covered it yet, the DefaultIfEmpty operator called in Listing 14-14 is not the same operator that was discussed in Chapter 4. As we will explain shortly, LINQ to SQL queries are translated into SQL statements, and those SQL statements are executed by the database. SQL Server has no way to call the DefaultIfEmpty standard query operator. Instead, that operator call will be translated into the appropriate SQL statement. This is why we wanted the DataContext logging to be enabled.

Also, notice that we access the city name from the Suppliers table instead of the temp collection. We did this because we know there will always be a record for the supplier, but for suppliers without a matching customer, there will be no city in the joined results in the temp collection. This is different from the previous example of the inner join where we obtained the city from the joined table. In that example, it didn't matter which of the tables we got the city from, because if a matching customer record didn't exist, there would be no record anyway since an inner join was performed.

Let's look at the results of Listing 14-14:

```
SELECT [t0].[CompanyName], [t1].[CompanyName] AS [value], [t0].[City]
FROM [dbo].[Suppliers] AS [t0]
LEFT OUTER JOIN [dbo].[Customers] AS [t1] ON [t0].[City] = [t1].[City]
-- Context: SqlProvider(Sql2005) Model: AttributedMetaModel Build: 3.5.20706.1

London: Exotic Liquids - Around the Horn
London: Exotic Liquids - B's Beverages
London: Exotic Liquids - Consolidated Holdings
London: Exotic Liquids - Eastern Connection
London: Exotic Liquids - North/South
London: Exotic Liquids - Seven Seas Imports
New Orleans: New Orleans Cajun Delights -
Ann Arbor: Grandma Kelly's Homestead -
Tokyo: Tokyo Traders -
Oviedo: Cooperativa de Quesos 'Las Cabras' -
Osaka: Mayumi's -
Melbourne: Pavlova, Ltd. -
Manchester: Specialty Biscuits, Ltd. -
Göteborg: PB Knäckebröd AB -
Sao Paulo: Refrescos Americanas LTDA - Comércio Mineiro
Sao Paulo: Refrescos Americanas LTDA - Familia Arquibaldo
Sao Paulo: Refrescos Americanas LTDA - Queen Cozinha
Sao Paulo: Refrescos Americanas LTDA - Tradiçao Hipermercados
Berlin: Heli Süßwaren GmbH & Co. KG - Alfreds Futterkiste
Frankfurt: Plutzer Lebensmittelgroßmärkte AG -
Cuxhaven: Nord-Ost-Fisch Handelsgesellschaft mbH -
Ravenna: Formaggi Fortini s.r.l. -
Sandvika: Norske Meierier -
Bend: Bigfoot Breweries -
Stockholm: Svensk Sjöföda AB -
Paris: Aux joyeux ecclésiastiques - Paris spécialités
```

```
Paris: Aux joyeux ecclésiastiques - Spécialités du monde
Boston: New England Seafood Cannery -
Singapore: Leka Trading -
Lyngby: Lyngbysild -
Zaandam: Zaanse Snoepfabriek -
Lappeenranta: Karkki Oy -
Sydney: G'day, Mate -
Montréal: Ma Maison - Mère Paillarde
Salerno: Pasta Buttini s.r.l. -
Montceau: Escargots Nouveaux -
Annecy: Gai pâturage -
Ste-Hyacinthe: Forêts d'érables -
```

As you can see in the output of Listing 14-14, we got at least one record for every supplier, and you can see that some suppliers do not have a matching customer, thereby proving the outer join was performed. But, if there is any doubt, you can see the actual generated SQL statement, and that clearly is performing an outer join.

To Flatten or Not to Flatten

In the examples in Listing 14-13 and Listing 14-14, we projected our query results into a flat structure. By this, we mean an object was created from an anonymous class where each field requested is a member of that anonymous class. Contrast this with the fact that, instead of creating a single anonymous class containing each field we wanted, we could have created an anonymous class composed of a Supplier object and matching Customer object. In that case, there would be the topmost level of the anonymous class, as well as a lower level containing a Supplier object and either a Customer object or the default value provided by the DefaultIfEmpty operator, which would be null.

If we take the flat approach, as we did in the two previous examples, because the projected output class is not an entity class, we will not be able to perform updates to the output objects by having the DataContext object manage persistence for the changes to the database for us. This is fine for data that will not be changed. However, sometimes you may be planning on allowing updates to the retrieved data. In this case, using the nonflat approach would allow you to make changes to the retrieved objects and have the DataContext object manage the persistence. We will cover this in more depth in Chapter 16. For now, let's just take a look at Listing 14-15, which contains an example that isn't flat.

Listing 14-15. *Returning Nonflat Results so the DataContext Can Manage Persistence*

```
Northwind db = new Northwind(@"Data Source=.\SQLEXPRESS;Initial
Catalog=Northwind");

var entities = from s in db.Suppliers
               join c in db.Customers on s.City equals c.City into temp
               from t in temp.DefaultIfEmpty()
               select new { s, t };

foreach (var e in entities)
```

```
{
  Console.WriteLine("{0}: {1} - {2}", e.s.City,
    e.s.CompanyName,
    e.t != null ? e.t.CompanyName : "");
}
```

In Listing 14-15, instead of returning the query results into a flat anonymous object with a member for each desired field, we return the query results in an anonymous object composed of the `Supplier` and potentially `Customer` entity objects. Also notice that in the `Console.WriteLine` method call, we still have to be concerned that the temporary result can be a `null` if no matching `Customer` object exists. Let's take a look at the results of Listing 14-15:

```
London: Exotic Liquids - Around the Horn
London: Exotic Liquids - B's Beverages
London: Exotic Liquids - Consolidated Holdings
London: Exotic Liquids - Eastern Connection
London: Exotic Liquids - North/South
London: Exotic Liquids - Seven Seas Imports
New Orleans: New Orleans Cajun Delights -
Ann Arbor: Grandma Kelly's Homestead -
Tokyo: Tokyo Traders -
Oviedo: Cooperativa de Quesos 'Las Cabras' -
Osaka: Mayumi's -
Melbourne: Pavlova, Ltd. -
Manchester: Specialty Biscuits, Ltd. -
Göteborg: PB Knäckebröd AB -
Sao Paulo: Refrescos Americanas LTDA - Comércio Mineiro
Sao Paulo: Refrescos Americanas LTDA - Familia Arquibaldo
Sao Paulo: Refrescos Americanas LTDA - Queen Cozinha
Sao Paulo: Refrescos Americanas LTDA - Tradiçao Hipermercados
Berlin: Heli Süßwaren GmbH & Co. KG - Alfreds Futterkiste
Frankfurt: Plutzer Lebensmittelgroßmärkte AG -
Cuxhaven: Nord-Ost-Fisch Handelsgesellschaft mbH -
Ravenna: Formaggi Fortini s.r.l. -
Sandvika: Norske Meierier -
Bend: Bigfoot Breweries -
Stockholm: Svensk Sjöföda AB -
Paris: Aux joyeux ecclésiastiques - Paris spécialités
Paris: Aux joyeux ecclésiastiques - Spécialités du monde
Boston: New England Seafood Cannery -
Singapore: Leka Trading -
Lyngby: Lyngbysild -
Zaandam: Zaanse Snoepfabriek -
Lappeenranta: Karkki Oy -
Sydney: G'day, Mate -
Montréal: Ma Maison - Mère Paillarde
Salerno: Pasta Buttini s.r.l. -
```

```
Montceau: Escargots Nouveaux -
Annecy: Gai pâturage -
Ste-Hyacinthe: Forêts d'érables -
```

In the output for Listing 14-15, you can see that some suppliers do not have customers in their cities. Unlike the sequence of anonymous objects returned by the query in Listing 14-14, the anonymous objects returned by the query in Listing 14-15 contain entity objects of type `Supplier` and `Customer`. Because these are entity objects, we can take advantage of the services provided by the `DataContext` to manage the changes to them and their persistence to the database.

Deferred Query Execution

You have probably read our explanation of deferred query execution a dozen times, but this is such an important topic that it bears some repetition in case you have skipped around the book to get to this point. Deferred query execution refers to the fact that a LINQ query of any type—be it a LINQ to SQL query, a LINQ to XML query, or a LINQ to Objects query—may not actually be executed at the time it is defined. Take the following query, for example:

```
IQueryable<Customer> custs = from c in db.Customers
                             where c.Country == "UK"
                             select c;
```

The database query is not actually performed when this statement is executed; it is merely defined and assigned to the variable `custs`. The query will not be performed until the `custs` sequence is enumerated.

Repercussions of Deferred Query Execution

One repercussion of deferred query execution is that your query can contain errors that will cause exceptions but only when the query is actually performed, not when defined. This can be very misleading when you step over the query in the debugger and all is well, but then, farther down in the code, an exception is thrown when enumerating the query sequence. Or, perhaps you call another operator on the query sequence that results in the query sequence being enumerated.

Another repercussion is that since the SQL query is performed when the query sequence is enumerated, enumerating it multiple times results in the SQL query being performed multiple times. This could certainly hamper performance. The way to prevent this is by calling one of the standard query operator conversion operators, `ToArray<T>`, `ToList<T>`, `ToDictionary<T, K>`, or `ToLookup<T, K>`, on a sequence. Each of these operators will convert the sequence on which it is called to a data structure of the type specified, which in effect caches the results for you. You can then enumerate that new data structure repeatedly without causing the SQL query to be performed again and the results potentially changing.

Taking Advantage of Deferred Query Execution

One advantage of deferred query execution is that performance can be improved while at the same time allowing you to reuse previously defined queries. Since the query is executed every time the query sequence is enumerated, you can define it once and enumerate it over and over, whenever the situation warrants. And, if the code flow takes some path that doesn't need to actually examine the query results by enumerating them, performance is improved because the query is never actually executed.

Another of the benefits of deferred query execution is that since the query isn't actually performed by merely defining it, we can append additional operators programmatically as needed. Imagine an application that allows the user to query customers. Also imagine that the user can filter the queried customers. Picture one of those filter-type interfaces that have a drop-down list for each column in the customer table. There is a drop-down list for the City column and another for the Country column. Each drop-down list has every city and country from all Customer records in the database. At the top of each drop-down list is an [ALL] option, which is the default for its respective database column. If the user hasn't changed the setting of either of those drop-down lists, no additional `where` clause is appended to the query for the respective column. Listing 14-16 contains an example programmatically building a query for such an interface.

Listing 14-16. *Programmatically Building a Query*

```
Northwind db = new Northwind(@"Data Source=.\SQLEXPRESS;Initial
Catalog=Northwind");

// Turn on the logging.
db.Log = Console.Out;

// Pretend the values below are not hardcoded, but instead, obtained by accessing
// a dropdown list's selected value.
string dropdownListCityValue = "Cowes";
string dropdownListCountryValue = "UK";

IQueryable<Customer> custs = (from c in db.Customers
                              select c);

if (!dropdownListCityValue.Equals("[ALL]"))
{
  custs = from c in custs
          where c.City == dropdownListCityValue
          select c;
}

if (!dropdownListCountryValue.Equals("[ALL]"))
{
  custs = from c in custs
          where c.Country == dropdownListCountryValue
          select c;
}

foreach (Customer cust in custs)
{
  Console.WriteLine("{0} - {1} - {2}", cust.CompanyName, cust.City, cust.Country);
}
```

In Listing 14-16, we simulate obtaining the user selected city and country from their drop-down lists, and only if they are not set to "[ALL]", we append an additional `where` operator to the query.

Because the query is not actually performed until the sequence is enumerated, we can programmatically build it, one portion at a time.

Let's take a look at the results of Listing 14-16:

```
SELECT [t0].[CustomerID], [t0].[CompanyName], [t0].[ContactName],
[t0].[ContactTitle], [t0].[Address], [t0].[City], [t0].[Region], [t0].[PostalCode],
[t0].[Country], [t0].[Phone], [t0].[Fax]
FROM [dbo].[Customers] AS [t0]
WHERE ([t0].[Country] = @p0) AND ([t0].[City] = @p1)
-- @p0: Input String (Size = 2; Prec = 0; Scale = 0) [UK]
-- @p1: Input String (Size = 5; Prec = 0; Scale = 0) [Cowes]
-- Context: SqlProvider(Sql2005) Model: AttributedMetaModel Build: 3.5.20706.1


Island Trading - Cowes - UK
```

Notice that since we specified that the selected city was Cowes and the selected country was UK, we got the records for the customers in Cowes in the United Kingdom. Also notice that there is a single SQL statement that was performed. And, because the query execution is deferred, we can continue to append to the query to further restrict it, or perhaps order it, without the expense of multiple SQL queries taking place.

For another test, in Listing 14-17, we'll change the value of the dropdownListCityValue variable to " [ALL]" and see what the executed SQL statement looks like then and what the results are. Since the default city of " [ALL]" is specified, the SQL query shouldn't even restrict the results set by the city.

Listing 14-17. Programmatically Building Another Query

```
Northwind db = new Northwind(@"Data Source=.\SQLEXPRESS;Initial
Catalog=Northwind");

// Turn on the logging.
db.Log = Console.Out;

// Pretend the values below are not hardcoded, but instead, obtained by accessing
// a dropdown list's selected value.
string dropdownListCityValue = "[ALL]";
string dropdownListCountryValue = "UK";

IQueryable<Customer> custs = (from c in db.Customers
                              select c);

if (!dropdownListCityValue.Equals("[ALL]"))
{
  custs = from c in custs
          where c.City == dropdownListCityValue
          select c;
}
```

```
if (!dropdownListCountryValue.Equals("[ALL]"))
{
  custs = from c in custs
          where c.Country == dropdownListCountryValue
          select c;
}

foreach (Customer cust in custs)
{
  Console.WriteLine("{0} - {1} - {2}", cust.CompanyName, cust.City, cust.Country);
}
```

Let's examine the output of Listing 14-17:

```
SELECT [t0].[CustomerID], [t0].[CompanyName], [t0].[ContactName],
[t0].[ContactTitle], [t0].[Address], [t0].[City], [t0].[Region], [t0].[PostalCode],
[t0].[Country], [t0].[Phone], [t0].[Fax]
FROM [dbo].[Customers] AS [t0]
WHERE [t0].[Country] = @p0
-- @p0: Input String (Size = 2; Prec = 0; Scale = 0) [UK]
-- Context: SqlProvider(Sql2005) Model: AttributedMetaModel Build: 3.5.20706.1

Around the Horn - London - UK
B's Beverages - London - UK
Consolidated Holdings - London - UK
Eastern Connection - London - UK
Island Trading - Cowes - UK
North/South - London - UK
Seven Seas Imports - London - UK
```

You can see that the where clause of the SQL statement no longer specifies the city, which is exactly what we wanted. You can also see in the output results that there are now customers from different cities in the United Kingdom.

Of course, you can always append a call to the ToArray<T>, ToList<T>, ToDictionary<T, K>, or ToLookup<T, K> standard query operators to force the query to execute when you want.

The SQL IN Statement with the Contains Operator

One of the SQL query capabilities that early incarnations of LINQ to SQL lacked was the ability to perform a SQL IN statement, such as the one in the following SQL query:

A SQL Query with an IN Statement

```
SELECT *
FROM Customers
WHERE (City IN ('London', 'Madrid'))
```

To alleviate this problem, Microsoft added the Contains operator. But it works in the opposite direction to what you might expect given how the SQL IN statement works. With SQL IN, we say some member of an entity class must be IN some set of values. Instead, Contains works in the opposite manner. Let's take a look at Listing 14-18 where we demonstrate the Contains operator.

Listing 14-18. *The Contains Operator*

```
Northwind db = new Northwind(@"Data Source=.\SQLEXPRESS;Initial
Catalog=Northwind");

db.Log = Console.Out;

string[] cities = { "London", "Madrid" };

IQueryable<Customer> custs = db.Customers.Where(c => cities.Contains(c.City));

foreach (Customer cust in custs)
{
  Console.WriteLine("{0} - {1}", cust.CustomerID, cust.City);
}
```

As you can see in Listing 14-18, instead of writing the query so that the customer's city must be in some set of values, you write the query so that some set of values contains the customer's city. In the case of Listing 14-18, we create an array of cities named cities. In our query, we then call the Contains operator on the cities array and pass it the customer's city. If the cities array contains the customer's city, true will be returned to the Where operator, and that will cause the Customer object to be included in the output sequence.

Let's take a look at the output of Listing 14-18:

```
SELECT [t0].[CustomerID], [t0].[CompanyName], [t0].[ContactName],
[t0].[ContactTitle], [t0].[Address], [t0].[City], [t0].[Region], [t0].[PostalCode],
[t0].[Country], [t0].[Phone], [t0].[Fax]
FROM [dbo].[Customers] AS [t0]
WHERE [t0].[City] IN (@p0, @p1)
-- @p0: Input String (Size = 6; Prec = 0; Scale = 0) [London]
-- @p1: Input String (Size = 6; Prec = 0; Scale = 0) [Madrid]
-- Context: SqlProvider(Sql2005) Model: AttributedMetaModel Build: 3.5.20706.1

AROUT - London
```

```
BOLID - Madrid
BSBEV - London
CONSH - London
EASTC - London
FISSA - Madrid
NORTS - London
ROMEY - Madrid
SEVES - London
```

Looking at the generated SQL statement, you can see that the `Contains` operator was translated into a SQL IN statementN statement.

Updates

Making database updates with LINQ to SQL is as easy as changing properties on an object, calling the `DataContext` object's `SubmitChanges` method, and handling any concurrency conflicts that may occur. Don't let the concurrency conflict handling intimidate you; there are several options for handling conflicts, and none of them is too painful. We will cover detecting and handling conflicts in detail in Chapter 17.

Of course, this simplicity is true only if you have written entity classes that are mapped to the database properly and maintain graph consistency. For more information about mapping the entity classes to the database, read the "Entity Class Attributes and Attribute Properties" section in Chapter 15. For more information about graph consistency, read the "Graph Consistency" section in that same chapter. However, SQLMetal and the Object Relational Designer handle all the necessary plumbing to make all this happen for you.

For a simple example of making an update to the database, look at the first example in Chapter 12, Listing 12-1.

Updating Associated Classes

By design, LINQ to SQL allows you to update either side of associated classes to remove the relationship between them. You could update a parent object's reference to one of its children, or you could update that child's reference to the parent. Obviously, the references at each end of that relationship must be updated, but *you* need to update only one side or the other.

It is not LINQ to SQL that keeps your object model's graph consistent when updating one side; it is the responsibility of the entity class to make this happen. Please read the "Graph Consistency" section in Chapter 15 for more information about how this should be implemented.

However, SQLMetal and the Object Relational Designer handle this for you if you allow them to create your entity classes.

Updating a Child's Parent Reference

Since we can update either side of the relationship, we could choose to update a child's parent reference. So, as an example, let's see how we would change the employee that gets credit for an order in the Northwind database by examining Listing 14-19. Because this example is more complex than many of the others, we will explain it as we go.

Listing 14-19. Changing a Relationship by Assigning a New Parent

```
Northwind db = new Northwind(@"Data Source=.\SQLEXPRESS;Initial
Catalog=Northwind");

Order order = (from o in db.Orders
              where o.EmployeeID == 5
              orderby o.OrderDate descending
              select o).First<Order>();

// Save off the current employee so we can reset it at the end.
Employee origEmployee = order.Employee;
```

In the preceding code, after obtaining the DataContext, we query for the most recent order of the employee whose EmployeeID is 5 by ordering that person's orders by date in descending order and calling the First operator. This will provide us with the most recent order. Next, just so we will have a reference to the original employee this order was credited to, so that we can restore it at the end of the example, we save the reference in a variable named origEmployee:

```
Console.WriteLine("Before changing the employee.");
Console.WriteLine("OrderID = {0} : OrderDate = {1} : EmployeeID = {2}",
  order.OrderID, order.OrderDate, order.Employee.EmployeeID);
```

Next, we display a line to the console letting you know we haven't changed the employee for the retrieved order yet, followed by displaying the order's ID, date, and credited employee to the screen. We should see that the order is credited to employee 5, since that is the employee we queried to obtain the order.

```
Employee emp = (from e in db.Employees
                where e.EmployeeID == 9
                select e).Single<Employee>();

// Now we will assign the new employee to the order.
order.Employee = emp;

db.SubmitChanges();
```

Next, we query for some other employee, the one whose EmployeeID is 9, that we then set to be the credited employee for the previously queried order. Then, we save the changes by calling the SubmitChanges method.

Now, to prove the change was really made at both ends, we could just show you the credited employee for the queried order, but that would be anticlimactic, since you just saw us set the Employee property of the order, and it wouldn't really prove to you that the change was made on the employee side of the relationship. It would be much more satisfying for us to find the order we just changed in the new employee's collection of orders, so that is what we will do.

```
Order order2 = (from o in emp.Orders
                where o.OrderID == order.OrderID
                select o).First<Order>();
```

In the preceding code, we query for the order we changed by its OrderID in the new employee's Orders. If it is found, that will prove the relationship between the employee and order was updated on both ends of the relationship.

```
Console.WriteLine("{0}After changing the employee.", System.Environment.NewLine);
Console.WriteLine("OrderID = {0} : OrderDate = {1} : EmployeeID = {2}",
  order2.OrderID, order2.OrderDate, order2.Employee.EmployeeID);
```

In the preceding code, we display to the console that we are about to display the order after changing it to the new employee emp. We then display that order. We should see that its employee is the employee whose EmployeeID is 9. Prior to the change, the EmployeeID was 5.

```
// Now we need to reverse the changes so the example can be run multiple times.
order.Employee = origEmployee;
db.SubmitChanges();
```

The last two lines of code, as well as the line that saves the order's original employee, are for resetting the database so the example can be run multiple times.

Now, let's examine the output for Listing 14-19:

```
Before changing the employee.
OrderID = 11043 : OrderDate = 4/22/1998 12:00:00 AM : EmployeeID = 5

After changing the employee.
OrderID = 11043 : OrderDate = 4/22/1998 12:00:00 AM : EmployeeID = 9
```

As you can see, the employee for the order before the change was the employee whose EmployeeID is 5. After the change, the order's credited EmployeeID is 9. What is significant is that we didn't just display the order's credited employee on the same order variable, order. We retrieved that order from the employee whose EmployeeID is 9. This proves that the order was indeed changed on the employee side of the relationship.

In this example, we updated the child object's parent reference, where the child was the order and the parent was the employee. There is yet another approach we could have taken to achieve the same result. We could have updated the parent object's child reference.

Updating a Parent's Child Reference

Another approach to changing the relationship between two objects is to remove the child object from the parent object's EntitySet<T> collection and add it to a different parent's EntitySet<T> collection. In Listing 14-20, we remove the order from the employee's collection of orders. Because this example is similar to Listing 14-19, we will be far briefer in the explanation, but the significant differences will be in bold.

Listing 14-20. Changing a Relationship by Removing and Adding a Child to a Parent's EntitySet

```
Northwind db = new Northwind(@"Data Source=.\SQLEXPRESS;Initial
Catalog=Northwind");

Order order = (from o in db.Orders
                where o.EmployeeID == 5
                orderby o.OrderDate descending
                select o).First<Order>();

// Save off the current employee so we can reset it at the end.
Employee origEmployee = order.Employee;

Console.WriteLine("Before changing the employee.");
Console.WriteLine("OrderID = {0} : OrderDate = {1} : EmployeeID = {2}",
  order.OrderID, order.OrderDate, order.Employee.EmployeeID);

Employee emp = (from e in db.Employees
                where e.EmployeeID == 9
                select e).Single<Employee>();

// Remove the order from the original employee's Orders.
origEmployee.Orders.Remove(order);

// Now add it to the new employee's orders.
emp.Orders.Add(order);

db.SubmitChanges();

Console.WriteLine("{0}After changing the employee.", System.Environment.NewLine);
Console.WriteLine("OrderID = {0} : OrderDate = {1} : EmployeeID = {2}",
  order.OrderID, order.OrderDate, order.Employee.EmployeeID);

// Now we need to reverse the changes so the example can be run multiple times.
order.Employee = origEmployee;
db.SubmitChanges();
```

In Listing 14-20, we retrieve the most recent order for the employee whose EmployeeID is 5, and we save off the retrieved order's employee in origEmployee so that we can restore it at the end of the example. Next, we display the order before the employee is changed. Then, we retrieve the employee whose EmployeeID is 9 and store the reference in the variable named emp. At this point, this code is the same as Listing 14-19.

Then, we remove the order from the original employee's collection of orders and add it to the new employee's collection of orders. We then call the SubmitChanges method to persist the changes to the database. Next, we display the order after the changes to the console. Last, we restore the order to its original condition so the example can be run more than once. Let's examine the results of Listing 14-20:

```
Before changing the employee.
OrderID = 11043 : OrderDate = 4/22/1998 12:00:00 AM : EmployeeID = 5

After changing the employee.
OrderID = 11043 : OrderDate = 4/22/1998 12:00:00 AM : EmployeeID = 9
```

Deletes

To delete a record from a database using LINQ to SQL, you must delete the entity object from the Table<T> of which it is a member with the Table<T> object's DeleteOnSubmit method. Then, of course, you must call the SubmitChanges method. Listing 14-21 contains an example.

■ **Caution** Unlike all the other examples in this chapter, this example will not restore the database at the end. This is because one of the tables involved contains an identity column, and it is not a simple matter to programmatically restore the data to its identical state prior to the example executing. Therefore, before running this example, make sure you have a backup of your database that you can restore from. If you downloaded the zipped extended version of the Northwind database, after running this example, you could just detach the Northwind database, reextract the database files, and reattach the database.

Listing 14-21. Deleting a Record by Deleting It from Its Table<T>

```
Northwind db = new Northwind(@"Data Source=.\SQLEXPRESS;Initial
Catalog=Northwind");

//  Retrieve a customer to delete.
Customer customer = (from c in db.Customers
                     where c.CompanyName == "Alfreds Futterkiste"
                     select c).Single<Customer>();

db.OrderDetails.DeleteAllOnSubmit(
  customer.Orders.SelectMany(o => o.OrderDetails));
db.Orders.DeleteAllOnSubmit(customer.Orders);
db.Customers.DeleteOnSubmit(customer);

db.SubmitChanges();

Customer customer2 = (from c in db.Customers
                      where c.CompanyName == "Alfreds Futterkiste"
                      select c).SingleOrDefault<Customer>();

Console.WriteLine("Customer {0} found.", customer2 != null ? "is" : "is not");.
```

This example is pretty straightforward, but there are some interesting facets to it. First, since the Order table contains a foreign key to the Customer table, you cannot delete a customer without first deleting the customer's orders. And, since the OrderDetails table contains a foreign key to the Orders table, you cannot delete an order without first deleting the order's order details. So, to delete a customer, we must first delete the order details for all the orders for the customer, then we can delete all the orders, and finally we can delete the customer.

Deleting all the orders is not difficult thanks to the DeleteAllOnSubmit operator that can delete a sequence of orders, but deleting all the order details for each order is a little trickier. Of course, we could enumerate through all the orders and call the DeleteAllOnSubmit operator on each order's sequence of order details, but that would be boring. Instead, we call the SelectMany operator to take a sequence of sequences of order details to create a single concatenated sequence of order details that we then pass to the DeleteAllOnSubmit operator.

After deleting the order details, orders, and the customer, we call the SubmitChanges method. To prove the customer is actually gone, we query for it and display a message to the console.

Let's take a look at the output of Listing 14-21:

```
Customer is not found.
```

That's not very exciting output, but it does prove the customer no longer exists. Although the point of Listing 14-21 is to demonstrate that to delete an entity object you must delete it from the appropriate Table<T>, we think the example became a cheerleader for the SelectMany operator as well.

■ **Note** Remember that this example did not restore the database at the end, so you should manually restore it now.

Deleting Attached Entity Objects

Unlike when an attached associated dependent entity object was automatically inserted into the database by the DataContext when the dependent entity object's associated parent object was inserted, as happened in Listing 14-3, our attached dependent entity objects are not automatically deleted if the parent entity object is deleted. By dependent, we mean the entity objects containing the foreign key. You saw this demonstrated in Listing 14-21, where we had to delete the OrderDetails records before the Orders records and the Orders records before the Customers record.

So, for example, with the Northwind database, if you attempt to delete an order, its order details will not automatically be deleted. This will cause a foreign key constraint violation when you attempt to delete the order. Therefore, before you can delete an entity object, you must delete all its attached associated child entity objects.

For examples of this, see Listing 14-21 and Listing 14-3. In each of these listings, we had to delete the associated attached entity objects before we could delete their parent object.

Deleting Relationships

To delete a relationship between two entity objects in LINQ to SQL, you reassign the entity object's reference to the related object to a different object or null. By assigning the reference to null, the entity object will have no relationship to an entity of that type. However, removing the relationship altogether by assigning the reference to null will not delete the record itself. Remember, to actually delete a record, its corresponding entity object must be deleted from the appropriate Table<T>. Listing 14-22 contains an example of removing the relationship.

Listing 14-22. Removing a Relationship Between Two Entity Objects

```
Northwind db = new Northwind(@"Data Source=.\SQLEXPRESS;Initial
Catalog=Northwind");

//  Retrieve an order to unrelate.
Order order = (from o in db.Orders
               where o.OrderID == 11043
               select o).Single<Order>();

//  Save off the original customer so we can set it back.
Customer c = order.Customer;

Console.WriteLine("Orders before deleting the relationship:");
foreach (Order ord in c.Orders)
{
  Console.WriteLine("OrderID = {0}", ord.OrderID);
}

//  Remove the relationship to the customer.
order.Customer = null;
db.SubmitChanges();

Console.WriteLine("{0}Orders after deleting the relationship:",
  System.Environment.NewLine);
foreach (Order ord in c.Orders)
{
  Console.WriteLine("OrderID = {0}", ord.OrderID);
}

//  Restore the database back to its original state.
order.Customer = c;
db.SubmitChanges();
```

In Listing 14-22, we query a specific order, one with an OrderID of 11043. We save that order's Customer, so we can restore it at the end of the example. We then display all of that customer's orders to the console and assign the retrieved order's customer to null and call the SubmitChanges method to persist the changes to the database. Then, we display all the customer's orders again, and this time, the order whose OrderID is 11043 is gone. Let's examine the output for Listing 14-22:

```
Orders before deleting the relationship:
OrderID = 10738
OrderID = 10907
OrderID = 10964
OrderID = 11043

Orders after deleting the relationship:
OrderID = 10738
OrderID = 10907
OrderID = 10964
```

As you can see, once we remove the relationship to the customer for the order whose OrderID is 11043, the order is no longer in the customer's collection of orders.

Overriding Database Modification Statements

If you have been thinking that using LINQ to SQL in your environment is not possible, perhaps because of requirements to use stored procedures for all modifications to the database, then you would be interested in knowing that the actual code that gets called to make the updates, including inserts and deletes, can be overridden.

Overriding the code called to insert, update, and delete is as simple as defining the appropriately named *partial* method with the appropriate signature. When you override this way, the DataContext change processor will call your partial method implementation for the database update, insert, or delete. Here is yet another way Microsoft is taking advantage of partial methods. You get the ability to hook into the code but with no overhead if you don't.

You must be aware, though, that if you take this approach, you will be responsible for concurrency conflict detection. Please read Chapter 17 thoroughly before you do this.

When you define these override methods, it is the name of the partial method and the entity type of the method's parameters that instruct the DataContext to call your override methods. Let's take a look at the method prototypes you must define to override the insert, update, and delete methods.

Overriding the Insert Method

You may override the method called to insert a record in the database by implementing a partial method prototyped as

```
partial void Insert[EntityClassName](T instance)
```

where [EntityClassName] is the name of the entity class whose insert method is being overridden and type T is that entity class.

Here is an example of the prototype to override the insert method for the Shipper entity class:

```
partial void InsertShipper(Shipper instance)
```

Overriding the Update Method

You may override the method called to update a record in the database by implementing a partial method prototyped as

```
partial void Update[EntityClassName](T instance)
```

where [EntityClassName] is the name of the entity class whose update method is being overridden and type T is that entity class.

Here is an example of the prototype to override the update method for the Shipper entity class:

```
partial void UpdateShipper(Shipper instance)
```

Overriding the Delete Method

You may override the method called to delete a record in the database by implementing a partial method prototyped as

```
partial void Delete[EntityClassName](T instance)
```

where [EntityClassName] is the name of the entity class whose delete method is being overridden and type T is that entity class.

Here is an example of the prototype to override the delete method for the Shipper entity class:

```
partial void DeleteShipper(Shipper instance)
```

Example

For an example demonstrating overriding the insert, update, and delete methods, instead of modifying our generated entity class file, we are going to create a new file for our override partial methods so that if we ever need to regenerate our entity class file, we will not lose our override partial methods. We have named our file NorthwindExtended.cs. Here is what it will look like:

The NorthwindExtended.cs File with Database Update Override Methods

```
using System;
using System.Data.Linq;

namespace nwind
{
  public partial class Northwind : DataContext
  {
    partial void InsertShipper(Shipper instance)
```

```
  {
    Console.WriteLine("Insert override method was called for shipper {0}.",
      instance.CompanyName);
  }

  partial void UpdateShipper(Shipper instance)
  {
    Console.WriteLine("Update override method was called for shipper {0}.",
      instance.CompanyName);
  }

  partial void DeleteShipper(Shipper instance)
  {
    Console.WriteLine("Delete override method was called for shipper {0}.",
      instance.CompanyName);
  }
 }
}
```

■ **Note** You will have to add the file containing this partial class definition to your Visual Studio project.

The first thing to notice about the override code is that the override methods are partial methods defined at the `DataContext` level. They are not defined in the entity class to which they relate.

As you can see, our override methods aren't doing anything except for informing us that they are getting called. In many situations, the override will be for the purpose of calling a stored procedure, but this is up to the developer.

Now, let's take a look at Listing 14-23, which contains code that will cause our override methods to be called.

Listing 14-23. An Example Where the Update, Insert, and Delete Methods Are Overridden

```
Northwind db = new Northwind(@"Data Source=.\SQLEXPRESS;Initial
Catalog=Northwind");

Shipper ship = (from s in db.Shippers
                where s.ShipperID == 1
                select s).Single<Shipper>();

ship.CompanyName = "Jiffy Shipping";

Shipper newShip =
  new Shipper
  {
    ShipperID = 4,
```

```
      CompanyName = "Vickey Rattz Shipping",
      Phone = "(800) SHIP-NOW"
   };

db.Shippers.InsertOnSubmit(newShip);

Shipper deletedShip = (from s in db.Shippers
                       where s.ShipperID == 3
                       select s).Single<Shipper>();

db.Shippers.DeleteOnSubmit(deletedShip);

db.SubmitChanges();
```

In Listing 14-23, first we retrieve the shipper whose ShipperID is 1, and then we update a field. Then, we insert another shipper, Vickey Rattz Shipping, and delete yet another, the one with a ShipperID of 3. Of course, since our override methods are getting called and they only display a message to the console, no change is actually persisted to the database. Here are the results of Listing 14-23:

```
Update override method was called for shipper Jiffy Shipping.
Insert override method was called for shipper Vickey Rattz Shipping.
Delete override method was called for shipper Federal Shipping.
```

From the results, you can see each of our override methods is called. Now the question becomes, what if you want to override the insert, update, and delete methods but you also want the default behavior to occur?

Because the code required would conflict with our partial methods for the previous example, we will not provide a working example of this, but we will explain how to do it. In your partial method implementations for the insert, update, and delete methods, you call the DataContext.ExecuteDynamicInsert, DataContext.ExecuteDynamicUpdate, or DataContext.ExecuteDynamicDelete method, respectively, to get the default method behavior.

For example, if, for the previous example, we want our log messages to be called *and* we want the normal LINQ to SQL code to be called to actually handle the persistence to the database, we could change our partial method implementations to the following:

Overriding the Insert, Update, and Delete Methods Plus Calling the Default Behavior

```
namespace nwind
{
  public partial class Northwind : DataContext
  {
    partial void InsertShipper(Shipper instance)
    {
      Console.WriteLine("Insert override method was called for shipper {0}.",
        instance.CompanyName);
      this.ExecuteDynamicInsert(instance);
```

```
    }

    partial void UpdateShipper(Shipper instance)
    {
      Console.WriteLine("Update override method was called for shipper {0}.",
        instance.CompanyName);
      this.ExecuteDynamicUpdate(instance);
    }

    partial void DeleteShipper(Shipper instance)
    {
      Console.WriteLine("Delete override method was called for shipper {0}.",
        instance.CompanyName);
      this.ExecuteDynamicDelete(instance);
    }
  }
}
```

Notice that in each of the partial methods we call the appropriate `ExecuteDynamicInsert`, `ExecuteDynamicUpdate`, or `ExecuteDynamicDelete` method. Now, we can extend the behavior when an entity class is called, we can modify it, or we can even create a wrapper for the existing default behavior. LINQ to SQL is very flexible.

Overriding in the Object Relational Designer

Don't forget, as we covered in Chapter 13, you can override the insert, update, and delete methods using the Object Relational Designer.

Considerations

Don't forget that when you override the update, insert, and delete methods, you take responsibility for performing concurrency conflict detection. This means you should be very familiar with how the currently implemented concurrency conflict detection works. For example, the way Microsoft has implemented it is to specify all relevant fields involved in update checks in the `where` clause of the update statement. The logic then checks to see how many records were updated by the statement. You should follow a similar pattern, and if a concurrency conflict is detected, you must throw a `ChangeConflictException` exception. Be sure to read Chapter 17 before attempting to override these methods.

SQL Translation

When writing LINQ to SQL queries, you may have noticed that when specifying expressions such as `where` clauses, the expressions are in the native programming language, as opposed to SQL. After all, this is part of the goal of LINQ, language integration. For this book, the expressions are in C#. If you haven't noticed, shame on you.

For example, in Listing 14-2, we have a query that looks like this:

An Example of a LINQ to SQL Query

```
Customer cust = (from c in db.Customers
                    where c.CustomerID == "LONEP"
                    select c).Single<Customer>();
```

Notice that the expression in the where clause is indeed C# syntax, as opposed to SQL syntax that would look more like this:

An Example of an Invalid LINQ to SQL Query

```
Customer cust = (from c in db.Customers
                    where c.CustomerID = 'LONEP'
                    select c).Single<Customer>();
```

Notice that instead of using the C# equality operator (==), the SQL equality operator (=) is used. Instead of enclosing the string literal in double quotes (""), single quotes (' ') enclose it. One of the goals of LINQ is to allow developers to program in their native programming languages. Remember, LINQ stands for Language Integrated Query. However, since the database won't be executing C# expressions, your C# expressions must be translated to valid SQL. Therefore, your queries must be translated to SQL.

Right off the bat, this means that what you can do does have limitations. But, in general, the translation is pretty good. Rather than attempt to re-create a reference similar to the MSDN help for this translation process and what can and cannot be translated, we want to show you what to expect when your LINQ to SQL query cannot be translated.

First, be aware that the untranslatable code may compile. A failed translation may not actually reveal itself until the time the query is actually performed. Because of deferred query execution, this also means the line of code defining the query may execute just fine. Only when the query is actually performed does the failed translation rear its ugly head, and it does so in the form of an exception similar to this:

```
Unhandled Exception: System.NotSupportedException: Method 'TrimEnd' has no
supported
translation to SQL.
…
```

That is a pretty clear error message. Let's examine the code in Listing 14-24 that produces this exception.

Listing 14-24. *A LINQ to SQL Query That Cannot Be Translated*

```
Northwind db = new Northwind(@"Data Source=.\SQLEXPRESS;Initial
Catalog=Northwind");

IQueryable<Customer> custs = from c in db.Customers
                                where c.CustomerID.TrimEnd('K') == "LAZY"
                                select c;
```

```
foreach (Customer c in custs)
{
  Console.WriteLine("{0}", c.CompanyName);
}
```

Notice that the TrimEnd method that caused the translation exception is called on the database field, not our local string literal. In Listing 14-25, I'll reverse the side we call the TrimEnd method on and see what happens.

Listing 14-25. *A LINQ to SQL Query That Can Be Translated*

```
Northwind db = new Northwind(@"Data Source=.\SQLEXPRESS;Initial
Catalog=Northwind");

IQueryable<Customer> custs = from c in db.Customers
                            where c.CustomerID == "LAZY".TrimEnd('K')
                            select c;

foreach (Customer c in custs)
{
  Console.WriteLine("{0}", c.CompanyName);
}
```

The output of Listing 14-25 looks like this:

OK, you got us; there is no output. But that is fine because this is the appropriate output for the query, and no SQL translation exception is thrown.

So, calling an unsupported method on a database column causes the exception, while calling that same method on the passed parameter is just fine. This makes sense. LINQ to SQL would have no problem calling the TrimEnd method on our parameter, because it can do this prior to binding the parameter to the query, which occurs in our process environment. Calling the TrimEnd method on the database column would have to be done in the database, and that means, instead of calling the method in our process environment, that call must be translated to a SQL statement that can be passed to the database and executed. Since the TrimEnd method is not supported for SQL translation, the exception is thrown.

One thing to keep in mind is that if you do need to call an unsupported method on a database column, perhaps you can instead call a method that has the mutually opposite effect on the parameter? Say, for example, you want to call the ToUpper method on the database column, and it's not supported; perhaps you could call the ToLower method on the parameter instead. However, in this case, the ToUpper method is supported, so the point is moot. Also, you must ensure that the method you call does indeed have a mutually opposite effect. In this case, the database column could have mixed case, so calling the ToLower method would still not have exactly the opposite effect. If your database column contained the value "Smith" and your parameter was "SMITH", and you were checking for equality, calling the ToUpper method on the database column would work and give you a match. However, if the

519

ToUpper method were not supported, trying to reverse the logic by calling the ToLower method on the parameter would still not yield a match.

You may be wondering how you would know that the TrimEnd method is not supported by SQL translation. Because the nature of which primitive types and methods are supported is so dynamic and subject to change, it is beyond the scope of this book to attempt to document them all. There are also a lot of restrictions and disclaimers to the translation. We suspect SQL translation will be an ongoing effort for Microsoft. For you to know what is supported, you should consult the MSDN documentation titled ".NET Framework Function Translation" for LINQ to SQL. However, as you can see from the previous examples, it is pretty easy to tell when a method is not supported.

Summary

We know this chapter has been a whirlwind tour of standard database operations using LINQ to SQL. We hope we kept the examples simple enough to allow you to focus on the basic steps necessary to perform inserts, queries, updates, and deletes to the database. We also pointed out the ways that LINQ to SQL queries differ from LINQ to Objects queries.

Bear in mind that any LINQ to SQL code that changes the database should detect and resolve concurrency conflicts, which we cover thoroughly in Chapter 17.

In addition to understanding how to perform these basic operations on entity objects, it is also important to understand how this affects an object's associated entity objects. Remember, when you insert an entity object into the database, any attached objects will be added automatically for you. However, this automation does not extend to deletes. To delete a parent entity object in an association relationship, you must first delete the child entity objects; otherwise, an exception will be thrown.

Next, we demonstrated how you can override the default methods generated to modify your entity object's corresponding database records. This allows a developer to control how database changes are made, which allows you to use stored procedures.

Finally, we covered the fact that LINQ to SQL queries must be translated to SQL statements. It is important to never forget that this translation takes place, and this does somewhat restrict what can be done.

We are conscious that we have mentioned entity classes repeatedly but have yet to explain them in any depth. It's high time we rectify this state of affairs. So, in the next chapter, Chapter 15, we plan to bore you to tears with them.

■ ■ ■

LINQ to SQL Entity Classes

In the previous LINQ to SQL chapters, we mentioned entity classes numerous times but did not define or describe them. In this chapter, we will define entity classes, as well as discuss the different ways they can be created. We will also discuss of the complexities and responsibilities should you decide to create your own entity classes.

But before we can begin, you must meet some prerequisites to be able to run the examples in this chapter.

Prerequisites for Running the Examples

To run the examples in this chapter, you will need to have obtained the extended version of the Northwind database and generated entity classes for it. Please read and follow the instructions in the "Prerequisites for Running the Examples" section of Chapter 12.

Entity Classes

Classes that are mapped to the SQL Server database using LINQ to SQL are known as *entity classes*. An instantiated object of an entity class is an entity of that type, and we will refer to it as an *entity object*. Entity classes are normal C# classes with additional LINQ to SQL attributes specified. Alternatively, rather than adding attributes, entity classes can be created by providing an XML mapping file when instantiating the DataContext object. Those attributes or mapping file entries dictate how the entity classes are to be mapped to a SQL Server database when using LINQ to SQL.

By using these entity classes, we can query and update the database using LINQ to SQL.

Creating Entity Classes

Entity classes are the basic building blocks utilized when performing LINQ to SQL queries. To begin using LINQ to SQL, entity classes are required. There are two ways to obtain entity classes; you can generate them, as we demonstrate in Chapter 12 and Chapter 13, or you can write them by hand. And, there is no reason you cannot do a combination of both.

If you do not already have business classes for the entities stored in the database, generating the entity classes is probably the best approach. If you already have an object model, writing the entity classes may be the best approach.

If you are starting a project from scratch, we recommend that you consider modeling the database first and generating the entity classes from the database, which will alleviate the burden of writing them correctly.

Generating Entity Classes

In Chapter 12, we demonstrate how to generate the entity classes for the Northwind database so you can try the examples in the LINQ to SQL chapters of this book. In Chapter 13, we discuss in detail how you can generate entity classes using either the command-line tool named SQLMetal or the GUI tool named the Object Relational Designer.

SQLMetal is very simple to use but does not provide any options for controlling the naming of the generated entity classes—although you can use it to produce an intermediate XML file, which you can edit. Further, SQLMetal generates entity classes for every table in the specified database and for every field in each table. The Object Relational Designer may take longer to create a complete object model for a database, but it has the benefit of allowing you to specify exactly which tables and fields you want to generate entity classes for, as well as allowing you to specify the names of the entity classes and their properties. We have already discussed SQLMetal and the Object Relational Designer in Chapter 13, so refer to that chapter for more details about using either of these two tools.

There is a difference between generating an entity class and using one. You might generate entity classes for all the tables in a database, but that doesn't mean you have to use them all.

And using generated entity classes doesn't mean that you can't add custom functionality to them. For example, a Customer class was generated by SQLMetal in Chapter 12. There is no reason that business methods or nonpersisted class members cannot be added to this Customer class. However, if you do this, make sure you do not actually modify the generated entity class code. Instead, create another Customer class module, and take advantage of the fact that entity classes are generated as partial classes. Partial classes are a great addition to C# and make it easier than ever to separate functionality into separate modules. This way, if the entity class gets regenerated for any reason, you will not lose your added methods or members.

Writing Entity Classes by Hand

Writing entity classes by hand is the most difficult approach. It requires a solid understanding of the LINQ to SQL attributes and/or the external mapping schema. However, writing entity classes by hand is a great way to really learn LINQ to SQL.

Where writing entity classes by hand really pays off is when you already have an object model to work with. It wouldn't be very beneficial to generate entity classes from a database, since you already have your object model used by the application. In such cases, you can either add the necessary attributes to your existing object model or create a mapping file. Thanks to the flexibility of LINQ to SQL, it is not necessary that your classes match the name of the table they are persisted in or that the names of the properties of the class match the column names in the table. This means that previously implemented classes can now be modified to persist in a SQL Server database.

To create entity classes by hand using attributes, you will need to add the appropriate attributes to your classes, be they existing business classes or new classes created specifically as entity classes. Read the "Entity Class Attributes and Attribute Properties" section in this chapter for a description of the available attributes and properties.

To create entity classes by using an external mapping file, you will need to create an XML file that conforms to the schema discussed in the "XML External Mapping File Schema" section later in this chapter. Once you have this external mapping file, you will use the appropriate DataContext constructor when instantiating the DataContext object to load the mapping file. There are two constructors that allow you to specify an external mapping file.

Additional Responsibilities of Entity Classes

Unfortunately, when writing entity classes by hand, it is not enough to understand the attributes and attribute properties. You must also know about some of the additional responsibilities of entity classes.

For example, you must be aware change notifications and how to implement them. You also must ensure graph consistency between your parent and child classes.

These additional responsibilities are all taken care of for you when using SQLMetal or the Object Relational Designer, but if you are creating your entity classes yourself, you must add the necessary code.

Change Notifications

Later, in Chapter 16, we will discuss change tracking. It turns out that change tracking is not very elegant or efficient without assistance from the entity classes themselves. If your entity classes are generated by SQLMetal or the Object Relational Designer, you can relax because these tools will take care of these inefficiencies by implementing code to participate in change notifications when they generate your entity classes. But if you are writing your entity classes, you need to understand change notifications and potentially implement the code to participate in the change notifications.

You can elect to have your entity classes participate in change notifications. If they do not participate in change notifications, the `DataContext` provides change tracking by keeping two copies of each entity object—one with the original values and one with the current values. It creates the copies the first time an entity is retrieved from the database when change tracking begins. You can make change tracking more efficient by making your handwritten entity classes implement the change notification interfaces, `System.ComponentModel.INotifyPropertyChanging` and `System.ComponentModel.INotifyPropertyChanged`.

As we will do often in the LINQ to SQL chapters, we will refer to the code that was generated by SQLMetal to show you the quintessential way to handle a situation. In this case, we will refer to the SQLMetal-generated code to handle change notifications. To implement the `INotifyPropertyChanging` and `INotifyPropertyChanged` interfaces, we need to do four things.

First, we need to define an entity class so that it implements the `INotifyPropertyChanging` and `INotifyPropertyChanged` interfaces:

From the Generated Customer Entity Class

```
[Table(Name="dbo.Customers")]
public partial class Customer : INotifyPropertyChanging, INotifyPropertyChanged
{ ... }
```

Because the entity class implements these two interfaces, the `DataContext` will know to register two event handlers for two events we will discuss in just a few paragraphs.

You can see that the `Table` attribute is specified in the preceding code. We will be displaying the related attributes for context purposes in this section and discuss them in detail later in this chapter. You can ignore them for the moment.

Second, we need to declare a `private static` variable of type `PropertyChangingEventArgs` and pass `String.Empty` to its constructor.

From the Generated Customer Entity Class

```
[Table(Name="dbo.Customers")]
public partial class Customer : INotifyPropertyChanging, INotifyPropertyChanged
{
  private static PropertyChangingEventArgs emptyChangingEventArgs =
    new PropertyChangingEventArgs(String.Empty);
```

```
  ...
}
```

The emptyChangingEventArgs object will be passed to one of the previously mentioned event handlers when the appropriate event is raised.

Third, we need to add two public event members, one of type System.ComponentModel.PropertyChangingEventHandler named PropertyChanging, and one of type System.ComponentModel.PropertyChangedEventHandler named PropertyChanged to the entity class.

From the Generated Customer Entity Class

```
[Table(Name="dbo.Customers")]
public partial class Customer : INotifyPropertyChanging, INotifyPropertyChanged
{
  private static PropertyChangingEventArgs emptyChangingEventArgs =
    new PropertyChangingEventArgs(String.Empty);
  ...
  public event PropertyChangingEventHandler PropertyChanging;

  public event PropertyChangedEventHandler PropertyChanged;
  ...
}
```

When the DataContext object initiates change tracking for an entity object, the DataContext object will register event handlers with these two events if the entity class implements the two change notification interfaces. If not, it will make a copy of the entity object as we previously mentioned.

Fourth, every time a mapped entity class property is changed, we need to raise the PropertyChanging event prior to changing the property and raise the PropertyChanged event after changing the property.

Although it is not necessary that we implement raising the events the following way, for conciseness, SQLMetal generates SendPropertyChanging and SendPropertyChanged methods for you.

From the Generated Customer Entity Class

```
  protected virtual void SendPropertyChanging()
  {
    if ((this.PropertyChanging != null))
    {
      this.PropertyChanging(this, emptyChangingEventArgs);
    }
  }

  protected virtual void SendPropertyChanged(String propertyName)
  {
    if ((this.PropertyChanged != null))
    {
```

```
        this.PropertyChanged(this, new PropertyChangedEventArgs(propertyName));
    }
}
```

Notice that in the raising of the PropertyChanged event, a new PropertyChangedEventArgs object is created and passed the name of the specific property that has been changed. This lets the DataContext object know exactly which property has been changed. So when the SendPropertyChanging method is called, it raises the PropertyChanging event, which results in the event handler the DataContext object registered being called. This same pattern and flow also applies to the SendPropertyChanged method and PropertyChanged event.

Of course, you could choose to embed similar logic in your code instead of creating methods that are reused, but that would be more of a hassle and create more code to maintain.

Then in each property's set method, we must call the two methods SendPropertyChanging and SendPropertyChanged just prior to and after changing a property.

From the Generated Customer Entity Class

```
[Column(Storage="_ContactName", DbType="NVarChar(30)")]
public string ContactName
{
  get
  {
    return this._ContactName;
  }
  set
  {
    if ((this._ContactName != value))
    {
      this.OnContactNameChanging(value);
      this.SendPropertyChanging();
      this._ContactName = value;
      this.SendPropertyChanged("ContactName");
      this.OnContactNameChanged();
    }
  }
}
```

Again, notice that in the call to the SendPropertyChanged method, the name of the property is passed, which in this case is ContactName. Once the SendPropertyChanged method is called, the DataContext object knows the ContactName property has been changed for this entity object.

We must also see to it that the appropriate events are raised in the set methods for properties that represent an association. So, on the *many* side of a one-to-many association, we need to add the following code that is bold:

From the Order Class Since Customer Has No EntityRef<T> Properties

```
[Association(Name="FK_Orders_Customers", Storage="_Customer",
  ThisKey="CustomerID", IsForeignKey=true)]
```

```
public Customer Customer
{
  get
  {
    return this._Customer.Entity;
  }
  set
  {
    Customer previousValue = this._Customer.Entity;
    if (((previousValue != value)
          || (this._Customer.HasLoadedOrAssignedValue == false)))
    {
      this.SendPropertyChanging();
      if ((previousValue != null))
      {
        this._Customer.Entity = null;
        previousValue.Orders.Remove(this);
      }
      this._Customer.Entity = value;
      if ((value != null))
      {
        value.Orders.Add(this);
        this._CustomerID = value.CustomerID;
      }
      else
      {
        this._CustomerID = default(string);
      }
      this.SendPropertyChanged("Customer");
    }
  }
}
```

and, on the *one* side of a one-to-many association, we need the following code that is bold:

From the Generated Customer Entity Class

```
public Customer()
{
  ...
  this._Orders =
    new EntitySet<Order>(new Action<Order>(this.attach_Orders),
                         new Action<Order>(this.detach_Orders));
}
...
private void attach_Orders(Order entity)
{
```

```
  this.SendPropertyChanging();
  entity.Customer = this;
  this.SendPropertyChanged("Orders");
}

private void detach_Orders(Order entity)
{
  this.SendPropertyChanging();
  entity.Customer = null;
  this.SendPropertyChanged("Orders");
}
```

In case you are unfamiliar with the Action generic delegate used in the preceding code, it exists in the System namespace and was added to the .NET Framework in version 2.0. The preceding code instantiates an Action delegate object for the Order entity class and passes it a delegate to the attach_Orders method. LINQ to SQL will use this delegate later to assign a Customer to an Order. Likewise, another Action delegate object is instantiated and passed a delegate to the detach_Orders method. LINQ to SQL will use this delegate later to remove the assignment of a Customer to an Order.

By implementing change notification in the manner just described, we can make change tracking more efficient. Now, the DataContext object knows when and which entity class properties are changed.

When we call the SubmitChanges method, the DataContext object forgets the original values of the properties, the current property values effectively become the original property values, and change tracking starts over. The SubmitChanges method is covered in detail in Chapter 16.

Of course, as we previously mentioned, if you allow SQLMetal or the Object Relational Designer to create your entity classes, you are relieved of these complexities, because they handle all this plumbing code for you. It is only when writing entity classes by hand that you need to be concerned with implementing change notifications.

Graph Consistency

In mathematics, when nodes are connected together, the network created by the connections is referred to as a *graph*. In the same way, the network representing the connections created by classes referencing other classes is also referred to as a *graph*. When you have two entity classes that participate in a relationship, meaning an Association has been created between them, since they each have a reference to the other, a graph exists.

When you are modifying a relationship between two entity objects, such as a Customer and an Order, the references on each side of the relationship must be properly updated so that each entity object properly references or no longer references the other. This is true whether you are creating the relationship or removing it. Since LINQ to SQL defines that the programmer writing code that uses entity classes need only modify one side of the relationship, something has to handle updating the other side, and, sadly, LINQ to SQL doesn't do that for us.

It is the responsibility of the entity class to handle updating the other side of the relationship. If you allowed SQLMetal or the Object Relational Designer to generate your entity classes, you are set because they do this for you. But, when you create your own entity classes, it is the entity class developer who must implement the code to make this happen.

By ensuring that each side of the relationship is properly updated, the graph remains consistent. Without it, the graph becomes inconsistent, and chaos ensues. A Customer may be related to an Order, but the Order might be related to a different Customer or no Customer at all. Fortunately, Microsoft provides a pattern we can use to make sure our entity classes properly implement graph consistency. Let's take a look at their implementation generated for the Northwind database by SQLMetal.

From the Generated Customer Entity Class

```
public Customer()
{
  ...
  this._Orders =
    new EntitySet<Order>(new Action<Order>(this.attach_Orders),
                         new Action<Order>(this.detach_Orders));
}
...
private void attach_Orders(Order entity)
{
  this.SendPropertyChanging();
  entity.Customer = this;
  this.SendPropertyChanged("Orders");
}

private void detach_Orders(Order entity)
{
  this.SendPropertyChanging();
  entity.Customer = null;
  this.SendPropertyChanged("Orders");
}
```

In this example, the Customer class will be the parent class, or the *one* side of the one-to-many relationship. The Order class will be the child class, or the *many* side of the one-to-many relationship.

In the preceding code, we can see that in the constructor of the parent class Customer, when the EntitySet<T> member for our child class collection _Orders is initialized, two Action<T> delegate objects are passed into the constructor.

The first Action<T> delegate object is passed a delegate to a callback method that will handle assigning the current Customer object, referenced with the this keyword, as the Customer of the Order that will be passed into the callback method. In the preceding code, the callback method we are referring to is the attach_Orders method.

The second parameter to the EntitySet<T> constructor is an Action<T> delegate object that is passed a delegate to a callback method that will handle removing the assignment of the passed Order object's Customer. In the preceding code, the callback method we are referring to is the detach_Orders method.

Even though the preceding code is in the parent class Customer, the assignment of the child class Order to the Customer is actually being handled by the Order object's Customer property. You can see that in both the attach_Orders and detach_Orders methods; all they really do is change the Order object's Customer property. You can see the entity.Customer property being set to this and null, respectively, to attach the current Customer and detach the currently assigned Customer. In the get and set methods for the child class, Order is where all the heavy lifting will be done to maintain graph consistency. We have effectively pawned off the real work to the child class this way. In the parent class, that is all there is to maintaining graph consistency.

However, before we proceed, notice that in the attach_Orders and detach_Orders methods, change notifications are being raised by calling the SendPropertyChanging and SendPropertyChanged methods.

Now, let's take a look at what needs to be done in the child class of the parent-to-child relation to maintain graph consistency.

From the Generated Order Entity Class

```
[Association(Name="FK_Orders_Customers", Storage="_Customer",
  ThisKey="CustomerID", IsForeignKey=true)]
public Customer Customer
{
  get
  {
    return this._Customer.Entity;
  }
  set
  {
    Customer previousValue = this._Customer.Entity;
    if (((previousValue != value)
         || (this._Customer.HasLoadedOrAssignedValue == false)))
    {
      this.SendPropertyChanging();
      if ((previousValue != null))
      {
        this._Customer.Entity = null;
        previousValue.Orders.Remove(this);
      }
      this._Customer.Entity = value;
      if ((value != null))
      {
        value.Orders.Add(this);
        this._CustomerID = value.CustomerID;
      }
      else
      {
        this._CustomerID = default(string);
      }
      this.SendPropertyChanged("Customer");
    }
  }
}
```

In the preceding code, we are concerned only with the Customer property's set method, especially since the parent side of the relationship put the burden of maintaining graph consistency on it. Because this method gets so complicated, we will present the code as we describe it.

```
set
{
  Customer previousValue = this._Customer.Entity;
```

You can see that in the first line of the set method code, a copy of the original Customer assigned to the Order is saved as previousValue. Don't let the fact that the code is referencing this._Customer.Entity confuse you. Remember that the _Customer member variable is actually an EntityRef<Customer>, not a Customer. So, to get the actual Customer object, the code must reference the EntityRef<T> object's Entity property. Since the EntityRef<T> is for a Customer, the type of Entity will be Customer; casting is not necessary.

```
    if (((previousValue != value)
          || (this._Customer.HasLoadedOrAssignedValue == false)))
    {
```

Next, the code checks to see whether the Customer currently being assigned to the Order via the passed value parameter is not the same Customer that is already assigned to the Order, because if it is, there is nothing that needs to be done unless the Customer has not been loaded or assigned a value yet. Not only is this logically sensible, when we get to the recursive nature of how this code works, this line of code will become very important, because it is what will cause the recursion to stop.

```
      this.SendPropertyChanging();
```

In the preceding line of code, the SendPropertyChanging method is called to raise the change notification event.

```
      if ((previousValue != null))
      {
```

Next, the code determines whether a Customer object, the parent object, is already assigned to the Order object, the child object, by comparing the previousValue to null. Remember, at this point, the Order object's Customer is still the same as the previousValue variable.

If a Customer is assigned to the Order—meaning the previousValue, which represents the assigned Customer, is not null—the code needs to set the Order object's Customer EntityRef<T> object's Entity property to null in the following line:

```
        this._Customer.Entity = null;
```

The Entity property is set to null in the preceding line of code to halt the recursion that will be set in motion in the next line of code. Since the Order object's Customer property's Entity property is now null and doesn't reference the actual Customer object but the Customer object's Orders property still contains this Order in its collection, the graph is inconsistent at this moment in time.

In the next line of code, the Remove method is called on the Customer object's Orders property, and the current Order is passed as the Order to be removed.

```
        previousValue.Orders.Remove(this);
      }
```

Calling the `Remove` method will cause the `Customer` class's `detach_Orders` method to get called and passed the `Order` that is to be removed. In the `detach_Orders` method, the passed `Order` object's `Customer` property is set to `null`. To refresh your memory, here is what the `detach_Orders` method looks like:

This Code Is a Separate Method Listed Here for Your Convenience

```
private void detach_Orders(Order entity)
{
  this.SendPropertyChanging();
  entity.Customer = null;
  this.SendPropertyChanged("Orders");
}
```

When the `detach_Orders` method is called, the passed `Order` has its `Customer` property set to `null`. This causes the passed `Order` object's `Customer` property's set method to be called, which is the method that invoked the code that invoked the `detach_Orders` method, so the very method that started this process of removing the `Order` gets called recursively, and the value of `null` is passed as the `value` to the set method. The flow of execution is now in a recursed call to the `Customer` set method.

The detach_Orders Method Causes the set Method to Be Called Recursively

```
set
{
  Customer previousValue = this._Customer.Entity;
  if (((previousValue != value)
        || (this._Customer.HasLoadedOrAssignedValue == false)))
  {
```

In the fourth line of the set method, the passed value is checked, and if it is equal to the currently assigned `Customer` property's `Entity` property, this recursed call to the set method returns without doing anything. Because in the previous line of code of the first, nonrecursed set method call the `Customer` property's `Entity` property was set to `null` and because `null` was passed as the `value` in the `detach_Orders` method, they are indeed equal: the recursed invocation of the set method exits without doing anything more, and the flow of control returns to the first invocation of the set method. This is what we meant in a previous paragraph when we said the `Entity` property was set to `null` to halt recursion. So, once the recursed call to the set method returned, flow returns to the last line in the initial invocation of the set method we were discussing.

This Line of Code Is Repeated from a Previous Snippet for Your Convenience

```
    previousValue.Orders.Remove(this);
}
```

Once the `Orders.Remove` method has completed, the `Customer` object's `Orders` property no longer contains a reference to this `Order`; therefore, the graph is now consistent again.

Obviously, if you are planning to write your entity classes, you had better plan to spend some time in the debugger on this. Just put breakpoints in the detach_Orders method and the set method, and watch what happens.

Next, the Order object's Customer object's Entity property is assigned to be the new Customer object that was passed to the set method in the value parameter.

```
this._Customer.Entity = value;
```

After all, this is the Customer property's set method. We were trying to assign the Order to a new Customer. And again, at this point, the Order has a reference to the newly assigned Customer, but the newly assigned Customer does not have a reference to the Order, so the graph is no longer consistent.

Next, the code checks to see whether the Customer being assigned to the Order is not null, because if it is not, the newly assigned Customer needs to be assigned to the Order.

```
if ((value != null))
{
```

If the Customer object passed in the value parameter is not null, add the current Order to the passed Customer object's collection of Order objects.

```
value.Orders.Add(this);
```

When the Order is added to the passed Customer object's Orders collection in the preceding line, the delegate that was passed to the callback method in the Customer object's EntitySet<T> constructor will be called. So, the result of making the assignment is that the Customer object's attach_Orders method gets called.

This, in turn, will assign the current Order object's Customer to the passed Customer resulting in the Order object's Customer property's set method being called again. The code recurses into the set method just like it did before. However, just two code statements prior to the previous code statement, and before we recursed, the Order object's Customer property's Entity property was set to the new Customer, and this is the Customer who is passed to the set method by the attach_Orders method. Again, the set method code is called recursively, and eventually the second line of code, which is listed next, is called:

The Following Line of Code Is from Another Invocation of the set Method

```
if ((((previousValue != value)
        || (this._Customer.HasLoadedOrAssignedValue == false)))
```

Since the Order object's current Customer object, which is now stored in previousValue, and the value parameter are the same, the set method returns without doing anything more, and the recursed call is over.

In the next line of code, the current Order object's CustomerID member is set to the new Customer object's CustomerID.

```
this._CustomerID = value.CustomerID;
}
```

If the newly assigned `Customer` was `null`, then the code sets the `Order` object's `CustomerID` member to the default value of the member's data type, which in this case is a `string`.

```
else
{
  this._CustomerID = default(string);
}
```

If the `CustomerID` member had been of type `int`, the code would have set it to `default(int)`.

In the very last line of the code, the `SendPropertyChanged` method is called and passed the name of the property being changed to raise the change notification event.

```
this.SendPropertyChanged("Customer");
}
```

This pattern is relevant for one-to-many relationships. For a one-to-one relationship, each side of the relationship would be implemented as the child side was in this example, with a couple of changes. Since in a one-to-one relationship there is no logical parent or child, let's pretend that the relationship between customers and orders is one-to-one. This will give me a name to use to reference each class since parent and child no longer apply.

If you are writing the entity classes by hand and the relationship between the `Customer` class and `Order` class is one-to-one, then each of those classes will contain a property that is of type `EntityRef<T>` where type T is the other entity class. The `Customer` class will contain an `EntityRef<Order>`, and the `Order` class will contain an `EntityRef<Customer>`. Since neither class contains an `EntitySet<T>`, there are no calls to the `Add` and `Remove` methods that exist in the pattern for one-to-many relationships as we previously described.

So, assuming a one-to-one relationship between orders and customers, the `Order` class `Customer` property `set` method would look basically like it does previously, except when we are removing the assignment of the current `Order` to the original `Customer`. Since that original `Customer` has a single `Order`, we will not be removing the current `Order` from a collection of `Order` objects; we will merely be assigning the `Customer` object's `Order` property to `null`.

So instead of this line of code

```
previousValue.Orders.Remove(this);
```

we would have this line of code:

```
previousValue.Order = null;
```

Likewise, when we assign the current `Order` to the new `Customer`, since it has a single `Order`, instead of calling the `Add` method on a collection of `Order` objects, we merely assign the new `Customer` object's `Order` property to the current `Order`.

So instead of this line of code

```
value.Orders.Add(this);
```

we would have this line of code:

```
            value.Order = this;
```

As you can see, handling graph consistency is not trivial, and it gets confusing. Fortunately, there are two tools that take care of all of this for you. Their names are SQLMetal and the Object Relational Designer. For maintaining graph consistency and properly implementing change notifications, they are worth their weight in, uh, metal. Perhaps the command-line tool should have been named SQLGold, but we suspect that the metal portion of the name came from the term *metalanguage*.

Calling the Appropriate Partial Methods

When Microsoft added partial methods to make extending generated code, such as entity classes, easier, it threw a little bit more responsibility your way if you are going to implement your entity classes yourself.

There are several partial methods you should declare in your handwritten entity classes:

```
partial void OnLoaded();
partial void OnValidate(ChangeAction action);
partial void OnCreated();
partial void On[Property]Changing(int value);
partial void On[Property]Changed();
```

You should have a pair of On[Property]Changing and On[Property]Changed methods for each entity class property.

For the OnLoaded and OnValidate methods, you do not need to add calls anywhere in your entity class code for them; they will be called by the DataContext for you.

You should add code to call the OnCreated method inside your entity class's constructor like this:

Calling the OnCreated Partial Method

```
public Customer()
{
  OnCreated();
  ...
}
```

Then, for each mapped entity class property, you should add a call to the On[Property]Changing and On[Property]Changed methods just prior to and just after a change to the entity class property like this:

An Entity Class Property set Method Calling the On[Property]Changing and On[Property]Changed Methods

```
public string CompanyName
{
  get
  {
    return this._CompanyName;
  }
```

```
  set
  {
    if ((this._CompanyName != value))
    {
      this.OnCompanyNameChanging(value);
      this.SendPropertyChanging();
      this._CompanyName = value;
      this.SendPropertyChanged("CompanyName");
      this.OnCompanyNameChanged();
    }
  }
}
```

Notice that the On[Property]Changing method is called before the SendPropertyChanging method is called, and the On[Property]Changed method is called after the SendPropertyChanged method.

By declaring and calling these partial methods, you are giving other developers easy extensibility with no performance cost should they choose to not take advantage of it. That's the beauty of partial methods.

EntityRef<T> Complications

Although the private class member data type for an associated class is of type EntityRef<T>, the public property for that private class member must return the type of the entity class, not EntityRef<T>.

Let's take a look at the way SQLMetal generates the property for an EntityRef<T> private member:

A Public Property for a Class Member Returning the Entity Class Type Instead of EntityRef<T>

```
[Table(Name="dbo.Orders")]
public partial class Order : INotifyPropertyChanging, INotifyPropertyChanged
{
  ...
  private EntityRef<Customer> _Customer;
  ...
  [Association(Name="FK_Orders_Customers", Storage="_Customer",
    ThisKey="CustomerID", IsForeignKey=true)]
  public Customer Customer
  {
    get
    {
      return this._Customer.Entity;
    }
    set
    {
      ...
    }
  }
}
```

```
    ...
}
```

As you can see, even though the private class member is of type `EntityRef<Customer>`, the `Customer` property returns the type `Customer`, not `EntityRef<Customer>`. This is important because any reference in a query to type `EntityRef<T>` will not get translated into SQL.

EntitySet<T> Complications

Although public properties for private class members of type `EntityRef<T>` should return a type `T` instead of `EntityRef<T>`, the same is not true for public properties for private class members of type `EntitySet<T>`. Let's take a look at the code SQLMetal generated for a private class member of type `EntitySet<T>`.

An EntitySet<T> Private Class Member and Its Property

```
[Table(Name="dbo.Customers")]
public partial class Customer : INotifyPropertyChanging, INotifyPropertyChanged
{
  ...
  private EntitySet<Order> _Orders;
  ...
  [Association(Name="FK_Orders_Customers", Storage="_Orders",
OtherKey="CustomerID",
      DeleteRule="NO ACTION")]
  public EntitySet<Order> Orders
  {
    get
    {
      return this._Orders;
    }
    set
    {
      this._Orders.Assign(value);
    }
  }
  ...
}
```

As you can see, the property return type is `EntitySet<Order>`, just like the private class member type. Since `EntitySet<T>` implements the `ICollection<T>` interface, you may have the property return the type of `ICollection<T>` if you want to hide the implementation details.

Another complication to keep in mind when writing your own entity classes is that when you write a public setter for an `EntitySet<T>` property, you should use its `Assign` method, as opposed to merely assigning the passed value to the `EntitySet<T>` class member. This will allow the entity object to continue using the original collection of associated entity objects, since the collection may already be getting tracked by the `DataContext` object's change tracking service.

Looking at the previous example code again, as you can see, instead of assigning the member variable this._Orders to the value of variable value, it calls the Assign method.

Entity Class Attributes and Attribute Properties

Entity classes are defined by the attributes and attribute properties that map the entity class to a database table and the entity class properties to database table columns. Attributes define the existence of a mapping, and the attribute properties provide the specifics on how to map. For example, it is the Table attribute that defines that a class is mapped to a database table, but it is the Name property that specifies the database table name to which to map the class.

There is no better way to understand the attributes and attribute properties, and how they work, than by examining the attributes generated by the experts. So, we will analyze the Customer entity object generated by SQLMetal.

Here is a portion of the Customer entity class:

A Portion of the SQLMetal Generated Customer Entity Class

```
[Table(Name="dbo.Customers")]
public partial class Customer : INotifyPropertyChanging, INotifyPropertyChanged
{
  ...

  [Column(Storage="_CustomerID", DbType="NChar(5) NOT NULL", CanBeNull=false,
      IsPrimaryKey=true)]
  public string CustomerID
  {
    get
    {
      return this._CustomerID;
    }
    set
    {
      if ((this._CustomerID != value))
      {
        this.OnCustomerIDChanging(value);
        this.SendPropertyChanging();
        this._CustomerID = value;
        this.SendPropertyChanged("CustomerID");
        this.OnCustomerIDChanged();
      }
    }
  }

  ...
```

```
  [Association(Name="FK_Orders_Customers", Storage="_Orders",
OtherKey="CustomerID",
      DeleteRule="NO ACTION")]
  public EntitySet<Order> Orders
  {
    get
    {
      return this._Orders;
    }
    set
    {
      this._Orders.Assign(value);
    }
  }

  ...

  }
}
```

For the sake of brevity, we have omitted all the parts of the entity class except those containing LINQ to SQL attributes. We have also eliminated any redundant attributes.

And here is a portion containing a stored procedure and user-defined function:

A Portion Containing a Stored Procedure and User-Defined Function

```
[Function(Name="dbo.Get Customer And Orders")]
[ResultType(typeof(GetCustomerAndOrdersResult1))]
[ResultType(typeof(GetCustomerAndOrdersResult2))]
public IMultipleResults GetCustomerAndOrders(
    [Parameter(Name="CustomerID", DbType="NChar(5)")] string customerID)
{
  ...
}


[Function(Name="dbo.MinUnitPriceByCategory", IsComposable=true)]
[return: Parameter(DbType="Money")]
public System.Nullable<decimal> MinUnitPriceByCategory(
    [Parameter(DbType="Int")] System.Nullable<int> categoryID)
{
  ...
}
```

In the preceding code fragments, the attributes are in bold type. We listed these code fragments to provide context for the discussion of attributes.

Database

The `Database` attribute specifies for a derived `DataContext` class the default name of the mapped database if the database name is not specified in the connection information when the `DataContext` is instantiated. If the `Database` attribute is not specified and the database is not specified in the connection information, the name of the derived `DataContext` class will be assumed to be the name of the database with which to connect.

So for clarity, the order of precedence for where the database name comes from, in highest priority order, follows:

1. The connection information provided when the derived `DataContext` class is instantiated

2. The database name specified in the `Database` attribute

3. The name of the derived `DataContext` class

Here is the relevant portion of the SQLMetal generated derived `DataContext` class named `Northwind`:

From the SQLMetal Generated Northwind Class

```
public partial class Northwind : System.Data.Linq.DataContext
{
```

As you can see, the `Database` attribute is not specified in the generated `Northwind` class that derives from the `DataContext` class. Since this class was generated by Microsoft, we assume this is intentional. If you were going to specify the `Database` attribute and you wanted it to default to a database named `NorthwindTest`, the code should look like this:

The Database Attribute

```
[Database(Name="NorthwindTest")]
public partial class Northwind : System.Data.Linq.DataContext
{
```

We cannot necessarily see a reason to omit specifying the `Database` attribute. Perhaps it is because if you specify the database in the connection information, that will override the derived `DataContext` class name and the `Database` attribute. Perhaps Microsoft thought if you don't specify the database name in the connection information, the derived `DataContext` class name will be used, and that is satisfactory.

We thought about this and came to the conclusion that we personally don't like the idea of the generated class derived from `DataContext` connecting to a database by default. We cringe at the thought of running an application, perhaps accidentally, that has not yet been configured and having it default to a database. That sounds like a potentially painful mistake just waiting to happen. In fact, we might just advocate specifying a `Database` attribute with an intentionally ludicrous name just to prevent it from connecting to a default database. Perhaps something like this:

A Derived DataContext Class Highly Unlikely to Actually Connect to a Database by Default

```
[Database(Name=" goopeygobezileywag ")]
public partial class Northwind : System.Data.Linq.DataContext
{
```

We can't see that connecting to a database unless we have specified one in the connection information passed to the DataContext during instantiation.

Name (string)

The Name attribute property is a string that specifies the name of the database with which to connect if the database name is not specified in the connection information when the class derived from the DataContext class is instantiated. If the Name attribute property is not specified and the database name is not specified in the connection information, the name of the derived DataContext class will be assumed to be the name of the database with which to connect.

Table

It is the Table attribute that specifies in which database table an entity class is to be persisted. The entity class name does not necessarily need to be the same as the table. Here is the relevant portion of the entity class:

The Table Attribute

```
[Table(Name="dbo.Customers")]
public partial class Customer : INotifyPropertyChanging, INotifyPropertyChanged
{
```

Notice that the Table attribute is specifying the name of the database table by specifying the Name attribute property. If the name of the entity class is the same as the name of the database table, the Name attribute property can be omitted, because the class name will be the default table name to which it is mapped.

In this example, because we specified the pluralize option when we used SQLMetal to generate the Northwind entity classes, the database table name, Customers, is converted to its singular form, Customer, for the class name. Since the class name does not match the database table name, the Name property must be specified.

Name (string)

The Name attribute property is a string that specifies the name of the table to which to map this entity class. If the Name attribute property is not specified, the entity class name will be mapped to a database table of the same name by default.

Column

The Column attribute defines that an entity class property is mapped to a database field. Here is the relevant portion of the entity class:

The Column Attribute

```
Private string _CustomerID;
...
[Column(Storage="_CustomerID", DbType="NChar(5) NOT NULL", CanBeNull=false,
    IsPrimaryKey=true)]
public string CustomerID
{
```

In this example, because the Storage attribute property is specified, LINQ to SQL can directly access the private member variable _CustomerID, bypassing the public property accessor CustomerID. If the Storage attribute property is not specified, the public accessors will be used. This can be useful for bypassing special logic that may exist in your public property accessors.

You can see that the database type for this field is specified by the DbType attribute as an NCHAR that is five characters long. Because the CanBeNull attribute is specified with a value of false, this field's value in the database cannot be NULL, and because the IsPrimaryKey attribute is specified with a value of true, this is a record identity column.

It is not necessary for every property of an entity class to be mapped to the database. You may have runtime data properties that you would not want to persist to the database, and this is perfectly fine. For those properties, you just wouldn't specify the Column attribute.

You can also have persisted columns that are read-only. This is accomplished by mapping the column and specifying the Storage attribute property to reference the private member variable but not implementing the set method of the class property. The DataContext can still access the private member, but since there is no set method for the entity class property, no one can change it.

AutoSync (AutoSync enum)

The AutoSync attribute property is an AutoSync enum that instructs the runtime to retrieve the mapped column's value after an insert or update database operation. The possible values are Default, Always, Never, OnInsert, and OnUpdate. We are going to let you guess which one is used by default. According to Microsoft documentation, the default behavior is Never.

This attribute property setting is overridden when either IsDbGenerated or IsVersion is set to true.

CanBeNull (bool)

The CanBeNull attribute property is a bool that specifies whether the mapped database column's value can be NULL. This attribute property defaults to true.

DbType (string)

The DbType attribute property is a string that specifies the data type of the column in the database to which this entity class property is mapped. If the DbType property is not specified, the database column type will be inferred from the data type of the entity class property. This attribute property is used to define the column only if the CreateDatabase method is called.

Expression (string)

The Expression attribute property is a string that defines a computed column in the database. It is used only if the CreateDatabase method is called. This attribute property defaults to String.Empty.

IsDbGenerated (bool)

The IsDbGenerated attribute property is a bool specifying that the database table column the class property is mapped to is automatically generated by the database. If a primary key is specified with its IsDbGenerated attribute property set to true, the class property's DbType attribute property must be set to IDENTITY.

A class property whose IsDbGenerated attribute property is set to true will be immediately synchronized after a record is inserted into the database regardless of the AutoSync attribute property setting, and the class property's synchronized value will be visible in the class property once the SubmitChanges method has successfully completed. This attribute property defaults to false.

IsDiscriminator (bool)

The IsDiscriminator attribute property is a bool that specifies that the mapped entity class property is the entity class property that stores the discriminator value for entity class inheritance. This attribute property defaults to false. Please read the section about the InheritanceMapping attribute later in this chapter, and see the "Entity Class Inheritance" section in Chapter 18 for more information.

IsPrimaryKey (bool)

The IsPrimaryKey attribute property is a bool specifying whether the database table column that this entity class property is mapped to is part of the database table's primary key. Multiple class properties may be specified to be part of the primary key. In that case, all the mapped database columns act as a composite primary key. For an entity object to be updateable, at least one entity class property must have an attribute property IsPrimaryKey set to true. Otherwise, the entity objects mapped to this table will be read-only. This attribute property defaults to false.

IsVersion (bool)

The IsVersion attribute property is a bool that specifies that the mapped database column is either a version number or a timestamp that provides version information for the record. By specifying the IsVersion attribute property and setting its value to true, the mapped database column will be incremented if it is a version number and updated if it is a timestamp, whenever the database table record is updated.

A class property whose IsVersion attribute property is set to true will be immediately synchronized after a record is inserted or updated in the database regardless of the AutoSync attribute property setting, and the class property's synchronized value will be visible in the class property once the SubmitChanges method has successfully completed. This attribute property defaults to false.

Name (string)

The Name attribute property is a string that specifies the name of the table column to which to map this class property. If the Name attribute property is not specified, the class property name will be mapped to a database table column of the same name by default.

Storage (string)

The Storage attribute property is a string that specifies the private member variable that the entity class property's value is stored in. This allows LINQ to SQL to bypass the property's public accessors and any business logic they contain and allows it to directly access the private member variable. If the Storage attribute property is not specified, the property's public accessors will be used by default.

UpdateCheck (UpdateCheck enum)

The UpdateCheck attribute property is an UpdateCheck enum that controls how optimistic concurrency detection behaves for the class property and its mapped database column if no entity class mapped property has an attribute property of IsVersion set to true. The three possible values are UpdateCheck.Always, UpdateCheck.WhenChanged, and UpdateCheck.Never. If no entity class property has an attribute property of IsVersion set to true, the value of the UpdateCheck attribute property will default to Always. Read Chapter 17 for more information about this attribute property and its effect.

Association

The Association attribute is used to define relationships between two tables, such as a primary key to foreign key relationship. In this context, the entity whose mapped table contains the primary key is referred to as the *parent*, and the entity whose mapped table contains the foreign key is the *child*. Here are the relevant portions of two entity classes containing an association:

The Association from the Parent (Customer) Entity Class

```
[Association(Name="FK_Orders_Customers", Storage="_Orders", OtherKey="CustomerID",
    DeleteRule="NO ACTION")]
public EntitySet<Order> Orders
{
```

The Association from the Child (Order) Entity Class

```
[Association(Name="FK_Orders_Customers", Storage="_Customer", ThisKey="CustomerID",
    IsForeignKey=true)]
public Customer Customer
{
```

For this discussion of the Association attribute and its properties, we are using the Customer entity class as the parent example, and the Order entity class as the child example. Therefore, we have provided the relevant Association attributes that exist in both the Customer and Order entity classes.

When discussing the Association attribute properties, some attribute properties will pertain to the class in which the Association attribute exists, and other attribute properties will pertain to the other associated entity class. In this context, the class in which the Association attribute exists is referred to as the *source* class, and the other associated entity class is the *target* class. So, if we are discussing the attribute properties for the Association attribute that is specified in the Customer entity class, the Customer entity class is the source class, and the Order entity class is the target. If we are discussing the attribute properties for the Association attribute that is specified in the Order entity class, the Order entity class is the source class, and the Customer entity class is the target.

The Association attribute defines that the source entity class, Customer, has a relationship to the target entity class, Order.

In the preceding examples, the Name attribute property is specified to provide a name for the relationship. The Name attribute property's value corresponds to the name of the foreign key constraint in the database and will be used to create the foreign key constraint if the CreateDatabase method is called. The Storage attribute property is also specified. Specifying the Storage attribute property allows LINQ to SQL to bypass the property's public accessors to get access to the entity class property's value.

With associations of the primary key to foreign key variety, an entity class that is the parent in the relationship will store the reference to the child entity class in an EntitySet<T> collection since there may be many children. The entity class that is the child will store the reference to the parent entity class in an EntityRef<T>, since there will be only one. Please read the sections titled "EntitySet<T>" and "EntityRef<T>" later in this chapter, and see "Deferred Loading" and "Immediate Loading with the DataLoadOptions Class" in Chapter 14 for more information about associations and their characteristics.

DeleteOnNull (bool)

The DeleteOnNull attribute property is a bool that, if set to true, specifies that an entity object on the child side of an association should be deleted if the reference to its parent is set to null.

This attribute property's value is inferred by SQLMetal if there is a "Cascade" Delete Rule specified for the foreign key constraint in the database and the foreign key column does not allow null.

DeleteRule (string)

The DeleteRule attribute property is a string that specifies the Delete Rule for a foreign key constraint. It is used by LINQ to SQL only when the constraint is created in the database by the CreateDatabase method.

The possible values are "NO ACTION", "CASCADE", "SET NULL", and "SET DEFAULT". Consult your SQL Server documentation for the definition of each.

IsForeignKey (bool)

The IsForeignKey attribute property is a bool that, if set to true, specifies that the source entity class is the side of the relationship containing the foreign key; therefore, it is the child side of the relationship. This attribute property defaults to false.

In the Association attribute examples shown previously for the Customer and Order entity classes, because the Association attribute specified for the Order entity class contains the IsForeignKey attribute property whose value is set to true, the Order class is the child class in this relationship.

IsUnique (bool)

The IsUnique attribute property is a bool that, if true, specifies that a uniqueness constraint exists on the foreign key, indicating a one-to-one relationship between the two entity classes. This attribute property defaults to false.

Name (string)

The Name attribute property is a string that specifies the name of the foreign key constraint. This will be used to create the foreign key constraint if the CreateDatabase method is called. It is also used to differentiate multiple relationships between the same two entities. In that case, if both sides of the parent and child relationship specify a name, they must be the same.

If you do not have multiple relationships between the same two entity classes and you do not call the CreateDatabase method, this attribute property is not necessary. There is no default value for this attribute property.

OtherKey (string)

The OtherKey attribute property is a string that is a comma-delimited list of all the entity class properties of the target entity class that make up the key, either primary or foreign, depending on which side of the relationship the target entity is. If this attribute property is not specified, the primary key members of the target entity class are used by default.

It is important to realize that the Association attribute specified on each side of the association relationship, Customer and Order, specify where both sides' keys are located. The Association attribute specified in the Customer entity class specifies which Customer entity class properties contain the key for the relationship and which Order entity class properties contain the key for the relationship. Likewise, the Association attribute specified in the Order entity class specifies which Order entity class properties contain the key for the relationship and which Customer entity class properties contain the key for the relationship.

It often may not look as though each side always specifies both sides' key locations. Because typically on the parent side of the relationship the table's primary key is the key used, the ThisKey attribute property need not be specified, since the primary key is the default. And on the child side, the OtherKey attribute property need not be specified, because the parent's primary key is the default. Therefore, it is common to see the OtherKey attribute property specified only on the parent side and the ThisKey attribute property specified on the child side. But because of the default values, both the parent and child know the keys on both sides.

Storage (string)

The Storage attribute property is a string that specifies the private member variable that the entity class property's value is stored in. This allows LINQ to SQL to bypass the entity class property's public accessors and directly access the private member variable. This allows any business logic in the accessors to be bypassed. If the Storage attribute property is not specified, the property's public accessors will be used by default.

Microsoft recommends that both members of an association relationship be entity class properties with separate entity class member variables for data storage and for the Storage attribute property to be specified.

ThisKey (string)

The ThisKey attribute property is a string that is a comma-delimited list of all the entity class properties of the source entity class that make up the key, either primary or foreign, depending on which side of the relationship the source entity is, which is determined by the IsForeignKey attribute property. If the ThisKey attribute property is not specified, the primary key members of the source entity class are used by default.

Since the example `Association` attribute shown previously for the `Customer` entity class does not contain the `IsForeignKey` attribute property, we know that the `Customer` entity class is the parent side of the relationship, the side containing the primary key. Because the `Association` attribute does not specify the `ThisKey` attribute property, we know the `Customer` table's primary key value will become the foreign key in the associated table, `Orders`.

Because the `Association` attribute shown previously for the `Order` entity class specifies the `IsForeignKey` attribute with a value of `true`, we know the `Orders` table will be the side of the association containing the foreign key. And, because the `Association` attribute does specify the `ThisKey` attribute property with a value of `CustomerID`, we know that the `CustomerID` column of the `Orders` table will be where the foreign key is stored.

It is important to realize that the `Association` attribute specified on each side of the association relationship, `Customer` and `Order`, specifies where both sides' keys are located. The `Association` attribute specified in the `Customer` entity class specifies which `Customer` entity class properties contain the key for the relationship and which `Order` entity class properties contain the key for the relationship. Likewise, the `Association` attribute specified in the `Order` entity class specifies which `Order` entity class properties contain the key for the relationship and which `Customer` entity class properties contain the key for the relationship.

It often may not look as though each side always specifies both sides' key locations. Because typically on the parent side of the relationship, the table's primary key is the key used, the `ThisKey` attribute property need not be specified since the primary key is the default. And on the child side, the `OtherKey` attribute property need not be specified, because the parent's primary key is the default. Therefore, it is common to see the `OtherKey` attribute property specified only on the parent side and the `ThisKey` attribute property specified on the child side. But because of the default values, both the parent and child know the keys on both sides.

Function

The `Function` attribute defines that a class method, when called, will call a stored procedure or scalar-valued or table-valued user-defined function. Here is the relevant portion of the derived `DataContext` class for a stored procedure:

A Function Attrbiute Mapping a Method to a Stored Procedure in the Northwind Database

```
[Function(Name="dbo.Get Customer And Orders")]
[ResultType(typeof(GetCustomerAndOrdersResult1))]
[ResultType(typeof(GetCustomerAndOrdersResult2))]
public IMultipleResults GetCustomerAndOrders(
    [Parameter(Name="CustomerID", DbType="NChar(5)")] string customerID)
{
  ...
}
```

From this, we can see that there is a method named `GetCustomerAndOrders` that will call the stored procedure named `Get Customer And Orders`. We know the method is being mapped to a stored procedure as opposed to a user-defined function because the `IsComposable` attribute property is not specified and therefore defaulting to false, thereby mapping the method to a stored procedure. We can also see that it returns multiple results shapes, because there are two `ResultType` attributes specified.

Writing your derived `DataContext` class so that it can call a stored procedure is not quite as trivial as mapping an entity class to a table. In addition to the appropriate attributes being specified, you must also call the appropriate version of the `DataContext` class's `ExecuteMethodCall` method. You will read about this method in Chapter 16.

Of course, as is typical, this is necessary only when writing your own `DataContext` class, because SQLMetal and the Object Relational Designer do it for you.

The relevant portion of the derived `DataContext` class for a user-defined function follows:

A Function Attribute Mapping a Method to a User-Defined Function in the Northwind Database

```
[Function(Name="dbo.MinUnitPriceByCategory", IsComposable=true)]
[return: Parameter(DbType="Money")]
public System.Nullable<decimal> MinUnitPriceByCategory(
    [Parameter(DbType="Int")] System.Nullable<int> categoryID)
{
  ...
}
```

From this, we can see that there is a method named `MinUnitPriceByCategory` that will call the user-defined function named `MinUnitPriceByCategory`. We know the method is being mapped to a user-defined function, as opposed to a stored procedure, because the `IsComposable` attribute property is set to `true`. We can also see from the `return` attribute that the user-defined function will return a value of type `Money`.

Writing your derived `DataContext` class so that it can call a user-defined function is not quite as trivial as mapping an entity class to a table. In addition to the appropriate attributes being specified, you must also call the `DataContext` class's `ExecuteMethodCall` method for scalar-valued user-defined functions or the `CreateMethodCallQuery` method for table-valued user-defined functions. You will read about these methods in Chapter 16 as well.

Of course, as is typical, this is necessary only when writing your own `DataContext` class, because SQLMetal and the Object Relational Designer do it for you.

IsComposable (bool)

The `IsComposable` attribute property is a `bool` that specifies whether the mapped function is calling a stored procedure or a user-defined function. If the value of `IsComposable` is `true`, the method is being mapped to a user-defined function. If the value of `IsComposable` is `false`, the method is being mapped to a stored procedure. This attribute property's value defaults to `false` if it is not specified, so a method mapped with the `Function` attribute defaults to a stored procedure if the `IsComposable` attribute property is not specified.

Name (string)

The `Name` attribute property is a `string` that specifies the actual name of the stored procedure or user-defined function in the database. If the `Name` attribute property is not specified, the name of the stored procedure or user-defined function is assumed to be the same as the name of the method.

return

The return attribute is used to specify the returned data type from a stored procedure or user-defined function. It typically contains a Parameter attribute.

A return Attribute from the Northwind Class

```
[Function(Name="dbo.MinUnitPriceByCategory", IsComposable=true)]
[return: Parameter(DbType="Money")]
public System.Nullable<decimal> MinUnitPriceByCategory(
    [Parameter(DbType="Int")] System.Nullable<int> categoryID)
{
 ...
}
```

In the preceding code, we can tell that the user-defined function being called will return a value of type Money because of the return attribute and the embedded Parameter attribute's specified DbType attribute property.

ResultType

The ResultType attribute maps the data type returned by a stored procedure to a .NET class in which to store the returned data. Stored procedures that return multiple shapes will specify multiple ResultType attributes in their respective order.

ResultType Attributes from the Northwind Class

```
[Function(Name="dbo.Get Customer And Orders")]
[ResultType(typeof(GetCustomerAndOrdersResult1))]
[ResultType(typeof(GetCustomerAndOrdersResult2))]
public IMultipleResults GetCustomerAndOrders(
    [Parameter(Name="CustomerID", DbType="NChar(5)")] string customerID)
{
 ...
}
```

From the preceding code, we can tell that the stored procedure this method is mapped to will first return a shape of type GetCustomerAndOrdersResult1 followed by a shape of type GetCustomerAndOrdersResult2. SQLMetal is kind enough to even generate entity classes for GetCustomerAndOrdersResult1 and GetCustomerAndOrdersResult2.

Parameter

The Parameter attribute maps a method parameter to a parameter of a database stored procedure or user-defined function. Here is the relevant portion of the derived DataContext class:

A Parameter Attribute from the Northwind Class

```
[Function(Name="dbo.Get Customer And Orders")]
[ResultType(typeof(GetCustomerAndOrdersResult1))]
[ResultType(typeof(GetCustomerAndOrdersResult2))]
public IMultipleResults GetCustomerAndOrders(
    [Parameter(Name="CustomerID", DbType="NChar(5)")] string customerID)
{
  ...
}
```

From this, we can see that the GetCustomerAndOrders method, which is mapped to a database stored procedure named Get Customer And Orders, passes the stored procedure a parameter of type NChar(5).

DbType (string)

The DbType attribute property is a string that specifies the database data type and modifiers of the database stored procedure or user-defined function parameter.

Name (string)

The Name attribute property is a string that specifies the actual name of the parameter of the stored procedure or user-defined function. If the Name attribute property is not specified, the name of the database stored procedure or user-defined function parameter is assumed to be the same as the name of the method parameter.

InheritanceMapping

The InheritanceMapping attribute is used to map a *discriminator code* to a base class or subclass of that base class. A discriminator code is the value of an entity class column for the column specified as the discriminator, which is defined as the entity class property whose IsDiscriminator attribute property is set to true.

For an example, let's examine an InheritanceMapping attribute:

An InheritanceMapping Attribute

```
[InheritanceMapping(Code = "G", Type = typeof(Shape), IsDefault = true)]
```

The preceding InheritanceMapping attribute defines that if a database record has the value "G" in the discriminator column, which means its discriminator code is "G", instantiate that record as a Shape object using the Shape class. Because the IsDefault attribute property is set to true, if the discriminator code of a record doesn't match any of the InheritanceMapping attributes' Code values, that record will be instantiated as a Shape object using the Shape class.

To use inheritance mapping, when a base entity class is declared, one of its entity class properties is given the Column attribute property of IsDiscriminator, and that property's value is set to true. This means that the value of this column will determine, by discrimination, which class, be it the base class or one of its subclasses, a database table record is an instance of. An InheritanceMapping attribute is specified on the base class for each of its subclasses, as well as one for the base class itself. Of those InheritanceMapping attributes, one and only one must be given an attribute property of IsDefault with a value of true. This is so a database table record whose discriminator column does not match any of the discriminator codes specified in any of the InheritanceMapping attributes can be instantiated into a class. It is probably most common for the base class's InheritanceMapping attribute to be specified as the default InheritanceMapping attribute.

Again, all the InheritanceMapping attributes are specified on the base class only and associate a discriminator code to the base class or one of its subclasses.

Since the Northwind database does not contain any tables used in this way, we will provide three example classes.

Some Example Classes Demonstrating Inheritance Mapping

```
[Table]
[InheritanceMapping(Code = "G", Type = typeof(Shape), IsDefault = true)]
[InheritanceMapping(Code = "S", Type = typeof(Square))]
[InheritanceMapping(Code = "R", Type = typeof(Rectangle))]
public class Shape
{
  [Column(IsPrimaryKey = true, IsDbGenerated = true,
      DbType = "Int NOT NULL IDENTITY")]
  public int Id;

  [Column(IsDiscriminator = true, DbType = "NVarChar(2)")]
  public string ShapeCode;

  [Column(DbType = "Int")]
  public int StartingX;

  [Column(DbType = "Int")]
  public int StartingY;
}

public class Square : Shape
{
  [Column(DbType = "Int")]
  public int Width;
}

public class Rectangle : Square
{
  [Column(DbType = "Int")]
  public int Length;
}
```

Here, we can see that we have mapped the Shape class to a table, and since we didn't specify the Name attribute property, the Shape class will be mapped by default to a table named Shape.

Next, you will see three `InheritanceMapping` attributes. The first one defines that if the value of a database `Shape` table record's discriminator column is `"G"`, then that record should be instantiated as a `Shape` object using the `Shape` class. For our purposes, we chose `"G"` for *generic*, meaning it is a generic undefined shape. Since it is the `ShapeCode` property in the `Shape` class that is the discriminator, meaning it has an attribute property of `IsDiscriminator` set to `true`, if a record has a `ShapeCode` value of `"G"`, that record will get instantiated into a `Shape` object.

Also, you can see that the first `InheritanceMapping` attribute has the `IsDefault` attribute property set to true, so if the value of a `Shape` record's `ShapeCode` column matches none of the discriminator codes specified—`"G"`, `"S"`, and `"R"`—the default mapping is used, and the record will be instantiated as a `Shape` object.

The second `InheritanceMapping` attribute associates a discriminator code of `"S"` to the `Square` class. So, if a record in the database `Shape` table has a `ShapeCode` of `"S"`, then that record will be instantiated into a `Square` object.

The third `InheritanceMapping` attribute associates a discriminator code of `"R"` to the `Rectangle` class. So, if a record in the database `Shape` table has a `ShapeCode` of `"R"`, then that record will be instantiated into a `Rectangle` object.

Any record with a `ShapeCode` different from those specified will get instantiated into a `Shape` object, because `Shape` is the default class as specified with the `IsDefault` attribute property.

■ **Note** Inheritance mapping is discussed and examples are provided in Chapter 18.

Code (object)

The `Code` attribute property specifies what the discriminator code is for the mapping to the specified class, which will be specified by the `Type` attribute property.

IsDefault (bool)

The `IsDefault` attribute property is a `bool` that specifies which `InheritanceMapping` attribute should be used if a database table record's discriminator column doesn't match any of the discriminator codes specified in any of the `InheritanceMapping` attributes.

Type (Type)

The `Type` attribute property specifies the class type to instantiate the record as when the discriminator column matches the mapped discriminator code.

Data Type Compatibility

Some of the entity class attributes have a `DbType` attribute property where you can specify the database column data type. This attribute property is used only when the database is created with the `CreateDatabase` method. Since the mapping between .NET data types and SQL Server data types is not one-to-one, you will need to specify the DbType attribute property if you plan on calling the CreateDatabase method.

Because the .NET Common Language Runtime (CLR) data types that are used in your LINQ code are not the same data types that the database uses, you should refer to the MSDN documentation for information about SQL-to-CLR type mapping (LINQ to SQL). There is a matrix in that documentation that defines the behavior when converting between CLR data types and SQL data types. You should be aware that some data type conversions are not supported, and others can cause a loss of data depending on the data types involved and the direction of the conversion.

However, we think that you will find the conversions work fine most of the time, and this will not typically be an issue. While writing the examples for the LINQ to SQL chapters, we never encountered an issue caused by the data type conversions. Of course, you should use common sense. If you are trying to map obviously incompatible types, such as a .NET numeric data type to a SQL character data type, you should expect some issues.

XML External Mapping File Schema

As we discuss in the section on SQLMetal in Chapter 13, not only can you map classes to the database with entity classes, but you can also use an XML external mapping file. You will learn how to use the XML external mapping file when we cover the constructors for the DataContext class in Chapter 16.

Also, as we discuss in Chapter 13, the easiest way to obtain an XML external mapping file is to call the SQLMetal program and specify the /map option, and one will be generated for you. However, if you intend to create the mapping file manually, you will need to know the schema.

Please refer to the MSDN documentation for the external mapping schema titled "External Mapping Reference (LINQ to SQL)."

Projecting into Entity Classes vs. Nonentity Classes

When performing LINQ to SQL queries, you have two options for projecting the returned results. You can project the results into an entity class, or you can project the results into a nonentity class, which could be a named or anonymous class. There is a major difference between projecting into an entity class versus a nonentity class.

When projecting into an entity class, that entity class gains the benefit of the DataContext object's identity tracking, change tracking, and change processing services. You may make changes to an entity class and persist them to the database with the SubmitChanges method.

When projecting into a nonentity class, barring one specialized exception, you do not get the benefits of the DataContext object's identity tracking, change tracking, and change processing services. This means you cannot change the nonentity class and have it persist using LINQ to SQL. This only makes sense, since the class will not have the necessary attributes or a mapping file to map the class to the database. And, if it does have the attributes or a mapping file, then by definition it *is* an entity class.

Here is an example of a query that projects into an entity class:

Projecting into an Entity Class Provides DataContext Services

```
IEnumerable<Customer> custs = from c in db.Customers
                              select c;
```

After that query, we could make changes to any of the Customer entity objects in the custs sequence, and we would be able to persist them by calling the SubmitChanges method.

Here is an example of a query that projects into a nonentity class:

Projecting into a Nonentity Class Does Not Provide DataContext Services

```
var custs = from c in db.Customers
            select new { Id = c.CustomerID, Name = c.ContactName };
```

By projecting into the anonymous class, we will not be able to persist any changes we make to each object in the custs sequence by calling the SubmitChanges method.

We mentioned that there is one specialized exception concerning gaining the benefits of identity tracking, change tracking, and change processing when projecting into nonentity classes. This exception occurs when the class projected into *contains* members that are entity classes. Listing 15-1 contains an example.

Listing 15-1. Projecting into a Nonentity Class Containing Entity Classes

```
Northwind db = new Northwind(@"Data Source=.\SQLEXPRESS;Initial
Catalog=Northwind");

var cusorders = from o in db.Orders
                where o.Customer.CustomerID == "CONSH"
                orderby o.ShippedDate descending
                select new { Customer = o.Customer, Order = o };

// Grab the first order.
Order firstOrder = cusorders.First().Order;

// Now, let's save off the first order's shipcountry so we can reset it later.
string shipCountry = firstOrder.ShipCountry;
Console.WriteLine("Order is originally shipping to {0}", shipCountry);

// Now, We'll change the order's ship country from UK to USA.
firstOrder.ShipCountry = "USA";
db.SubmitChanges();

// Query to see that the country was indeed changed.
string country = (from o in db.Orders
                  where o.Customer.CustomerID == "CONSH"
                  orderby o.ShippedDate descending
                  select o.ShipCountry).FirstOrDefault<string>();

Console.WriteLine("Order is now shipping to {0}", country);

// Reset the order in the database so example can be re-run.
firstOrder.ShipCountry = shipCountry;
db.SubmitChanges();
```

In Listing 15-1, we query for the orders whose customer is "CONSH". We project the returned orders into an anonymous type containing the Customer and each Order. The anonymous class itself does not receive the DataContext services such as identity tracking, change tracking, and change processing, but its components Customer and Order do, because they are entity classes. We then perform another query on the previous query's results to get the first Order. We then save a copy of the Order object's original ShipCountry, so we can restore it at the end of the example, and we display the original ShipCountry to the screen. Next, we change the ShipCountry on the Order and save the change by calling the SubmitChanges method. Then, we query the ShipCountry for this order from the database again and display it just to prove that it was indeed changed in the database. This proves that the SubmitChanges method worked, and that the entity class components of our anonymous type did gain the services of the DataContext object. Then, we reset the ShipCountry to the original value and save so that the example can be run again and no subsequent examples will be affected.

Here are the results of Listing 15-1:

```
Order is originally shipping to UK
Order is now shipping to USA
```

Listing 15-1 is an example where we projected the query results into a nonentity class type, but because it was comprised of an entity class, we were able to gain the benefits of identity tracking, change tracking, and change processing by the DataContext.

There is one interesting note about the preceding code. You will notice that the query that obtains a reference to the first Order is in bold. We did this to catch your attention. Notice that we call the First operator before selecting the portion of the sequence element we are interested in, the Order member. We do this for performance enhancement, because in general the earlier you can narrow the results, the better the performance.

Prefer Object Initialization to Parameterized Construction When Projecting

You are free to project into classes prior to the end of the query for subsequent query operations, but when you do, prefer object initialization to parameterized construction. To understand why, let's take a look at Listing 15-2, which uses object initialization in the projection.

Listing 15-2. Projecting Using Object Initialization

```
Northwind db = new Northwind(@"Data Source=.\SQLEXPRESS;Initial
Catalog=Northwind");

db.Log = Console.Out;

var contacts = from c in db.Customers
               where c.City == "Buenos Aires"
               select new { Name = c.ContactName, Phone = c.Phone } into co
               orderby co.Name
               select co;

foreach (var contact in contacts)
{
  Console.WriteLine("{0} - {1}", contact.Name, contact.Phone);
}
```

Notice that, in Listing 15-2, we projected into an anonymous class and used object initialization to populate the anonymous objects that get created. Let's take a look at the output of Listing 15-2:

```
SELECT [t0].[ContactName] AS [Name], [t0].[Phone]
FROM [dbo].[Customers] AS [t0]
WHERE [t0].[City] = @p0
ORDER BY [t0].[ContactName]
-- @p0: Input String (Size = 12; Prec = 0; Scale = 0) [Buenos Aires]
-- Context: SqlProvider(Sql2008) Model: AttributedMetaModel Build: 3.5.30729.4926

Patricio Simpson - (1) 135-5555
Sergio Gutiérrez - (1) 123-5555
Yvonne Moncada - (1) 135-5333
```

We are not interested in the output of the query's results. We really want to see the SQL query that was generated. So, you might ask, "Why the need for the foreach loop?" Well, without it, because of query execution being deferred, the query would not actually execute.

The significant parts of the LINQ to SQL query for this discussion are the select and orderby statements. In our LINQ to SQL query, we instruct the query to create a member in the anonymous class named Name that is populated with the ContactName field from the Customers table. We then tell the query to sort by the Name member of the anonymous object into which we projected. The DataContext object has all of that information passed to it. The object initialization is effectively mapping a source field, ContactName, from the Customer class to the destination field, Name, in the anonymous class, and the DataContext object is privy to that mapping. From that information, it is able to know that we are effectively sorting the Customers by the ContactName field, so it can generate the SQL query to do just that. When you look at the generated SQL query, you can see that is exactly what it is doing.

Now let's take a look at what happens when we project into a named class using parameterized construction. First, we will need a named class. We will use this one:

The Named Class Used in Listing 15-3

```
class CustomerContact
{
  public string Name;
  public string Phone;

  public CustomerContact(string name, string phone)
  {
    Name = name;
    Phone = phone;
  }
}
```

Notice that there is a single constructor that takes two parameters, name and phone. Now, let's take a look at the same code as in Listing 15-2, except in Listing 15-3, the code will be modified to project into the CustomerContact class using parameterized construction.

Listing 15-3. *Projecting Using Parameterized Construction*

```
Northwind db = new Northwind(@"Data Source=.\SQLEXPRESS;Initial
Catalog=Northwind");

db.Log = Console.Out;

var contacts = from c in db.Customers
               where c.City == "Buenos Aires"
               select new CustomerContact(c.ContactName, c.Phone) into co
               orderby co.Name
               select co;

foreach (var contact in contacts)
{
  Console.WriteLine("{0} - {1}", contact.Name, contact.Phone);
}
```

Again, we are focusing on the select and orderby statements. As you can see in Listing 15-3, instead of projecting into an anonymous class, we are projecting into the CustomerContact class. And, instead of using object initialization to initialize the created objects, we are using a parameterized constructor. This code compiles just fine, but what happens when we run the example? The following exception is thrown:

```
Unhandled Exception: System.NotSupportedException: The member
'LINQChapter15.CustomerContact.Name' has no supported translation to SQL.…
```

So, what happened? Looking at the preceding LINQ to SQL query, ask yourself, "How does the DataContext know which field in the Customer class gets mapped to the CustomerContact.Name member that we are trying to order by?" In Listing 15-2, because we passed it the field names of the anonymous class, it knew the source field in the Customer class was ContactName, and it knew the destination field in the anonymous class was Name. In Listing 15-3, that mapping does not occur in the LINQ to SQL query, it happens in the constructor of the CustomerContact class, which the DataContext is not privy to. Therefore, it has no idea what field in the source class, Customer, to order by when it generates the SQL statement. And that spells trouble.

However, it is safe to use parameterized construction so long as nothing in the query after the projection references the named class's members, as Listing 15-4 demonstrates.

Listing 15-4. *Projecting Using Parameterized Construction Without Referencing Members*

```
Northwind db = new Northwind(@"Data Source=.\SQLEXPRESS;Initial
Catalog=Northwind");
```

```
db.Log = Console.Out;

var contacts = from c in db.Customers
               where c.City == "Buenos Aires"
               select new CustomerContact(c.ContactName, c.Phone);

foreach (var contact in contacts)
{
  Console.WriteLine("{0} - {1}", contact.Name, contact.Phone);
}
```

In Listing 15-4, since we are using query expression syntax and since query expression syntax requires that the query end with a `select` statement, we are safe using parameterized construction in that last `select` statement of the query. We're safe, because nothing can come after the `select` statement containing the parameterized constructor call that references the named class members. Here are the results of Listing 15-4:

```
SELECT [t0].[ContactName], [t0].[Phone]
FROM [dbo].[Customers] AS [t0]
WHERE [t0].[City] = @p0
-- @p0: Input String (Size = 12; Prec = 0; Scale = 0) [Buenos Aires]
-- Context: SqlProvider(Sql2008) Model: AttributedMetaModel Build: 3.5.30729.4926

Patricio Simpson - (1) 135-5555
Yvonne Moncada - (1) 135-5333
Sergio Gutiérrez - (1) 123-5555
```

However, since using standard dot notation syntax does not require the query to end with a `select` statement, it is not safe to assume that the query will work just because the projection into a named class using parameterized construction occurs in the last projection. Listing 15-5 is an example using standard dot notation syntax with the last projection using parameterized construction, but because a subsequent part of the query references the named class members, the query throws an exception.

Listing 15-5. *Projecting Using Parameterized Construction Referencing Members*

```
Northwind db = new Northwind(@"Data Source=.\SQLEXPRESS;Initial
Catalog=Northwind");

db.Log = Console.Out;

var contacts = db.Customers.Where(c => c.City == "Buenos Aires").
               Select(c => new CustomerContact(c.ContactName, c.Phone)).
               OrderBy(c => c.Name);

foreach (var contact in contacts)
```

```
{
  Console.WriteLine("{0} - {1}", contact.Name, contact.Phone);
}
```

The query in Listing 15-5 is very similar to the query in Listing 15-4 except we are using standard dot notation syntax instead of query expression syntax, and we have tacked a call to the `OrderBy` operator onto the end of the query. We are using parameterized construction in the final projection, but this doesn't work because the `OrderBy` operator is referencing a member of the named class. Here are the results of Listing 15-5:

```
Unhandled Exception: System.NotSupportedException: The member
'LINQChapter15.CustomerContact.Name' has no supported translation to SQL....
```

Because of these complexities, we recommend using object initialization instead of parameterized construction whenever possible.

Extending Entity Classes with Partial Methods

In Chapter 2, we told you about partial methods, and this is where they become incredibly useful. Microsoft determined where in the lifetime of an entity class developers were most likely interested in being notified and therefore added calls to partial methods. Here is a list of the supported partial methods that are called:

The Supported Partial Methods for an Entity Class

```
partial void OnLoaded();
partial void OnValidate(ChangeAction action);
partial void OnCreated();
partial void On[Property]Changing([Type] value);
partial void On[Property]Changed();
```

The last two methods listed will have the name of a property where we show "`[Property]`" and will have the property's data type where we have "`[Type]`". To demonstrate some of the partial methods supported by entity classes, we will add the following class code for the `Contact` entity class:

An Additional Declaration for the Contact Class to Implement Some Partial Methods

```
namespace nwind
{
  public partial class Contact
  {
    partial void OnLoaded()
    {
      Console.WriteLine("OnLoaded() called.");
    }
```

```
    partial void OnCreated()
    {
      Console.WriteLine("OnCreated() called.");
    }

    partial void OnCompanyNameChanging(string value)
    {
      Console.WriteLine("OnCompanyNameChanging() called.");
    }

    partial void OnCompanyNameChanged()
    {
      Console.WriteLine("OnCompanyNameChanged() called.");
    }
  }
}
```

Notice that we specified the namespace as nwind. This is necessary because the namespace for our declaration of the class must match the namespace of the class we are extending. Because we specified the namespace nwind when we generated our entity classes with SQLMetal, we must declare our partial Contact class to be in the nwind namespace too. In your production code, you would probably want to create a separate module in which to keep this partial class declaration.

We have provided simple implementations for the OnLoaded, OnCreated, OnCompanyNameChanging, and OnCompanyNameChanged methods that display a message to the console. Now, let's take a look at some code demonstrating the partial methods. In Listing 15-6, we query a Contact record from the database and change its CompanyName property.

Listing 15-6. Querying a Class with Implemented Partial Methods

```
Northwind db = new Northwind(@"Data Source=.\SQLEXPRESS;Initial
Catalog=Northwind");

Contact contact = db.Contacts.Where(c => c.ContactID == 11).SingleOrDefault();
Console.WriteLine("CompanyName = {0}", contact.CompanyName);

contact.CompanyName = "Joe's House of Booze";
Console.WriteLine("CompanyName = {0}", contact.CompanyName);
```

There is nothing special about the preceding code except that we have implemented some of the partial methods that entity classes support. First, we query a contact and display its company's name to the console. Then, we change the contact's company name and display it again to the console. Let's press Ctrl+F5 to see the output:

```
OnCreated() called.
OnLoaded() called.
CompanyName = B's Beverages
```

```
OnCompanyNameChanging() called.
OnCreated() called.
OnCompanyNameChanged() called.
CompanyName = Joe's House of Booze
```

As you can see, the OnCreated method was called, followed by the OnLoaded method. At this point, the record has been retrieved from the database and loaded into a Contact entity object. You can then see the output of the company's name we sent to the console. Next, the OnCompanyNameChanging method is called, followed by the only surprise to us, another call to the OnCreated method. Obviously, the DataContext is creating another Contact entity object as part of its change tracking procedure. Next, the OnCompanyNameChanged method is called, followed by our output of the new company name to the console.

This demonstrates how you can extend entity classes using partial methods without modifying the generated code.

Important System.Data.Linq API Classes

There are a handful of classes in the System.Data.Linq namespace that you will use on a regular basis when using LINQ to SQL. The following section is meant to provide a brief overview of these classes, their purposes, and where they fit in the scheme of LINQ to SQL.

EntitySet<T>

An entity class on the *one* side of a one-to-many relationship stores its associated *many* entity classes in a class member of type EntitySet<T> where type T is the type of the associated entity class.

Since, in the Northwind database, the relationship between Customers and Orders is one-to-many, in the Customer class, the Orders are stored in an EntitySet<Order>.

```
private EntitySet<Order> _Orders;
```

The EntitySet<T> class is a special collection used by LINQ to SQL. It implements the IEnumerable<T> interface, which allows you to perform LINQ queries on it. It also implements the ICollection<T> interface.

EntityRef<T>

An entity class on the *many* side of a one-to-many relationship stores its associated *one* entity class in a class member of type EntityRef<T> where type T is the type of the associated entity class.

Since in the Northwind database, the relationship between Customers and Orders is one-to-many, the Customer is stored in an EntityRef<Customer> in the Order class.

```
private EntityRef<Customer> _Customer;
```

Entity

When we are referencing an associated entity class that is on the *one* side of a one-to-many or one-to-one relationship, we tend to think of the member variable as being the same type as the entity class. For example, when we refer to an `Order` object's `Customer`, we tend to think the `Customer` object is stored in a `Customer` class member of the `Order` class. You should remember though that, in reality, the `Customer` is stored in an `EntityRef<Customer>`. Should you need to actually reference the `Customer` object referenced by the `EntityRef<Customer>` member, it can be referenced using the `EntityRef<Customer>` object's `Entity` property.

There are times when it is important to be cognizant of this fact, such as when writing your own entity classes. If you look at the `Order` class generated by SQLMetal, you will notice that the public property get and set methods for the `Customer` property use the `EntityRef<Customer>` object's `Entity` property to reference the `Customer`.

A Public Property Using the EntityRef<T>.Entity Property to Access the Actual Entity Object

```
private EntityRef<Customer> _Customer;
...
public Customer Customer
{
  get
  {
    return this._Customer.Entity;
  }
  set
  {
    Customer previousValue = this._Customer.Entity;
    ...
  }
}
```

HasLoadedOrAssignedValue

This property is a `bool` that lets you know if an entity class property stored in an `EntityRef<T>` has been assigned a value or if one has been loaded into it.

It is typically used in the set methods for references to the *one* side of a one-to-many association to prevent the entity class property containing the *one* side's ID from becoming inconsistent with the `EntityRef<T>` containing the reference to the *one*.

For example, let's look at the set methods for the `Order` entity class properties `CustomerID` and `Customer`:

The CustomerId set Method

```
public string CustomerID
{
  get
  {
    return this._CustomerID;
  }
  set
```

```
    {
      if ((this._CustomerID != value))
      {
        if (this._Customer.HasLoadedOrAssignedValue)
        {
          throw new System.Data.Linq.ForeignKeyReferenceAlreadyHasValueException();
        }
        this.OnCustomerIDChanging(value);
        this.SendPropertyChanging();
        this._CustomerID = value;
        this.SendPropertyChanged("CustomerID");
        this.OnCustomerIDChanged();
      }
    }
  }
}
```

Notice that in the set method for the CustomerID property, if the EntityRef<T> storing the Customer has the HasLoadedOrAssignedValue property set to true, an exception is thrown. This prevents a developer from changing the CustomerID of an Order entity object if that Order already has a Customer entity assigned to it. We cannot cause the Order entity object's CustomerID and Customer to become inconsistent because of this safeguard.

Contrast this with the fact that in the set method for the Customer property, the Customer reference can be assigned if the HasLoadedOrAssignedValue property is set to false:

The Customer set Method

```
public Customer Customer
{
  get
  {
    return this._Customer.Entity;
  }
  set
  {
    Customer previousValue = this._Customer.Entity;
    if (((previousValue != value)
          || (this._Customer.HasLoadedOrAssignedValue == false)))
    {
      this.SendPropertyChanging();
      if ((previousValue != null))
      {
        this._Customer.Entity = null;
        previousValue.Orders.Remove(this);
      }
      this._Customer.Entity = value;
      if ((value != null))
      {
```

```
      value.Orders.Add(this);
      this._CustomerID = value.CustomerID;
    }
    else
    {
      this._CustomerID = default(string);
    }
    this.SendPropertyChanged("Customer");
  }
 }
}
```

Checking the HasLoadedOrAssignedValue property in each of these set methods prevents the developer from causing the reference to become inconsistent between the CustomerID and the Customer references.

Table<T>

This is the data type LINQ to SQL uses to interface with a table or view in a SQL Server database. Typically, the derived DataContext class, often referred to as [Your]DataContext in the LINQ to SQL chapters, will have a public property of type Table<T>, where type T is an entity class, for each database table mapped in the derived DataContext.

So to reference the Customers database table of the Northwind database, there will typically be a public property of type Table<Customer> named Customers in the derived DataContext. It would look like this:

A Table<t> Property for the Customers Database Table

```
public System.Data.Linq.Table<Customer> Customers
{
  get
  {
    return this.GetTable<Customer>();
  }
}
```

Table<T> implements the IQueryable<T> interface, which itself implements IEnumerable<T>. This means you can perform LINQ to SQL queries on it. This is the initial data source for most LINQ to SQL queries.

IExecuteResult

When a stored procedure or user-defined function is called with the ExecuteMethodCall method, the results are returned in an object implementing the IExecuteResult interface, like this:

The ExecuteMethodCall Method Returns an IExecuteResult

```
IExecuteResult result = this.ExecuteMethodCall(...);
```

The `IExecuteResult` interface provides one property named `ReturnValue` and one method named `GetParameterValue` for accessing the returned value and output parameters, respectively.

ReturnValue

All stored procedure results other than output parameters and scalar-valued user-defined function results are returned via the `IExecuteResult.ReturnValue` variable.

To obtain access to the return value of a stored procedure or scalar-valued user-defined function, you reference the returned object's `ReturnValue` member. Your code should look something like this:

Accessing the Returned Value from a Stored Procedure Returning an Integer

```
IExecuteResult result = this.ExecuteMethodCall(...);
int returnCode = (int)(result.ReturnValue);
```

In Chapter 16, we will discuss the `ExecuteMethodCall` method and provide an example returning a stored procedure's returned integer.

If a stored procedure is returning data other than its return value, the `ReturnValue` variable will implement either the `ISingleResult<T>` or `IMultipleResults` interface, whichever is appropriate depending on how many data shapes are returned from the stored procedure.

GetParameterValue

To obtain access to a stored procedure's output parameters, you call the `GetParameterValue` method on the returned object, passing the method the zero-based index number of the parameter for which you want the value. Assuming the stored procedure is returning the `CompanyName` in the third parameter, your code should look something like this:

Accessing the Returned Paramters from a Stored Procedure

```
IExecuteResult result = this.ExecuteMethodCall(..., param1, param2, companyName);
string CompanyName = (string)(result.GetParameterValue(2));
```

In Chapter 16, we will discuss the `ExecuteMethodCall` method and provide an example accessing a stored procedure's output parameters.

ISingleResult<T>

When a stored procedure returns its results in a single shape, the results are returned in an object that implements the `ISingleResult<T>` interface, where T is an entity class. That returned object implementing `ISingleResult<T>` is the `IExecuteResult.ReturnValue` variable. Your code should look similar to this:

Accessing the Returned Results When There Is One Shape

```
IExecuteResult result = this.ExecuteMethodCall(...);
ISingleResult<CustOrdersOrdersResult> results =
  (ISingleResult<CustOrdersOrdersResult>)(result.ReturnValue);
```

Notice that we simply cast the `IExecuteResult` object's `ReturnValue` member to an `ISingleResult<T>` to get access to the results.

Since `ISingleResult<T>` inherits from `IEnumerable<T>`, the good news is that you access the returned results just as you would any other LINQ sequence.

Accessing the Results from ISingleResult<T>

```
foreach (CustomersByCityResult cust in results)
{
  ...
}
```

In Chapter 16, we will discuss the `ExecuteMethodCall` method and provide an example accessing a stored procedure's results when the stored procedure returns a single shape.

ReturnValue

The `ISingleResult<T>` interface provides a `ReturnValue` property that works just as it does in the `IExecuteResult` interface. Please read the previous section for the `IExecuteResult ReturnValue` property to understand how to access this property.

IMultipleResults

When a stored procedure returns its results in multiple shapes, the results are returned in an object that implements the `IMultipleResults` interface. That returned object implementing `IMultipleResults` is the `IExecuteResult.ReturnValue` variable. Your code should look similar to this:

Accessing the Returned Results When There Are Multiple Shapes

```
IExecuteResult result = this.ExecuteMethodCall(...);
IMultipleResults results = (IMultipleResults)(result.ReturnValue);
```

To obtain access to the multiple shapes that are returned, call the `IMultipleResults.GetResult<T>` method we discuss below.

In Chapter 16, we will discuss the `ExecuteMethodCall` method and provide an example accessing a stored procedure's results when the stored procedure returns multiple shapes.

The `IMultipleResults` interface provides one property named `ReturnValue` for accessing the stored procedure's returned value and one method named `GetResult<T>` for retrieving an `IEnumerable<T>` for each returned shape where type `T` is an entity class corresponding to the shape.

ReturnValue

The IMultipleResults interface provides a ReturnValue property that works just as it does in the IExecuteResults interface. Please read the previous section for the IExecuteResults ReturnValue property to understand how to access this property.

GetResult<T>

The IMultipleResults interface provides a GetResult<T> method where type T represents the data type storing the shape returned. The GetResult<T> method is used to obtain the repeating records of the specified result shape, and the records are returned in an IEnumerable<T> where T is the entity class used to store the shape record. Your code should look something like this:

Accessing Multiple Shapes Returned by a Stored Procedure

```
[StoredProcedure(Name="A Stored Procedure")]
[ResultType(typeof(Shape1))]
[ResultType(typeof(Shape2))]
...
IExecuteResult result = this.ExecuteMethodCall (...);
IMultipleResults results = (IMultipleResults)(result.ReturnValue);

foreach(Shape1 x in results.GetResult<Shape1>()) {…}

foreach(Shape2 y in results.GetResult<Shape2>()) {…}
```

We have included the attributes that would be before the method containing this code so that you can see the context of the ResultType attributes and the shapes that are returned by the stored procedure.

In the preceding code, we know that records that will be mapped to data type Shape1 will be returned by the stored procedure first, followed by records mapped to data type Shape2. So, we enumerate through the IEnumerable<Shape1> sequence that is returned from the first call to the GetResult<T> method first, followed by enumerating through the IEnumerable<Shape2> sequence that is returned by the second call to the GetResult<T> method. It is important that we know Shape1 records are returned first, followed by Shape2 records, and that we retrieve them with the GetResult<T> method in that same order.

In Chapter 16, we will discuss the ExecuteMethodCall method and provide an example accessing a stored procedure's returned multiple shapes.

Summary

This chapter provided an in-depth examination of LINQ to SQL entity classes, the complications of writing your own, and their attributes and attribute properties.

It is important to remember that if you write your own entity classes, you will be responsible for implementing change notifications and ensuring graph consistency. These are not trivial details and can become complex to implement. Fortunately, both SQLMetal and the Object Relational Designer take care of these complications for you.

Also, to write your own entity classes, you must have a thorough knowledge of the entity class attributes and their properties. We covered each of these in this chapter and provided the quintessential implementation of each by discussing the SQLMetal-generated entity classes for the Northwind database.

We also covered the benefits of projecting your query results into entity classes as opposed to nonentity classes. If you have no need to modify the data and persist the changes, nonentity classes are generally fine. But if you want to be able to change the data that is returned and persist it back to the database, projecting into entity classes is the way to go.

Last, we discussed some of the often-used classes in the System.Data.Linq namespace and how they are used by LINQ to SQL.

At this point, you should be an expert on the anatomy of entity classes. We have discussed them in depth and explained to you the generated code. Of course, these entity classes are typically referenced by a class derived from the DataContext class, which we have yet to discuss in detail. Therefore, in the next chapter, we will discuss the DataContext class in full detail.

CHAPTER 16

The LINQ to SQL DataContext

In this chapter, we explain the DataContext class, what it can do for you, and how to make the most of it. We discuss all of its major methods and provide examples of each. Understanding the DataContext class is necessary to successfully employ LINQ to SQL, and by the time you have read this chapter, you should be a master of the DataContext class.

Prerequisites for Running the Examples

To run the examples in this chapter, you will need to have obtained the extended version of the Northwind database and generated entity classes for it. Please read and follow the instructions in Chapter 12's "Prerequisites for Running the Examples" section.

Some Common Methods

To run the examples in this chapter, you will need some common methods that will be utilized by the examples. Please read and follow the instructions in Chapter 12's "Some Common Methods" instructions.

Using the LINQ to SQL API

To run the examples in this chapter, you may need to add the appropriate references and using directives to your project. Please read and follow the instructions in Chapter 12's "Using the LINQ to SQL API" section.

Additionally, for some of the examples in this chapter, you will also need to add a using directive for the System.Data.Linq.Mapping namespace like this:

```
using System.Data.Linq.Mapping;
```

[Your]DataContext Class

Although we haven't covered it yet, one of the LINQ to SQL classes you will frequently use is the System.Data.Linq.DataContext class. This is the class you will use to establish your database connection. When creating or generating entity classes, it is common for a class to be created that derives from the DataContext class. This derived class will typically take on the name of the database it will be connecting to. Since we are using the Northwind database for the examples in this chapter, our derived database class will be named `Northwind`. However, since the name of the derived class changes with the database being used, the name of the class will vary from code to code. For ease of reference in the LINQ to SQL chapters, we will often refer to this derived class as the `[Your]DataContext` class. This is your clue that we are talking about your created or generated class that is derived from the `DataContext` class.

The DataContext Class

The `DataContext` class handles your connection to the database. It also handles database queries, updates, inserts, identity tracking, change tracking, change processing, transactional integrity, and even database creation. The `DataContext` class translates your queries of entity classes into SQL statements that are performed on the connected database. It is a busy class.

Deriving the `[Your]DataContext` class from the `DataContext` class gives `[Your]DataContext` class access to a host of common database methods, such as `ExecuteQuery`, `ExecuteCommand`, and `SubmitChanges`. In addition to these inherited methods, the `[Your]DataContext` class will contain properties of type `System.Data.Linq.Table<T>` for each table and view in the database for which you desire to use LINQ to SQL, where each type `T` is an entity class mapped to a particular table or view.

For example, let's take a look at the `Northwind` class that was generated for us by the SQLMetal tool. It is the `[Your]DataContext` class for the Northwind database. Here is what a portion of ours looks like, with the noteworthy portions in bold:

A Portion of the Generated Northwind Class

```
public partial class Northwind : System.Data.Linq.DataContext
{
  ...

  static Northwind()
  {
  }

  public Northwind(string connection) :
      base(connection, mappingSource)
  {
    OnCreated();
  }

  public Northwind(System.Data.IDbConnection connection) :
      base(connection, mappingSource)
  {
    OnCreated();
  }

  public Northwind(string connection,
                   System.Data.Linq.Mapping.MappingSource mappingSource) :
```

```
      base(connection, mappingSource)
{
  OnCreated();
}

public Northwind(System.Data.IDbConnection connection,
                 System.Data.Linq.Mapping.MappingSource mappingSource) :
      base(connection, mappingSource)
{
  OnCreated();
}

...

public System.Data.Linq.Table<Customer> Customers
{
  get
  {
    return this.GetTable<Customer>();
  }
}

...

}
```

As you can see, this class does indeed inherit from the DataContext class. You can also see that there are five constructors. The default constructor is private since the visibility modifier is not specified, so you won't be instantiating a [Your]DataContext without parameters. Each of the public [Your]DataContext constructors matches one of the inherited DataContext constructors and calls the base DataContext class's equivalent constructor in the initializer. In the body of the constructors, the only code is a call to the OnCreated partial method. This allows the developer to implement an OnCreated partial method that is called every time a [Your]DataContext object is instantiated.

Also in the Northwind class, there is a property named Customers of type Table<Customer> where type Customer is an entity class. It is the Customer entity class that is mapped to the Northwind database's Customers table.

It is not necessary to actually write code that uses the [Your]DataContext class; it is possible to work with the standard DataContext class instead. However, using the [Your]DataContext class does make writing the code more convenient. For example, if you use the [Your]DataContext class, each table is a property that can be accessed directly off the [Your]DataContext object. Listing 16-1 contains an example.

Listing 16-1. *An Example Demonstrating Table Access with a Property*

```
Northwind db =
  new Northwind(@"Data Source=.\SQLEXPRESS;Initial Catalog=Northwind");
```

```
IQueryable<Customer> query = from cust in db.Customers
                            where cust.Country == "USA"
                            select cust;

foreach(Customer c in query)
{
    Console.WriteLine("{0}", c.CompanyName);
}
```

■ **Note** You may need to change the connection strings in the examples in this chapter for them to work.

In the preceding code, since we connect using the [Your]DataContext class, Northwind, we can access the customers Table<Customer> as a property, Customers, of the [Your]DataContext class. Here are the results of the code:

```
Great Lakes Food Market
Hungry Coyote Import Store
Lazy K Kountry Store
Let's Stop N Shop
Lonesome Pine Restaurant
Old World Delicatessen
Rattlesnake Canyon Grocery
Save-a-lot Markets
Split Rail Beer & Ale
The Big Cheese
The Cracker Box
Trail's Head Gourmet Provisioners
White Clover Markets
```

If, instead, we connect using the DataContext class itself, we must use the GetTable<T> method of the DataContext object, as in Listing 16-2.

Listing 16-2. An Example Demonstrating Table Access with the GetTable<T> Method

```
DataContext dc =
  new DataContext(@"Data Source=.\SQLEXPRESS;Initial Catalog=Northwind");

IQueryable<Customer> query = from cust in dc.GetTable<Customer>()
                            where cust.Country == "USA"
                            select cust;

foreach(Customer c in query)
```

```
{
    Console.WriteLine("{0}", c.CompanyName);
}
```

This code gives us the same results, though:

```
Great Lakes Food Market
Hungry Coyote Import Store
Lazy K Kountry Store
Let's Stop N Shop
Lonesome Pine Restaurant
Old World Delicatessen
Rattlesnake Canyon Grocery
Save-a-lot Markets
Split Rail Beer & Ale
The Big Cheese
The Cracker Box
Trail's Head Gourmet Provisioners
White Clover Markets
```

So, using the [Your]DataContext class is merely a convenience, but it's one worth taking advantage of whenever possible.

The DataContext Class Implements IDisposable

The DataContext class implements the IDisposable interface, and because of this, it shouldbe treated properly as a disposable object. This means that if you create a new class that is composed of a DataContext or [Your]DataContext class, meaning there is a has-a relationship between your new class and the DataContext or [Your]DataContext class, the new class should implement the IDisposable interface too. Designing classes to properly implement the IDisposable interface is beyond the scope of this book, but many resources online delve into this topic. Another benefit of the DataContext class implementing the IDisposable interface is that you can now utilize a using statement to manage the DataContext or [Your]DataContext object.

Primary Purposes

In addition to all the methods we cover in this chapter, the DataContext class provides three main services: identity tracking, change tracking, and change processing.

Identity Tracking

One of the issues that LINQ to SQL is designed to overcome is referred to as the *object-relational impedance mismatch*. This term refers to the inherent difficulties caused by the fact that the most commonly used databases are relational, while most modern programming languages are object oriented. Because of this difference, problems arise.

One such manifestation of the object-relational impedance mismatch is the way we expect identity to behave. If we query the same record from a database in multiple places in our code, we expect that the returned data will be stored in different locations in memory. We expect that modifying a record's fields in one part of the code will not affect that same record's fields that were retrieved in another part of the code. We expect this because we know that retrieved data is stored in different variables living at different addresses in memory.

Contrast this with the way we expect objects to behave. We expect that when we have an object in memory, say a `Customer` object, we expect that all places in the code having a reference to that same customer will actually have a reference to the same location in memory. If we update that customer object's name property in one location of our program, we expect the customer we have a reference to in another part of the code will have the new name.

The `DataContext` class identity tracking service is what provides this behavior for us. When a record is queried from the database for the first time since the instantiation of the `DataContext` object, that record is recorded in an identity table using its primary key, and an entity object is created and stored in a cache. Subsequent queries that determine that the same record should be returned will first check the identity table, and if the record exists in the identity table, the already existing entity object will be returned from the cache. That is an important concept to understand, so we will reiterate it in a slightly different way. When a query is executed, if a record in the database matches the search criteria *and* its entity object is already cached, the already cached entity object is returned. This means that the actual data returned by the query may not be the same as the record in the database. The query determines *which* entities will be returned based on data in the database. But the `DataContext` object's identity tracking service determines *what* data is returned. This can lead to a problem we call the *results set cache mismatch*.

The Results Set Cache Mismatch

The results set cache mismatch can occur when a record in the database is inconsistent with that same record's entity object in your `DataContext` object's cache. When you perform a query, the actual database is queried for records matching the query. If a record in the database matches the search criteria for the query, that record's entity object will be included in the returned results set. However, if a record from the results set is already cached in the `DataContext` object's cache of entity objects, the cached entity object will be returned by the query, as opposed to reading the latest version from the database.

The result is that if you have an entity object cached in your `DataContext`, if another context updates a field for that entity object's record in the database, and if you perform a LINQ query specifying that field in the search criteria so that it matches the new value in the database, the record will be included in the results set. However, since you already have it cached, you get the cached entity object returned with the field not matching your search criteria.

It will probably be clearer if we provide an example. What we will do is first query for a specific customer that we know will not match the search criteria we will provide for a subsequent query. We will use customer `LONEP`. The region for customer `LONEP` is `OR`, so we will search for customers whose region is `WA`. We will then display those customers whose region is `WA`. Next, we will update the region for customer `LONEP` to `WA` using ADO.NET, just as if some other context did it externally to our process. At this point, `LONEP` will have a region of `OR` in our entity object but `WA` in the database. Next, we will perform that very same query again to retrieve all the customers whose region is `WA`. When you look in the code, you will not see the query defined again, though. You will merely see us enumerate through the returned sequence of `custs`. Remember that, because of deferred query execution, we need only enumerate the results to cause the query to be executed again. Since the region for `LONEP` is `WA` in the database, that record will be included in the results set. But, since that record's entity object is already cached, it will be the cached entity object that is returned, and that object still has a region of `OR`. We will then display each returned entity object's region. When customer LONEP is displayed, its region will be OR, despite that our query specified it wanted customers whose region is WA. Listing 16-3 provides the code to demonstrate this mismatch.

Listing 16-3. An Example Demonstrating the Results Set Cache Mismatch

```
Northwind db = new Northwind(@"Data Source=.\SQLEXPRESS;Initial
Catalog=Northwind");

// Let's get a cutomer to modify that will be outside our query of region == 'WA'.
Customer cust = (from c in db.Customers
                where c.CustomerID == "LONEP"
                select c).Single<Customer>();

Console.WriteLine("Customer {0} has region = {1}.{2}",
  cust.CustomerID, cust.Region, System.Environment.NewLine);

// Ok, LONEP's region is OR.

// Now, let's get a sequence of customers from 'WA', which will not include LONEP
// since his region is OR.
IEnumerable<Customer> custs = (from c in db.Customers
                              where c.Region == "WA"
                              select c);

Console.WriteLine("Customers from WA before ADO.NET change - start ...");
foreach(Customer c in custs)
{
  // Display each entity object's Region.
  Console.WriteLine("Customer {0}'s region is {1}.", c.CustomerID, c.Region);
}
Console.WriteLine("Customers from WA before ADO.NET change - end.{0}",
  System.Environment.NewLine);

// Now we will change LONEP's region to WA, which would have included it
// in that previous query's results.

// Change the customers' region through ADO.NET.
Console.WriteLine("Updating LONEP's region to WA in ADO.NET...");
ExecuteStatementInDb(
  "update Customers set Region = 'WA' where CustomerID = 'LONEP'");
Console.WriteLine("LONEP's region updated.{0}", System.Environment.NewLine);

Console.WriteLine("So LONEP's region is WA in database, but ...");
Console.WriteLine("Customer {0} has region = {1} in entity object.{2}",
  cust.CustomerID, cust.Region, System.Environment.NewLine);
```

```
//  Now, LONEP's region is WA in database, but still OR in entity object.

//  Now, let's perform the query again.
//  Display the customers entity object's region again.
Console.WriteLine("Query entity objects after ADO.NET change - start ...");
foreach(Customer c in custs)
{
  //  Display each entity object's Region.
  Console.WriteLine("Customer {0}'s region is {1}.", c.CustomerID, c.Region);
}
Console.WriteLine("Query entity objects after ADO.NET change - end.{0}",
  System.Environment.NewLine);

//  We need to reset the changed values so that the code can be run
//  more than once.
Console.WriteLine("{0}Resetting data to original values.",
  System.Environment.NewLine);
ExecuteStatementInDb(
  "update Customers set Region = 'OR' where CustomerID = 'LONEP'");
```

Here are the results:

```
Customer LONEP has region = OR.

Customers from WA before ADO.NET change - start ...
Customer LAZYK's region is WA.
Customer TRAIH's region is WA.
Customer WHITC's region is WA.
Customers from WA before ADO.NET change - end.

Updating LONEP's region to WA in ADO.NET...
Executing SQL statement against database with ADO.NET ...
Database updated.
LONEP's region updated.

So LONEP's region is WA in database, but ...
Customer LONEP has region = OR in entity object.

Query entity objects after ADO.NET change - start ...
Customer LAZYK's region is WA.
Customer LONEP's region is OR.
Customer TRAIH's region is WA.
Customer WHITC's region is WA.
Query entity objects after ADO.NET change - end.
```

```
Resetting data to original values.
Executing SQL statement against database with ADO.NET ...
Database updated.
```

As you can see, even though we queried for customers in WA, LONEP is included in the results despite that its region is OR. Sure, it's true that in the database LONEP has a region of WA, but it does not in the object we have a reference to in our code. Is anyone else getting a queasy feeling?

Another aspect of this behavior is that inserted entities cannot be queried back out, but deleted entities can be, prior to calling the SubmitChanges method. Again, this is because even though we have inserted an entity, when the query executes, the results set is determined by what is in the actual database, not the DataContext object's cache. Since the changes have not been submitted, the inserted entity is not yet in the database. The opposite applies to deleted entities. Listing 16-4 contains an example demonstrating this behavior.

Listing 16-4. *Another Example Demonstrating the Results Set Cache Mismatch*

```
Northwind db = new Northwind(@"Data Source=.\SQLEXPRESS;Initial
Catalog=Northwind");

Console.WriteLine("First we will add customer LAWN.");
db.Customers.InsertOnSubmit(
  new Customer
  {
    CustomerID = "LAWN",
    CompanyName = "Lawn Wranglers",
    ContactName = "Mr. Abe Henry",
    ContactTitle = "Owner",
    Address = "1017 Maple Leaf Way",
    City = "Ft. Worth",
    Region = "TX",
    PostalCode = "76104",
    Country = "USA",
    Phone = "(800) MOW-LAWN",
    Fax = "(800) MOW-LAWO"
  });

Console.WriteLine("Next we will query for customer LAWN.");
Customer cust = (from c in db.Customers
                 where c.CustomerID == "LAWN"
                 select c).SingleOrDefault<Customer>();
Console.WriteLine("Customer LAWN {0}.{1}",
  cust == null ? "does not exist" : "exists",
  System.Environment.NewLine);

Console.WriteLine("Now we will delete customer LONEP");
```

```
cust = (from c in db.Customers
        where c.CustomerID == "LONEP"
        select c).SingleOrDefault<Customer>();
db.Customers.DeleteOnSubmit(cust);

Console.WriteLine("Next we will query for customer LONEP.");
cust = (from c in db.Customers
        where c.CustomerID == "LONEP"
        select c).SingleOrDefault<Customer>();
Console.WriteLine("Customer LONEP {0}.{1}",
  cust == null ? "does not exist" : "exists",
  System.Environment.NewLine);

// No need to reset database since SubmitChanges() was not called.
```

In the previous code, we insert a customer, LAWN, and then query to see whether it exists. We then delete a different customer, LONEP, and query to see whether it exists. We do all this without calling the SubmitChanges method so that the cached entity objects have not been persisted to the database. Here are the results of this code:

```
First we will add customer LAWN.
Next we will query for customer LAWN.
Customer LAWN does not exist.

Now we will delete customer LONEP
Next we will query for customer LONEP.
Customer LONEP exists.
```

We have been told by a Microsoft developer that this is intentional behavior, that the data retrieved by a query is considered to be stale the moment you retrieve it, and that the data cached by the DataContext is not meant to be cached for long periods of time. If you need better isolation and consistency, he recommended you wrap it all in a transaction. Please read the section titled "Pessimistic Concurrency" in Chapter 17 to see an example of doing this.

Change Tracking

Once the identity tracking service creates an entity object in its cache, change tracking begins for that object. Change tracking works by storing the original values of an entity object. Change tracking for an entity object continues until you call the SubmitChanges method. Calling the SubmitChanges method causes the entity objects' changes to be saved to the database, the original values to be forgotten, and the changed values to become the original values. This allows change tracking to start over.

This works fine as long as the entity objects are retrieved from the database. However, merely creating a new entity object by instantiating it will not provide any identity or change tracking until the DataContext is aware of its existence. To make the DataContext aware of the entity object's existence, simply insert the entity object into one of the Table<T> properties. For example, in our Northwind class, we have a Table<Customer> property named Customers. We can call the InsertOnSubmit method on the `Customers` property to insert the entity object, a `Customer`, to the `Table<Customer>`. When this is done, the `DataContext` will begin identity and change tracking on that entity object. Here is example code inserting a customer:

```
db.Customers.InsertOnSubmit(
  new Customer {
    CustomerID = "LAWN",
    CompanyName = "Lawn Wranglers",
    ContactName = "Mr. Abe Henry",
    ContactTitle = "Owner",
    Address = "1017 Maple Leaf Way",
    City = "Ft. Worth",
    Region = "TX",
    PostalCode = "76104",
    Country = "USA",
    Phone = "(800) MOW-LAWN",
    Fax = "(800) MOW-LAWO"});
```

Once we call the `InsertOnSubmit` method, identity and change tracking for customer `LAWN` begins.

Initially, we found change tracking a little confusing. Understanding the basic concept is simple enough, but feeling comfortable about how it was working did not come easy. Understanding change tracking becomes even more important if you are writing your entity classes by hand. Be sure to read the section titled "Change Notifications" in Chapter 15 to gain a complete understanding of how change tracking works.

Change Processing

One of the more significant services the `DataContext` provides is change tracking for entity objects. When you insert, change, or delete an entity object, the `DataContext` is monitoring what is happening. The changes are cached by the `DataContext` until you call the `SubmitChanges` method.

When you call the `SubmitChanges` method, the `DataContext` object's change processor manages the update of the database. First, the change processor will insert any newly inserted entity objects to its list of tracked entity objects. Next, it will order all changed entity objects based on their dependencies resulting from foreign keys and unique constraints. Then, if no transaction is in scope, it will create a transaction so that all SQL commands carried out during this invocation of the `SubmitChanges` method will have transactional integrity. It uses SQL Server's default isolation level of `ReadCommitted`, which means that the data read will not be physically corrupted and only committed data will be read, but since the lock is shared, nothing prevents the data from being changed before the end of the transaction. Last, it enumerates through the ordered list of changed entity objects, creates the necessary SQL statements, and executes them.

If any errors occur while enumerating the changed entity objects and, if the `SubmitChanges` method is using a `ConflictMode` of `FailOnFirstConflict`, then the enumeration process aborts, the transaction is rolled back (undoing all changes to the database), and an exception is thrown. If a `ConflictMode` of `ContinueOnConflict` is specified, all changed entity objects will be enumerated and processed despite any conflicts that occur, while the `DataContext` builds a list of the conflicts. But again, the transaction is rolled back, undoing all changes to the database, and an exception is thrown. However, although the changes have not persisted to the database, all of the entity objects' changes still exist in the entity objects. This gives the developer the opportunity to try to resolve the problem and to call the `SubmitChanges` method again.

If all the changes are made to the database successfully, the transaction is committed, and the change tracking information for the changed entity objects is deleted so that change tracking can restart fresh.

The Data Context Lifetime

One of the questions that is asked regularly is how long a DataContext object should be kept alive and utilized. As we mentioned in "The Results Set Cache Mismatch" section, data retrieved and cached by the DataContext is considered stale the moment it is retrieved. This means the longer you keep a DataContext object alive, the staler the data can become. Not only does this create additional overhead, it creates a greater likelihood of a results set cache mismatch occurring. Therefore it is highly recommended to keep DataContext objects as short-lived as possible.

We recommend creating a DataContext object each time it is needed and then allowing it to go out of scope after the SubmitChanges method has been called. Of course every situation is different, so this is a judgment call. We would not create a single DataContext object and try to use it for the lifetime of a desktop application. A good rule of thumb would be that a DataContext object should live for seconds, not minutes or hours.

Some developers may be tempted to keep a DataContext object alive for longer periods of time and rely on the Refresh method that we cover at the end of this chapter to prevent results set cache mismatches from occurring. We think this a poor approach because then you are left with the decision of how often and when you should call the Refresh method. Would you call it every time you use the DataContext object? Unnecessarily calling the Refresh method will cause all of the cached data to be refreshed from the database. This could lead to performance issues if a DataContext lives long enough. That is a large price to pay just to eliminate the cost of instantiating a DataContext.

DataContext() and [Your]DataContext()

The DataContext class is typically derived from to create the [Your]DataContext class. It exists for the purpose of connecting to the database and handling all database interaction. You will use one of the following constructors to instantiate a DataContext or [Your]DataContext object.

Prototypes

The DataContext constructor has four prototypes we will cover.

The First DataContext Constructor Prototype

```
DataContext(string fileOrServerOrConnection);
```

This prototype of the constructor takes an ADO.NET connection string and is probably the one you will use the majority of the time. This prototype is the one used by most of the LINQ to SQL examples in this book.

The Second DataContext Constructor Prototype

```
DataContext (System.Data.IDbConnection connection);
```

Because `System.Data.SqlClient.SqlConnection` inherits from
`System.Data.Common.DbConnection`, which implements `System.Data.IDbConnection`, you can
instantiate a `DataContext` or `[Your]DataContext` with a `SqlConnection` that you have already created.
This prototype of the constructor is useful when mixing LINQ to SQL code with already existing
ADO.NET code.

The Third DataContext Constructor Prototype

```
DataContext(string fileOrServerOrConnection,
            System.Data.Linq.MappingSource mapping);
```

This prototype of the constructor is useful when you don't have a `[Your]DataContext` class and
instead have an XML mapping file. Sometimes, you may have an already existing business class to which
you cannot add the appropriate LINQ to SQL attributes. Perhaps you don't even have the source code for
it. You can generate a mapping file with SQLMetal or write one by hand to work with an already existing
business class, or any other class for that matter. You provide a normal ADO.NET connection string to
establish the connection.

The Fourth DataContext Constructor Prototype

```
DataContext (System.Data.IDbConnection connection,
             System.Data.Linq.MappingSource mapping)
```

This prototype allows you to create a LINQ to SQL connection from an already existing ADO.NET
connection and to provide an XML mapping file. This version of the prototype is useful for those times
when you are combining LINQ to SQL code with already existing ADO.NET code and you don't have
entity classes decorated with attributes.

Examples

For an example of the first `DataContext` constructor prototype, in Listing 16-5, we will connect to a
physical `.mdf` file using an ADO.NET type connection string.

Listing 16-5. The First DataContext Constructor Prototype Connecting to a Database File

```
DataContext dc = new DataContext(@"C:\Northwind.mdf");

IQueryable<Customer> query = from cust in dc.GetTable<Customer>()
                             where cust.Country == "USA"
                             select cust;

foreach (Customer c in query)
{
```

```
    Console.WriteLine("{0}", c.CompanyName);
}
```

■ **Note** You will need to modify the path passed to the `DataContext` constructor so that it can find your `.mdf` file.

We provide the path to the `.mdf` file to instantiate the `DataContext` object. Since we are creating a `DataContext` and not a `[Your]DataContext` object, we must call the `GetTable<T>` method to access the customers in the database. Here are the results:

```
Great Lakes Food Market
Hungry Coyote Import Store
Lazy K Kountry Store
Let's Stop N Shop
Lonesome Pine Restaurant
Old World Delicatessen
Rattlesnake Canyon Grocery
Save-a-lot Markets
Split Rail Beer & Ale
The Big Cheese
The Cracker Box
Trail's Head Gourmet Provisioners
White Clover Markets
```

Next we want to demonstrate the same basic code, except this time, in Listing 16-6, we will use our `[Your]DataContext` class, which in this case is the `Northwind` class.

Listing 16-6. *The First [Your]DataContext Constructor Prototype Connecting to a Database File*

```
Northwind db = new Northwind(@"C:\Northwind.mdf");

IQueryable<Customer> query = from cust in db.Customers
                             where cust.Country == "USA"
                             select cust;

foreach(Customer c in query)
{
    Console.WriteLine("{0}", c.CompanyName);
}
```

Notice that instead of calling the `GetTable<T>` method, we can reference the `Customers` property to access the customers in the database. Unsurprisingly, this code provides the same results:

```
Great Lakes Food Market
Hungry Coyote Import Store
Lazy K Kountry Store
Let's Stop N Shop
Lonesome Pine Restaurant
Old World Delicatessen
Rattlesnake Canyon Grocery
Save-a-lot Markets
Split Rail Beer & Ale
The Big Cheese
The Cracker Box
Trail's Head Gourmet Provisioners
White Clover Markets
```

For the sake of completeness, we will provide one more example of the first prototype, but this time we will use a connection string to actually connect to a SQL Express database server containing the attached Northwind database. And, because our normal practice will be to use the [Your]DataContext class, we will use it in Listing 16-7.

Listing 16-7. The First [Your]DataContext Constructor Prototype Connecting to a Database

```
Northwind db = new Northwind(@"Data Source=.\SQLEXPRESS;Initial
Catalog=Northwind");

IQueryable<Customer> query = from cust in db.Customers
                             where cust.Country == "USA"
                             select cust;

foreach(Customer c in query)
{
    Console.WriteLine("{0}", c.CompanyName);
}
```

And the results are still the same:

```
Great Lakes Food Market
Hungry Coyote Import Store
Lazy K Kountry Store
Let's Stop N Shop
Lonesome Pine Restaurant
Old World Delicatessen
Rattlesnake Canyon Grocery
Save-a-lot Markets
Split Rail Beer & Ale
The Big Cheese
```

```
The Cracker Box
Trail's Head Gourmet Provisioners
White Clover Markets
```

The second prototype for the DataContext class is useful when combining LINQ to SQL code with ADO.NET code, and that is what Listing 16-8 does. First, we will create a SqlConnection and insert a record in the Customers table using it. Then, we will use the SqlConnection to instantiate a [Your]DataContext class. We will query the Customers table with LINQ to SQL and display the results. Lastly, using ADO.NET, we will delete the record from the Customers table we inserted, query the Customers table one last time using LINQ to SQL, and display the results.

Listing 16-8. *The Second [Your]DataContext Constructor Prototype Connecting with a Shared ADO.NET Connection*

```
System.Data.SqlClient.SqlConnection sqlConn =
  new System.Data.SqlClient.SqlConnection(
  @"Data Source=.\SQLEXPRESS;Initial Catalog=Northwind;Integrated Security=SSPI;");

string cmd = @"insert into Customers values ('LAWN', 'Lawn Wranglers',
  'Mr. Abe Henry', 'Owner', '1017 Maple Leaf Way', 'Ft. Worth', 'TX',
  '76104', 'USA', '(800) MOW-LAWN', '(800) MOW-LAWO')";

System.Data.SqlClient.SqlCommand sqlComm =
  new System.Data.SqlClient.SqlCommand(cmd);

sqlComm.Connection = sqlConn;
try
{
  sqlConn.Open();
  //  Insert the record.
  sqlComm.ExecuteNonQuery();

  Northwind db = new Northwind(sqlConn);

  IQueryable<Customer> query = from cust in db.Customers
                               where cust.Country == "USA"
                               select cust;

  Console.WriteLine("Customers after insertion, but before deletion.");
  foreach (Customer c in query)
  {
    Console.WriteLine("{0}", c.CompanyName);
  }
```

```
sqlComm.CommandText = "delete from Customers where CustomerID = 'LAWN'";
// Delete the record.
sqlComm.ExecuteNonQuery();

Console.WriteLine("{0}{0}Customers after deletion.", System.Environment.NewLine);
foreach (Customer c in query)
{
  Console.WriteLine("{0}", c.CompanyName);
}
}
finally
{
// Close the connection.
sqlComm.Connection.Close();
}
```

Notice that we defined the LINQ query only once, but we caused it to be performed twice by enumerating the returned sequence twice. Remember, because of deferred query execution, the definition of the LINQ query does not actually result in the query being performed. The query is performed only when the results are enumerated. This is demonstrated by the fact that the results differ between the two enumerations. Listing 16-8 also shows a nice integration of ADO.NET and LINQ to SQL and just how well they can play together. Here are the results:

```
Customers after insertion, but before deletion.
Great Lakes Food Market
Hungry Coyote Import Store
Lawn Wranglers
Lazy K Kountry Store
Let's Stop N Shop
Lonesome Pine Restaurant
Old World Delicatessen
Rattlesnake Canyon Grocery
Save-a-lot Markets
Split Rail Beer & Ale
The Big Cheese
The Cracker Box
Trail's Head Gourmet Provisioners
White Clover Markets


Customers after deletion.
Great Lakes Food Market
Hungry Coyote Import Store
Lazy K Kountry Store
Let's Stop N Shop
Lonesome Pine Restaurant
```

```
Old World Delicatessen
Rattlesnake Canyon Grocery
Save-a-lot Markets
Split Rail Beer & Ale
The Big Cheese
The Cracker Box
Trail's Head Gourmet Provisioners
White Clover Markets
```

For an example of the third prototype, we won't even use the Northwind entity classes. Pretend we don't even have them. Instead, we will use a Customer class we have written by hand and an abbreviated mapping file. In truth, our handwritten Customer class is the SQLMetal-generated Customer class that we have gutted to remove all LINQ to SQL attributes. Let's take a look at our handwritten Customer class:

My Handwritten Customer Class

```
namespace Linqdev
{
  public partial class Customer
  {
    private string _CustomerID;
    private string _CompanyName;
    private string _ContactName;
    private string _ContactTitle;
    private string _Address;
    private string _City;
    private string _Region;
    private string _PostalCode;
    private string _Country;
    private string _Phone;
    private string _Fax;

    public Customer()
    {
    }

    public string CustomerID
    {
      get
      {
        return this._CustomerID;
      }
      set
      {
        if ((this._CustomerID != value))
```

```
    {
      this._CustomerID = value;
    }
  }
}

public string CompanyName
{
  get
  {
    return this._CompanyName;
  }
  set
  {
    if ((this._CompanyName != value))
    {
      this._CompanyName = value;
    }
  }
}

public string ContactName
{
  get
  {
    return this._ContactName;
  }
  set
  {
    if ((this._ContactName != value))
    {
      this._ContactName = value;
    }
  }
}

public string ContactTitle
{
  get
  {
    return this._ContactTitle;
  }
  set
  {
    if ((this._ContactTitle != value))
    {
      this._ContactTitle = value;
```

```csharp
        }
      }
    }

    public string Address
    {
      get
      {
        return this._Address;
      }
      set
      {
        if ((this._Address != value))
        {
          this._Address = value;
        }
      }
    }

    public string City
    {
      get
      {
        return this._City;
      }
      set
      {
        if ((this._City != value))
        {
          this._City = value;
        }
      }
    }

    public string Region
    {
      get
      {
        return this._Region;
      }
      set
      {
        if ((this._Region != value))
        {
          this._Region = value;
        }
      }
```

```
    }

    public string PostalCode
    {
      get
      {
        return this._PostalCode;
      }
      set
      {
        if ((this._PostalCode != value))
        {
          this._PostalCode = value;
        }
      }
    }

    public string Country
    {
      get
      {
        return this._Country;
      }
      set
      {
        if ((this._Country != value))
        {
          this._Country = value;
        }
      }
    }

    public string Phone
    {
      get
      {
        return this._Phone;
      }
      set
      {
        if ((this._Phone != value))
        {
          this._Phone = value;
        }
      }
    }
```

```
    public string Fax
    {
      get
      {
        return this._Fax;
      }
      set
      {
        if ((this._Fax != value))
        {
          this._Fax = value;
        }
      }
    }
  }
}
```

Now this is probably the worst handwritten entity class of all time. We don't handle change notifications, and we have deleted many of the portions of code that would make this a well-behaved entity class. Please read Chapter 15 to learn how to write well-behaved entity classes.

We have specified that this class lives in the Linqdev namespace. This is important, because not only will we need to specify this in our example code to differentiate between this Customer class and the one in the nwind namespace, but this namespace must also be specified in the external mapping file.

What is important for this example, though, is that there is a property for each database field mapped in the external mapping file. Now, let's take a look at the external mapping file we will be using for this example:

An Abbreviated External XML Mapping File

```xml
<?xml version="1.0" encoding="utf-8"?>
<Database Name="Northwind"
  xmlns="http://schemas.microsoft.com/linqtosql/mapping/2007">
  <Table Name="dbo.Customers" Member="Customers">
    <Type Name="Linqdev.Customer">
      <Column Name="CustomerID" Member="CustomerID" Storage="_CustomerID"
        DbType="NChar(5) NOT NULL" CanBeNull="false" IsPrimaryKey="true" />
      <Column Name="CompanyName" Member="CompanyName" Storage="_CompanyName"
        DbType="NVarChar(40) NOT NULL" CanBeNull="false" />
      <Column Name="ContactName" Member="ContactName" Storage="_ContactName"
        DbType="NVarChar(30)" />
      <Column Name="ContactTitle" Member="ContactTitle" Storage="_ContactTitle"
        DbType="NVarChar(30)" />
      <Column Name="Address" Member="Address" Storage="_Address"
        DbType="NVarChar(60)" />
      <Column Name="City" Member="City" Storage="_City" DbType="NVarChar(15)" />
      <Column Name="Region" Member="Region" Storage="_Region"
        DbType="NVarChar(15)" />
```

```
        <Column Name="PostalCode" Member="PostalCode" Storage="_PostalCode"
          DbType="NVarChar(10)" />
        <Column Name="Country" Member="Country" Storage="_Country"
          DbType="NVarChar(15)" />
        <Column Name="Phone" Member="Phone" Storage="_Phone" DbType="NVarChar(24)" />
        <Column Name="Fax" Member="Fax" Storage="_Fax" DbType="NVarChar(24)" />
    </Type>
  </Table>
</Database>
```

Notice that we have specified that the `Customer` class this mapping applies to is in the `Linqdev` namespace.

We have placed this XML in a file named `abbreviatednorthwindmap.xml` and placed that file in our `bin\Debug` directory.

In Listing 16-9 we will use this handwritten `Customer` class and external mapping file to perform a LINQ to SQL query without using any attributes.

Listing 16-9. *The Third DataContext Constructor Prototype Connecting to a Database and Using a Mapping File*

```
string mapPath = "abbreviatednorthwindmap.xml";
XmlMappingSource nwindMap =
  XmlMappingSource.FromXml(System.IO.File.ReadAllText(mapPath));

DataContext db = new DataContext(
  @"Data Source=.\SQLEXPRESS;Initial Catalog=Northwind;Integrated Security=SSPI;",
  nwindMap);

IQueryable<Linqdev.Customer> query =
  from cust in db.GetTable<Linqdev.Customer>()
  where cust.Country == "USA"
  select cust;

foreach (Linqdev.Customer c in query)
{
  Console.WriteLine("{0}", c.CompanyName);
}
```

■ **Note** We placed the `abbreviatednorthwindmap.xml` file in our Visual Studio project's `bin\Debug` directory for this example, since we are compiling and running with the Debug configuration.

As you can see, we instantiate the `XmlMappingSource` object from the mapping file and pass that `XmlMappingSource` into the `DataContext` constructor. Also notice that we cannot simply access the `Customers Table<Customer>` property in our `DataContext` object for the LINQ to SQL query, because we are using the base `DataContext` class, as opposed to our `[Your]DataContext` class, and it doesn't exist.

Also notice that everywhere we reference the `Customer` class, we also explicitly state the `Linqdev` namespace just to be sure we are not using the SQLMetal-generated `Customer` class that most of the other examples are using.

Here are the results of Listing 16-9:

```
Great Lakes Food Market
Hungry Coyote Import Store
Lazy K Kountry Store
Let's Stop N Shop
Lonesome Pine Restaurant
Old World Delicatessen
Rattlesnake Canyon Grocery
Save-a-lot Markets
Split Rail Beer & Ale
The Big Cheese
The Cracker Box
Trail's Head Gourmet Provisioners
White Clover Markets
```

Although this example uses a crude `Customer` class missing most of the code that makes a class a well-behaved entity class, we wanted to show you one example using a mapping file and a class without LINQ to SQL attributes.

The fourth prototype is a combination of the second and third prototypes, and Listing 16-10 contains an example.

Listing 16-10. *The Fourth DataContext Constructor Prototype Connecting to a Database with a Shared ADO.NET Connection and Using a Mapping File*

```
System.Data.SqlClient.SqlConnection sqlConn =
  new System.Data.SqlClient.SqlConnection(
  @"Data Source=.\SQLEXPRESS;Initial Catalog=Northwind;Integrated Security=SSPI;");

string cmd = @"insert into Customers values ('LAWN', 'Lawn Wranglers',
  'Mr. Abe Henry', 'Owner', '1017 Maple Leaf Way', 'Ft. Worth', 'TX',
  '76104', 'USA', '(800) MOW-LAWN', '(800) MOW-LAWO')";

System.Data.SqlClient.SqlCommand sqlComm =
  new System.Data.SqlClient.SqlCommand(cmd);

sqlComm.Connection = sqlConn;
try
{
  sqlConn.Open();
  // Insert the record.
```

```
    sqlComm.ExecuteNonQuery();

    string mapPath = "abbreviatednorthwindmap.xml";
    XmlMappingSource nwindMap =
      XmlMappingSource.FromXml(System.IO.File.ReadAllText(mapPath));

    DataContext db = new DataContext(sqlConn, nwindMap);

    IQueryable<Linqdev.Customer> query =
      from cust in db.GetTable<Linqdev.Customer>()
      where cust.Country == "USA"
      select cust;

    Console.WriteLine("Customers after insertion, but before deletion.");
    foreach (Linqdev.Customer c in query)
    {
      Console.WriteLine("{0}", c.CompanyName);
    }

    sqlComm.CommandText = "delete from Customers where CustomerID = 'LAWN'";
    //  Delete the record.
    sqlComm.ExecuteNonQuery();

    Console.WriteLine("{0}{0}Customers after deletion.", System.Environment.NewLine);
    foreach (Linqdev.Customer c in query)
    {
      Console.WriteLine("{0}", c.CompanyName);
    }
}
finally
{
  //  Close the connection.
  sqlComm.Connection.Close();
}
```

Listing 16-10 depends on the Linqdev.Customer class and abbreviatednorthwindmap.xml external mapping file just at Listing 16-9 does.

This is a nice example of using LINQ to SQL to query a database without attribute-decorated entity class code and integrating with ADO.NET code. And, the results are just as we would expect:

```
Customers after insertion, but before deletion.
Great Lakes Food Market
Hungry Coyote Import Store
Lawn Wranglers
Lazy K Kountry Store
Let's Stop N Shop
Lonesome Pine Restaurant
```

```
Old World Delicatessen
Rattlesnake Canyon Grocery
Save-a-lot Markets
Split Rail Beer & Ale
The Big Cheese
The Cracker Box
Trail's Head Gourmet Provisioners
White Clover Markets


Customers after deletion.
Great Lakes Food Market
Hungry Coyote Import Store
Lazy K Kountry Store
Let's Stop N Shop
Lonesome Pine Restaurant
Old World Delicatessen
Rattlesnake Canyon Grocery
Save-a-lot Markets
Split Rail Beer & Ale
The Big Cheese
The Cracker Box
Trail's Head Gourmet Provisioners
White Clover Markets
```

As you can see from the previous examples, getting a connected DataContext or [Your]DataContext is not difficult.

SubmitChanges()

The DataContext will cache all changes made to entity objects until the SubmitChanges method is called. The SubmitChanges method will initiate the change processor, and the changes to entity objects will be persisted to the database.

If an ambient transaction is not available for the DataContext object to enlist with during the SubmitChanges method call, a transaction will be created, and all changes will be made within the transaction. This way if one transaction fails, all database changes can be rolled back.

If concurrency conflicts occur, a ChangeConflictException will be thrown, allowing you the opportunity to try to resolve any conflicts and resubmit. And, what is really nice is that the DataContext contains a ChangeConflicts collection that provides a ResolveAll method to do the resolution for you. How cool is that?

Concurrency conflicts are covered in excruciating detail in Chapter 17.

Prototypes

The SubmitChanges method has two prototypes we will cover.

The First SubmitChanges Prototype

```
void SubmitChanges()
```

This prototype of the method takes no arguments and defaults to `FailOnFirstConflict` for the `ConflictMode`.

The Second SubmitChanges Prototype

```
void SubmitChanges(ConflictMode failureMode)
```

This prototype of the method allows you to specify the `ConflictMode`. The possible values are `ConflictMode.FailOnFirstConflict` and `ConflictMode.ContinueOnConflict`. `ConflictMode.FailOnFirstConflict` behaves just as it sounds, causing the `SubmitChanges` method to throw a `ChangeConflictException` on the very first conflict that occurs. `ConflictMode.ContinueOnConflict` attempts to make all the database updates so that they may all be reported and resolved at once when the `ChangeConflictException` is thrown.

Conflicts are counted in terms of the number of records conflicting, not the number of fields conflicting. You could have two fields from one record that conflict, but that causes only one conflict.

Examples

Since many of the examples in Chapter 14 call the `SubmitChanges` method, a trivial example of this method is probably old hat to you by now. Instead of boring you with another basic example calling the `SubmitChanges` method to merely persist changes to the database, we want to get a little more complex.

For an example of the first `SubmitChanges` prototype, we want to prove to you that the changes are not made to the database until the `SubmitChanges` method is called. Because this example is more complex than many of the previous examples, we will explain it as we go. Listing 16-11 contains the example.

Listing 16-11. *An Example of the First SubmitChanges Prototype*

```
System.Data.SqlClient.SqlConnection sqlConn =
  new System.Data.SqlClient.SqlConnection(
  @"Data Source=.\SQLEXPRESS;Initial Catalog=Northwind;Integrated Security=SSPI;");

try
{
  sqlConn.Open();

  string sqlQuery = "select ContactTitle from Customers where CustomerID =
'LAZYK'";
  string originalTitle = GetStringFromDb(sqlConn, sqlQuery);
  string title = originalTitle;
  Console.WriteLine("Title from database record: {0}", title);

  Northwind db = new Northwind(sqlConn);
```

```
    Customer c = (from cust in db.Customers
                  where cust.CustomerID == "LAZYK"
                  select cust).
                  Single<Customer>();
    Console.WriteLine("Title from entity object : {0}", c.ContactTitle);
```

In the previous code, we create an ADO.NET database connection and open it. Next, we query the database for the LAZYK customer's ContactTitle using our common GetStringFromDb method and display it. Then, we create a Northwind object using the ADO.NET database connection, query the same customer using LINQ to SQL, and display their ContactTitle. At this point, the ContactTitle of each should match.

```
    Console.WriteLine(String.Format(
      "{0}Change the title to 'Director of Marketing' in the entity object:",
      System.Environment.NewLine));
    c.ContactTitle = "Director of Marketing";

    title = GetStringFromDb(sqlConn, sqlQuery);
    Console.WriteLine("Title from database record: {0}", title);

    Customer c2 = (from cust in db.Customers
                   where cust.CustomerID == "LAZYK"
                   select cust).
                   Single<Customer>();
    Console.WriteLine("Title from entity object : {0}", c2.ContactTitle);
```

In the previous code, we change the ContactTitle of the customer's LINQ to SQL entity object. Then, we query the ContactTitle from the database and the entity object again and display them. The ContactTitle values should not match this time, because the change has not yet been persisted to the database.

```
    db.SubmitChanges();
    Console.WriteLine(String.Format(
      "{0}SubmitChanges() method has been called.",
      System.Environment.NewLine));

    title = GetStringFromDb(sqlConn, sqlQuery);
    Console.WriteLine("Title from database record: {0}", title);

    Console.WriteLine("Restoring ContactTitle back to original value ...");
    c.ContactTitle = "Marketing Manager";
    db.SubmitChanges();
    Console.WriteLine("ContactTitle restored.");
}
finally
{
    sqlConn.Close();
}
```

We call the SubmitChanges method and then retrieve the ContactTitle from the database to display again. This time, the value from the database should be updated, because the SubmitChanges method has persisted the change to the database.

Last, we set the ContactTitle to the original value and persist it to the database using the SubmitChanges method to restore the database to its original state so this example can be run multiple times and no other examples will be affected.

That code is doing a lot, but its intent is to prove that the changes made to the entity object are not persisted to the database until the SubmitChanges method is called. When you see a call to the GetStringFromDb method, it is retrieving the ContactTitle directly from the database using ADO.NET. Here are the results:

```
Title from database record: Marketing Manager
Title from entity object : Marketing Manager

Change the title to 'Director of Marketing' in the entity object:
Title from database record: Marketing Manager
Title from entity object : Director of Marketing

SubmitChanges() method has been called.
Title from database record: Director of Marketing
Restoring ContactTitle back to original value ...
ContactTitle restored.
```

As you can see in the previous results, the ContactTitle value is not changed in the database until the SubmitChanges method is called.

For an example of the second SubmitChanges prototype, we intentionally induce concurrency errors on two records by updating them with ADO.NET between the time we query the records with LINQ to SQL, and the time we try to update them with LINQ to SQL. We will create *two* record conflicts to demonstrate the difference between ConflictMode.FailOnFirstConflict and ConflictMode.ContinueOnConflict.

Also, you will see code toward the bottom that will reset the ContactTitle values to their original values in the database. This is to allow the code to be run multiple times. If, while running the code in the debugger, you prevent the entire code from running, you may need to manually reset these values.

In the first example of the second prototype of the SubmitChanges method, Listing 16-12, we will set the ConflictMode to ContinueOnConflict so that you can see it handle multiple conflicts first. Because this example is complex, we will explain it a portion at a time.

Listing 16-12. The Second SubmitChanges Prototype Demonstrating ContinueOnConflict

```
Northwind db = new Northwind(@"Data Source=.\SQLEXPRESS;Initial
Catalog=Northwind");

Console.WriteLine("Querying for the LAZYK Customer with LINQ.");
Customer cust1 = (from c in db.Customers
                  where c.CustomerID == "LAZYK"
```

```
                    select c).Single<Customer>();

Console.WriteLine("Querying for the LONEP Customer with LINQ.");
Customer cust2 = (from c in db.Customers
                    where c.CustomerID == "LONEP"
                    select c).Single<Customer>();
```

In the previous code, we create a Northwind DataContext and query two customers, LAZYK and LONEP.

```
string cmd = @"update Customers set ContactTitle = 'Director of Marketing'
                    where CustomerID = 'LAZYK';
                update Customers set ContactTitle = 'Director of Sales'
                    where CustomerID = 'LONEP'";
ExecuteStatementInDb(cmd);
```

Next, in the preceding code, we update the ContactTitle value in the database for both customers using our ExecuteStatementInDb common method, which uses ADO.NET to make the changes. At this point, we have created the potential for concurrency conflicts for each record.

```
Console.WriteLine("Change ContactTitle in entity objects for LAZYK and LONEP.");
cust1.ContactTitle = "Vice President of Marketing";
cust2.ContactTitle = "Vice President of Sales";
```

In the previous code, we update the ContactTitle for each customer so that when we call the SubmitChanges method in the next portion of code, the DataContext object's change processor will try to persist the changes for these two customers and detect the concurrency conflicts.

```
try
{
  Console.WriteLine("Calling SubmitChanges() ...");
  db.SubmitChanges(ConflictMode.ContinueOnConflict);
  Console.WriteLine("SubmitChanges() called successfully.");
}
```

In the previous code, we call the SubmitChanges method. This will cause the DataContext change processor to try to persist these two customers, but since the value for each customer's ContactTitle will be different in the database than when initially loaded from the database, a concurrency conflict will be detected.

```
catch (ChangeConflictException ex)
{
  Console.WriteLine("Conflict(s) occurred calling SubmitChanges(): {0}.",
    ex.Message);

  foreach (ObjectChangeConflict objectConflict in db.ChangeConflicts)
  {
    Console.WriteLine("Conflict for {0} occurred.",
      ((Customer)objectConflict.Object).CustomerID);
```

```
    foreach (MemberChangeConflict memberConflict in objectConflict.MemberConflicts)
    {
      Console.WriteLine("  LINQ value = {0}{1}  Database value = {2}",
        memberConflict.CurrentValue,
        System.Environment.NewLine,
        memberConflict.DatabaseValue);
    }
  }
}
```

In the preceding code, we catch the `ChangeConflictException` exception. This is where things get interesting. Notice that first we enumerate the `ChangeConflicts` collection of the `DataContext` object, db. This collection will store `ObjectChangeConflict` objects. Notice that an `ObjectChangeConflict` object has a property named `Object` that references the actual entity object that the concurrency conflict occurred during the persistence thereof. We simply cast that `Object` member as the data type of the entity class to reference property values of the entity object. In this case, we access the `CustomerID` property.

Then, for each `ObjectChangeConflict` object, we enumerate through its collection of `MemberChangeConflict` objects and display the information from each that we are interested in. In this case, we display the LINQ value and the value from the database.

```
Console.WriteLine("{0}Resetting data to original values.",
  System.Environment.NewLine);

cmd = @"update Customers set ContactTitle = 'Marketing Manager'
          where CustomerID = 'LAZYK';
        update Customers set ContactTitle = 'Sales Manager'
          where CustomerID = 'LONEP'";
ExecuteStatementInDb(cmd);
```

In the previous code, we simply restore the database to its original state so the example can be run multiple times.

That is a lot of code to demonstrate this. Keep in mind that none of this enumeration through the various conflict collections is necessary. We are merely demonstrating how you would do it and showing some of the conflict information available, should you care.

Also, please notice that we are doing nothing in this example to resolve the conflicts. We are merely reporting them.

Here are the results of the code:

```
Querying for the LAZYK Customer with LINQ.
Querying for the LONEP Customer with LINQ.
Executing SQL statement against database with ADO.NET ...
Database updated.
Change ContactTitle in entity objects for LAZYK and LONEP.
Calling SubmitChanges() ...
```

```
Conflict(s) occurred calling SubmitChanges(): 2 of 2 updates failed.
Conflict for LAZYK occurred.
  LINQ value = Vice President of Marketing
  Database value = Director of Marketing
Conflict for LONEP occurred.
  LINQ value = Vice President of Sales
  Database value = Director of Sales

Resetting data to original values.
Executing SQL statement against database with ADO.NET ...
Database updated.
```

As you can see, there were two conflicts, one for each of the two records for which we created a conflict. This demonstrates that the change processor did *not* stop trying to persist the changes to the database after the first conflict. This is because we passed a ConflictMode of ContinueOnConflict when we called the SubmitChanges method.

Listing 16-13 is the same code except we pass a ConflictMode of FailOnFirstConflict when we call the SubmitChanges method.

Listing 16-13. *The Second SubmitChanges Prototype Demonstrating FailOnFirstConflict*

```
Northwind db = new Northwind(@"Data Source=.\SQLEXPRESS;Initial
Catalog=Northwind");

Console.WriteLine("Querying for the LAZYK Customer with LINQ.");
Customer cust1 = (from c in db.Customers
                  where c.CustomerID == "LAZYK"
                  select c).Single<Customer>();

Console.WriteLine("Querying for the LONEP Customer with LINQ.");
Customer cust2 = (from c in db.Customers
                  where c.CustomerID == "LONEP"
                  select c).Single<Customer>();

string cmd = @"update Customers set ContactTitle = 'Director of Marketing'
                  where CustomerID = 'LAZYK';
               update Customers set ContactTitle = 'Director of Sales'
                  where CustomerID = 'LONEP'";
ExecuteStatementInDb(cmd);

Console.WriteLine("Change ContactTitle in entity objects for LAZYK and LONEP.");
cust1.ContactTitle = "Vice President of Marketing";
cust2.ContactTitle = "Vice President of Sales";

try
{
```

```
      Console.WriteLine("Calling SubmitChanges() ...");
      db.SubmitChanges(ConflictMode.FailOnFirstConflict);
      Console.WriteLine("SubmitChanges() called successfully.");
}
catch (ChangeConflictException ex)
{
      Console.WriteLine("Conflict(s) occurred calling SubmitChanges(): {0}",
        ex.Message);

      foreach (ObjectChangeConflict objectConflict in db.ChangeConflicts)
      {
        Console.WriteLine("Conflict for {0} occurred.",
          ((Customer)objectConflict.Object).CustomerID);

        foreach (MemberChangeConflict memberConflict in objectConflict.MemberConflicts)
        {
          Console.WriteLine("  LINQ value = {0}{1}  Database value = {2}",
            memberConflict.CurrentValue,
            System.Environment.NewLine,
            memberConflict.DatabaseValue);
        }
      }
}

Console.WriteLine("{0}Resetting data to original values.",
  System.Environment.NewLine);
cmd = @"update Customers set ContactTitle = 'Marketing Manager'
          where CustomerID = 'LAZYK';
          update Customers set ContactTitle = 'Sales Manager'
          where CustomerID = 'LONEP'";
ExecuteStatementInDb(cmd);
```

This time, the results should indicate that the processing of changes to the entity objects halts once the first concurrency conflict is detected. Let's take a look at the results:

```
Querying for the LAZYK Customer with LINQ.
Querying for the LONEP Customer with LINQ.
Executing SQL statement against database with ADO.NET ...
Database updated.
Change ContactTitle in entity objects for LAZYK and LONEP.
Calling SubmitChanges() ...
Conflict(s) occurred calling SubmitChanges(): Row not found or changed.
Conflict for LAZYK occurred.
  LINQ value = Vice President of Marketing
  Database value = Director of Marketing
```

```
Resetting data to original values.
Executing SQL statement against database with ADO.NET ...
Database updated.
```

As you can see, even though we induced two conflicts, the change processor stopped trying to persist changes to the database once a conflict occurred, as evidenced by only one conflict being reported.

DatabaseExists()

The DatabaseExists method can be used to determine whether a database already exists. The determination of database existence is based on the connection string specified when instantiating the DataContext. If you specify a path for an .mdf file, it will look for the database in that path with the specified name. If you specify a server, it will check that server.

The DatabaseExists method is often used in conjunction with the DeleteDatabase and CreateDatabase methods.

Prototypes

The DatabaseExists method has one prototype we will cover.

The Only DatabaseExists Prototype

```
bool DatabaseExists()
```

This method will return true if the database specified in the connection string when instantiating the DataContext exists. Otherwise, it returns false.

Examples

Thankfully, this is a fairly simple method to demonstrate. In Listing 16-14, we will just instantiate a DataContext and call the DatabaseExists method to see whether the Northwind database exists. And of course, we already know that it does.

Listing 16-14. *An Example of the DatabaseExists Method*

```
Northwind db = new Northwind(@"Data Source=.\SQLEXPRESS;Initial
Catalog=Northwind");

Console.WriteLine("The Northwind database {0}.",
    db.DatabaseExists() ? "exists" : "does not exist");
```

Here are the results:

```
The Northwind database exists.
```

For kicks, if you detach your `Northwind` database and run the example again, you will get these results:

```
The Northwind database does not exist.
```

If you tried that, don't forget to attach your `Northwind` database back so the other examples will work.

CreateDatabase()

To make things even slicker, since the entity classes know so much about the structure of the database to which they are mapped, Microsoft provides a method named `CreateDatabase` to actually create the database.

You should realize, though, that it can only create the parts of the database that it knows about via the entity class attributes or a mapping file. So, the *content* of things such as stored procedures, triggers, user-defined functions, and check constraints will not be produced in a database created in this manner, since there are no attributes specifying this information. For simple applications, this may be perfectly acceptable, though.

■ **Caution** Unlike most other changes that you make to a database through the `DataContext`, the `CreateDatabase` method executes immediately. There is no need to call the `SubmitChanges` method, and the execution is not deferred. This gives you the benefit of being able to create the database and begin inserting data immediately.

Prototypes

The `CreateDatabase` method has one prototype we will cover.

The Only CreateDatabase Prototype

```
void CreateDatabase()
```

This method takes no arguments and returns nothing.

Examples

Again, this is a simple method to demonstrate, and Listing 16-15 contains the code.

Listing 16-15. An Example of the CreateDatabase Method

```
Northwind db = new Northwind(@"C:\Northwnd.mdf");
db.CreateDatabase();
```

■ **Note** We have intentionally spelled Northwnd without the letter *i* in Listing 16-15 so that it does not impact a Northwind (with the letter *i*) database should you have one.

This code doesn't produce any screen output, so there are no results to show. However, if we look in the C:\ directory, we can see the Northwnd.mdf and Northwnd.ldf files. Also, if we look in SQL Server Management Studio, we can see that the C:\Northwnd.mdf file is attached. This method would be best combined with the DatabaseExists method. If you attempt to call the CreateDatabase method and the database already exists, an exception will be thrown. To demonstrate this, merely run the code in Listing 16-15 a second time, without deleting or detaching it from your SQL Server Management Studio or Enterprise Manager, and you will get this output:

```
Unhandled Exception: System.Data.SqlClient.SqlException: Database 'C:\Northwnd.mdf'
already exists. Choose a different database name.
...
```

Also, don't make the mistake of assuming you can just delete the two Northwind database files that were created from the file system to eliminate the database so that you can run the example again. SQL Server will still have it cataloged. You must delete or detach the database in a proper manner for the CreateDatabase method to succeed.

You may want to delete or detach that newly created database to prevent confusion at some future point, or you could just leave it in place for the next example, Listing 16-16, to delete.

DeleteDatabase()

LINQ to SQL gives us the ability to delete a database with the DataContext object's DeleteDatabase method. Attempting to delete a database that does not exist will throw an exception, so it would be best to call this method only after checking for the existence of the database with the DatabaseExists method.

■ **Caution** Unlike most other changes that you make to a database through the DataContext, the DeleteDatabase method executes immediately. There is no need to call the SubmitChanges method, and the execution is not deferred.

Prototypes

The DeleteDatabase method has one prototype we will cover.

The Only DeleteDatabase Prototype

```
void DeleteDatabase()
```

This method takes no arguments and returns nothing.

Examples

In Listing 16-16, we will delete the database we just created in Listing 16-15.

Listing 16-16. *An Example of the DeleteDatabase Method*

```
Northwind db = new Northwind(@"C:\Northwnd.mdf");
db.DeleteDatabase();
```

This example doesn't create any screen output when run, as long as the database specified exists, but after running it, you will find that the two database files that were created when calling the CreateDatabase method are gone.

Calling this method when the database does not exist will cause the following exception to be thrown:

```
Unhandled Exception: System.Data.SqlClient.SqlException: An attempt to attach an
auto-named database for file C:\Northwnd.mdf failed. A database with the same name
exists, or specified file cannot be opened, or it is located on UNC share.
...
```

CreateMethodCallQuery()

The first thing you need to know about the CreateMethodCallQuery method is that it is a protected method. This means you are not able to call this method from your application code and that you must derive a class from the DataContext class to be able to call it.

The CreateMethodCallQuery method is used to call *table-valued* user-defined functions. The ExecuteMethodCall method is used to call *scalar-valued* user-defined functions, and we will discuss it later in this chapter.

Prototypes

The CreateMethodCallQuery method has one prototype we will cover.

The Only CreateMethodCallQuery Prototype

```
protected internal IQueryable<T> CreateMethodCallQuery<T>(
  object instance,
  System.Reflection.MethodInfo methodInfo,
  params object[] parameters)
```

The CreateMethodCallQuery method is passed a reference to the DataContext or [Your]DataContext object of which the method that is calling the CreateMethodCallQuery method is a member, the MethodInfo object for that calling method, and a params array of the parameters for the table-valued user-defined function.

Examples

Because the CreateMethodCallQuery method is protected and can be called only from the DataContext class or one derived from it, instead of providing an example that actually calls the CreateMethodCallQuery method, we will discuss the method that SQLMetal generated for the extended Northwind database's ProductsUnderThisUnitPrice table-valued user-defined function. Here is that method:

The SQLMetal-Generated Method Calling CreateMethodCallQuery

```
[Function(Name="dbo.ProductsUnderThisUnitPrice", IsComposable=true)]
public IQueryable<ProductsUnderThisUnitPriceResult>
  ProductsUnderThisUnitPrice(
    [Parameter(DbType="Money")] System.Nullable<decimal> price)
{
  return this.CreateMethodCallQuery<ProductsUnderThisUnitPriceResult>(
    this, ((MethodInfo)(MethodInfo.GetCurrentMethod())), price);
}
```

In the previous code, you can see that the ProductsUnderThisUnitPrice method is attributed with the Function attribute, so we know it is going to call either a stored procedure or a user-defined function named ProductsUnderThisUnitPrice. Because the IsComposable attribute property is set to true, we know it is a user-defined function and not a stored procedure. Because the code that was generated calls the CreateMethodCallQuery method, we know that the specified user-defined function ProductsUnderThisUnitPrice is a table-valued user-defined function, not a *scalar-valued* user-defined function.

For the arguments passed to the CreateMethodCallQuery method, the first argument is a reference to the derived DataContext class SQLMetal generated. The second argument passed is the current method's MethodInfo object. This will allow the CreateMethodCallQuery method access to the attributes, so it knows the necessary information to call the *table-valued* user-defined function, such as its name. The third argument passed to the CreateMethodCallQuery method is the only parameter the specified user-defined function accepts, which in this case is a price.

The value returned by the call to the CreateMethodCallQuery method will be returned by the ProductsUnderThisUnitPrice method, and that is a sequence of

ProductsUnderThisUnitPriceResult objects. SQLMetal was nice enough to generate the ProductsUnderThisUnitPriceResult class for us as well.

The code we discuss previously shows how to call the CreateMethodCallQuery method, but just to provide some context, let's look at an example calling the generated ProductsUnderThisUnitPriceResult method, so you can see it all in action.

In Listing 16-17, we will make a simple call to the ProductsUnderThisUnitPriceResult method.

Listing 16-17. An Example Calling the ProductsUnderThisUnitPrice Method

```
Northwind db = new Northwind(@"Data Source=.\SQLEXPRESS;Initial
Catalog=Northwind");

IQueryable<ProductsUnderThisUnitPriceResult> results =
  db.ProductsUnderThisUnitPrice(new Decimal(5.50m));

foreach(ProductsUnderThisUnitPriceResult prod in results)
{
  Console.WriteLine("{0} - {1:C}", prod.ProductName, prod.UnitPrice);
}
```

Here are the results of this example:

```
Guaranà¡ Fantà¡stica - $4.50
Geitost - $2.50
```

ExecuteQuery()

There is no doubt that LINQ to SQL is awesome. Using the LINQ standard dot notation or expression syntax makes crafting LINQ queries fun. But, at one time or another, we think we have all experienced the desire to just perform a SQL query. Well, you can do that too with LINQ to SQL. In fact, you can do that and still get back entity objects.

The ExecuteQuery method allows you to specify a SQL query as a string and to even provide parameters for substitution into the string, just as you would when calling the String.Format method, and it will translate the query results into a sequence of entity objects.

It's just that simple. We hear what you are saying. What about SQL injection errors? Doesn't the appropriate way to do this require using parameters? Yes, it does. And, the ExecuteQuery method is handling all that for you! We know you must be saying, "Show us an example, and pronto!"

Prototypes

The ExecuteQuery method has one prototype we will cover.

The Only ExecuteQuery Prototype

```
IEnumerable<T> ExecuteQuery<T>(string query, params object[] parameters)
```

This method takes at least one argument, a SQL query, and zero or more parameters. The query string and optional parameters work just like the `String.Format` method. The method returns a sequence of type T, where type T is an entity class.

Be aware that if you specify the value of a column for a `where` clause in the query string, you must enclose char-based type columns with single quotes just as you would if you were making a normal SQL query. But, if you provide the column's value as a parameter, there is no need to enclose the parameter specifier, such as {0}, in single quotes.

For a column in the query to be propagated into an actual entity object, the column's name must match one of the entity object's mapped fields. Of course, you can accomplish this by appending `"as <columnname>"` to the actual column name, where `<columnname>` is a mapped column in the entity object.

Every mapped field does not need to be returned by the query, but primary keys certainly do. And, you can retrieve fields in the query that do not map to any mapped field in the entity object, but they will not get propagated to the entity object.

Examples

For a simple example calling the `ExecuteQuery` method, in Listing 16-18 we will query the `Customers` table.

Listing 16-18. A Simple Example of the ExecuteQuery Method

```
Northwind db = new Northwind(@"Data Source=.\SQLEXPRESS;Initial
Catalog=Northwind");

IEnumerable<Customer> custs = db.ExecuteQuery<Customer>(
  @"select CustomerID, CompanyName, ContactName, ContactTitle
    from Customers where Region = {0}", "WA");

foreach (Customer c in custs)
{
  Console.WriteLine("ID = {0} : Name = {1} : Contact = {2}",
    c.CustomerID, c.CompanyName, c.ContactName);
}
```

There isn't much to this example. Again notice that, because we are using the parameter substitution feature of the method by specifying "WA" as a parameter instead of hard-coding it in the query, we do not need to enclose the format specifier in single quotes. Here are the results:

```
ID = LAZYK : Name = Lazy K Kountry Store : Contact = John Steel
ID = TRAIH : Name = Trail's Head Gourmet Provisioners : Contact = Helvetius Nagy
ID = WHITC : Name = White Clover Markets : Contact = Karl Jablonski
```

If we want to make that same query, but without using parameter substitution, we would have to enclose the "WA" portion in single quotes like a normal SQL query. Listing 16-19 contains the code.

Listing 16-19. Another Simple Example of the ExecuteQuery Method

```
Northwind db = new Northwind(@"Data Source=.\SQLEXPRESS;Initial
Catalog=Northwind");

IEnumerable<Customer> custs = db.ExecuteQuery<Customer>(
  @"select CustomerID, CompanyName, ContactName, ContactTitle
    from Customers where Region = 'WA'");

foreach (Customer c in custs)
{
  Console.WriteLine("ID = {0} : Name = {1} : Contact = {2}",
    c.CustomerID, c.CompanyName, c.ContactName);
}
```

In case it is hard to detect, WA is enclosed in single quotes in that query string. The results of this code are the same as for the previous example:

```
ID = LAZYK : Name = Lazy K Kountry Store : Contact = John Steel
ID = TRAIH : Name = Trail's Head Gourmet Provisioners : Contact = Helvetius Nagy
ID = WHITC : Name = White Clover Markets : Contact = Karl Jablonski
```

In addition to this, you can append a specified column name if the real column name doesn't match the column name in the database. Since you can perform joins in the query string, you could query columns with a different name from a different table but specify their name as one of the mapped fields in the entity class. Listing 16-20 contains an example.

Listing 16-20. An Example of the ExecuteQuery Method Specifying a Mapped Field Name

```
Northwind db = new Northwind(@"Data Source=.\SQLEXPRESS;Initial
Catalog=Northwind");

IEnumerable<Customer> custs = db.ExecuteQuery<Customer>(
  @"select CustomerID, Address + ', ' + City + ', ' + Region as Address
    from Customers where Region = 'WA'");

foreach (Customer c in custs)
{
  Console.WriteLine("Id = {0} : Address = {1}",
      c.CustomerID, c.Address);
}
```

The interesting part of this example is that we are concatenating multiple database columns and string literals and specifying a mapped field name to get the address, city, and region into the single Address member of the entity object. In this case, all the fields come from the same table, but they could have come from a join on another table. Here are the results:

```
Id = LAZYK : Address = 12 Orchestra Terrace, Walla Walla, WA
Id = TRAIH : Address = 722 DaVinci Blvd., Kirkland, WA
Id = WHITC : Address = 305 - 14th Ave. S. Suite 3B, Seattle, WA
```

Of course, if you utilize this type of chicanery, don't forget that if one of those returned entity objects is modified and the SubmitChanges method is called, you could end up with some database records containing questionable data. But used properly, this could be a very handy technique.

Translate()

The Translate method is similar to the ExecuteQuery method in that it translates the results of a SQL query into a sequence of entity objects. Where it differs is that instead of passing a string containing a SQL statement, you pass it an object of type System.Data.Common.DbDataReader, such as a SqlDataReader. This method is useful for integrating LINQ to SQL code into existing ADO.NET code

Prototypes

The Translate method has one prototype we will cover.

The Only Translate Prototype

```
IEnumerable<T> Translate<T>(System.Data.Common.DbDataReader reader)
```

You pass the Translate method an object of type System.Data.Common.DbDataReader, and the Translate method returns a sequence of the specified entity objects.

Examples

In Listing 16-21, we will create and execute a query using ADO.NET. We will then use the Translate method to translate the results from the query into a sequence of Customer entity objects. Because Listing 16-21 is somewhat more complex than typical, we will explain it as we go.

Listing 16-21. An Example of the Translate Method

```
System.Data.SqlClient.SqlConnection sqlConn =
  new System.Data.SqlClient.SqlConnection(
  @"Data Source=.\SQLEXPRESS;Initial Catalog=Northwind;Integrated Security=SSPI;");

string cmd = @"select CustomerID, CompanyName, ContactName, ContactTitle
               from Customers where Region = 'WA'";

System.Data.SqlClient.SqlCommand sqlComm =
  new System.Data.SqlClient.SqlCommand(cmd);
```

```
sqlComm.Connection = sqlConn;
try
{
  sqlConn.Open();
  System.Data.SqlClient.SqlDataReader reader = sqlComm.ExecuteReader();
```

For this example, let's pretend all the previous code already existed. Pretend this is legacy code that we need to update, and we would like to take advantage of LINQ to accomplish our new task. As you can see, there are no references to LINQ in the previous code. A SqlConnection is established, a query is formed, a SqlCommand is created, the connection is opened, and the query is performed—all pretty much a run-of-the-mill ADO.NET database query. Now, let's add some LINQ code to do something.

```
Northwind db = new Northwind(sqlConn);

IEnumerable<Customer> custs = db.Translate<Customer>(reader);

foreach (Customer c in custs)
{
  Console.WriteLine("ID = {0} : Name = {1} : Contact = {2}",
      c.CustomerID, c.CompanyName, c.ContactName);
}
```

In the previous code, we instantiate our Northwind DataContext using our ADO.NET SqlConnection. We then call the Translate method, passing the already created reader so that the query results can be converted into a sequence of entity objects that we can then enumerate and display the results of.

Normally, since this is legacy code, there would be some more code doing something with the results, but for this example, there is no point to have that code. All that is left is the method cleanup code.

```
}
finally
{
  sqlComm.Connection.Close();
}
```

The previous code simply closes the connection. This example demonstrates how nicely LINQ to SQL can play with ADO.NET. Let's take a look at the results of Listing 16-21:

```
ID = LAZYK : Name = Lazy K Kountry Store : Contact = John Steel
ID = TRAIH : Name = Trail's Head Gourmet Provisioners : Contact = Helvetius Nagy
ID = WHITC : Name = White Clover Markets : Contact = Karl Jablonski
```

ExecuteCommand()

Like the ExecuteQuery method, the ExecuteCommand method allows you to specify an actual SQL statement to execute against the database. This means you can use it to execute insert, update, or delete statements, as well as execute stored procedures. Also, like with the `ExecuteQuery` method, you can pass parameters into the method.

One thing to be aware of when calling the `ExecuteCommand` method is that it executes immediately, and the `SubmitChanges` method does not need to be called.

Prototypes

The `ExecuteCommand` method has one prototype we will cover.

The Only ExecuteCommand Prototype

```
int ExecuteCommand(string command, params object[] parameters)
```

This method accepts a `command` string and zero or more optional parameters and returns an integer indicating how many rows were affected by the query.

Be aware that if you specify the value of a column for a `where` clause in the `command` string itself, you must enclose `char`-based type columns with single quotes just as you would if you were making a normal SQL query. But, if you provide the column's value as a parameter, there is no need to enclose the parameter specifier, such as `{0}`, in single quotes.

Examples

In Listing 16-22, we will insert a record using the `ExecuteCommand` method. Since we always reverse any changes we make to the database so subsequent examples are not affected, we will also use the `ExecuteCommand` method to delete the inserted record.

Listing 16-22. An Example of the ExecuteCommand Method Used to Insert and Delete a Record

```
Northwind db = new Northwind(@"Data Source=.\SQLEXPRESS;Initial
Catalog=Northwind");

Console.WriteLine("Inserting customer ...");
int rowsAffected = db.ExecuteCommand(
  @"insert into Customers values ({0}, 'Lawn Wranglers',
    'Mr. Abe Henry', 'Owner', '1017 Maple Leaf Way', 'Ft. Worth', 'TX',
    '76104', 'USA', '(800) MOW-LAWN', '(800) MOW-LAWO')",
  "LAWN");
Console.WriteLine("Insert complete.{0}", System.Environment.NewLine);

Console.WriteLine("There were {0} row(s) affected.  Is customer in database?",
  rowsAffected);

Customer cust = (from c in db.Customers
                 where c.CustomerID == "LAWN"
```

```
               select c).DefaultIfEmpty<Customer>().Single<Customer>();

Console.WriteLine("{0}{1}",
  cust != null ?
    "Yes, customer is in database." : "No, customer is not in database.",
  System.Environment.NewLine);

Console.WriteLine("Deleting customer ...");
rowsAffected =
  db.ExecuteCommand(@"delete from Customers where CustomerID = {0}", "LAWN");

Console.WriteLine("Delete complete.{0}", System.Environment.NewLine);
```

As you can see, there is not much to this example. We call the ExecuteCommand method and pass the command string plus any parameters. We then perform a query using LINQ to SQL just to make sure the record is indeed in the database and display the results of the query to the console. To clean up the database, we call the ExecuteCommand method to delete the inserted record. This code produces the following results:

```
Inserting customer ...
Insert complete.

There were 1 row(s) affected.  Is customer in database?
Yes, customer is in database.

Deleting customer ...
Delete complete.
```

ExecuteMethodCall()

The first thing you need to know about the ExecuteMethodCall method is that it is a protected method. This means you are not able to call this method from your application code and that you must derive a class from the DataContext class to be able to call it.

The ExecuteMethodCall method is used to call stored procedures and scalar-valued user-defined functions. To call table-valued user-defined functions, please read the section in this chapter about the CreateMethodCallQuery method.

Prototypes

The ExecuteMethodCall method has one prototype we will cover.

The Only ExecuteMethodCall Prototype

```
protected internal IExecuteResult ExecuteMethodCall(
  object instance,
```

```
System.Reflection.MethodInfo methodInfo,
params object[] parameters)
```

The `ExecuteMethodCall` method is passed a reference to the `DataContext` or `[Your]DataContext` object of which the method that is calling the `ExecuteMethodCall` method is a member, the `MethodInfo` object for that calling method, and a `params` array of the parameters for the stored procedure or scalar-valued user-defined function.

Since we must pass a `MethodInfo` object, notice that our method must be decorated with the appropriate stored procedure or user-defined function attribute and attribute properties. LINQ to SQL then uses the `MethodInfo` object to access the method's `Function` attribute to obtain the name of the stored procedure or scalar-valued user-defined function. It also uses the `MethodInfo` object to obtain the parameter names and types.

The `ExecuteMethodCall` method returns an object implementing the `IExecuteResult` interface. We cover this interface in Chapter 15.

If you use SQLMetal to generate your entity classes, it will create entity class methods that call the `ExecuteMethodCall` method for the database's stored procedures if you specify the `/sprocs` option, and for the database's user-defined functions if you specify the `/functions` option.

Examples

Before we discuss the code for the first example, we want to discuss the method named `CustomersCountByRegion` that SQLMetal generated to call the database's `Customers Count By Region` stored procedure. Here is what the generated method looks like:

Using the ExecuteMethodCall Method to Call a Stored Procedure

```
[Function(Name="dbo.Customers Count By Region")]
[return: Parameter(DbType="Int")]
public int CustomersCountByRegion([Parameter(DbType="NVarChar(15)")] string param1)
{
  IExecuteResult result =
    this.ExecuteMethodCall(
      this,
      ((MethodInfo)(MethodInfo.GetCurrentMethod())),
      param1);
  return ((int)(result.ReturnValue));
}
```

As you can see, the `CustomersCountByRegion` method is passed a `string` parameter that is passed as a parameter into the `ExecuteMethodCall` method, which is passed as a parameter to the `Customers Count By Region` stored procedure.

The `ExecuteMethodCall` method returns a variable implementing `IExecuteResult`. To obtain the integer return value, the `CustomersCountByRegion` method merely references the returned object's `ReturnValue` property and casts it to an `int`.

Now, let's take a look at Listing 16-23 to see some code calling the generated `CustomersCountByRegion` method.

Listing 16-23. An Example Calling the Generated CustomersCountByRegion Method

```
Northwind db = new Northwind(@"Data Source=.\SQLEXPRESS;Initial
Catalog=Northwind");
int rc = db.CustomersCountByRegion("WA");
Console.WriteLine("There are {0} customers in WA.", rc);
```

This is a very trivial example with no surprises. Here is the result:

```
There are 3 customers in WA.
```

Now, we want to discuss calling a stored procedure that returns an output parameter. Again, looking at the SQLMetal-generated entity classes for the Northwind database, we will discuss the CustOrderTotal method SQLMetal generated to call the CustOrderTotal stored procedure:

An Example Using the ExecuteMethodCall Method to Call a Stored Procedure That Returns an Output Parameter

```
[Function(Name="dbo.CustOrderTotal")]
[return: Parameter(DbType="Int")]
public int CustOrderTotal(
  [Parameter(Name="CustomerID", DbType="NChar(5)")] string customerID,
  [Parameter(Name="TotalSales", DbType="Money")] ref System.Nullable<decimal>
    totalSales)
{
  IExecuteResult result =
    this.ExecuteMethodCall(
      this,
      ((MethodInfo)(MethodInfo.GetCurrentMethod())),
      customerID,
      totalSales);

  totalSales = ((System.Nullable<decimal>)(result.GetParameterValue(1)));
  return ((int)(result.ReturnValue));
}
```

Notice that the CustOrderTotal method's second parameter, totalSales, specifies the ref keyword. This is a clue that the stored procedure is going to return this value. Notice that to get the value after the call to the ExecuteMethodCall method, the code calls the GetParameterValue method on the returned object implementing IExecuteResult and passes it 1, since we are interested in the second parameter. Listing 16-24 calls the CustOrderTotal method.

Listing 16-24. An Example Calling the Generated CustOrderTotal Method

```
Northwind db = new Northwind(@"Data Source=.\SQLEXPRESS;Initial
Catalog=Northwind");
decimal? totalSales = 0;
int rc = db.CustOrderTotal("LAZYK", ref totalSales);
Console.WriteLine("Customer LAZYK has total sales of {0:C}.", totalSales);
```

Notice that we had to specify the ref keyword for the second parameter, totalSales. Here is the result:

```
Customer LAZYK has total sales of $357.00.
```

Now, let's take a look at an example that calls a stored procedure that returns its results in a single shape. Since the Northwind database contains a stored procedure named Customers By City that returns a single shape, that is the stored procedure we will discuss.

Let's look at the SQLMetal-generated method that calls this stored procedure by calling the ExecuteMethodCall method.

An Example Using the ExecuteMethodCall Method to Call a Stored Procedure That Returns a Single Shape

```
[Function(Name="dbo.Customers By City")]
public ISingleResult<CustomersByCityResult>
  CustomersByCity([Parameter(DbType="NVarChar(20)")] string param1)
{
  IExecuteResult result =
    this.ExecuteMethodCall(
      this,
      ((MethodInfo)(MethodInfo.GetCurrentMethod())),
      param1);

  return ((ISingleResult<CustomersByCityResult>)(result.ReturnValue));
}
```

Notice that the generated method returns an object of type ISingleResult<CustomersByCityResult>. The generated method obtains this object by casting the returned object's ReturnValue property to that type. SQLMetal was kind enough to even generate the CustomersByCityResult class for us as well, although we won't discuss it here. Listing 16-25 contains code calling the generated CustomersByCity method.

Listing 16-25. An Example Calling the Generated CustomersByCity Method

```
Northwind db = new Northwind(@"Data Source=.\SQLEXPRESS;Initial
Catalog=Northwind");
```

```
ISingleResult<CustomersByCityResult> results = db.CustomersByCity("London");

foreach (CustomersByCityResult cust in results)
{
  Console.WriteLine("{0} - {1} - {2} - {3}", cust.CustomerID, cust.CompanyName,
    cust.ContactName, cust.City);
}
```

As you can see, we enumerate through the returned object of type
ISingleResult<CustomersByCityResult> just as though it is a LINQ sequence. This is because it is
derived from IEnumerable<T>, as we mentioned in Chapter 15. We then display the results to the
console. Here are the results:

```
AROUT - Around the Horn - Thomas Hardy - London
BSBEV - B's Beverages - Victoria Ashworth - London
CONSH - Consolidated Holdings - Elizabeth Brown - London
EASTC - Eastern Connection - Ann Devon - London
NORTS - North/South - Simon Crowther - London
SEVES - Seven Seas Imports - Hari Kumar - London
```

Now let's take a look at some examples returning multiple result shapes. For those unfamiliar with
the term *shape* in this context, the shape of the results is dictated by the types of data that are returned.
When a query returns a customer's ID and name, this is a shape. If a query returns an order ID, order
date, and shipping code, this is yet another shape. If a query returns both, a record containing a
customer's ID and name and another, or perhaps more than one, record containing the order ID, order
date, and shipping code, this query returns multiple result shapes. Since stored procedures have this
ability, LINQ to SQL needs a way to address this, and it has one.

For the first example returning multiple shapes, let's take the scenario where the shape of the result
is conditional. Fortunately, the extended Northwind database has a stored procedure of this type. The
name of that stored procedure is Whole Or Partial Customers Set. SQLMetal generated a method to
call that stored procedure for us named WholeOrPartialCustomersSet. Here it is:

*An Example Using the ExecuteMethodCall Method to Call a Stored Procedure That Conditionally
Returns Different Shapes*

```
[Function(Name="dbo.Whole Or Partial Customers Set")]
[ResultType(typeof(WholeOrPartialCustomersSetResult1))]
[ResultType(typeof(WholeOrPartialCustomersSetResult2))]
public IMultipleResults WholeOrPartialCustomersSet(
  [Parameter(DbType="Int")] System.Nullable<int> param1)
{
  IExecuteResult result =
    this.ExecuteMethodCall(
      this,
      ((MethodInfo)(MethodInfo.GetCurrentMethod())),
```

```
    param1);

  return ((IMultipleResults)(result.ReturnValue));
}
```

Notice that there are two `ResultType` attributes specifying the two possible result shapes. SQLMetal was also kind enough to generate the two specified classes for us. The developer calling the `WholeOrPartialCustomersSet` method must be aware that the stored procedure returns a different result shape based on the value of `param1`. Because we have examined the stored procedure, we know that if `param1` is equal to 1, the stored procedure will return all fields from the `Customers` table and therefore will return a sequence of objects of type `WholeOrPartialCustomersSetResult1`. If the value of `param1` is equal to 2, an abbreviated set of fields will be returned in a sequence of objects of type `WholeOrPartialCustomersSetResult2`.

Also notice that the return type from the `WholeOrPartialCustomersSet` method is `IMultipleResults`. The method obtains this by casting the `ReturnValue` property of the object returned by the `ExecuteMethodCall` method to an `IMultipleResults`. We discuss this interface in Chapter 15.

In Listing 16-26, we provide an example calling the `WholeOrPartialCustomersSet` method.

Listing 16-26. *An Example Calling the Generated WholeOrPartialCustomersSet Method*

```
Northwind db = new Northwind(@"Data Source=.\SQLEXPRESS;Initial
Catalog=Northwind");

IMultipleResults results = db.WholeOrPartialCustomersSet(1);

foreach (WholeOrPartialCustomersSetResult1 cust in
    results.GetResult<WholeOrPartialCustomersSetResult1>())
{
  Console.WriteLine("{0} - {1} - {2} - {3}", cust.CustomerID, cust.CompanyName,
    cust.ContactName, cust.City);
}
```

Notice that the results are of type `IMultipleResults`. We passed the value 1, so we know we will be getting a sequence of type `WholeOrPartialCustomersSetResult1`. Also notice that to get to the results, we call the `GetResult<T>` method on the `IMultipleResults` variable, where type `T` is the type of the returned data. Here are the results:

```
LAZYK - Lazy K Kountry Store - John Steel - Walla Walla
TRAIH - Trail's Head Gourmet Provisioners - Helvetius Nagy – Kirkland
WHITC - White Clover Markets - Karl Jablonski – Seattle
```

That stored procedure retrieves only those customers whose region is "WA". Had we passed a value of 2 when we called the `WholeOrPartialCustomersSet` method, we would have gotten a sequence of type `WholeOrPartialCustomersSetResult2`, so every place in the preceding code where we specified a type of `WholeOrPartialCustomersSetResult1` would have to be changed to `WholeOrPartialCustomersSetResult2`.

This just leaves us with the case of a stored procedure returning multiple shapes for the same call. Here again, the extended `Northwind` database has just such a stored procedure, and its name is `Get Customer And Orders`. First, let's look at the method SQLMetal generated to call that stored procedure:

An Example Using the ExecuteMethodCall Method to Call a Stored Procedure That Returns Multiple Shapes

```
[Function(Name="dbo.Get Customer And Orders")]
[ResultType(typeof(GetCustomerAndOrdersResult1))]
[ResultType(typeof(GetCustomerAndOrdersResult2))]
public IMultipleResults GetCustomerAndOrders(
  [Parameter(Name="CustomerID", DbType="NChar(5)")] string customerID)
{
  IExecuteResult result =
    this.ExecuteMethodCall(
      this,
      ((MethodInfo)(MethodInfo.GetCurrentMethod())),
      customerID);

  return ((IMultipleResults)(result.ReturnValue));
}
```

As you can see, the return type of the method is `IMultipleResults`. Since the stored procedure returns multiple result shapes, it is our responsibility to know the order of the shapes being returned. Because we have examined the `Get Customer And Orders` stored procedure, we know it will return the record from the `Customers` table first, followed by the related records from the `Orders` table.

Listing 16-27 calls the generated method from the previous code.

Listing 16-27. An Example Calling the Generated GetCustomerAndOrders Method

```
Northwind db = new Northwind(@"Data Source=.\SQLEXPRESS;Initial
Catalog=Northwind");

IMultipleResults results = db.GetCustomerAndOrders("LAZYK");

GetCustomerAndOrdersResult1 cust =
  results.GetResult<GetCustomerAndOrdersResult1>().Single();

Console.WriteLine("{0} orders:", cust.CompanyName);

foreach (GetCustomerAndOrdersResult2 order in
    results.GetResult<GetCustomerAndOrdersResult2>())
{
  Console.WriteLine("{0} - {1}", order.OrderID, order.OrderDate);
}
```

Because we know the stored procedure will return a single recording matching type GetCustomerAndOrdersResult1, we know we can call the `Single` operator on the sequence containing that type as long as we are confident the customer exists for the passed `CustomerID`. We could always call the `SingleOrDefault` operator if we were not confident. We also know that after the single GetCustomerAndOrdersResult1 object is returned, zero or more GetCustomerAndOrdersResult2 objects will be returned, so we enumerate through them displaying the data we are interested in. Here are the results:

```
Lazy K Kountry Store orders:
10482 - 3/21/1997 12:00:00 AM
10545 - 5/22/1997 12:00:00 AM
```

This completes the stored procedure examples for the `ExecuteMethodCall` method. At the beginning of the section on the `ExecuteMethodCall` method, we said this method was used to call scalar-valued user-defined functions. So, let's take a look at an example calling a scalar-valued user-defined function.

First, let's look at a SQLMetal-generated method calling the `ExecuteMethodCall` method to call a scalar-valued user-defined function:

An Example Using the ExecuteMethodCall Method to Call a Scalar-Valued User-Defined Function

```
[Function(Name="dbo.MinUnitPriceByCategory", IsComposable=true)]
[return: Parameter(DbType="Money")]
public System.Nullable<decimal> MinUnitPriceByCategory(
  [Parameter(DbType="Int")] System.Nullable<int> categoryID)
{
  return ((System.Nullable<decimal>)(this.ExecuteMethodCall(this,
    ((MethodInfo)(MethodInfo.GetCurrentMethod())), categoryID).ReturnValue));
}
```

Notice that the scalar value returned by the stored procedure is obtained by referencing the `ReturnValue` property of the object returned by the `ExecuteMethodCall` method.

We could create a simple example calling the generated `MinUnitPriceByCategory` method. However, all the fun of a user-defined function comes when embedding it in a query like it was a built-in SQL function.

Let's take a look at an example, Listing 16-28, that embeds the `MinUnitPriceByCategory` method in a query to identify all products that are the least expensive in their category.

Listing 16-28. *An Example Embedding a User-Defined Function Within a Query*

```
Northwind db = new Northwind(@"Data Source=.\SQLEXPRESS;Initial
Catalog=Northwind");

IQueryable<Product> products = from p in db.Products
                               where p.UnitPrice ==
                                 db.MinUnitPriceByCategory(p.CategoryID)
                               select p;
```

```
foreach (Product p in products)
{
  Console.WriteLine("{0} - {1:C}", p.ProductName, p.UnitPrice);
}
```

In this example, we embed the call to the `MinUnitPriceByCategory` method—which in turn causes a call to the scalar-valued user-defined function of the same name—in the `where` clause. Here are the results:

```
Aniseed Syrup - $10.00
Konbu - $6.00
Teatime Chocolate Biscuits - $9.20
Guaranà¡ Fantà¡stica - $4.50
Geitost - $2.50
Filo Mix - $7.00
Tourtière - $7.45
Longlife Tofu - $10.00
```

GetCommand()

One potentially useful method is the `GetCommand` method. When the `GetCommand` method is called on the `DataContext` object and passed a LINQ to SQL `IQueryable`, an object of type `System.Data.Common.DbCommand` is returned. The returned `DbCommand` object contains access to several key components that will be used by the passed query.

By retrieving the `DbCommand` object with the `GetCommand` method, you can obtain a reference to the `CommandText`, `CommandTimeout`, `Connection`, `Parameters`, and `Transaction` objects, as well as others, for the passed query. This allows you to not only examine those objects but to also modify them from their default values *without* modifying the same values for all queries that will be performed by the current instance of the `DataContext`. Perhaps for a particular query, you would like to increase the `CommandTimeout` value, but you don't want all the queries executed with the `DataContext` object to be allowed this extended timeout period.

Prototypes

The `GetCommand` method has one prototype we will cover.

The Only GetCommand Prototype

```
System.Data.Common.DbCommand GetCommand(IQueryable query)
```

This method is passed a LINQ to SQL query in the form of an `IQueryable` and returns a `System.Data.Common.DbCommand` for the passed LINQ query.

Examples

In Listing 16-29, we will obtain the DbCommand object to change the CommandTimeout for a query and to display the CommandText, which will be the SQL query itself.

Listing 16-29. An Example of the GetCommand Method

```
Northwind db = new Northwind(@"Data Source=.\SQLEXPRESS;Initial
Catalog=Northwind");

IQueryable<Customer> custs = from c in db.Customers
                            where c.Region == "WA"
                            select c;

System.Data.Common.DbCommand dbc = db.GetCommand(custs);

Console.WriteLine("Query's timeout is: {0}{1}", dbc.CommandTimeout,
  System.Environment.NewLine);

dbc.CommandTimeout = 1;

Console.WriteLine("Query's SQL is: {0}{1}",
  dbc.CommandText, System.Environment.NewLine);

Console.WriteLine("Query's timeout is: {0}{1}", dbc.CommandTimeout,
  System.Environment.NewLine);

foreach (Customer c in custs)
{
  Console.WriteLine("{0}", c.CompanyName);
}
```

There isn't much to this example. We merely declare a query and pass it to the GetCommand method. We then display the CommandTimeout value for the DbCommand object that was returned. Next, we set the CommandTimeout value to 1 and display the SQL query itself and the new CommandTimeout value. Last, we enumerate through the results returned by the query.

Here are the results of the code running on our machine:

```
Query's timeout is: 30

Query's SQL is: SELECT [t0].[CustomerID], [t0].[CompanyName], [t0].[ContactName],
[t0].[ContactTitle], [t0].[Address], [t0].[City], [t0].[Region], [t0].[PostalCode],
[t0].[Country], [t0].[Phone], [t0].[Fax]
FROM [dbo].[Customers] AS [t0]
WHERE [t0].[Region] = @p0
```

```
Query's timeout is: 1

Lazy K Kountry Store
Trail's Head Gourmet Provisioners
White Clover Markets
```

Of course, if that query takes too long to execute on your machine, the query could time out, and you would get different results.

GetChangeSet()

Sometimes, it may be useful to be able to obtain a list of all the entity objects that *will be* inserted, changed, or deleted once the SubmitChanges method is called. The GetChangeSet method does just that.

Prototypes

The GetChangeSet method has one prototype we will cover.

The Only GetChangeSet Prototype

```
ChangeSet GetChangeSet()
```

This method is passed nothing and returns a ChangeSet object. The ChangeSet object contains collections of type IList<T> for the inserted, modified, and deleted entity objects, where type T is an entity class. These collection properties are named Inserts, Updates, and Deletes, respectively.

You can then enumerate through each of these collections to examine the contained entity objects.

Examples

In Listing 16-30, we will modify, insert, and delete an entity object. We will then retrieve the ChangeSet using the GetChangeSet method and enumerate through each collection.

Listing 16-30. An Example of the GetChangeSet Method

```
Northwind db = new Northwind(@"Data Source=.\SQLEXPRESS;Initial
Catalog=Northwind");

Customer cust = (from c in db.Customers
                 where c.CustomerID == "LAZYK"
                 select c).Single<Customer>();
cust.Region = "Washington";

db.Customers.InsertOnSubmit(
  new Customer
```

```
    {
      CustomerID = "LAWN",
      CompanyName = "Lawn Wranglers",
      ContactName = "Mr. Abe Henry",
      ContactTitle = "Owner",
      Address = "1017 Maple Leaf Way",
      City = "Ft. Worth",
      Region = "TX",
      PostalCode = "76104",
      Country = "USA",
      Phone = "(800) MOW-LAWN",
      Fax = "(800) MOW-LAWO"
    });

Customer cust2 = (from c in db.Customers
                  where c.CustomerID == "LONEP"
                  select c).Single<Customer>();
db.Customers.DeleteOnSubmit(cust2);
cust2 = null;

ChangeSet changeSet = db.GetChangeSet();

Console.WriteLine("{0}First, the added entities:", System.Environment.NewLine);
foreach (Customer c in changeSet.Inserts)
{
  Console.WriteLine("Customer {0} will be added.", c.CompanyName);
}

Console.WriteLine("{0}Second, the modified entities:", System.Environment.NewLine);
foreach (Customer c in changeSet.Updates)
{
  Console.WriteLine("Customer {0} will be updated.", c.CompanyName);
}

Console.WriteLine("{0}Third, the removed entities:", System.Environment.NewLine);
foreach (Customer c in changeSet.Deletes)
{
  Console.WriteLine("Customer {0} will be deleted.", c.CompanyName);
}
```

In the previous example, we first modify the LAZYK customer's Region. We then insert a customer, LAWN, and delete customer LONEP. Next, we obtain the ChangeSet by calling the GetChangeSet method. Then, we enumerate through each collection—Inserts, Updates, and Deletes—and display each entity object in the respective collection.

Here are the results:

```
First, the added entities:
Customer Lawn Wranglers will be added.

Second, the modified entities:
Customer Lazy K Kountry Store will be updated.

Third, the removed entities:
Customer Lonesome Pine Restaurant will be deleted.
```

Of course, in the preceding example, we can enumerate through each of the collections assuming every element is a Customer object, because we know they are. In many cases, though, there could be more than one type of object in a collection, and you can't make that assumption. In these situations, you will have to write your enumeration code to handle multiple data types. The OfType operator could be helpful for this purpose.

GetTable()

The GetTable method is used to get a reference to a Table sequence from a DataContext for a specific mapped database table. This method is typically used only when the actual DataContext class is used, as opposed to [Your]DataContext. Using [Your]DataContext class is the preferred technique, because it will have a Table sequence property already having a reference for each mapped table.

Prototypes

The GetTable method has two prototypes we will cover.

The First GetTable Prototype

```
Table<T> GetTable<T>()
```

This method is provided a specified mapped entity type T and returns a Table sequence of type T.

The Second GetTable Prototype

```
ITable GetTable(Type type)
```

This method is passed a Type of entity object and returns the interface to the table. You can then use this ITable interface as you desire. If you want to use the ITable interface as though it were a table, be sure to cast it to an IQueryable<T>.

Examples

For an example of the first prototype, in Listing 16-31, we will use the standard DataContext class, as opposed to our [Your]DataContext class, Northwind, to retrieve a specific customer.

Listing 16-31. An Example of the First GetTable Prototype

```
DataContext db =
  new DataContext(@"Data Source=.\SQLEXPRESS;Initial Catalog=Northwind");

Customer cust = (from c in db.GetTable<Customer>()
                 where c.CustomerID == "LAZYK"
                 select c).Single<Customer>();

Console.WriteLine("Customer {0} retrieved.", cust.CompanyName);
```

Here, we call the GetTable method to get a reference to the Customer table so that we can retrieve a specific customer. Here are the results:

```
Customer Lazy K Kountry Store retrieved.
```

For an example of the second prototype of the GetTable method, we will use a DataContext instead of our [Your]DataContext. Listing 16-32 will be the same basic example as the previous except using the second prototype.

Listing 16-32. An Example of the Second GetTable Prototype

```
DataContext db =
  new DataContext(@"Data Source=.\SQLEXPRESS;Initial Catalog=Northwind");

Customer cust = (from c in ((IQueryable<Customer>)db.GetTable(typeof(Customer)))
                 where c.CustomerID == "LAZYK"
                 select c).Single<Customer>();

Console.WriteLine("Customer {0} retrieved.", cust.CompanyName);
```

It should come as no surprise that the results for Listing 16-32 are the same as for Listing 16-31:

```
Customer Lazy K Kountry Store retrieved.
```

Refresh()

The Refresh method allows you to manually refresh entity objects from the database. In some situations, this is done for you when you call the DataContext object's ChangeConflicts collection's ResolveAll method if concurrency conflicts occur during a call to the SubmitChanges method. However, there may be situations where you will never call the SubmitChanges method but want to get updates from the database.

An example might be an application that displays read-only type status data for some entity, system, or process. You may want the data refreshed from the database on some interval of time. The Refresh method could be used for this purpose.

With the Refresh method, you can refresh a single entity object, or a sequence of entity objects, meaning the results of a LINQ to SQL query.

Prototypes

The Refresh method has three prototypes we will cover.

The First Refresh Prototype

```
void Refresh(RefreshMode mode, object entity)
```

This method takes a refresh mode and a single entity object and returns nothing.

The Second Refresh Prototype

```
void Refresh(RefreshMode mode, params object[] entities)
```

This method takes a refresh mode and a params array of entity objects and returns nothing.

The Third Refresh Prototype

```
void Refresh(RefreshMode mode, System.Collections.IEnumerable entities)
```

This method takes a refresh mode and a sequence of entity objects and returns nothing.

The RefreshMode enumeration has three possible values: KeepChanges, KeepCurrentValues, and OverwriteCurrentValues. The Visual Studio documentation for the RefreshMode enumeration defines these values as outlined in Table 16-1.

Table 16-1. The RefreshMode Enumeration

Member name	Description
KeepCurrentValues	Forces the Refresh method to swap the original value with the values retrieved from the database
KeepChanges	Forces the Refresh method to keep the current value that has been changed but updates the other values with the database values
OverwriteCurrentValues	Forces the Refresh method to override all the current values with the values from the database

The behavior of each of these settings is discussed in more detail in Chapter 17.

Examples

For an example of the first prototype, in Listing 16-33, we will query a customer using LINQ to SQL and display its contact name and contact title. We will then change that customer's contact name in the database using ADO.NET. We will change the contact title in the entity object. Just to convince you that the current entity object is not aware of the change to the database but does have the changed contact title we just made, we will display the entity's contact name and contact title again, and you will see the contact name is unchanged, and the contact title is changed.

We will then call the Refresh method with a RefreshMode of KeepChanges and display the entity object's contact name and contact title once more, and you will see that it does indeed have the new value of the contact name from the database, while at the same time maintaining our change to the contact title.

We will then reset the contact name back to its original value just so the example can be run multiple times. Listing 16-33 shows the code.

Listing 16-33. An Example of the First Refresh Method Prototype

```
Northwind db = new Northwind(@"Data Source=.\SQLEXPRESS;Initial
Catalog=Northwind");

Customer cust = (from c in db.Customers
                 where c.CustomerID == "GREAL"
                 select c).Single<Customer>();

Console.WriteLine("Customer's original name is {0}, ContactTitle is {1}.{2}",
  cust.ContactName, cust.ContactTitle, System.Environment.NewLine);

ExecuteStatementInDb(String.Format(
  @"update Customers set ContactName = 'Brad Radaker' where CustomerID =
'GREAL'"));

cust.ContactTitle = "Chief Technology Officer";

Console.WriteLine("Customer's name before refresh is {0}, ContactTitle is {1}.{2}",
  cust.ContactName, cust.ContactTitle, System.Environment.NewLine);

db.Refresh(RefreshMode.KeepChanges, cust);

Console.WriteLine("Customer's name after refresh is {0}, ContactTitle is {1}.{2}",
  cust.ContactName, cust.ContactTitle, System.Environment.NewLine);

// we need to reset the changed values so that the code can be run
// more than once.
Console.WriteLine("{0}Resetting data to original values.",
  System.Environment.NewLine);
ExecuteStatementInDb(String.Format(
  @"update Customers set ContactName = 'John Steel' where CustomerID = 'GREAL'"));
```

In the previous code, we make a LINQ to SQL query to obtain a reference to the `Customer` object. We then display that `Customer` object's `ContactName` and `ContactTitle`.

Next, we update that customer's `ContactName` in the database using ADO.NET and update the `ContactTitle` on our retrieved `Customer` entity object. At this point, our `Customer` entity object is unaware that the `ContactName` has been changed in the database, and we prove this by displaying the `Customer` object's `ContactName` and `ContactTitle` to the console.

Then, we call the `RefreshMethod` with the `KeepChanges` `RefreshMode`. This should cause any `Customer` object properties that have been changed in the database to be loaded into our entity object as long as we have not changed them. In this case, since the `ContactName` has been changed in the database, it should be refreshed from the database.

We then display the `Customer` object's `ContactName` and `ContactTitle`, and this should show the `ContactName` from the database and the `ContactTitle` we changed in our entity object.

Last, we clean up the database so the example can be run again and no subsequent examples are affected.

Let's take a look at the results of Listing 16-33:

```
Customer's original name is John Steel, ContactTitle is Marketing Manager.

Executing SQL statement against database with ADO.NET ...
Database updated.
Customer's name before refresh is John Steel, ContactTitle is Chief Technology
Officer.

Customer's name after refresh is Brad Radaker, ContactTitle is Chief Technology
Officer.


Resetting data to original values.
Executing SQL statement against database with ADO.NET ...
Database updated.
```

As you can see, the entity object is not aware that we changed the `ContactName` to `"Brad Radaker"` in the database before we called the `Refresh` method, but once we call the `Refresh` method, it is.

For an example of the second prototype, in Listing 16-34, we will retrieve the customers whose region is `"WA"` using LINQ to SQL. We will enumerate through the returned sequence of `Customer` objects and display their `CustomerID`, `Region`, and `Country`. Then, using ADO.NET, we will update the `Country` field for each customer in the database whose region is `"WA"`. At this point, the value for the `Country` field for those customers is different in the database than it is in the entity objects that have been retrieved. We will enumerate through the sequence of retrieved customers again just to prove that the entity objects are unaware of the change to the `Region` field in the database.

Next, we will call the `ToArray` operator on the sequence of `Customer` objects to obtain an array containing `Customer` objects. We then call the `Refresh` method passing a `RefreshMode` of `KeepChanges` and pass the first, second, and third elements of the array of `Customer` objects.

We then enumerate through the sequence of `Customer` entity objects one last time displaying each `Customer` object's `CustomerID`, `Region`, and `Country` to prove that the `Country` field has indeed been refreshed from the database.

Of course, we still have to restore the database to its original state, so we then use ADO.NET to set the customer's Country back to its original value in the database.

Here is the code for Listing 16-34.

Listing 16-34. *An Example of the Second Refresh Method Prototype*

```
Northwind db = new Northwind(@"Data Source=.\SQLEXPRESS;Initial
Catalog=Northwind");

IEnumerable<Customer> custs = (from c in db.Customers
                               where c.Region == "WA"
                               select c);

Console.WriteLine("Entity objects before ADO.NET change and Refresh() call:");
foreach (Customer c in custs)
{
  Console.WriteLine("Customer {0}'s region is {1}, country is {2}.",
    c.CustomerID, c.Region, c.Country);
}

Console.WriteLine("{0}Updating customers' country to United States in ADO.NET...",
  System.Environment.NewLine);
ExecuteStatementInDb(String.Format(
  @"update Customers set Country = 'United States' where Region = 'WA'"));
Console.WriteLine("Customers' country updated.{0}", System.Environment.NewLine);

Console.WriteLine("Entity objects after ADO.NET change but before Refresh()
call:");
foreach (Customer c in custs)
{
  Console.WriteLine("Customer {0}'s region is {1}, country is {2}.",
    c.CustomerID, c.Region, c.Country);
}

Customer[] custArray = custs.ToArray();
Console.WriteLine("{0}Refreshing params array of customer entity objects ...",
  System.Environment.NewLine);
db.Refresh(RefreshMode.KeepChanges, custArray[0], custArray[1], custArray[2]);
Console.WriteLine("Params array of Customer entity objects refreshed.{0}",
  System.Environment.NewLine);

Console.WriteLine("Entity objects after ADO.NET change and Refresh() call:");
foreach (Customer c in custs)
{
  Console.WriteLine("Customer {0}'s region is {1}, country is {2}.",
    c.CustomerID, c.Region, c.Country);
}
```

```
//  We need to reset the changed values so that the code can be run
//  more than once.
Console.WriteLine("{0}Resetting data to original values.",
  System.Environment.NewLine);
ExecuteStatementInDb(String.Format(
  @"update Customers set Country = 'USA' where Region = 'WA'"));
```

The previous code doesn't start getting interesting until the call to the ToArray operator. Once we obtain the array of Customer objects, we call the RefreshMethod and pass custArray[0], custArray[1], and custArray[2].

Let's take a look at the results:

```
Entity objects before ADO.NET change and Refresh() call:
Customer LAZYK's region is WA, country is USA.
Customer TRAIH's region is WA, country is USA.
Customer WHITC's region is WA, country is USA.

Updating customers' country to United States in ADO.NET...
Executing SQL statement against database with ADO.NET ...
Database updated.
Customers' country updated.

Entity objects after ADO.NET change but before Refresh() call:
Customer LAZYK's region is WA, country is USA.
Customer TRAIH's region is WA, country is USA.
Customer WHITC's region is WA, country is USA.

Refreshing params array of customer entity objects ...
Params array of Customer entity objects refreshed.

Entity objects after ADO.NET change and Refresh() call:
Customer LAZYK's region is WA, country is United States.
Customer TRAIH's region is WA, country is United States.
Customer WHITC's region is WA, country is United States.

Resetting data to original values.
Executing SQL statement against database with ADO.NET ...
Database updated.
```

As you can see in the previous results, the changes we made to the Country field in the database are not reflected in the Customer entity objects until we call the Refresh method.

In Listing 16-34, each entity object we refreshed was of the same data type, Customer. For the second prototype of the Refresh method, it is not necessary that every entity object passed be the same data type. We could have passed entity objects of different data types. In the case of Listing 16-34, it would have actually been easier if we could have just passed a sequence of entity objects to the Refresh method, because a sequence is what we had. Fortunately, the third prototype of the Refresh method allows you to pass a sequence.

So, for an example of the third prototype, in Listing 16-35 we will use the same basic code as Listing 16-34, except instead of creating an array and passing explicitly stated elements to the Refresh method, we will pass the sequence of retrieved Customer objects.

Listing 16-35. *An Example of the Third Refresh Method Prototype*

```
Northwind db = new Northwind(@"Data Source=.\SQLEXPRESS;Initial
Catalog=Northwind");

IEnumerable<Customer> custs = (from c in db.Customers
                               where c.Region == "WA"
                               select c);

Console.WriteLine("Entity objects before ADO.NET change and Refresh() call:");
foreach (Customer c in custs)
{
  Console.WriteLine("Customer {0}'s region is {1}, country is {2}.",
    c.CustomerID, c.Region, c.Country);
}

Console.WriteLine("{0}Updating customers' country to United States in ADO.NET...",
  System.Environment.NewLine);
ExecuteStatementInDb(String.Format(
  @"update Customers set Country = 'United States' where Region = 'WA'"));
Console.WriteLine("Customers' country updated.{0}", System.Environment.NewLine);

Console.WriteLine("Entity objects after ADO.NET change but before Refresh()
call:");
foreach (Customer c in custs)
{
  Console.WriteLine("Customer {0}'s region is {1}, country is {2}.",
    c.CustomerID, c.Region, c.Country);
}

Console.WriteLine("{0}Refreshing sequence of customer entity objects ...",
  System.Environment.NewLine);
db.Refresh(RefreshMode.KeepChanges, custs);
Console.WriteLine("Sequence of Customer entity objects refreshed.{0}",
  System.Environment.NewLine);

Console.WriteLine("Entity objects after ADO.NET change and Refresh() call:");
foreach (Customer c in custs)
{
  Console.WriteLine("Customer {0}'s region is {1}, country is {2}.",
    c.CustomerID, c.Region, c.Country);
```

```
}

// We need to reset the changed values so that the code can be run
// more than once.
Console.WriteLine("{0}Resetting data to original values.",
  System.Environment.NewLine);
ExecuteStatementInDb(String.Format(
  @"update Customers set Country = 'USA' where Region = 'WA'"));
```

The code in Listing 16-35 is the same as Listing 16-34 except that when we call the Refresh method, we pass the custs sequence. Let's take a look at the results:

```
Entity objects before ADO.NET change and Refresh() call:
Customer LAZYK's region is WA, country is USA.
Customer TRAIH's region is WA, country is USA.
Customer WHITC's region is WA, country is USA.

Updating customers' country to United States in ADO.NET...
Executing SQL statement against database with ADO.NET ...
Database updated.
Customers' country updated.

Entity objects after ADO.NET change but before Refresh() call:
Customer LAZYK's region is WA, country is USA.
Customer TRAIH's region is WA, country is USA.
Customer WHITC's region is WA, country is USA.

Refreshing sequence of customer entity objects ...
Sequence of Customer entity objects refreshed.

Entity objects after ADO.NET change and Refresh() call:
Customer LAZYK's region is WA, country is United States.
Customer TRAIH's region is WA, country is United States.
Customer WHITC's region is WA, country is United States.

Resetting data to original values.
Executing SQL statement against database with ADO.NET ...
Database updated.
```

As you can see, despite that we updated the Country for the retrieved customers to "United States" in the database, we didn't see that change in the entity objects until we called the Refresh method.

Summary

We know it took a long time to get to the point of knowing what the DataContext class can do for you. LINQ to SQL is not trivial because it encapsulates an understanding of LINQ with an understanding of database queries and SQL. Because of this, there is a lot to know about LINQ to SQL, and much of what there is to understand about the DataContext class is intertwined with entity classes; therefore, something has to come first, and something has to come last.

Although there is a lot of information in this chapter, probably the most important topics to leave this chapter understanding are how the three DataContext services—identity tracking, change tracking, and change processing—work. Of course, none of those services has any value if you cannot even instantiate a DataContext or [Your]DataContext object, so the constructors for the DataContext and [Your]DataContext class are important as well.

Other than the DataContext and [Your]DataContext constructors, the DataContext method you will most likely use the most is the SubmitChanges method, because it is the method that you will call to persist your changes to the database.

It is important to remember that, when you attempt to persist your changes to the database, sometimes a concurrency conflict may arise and throw an exception. We have mentioned concurrency conflicts many times so far in the LINQ to SQL chapters, but we have yet to discuss them in detail. Therefore, in the next chapter, we will cover concurrency conflicts in depth.

■ ■ ■

CHAPTER 17

LINQ to SQL Concurrency Conflicts

How many times have you heard us say that you must detect concurrency conflicts and resolve them? In most of the preceding LINQ to SQL chapters, we mentioned concurrency conflicts, but we have yet to discuss them in the level of detail they deserve. In this chapter, we will resolve that deficiency.

Prerequisites for Running the Examples

To run the examples in this chapter, you will need to have obtained the extended version of the Northwind database and generated entity classes for it. Please read and follow the instructions in Chapter 12 titled "Prerequisites for Running the Examples."

Some Common Methods

Additionally, to run the examples in this chapter, you will need some common methods that will be utilized by the examples. Please read and follow the instructions in Chapter 12's "Some Common Methods" section.

Using the LINQ to SQL API

To run the examples in this chapter, you may need to add the appropriate references and using directives to your project. Please read and follow the instructions in Chapter 12's "Using the LINQ to SQL API" section.

Concurrency Conflicts

When one database connection attempts to update a piece of data that has been changed by another database connection since the record was read by the first database connection, a concurrency conflict occurs. That is to say that if process 1 reads the data, followed by process 2 reading the same data, and process 2 updates that same data before process one can, a concurrency conflict occurs when process 1 attempts to update the data. It is also true though that, if process 1 updates the data before process 2, process 2 will get a concurrency conflict when it attempts to update the data. If multiple connections can access a database and make changes, it is only a matter of time and luck before a concurrency conflict occurs.

When a conflict occurs, an application must take some action to resolve it. For example, a web site administrator may be on a page displaying data for a normal user that allows the administrator to update that normal user's data. If after the administrator's page reads the normal user's data from the database, the normal user goes to a page displaying her data and makes a change, a conflict will occur when the administrator saves his changes to the database. If a conflict did not occur, the normal user's changes would be overwritten and lost. An alternative is that the normal user's changes could be saved, and the administrator's changes are lost. Which is the correct behavior at any given time is a complex problem. The first step is to detect it. The second step is to resolve it.

There are two basic approaches for handling concurrency conflicts, *optimistic* and *pessimistic*.

Optimistic Concurrency

As the name would suggest, optimistic concurrency conflict handling takes the optimistic approach that most of the time, a concurrency conflict will not happen. Therefore, no locks will be placed on the data during a read of the database. If there is a conflict when attempting to update that same data, we will address the conflict then. Optimistic concurrency conflict handling is more complicated than pessimistic concurrency conflict handling, but it works better for most modern-day applications with very large-scale quantities of users. Imagine how frustrating it would be if every time you wanted to view an item at your favorite auction site, you couldn't because someone else was looking at that same item and the record was locked because that person might make a bid on that item. You wouldn't be a happy user for very long.

LINQ to SQL takes the optimistic concurrency conflict handling approach. Fortunately, LINQ to SQL makes the detection and resolution of concurrency conflicts as simple as seems feasibly possible. It even provides a method to handle the resolution for you if you like.

Conflict Detection

As we previously mentioned, the first step is detecting the conflict. LINQ to SQL has two approaches it uses to detect concurrency conflicts. If the IsVersion Column attribute property is specified on an entity class property and its value is true, then the value of that entity class property, and that property alone will be used to determine whether a concurrency conflict occurred.

If no entity class property has an IsVersion attribute property set to true, LINQ to SQL allows you to control which entity class properties participate in concurrency conflict detection with the Column attribute UpdateCheck property specified on an entity class's mapped property. The UpdateCheck enumeration provides three possible values: Never, Always, and WhenChanged.

UpdateCheck

If the UpdateCheck attribute property for a mapped entity class property is set to UpdateCheck.Never, that entity class property will not participate in concurrency conflict detection. If the UpdateCheck property is set to UpdateCheck.Always, the entity class property will always participate in the concurrency conflict detection regardless of whether the property's value has changed since initially being retrieved and cached by the DataContext. If the UpdateCheck property is set to UpdateCheck.WhenChanged, the entity class property will participate in the update check only if its value has been changed since being loaded into the DataContext object's cache. If the UpdateCheck attribute is not specified, it defaults to UpdateCheck.Always.

To understand how conflict detection technically works, it may help you to understand how it is currently implemented. When you call the SubmitChanges method, the change processor generates the necessary SQL statements to persist all changes in the entity objects to the database. When it needs to update a record, instead of merely supplying the record's primary key in the where clause to find the appropriate record to update, it specifies the primary key, as well as potentially all columns participating in conflict detection. If an entity class property's UpdateCheck attribute property is specified as UpdateCheck.Always, that property's mapped column and its original value will always be specified in the where clause. If the entity class property's UpdateCheck property is specified as UpdateCheck.WhenChanged, then only if the entity object's current value for a property has been changed from its original value will that property's mapped column, and its original value be specified in the where clause. If an entity class property's UpdateCheck property is specified as UpdateCheck.Never, that entity class property's mapped column will not be specified in the where clause.

For example, assume that the Customer entity object specifies the UpdateCheck property for CompanyName as UpdateCheck.Always, ContactName as UpdateCheck.WhenChanged, and ContactTitle as UpdateCheck.Never. If all three of those entity class properties were modified in the entity object for a customer, the generated SQL statement would look like this:

```
Update Customers
Set CompanyName = 'Art Sanders Park',
  ContactName = 'Samuel Arthur Sanders',
  ContactTitle = 'President'
Where CompanyName = 'Lonesome Pine Restaurant' AND
  ContactName = 'Fran Wilson' AND
  CustomerID = 'LONEP'
```

In that example, the column values in the where clause are the properties' original values as read from the database when the entity object was first retrieved, a SubmitChanges method call successfully completed, or the Refresh method was called.

You can see that, since the CompanyName property's UpdateCheck property is specified as UpdateCheck.Always, it will be in the where clause whether or not it has changed in the entity object. Since the ContactName property's UpdateCheck property is specified as UpdateCheck.WhenChanged and that entity class property's value has changed in the entity object, it is included in the where clause. And, since the ContactTitle property's UpdateCheck property is specified as UpdateCheck.Never, it was not specified in the where clause despite that the entity class property's value has changed.

When that SQL statement is executed, if any of the entity class properties' values specified in the where clause do not match what is in the database, the record will not be found, so it will not get updated. This is how concurrency conflicts are detected. If a conflict occurs, a ChangeConflictException is thrown. Let's examine Listing 17-1 to see exactly what the generated update statement looks like.

Listing 17-1. Causing a Database Update to See How Concurrency Conflicts Are Detected

```
Northwind db = new Northwind(@"Data Source=.\SQLEXPRESS;Initial
Catalog=Northwind");

db.Log = Console.Out;

Customer cust = db.Customers.Where(c => c.CustomerID == "LONEP").SingleOrDefault();
string name = cust.ContactName; // to restore later.

cust.ContactName = "Neo Anderson";

db.SubmitChanges();
```

```
//  Restore database.
cust.ContactName = name;
db.SubmitChanges();
```

There isn't much to this query. In fact, the only thing worth pointing out about the query is that we call the SingleOrDefault operator instead of the Single operator, like we typically have, just to provide more protection against a record not being found. In this case, we know the record will be found, but we want to start reminding you that you need to make sure the code safely handles these situations.

All that we are really interested in seeing is the generated update statement. Let's look at the results:

```
SELECT [t0].[CustomerID], [t0].[CompanyName], [t0].[ContactName],
[t0].[ContactTitle], [t0].[Address], [t0].[City], [t0].[Region], [t0].[PostalCode],
[t0].[Country], [t0].[Phone], [t0].[Fax]
FROM [dbo].[Customers] AS [t0]
WHERE [t0].[CustomerID] = @p0
-- @p0: Input String (Size = 5; Prec = 0; Scale = 0) [LONEP]
-- Context: SqlProvider(Sql2008) Model: AttributedMetaModel Build: 3.5.30729.4926
UPDATE [dbo].[Customers]
SET [ContactName] = @p11
WHERE ([CustomerID] = @p0) AND ([CompanyName] = @p1) AND ([ContactName] = @p2) AND
([ContactTitle] = @p3) AND ([Address] = @p4) AND ([City] = @p5) AND ([Region] =
@p6)
AND ([PostalCode] = @p7) AND ([Country] = @p8) AND ([Phone] = @p9) AND ([Fax] =
@p10)
-- @p0: Input StringFixedLength (Size = 5; Prec = 0; Scale = 0) [LONEP]
-- @p1: Input String (Size = 24; Prec = 0; Scale = 0) [Lonesome Pine Restaurant]
-- @p2: Input String (Size = 11; Prec = 0; Scale = 0) [Fran Wilson]
-- @p3: Input String (Size = 13; Prec = 0; Scale = 0) [Sales Manager]
-- @p4: Input String (Size = 18; Prec = 0; Scale = 0) [89 Chiaroscuro Rd.]
-- @p5: Input String (Size = 8; Prec = 0; Scale = 0) [Portland]
-- @p6: Input String (Size = 2; Prec = 0; Scale = 0) [OR]
-- @p7: Input String (Size = 5; Prec = 0; Scale = 0) [97219]
-- @p8: Input String (Size = 3; Prec = 0; Scale = 0) [USA]
-- @p9: Input String (Size = 14; Prec = 0; Scale = 0) [(503) 555-9573]
-- @p10: Input String (Size = 14; Prec = 0; Scale = 0) [(503) 555-9646]
-- @p11: Input String (Size = 12; Prec = 0; Scale = 0) [Neo Anderson]
-- Context: SqlProvider(Sql2005) Model: AttributedMetaModel Build: 3.5.20706.1

UPDATE [dbo].[Customers]
SET [ContactName] = @p11
WHERE ([CustomerID] = @p0) AND ([CompanyName] = @p1) AND ([ContactName] = @p2) AND
([ContactTitle] = @p3) AND ([Address] = @p4) AND ([City] = @p5) AND ([Region] =
@p6)
AND ([PostalCode] = @p7) AND ([Country] = @p8) AND ([Phone] = @p9) AND ([Fax] =
@p10)
-- @p0: Input StringFixedLength (Size = 5; Prec = 0; Scale = 0) [LONEP]
```

```
-- @p1: Input String (Size = 24; Prec = 0; Scale = 0) [Lonesome Pine Restaurant]
-- @p2: Input String (Size = 12; Prec = 0; Scale = 0) [Neo Anderson]
-- @p3: Input String (Size = 13; Prec = 0; Scale = 0) [Sales Manager]
-- @p4: Input String (Size = 18; Prec = 0; Scale = 0) [89 Chiaroscuro Rd.]
-- @p5: Input String (Size = 8; Prec = 0; Scale = 0) [Portland]
-- @p6: Input String (Size = 2; Prec = 0; Scale = 0) [OR]
-- @p7: Input String (Size = 5; Prec = 0; Scale = 0) [97219]
-- @p8: Input String (Size = 3; Prec = 0; Scale = 0) [USA]
-- @p9: Input String (Size = 14; Prec = 0; Scale = 0) [(503) 555-9573]
-- @p10: Input String (Size = 14; Prec = 0; Scale = 0) [(503) 555-9646]
-- @p11: Input String (Size = 11; Prec = 0; Scale = 0) [Fran Wilson]
-- Context: SqlProvider(Sql2005) Model: AttributedMetaModel Build: 3.5.20706.1
```

Notice that in the first update statement, the where clause has specified that the ContactName must equal "Fran Wilson", the original value of the ContactName. If some other process had changed the ContactName since we read it, no record would have matched the where clause, so no record would have been updated.

Since none of the entity class properties in the Customer entity class specifies the UpdateCheck attribute property, they all default to UpdateCheck.Always, so all of the mapped entity class properties are specified in the where clause of that update statement.

SubmitChanges()

The concurrency conflict detection occurs when the SubmitChanges method is called. When you call the SubmitChanges method, you have the ability to specify whether the process of saving the changes to the database should abort on the first conflict that occurs or whether it should attempt all changes, collecting the conflicts. You control this behavior with the ConflictMode argument that may be passed to the SubmitChanges method. If you pass ConflictMode.FailOnFirstConflict, as the name suggests, the process will abort after the first conflict occurs. If you pass ConflictMode.ContinueOnConflict, then the process will attempt all the necessary changes even if a conflict occurs. If you choose not to specify a ConflictMode, the SubmitChanges method will default to ConflictMode.FailOnFirstConflict.

Regardless of the ConflictMode you specify, if an ambient transaction is *not* in scope when the SubmitChanges method is called, a transaction will be created for all database changes attempting to be made during the invocation of the SubmitChanges method. If an ambient transaction *is* in scope, the DataContext will enlist in the ambient transaction. If an exception is thrown during the SubmitChanges method call, the transaction will be rolled back. This means that even the unconflicted entity objects whose changes were successfully persisted to the database will be rolled back.

ChangeConflictException

If a concurrency conflict occurs, regardless of whether the ConflictMode is FailOnFirstConflict or ContinueOnConflict, a ChangeConflictException will be thrown.

Catching the ChangeConflictException is how you detect when a concurrency conflict occurs.

Conflict Resolution

Once you have detected the concurrency conflict by catching the `ChangeConflictException`, the next step is most likely to resolve any conflicts. You could choose to take some other action, but resolving the conflicts is the most likely one. When we first read that we would have to resolve conflicts, we envisioned horribly complex code attempting to analyze what to do with each piece of data for every possible circumstance. Fortunately, LINQ to SQL makes this easy by providing a `ResolveAll` and two `Resolve` methods.

RefreshMode

When we actually resolve a conflict using the built-in LINQ to SQL resolution functionality by calling the `ResolveAll` or a `Resolve` method, we control how the conflict is resolved by specifying a `RefreshMode`. The three possible options are `KeepChanges`, `KeepCurrentValues`, and `OverwriteCurrentValues`. These options control which data is retained in the entity object properties' current values when the `DataContext` object performs the resolution.

The `RefreshMode.KeepChanges` option tells the `ResolveAll` or a `Resolve` method to load the changes from the database into the entity class properties' current value for any column changed since the data was initially loaded, unless the current user has also changed the property, in which case that value will be kept. The order of priority of retaining the data, from lowest to highest, is as follows: original entity class property values, reloaded changed database column values, current user's changed entity class property values.

The `RefreshMode.KeepCurrentValues` option tells the `ResolveAll` or `Resolve` method to keep the current user's original entity class property values and changes and to disregard any changes made to the database since the data was initially loaded. The order of priority of retaining the data, from lowest to highest, is as follows: original entity class property values, current user's changed entity class property values.

The `RefreshMode.OverwriteCurrentValues` option tells the `ResolveAll` or a `Resolve` method to load the changes from the database for any columns changed since the data was initially loaded and to disregard the current user's entity class property changes. The order of priority of retaining the data, from lowest to highest, is original entity class property values then reloaded changed column values.

Resolving Conflicts

There are three approaches to resolving conflicts: easiest, easy, and manual. The easiest approach is to merely call the `ResolveAll` method on the `DataContext.ChangeConflicts` collection, passing a `RefreshMode` and an optional `bool` specifying whether to automatically resolve deleted records.

Automatically resolving deleted records means to mark the corresponding deleted entity object as being successfully deleted, even though it wasn't because of the concurrency conflict so that the next time the `SubmitChanges` method is called, the `DataContext` will not attempt to delete the deleted entity object's matching database record again. In essence, we are telling LINQ to SQL to pretend like it was successfully deleted because someone else deleted it first, and that is alright.

The easy approach is to enumerate through each `ObjectChangeConflict` in the `DataContext.ChangeConflicts` collection and call the `Resolve` method on each `ObjectChangeConflict`.

If, however, you need some special handling, you always have the option to handle the resolution yourself by enumerating through the `DataContext` object's `ChangeConflicts` collection and then enumerating through each `ObjectChangeConflict` object's `MemberConflicts` collection, calling the

Resolve method on each MemberChangeConflict object in that collection. Even with manual resolution, methods are provided to make this easy.

DataContext.ChangeConflicts.ResolveAll()

Resolving conflicts gets no easier than this. You merely catch the ChangeConflictException and call the ResolveAll method on the DataContext.ChangeConflicts collection. All you have to do is decide which RefreshMode to use and if you want to automatically resolve deleted records.

Using this approach will cause all conflicts to be resolved the same way based on the RefreshMode passed. If you need more granular control when resolving the conflicts, use one of the slightly more complex approaches we will cover after this approach.

In Listing 17-2, we will resolve conflicts using this approach. Because this example is somewhat complex, we will describe it as we go.

Listing 17-2. An Example Resolving Conflicts with DataContext.ChangeConflicts.ResolveAll()

```
Northwind db = new Northwind(@"Data Source=.\SQLEXPRESS;Initial
Catalog=Northwind");

Customer cust = db.Customers.Where(c => c.CustomerID == "LAZYK").SingleOrDefault();

ExecuteStatementInDb(String.Format(
  @"update Customers
    set ContactName = 'Samuel Arthur Sanders'
    where CustomerID = 'LAZYK'"));
```

We create the Northwind DataContext, query a customer using LINQ to SQL, and make a change to the retrieved customer's ContactName column value in the database using ADO.NET. We have now set up a potential concurrency conflict.

Now, we just need to make a change to our entity object and try to persist it to the database.

```
cust.ContactTitle = "President";
try
{
  db.SubmitChanges(ConflictMode.ContinueOnConflict);
}
catch (ChangeConflictException)
{
```

Notice that we wrap the call to the SubmitChanges method in a try/catch block. To properly detect concurrency conflicts, we catch the ChangeConflictException exception. Now, we just need to call the ResolveAll method and try to persist the changes again.

```
  db.ChangeConflicts.ResolveAll(RefreshMode.KeepChanges);
  try
  {
    db.SubmitChanges(ConflictMode.ContinueOnConflict);
    cust = db.Customers.Where(c => c.CustomerID == "LAZYK").SingleOrDefault();
```

```
      Console.WriteLine("ContactName = {0} : ContactTitle = {1}",
        cust.ContactName, cust.ContactTitle);
  }
  catch (ChangeConflictException)
  {
    Console.WriteLine("Conflict again, aborting.");
  }
}
```

In the preceding code, we call the ResolveAll method and pass a RefreshMode of KeepChanges. We then call the SubmitChanges method again, which is wrapped in its own try/catch block. Then, we query the customer from the database again and display the customer's ContactName and ContactTitle just to prove that neither the ADO.NET change nor our LINQ to SQL change was lost. If that call to the SubmitChanges method throws an exception, we will just report it and abort the effort.

All that is left to do is to restore the database so the example can be run more than once.

```
//  Reset the database.
ExecuteStatementInDb(String.Format(
  @"update Customers
    set ContactName = 'John Steel', ContactTitle = 'Marketing Manager'
    where CustomerID = 'LAZYK'"));
```

If you look closely, disregarding the code to cause the conflict, which you wouldn't normally write, and the code to restore the database at the end of the example, which you also wouldn't normally write, resolving concurrency conflicts with this approach is pretty simple. You wrap the call to the SubmitChanges method in a try/catch block, catch the ChangeConflictException exception, call the ResolveAll method, and repeat the call to the SubmitChanges method. That's about all there is to it. Let's look at the results of Listing 17-2.

```
Executing SQL statement against database with ADO.NET ...
Database updated.
ContactName = Samuel Arthur Sanders : ContactTitle = President
Executing SQL statement against database with ADO.NET ...
Database updated.
```

As you can see in the results, both the ADO.NET change to the ContactName and our LINQ to SQL change to the ContactTitle were persisted to the database. This is a very simple approach for resolving concurrency conflicts.

ObjectChangeConflict.Resolve()

If resolving all conflicts with the same RefreshMode isn't going to work for you, you can take the approach of enumerating through all the conflicts in the DataContext.ChangeConflicts collection and handling each individually. You would handle each one by calling the Resolve method on it. This allows you the ability to pass a different RefreshMode value for each conflict.

Resolving conflicts at this level is akin to resolving them at the entity object level. The `RefreshMode` passed will apply to every entity class property in a conflicted entity object. If you need more control than this allows, consider using the manual approach that we will discuss after this approach.

In Listing 17-3, we demonstrate this approach. The code will be the same as Listing 17-2 except that the call to the `DataContext.ChangeConflicts.ResolveAll` method will be replaced with an enumeration of the `ChangeConflicts` collection.

Listing 17-3. An Example Resolving Conflicts with ObjectChangeConflict.Resolve()

```
Northwind db = new Northwind(@"Data Source=.\SQLEXPRESS;Initial
Catalog=Northwind");

Customer cust = db.Customers.Where(c => c.CustomerID == "LAZYK").SingleOrDefault();

ExecuteStatementInDb(String.Format(
  @"update Customers
    set ContactName = 'Samuel Arthur Sanders'
    where CustomerID = 'LAZYK'"));

cust.ContactTitle = "President";
try
{
  db.SubmitChanges(ConflictMode.ContinueOnConflict);
}
catch (ChangeConflictException)
{
  foreach (ObjectChangeConflict conflict in db.ChangeConflicts)
  {
    Console.WriteLine("Conflict occurred in customer {0}.",
      ((Customer)conflict.Object).CustomerID);
    Console.WriteLine("Calling Resolve ...");
    conflict.Resolve(RefreshMode.KeepChanges);
    Console.WriteLine("Conflict resolved.{0}", System.Environment.NewLine);
  }

  try
  {
    db.SubmitChanges(ConflictMode.ContinueOnConflict);
    cust = db.Customers.Where(c => c.CustomerID == "LAZYK").SingleOrDefault();
    Console.WriteLine("ContactName = {0} : ContactTitle = {1}",
      cust.ContactName, cust.ContactTitle);
  }
  catch (ChangeConflictException)
  {
    Console.WriteLine("Conflict again, aborting.");
  }
```

```
    }

    //  Reset the database.
    ExecuteStatementInDb(String.Format(
      @"update Customers
        set ContactName = 'John Steel', ContactTitle = 'Marketing Manager'
        where CustomerID = 'LAZYK'"));
```

Notice that, instead of calling the `DataContext.ChangeConflicts.ResolveAll` method, we enumerate the `ChangeConflicts` collection and call the `Resolve` method on each `ObjectChangeConflict` object in the collection. Then, as in the previous listing, we call the `SubmitChanges` method again, query the customer again, and display the relevant entity class properties. Of course, we then restore the database.

Here are the results of Listing 17-3:

```
Executing SQL statement against database with ADO.NET ...
Database updated.
Conflict occurred in customer LAZYK.
Calling Resolve ...
Conflict resolved.

ContactName = Samuel Arthur Sanders : ContactTitle = President
Executing SQL statement against database with ADO.NET ...
Database updated.
```

That worked just as we would want. In real production code, you may want to loop on the call to the `SubmitChanges` method and the conflict resolution just to handle the case of bad luck with additional conflicts occurring in that small window of opportunity. If you do, we would make sure you limit the loop to prevent getting stuck in an infinite loop, just in case something is seriously wrong.

MemberChangeConflict.Resolve()

In the first approach, we call a method to resolve all conflicts the same way. This is the easiest approach to resolve conflicts. In the second approach, we call a method to resolve a conflict for a single conflicted entity object. This provides the flexibility of resolving each entity object in a different manner. This is the easy way. What's left? The manual way is the only approach left.

Don't let our description intimidate you. Even with the manual approach, concurrency conflict detection is simpler than you might expect. Taking this approach allows you to apply different `RefreshMode` values to individual entity object properties.

Like the second resolution approach, we will enumerate through the `DataContext.ChangeConflicts` collection's `ObectChangeConflict` objects. But, instead of calling the `Resolve` method on each `ObectChangeConflict` object, we will enumerate through its `MemberConflicts` collection and call each `MemberChangeConflict` object's `Resolve` method.

At this level, a `MemberChangeConflict` object pertains to a specific entity class property from a conflicted entity class object. This allows you to deviate from a common `RefreshMode` for any entity class property you choose.

This `Resolve` method allows you to pass either a `RefreshMode` or the actual value you want the current value to be. This allows great flexibility.

For an example of manual conflict resolution, in Listing 17-4 let's pretend there is a requirement that if there is ever a conflict with the `ContactName` column in the database, the code must leave the database value as it is, but any other column in a record may be updated.

To implement this, we will use the same basic code as in Listing 17-3, but instead of calling the Resolve method on the `ObjectChangeConflict` object, we will enumerate through each object's `MemberConflicts` collection. Then, for each `MemberChangeConflict` object in that collection, if the entity object property in conflict is the `ContactName` property, we will maintain the value in the database by passing a `RefreshMode` of `RefreshMode.OverwriteCurrentValues` to the `Resolve` method. If the conflicted entity object property is not the `ContactName` property, we will maintain our value by passing a `RefreshMode` of `RefreshMode.KeepChanges` to the `Resolve` method.

Also, to make the example more interesting, when we update the database with ADO.NET to create a conflict, we will also update the `ContactTitle` column too. This will cause two entity object properties to be conflicted. One, the `ContactName`, should be handled so that the database value is maintained. The other, the `ContactTitle`, should be handled so that the LINQ to SQL value is maintained.

Let's look at Listing 17-4.

Listing 17-4. *An Example of Manually Resolving Conflicts*

```
Northwind db = new Northwind(@"Data Source=.\SQLEXPRESS;Initial
Catalog=Northwind");

Customer cust = db.Customers.Where(c => c.CustomerID == "LAZYK").SingleOrDefault();

ExecuteStatementInDb(String.Format(
  @"update Customers
    set ContactName = 'Samuel Arthur Sanders',
      ContactTitle = 'CEO'
    where CustomerID = 'LAZYK'"));

cust.ContactName = "Viola Sanders";
cust.ContactTitle = "President";
try
{
  db.SubmitChanges(ConflictMode.ContinueOnConflict);
}
catch (ChangeConflictException)
{
  foreach (ObjectChangeConflict conflict in db.ChangeConflicts)
  {
    Console.WriteLine("Conflict occurred in customer {0}.",
      ((Customer)conflict.Object).CustomerID);
    foreach (MemberChangeConflict memberConflict in conflict.MemberConflicts)
    {
      Console.WriteLine("Calling Resolve for {0} ...",
        memberConflict.Member.Name);
```

```
      if (memberConflict.Member.Name.Equals("ContactName"))
      {
        memberConflict.Resolve(RefreshMode.OverwriteCurrentValues);
      }
      else
      {
        memberConflict.Resolve(RefreshMode.KeepChanges);
      }

      Console.WriteLine("Conflict resolved.{0}", System.Environment.NewLine);
    }
  }

  try
  {
    db.SubmitChanges(ConflictMode.ContinueOnConflict);
    cust = db.Customers.Where(c => c.CustomerID == "LAZYK").SingleOrDefault();
    Console.WriteLine("ContactName = {0} : ContactTitle = {1}",
      cust.ContactName, cust.ContactTitle);
  }
  catch (ChangeConflictException)
  {
    Console.WriteLine("Conflict again, aborting.");
  }
}

// Reset the database.
ExecuteStatementInDb(String.Format(
  @"update Customers
    set ContactName = 'John Steel', ContactTitle = 'Marketing Manager'
    where CustomerID = 'LAZYK'"));
```

One of the significant changes is that we also update the ContactTitle with ADO.NET. This causes two entity object properties to be conflicted when we call the SubmitChanges method. Then, instead of calling the Resolve method on the ObjectChangeConflict object, we enumerate through its MemberConflicts collection examining each entity object property. If the property is the ContactName entity object property, we call the Resolve method with a RefreshMode of RefreshMode.OverwriteCurrentValues to maintain the value from the database. If the entity object property is not the ContactName property, we call the Resolve method with a RefreshMode of RefreshMode.KeepChanges to maintain the value set in our LINQ to SQL code.

We know you can hardly wait. Let's look at the results of Listing 17-4:

```
Executing SQL statement against database with ADO.NET ...
Database updated.
Conflict occurred in customer LAZYK.
```

```
Calling Resolve for ContactName ...
Conflict resolved.

Calling Resolve for ContactTitle ...
Conflict resolved.

ContactName = Samuel Arthur Sanders : ContactTitle = President
Executing SQL statement against database with ADO.NET ...
Database updated.
```

You can see in the results that both the ContactName and ContactTitle entity object properties were conflicted and resolved. Also, by examining the output of the ContactName and ContactTitle properties at the end, you can see that the value from the database was maintained for the ContactName property, but the value for the ContactTitle from the database was ignored, and the value set by LINQ to SQL was maintained. This is just exactly what we were looking for.

The actual code handling the conflict resolution manually is really not that bad. But, of course, all this effort is only necessary for specialized conflict resolution.

Pessimistic Concurrency

Just as its name implies, pessimistic concurrency assumes the worst—that you can just count on the fact that a record you read will be conflicted by the time you can update it. Fortunately, we have the ability to do this as well. It's as simple as wrapping the read and the update to the database in a transaction.

With the pessimistic concurrency approach, there are no actual conflicts to resolve, because the database is locked by your transaction, so no one else can be modifying it behind your back.

To test this, we will create a TransactionScope object and obtain an entity object for customer LAZYK. Then, we will create another TransactionScope object with a TransactionScopeOption of RequiresNew. We do this so the ADO.NET code does not participate in the ambient transaction created by the previously created TransactionScope object. After that, we will attempt to update that same record in the database using ADO.NET. Since there is already an open transaction locking the database, the ADO.NET update statement will be blocked and eventually timeout. Next, we will update the entity object's ContactName, call the SubmitChanges method, query the customer again to display the ContactName to prove it was updated by LINQ to SQL, and complete the transaction.

■ **Note** You must add a reference to the System.Transactions.dll assembly to your project for the following example to compile.

Listing 17-5 contains the code for this example.

Listing 17-5. An Example of Pessimistic Concurrency

```
Northwind db = new Northwind(@"Data Source=.\SQLEXPRESS;Initial
Catalog=Northwind");

using (System.Transactions.TransactionScope transaction =
  new System.Transactions.TransactionScope())
{
  Customer cust =
    db.Customers.Where(c => c.CustomerID == "LAZYK").SingleOrDefault();

  try
  {
    Console.WriteLine("Let's try to update LAZYK's ContactName with ADO.NET.");
    Console.WriteLine("  Please be patient, we have to wait for timeout ...");
    using (System.Transactions.TransactionScope t2 =
      new System.Transactions.TransactionScope(
        System.Transactions.TransactionScopeOption.RequiresNew))
    {
      ExecuteStatementInDb(String.Format(
        @"update Customers
          set ContactName = 'Samuel Arthur Sanders'
          where CustomerID = 'LAZYK'"));

      t2.Complete();
    }

    Console.WriteLine("LAZYK's ContactName updated.{0}",
      System.Environment.NewLine);
  }
  catch (Exception ex)
  {
    Console.WriteLine(
      "Exception occurred trying to update LAZYK with ADO.NET:{0}  {1}{0}",
      System.Environment.NewLine, ex.Message);
  }

  cust.ContactName = "Viola Sanders";
  db.SubmitChanges();

  cust = db.Customers.Where(c => c.CustomerID == "LAZYK").SingleOrDefault();
  Console.WriteLine("Customer Contact Name: {0}", cust.ContactName);

  transaction.Complete();
}
```

```
//  Reset the database.
ExecuteStatementInDb(String.Format(
  @"update Customers
    set ContactName = 'John Steel',
      ContactTitle = 'Marketing Manager'
    where CustomerID = 'LAZYK'"));
```

■ **Tip** If you get an exception of type "MSDTC on server '[server]\SQLEXPRESS' is unavailable" when working with any of the examples using the `TransactionScope` object, make sure the service named Distributed Transaction Coordinator is started.

This code is not quite as complex as it may look at first. The first thing we do is create a `TransactionScope` object. We have now taken a pessimistic concurrency approach, preventing anyone from modifying our data. Next, we query our customer using LINQ to SQL. Then, we create another `TransactionScope` object to prevent the ADO.NET code we are about to call from participating in our original `TransactionScope` object's transaction. After creating the second `TransactionScope` object, we attempt to update the customer in the database using ADO.NET. The ADO.NET code will not be able to perform the update because of our initial transaction and a timeout exception will be thrown. We then change the `ContactName` for the customer, persist that change to the database by calling the `SubmitChanges` method, query the customer again, and display the customer's `ContactName` to prove the change was persisted. We then complete the original transaction by calling the `Complete` method on it.

Of course, as always, we reset the database at the end of the code. Here are the results of Listing 17-5:

```
Let's try to update LAZYK's ContactName with ADO.NET.
  Please be patient, we have to wait for timeout ...
Executing SQL statement against database with ADO.NET ...
Exception occurred trying to update LAZYK with ADO.NET:
  Timeout expired.  The timeout period elapsed prior to completion of the operation
or the server is not responding.
The statement has been terminated.

Customer Contact Name: Viola Sanders
Executing SQL statement against database with ADO.NET ...
Database updated.
```

Notice that when we attempt to update the database with ADO.NET, a timeout exception occurs.

Don't get fooled by deferred query execution. Remember that many of the LINQ operators are deferred. In the case of this example, our LINQ to SQL query is calling the `SingleOrDefault` operator, so the query is not deferred, thereby requiring that the query must be declared inside the scope of the `TransactionScope` object. Had we not called the `SingleOrDefault` operator, that query could have been declared before the creation of the `TransactionScope` object, as long as the actual query got executed inside the `TransactionScope` object's scope. Therefore, we could have merely had the LINQ query return an `IEnumerable<T>` sequence prior to the creation of the `TransactionScope` object and then inside the scope of the `TransactionScope` object call the `SingleOrDefault` operator on that returned sequence, returning the single `Customer` matching our query.

When using this approach, you should always be conscious of just how much work you are doing inside the scope of the `TransactionScope` object because you will have the relevant records in the database locked during that time.

An Alternative Approach for Middle Tiers and Servers

An alternative approach exists for handling concurrency conflicts when they occur on a middle tier or server. Sometimes, when a concurrency conflict occurs, it may be easier to just create a new `DataContext`, apply changes, and call the `SubmitChanges` method again.

Consider for example an ASP.NET web application. Because of the connectionless nature of the browser client to web server communication, you very well may be creating the `DataContext` new every time an HTTP post is made to the web server and a LINQ to SQL query needs to be made. Remember that since data read from the database is immediately considered stale, it is not a good idea to keep a `DataContext` object open for very long with the intent to make changes.

When a user first goes to a web page and the data is retrieved, it may not make sense to hang on to the `DataContext` object waiting for a postback to attempt to update that data. The `DataContext` will not survive while waiting for the postback anyway, unless it is somehow persisted between connections, such as in session state. But even if it does survive, the delay between the connections could be very long and may never even occur. The longer you wait between the database read that occurred when first rendering the page and the attempted database update on a subsequent postback, the more stale your data is going to be. Rather than attempting to hold onto the `DataContext` for this type of scenario, it may make more sense to just create a `DataContext` on each postback when data needs to be saved. If this is the case and a concurrency conflict occurs, there may be little harm in creating another `DataContext`, reapplying the changes, and calling the `SubmitChanges` method again. And because the delay will be so short between the time you first read the data on the postback, apply your changes, and call the `SubmitChanges` method, it is unlikely that you will have concurrency conflicts in the first attempt, much less a second.

If you decide to take this approach, on the postback, after constructing the new `DataContext`, you could retrieve the necessary entity object as we just discussed, or there is another approach. Instead of retrieving the entity object, you could create a new entity object, populate the necessary properties with the appropriate values, and attach it to the appropriate table using the `Table<T>` object's `Attach` method. At this point, it's as though the entity object *was* retrieved from the database barring the fact that every field in the object may not be populated.

Prior to attaching an entity object to a `Table<T>`, you must set the necessary entity class properties to the appropriate values. This doesn't mean you have to query the database to get the values; they could come from anywhere, such as another tier. The necessary entity class properties include all entity class properties making up the primary key or establishing identity, all entity class properties you are going to change, and all entity class properties that participate in the update check. You must include the entity class properties establishing identity so that the `DataContext` can properly track identity of the entity class object. You must include all entity class properties you are going to change so that they can be updated and so concurrency conflict detection can work properly. Also, you must include all the entity class properties participating in the update check for the concurrency conflict detection. If the entity class has an entity class property specifying the `IsVersion` attribute property with a value of `true` for the `Column` attribute, that entity class property must be set prior to calling the `Attach` method.

Let's take a look at how this is done in Listing 17-6.

Listing 17-6. An Example of Using Attach() to Attach a Newly Constructed Entity Object

```
Northwind db = new Northwind(@"Data Source=.\SQLEXPRESS;Initial
Catalog=Northwind");

//  Create an entity object.
Console.WriteLine("Constructing an empty Customer object.");
Customer cust = new Customer();

//  First, all fields establishing identity must get set.
Console.WriteLine("Setting the primary keys.");
cust.CustomerID = "LAZYK";

//  Next, every field that will change must be set.
Console.WriteLine("Setting the fields we will change.");
cust.ContactName = "John Steel";

//  Last, all fields participating in update check must be set.
//  Unfortunately, for the Customer entity class, that is all of them.
Console.WriteLine("Setting all fields participating in update check.");
cust.CompanyName = "Lazy K Kountry Store";
cust.ContactTitle = "Marketing Manager";
cust.Address = "12 Orchestra Terrace";
cust.City = "Walla Walla";
cust.Region = "WA";
cust.PostalCode = "99362";
cust.Country = "USA";
cust.Phone = "(509) 555-7969";
cust.Fax = "(509) 555-6221";

//  Now let's attach to the Customers Table<T>.
Console.WriteLine("Attaching to the Customers Table<Customer>.");
db.Customers.Attach(cust);

//  At this point we can make our changes and call SubmitChanges().
Console.WriteLine("Making our changes and calling SubmitChanges().");
cust.ContactName = "Vickey Rattz";
db.SubmitChanges();

cust = db.Customers.Where(c => c.CustomerID == "LAZYK").SingleOrDefault();
Console.WriteLine("ContactName in database = {0}", cust.ContactName);

Console.WriteLine("Restoring changes and calling SubmitChanges().");
cust.ContactName = "John Steel";
db.SubmitChanges();
```

As you can see, we set our primary key entity class properties, the entity class properties we are going to change, and the entity class properties participating in update check. As we mentioned previously, we must set these properties to the appropriate values. That doesn't mean that we have to query the database, though. Perhaps we stored them in hidden variables or view state, or they were passed from another tier. We then call the `Attach` method on the `Customers Table<Customer>`. Next, we make our changes and finally call the `SubmitChanges` method. Next, we query the customer from the database and display the `ContactName` just to prove it was indeed changed in the database. Then, as always, we restore the database to its previous state. Let's look at the output of Listing 17-6:

```
Constructing an empty Customer object.
Setting the primary keys.
Setting the fields we will change.
Setting all fields participating in update check.
Attaching to the Customers Table<Customer>.
Making our changes and calling SubmitChanges().
ContactName in database = Vickey Rattz
Restoring changes and calling SubmitChanges().
```

Inserting or deleting entity class objects does not require this approach. You may merely insert or delete an entity class object prior to calling the `SubmitChanges` method. See the sections "Inserts" and "Deletes" in Chapter 14.

Summary

Well, it was a long time coming. We mentioned concurrency conflict detection and resolution countless times in the preceding LINQ to SQL chapters. It was time for us to pay the piper and give you the scoop.

We are quite impressed with how simple LINQ to SQL has made detecting and resolving concurrency conflicts, and we hope you are too. We hope you have found an inner peace with this often intimidating topic.

We are nearly finished with our LINQ to SQL journey. In the next and final chapter, we will try to wrap up LINQ to SQL with \some miscellaneous information.

■ ■ ■

CHAPTER 18

Additional LINQ to SQL Capabilities

In this final LINQ to SQL chapter, we will finish up with just a few miscellaneous topics. First on the list are database views, followed by entity class inheritance, and finally, we want to talk a little more about transactions.

Prerequisites for Running the Examples

To run the examples in this chapter, you will need to have obtained the extended version of the Northwind database and generated entity classes for it. Please read and follow the instructions in Chapter 12's "Prerequisites for Running the Examples" section.

Using the LINQ to SQL API

To run the examples in this chapter, you may need to add the appropriate references and using directives to your project. Please read and follow the instructions in Chapter 12's "Using the LINQ to SQL API" section.

Using the LINQ to XML API

Some of the examples in this chapter require the addition of a using directive for the System.Xml.Linq namespace.

Database Views

When we generate the entity classes for the Northwind database in Chapter 12, we specify the /views option to have entity class mappings for database views created, but we have yet to mention views and how to query them. The entity class generation tools, SQLMetal and the Object Relational Designer, declare a Table<T> property in the [Your]DataContext class for each database view and create a corresponding entity class T. You query them just like tables. In general, they behave just like tables except that they are read-only.

Because the entity classes generated for views do not contain entity class properties that are mapped as primary keys, they are read-only. If you consider that without primary keys, the DataContext has no effective way to provide identity tracking, this makes sense.

For example, the Northwind database has a view named Category Sales for 1997. Because of this, SQLMetal generated a public property named CategorySalesFor1997s:

A Public Property for a Database View

```
public System.Data.Linq.Table<CategorySalesFor1997> CategorySalesFor1997s
{
  get
  {
    return this.GetTable<CategorySalesFor1997>();
  }
}
```

SQLMetal also generated a `CategorySalesFor1997` entity class for us. Let's take a look at querying a database view in Listing 18-1.

Listing 18-1. *Querying a Database View*

```
Northwind db = new Northwind(@"Data Source=.\SQLEXPRESS;Initial
Catalog=Northwind");

IQueryable<CategorySalesFor1997> seq = from c in db.CategorySalesFor1997s
                                       where c.CategorySales > (decimal)100000.00
                                       orderby c.CategorySales descending
                                       select c;

foreach (CategorySalesFor1997 c in seq)
{
  Console.WriteLine("{0} : {1:C}", c.CategoryName, c.CategorySales);
}
```

Notice that in Listing 18-1, we query the view just like a table. Let's take a look at the results:

```
Dairy Products : $114,749.78
Beverages : $102,074.31
```

As we mentioned, views are read-only. In Listing 18-2, we will attempt to insert a record into a view.

Listing 18-2. *Attempting to Insert a Record into a View That Will Not Succeed*

```
Northwind db = new Northwind(@"Data Source=.\SQLEXPRESS;Initial
Catalog=Northwind");

db.CategorySalesFor1997s.InsertOnSubmit(
  new CategorySalesFor1997
    { CategoryName = "Legumes", CategorySales = 79043.92m });
```

Notice that in Listing 18-2 we do not even bother to call the `SubmitChanges` method. This is because we know the code will not make it that far without an exception being thrown. Let's look at the results:

```
Unhandled Exception: System.InvalidOperationException: Can't perform Create, Update
or Delete operations on 'Table(CategorySalesFor1997)' because it has no primary
key.

...
```

Allow us to provide a warning, though. Although the InsertOnSubmit and DeleteOnSubmit methods will throw exceptions when called on a Table<T> mapped to a database view, nothing will prevent you from making changes to a view's entity object's property. You can change the property's value and even call the SubmitChanges method without an exception being thrown, but the change to the view's entity object property will not be persisted to the database.

Entity Class Inheritance

So far, in all our LINQ to SQL discussion, there has been a single entity class mapped to a single table for any table that has an entity class mapped to it. Thus, the mapping between entity classes and tables has been one-to-one so far.

■ **Caution** The example used in this section creates a data model containing Square and Rectangle classes. Geometrically speaking, a square is a rectangle, but a rectangle is not necessarily a square. However, in the data model created for this example, the reverse relationship is true. This class model defines a rectangle to be derived from a square. Therefore, a rectangle is a square, but a square is not necessarily a rectangle. The reasoning for this is explained in the text.

LINQ to SQL also offers an alternative to this, known as *entity class inheritance*. Entity class inheritance allows a class hierarchy to be mapped to a single database table. For that single database table, there must be a base entity class, and the appropriate entity class attribute mappings for the database table must be specified. That base class will contain all properties common to every class in the hierarchy deriving from the base class, while the derived classes will contain only the properties that are specific to that derived class, as is typical with any object model. Here is an example of a base entity class without mapped derived classes:

Our Base Entity Class Without Mapped Derived Classes

```
[Table]
public class Shape
{
  [Column(IsPrimaryKey = true, IsDbGenerated = true,
    DbType = "Int NOT NULL IDENTITY")]
  public int Id;
```

```
[Column(IsDiscriminator = true, DbType = "NVarChar(2)")]
public string ShapeCode;

[Column(DbType = "Int")]
public int StartingX;

[Column(DbType = "Int")]
public int StartingY;
}
```

As you can see, we have specified the Table attribute, and since no Name attribute property has been specified, the base entity class is mapped to the table by the same name as the class, so it is mapped to the Shape table. Don't worry that you do not have a Shape table at this time. We will use the DataContext object's CreateDatabase method later to create the database for us. At this time, no derived classes have been mapped. Later, we will return to this base entity class to map some derived classes.

The idea behind entity class inheritance is that the single database table, Shape, has a database column whose value indicates which entity class the record should be constructed into when it is retrieved by LINQ to SQL. That column is known as the *discriminator column* and is specified using the Column attribute's IsDiscriminator attribute property.

A value in the discriminator column is known as the *discriminator value* or *discriminator code*. When mapping your base entity class to the database table, in addition to the Table attribute, you specify InheritanceMapping attributes to map discriminator codes to classes derived from the base entity class. But at this time, in the preceding Shape class, no inheritance has been mapped.

Notice that we have several public members, each being mapped to a database column, and the database column types have been specified. Specifying the database column types is necessary in our case, because we will be calling the CreateDatabase method later, and to do so, it must know the appropriate type. Also notice that for the ShapeCode member, we have specified that the IsDiscriminator attribute property is set to true, thereby making it the discriminator column. This means the ShapeCode database column will dictate the entity class type used to construct each record into an entity class object.

In this class, we have members for the Id, the ShapeCode, and the starting X and Y coordinates for the shape on the screen. At this time, those are the only members we foresee being common to every shape.

You may then create a class hierarchy by deriving classes from this base class. The derived classes must inherit from the base entity class. The derived classes will not specify the Table attribute but will specify Column attributes for each public member that will be mapped to the database. Here are our derived entity classes:

Our Derived Entity Classes

```
public class Square : Shape
{
    [Column(DBType = "Int")]
    public int Width;
}


public class Rectangle : Square
```

```
{
    [Column(DBType = "Int")]
    public int Length;
}
```

First, for this example, you must forget about the geometric definition for square and rectangle; that is, geometrically speaking, a square is a rectangle, but a rectangle is not necessarily a square. In this entity class inheritance example, because a square's sides must be equal, only one dimension value is needed, width. Since a rectangle needs a width and a length, it will inherit from the square and add a member for the length. In this sense, from a class inheritance perspective, a rectangle is a square, but a square is not a rectangle. Although this is backward from the geometric definition, it fits our inheritance entity class model.

The public members of each of those classes are the members deemed specific to each class. For example, since a Square needs a width, it has a Width property. Since the Rectangle inherits from the Square, in addition to the inherited Width property, it needs a Length property.

We now have our derived classes. All we are missing is the mapping between the discriminator values, and the base and derived entity classes. Adding the necessary InheritanceMapping attributes, our base class now looks like this:

Our Base Entity Class with Derived Class Mappings

```
[Table]
[InheritanceMapping(Code = "G", Type = typeof(Shape), IsDefault = true)]
[InheritanceMapping(Code = "S", Type = typeof(Square))]
[InheritanceMapping(Code = "R", Type = typeof(Rectangle))]
public class Shape
{
  [Column(IsPrimaryKey = true, IsDbGenerated = true,
    DbType = "Int NOT NULL IDENTITY")]
  public int Id;

  [Column(IsDiscriminator = true, DbType = "NVarChar(2)")]
  public string ShapeCode;

  [Column(DbType = "Int")]
  public int StartingX;

  [Column(DbType = "Int")]
  public int StartingY;
}
```

The added mappings map the different discriminator values of the discriminator column to entity classes. Since the ShapeCode column is the discriminator column, if a record has the value "G" in that column, that record will get constructed into a Shape class. If a record has an "S" value in the ShapeCode column, that record will get constructed into a Square class. And, if a record has an "R" value in the ShapeCode column, that record will get constructed into a Rectangle class.

Additionally, there must always be a default mapping for when the discriminator column value does not match any discriminator value mapped to an entity class. You specify which mapping is the default with the IsDefault attribute property. In this example, the mapping to the Shape class is the default. So, if a record has the value "Q" in the ShapeCode column, that record will get constructed into a Shape object by default since it doesn't match any of the specified discriminator codes.

That pretty much covers the concept and mappings of entity class inheritance. Now, let's take a look at the entire DataContext:

Our Entire DataContext Class

```
public partial class TestDB : DataContext
{
  public Table<Shape> Shapes;

  public TestDB(string connection) :
    base(connection)
  {
  }

  public TestDB(System.Data.IDbConnection connection) :
    base(connection)
  {
  }

  public TestDB(string connection,
                System.Data.Linq.Mapping.MappingSource mappingSource) :
    base(connection, mappingSource)
  {
  }

  public TestDB(System.Data.IDbConnection connection,
                System.Data.Linq.Mapping.MappingSource mappingSource) :
    base(connection, mappingSource)
  {
  }
}

[Table]
[InheritanceMapping(Code = "G", Type = typeof(Shape), IsDefault = true)]
[InheritanceMapping(Code = "S", Type = typeof(Square))]
[InheritanceMapping(Code = "R", Type = typeof(Rectangle))]
public class Shape
{
  [Column(IsPrimaryKey = true, IsDbGenerated = true,
    DbType = "Int NOT NULL IDENTITY")]
  public int Id;

  [Column(IsDiscriminator = true, DbType = "NVarChar(2)")]
  public string ShapeCode;
```

```
  [Column(DbType = "Int")]
  public int StartingX;

  [Column(DbType = "Int")]
  public int StartingY;
}

public class Square : Shape
{
  [Column(DbType = "Int")]
  public int Width;
}

public class Rectangle : Square
{
  [Column(DbType = "Int")]
  public int Length;
}
```

There is nothing new here other than putting the previously mentioned classes in a [Your]DataContext named TestDB and adding some constructors for it. Now, in Listing 18-3, we will call some code to actually create the database.

Listing 18-3. *Code Creating Our Entity Class Inheritance Sample Database*

```
TestDB db = new TestDB(@"Data Source=.\SQLEXPRESS;Initial Catalog=TestDB");
db.CreateDatabase();
```

That code doesn't have any screen output, but if you check your database server, you should see a database named TestDB with a single table named Shape. Check the Shape table to convince yourself that no records exist. Now that we have a table, let's create some data using LINQ to SQL in Listing 18-4.

Listing 18-4. *Code Creating Some Data for Our Entity Class Inheritance Sample Database*

```
TestDB db = new TestDB(@"Data Source=.\SQLEXPRESS;Initial Catalog=TestDB");

db.Shapes.InsertOnSubmit(new Square { Width = 4 });
db.Shapes.InsertOnSubmit(new Rectangle { Width = 3, Length = 6 });
db.Shapes.InsertOnSubmit(new Rectangle { Width = 11, Length = 5 });
db.Shapes.InsertOnSubmit(new Square { Width = 6 });
db.Shapes.InsertOnSubmit(new Rectangle { Width = 4, Length = 7 });
db.Shapes.InsertOnSubmit(new Square { Width = 9 });

db.SubmitChanges();
```

There is nothing new in that code. We create our `DataContext` and entity class objects and insert those objects into the `Shapes` table. Then, we call the `SubmitChanges` method to persist them to the database. After running this code, you should see the records in Table 18-1 in the `Shape` table in the `TestDB` database.

Table 18-1. The Results of the Previous Example

Id	ShapeCode	StartingX	StartingY	Length	Width
1	S	0	0	NULL	4
2	R	0	0	6	3
3	R	0	0	5	11
4	S	0	0	NULL	6
5	R	0	0	7	4
6	S	0	0	NULL	9

Since the Id column is an identity column, the values will change if you run the code more than once.

Now, we will perform a couple of queries on the table. First, in Listing 18-5, we will query for the squares, which will include rectangles since rectangles inherit from squares. Then we will query for just the rectangles:

Listing 18-5. Code Querying Our Entity Class Inheritance Sample Database

```
TestDB db = new TestDB(@"Data Source=.\SQLEXPRESS;Initial Catalog=TestDB");

// First we get all squares which will include rectangles.
IQueryable<Shape> squares = from s in db.Shapes
                            where s is Square
                            select s;

Console.WriteLine("The following squares exist.");
foreach (Shape s in squares)
{
  Console.WriteLine("{0} : {1}", s.Id, s.ToString());
}

//  Now I'll get just the rectangles.
IQueryable<Shape> rectangles = from r in db.Shapes
                               where r is Rectangle
                               select r;
```

```
Console.WriteLine("{0}The following rectangles exist.",
System.Environment.NewLine);
foreach (Shape r in rectangles)
{
  Console.WriteLine("{0} : {1}", r.Id, r.ToString());
}
```

In Listing 18-5, we basically perform the same query twice, except in the first one, we query only those records that get instantiated into squares, which includes rectangles because of our class inheritance. In the second query, we query the records that get instantiated into rectangles, which will exclude squares. Here are the results:

```
The following squares exist.
1 : LINQChapter18.Square
2 : LINQChapter18.Rectangle
3 : LINQChapter18.Rectangle
4 : LINQChapter18.Square
5 : LINQChapter18.Rectangle
6 : LINQChapter18.Square

The following rectangles exist.
2 : LINQChapter18.Rectangle
3 : LINQChapter18.Rectangle
5 : LINQChapter18.Rectangle
```

Entity class inheritance can be a useful technique for constructing an entity hierarchy from the database.

Transactions

We have already told you that when the SubmitChanges method is called, if a transaction is not already in scope, the SubmitChanges method will create a transaction for you. In doing so, all database modifications attempted during a single SubmitChanges call will be wrapped within a single transaction. This is very convenient, but what if you need the transaction to extend beyond the scope of a single SubmitChanges method call?

We want to provide an example demonstrating how you would make updates made by multiple SubmitChanges method calls enlist in the same transaction. Even better, we want the SubmitChanges method calls to be updating different databases. In Listing 18-6, we will make changes to a record in both the Northwind database and the TestDB database we just created in the "Entity Class Inheritance" section. Normally, each call to the SubmitChanges method on each of those DataContext objects would be wrapped in its own individual transaction. In our example, we want both calls to the SubmitChanges method to be enlisted in the same transaction.

Since Listing 18-6 will have a little more going on than the typical example does, we will explain it as we go.

■ **Note** For the next example, a reference to the `System.Transactions.dll` assembly must be added to your project.

Listing 18-6. Enlisting in Ambient Transactions

```
Northwind db = new Northwind(@"Data Source=.\SQLEXPRESS;Initial
Catalog=Northwind");
TestDB testDb = new TestDB(@"Data Source=.\SQLEXPRESS;Initial Catalog=TestDB");

Customer cust = db.Customers.Where(c => c.CustomerID == "LONEP").SingleOrDefault();
cust.ContactName = "Barbara Penczek";

Rectangle rect = (Rectangle)testDb.Shapes.Where(s => s.Id == 3).SingleOrDefault();
rect.Width = 15;
```
In the preceding code, we create our `DataContext` object for each database. We then query an entity object from each and make a change to each entity object.
```
try
{
  using (System.Transactions.TransactionScope scope =
    new System.Transactions.TransactionScope())
  {
    db.SubmitChanges();
    testDb.SubmitChanges();
    throw (new Exception("Just to rollback the transaction."));
    //  A warning will result because the next line cannot be reached.
    scope.Complete();
  }
}
catch (Exception ex)
{
  Console.WriteLine(ex.Message);
}
```

■ **Note** Please be aware that since there is code after the exception is thrown, a compiler warning will be produced since the `scope.Complete` method call is unreachable code.

In the preceding code, we instantiate a `TransactionScope` object so that there is an ambient transaction for the `DataContext` objects to enlist in for each call to the `SubmitChanges` method. After we call the `SubmitChanges` method on each `DataContext`, we intentionally throw an exception so that the `scope.Complete` method is not called and the transaction is rolled back.

Had we not wrapped the calls to the SubmitChanges method within the scope of the TransactionScope object, each SubmitChanges method call would have had its own transaction, and its changes would have been committed once the call successfully completed.

Once the exception is thrown in the preceding code, the transaction goes out of scope, and since the Complete method was not called, the transaction is rolled back. At this point, all of the changes made to the database have been rolled back.

```
db.Refresh(System.Data.Linq.RefreshMode.OverwriteCurrentValues, cust);
Console.WriteLine("Contact Name = {0}", cust.ContactName);

testDb.Refresh(System.Data.Linq.RefreshMode.OverwriteCurrentValues, rect);
Console.WriteLine("Rectangle Width = {0}", rect.Width);
```

It is important to remember that, even though the changes were not successfully persisted to the database, the entity objects still contain the modified data. Remember, even when the SubmitChanges method does not complete successfully, the changes are maintained in the entity objects so that you can resolve concurrency conflicts and call the SubmitChanges method again. In this case, the SubmitChanges methods even completed successfully. Also, as you may recall from the "The Results Set Cache Mismatch" section in Chapter 16, querying the objects from the database again will not result in getting the current values from the database. The database query will only determine which entities should be included in the results set for the query. If those entities are already cached in the DataContext, the cached entity objects will be returned. So, to truly know what the values for the previously queried entity objects are in the database, the entity objects must first be refreshed by calling the Refresh method.

So, for each of the two retrieved entity objects, we first refresh it and then display to the console the entity object property we changed to prove that the changes were indeed rolled back. Let's look at the results:

```
Just to rollback the transaction.
Contact Name = Fran Wilson
Rectangle Width = 11
```

As you can see, the values were rolled back in the database.

■ **Tip** If you get an exception of type "MSDTC on server [server]\SQLEXPRESS' is unavailable" when working with any of the examples using the TransactionScope object, make sure the service named Distributed Transaction Coordinator is started.

Summary

In this chapter, we demonstrated how to perform queries on database views. Remember, they effectively get mapped as read-only tables, so you already know how to query them.

Next, we covered entity class inheritance. This is a convenient technique to allow records from a single table to be instantiated into differing but related by inheritance class objects. Last, we delved a little deeper into transactions by demonstrating how to make your LINQ to SQL database updates enlist in ambient transactions.

P A R T 6

■ ■ ■

LINQ to Entities

CHAPTER 19

■ ■ ■

LINQ to Entities Introduction

Listing 19-1. A Simple Example Updating the ContactName of a Customer in the Northwind Database

```
// create the ObjectContext
NorthwindEntities context = new NorthwindEntities();

// retrieve customer LAZY K
Customer cust = (from c in context.Customers
                 where c.CustomerID == "LAZYK"
                 select c).Single<Customer>();

// Update the contact name
cust.ContactName = "Ned Plimpton";

// save the changes
try {
    context.SaveChanges();
} catch (OptimisticConcurrencyException) {
    context.Refresh(RefreshMode.ClientWins,
        context.Customers);
    context.SaveChanges();
}
```

■ **Note** This example requires generation of an entity data model, which we will cover later in this chapter.

In Listing 19-1, we used LINQ to Entities to query the record whose `CustomerID` field is `"LAZYK"` from the Northwind database's Customers table and to return a `Customer` object representing that record. We then updated the `Customer` object's `ContactName` property and saved the change to the database by calling the `SaveChanges` method. Press Ctrl+F5 to run Listing 19-1. There is no console output, but if you check the database, you should see that the `ContactName` for customer LAZYK is now `"Ned Plimpton"`.

■ **Note** This example makes a change to the data in the database without changing it back. The original value of the `ContactName` for customer `LAZYK` is `"John Steel"`. You should change this back so that no subsequent examples behave improperly. You can change it manually, or you can just change the example code and run the example again.

This book uses an extended version of the Northwind database. Please read the "Obtaining the Appropriate Version of the Northwind Database" section later in this chapter for details.

Introducing LINQ to Entities

In Chapter 12, we explained that LINQ to SQL is an entry-level object/relational mapping system. LINQ to Entities is part of the ADO.NET Entity Framework, which offers more flexibility and more features than LINQ to SQL does but which has lingered behind LINQ to SQL in terms of adoption because of increased complexity and earlier releases that lacked key features.

Listing 19-1 does the same thing as Listing 12-1, which we used to introduce LINQ to SQL. Take a moment to compare Listings 19-1 and 12-1, and you'll see that they look pretty similar.

The Entity Framework is designed to work with any ADO-supported database out of the box (rather than just SQL Server) and even has its own dialect of vendor-neutral SQL that you can use as an alternative to LINQ. In fact, the Entity Framework does so much that it could fill its own book. In this book, we'll show you how to get up and running with an emphasis on the parts of the Entity Framework that relate to LINQ to Entities, but we will be barely scratching the surface of all the Entity Framework features.

You might be confused about the names. After all, didn't we just spend the past few chapters talking about entity classes as part of LINQ to SQL? The answer is yes—LINQ to SQL and the Entity Framework do some of the same things, so some terms are common to both.

Much as with LINQ to SQL, LINQ to Entities lets you work with objects that represent the data in your database—perform LINQ queries, change values, and add and delete objects. And, just as with LINQ to SQL, the first step toward using these features is to generate the classes that map the contents of your database into objects—something we do by creating an entity data model (EDM). The EDM contains the set of objects and properties that we will use to interact with our data.

In Listing 19-1, we first had to instantiate an instance of the `NorthwindEntities` class. That class is derived from the `System.Data.Objects.ObjectContext` class, and we will cover this class in-depth in the following chapters. This is the entry point into the EDM—much like the `DataContext` class is for LINQ to SQL. The `NorthwindEntities` class creates the connection to the database for us when we create a new instance and takes care of storing changes for us when we call the `SaveChanges` method.

Next, we retrieved a single customer from the database into a `Customer` object. That `Customer` object is an instantiation of the `Customer` entity class, which is part of the entity data model. We show you how to generate the EDM for the Northwind database later in this chapter. After we retrieved the `Customer`, we updated one of the object's properties and called the `SaveChanges` method to write the changes to the database. We wrapped the `SaveChanges` method in a `try/catch` block to deal with any potential concurrency conflicts—we'll show you how to handle concurrency issues in Chapter 20.

Before you can run this example or any of the others in this chapter, you will need to create an entity data model for the Northwind database. Please read the "Prerequisites for Running the Examples" section for details.

As we did with LINQ to SQL, we will start off by giving you an overview of the key parts of LINQ to Entities. Some of what we say about LINQ to Entities will be in the form of comparison to LINQ to SQL, so if you have not read those chapters, you should do so before proceeding. In the first example at the beginning of this chapter, we are using a derived `ObjectContext` class, which is the `NorthwindEntities` class; an entity class, which is the `Customer` class; concurrency conflict detection and resolution; and database updates via the `SaveChanges` method. We need to give you some background on each of these components before we begin so that you will have a basic understanding of the foundation of LINQ to Entities and the broader ADO.NET Entity Framework.

The ObjectContext

The `ObjectContext` class is the key to accessing an entity data model and is the equivalent of the `DataContext` class that we saw in LINQ to SQL. The `ObjectContext` class is responsible for creating and managing the connection to the database, tracking changes, and managing persistence. We'll go into etail later, but for now it is enough to know that it is the `ObjectContext` class that is connecting us to the database when we create a new instance of `NorthwindEntities`, and it is the same class that tracks the changes we made to the `Customer` object and that translates it to a SQL statement that persisted our change when we called the `SaveChanges` method.

Usually, you use a class derived from `ObjectContext`, created for you when you generate the EDM from a database. We show you how to do this for the Northwind database later in this chapter. The name is chosen for you based on the name of the database, in the form `[Database]Entities`. You can see from Listing 19-1 that we ended up with a class called `NorthwindEntities` for the Northwind database.

The derived class, `[Database]Entities`, will have an `ObjectSet<T>` property for each database table you select when you create the EDM, where `T` is the type of entity class that is created to represent a record in that table. For example, the `NorthwindEntities` class we used in Listing 19-1 has a public property called `Customers`, which is an `OrderSet<Customer>`. We used this in the listing to perform a LINQ query against the set of customers.

Entity Classes

Entity classes in the Entity Framework have a lot in common with those we covered in the LINQ to SQL chapter. They are .NET types that provide a mapping to the relational data structure of the database. The Entity Framework allows for very sophisticated mapping between entity classes and relational data, which can span different databases and be abstracted in some interesting ways. We are going to keep things simple in this book because we want to focus on the LINQ aspects—but if you need heavy-duty ORM features, the Entity Framework is a candidate you should consider.

You will be able to detect the existence of entity classes in our examples when you see classes or objects that have the singular form of a Northwind database table name. For example, in Listing 19-1, we use a class named `Customer`. Because *Customer* is the singular form of *Customers* and the Northwind database has a table named Customers, this is your clue that the `Customer` class is an entity class for the Northwind database's Customers table.

The entity data model Wizard, which you'll see shortly, has an option to pluralize the names of tables when creating entity classes—so when it finds a database table called Customers, it creates an entity class called `Customer` to represent an item in that table. This is the same approach as with the `/pluralize` option for SQLMetal that you saw in Chapter 12, and it can really make a difference to code readability when it is used.

Associations

An *association* is the term used to designate a primary key to foreign key relationship between two entity classes. In a one-to-many relationship, the result of an association is that the parent class, the class containing the primary key, contains a collection of the child classes, the classes having the foreign key.

The collection is stored in an `EntityCollection<T>`, where `T` is the type of the child entity class. For many-to-many relationships, each entity class maintains an `EntityCollection<T>`, where `T` is the other entity type in the relationship.

The entity collections are accessible using public properties with the name of the foreign key. So, for example, to access orders associated with a customer in the Northwind database, you would access the `Customer.Orders` property, which will return an `EntityCollection<Order>`.

The benefit of associations between entity types is that it allows you to navigate through your data seamlessly and without having to take into account the fact that the data may be contained in multiple tables or even across multiple databases.

Prerequisites for Running the Examples

This and the following LINQ to Entities chapters use the same *extended* Northwind database that we used for the LINQ to SQL chapters. We need to generate an entity data model for the Northwind database.

Obtaining the Appropriate Version of the Northwind Database

For consistency, we have used the same extended version of Microsoft's Northwind sample database that we used for the LINQ to SQL chapters. We have included the extended version of the Northwind database with the source code for this book, which you can download from the Apress site.

Generating the Northwind Entity Data Model

You can generate EDMs either using the `EdmGen` command-line tool or using Visual Studio 2010. We will show you how to use the graphical Visual Studio wizard. First, right-click your project, select Add ➤ New Item from the pop-up context menu, and then select ADO.NET Entity Data Model from the list. Edit the name of the data model. Since we are using the Northwind database, we used the name `NorthwindDataModel.edmx`. Click the Add button, and the Entity Data Model Wizard will start, as shown by Figure 19-1.

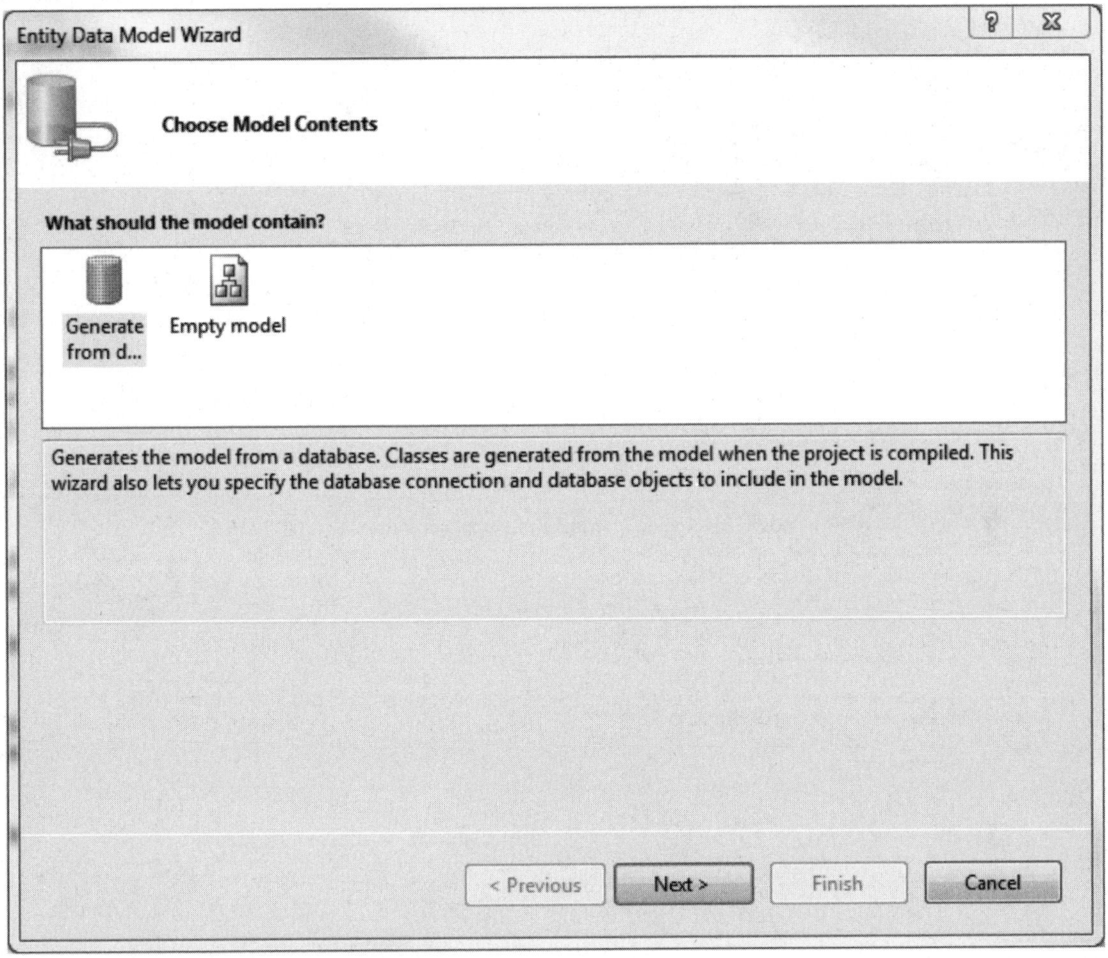

Figure 19-1. *The first screen of the Entity Data Model Wizard*

You can create an entity data model from scratch or have one generated from a database. We want to generate an EDM for the Northwind database, so select the "Generate from database" option in the wizard, and click Next to move to the data connection screen, shown by Figure 19-2.

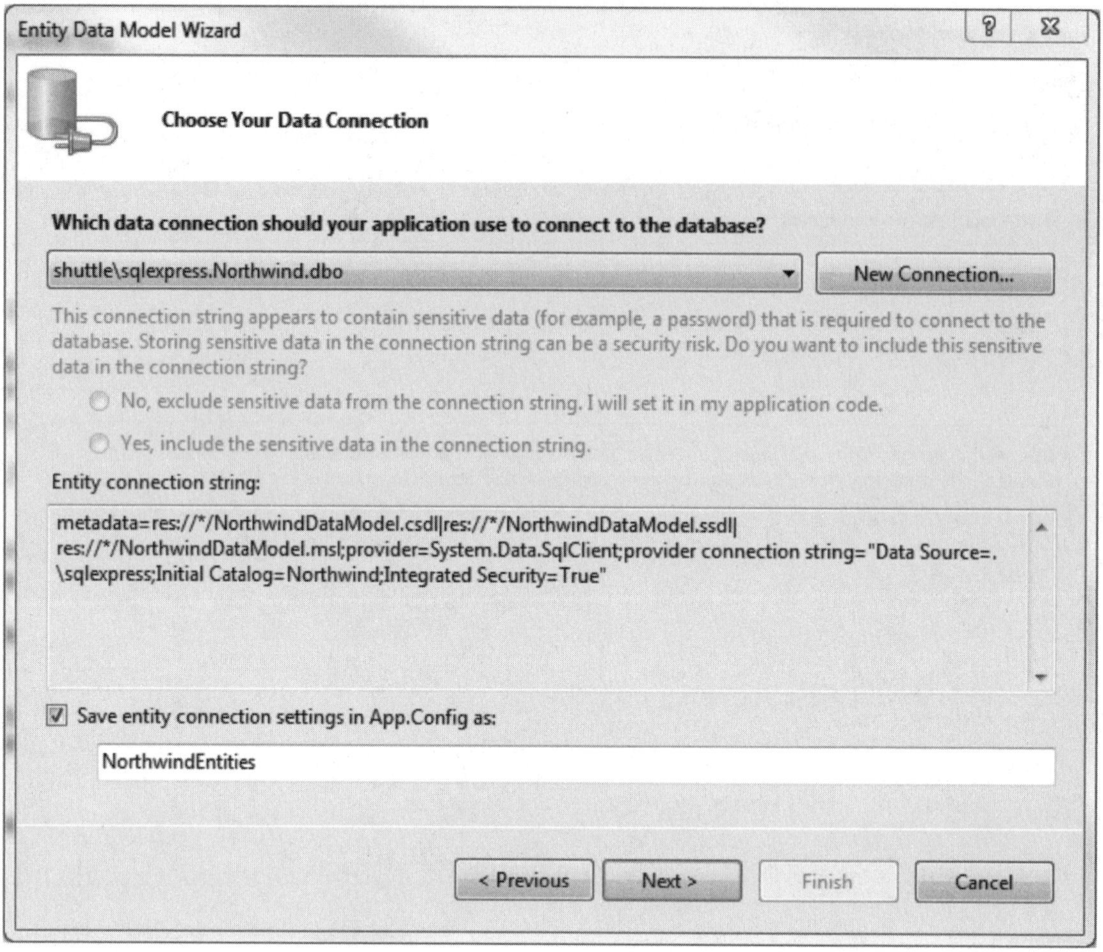

Figure 19-2. The data connection screen from the Entity Data Model Wizard

You use this screen to select the database from which the EDM will be generated. In the figure, we have selected the extended Northwind database, which we have previously attached to SQL Server 2008. What you see will differ based on the location of your database. You will at least see a server name other than `shuttle`, which is one of our development machines. Select the connection you want, and click Next to move to the next wizard screen, shown by Figure 19-3.

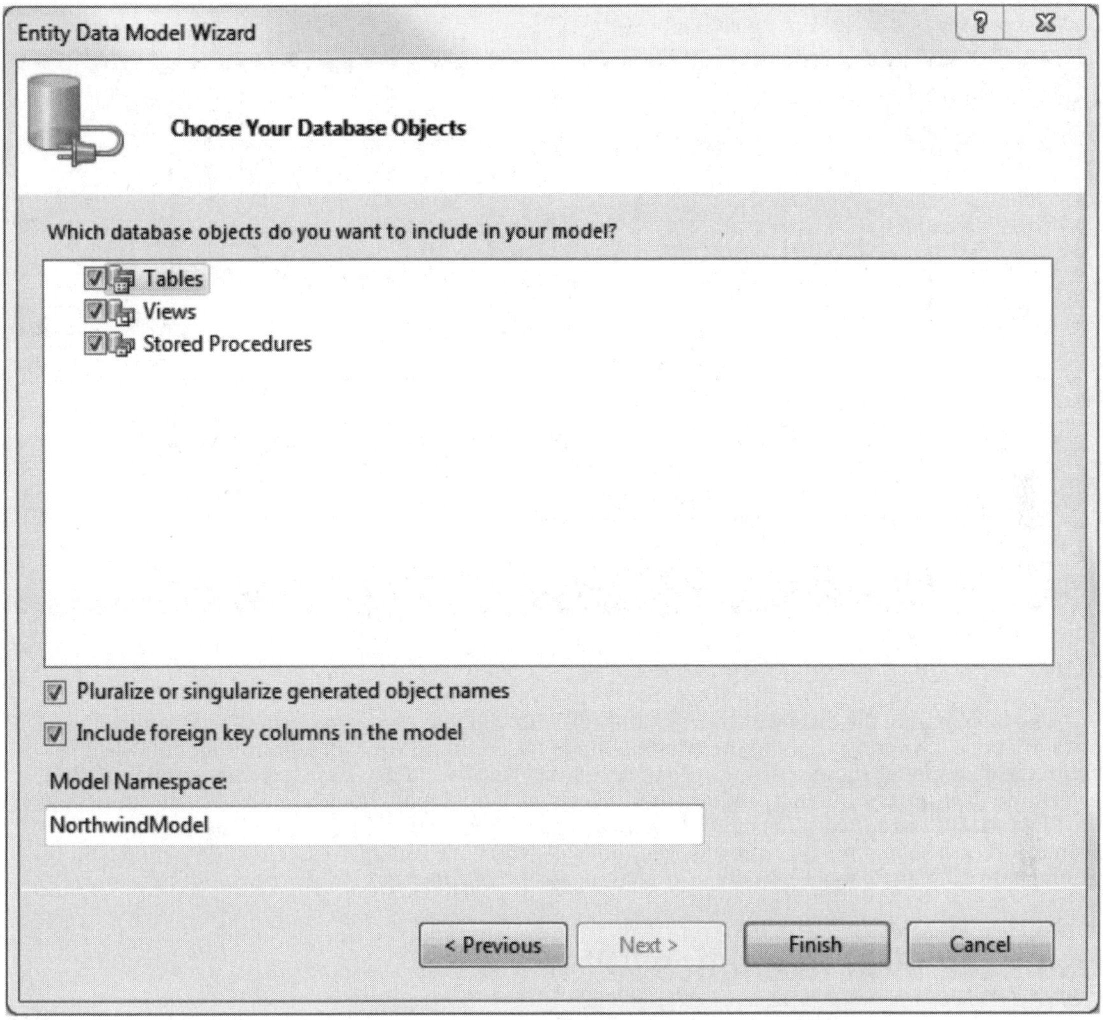

Figure 19-3. *The entity data model database objects screen*

In this view, you select the tables, views, and stored procedures from the database that will be included in your EDM. You can also elect to have object names pluralized or singularized (so that objects generated from the Customers table are called `Customer`, for example) and include foreign keys. For our purposes, we want everything from the database in the model, so select all the boxes you see in Figure 19-3. Click Finish to close the wizard and generate the model. It can take a few minutes to generate the model, but when the process has been completed, your Visual Studio should look something like Figure 19-4.

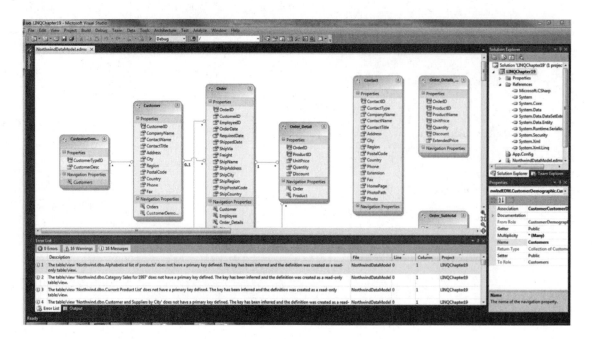

Figure 19-4. The Northwind EDM

The main part of the display shows you the entity model that has been created. You can see the properties of each entity class and the relationship between them. You will see a number of warnings about the data model; these arise because the extended Northwind database has some omissions. We will ignore these errors, but in a production project, you should read them carefully. Finally, note that the EDM wizard has added some new references to your project; these are required by the Entity Framework and should not be removed. And that's it—you have generated an entity data model for the extended Northwind database. In the next section, we'll give you a very brief overview of how to use it.

Using the LINQ to Entities API

The assemblies that you need to use LINQ to Entities are added to your project automatically when you generate the entity data model. And, unlike LINQ to SQL, you don't need to import a namespace to use the entity classes—the Entity Data Model Wizard generates the entity data models in the default namespace for your project.

IQueryable<T>

You will see that in many of the examples in this chapter and the subsequent LINQ to Entities chapters, we work with sequences of type `IQueryable<T>`, where `T` is the type of an entity class. These are the type of sequences that are typically returned by LINQ to Entities queries—just like they are for LINQ to SQL. They will often appear to work just like an `IEnumerable<T>` sequence, and that is no coincidence. The

`IQueryable<T>` interface implements the `IEnumerable<T>` interface. Here is the definition of `IQueryable<T>`:

```
interface IQueryable<T> : IEnumerable<T>, IQueryable
```

Because of this inheritance, you can treat an `IQueryable<T>` sequence like an `IEnumerable<T>` sequence.

Some Common Methods

As we demonstrate some of the features of LINQ to Entities, we need to be able to query or modify the database external to the Entity Framework. To highlight the LINQ to Entities code and to eliminate as many of the trivial details as possible (while at the same time providing useful examples), we have created some common methods. Be sure to add these common methods to your source modules as appropriate when testing the examples in the LINQ to SQL chapters.

GetStringFromDb()

A common method that will come in handy is a method to obtain a simple string from the database using standard ADO.NET (Listing 19-2). This will allow us to examine what is actually in the database, as opposed to what LINQ to Entities is showing us.

Listing 19-2. GetStringFromDb: A Method for Retrieving a String Using ADO.NET

```
static private string GetStringFromDb(string sqlQuery) {

    string connection =
        @"Data Source=.\SQLEXPRESS;Initial Catalog=Northwind;Integrated
Security=SSPI;";

    System.Data.SqlClient.SqlConnection sqlConn =
      new System.Data.SqlClient.SqlConnection(connection);


    if (sqlConn.State != ConnectionState.Open) {
        sqlConn.Open();
    }

    System.Data.SqlClient.SqlCommand sqlCommand =
      new System.Data.SqlClient.SqlCommand(sqlQuery, sqlConn);

    System.Data.SqlClient.SqlDataReader sqlDataReader = sqlCommand.ExecuteReader();
    string result = null;

    try {
        if (!sqlDataReader.Read()) {
```

```
                    throw (new Exception(
                       String.Format("Unexpected exception executing query [{0}].",
sqlQuery))));
            } else {
                if (!sqlDataReader.IsDBNull(0)) {
                    result = sqlDataReader.GetString(0);
                }
            }
        } finally {
            // always call Close when done reading.
            sqlDataReader.Close();
            sqlConn.Close();
        }

        return (result);
}
```

To call the GetStringFromDb method, a string containing a SQL query is passed into the method. The method creates and opens a new connection to the database.

Next, a SqlCommand is created by passing the query and connection into the constructor. Then, a SqlDataReader is obtained by calling the ExecuteReader method on the SqlCommand. The SqlDataReader is read by calling its Read method, and if data was read and the returned first column's value is not null, then the returned first column value is retrieved with the GetString method. Finally, the SqlDataReader and the SqlConnection are closed, and the first column value is returned to the calling method.

ExecuteStatementInDb()

Sometimes, we will need to execute nonquery SQL statements such as insert, update, and delete in ADO.NET to modify the state of the database external to the Entity Framework. For that purpose, we have created the ExecuteStatementInDb method (see Listing 19-3).

Listing 19-3. *ExecuteStatementInDb: A Method for Executing Insert, Updates, and Deletes in ADO.NET*

```
static private void ExecuteStatementInDb(string cmd) {
    string connection =
      @"Data Source=.\SQLEXPRESS;Initial Catalog=Northwind;Integrated
Security=SSPI;";

    System.Data.SqlClient.SqlConnection sqlConn =
      new System.Data.SqlClient.SqlConnection(connection);

    if (sqlConn.State != ConnectionState.Open) {
        sqlConn.Open();
    }
```

```
    System.Data.SqlClient.SqlCommand sqlComm =
      new System.Data.SqlClient.SqlCommand(cmd);

    sqlComm.Connection = sqlConn;
    try {
        Console.WriteLine("Executing SQL statement against database with ADO.NET
...");
        sqlComm.ExecuteNonQuery();
        Console.WriteLine("Database updated.");
    } finally {
        //  Close the connection.
        sqlComm.Connection.Close();
    }
}
```

To call the ExecuteStatementInDb method, a string is passed containing a SQL command. A SqlConnection is created followed by a SqlCommand. The SqlConnection is assigned to the SqlCommand. The SqlConnection is then opened, and the SQL command is executed by calling the SqlCommand object's ExecuteNonQuery method. Finally, the SqlConnection is closed.

Summary

In this chapter, we have introduced you to the Entity Framework and LINQ to Entities, as well as to some of the basic elements, such as ObjectContext objects, entity classes, and associations.

We showed you how to generate an entity data model for the extended Northwind database, which contains the entity classes you will use to work with the Northwind data. These entity classes will be used throughout the LINQ to Entities examples. We also provided a couple of common methods that some of the examples in the subsequent LINQ to Entities chapters will rely on. The next step is to show you how to use LINQ to Entities and the Entity Framework to perform common database operations, and that is exactly what the next chapter is about.

■ ■ ■

CHAPTER 20

LINQ to Entities Operations

In this chapter, we'll show you how to perform the typical database operations with LINQ to Entities. We'll show you how to perform the following:

- Inserts
- Queries
- Updates
- Deletes

To show you how to perform these operations, we'll need to use the `ObjectContext` class and features of the entity classes. We explain these in detail in Chapter 21, but for now just remember that the `ObjectContext` class maintains and manages our connection to the database, and the entity classes represent data in database tables and the relationships between tables.

If you have read the LINQ to SQL chapters, then you will already understand a lot of the principles that you will see in this chapter. If you have not read the LINQ to SQL part of this book, you might like to do so now. For ease of comparison, we use the same examples when describing LINQ to Entities as we did for LINQ to SQL wherever possible.

Prerequisites for Running the Examples

To run the examples in this chapter, you will need to have obtained the extended version of the Northwind database and generated an entity data model for it. Please read and follow Chapter 19's "Prerequisites for Running the Examples" section.

Some Common Methods

Additionally, to run the examples in this chapter, you will need some common methods that will be utilized by the examples. Please read and follow Chapter 19's "Some Common Methods" sections.

Standard Database Operations

In this section, we show you how to perform some standard database operations. These examples are meant to demonstrate the basic concepts. As such, they do not include error checking or exception handling.

For example, since many of the basic operations we discuss make changes to the database, those that make changes should detect and resolve concurrency conflicts. But, for the sake of simplicity, these examples will not demonstrate these principles until we reach the "Managing Concurrency" section at the end of the chapter.

Inserts

Four steps are required to perform an insert. The first is to create an `ObjectContext`. This is the first step for all LINQ to Entities operations, and you'll see us do this in all of the examples. Once you have an object context, you can create a new instance of an entity type, for example the `Customer` type, and populate its fields. The populated entity type is then added to the `ObjectSet<T>`. The final step is to save the new data using the `SaveChanges` method. Listing 20-1 demonstrates these four steps.

Listing 20-1. *The Four Steps for Inserting a Record*

```
// step 1. Create the ObjectContext
NorthwindEntities context = new NorthwindEntities();

// Step 2. Create a new customer object
Customer cust = new Customer() {
    CustomerID = "LAWN",
    CompanyName = "Lawn Wranglers",
    ContactName = "Mr. Abe Henry",
    ContactTitle = "Owner",
    Address = "1017 Maple Leaf Way",
    City = "Ft. Worth",
    Region = "TX",
    PostalCode = "76104",
    Country = "USA",
    Phone = "(800) MOW-LAWN",
    Fax = "(800) MOW-LAWO"
};

// Step 3. Add to the ObjectSet<Customer>
context.Customers.AddObject(cust);

// Step 4. Save the changes
context.SaveChanges();

//  Query the record.
Customer customer = context.Customers.Where(c => c.CustomerID == "LAWN").First();
Console.WriteLine("{0} - {1}", customer.CompanyName, customer.ContactName);

//  Reset the database so the example can be run more than once.
```

```
Console.WriteLine("Deleting the added customer LAWN.");
context.DeleteObject(customer);
context.SaveChanges();
```

You can see that we have numbered the steps in the example code. For the first step, we create an `ObjectContext` by creating a new instance of our derived class `NorthwindEntities`. For the second step, we create a new instance of the `Customer` entity type and use object initialization to populate the fields. In the third set, we add the new `Customer` instance to the collection of `Customers` by calling the `AddObject` method on the `Customers` property of the `ObjectContext`. Remember from Chapter 19 that this property is the `ObjectSet<Customer>` for our database. For the final step, we call the `SaveChanges` method to store the new record in the database.

The remainder of the code queries the data to ensure that our new record has been created and then deletes it so that you can run the example repeatedly without any problems. Wherever possible, we will reset the database at the end of our examples.

Creating Partially Populated Entity Types

In Listing 20-1, we create a new entity type explicitly, but we could have used a different technique. Entity Framework entity types include a static method called `Create[T]`, where `[T]` is the name of the type. For example, the `Customer` entity type will include a method called `CreateCustomer`, and the `Order` entity type will include a method called `CreateOrder`. These methods have parameters for each entity type field that cannot be set to null. Figure 20-1 shows the Northwind Customers table in the SQL Server Management Studio. You can see that all the columns can contain null values except for `CustomerID` and `CompanyName`.

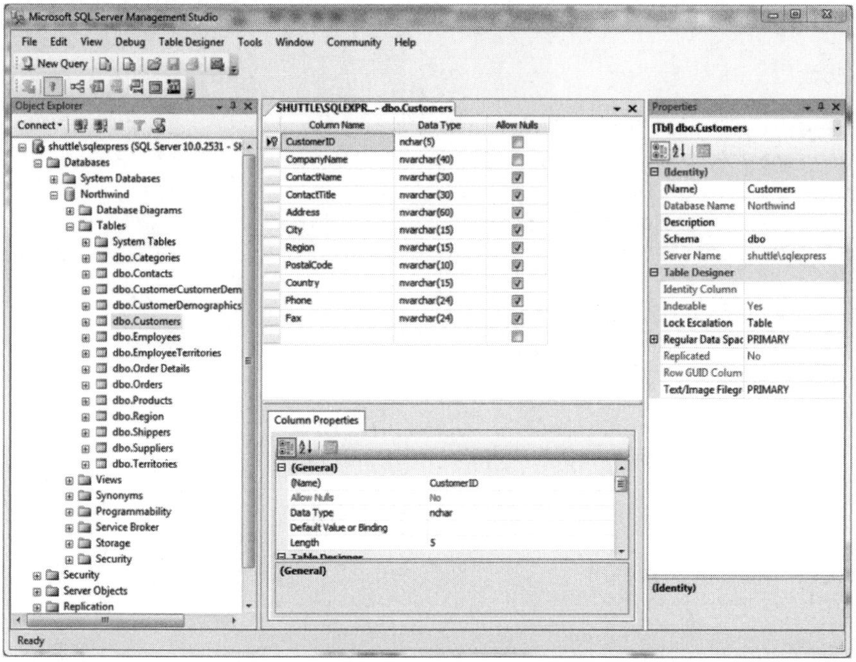

Figure 20-1. The Northwind Customers table

So, the static `Customer.CreateCustomer` method has the following signature, with required parameters for the field that cannot be left without values.

```
public static Customer CreateCustomer(
    String customerID,
    String companyName);
```

The advantage of using the `Create[T]` methods is avoid the prospect of exceptions when trying to persist an entity type that has null for a non-nullable field. Listing 20-2 demonstrates how to create and add a record using this technique.

Listing 20-2. Creating an Entity Type with the Create[T] Method

```
// create the ObjectContext
NorthwindEntities context = new NorthwindEntities();

// create a new customer object
Customer cust = Customer.CreateCustomer("LAWN", "Lawn Wranglers");

// populate the nullable fields
cust.ContactName = "Mr. Abe Henry";
cust.ContactTitle = "Owner";
cust.Address = "1017 Maple Leaf Way";
cust.City = "Ft. Worth";
cust.Region = "TX";
cust.PostalCode = "76104";
cust.Country = "USA";
cust.Phone = "(800) MOW-LAWN";
cust.Fax = "(800) MOW-LAWO";

// add the new customer to the Customers ObjectSet
context.Customers.AddObject(cust);

// save the changes
context.SaveChanges();

//  Query the record.
Customer customer = context.Customers.Where(c => c.CustomerID == "LAWN").First();
Console.WriteLine("{0} - {1}", customer.CompanyName, customer.ContactName);

//  Reset the database so the example can be run more than once.
Console.WriteLine("Deleting the added customer LAWN.");
context.DeleteObject(customer);
context.SaveChanges();
```

You can see that we create the new Customer instance using the static CreateCustomer method, supplying values for the two fields that cannot be null. We then use the public properties of the Customer type to set the other values we need.

Inserting Attached Entity Objects

The ObjectContext class detects attachments between entity objects and ensures that they are persisted to the database automatically when you call the SaveChanges method. Remember that entity objects are attached when there is a foreign key relationship between them. Listing 20-3 demonstrates how this works.

Listing 20-3. Inserting an Attached Entity Object

```
// create the ObjectContext
NorthwindEntities context = new NorthwindEntities();

Customer cust = new Customer {
    CustomerID = "LAWN",
    CompanyName = "Lawn Wranglers",
    ContactName = "Mr. Abe Henry",
    ContactTitle = "Owner",
    Address = "1017 Maple Leaf Way",
    City = "Ft. Worth",
    Region = "TX",
    PostalCode = "76104",
    Country = "USA",
    Phone = "(800) MOW-LAWN",
    Fax = "(800) MOW-LAWO",
    Orders = {
      new Order {
        CustomerID = "LAWN",
        EmployeeID = 4,
        OrderDate = DateTime.Now,
        RequiredDate = DateTime.Now.AddDays(7),
        ShipVia = 3,
        Freight = new Decimal(24.66),
        ShipName = "Lawn Wranglers",
        ShipAddress = "1017 Maple Leaf Way",
        ShipCity = "Ft. Worth",
        ShipRegion = "TX",
        ShipPostalCode = "76104",
        ShipCountry = "USA"
      }
    }
};

// add the new Customer
context.Customers.AddObject(cust);
```

```
// save the changes
context.SaveChanges();

// query to make sure the record is there
Customer customer = context.Customers.Where(c => c.CustomerID == "LAWN").First();
Console.WriteLine("{0} - {1}", customer.CompanyName, customer.ContactName);
foreach (Order order in customer.Orders) {
    Console.WriteLine("{0} - {1}", order.CustomerID, order.OrderDate);
}

//  This part of the code resets the database
context.DeleteObject(cust);
context.SaveChanges();
```

In the example, we created a new Customer object and initialized the Orders collection property with a single new order. When we called the SaveChanges method, the ObjectContext persisted both the Customer and the Order—we didn't have to explicitly add the Order to the Orders ObjectSet.

You don't have to create attached objects together in this way. You can create them separately and then associate them with each other later. Listing 20-4 demonstrates how to do this.

Listing 20-4. *Attaching Objects After They Have Been Created*

```
// create the ObjectContext
NorthwindEntities context = new NorthwindEntities();

// create the new customer
Customer cust = new Customer {
    CustomerID = "LAWN",
    CompanyName = "Lawn Wranglers",
    ContactName = "Mr. Abe Henry",
    ContactTitle = "Owner",
    Address = "1017 Maple Leaf Way",
    City = "Ft. Worth",
    Region = "TX",
    PostalCode = "76104",
    Country = "USA",
    Phone = "(800) MOW-LAWN",
    Fax = "(800) MOW-LAWO"
};

// create the new order
Order ord = new Order {
        CustomerID = "LAWN",
        EmployeeID = 4,
        OrderDate = DateTime.Now,
        RequiredDate = DateTime.Now.AddDays(7),
```

```
        ShipVia = 3,
        Freight = new Decimal(24.66),
        ShipName = "Lawn Wranglers",
        ShipAddress = "1017 Maple Leaf Way",
        ShipCity = "Ft. Worth",
        ShipRegion = "TX",
        ShipPostalCode = "76104",
        ShipCountry = "USA"
};

// attach the order to the customer
cust.Orders.Add(ord);

// add the new Customer
context.Customers.AddObject(cust);

// save the changes
context.SaveChanges();

// query to make sure the record is there
Customer customer = context.Customers.Where(c => c.CustomerID == "LAWN").First();
Console.WriteLine("{0} - {1}", customer.CompanyName, customer.ContactName);
foreach (Order order in customer.Orders) {
    Console.WriteLine("{0} - {1}", order.CustomerID, order.OrderDate);
}

//  This part of the code resets the database
context.DeleteObject(cust);
context.SaveChanges();
```

We created the Customer and Order objects separately and then attached them by calling the Orders.Add method to place the Order in the ObjectSet<Order> collection maintained by the Customer. When we called the SaveChanges method, the ObjectContext detected the new Order and persisted it to the database.

In Listings 20-3 and 20-4, we associated objects in a one-to-many relationship by calling the AddObject method on the Customer object (the one) and passed in the new Order object (the many). You can make the association in the other direction. For example, set the value of the Order.Customer property to be the new Customer object. The ObjectContext will still detect both new entity objects and persist them for you. Listing 20-5 demonstrates this.

Listing 20-5. *Attaching Objects in the Other Direction*

```
// create the ObjectContext
NorthwindEntities context = new NorthwindEntities();

// create the new customer
Customer cust = new Customer {
```

```
        CustomerID = "LAWN",
        CompanyName = "Lawn Wranglers",
        ContactName = "Mr. Abe Henry",
        ContactTitle = "Owner",
        Address = "1017 Maple Leaf Way",
        City = "Ft. Worth",
        Region = "TX",
        PostalCode = "76104",
        Country = "USA",
        Phone = "(800) MOW-LAWN",
        Fax = "(800) MOW-LAWO"
    };

    // create the new order
    Order ord = new Order {
        CustomerID = "LAWN",
        EmployeeID = 4,
        OrderDate = DateTime.Now,
        RequiredDate = DateTime.Now.AddDays(7),
        ShipVia = 3,
        Freight = new Decimal(24.66),
        ShipName = "Lawn Wranglers",
        ShipAddress = "1017 Maple Leaf Way",
        ShipCity = "Ft. Worth",
        ShipRegion = "TX",
        ShipPostalCode = "76104",
        ShipCountry = "USA"
    };

    // attach the customer to the order
    ord.Customer = cust;

    // add the new Order to the context
    context.Orders.AddObject(ord);

    // save the changes
    context.SaveChanges();

    // query to make sure the record is there
    Customer customer = context.Customers.Where(c => c.CustomerID == "LAWN").First();
    Console.WriteLine("{0} - {1}", customer.CompanyName, customer.ContactName);
    Console.WriteLine("Customer has {0} orders", customer.Orders.Count());

    //  This part of the code resets the database
    context.DeleteObject(ord);
    context.DeleteObject(cust);
    context.SaveChanges();
```

You will see that we had to delete the `Customer` and `Order` objects separately this time. If you make the association in this direction, you have to take responsibility for deleting them explicitly. If we compile and run this code, we get the some surprising results:

```
Lawn Wranglers - Mr. Abe Henry
Customer has 0 orders
Press any key to continue . . .
```

Huh? The `Customer` was found, but what happened to our `Order`? Well, you'll have to wait until Chapter 21 for an explanation. For the moment, know that the best way to attach objects in a one-to-many relationship is by adding them to the appropriate `ObjectSet` on the parent side of the relationship. Also, just because you *can* do something doesn't mean you *should*.

Queries

Querying using LINQ to Entities is very similar to using LINQ to SQL. However, there are some wrinkles and differences.

Basic Queries

Just like LINQ to SQL, LINQ to Entities queries return an `IQueryable<T>`. You can use the result of a LINQ to Entities query just as you would a LINQ to SQL query. Listing 20-6 contains a demonstration.

Listing 20-6. *Obtaining an IQueryable<T> Result from LINQ to Entities*

```
// create the ObjectContext
NorthwindEntities context = new NorthwindEntities();

IQueryable<Customer> custs = from c in context.Customers
                             where c.City == "London"
                             select c;

foreach (Customer cust in custs) {
    Console.WriteLine("Customer: {0}", cust.CompanyName);
}
```

As you can see, we perform a query using the `Customers` property of the `ObjectContext` as the source and receive an `IQueryable<Customer>` as the result. Here is the output from compiling and running Listing 20-6:

```
Customer: Around the Horn
Customer: B's Beverages
Customer: Consolidated Holdings
Customer: Eastern Connection
Customer: North/South
```

Customer: Seven Seas Imports

Compiled Queries

LINQ to Entities supports compiling queries to improve performance. The static
CompiledQuery.Compile method takes a query and returns a Func that accepts an ObjectContext and
up to 16 parameters that you can use in the query. The best way of explaining this is with an example.
Listing 20-7 contains two LINQ to Entities queries that obtain the set of customers based in London and
Paris.

Listing 20-7. Similar LINQ to Entities Queries

```
// create the ObjectContext
NorthwindEntities context = new NorthwindEntities();

// query for London-based customers
IQueryable<Customer> londonCustomers = from customer in context.Customers
                                       where customer.City == "LONDON"
                                       select customer;
// print out the names of the london customers
foreach (Customer cust in londonCustomers) {
    Console.WriteLine("London customer: {0}", cust.CompanyName);
}

// query for Paris-based customers
IQueryable<Customer> parisCustomers = from customer in context.Customers
                                      where customer.City == "PARIS"
                                      select customer;
// print out the names of the Paris customers
foreach (Customer cust in parisCustomers) {
    Console.WriteLine("Paris customer: {0}", cust.CompanyName);
}
```

We define the same query for each city—only the name of the city changes. Running the code in
Listing 20-7 produces the following results:

```
London customer: Around the Horn
London customer: B's Beverages
London customer: Consolidated Holdings
London customer: Eastern Connection
London customer: North/South
London customer: Seven Seas Imports
Paris customer: Paris spécialités
Paris customer: Spécialités du monde
```

To create a compiled version of the query in Listing 20-7, we call the `CompiledQuery.Compile` method, as shown next. The first argument is always the `ObjectContext` for your entity data model. The last argument is the result from the query—in our case, an `IQueryable<Customer>`. The other arguments are the parameters you want to pass to the query to make it reusable. After all, there is no point compiling a query if you can't use it more than once. For our example, we want to be able to specify different cities, so we have one `string` argument.

```
Func<NorthwindEntities, string, IQueryable<Customer>> compiledQuery
    = CompiledQuery.Compile<NorthwindEntities, string, IQueryable<Customer>>(
        (ctx, city) =>
            from customer in ctx.Customers
            where customer.City == city
            select customer);
```

The return type from the `Compile` method is a `Func` that is strongly typed to match the types you specified for the `Compile` method itself. In our case, we get a `Func<NorthwindEntities, string, IQueryable<Customer>>`. Now to reuse this query, we simply call the function and supply the parameters. Listing 20-8 shows you how to do this.

Listing 20-8. *Using a Compiled LINQ to Entities Query*

```
// define the compiled query
Func<NorthwindEntities, string, IQueryable<Customer>> compiledQuery
    = CompiledQuery.Compile<NorthwindEntities, string, IQueryable<Customer>>(
        (ctx, city) =>
            from customer in ctx.Customers
            where customer.City == city
            select customer);

// create the ObjectContext
NorthwindEntities context = new NorthwindEntities();

// define the cities we are interested in
string[] cities = new string[] { "London", "Paris" };

// call the compiled query for each city
foreach (string city in cities) {
    IQueryable<Customer> custs = compiledQuery(context, city);
    foreach (Customer cust in custs) {
        Console.WriteLine("{0} customer: {1}", city, cust.CompanyName);
    }
}
```

We define the compiled query function and then call it for each city that we are interested in. The query is compiled the first time that we use it, which can offer a performance improvement, especially for complex queries. The results from Listing 20-8 are shown here:

```
London customer: Around the Horn
London customer: B's Beverages
London customer: Consolidated Holdings
London customer: Eastern Connection
London customer: North/South
London customer: Seven Seas Imports
Paris customer: Paris spécialités
Paris customer: Spécialités du monde
```

Seeing the SQL Statement

It can often be useful to see the SQL statement that your LINQ to Entities query is translated into. Unfortunately, there is no convenient way of doing this for all SQL statements that are created by an ObjectContext instance. You can, however, see the SQL statement that a single LINQ to Entities query will generate by casting the IQueryable<T> result from a LINQ to Entities query to the concrete ObjectQuery class and calling the ToTraceString method. Listing 20-9 demonstrates how to do this.

Listing 20-9. *Displaying the SQL Statement*

```
// create the ObjectContext
NorthwindEntities context = new NorthwindEntities();

// query for London-based customers
IQueryable<Customer> londonCustomers = from customer in context.Customers
                                       where customer.City == "LONDON"
                                       select customer;

// ensure that the database connection is open
if (context.Connection.State != ConnectionState.Open) {
    context.Connection.Open();
}

// display the sql statement
string sqlStatement = (londonCustomers as ObjectQuery).ToTraceString();
Console.WriteLine(sqlStatement);
```

In Listing 20-9, we define a query that will select all the Northwind customers that are based in London. We then make sure that there is an open connection to the database. We'll cover the ObjectContext members we used to do this in detail in Chapter 21, but for now just know that you will get an exception if you try to get the SQL statement from a query without an open connection.

To get the SQL statement, we cast the IQueryable<Customer> that is the result enumeration from the LINQ query to an ObjectQuery and call the ToTraceString method. This returns a string containing the SQL statement that our query is translated into, which we write to the console. Compiling and running the code in Listing 20-9 gives the following output:

```
SELECT
[Extent1].[CustomerID] AS [CustomerID],
[Extent1].[CompanyName] AS [CompanyName],
[Extent1].[ContactName] AS [ContactName],
[Extent1].[ContactTitle] AS [ContactTitle],
[Extent1].[Address] AS [Address],
[Extent1].[City] AS [City],
[Extent1].[Region] AS [Region],
[Extent1].[PostalCode] AS [PostalCode],
[Extent1].[Country] AS [Country],
[Extent1].[Phone] AS [Phone],
[Extent1].[Fax] AS [Fax]
FROM [dbo].[Customers] AS [Extent1]
WHERE N'LONDON' = [Extent1].[City]
```

Getting hold of the SQL statement this way doesn't execute the query—it just translates from a LINQ to Entities query to a SQL statement. We'll readily admit that this is an inelegant technique. Although we do use this approach, we tend to favor the SQL Server Profiler. If you don't have this tool (it is not included with the Express edition that ships with Visual Studio 2010, for example), then we recommend the free, open source SQL profiler from Anjlab, which you can find at `http://sites.google.com/site/sqlprofiler`. Using a profiler allows you to see all the SQL statements sent to your database and not just do so on a per-query basis.

Loading Related Objects

Entity types are associated when there is a foreign-key relationship between them. Entity objects (that is, instances of entity types) are related to one another through a specific foreign key value. For example, the Northwind `Customer` and `Order` entity types are associated, and the `Customer` object for `Round the Horn` and the `Order` objects for `Round the Horn` are related. LINQ to Entities makes it easy to navigate through your data by automatically dealing associations for you . Behind-the-scenes related objects are loaded so that your code work seamlessly. However, it is worth paying attention to how related objects are being loaded.

Lazy Loading

Lazy object loading is the default behavior for LINQ to Entities. Related objects are loaded only from the database when you access the association property in an entity type. You never load data that you don't want—this is a *just-in-time* loading strategy—but it means that you can end up with a surprising number of SQL queries being generated by your code. Listing 20-10 demonstrates this issue.

Listing 20-10. The Effect of Lazy Object Loading

```
// create the ObjectContext
NorthwindEntities context = new NorthwindEntities();

IQueryable<Customer> custs = from c in context.Customers
                             where c.Country == "UK" &&
                                 c.City == "London"
```

```
                    orderby c.CustomerID
                    select c;

foreach (Customer cust in custs) {
    Console.WriteLine("{0} - {1}", cust.CompanyName, cust.ContactName);
    Order firstOrder = cust.Orders.First();
    Console.WriteLine("    {0}", firstOrder.OrderID);
}
```

In Listing 20-10, we query for customers who are in London, UK and order the results by the CustomerID field. We then write out the company name and contact name for each company, along with the OrderID of the first order associated with the customer. Compiling and running the code in Listing 20-10 produces the following results—there are six matching customers:

```
Around the Horn - Thomas Hardy
    10355
B's Beverages - Victoria Ashworth
    10289
Consolidated Holdings - Elizabeth Brown
    10435
Eastern Connection - Ann Devon
    10364
North/South - Simon Crowther
    10517
Seven Seas Imports - Hari Kumar
    10359
```

Cleverly, the Orders related to each Customer are not loaded until we access the Customer.Orders field. When we do this, the Entity Framework seamlessly queries the database and loads the data we want—nice and easy. None of the other entity objects related to the Customer type has been loaded.

Depending on your project, this approach is either genius or total madness. It can be genius because you get just what you need from the database just when you need it. It can be madness because even a simple LINQ query can result in many queries to the database. In the case of Listing 20-10, we end up generating up to seven SQL queries—one to get the list of London, UK–based customers and then six to get the set of orders for customer that matched. For some projects, seven queries for such a simple piece of code would be too many, and in the following sections, we'll show you some alternative approaches.

We said *up to* seven queries for Listing 20-10 because the Entity Framework caches data to improve performance. Some of the data that would otherwise have led to a request may already be cached. You can disable lazy loading by setting an option in the ObjectContext as follows:

```
context.ContextOptions.LazyLoadingEnabled = false;
```

You will cause an exception if you disable lazy loading and attempt to access a related entity object—unless you use one of the other techniques shown next to ensure that the data is loaded.

Eager Loading

When you know exactly what data you require when you code, as we did in the previous listing, you can use the `Include` method to load related entity objects as part of your LINQ to Entities query. You apply the `Include` method to your query, specifying the name of the association property between the type you are querying and the type you want to load as a string—in our case, the property that associated the `Customer` type with the `Order` type is the `Orders` property, so we would call the `Include` method with the string argument `"Orders"`. Listing 20-11 demonstrates eager loading for the query we used in Listing 20-10.

Listing 20-11. *Eager Loading of the Orders Data*

```
// create the ObjectContext
NorthwindEntities context = new NorthwindEntities();

IQueryable<Customer> custs = from c in context.Customers
                        .Include("Orders")
                        where c.Country == "UK" &&
                          c.City == "London"
                        orderby c.CustomerID
                        select c;

foreach (Customer cust in custs) {
    Console.WriteLine("{0} - {1}", cust.CompanyName, cust.ContactName);
    Order firstOrder = cust.Orders.First();
    Console.WriteLine("    {0}", firstOrder.OrderID);
}
```

When we compile and run the code in Listing 20-11, we get the same results as for Listing 20-10, but only one SQL query is issued to the database, shown here:

```
[Project1].[Freight] AS [Freight],
[Project1].[ShipName] AS [ShipName],
[Project1].[ShipAddress] AS [ShipAddress],
[Project1].[ShipCity] AS [ShipCity],
[Project1].[ShipRegion] AS [ShipRegion],
[Project1].[ShipPostalCode] AS [ShipPostalCode],
[Project1].[ShipCountry] AS [ShipCountry]
FROM ( SELECT
        [Extent1].[CustomerID] AS [CustomerID],
        [Extent1].[CompanyName] AS [CompanyName],
        [Extent1].[ContactName] AS [ContactName],
        [Extent1].[ContactTitle] AS [ContactTitle],
        [Extent1].[Address] AS [Address],
        [Extent1].[City] AS [City],
        [Extent1].[Region] AS [Region],
        [Extent1].[PostalCode] AS [PostalCode],
        [Extent1].[Country] AS [Country],
```

```
        [Extent1].[Phone] AS [Phone],
        [Extent1].[Fax] AS [Fax],
        1 AS [C1],
        [Extent2].[OrderID] AS [OrderID],
        [Extent2].[CustomerID] AS [CustomerID1],
        [Extent2].[EmployeeID] AS [EmployeeID],
        [Extent2].[OrderDate] AS [OrderDate],
        [Extent2].[RequiredDate] AS [RequiredDate],
        [Extent2].[ShippedDate] AS [ShippedDate],
        [Extent2].[ShipVia] AS [ShipVia],
        [Extent2].[Freight] AS [Freight],
        [Extent2].[ShipName] AS [ShipName],
        [Extent2].[ShipAddress] AS [ShipAddress],
        [Extent2].[ShipCity] AS [ShipCity],
        [Extent2].[ShipRegion] AS [ShipRegion],
        [Extent2].[ShipPostalCode] AS [ShipPostalCode],
        [Extent2].[ShipCountry] AS [ShipCountry],
        CASE WHEN ([Extent2].[OrderID] IS NULL) THEN CAST(NULL AS int) ELSE 1 END AS
[C2]
        FROM   [dbo].[Customers] AS [Extent1]
        LEFT OUTER JOIN [dbo].[Orders] AS [Extent2] ON [Extent1].[CustomerID] =
[Extent2].[CustomerID]
        WHERE (N'UK' = [Extent1].[Country]) AND (N'London' = [Extent1].[City])
)  AS [Project1]
ORDER BY [Project1].[CustomerID] ASC, [Project1].[C2] ASC
```

You can eagerly load any number of related entity types by applying the Include method for each type you want to eagerly load. Listing 20-12 shows a query for Orders that eagerly loads the related Shipper and Customer entity types.

Listing 20-12. *Eagerly Loading Multiple Related Entity Types*

```
// create the ObjectContext
NorthwindEntities context = new NorthwindEntities();

IQueryable<Order> orders = context.Orders
    .Include("Shipper")
    .Include("Customer")
    .Where(c => c.ShipCountry == "France")
    .Select(c => c);

foreach (Order ord in orders) {
    Console.WriteLine("OrderID: {0}, Shipper: {1}, Contact: {2}",
        ord.OrderID,
        ord.Shipper.CompanyName,
```

```
        ord.Customer.ContactName);
}
```

In the LINQ query, we Include the Shipper and Customer entity types, which results in one SQL query to the database, even though we access fields from three different entity types. The results from running this query are shown here:

```
OrderID: 10248, Shipper: Federal Shipping, Contact: Paul Henriot
OrderID: 10251, Shipper: Speedy Express, Contact: Mary Saveley
OrderID: 10265, Shipper: Speedy Express, Contact: Frédérique Citeaux
OrderID: 10274, Shipper: Speedy Express, Contact: Paul Henriot
OrderID: 10295, Shipper: United Package, Contact: Paul Henriot
OrderID: 10297, Shipper: United Package, Contact: Frédérique Citeaux
OrderID: 10311, Shipper: Federal Shipping, Contact: Janine Labrune
OrderID: 10331, Shipper: Speedy Express, Contact: Laurence Lebihan
...
```

Explicit Loading

If you want total control, then explicit loading is for you. You specify which related entity objects are loaded by using the EntityCollection.Load method. Listing 20-13 demonstrates how to selectively load related entity objects.

Listing 20-13. *Explicit Loading to Control Database Queries*

```
// create the ObjectContext
NorthwindEntities context = new NorthwindEntities();

// disable lazy loading
context.ContextOptions.LazyLoadingEnabled = false;

IQueryable<Customer> custs = context.Customers
    .Where(c => c.Country == "UK" && c.City == "London")
    .OrderBy(c => c.CustomerID)
    .Select(c => c);

// explicitly load the orders for each customer
foreach (Customer cust in custs) {
    if (cust.CompanyName != "North/South") {
        cust.Orders.Load();
    }
}

foreach (Customer cust in custs) {
    Console.WriteLine("{0} - {1}", cust.CompanyName, cust.ContactName);
    // check to see that the order data is loaded for this customer
```

```
if (cust.Orders.IsLoaded) {
    Order firstOrder = cust.Orders.First();
    Console.WriteLine("   {0}", firstOrder.OrderID);
} else {
    Console.WriteLine("   No order data loaded");
}
```

To use explicit loading, you must disable lazy loading. Otherwise, the Entity Framework will load related objects automatically for you anyway. In the example, we perform a LINQ query for all London, UK customers and then explicitly load the related Orders for all of them except the one called North/South. We then enumerate the results again and print out the data we require, using the IsLoaded method to determine whether the related objects have been loaded. Using explicit loading can be error-prone unless you carefully check that objects have been loaded before accessing them. But if you need full control over which data is loaded, then this is an ideal solution.

Querying Views

When you generate an entity data model for your database, you can elect to include support for any views that might exist. If you followed our instructions in the previous chapter, you selected all the views in the Northwind database when generating the entity data model for the examples.

Querying a view is just like querying a table. Listing 20-14 demonstrates the use of the Customers and Suppliers by City view from the Northwind database.

Listing 20-14. Using LINQ to Query a Database View

```
// create the ObjectContext
NorthwindEntities context = new NorthwindEntities();

IQueryable<Customer_and_Suppliers_by_City> res
    = context.Customer_and_Suppliers_by_Cities
    .Where(c => c.City == "LONDON")
    .Select(c => c);

foreach (Customer_and_Suppliers_by_City r in res) {
    Console.WriteLine("{0}, {1}", r.CompanyName, r.ContactName);
}
```

The entity data model defines an entity type called Customer_and_Suppliers_by_City, which is collected in the ObjectContext property Customer_and_Suppliers_by_Cities. The view name has been pluralized by the Entity Data Model Wizard, and this can be disabled when the model is generated. Aside from the unwieldy type names, querying a view is just like querying a table—the results of compiling and running the code in Listing 20-14 are shown here:

```
Around the Horn, Thomas Hardy
B's Beverages, Victoria Ashworth
Consolidated Holdings, Elizabeth Brown
Eastern Connection, Ann Devon
Exotic Liquids, Charlotte Cooper
```

North/South, Simon Crowther
Seven Seas Imports, Hari Kumar

Querying Stored Procedures

Using stored procedures is not as simple as using views. You have to explicitly import a stored procedure into your entity data model. But don't worry—Visual Studio does most of the hard work for you. The first step to importing a stored procedure is to open the Model Browser window in Visual Studio 2010. Select View ➤ Other Windows ➤ Entity Data Model Browser. Figure 20-2 shows you the browser for the Northwind entity data model.

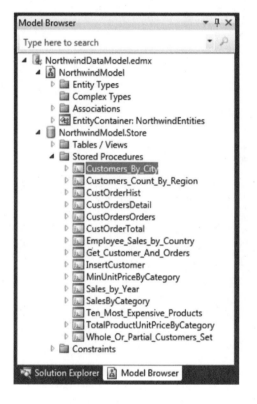

Figure 20-2. *The Visual Studio Model Browser*

We are going to import and use the `Customers_By_City` stored procedure, which is highlighted in Figure 20-2. To start the import, simply double-click the stored procedure name to open the Add Function Import dialog box, which is shown in Figure 20-3.

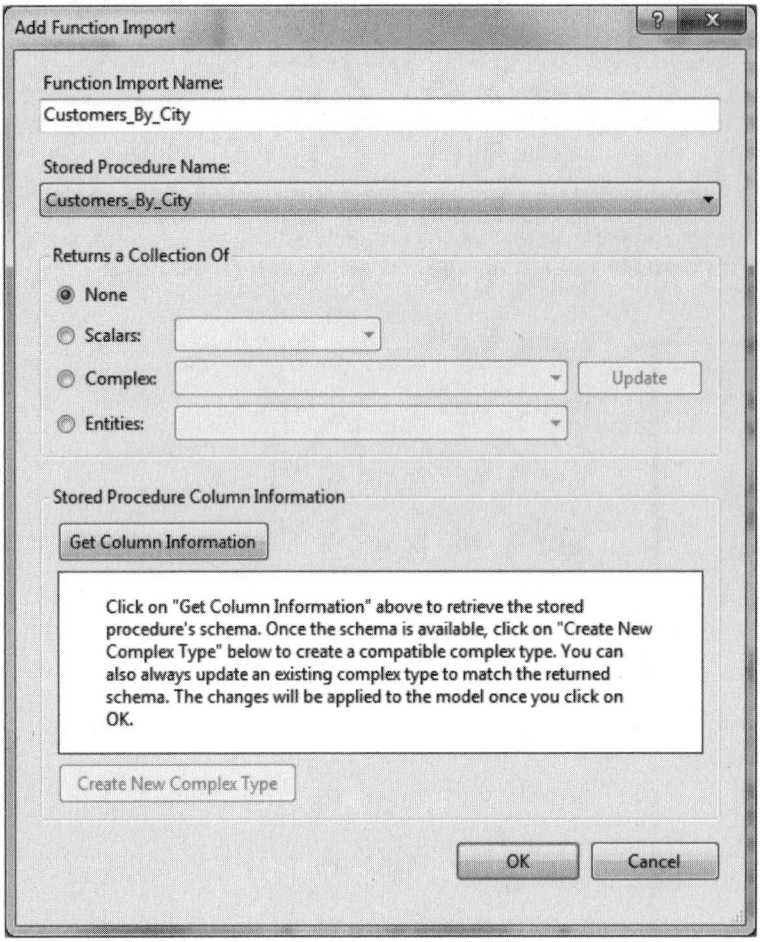

Figure 20-3. *The Add Function Import dialog box*

You can set the name of the `ObjectContext` property that will be used to call the stored procedure by changing the `Function Import Name` value. We are happy with the default name for this example. The most important thing is to set the result type for the stored procedure. If the procedure returns the fields required to populate a preexisting entity type, then you can select that type from the drop-down box. Equally, if there is no return type or the procedure returns a collection of scalar types, you can specify that behavior in this dialog box.

The stored procedure we want to use doesn't map conveniently to an existing entity type—so we will have a new type created as part of the procedure import. To do this, click the Get Column Information button, and then click the Create New Complex Type button. The dialog box should look something like the one shown in Figure 20-4.

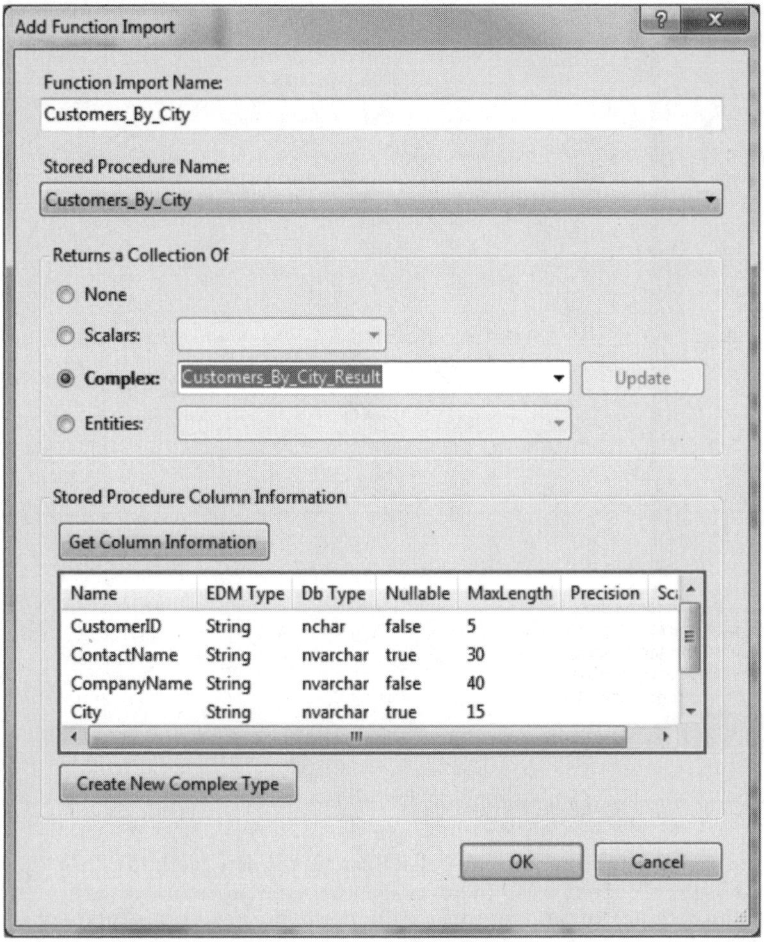

Figure 20-4. *Generating a new complex type to support a stored procedure*

You can change the name of the new type, but we are happy with the default. All that remains now is to click the OK button. You should now see two new entries in the Model Browser—one for the imported procedure and one for the new result type. You can see this in Figure 20-5.

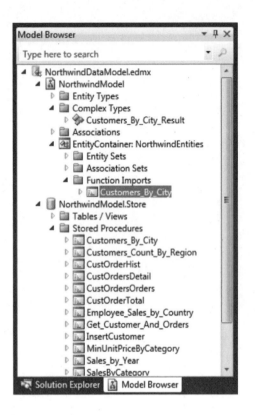

Figure 20-5. *An imported stored procedure and a new complex result type*

Now that we have imported the stored procedure, we can call it through the new method `Customers_By_City` in the derived `ObjectContext` class. In our case, our stored procedure takes a single parameter (the name of the city to query for) and returns a sequence of the new complex type that was created for us—an `IEnumerable<Customers_By_City_Result>` in this case. Listing 20-15 demonstrates how to use the stored procedure to get the details of the customers based in London.

Listing 20-15. *Querying an Imported Stored Procedure*

```
// create the ObjectContext
NorthwindEntities context = new NorthwindEntities();

IEnumerable<Customers_By_City_Result> custs = context.Customers_By_City("London");

foreach (Customers_By_City_Result cust in custs) {
    Console.WriteLine("{0}, {1}", cust.CompanyName, cust.ContactName);
}
```

Joins

The way that the Entity Framework handles associations and related objects can be incredibly intuitive and useful, but it works only where there are foreign-key relationships in the database. When you need to query between types that are not associated, then you will need to explicitly join tables.

Inner Joins

Performing joins with LINQ to Entities is just like you saw with LINQ to SQL in Chapter 14; you use the join operator. As is typical with an inner join, any records in the outer results set will be omitted if a matching record does not exist in the inner results set. Listing 20-16 contains an example.

Listing 20-16. *A LINQ to Entities Inner Join*

```
// create the ObjectContext
NorthwindEntities context = new NorthwindEntities();

var entities = from s in context.Suppliers
               join c in context.Customers on s.City equals c.City
               select new {
                   SupplierName = s.CompanyName,
                   CustomerName = c.CompanyName,
                   City = c.City
               };

foreach (var e in entities) {
    Console.WriteLine("{0}: {1} - {2}", e.City, e.SupplierName, e.CustomerName);
}
```

In Listing 20-16, we performed an inner join on the suppliers and the customers. If a customer record doesn't exist with the same city as a supplier, the supplier record will be omitted from the results set. Here are the results of Listing 20-16:

```
London: Exotic Liquids - Around the Horn
London: Exotic Liquids - B's Beverages
London: Exotic Liquids - Consolidated Holdings
London: Exotic Liquids - Eastern Connection
London: Exotic Liquids - North/South
London: Exotic Liquids - Seven Seas Imports
Sao Paulo: Refrescos Americanas LTDA - Comércio Mineiro
Sao Paulo: Refrescos Americanas LTDA - Familia Arquibaldo
Sao Paulo: Refrescos Americanas LTDA - Queen Cozinha
Sao Paulo: Refrescos Americanas LTDA - Tradição Hipermercados
Berlin: Heli Süßwaren GmbH & Co. KG - Alfreds Futterkiste
Paris: Aux joyeux ecclésiastiques - Paris spécialités
Paris: Aux joyeux ecclésiastiques - Spécialités du monde
Montréal: Ma Maison - Mère Paillarde
```

As you can see, despite that some suppliers are in the output with multiple matching customers, some suppliers are not in the list at all. This is because there were no customers in the same city as the missing suppliers. If we need to still see the supplier regardless of whether there is a matching customer, we need to perform an outer join.

Outer Joins

As with LINQ to SQL, the DefaultIfEmpty standard query operator can be used in LINQ to Entities to perform outer joins. In Listing 20-17, we will use the into clause to direct the matching join results into a temporary sequence that we will subsequently call the DefaultIfEmpty operator on. This way, if the record is missing from the joined results, a default value will be provided.

Listing 20-17. A LINQ to Entities Outer Join

```
// create the ObjectContext
NorthwindEntities context = new NorthwindEntities();

var entities =
  from s in context.Suppliers
  join c in context.Customers on s.City equals c.City into temp
  from t in temp.DefaultIfEmpty()
  select new {
      SupplierName = s.CompanyName,
      CustomerName = t.CompanyName,
      City = s.City
  };

foreach (var e in entities) {
    Console.WriteLine("{0}: {1} - {2}", e.City, e.SupplierName, e.CustomerName);
}
```

Notice that in the join statement in Listing 20-17, we direct the join results into the temporary sequence named temp. That temporary sequence name can be whatever you want, as long as it doesn't conflict with any other name or keyword. Then we perform a subsequent query on the results of the temp sequence passed to the DefaultIfEmpty operator. If we trace the SQL statement sent to the database, we see the following:

```
SELECT
1 AS [C1],
[Extent1].[CompanyName] AS [CompanyName],
[Extent2].[CompanyName] AS [CompanyName1],
[Extent1].[City] AS [City]
FROM  [dbo].[Suppliers] AS [Extent1]
LEFT OUTER JOIN [dbo].[Customers] AS [Extent2] ON ([Extent1].[City] =
[Extent2].[City]) OR ((([Extent1].[City] IS NULL) AND ([Extent2].[City] IS NULL))
```

If you compare this to the SQL statement generated by LINQ to SQL in Chapter 14 for the same outer query, you will notice that LINQ to Entities translates the query differently. Running the code in Listing 20-17 gives us the following results:

```
London: Exotic Liquids - Around the Horn
London: Exotic Liquids - B's Beverages
London: Exotic Liquids - Consolidated Holdings
London: Exotic Liquids - Eastern Connection
London: Exotic Liquids - North/South
London: Exotic Liquids - Seven Seas Imports
New Orleans: New Orleans Cajun Delights -
Ann Arbor: Grandma Kelly's Homestead -
Tokyo: Tokyo Traders -
Oviedo: Cooperativa de Quesos 'Las Cabras' -
Osaka: Mayumi's -
Melbourne: Pavlova, Ltd. -
Manchester: Specialty Biscuits, Ltd. -
Göteborg: PB Knäckebröd AB -
Sao Paulo: Refrescos Americanas LTDA - Comércio Mineiro
Sao Paulo: Refrescos Americanas LTDA - Familia Arquibaldo
Sao Paulo: Refrescos Americanas LTDA - Queen Cozinha
Sao Paulo: Refrescos Americanas LTDA - Tradição Hipermercados
Berlin: Heli Süßwaren GmbH & Co. KG - Alfreds Futterkiste
Frankfurt: Plutzer Lebensmittelgroßmärkte AG -
Cuxhaven: Nord-Ost-Fisch Handelsgesellschaft mbH -
Ravenna: Formaggi Fortini s.r.l. -
Sandvika: Norske Meierier -
Bend: Bigfoot Breweries -
Stockholm: Svensk Sjöföda AB -
Paris: Aux joyeux ecclésiastiques - Paris spécialités
Paris: Aux joyeux ecclésiastiques - Spécialités du monde
Boston: New England Seafood Cannery -
Singapore: Leka Trading -
Lyngby: Lyngbysild -
Zaandam: Zaanse Snoepfabriek -
Lappeenranta: Karkki Oy -
Sydney: G'day, Mate -
Montréal: Ma Maison - Mère Paillarde
Salerno: Pasta Buttini s.r.l. -
Montceau: Escargots Nouveaux -
Annecy: Gai pâturage -
Ste-Hyacinthe: Forêts d'érables -
: Sharp As You Like -
```

As you can see in the output of Listing 20-17, we got at least one record for every supplier, and you can see that some suppliers do not have a matching customer, thereby proving the outer join was performed. But, if there is any doubt, you can see the actual generated SQL statement, and that clearly is performing an outer join.

Updates

Updating entity types is as simple as changing the properties of an entity object, calling the SaveChanges method of the ObjectContext and, if needed, resolving any concurrency conflicts. We explain how the Entity Framework handles concurrency issues later in this chapter. Listing 20-18 shows a simple example of an update.

Listing 20-18. A Simple Entity Object Update

```
// create the ObjectContext
NorthwindEntities context = new NorthwindEntities();

//  Retrieve customer LAZYK.
Customer cust = (from c in context.Customers
                where c.CustomerID == "LAZYK"
                select c).Single<Customer>();

//  Update the contact name.
cust.ContactName = "Ned Plimpton";

// save the changes
context.SaveChanges();

// restore the database
cust.ContactName = "John Steel";
context.SaveChanges();
```

In Listing 20-18, we query to find the Customer with the CustomerID of LAZYK and change the ContactName value to Ned Plimpton. We then call the SaveChanges method to persist this change to the database. We want to restore the database, so we change the ContactName back to John Steel and call the SaveChanges method again, leaving the database as we found it.

Updating Associated Objects

The Entity Framework takes care of managing the relationships between associated data types. You simply have to make the changes you require and call the SaveChanges method. Listing 20-19 contains an example.

Listing 20-19. Updating an Associated Type Relationship

```
// create the ObjectContext
NorthwindEntities context = new NorthwindEntities();

Order order = (from o in context.Orders
                where o.EmployeeID == 5
```

```
            orderby o.OrderDate descending
            select o).First<Order>();

// Save off the current employee so we can reset it at the end.
Employee origEmployee = order.Employee;

Console.WriteLine("Before changing the employee.");
Console.WriteLine("OrderID = {0} : OrderDate = {1} : EmployeeID = {2}",
  order.OrderID, order.OrderDate, order.Employee.EmployeeID);

Employee emp = (from e in context.Employees
            where e.EmployeeID == 9
            select e).Single<Employee>();

// Now we will assign the new employee to the order.
order.Employee = emp;

context.SaveChanges();

Order order2 = (from o in emp.Orders
            where o.OrderID == order.OrderID
            select o).First<Order>();

Console.WriteLine("{0}After changing the employee.", System.Environment.NewLine);
Console.WriteLine("OrderID = {0} : OrderDate = {1} : EmployeeID = {2}",
  order2.OrderID, order2.OrderDate, order2.Employee.EmployeeID);

// Now we need to reverse the changes so the example can be run multiple times.
order.Employee = origEmployee;
context.SaveChanges();
```

Listing 20-19 is the same example that we used to demonstrate updating associated classes for LINQ to SQL, but it updates the code to use the LINQ to Entities. We query to find an Order and update the relationship with the Employee type before restoring the database to its original state. As with LINQ to SQL, LINQ to Entities takes care of managing the changes in the relational data based on the associations in your entity objects.

Deletes

To delete a record from the database, you simply pass the entity object that represent that record as an argument to the ObjectContext.DeleteObject method. Listing 20-20 shows an example of using this method.

■ **Caution** The examples in this section do not restore the database to its original state. You should detach your Northwind database from SQL Server 2008 and attach the original version you downloaded so that you can run the other examples without getting unexpected results.

Listing 20-20. Deleting a Record by Deleting an Entity Object

```
// create the ObjectContext
NorthwindEntities context = new NorthwindEntities();

// get the order details for order 10248
IQueryable<Order_Detail> ods = from o in context.Order_Details
                               where o.OrderID == 10248
                               select o;

// print out the query results
Console.WriteLine("Before deletion");
foreach (Order_Detail od in ods) {
    Console.WriteLine("Order detail {0}, {1}, {2}",
        od.ProductID, od.UnitPrice, od.Quantity);
}

// delete the first order detail
context.DeleteObject(ods.First());

// save the changes
context.SaveChanges();

// print out the query results
Console.WriteLine("After deletion");
foreach (Order_Detail od in ods) {
    Console.WriteLine("Order detail {0}, {1}, {2}",
        od.ProductID, od.UnitPrice, od.Quantity);
}
```

In Listing 20-20, we query for all the Order_Detail entity objects with an OrderID value of 10248. We select the first of these with the First method and then pass it as an argument to the ObjectContext.DeleteObject method. To make the change persistent, we call the ObjectContext.SaveChanges method, which issues the delete command to the database.

The EntitySet class also has a DeleteObject method, which means you can get the same effect as in Listing 20-20 by using the entity object that represents the table you want to delete a record from. Listing 20-21 contains an example of this.

Listing 20-21. Deleting a Record Using the EntitySet Class

```
// create the ObjectContext
NorthwindEntities context = new NorthwindEntities();

// get the order details for order 10248
IQueryable<Order_Detail> ods = from o in context.Order_Details
                               where o.OrderID == 10248
                               select o;

// print out the query results
Console.WriteLine("Before deletion");
foreach (Order_Detail od in ods) {
    Console.WriteLine("Order detail {0}, {1}, {2}",
        od.ProductID, od.UnitPrice, od.Quantity);
}

// delete the first order detail
context.Order_Details.DeleteObject(ods.First());

// save the changes
context.SaveChanges();

// print out the query results
Console.WriteLine("After deletion");
foreach (Order_Detail od in ods) {
    Console.WriteLine("Order detail {0}, {1}, {2}",
        od.ProductID, od.UnitPrice, od.Quantity);
}
```

In Listing 20-21 we perform the same query as in Listing 20-20 but use the `EntitySet.DeleteObject` method. Since we want to delete an instance of the `Order_Detail` entity type, we call the `DeleteObject` method on the `Order_Details` property of the `ObjectContext`, which is the `EntitySet` that represents the `Order_Details` table in the database. Compiling and running the code in Listings 20-20 and 20-21 gives us the same results, as shown here:

```
Before deletion
Order detail 11, 14.0000, 12
Order detail 42, 9.8000, 10
Order detail 72, 34.8000, 5
After deletion
Order detail 42, 9.8000, 10
Order detail 72, 34.8000, 5
```

Deleting Related Objects

Deleting an entity object in the Entity Framework doesn't automatically delete related objects. You must be careful when deleting an entity object that has related objects—depending on the schema for your database, you will either create orphaned data (data that has a foreign key reference to a primary key that no longer exists) or receive an exception for violating a constrain in your schema.

Listing 20-22 demonstrates what happens when you delete an object without handling any related objects. In this case, we have tried to delete an Order entity object.

Listing 20-22. *Deleting an Entity Object Without Dealing with Related Objects*

```
// create the ObjectContext
NorthwindEntities context = new NorthwindEntities();

// query for the first order for LAZYK
Order firstOrder = context.Orders
    .Where(o => o.CustomerID == "LAZYK")
    .Select(o => o)
    .First();

// delete the order
context.DeleteObject(firstOrder);

// save the changes
context.SaveChanges();
```

Compiling and running the code in Listing 20-22 gives us the following exception:

```
Unhandled Exception: System.Data.UpdateException: An error occurred while updating
the entries. See the inner exception
for details. ---> System.Data.SqlClient.SqlException: The DELETE statement
conflicted with the REFERENCE constraint "FK_
Order_Details_Orders". The conflict occurred in database "Northwind", table
"dbo.Order Details", column 'OrderID'.
The statement has been terminated.
```

What has happened? Well, we violated a schema constraint in the database. The exception tells us that there is a constraint called FK_Order_Details_Orders in the Order Details table. Figure 20-6 shows us that if we look at the database using SQL Server Management Studio, we can see that the Enforce Foreign Key Constraint option is set to Yes, meaning that we can't delete an Order while there are still related records in the Order Details table.

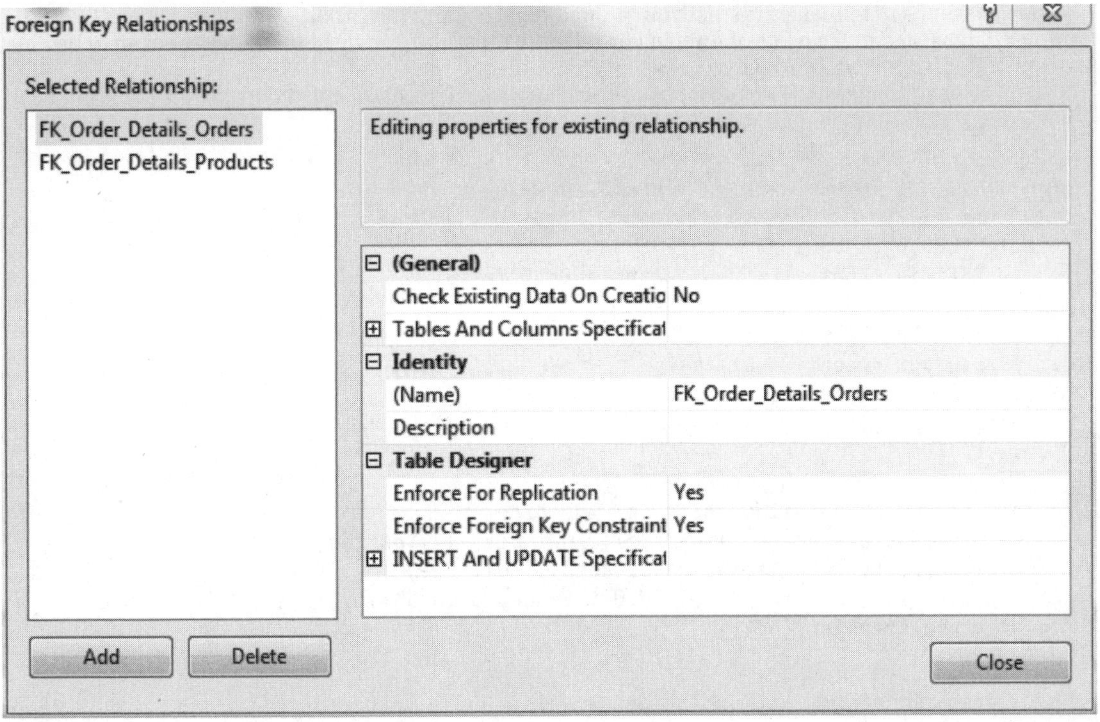

Figure 20-6. *A foreign key constraint*

■ **Tip** SQL Server Management Studio isn't installed with SQL Server Express when you use the Visual Studio 2010 installer. You can download SQL Server Management Studio free of charge from Microsoft.

There are two approaches to safely deleting related objects. You can do it manually, or you can use cascade deletes in the database and your entity data model to handle it automatically. We prefer the automatic approach, but since there are times when you can't modify the database schema, we find that we often have to use the manual approach anyway. We'll show you both methods now.

Manually Deleting Related Objects

Perhaps the simplest way of deleting related objects is to simply pass each of them to the `ObjectContext.DeleteObject` method. You need to be careful when doing this. First, you need to make sure that the order you delete them in doesn't violate a scheme constraint. For example, if we want to delete an `Order`, we have to delete the related `Order_Detail` objects first and then delete the `Order`. You'll get an exception just like the one we saw earlier if you do it the other way around.

Second, you need to make sure you delete them all—you can't leave any behind; otherwise, you'll get an exception or create some rows of orphaned data.

Finally, you need to make sure that your related objects don't have their own related objects. Complex databases can have lots of foreign key relationships, and you need to unpick them all to be able to delete a graph of objects correctly.

So, if we want to manually delete an Order, we have to delete all the related Order_Detail objects first. Listing 20-23 shows you how this is done.

Listing 20-23. *Manually Deleting a Graph of Related Objects*

```
// create the ObjectContext
NorthwindEntities context = new NorthwindEntities();

// query for the first order for LAZYK
Order firstOrder = context.Orders
    .Where(o => o.OrderID == 10248)
    .Select(o => o)
    .First();

// delete the Order_Detail objects for the order
foreach (Order_Detail od in firstOrder.Order_Details.ToArray()) {
    Console.WriteLine("Deleting order detail {0}, {1}, {2}, {3}",
        od.OrderID, od.ProductID, od.UnitPrice, od.Quantity);
    context.DeleteObject(od);
}

// delete the order
context.DeleteObject(firstOrder);

// save the changes
context.SaveChanges();
```

In this example, we query for the Order object that has the OrderID of 10248. We have picked this one because it has more than one related Order_Detail in the database. We enumerate the Order_Detail objects and delete them one by one, before then deleting the Order.

You'll notice that we call the ToArray method on the Order_Details EntityCollection and enumerated the result. If we had not done this, we would have been deleting objects from the enumeration we were processing and received an exception after deleting the first Order_Details object.

Cascade Deleting Related Objects

The other way of handling related object deletion is to use cascade deletes. A cascade delete means that when we delete a record from the database, such as for an Order, related rows that have a foreign key relationship, such as Order Details, will also be deleted automatically. To demonstrate how this would work for the deletion in Listing 20-23, we need to enable the cascade deletes feature on the database and in the EDM. We'll show you how to do this for our Northwind examples, but the fine detail is likely to be slightly different for your own projects.

■ **Note** You must enable cascade deletes in the database and in your entity data model for each foreign key relationship you want to change.

Enabling Cascade Deletes in the Northwind Database

Connect to your SQL Server using the SQL Server Management Studio, and navigate to `FK_Order_Details_Orders` in the `Database/NorthwindTables/dbo.Order Details/Keys` folder, as shown by Figure 20-7.

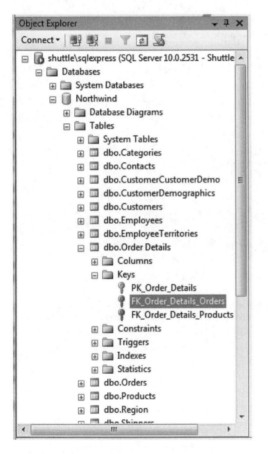

Figure 20-7. The FK_Order_Details_Orders key item

We know that this is the item we want because it was the one mentioned in the exception we got from Listing 20-22. Right-click and select Modify. Expand the `INSERT and UPDATE Specification` part of the tree, and change the setting for Delete Rule to be Cascade. Figure 20-8 shows you what this looks like.

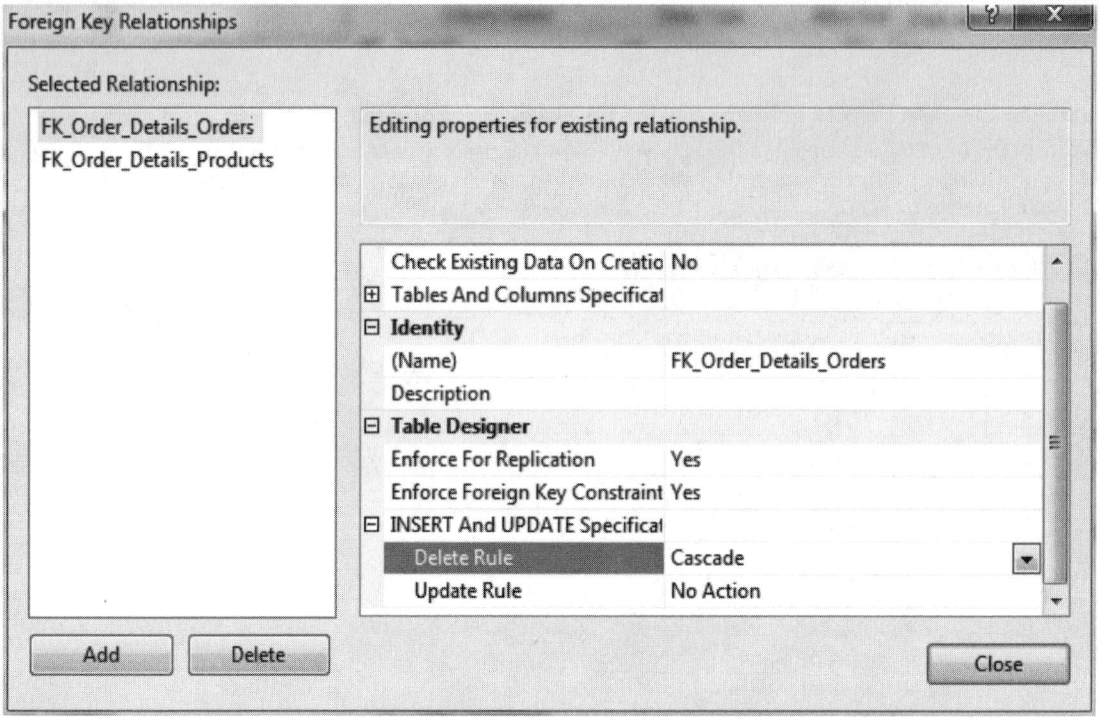

Figure 20-8. Modifying a key constraint with SQL Server Management Studio

Once you have made the change, click the Close button, and then select Save Order Details or Save All from the File menu. We have now told the database that when we delete a row from the Orders table, we want it to automatically delete rows from the Order Details table that use the same key/foreign key value.

Enabling Cascade Deletes in the Entity Data Model

We have enabled the cascade deletes for the Order_Details table in the database, and now we have to do the same for the Order_Detail entity type in the entity data model. It would be nice if the Entity Data Model Wizard would detect cascade deletes for us when it generates or updates the model, but sadly, it doesn't, so we have to do it ourselves.

We need to modify the model to match the database so that the data cached by the Entity Framework is handled properly. If you change the database but not the entity data model, then you end up with cached entity objects that do not map to rows in the database—not good.

First, open the entity data model by double-clicking the EDMX file in the Solution Explorer. Open the Model Browser window by selecting View ➤ Other Windows ➤ Entity Data Model Browser in Visual Studio 2010. Open to tree view to NorthwindDataModel/NorthwindModel/Associations. You will see the FK_Order_Details_Orders item in the list, as shown in Figure 20-9.

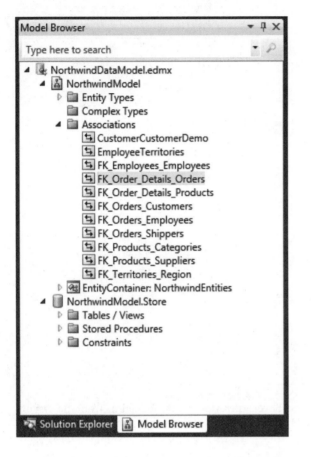

Figure 20-9. *Browsing the foreign key constraint*

Select the FK_Order_Details_Orders item to open the details in the Properties window, and change the value of End1 OnDelete to Cascade, as shown by Figure 20-10.

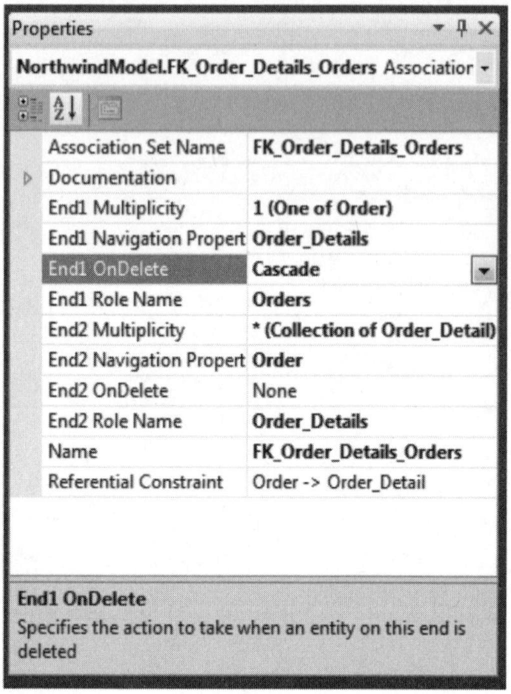

Figure 20-10. Changing the OnDelete action

Once you have made the change, be sure to select Save NorthwindDataModel.edmx from the Visual Studio 2010 File menu. Now that we have changed both the database and the data model, we can delete `Order` entity objects, and the related `Order_Details` will be deleted for us automatically. Listing 20-24 demonstrates this.

Listing 20-24. Deleting with Cascades Enabled

```
// create the ObjectContext
NorthwindEntities context = new NorthwindEntities();

// query for the order
Order firstOrder = context.Orders
    .Where(o => o.OrderID == 10248)
    .Select(o => o)
    .First();

// delete the order
context.DeleteObject(firstOrder);

// save the changes
context.SaveChanges();
```

Managing Concurrency

By default, the Entity Framework uses an optimistic concurrency model. It's optimistic in the sense that it hopes that no one else will modify your data while you are using it and saves changes to the database without checking to see whether anyone else has changed it. Listing 20-25 demonstrates this behavior.

Listing 20-25. An Example of a Concurrency Problem

```
// create the ObjectContext
NorthwindEntities context = new NorthwindEntities();

Customer cust = context.Customers
    .Where(c => c.CustomerID == "LAZYK")
    .Select(c => c)
    .First();

Console.WriteLine("Initial value {0}", cust.ContactName);

// change the record outside of the entity framework
ExecuteStatementInDb(String.Format(
        @"update Customers
        set ContactName = 'Samuel Arthur Sanders'
        where CustomerID = 'LAZYK'"));

// get the database value outside of the Entity Framework
string dbValue = GetStringFromDb(String.Format(
    @"select ContactName from Customers
    where CustomerID = 'LAZYK'"));

Console.WriteLine("Database value: {0}", dbValue);

// modify the customer
cust.ContactName = "John Doe";

// save the changes
context.SaveChanges();
```

We use LINQ to Entities to load an entity object for the Customer with the CustomerID of LAZYK. Then, we update the record directly, outside the Entity Framework, so that the ContactName value is Samuel Arthur Sanders, and then read the value back from the database, also outside the Entity Framework, meaning that the Customer entity object is now out of synchronization with the database.

Using the Customer entity object, we change the ContactName value to John Doe and call SaveChanges. The Entity Framework writes out the change we made to the database and—because optimistic concurrency means that we hope no one else has changed the data—overwrites the change we made outside the Entity Framework.

Enabling Concurrency Checks

You can have the Entity Framework check to see whether the database has been modified by another party before it writes changes. This is still optimistic concurrency because nothing is locked in the database while you are working with the entity objects, but it does help stop the kind of problem that we saw in Listing 20-25 by alerting you to concurrency issues.

You have to enable concurrency checking on a per-field basis. If you want all the fields of an entity object to be checked for concurrency conflicts...well, then you need to be sure that you have edited all of the fields. There is no way of telling the Entity Framework that you want every change to an entity type or even every change to the entire entity data model to be checked automatically.

To solve the problem we saw in Listing 20-25, we need to enable concurrency checking on the ContactName field of the Customer entity type. The first step is to open the EDMX file by double-clicking it in your Solution Explorer window and find the Customer entity in the designer view. Figure 20-11 shows you what this should look like.

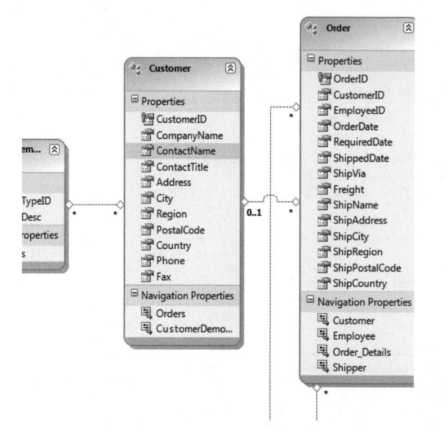

Figure 20-11. The Customer entity type

Click the `ContactName` property to open the details in the `Properties` window, and change the value for `Concurrency Mode` to `Fixed`, as shown by Figure 20-12.

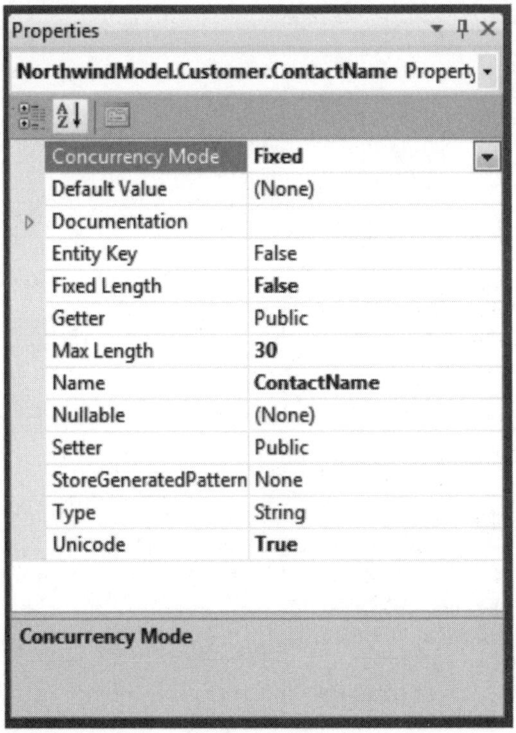

Figure 20-12. Setting the concurrency mode for the ContactName property

Lastly, make sure you save the changes by selecting File ➤ Save NorthwindEntityModel.edmx in Visual Studio.

Handling Concurrency Conflicts

Once you have enabled concurrency conflict checking for an entity object field, you will receive an `OptimisticConcurrencyException` when you try to update data that has been modified since you loaded your entity objects. Listing 20-26 demonstrates this.

Listing 20-26. Handling a Concurrency Conflict

```
// create the ObjectContext
NorthwindEntities context = new NorthwindEntities();

Customer cust = context.Customers
    .Where(c => c.CustomerID == "LAZYK")
```

```
        .Select(c => c)
        .First();

Console.WriteLine("Initial value {0}", cust.ContactName);

// change the record outside of the entity framework
ExecuteStatementInDb(String.Format(
        @"update Customers
        set ContactName = 'Samuel Arthur Sanders'
        where CustomerID = 'LAZYK'"));

// modify the customer
cust.ContactName = "John Doe";

// save the changes
try {
    context.SaveChanges();
} catch (OptimisticConcurrencyException) {
    Console.WriteLine("Detected concurrency conflict - giving up");
} finally {
    string dbValue = GetStringFromDb(String.Format(
        @"select ContactName from Customers
    where CustomerID = 'LAZYK'"));
    Console.WriteLine("Database value: {0}", dbValue);
    Console.WriteLine("Cached value: {0}", cust.ContactName);
}
```

We perform the same query sequence as in Listing 20-25. We obtain the Customer entity object for the record with the CustomerID of LAZYK, change the ContactName field outside of the Entity Framework, make the same change using the Entity Framework, and then call SaveChanges.

We wrap the SaveChanges call in a try...catch...finally block. Since we have enabled concurrency checking on the ContactName field, we know that we will receive an OptimisticConcurrencyException when we try to update the database. In the finally block, we print the ContactName value in the database and the value from the entity object. Compiling and running the code in Listing 20-26 gives us the following output:

```
Initial value John Doe
Executing SQL statement against database with ADO.NET ...
Database updated.
Detected concurrency conflict - giving up
Database value: Samuel Arthur Sanders
Cached value: John Doe
```

We end up with a database that has one value and a cached entity object that has a conflicting value for the same data. That's a step forward—at least we didn't write back an update to the database without checking first. But now we need to resolve the differences in the data values so we are back in sync and can (optionally) try to update again. We do this by using the `ObjectContext.Refresh` method. Listing 20-27 contains an example.

***Listing 20-27.** Using the Refresh Method*

```
// create the ObjectContext
NorthwindEntities context = new NorthwindEntities();

Customer cust = context.Customers
    .Where(c => c.CustomerID == "LAZYK")
    .Select(c => c)
    .First();

Console.WriteLine("Initial value {0}", cust.ContactName);

// change the record outside of the entity framework
ExecuteStatementInDb(String.Format(
        @"update Customers
        set ContactName = 'Samuel Arthur Sanders'
        where CustomerID = 'LAZYK'"));

// modify the customer
cust.ContactName = "John Doe";

// save the changes
try {
    context.SaveChanges();
} catch (OptimisticConcurrencyException) {
    Console.WriteLine("Detected concurrency conflict - refreshing data");
    context.Refresh(RefreshMode.StoreWins, cust);
} finally {
    string dbValue = GetStringFromDb(String.Format(
        @"select ContactName from Customers
        where CustomerID = 'LAZYK'"));
    Console.WriteLine("Database value: {0}", dbValue);
    Console.WriteLine("Cached value: {0}", cust.ContactName);
}
```

In this example, we call the `Refresh` method when we catch the `OptimisticConcurrencyException`. The `Refresh` method takes two arguments. The first is a value from the `RefreshMode` enumeration, and the second is the object that you want to refresh. The `RefreshMode` enumeration has two values—`StoreWins` and `ClientWins`. The `StoreWins` value refreshes the values for the object you specified using the data in the database. So, in our example, we would expect both the value in the entity object and the value in the database to be `Samuel Arthur Adams`. Compiling and running the code gives us the expected results:

```
Initial value John Steel
Executing SQL statement against database with ADO.NET ...
Database updated.
Detected concurrency conflict - refreshing data
Database value: Samuel Arthur Sanders
Cached value: Samuel Arthur Sanders
```

Let's just recap what happened there. We tried to write an update on a database row that had been modified by someone else. The Entity Framework detected a concurrency conflict and threw an `OptimisticConcurrencyException` to let us know that there was a problem. We refreshed the entity object we modified using the data in the database, which put us back to a consistent state.

But what happened to our update? Well, nothing—we didn't apply it. If you want to apply your changes even when someone else has modified the same data you are using, then you need to use the `ClientWins` value of the `RefreshMode` enumeration and call `SaveChanges` again. Listing 20-28 contains an example.

Listing 20-28. *Writing an Update Following a Concurrency Conflict*

```
// create the ObjectContext
NorthwindEntities context = new NorthwindEntities();

Customer cust = context.Customers
    .Where(c => c.CustomerID == "LAZYK")
    .Select(c => c)
    .First();

Console.WriteLine("Initial value {0}", cust.ContactName);

// change the record outside of the entity framework
ExecuteStatementInDb(String.Format(
        @"update Customers
        set ContactName = 'Samuel Arthur Sanders'
        where CustomerID = 'LAZYK'"));

// modify the customer
cust.ContactName = "John Doe";

// save the changes
try {
    context.SaveChanges();
} catch (OptimisticConcurrencyException) {
    Console.WriteLine("Detected concurrency conflict - refreshing data");
    context.Refresh(RefreshMode.ClientWins, cust);
    context.SaveChanges();
} finally {
    string dbValue = GetStringFromDb(String.Format(
        @"select ContactName from Customers
```

```
        where CustomerID = 'LAZYK'"));
    Console.WriteLine("Database value: {0}", dbValue);
    Console.WriteLine("Cached value: {0}", cust.ContactName);
}
```

This time, we have specified the ClientWins value, which is like saying "I know there is a concurrency conflict, but I want to keep my changes." You need to call SaveChanges again. The call to the Refresh method just clears the concurrency conflict for the Entity Framework and doesn't write the changes for you. If we compile and run the code in Listing 20-28, we get the following results:

```
Initial value John Steel
Executing SQL statement against database with ADO.NET ...
Database updated.
Detected concurrency conflict - refreshing data
Database value: John Doe
Cached value: John Doe
```

We can see that the change that we made using the Entity Framework has been written to the database. There is one point we want to make about dealing with a concurrency conflict properly—someone may have changed the data again while we were refreshing our entity objects. That means that our second call to SaveChanges may result in another OptimisticConcurrencyException. To deal with this, we can use a loop that tries to apply our update repeatedly. Listing 20-29 shows you this approach.

Listing 20-29. *Repeating a Save Request*

```
// create the ObjectContext
NorthwindEntities context = new NorthwindEntities();

Customer cust = context.Customers
    .Where(c => c.CustomerID == "LAZYK")
    .Select(c => c)
    .First();

Console.WriteLine("Initial value {0}", cust.ContactName);

// change the record outside of the entity framework
ExecuteStatementInDb(String.Format(
        @"update Customers
        set ContactName = 'Samuel Arthur Sanders'
        where CustomerID = 'LAZYK'"));

// modify the customer
cust.ContactName = "John Doe";
```

```
int maxAttempts = 5;
bool recordsUpdated = false;

for (int i = 0; i < maxAttempts && !recordsUpdated; i++) {
    Console.WriteLine("Performing write attempt {0}", i);
    // save the changes
    try {
        context.SaveChanges();
        recordsUpdated = true;
    } catch (OptimisticConcurrencyException) {
        Console.WriteLine("Detected concurrency conflict - refreshing data");
        context.Refresh(RefreshMode.ClientWins, cust);
    }
}

string dbValue = GetStringFromDb(String.Format(
    @"select ContactName from Customers
    where CustomerID = 'LAZYK'"));
Console.WriteLine("Database value: {0}", dbValue);
Console.WriteLine("Cached value: {0}", cust.ContactName);
```

We use a loop to try applying our update to the database several times. The bool recordsUpdated will be set to true only if the SaveChanges method doesn't throw an exception. This can be a useful technique, but it should be used carefully.

First, the more attempts we make to write our changes, the more updates from others we are ignoring. We have to be very confident that our update is more important than all the others to keep trying to save our changes.

Second, you will see that we used a loop counter to try writing our update five times and no more. There are very few situations in which you should try to save your changes in an infinite loop. Not only do you have to be super-confident that you have the best data, but there comes a point where you have to question the design of your code or the value of the data you are generating. If the same rows are being updated again and again, the chances are that most of the updates are being discarded as processes keep forcing their changes into the database. So, as a word to the wise, we think you should be very careful when automatically trying to save changes when you encounter a concurrency conflict.

Summary

In this chapter, we have introduced you to the core database operations you can perform with the Entity Framework and LINQ to Entities. We showed you how to query for data using LINQ to Entities, as well as inserting, modifying, and deleting using the Entity Framework. We also showed you how to handle concurrency conflicts—something that you will find increasingly important as your database server becomes busier and busier. In the next chapter, we'll walk you through some of the key Entity Framework classes and show you how to get more control over how your entity objects are created and used.

CHAPTER 21

LINQ to Entities Classes

In the previous chapters, we used a number of Entity Framework classes to demonstrate LINQ to Entities features without fully defining them. In this chapter, we set that right by detailing the key members of the most important Entity Framework classes.

As we have already explained, the Entity Framework is an expensive and complex toolset, so we have had to skim the surface somewhat to be able to keep our focus on the LINQ to Entities side of things. Our skimming continues in this chapter. We have been selective about the classes and members we describe, choosing to focus on the ones that we have used in previous chapters and those that you need to get started with the Entity Framework and LINQ to Entities in particular.

Prerequisites for Running the Examples

To run the examples in this chapter, you will need to have obtained the extended version of the Northwind database and generated an entity data model for it. Please read the instructions in Chapter 19's "Prerequisites for Running the Examples" section. Additionally, to run the examples in this chapter, you will need some common methods that will be utilized by the examples. Please read the instructions in Chapter 19's "Some Common Methods" section.

■ **Warning** Some of the example in this chapter modify (and even delete) the database. If you run these examples, you should detach the Northwind database from SQL Server and attach the original version you downloaded with the source code to the examples from Apress.com.

The ObjectContext Class

The `ObjectContext` class is at the heart of the Entity Framework and LINQ to Entities. When you create an entity data model, a class derived from `ObjectContext` is created for you with properties that represent the entity types and collections that are specific to your database. In the `Northwind` entity data model we created in Chapter 19, the derived class was called `NorthwindEntities`. We have been using this class throughout our LINQ to Entities examples to handle our connection to the database, load our entity objects, and save changes to the database when we make modifications. And, since this is the derived class, `NorthwindEntities` has public properties for the collections of entity objects used to represent the contents of the Northwind database. You will find the `ObjectContext` class in the `System.Data.Objects` namespace.

Constructor

You must create a new instance of the derived `ObjectContext` class before you can use any of the Entity Framework or LINQ to Entity features that we described in the previous chapters. The instance you create is responsible for managing the connection to the database and is used to load data from and save changes to the database.

Prototypes

There are two derived `ObjectContext` constructor prototypes that we will cover.

The First Derived ObjectContext Constructor

```
public NorthwindEntities();
```

This is the default constructor that creates a new instance of the derived `ObjectContext` class using the database construction string that we added to the `App.Config` file when the entity data model was created. This is the prototype that we have used in the examples throughout the LINQ to Entities chapters.

The Second Derived ObjectConText Constructor

```
public NorthwindEntities(string connectionString);
```

This constructor prototype allows you to specify a string containing the details that will be used to connect to the database or the name of the connection string in the `App.Config` file.

Examples

Listing 21-1 uses the default constructor prototype to create a new derived `ObjectContext` instance, which is then used to query `Customer` data.

Listing 21-1. Using the Default Derived ObjectContext Constructor

```
NorthwindEntities context = new NorthwindEntities();

IQueryable<Customer> custs = context.Customers
    .Where(c => c.City == "London")
    .Select(c => c);

foreach (Customer cust in custs) {
    Console.WriteLine("Customer name: {0}", cust.CompanyName);
}
```

Listing 21-2 uses the second constructor prototype to specify the name of the connection string in the App.Config file. The resulting derived ObjectContext instance is then used to query the database.

Listing 21-2. Specifying the Name of the Connection String Property

```
string connectionString = "name=NorthwindEntities";

NorthwindEntities context = new NorthwindEntities(connectionString);

IQueryable<Customer> custs = context.Customers
    .Where(c => c.City == "London")
    .Select(c => c);

foreach (Customer cust in custs) {
    Console.WriteLine("Customer name: {0}", cust.CompanyName);
}
```

You can also use the second constructor prototype to supply a completely custom connection string. The easiest way to do this is with the EntityConnectionStringBuilder and SqlConnectionStringBuilder classes, which you can find in the System.Data.EntityClient and System.Data.SqlClient namespaces, respectively. Listing 21-3 shows you how to use these classes to create the same connection string placed in the App.Config file when we created the Northwind entity data model in Chapter 19.

Listing 21-3. Creating and Using a Custom Connection String

```
SqlConnectionStringBuilder scsb = new SqlConnectionStringBuilder();
scsb.DataSource = @".\sqlexpress";
scsb.InitialCatalog = "Northwind";
scsb.IntegratedSecurity = true;
scsb.MultipleActiveResultSets = true;

EntityConnectionStringBuilder ecsb = new EntityConnectionStringBuilder();
ecsb.Provider = "System.Data.SqlClient";
ecsb.ProviderConnectionString = scsb.ToString();
ecsb.Metadata = @"res://*/NorthwindEntityModel.csdl|
        res://*/NorthwindEntityModel.ssdl
        |res://*/NorthwindEntityModel.msl";

NorthwindEntities context = new NorthwindEntities(ecsb.ToString());

IQueryable<Customer> custs = context.Customers
    .Where(c => c.City == "London")
    .Select(c => c);

foreach (Customer cust in custs) {
```

```
    Console.WriteLine("Customer name: {0}", cust.CompanyName);
}
```

DatabaseExists()

The DatabaseExists method returns true if the database specified in the connection string used to create the ObjectContext exists and false if it does not.

Prototypes

The DatabaseExists method has one prototype that we will cover.

The Sole DatabaseExists Prototype

```
public bool DatabaseExists();
```

The DatabaseExists method returns true if the database specified in the connection string used to create the ObjectContext exists and false if it does not.

Examples

Listing 21-4 creates an instance of the derived ObjectContext class for the Northwind database and uses the DatabaseExists method.

Listing 21-4. Using the DatabaseExists Method

```
NorthwindEntities context = new NorthwindEntities();

bool databaseExists = context.DatabaseExists();
Console.WriteLine("Database exists: {0}", databaseExists);
```

DeleteDatabase()

The DeleteDatabase method deletes the database specified in the connection string used to create the derived ObjectContext instance. This method is typically used in conjunction with the DatabaseExists method.

Prototypes

The DeleteDatabase method has one prototype.

```
public void DeleteDatabase();
```

Examples

Listing 21-5 uses the DeleteDatabase method to delete the Northwind database.

■ **Caution** You will need to restore the original version of the Northwind database if you compile and run Listing 21-5.

Listing 21-5. Deleting a Database

```
NorthwindEntities context = new NorthwindEntities();

if (context.DatabaseExists()) {
    context.DeleteDatabase();
}
```

CreateDatabase()

The CreateDatabase method uses the entity data model to create a new database, although there will be no data, of course. This method is usually used in conjunction with the DatabaseExists method.

Prototypes

The CreateDatabase method has one prototype.

```
public void CreateDatabase();
```

Examples

Listing 21-6 creates a new database using the Northwind entity data model.

Listing 21-6. Creating a New Database

```
NorthwindEntities context = new NorthwindEntities();

if (!context.DatabaseExists()) {
    context.CreateDatabase();
}
```

SaveChanges()

The SaveChanges method persists modifications made to entity objects to the database. This method will throw an OptimisticConcurrencyException if concurrency checking is enabled and there is an update conflict. See Chapter 20 for details of how to manage Entity Framework concurrency issues.

Prototypes

The SaveChanges method has one prototype we will cover.

The SaveChanges Prototype

```
public int SaveChanges();
```

The return value indicates how many entity objects were added, updated, or deleted.

Examples

Listing 21-7 modifies the ContactName field of the Customer entity type and calls the SaveChanges method to persist the modification to the database.

Listing 21-7. Using the SaveChanges Method

```
NorthwindEntities context = new NorthwindEntities();

Customer cust = (from c in context.Customers
                 where c.CustomerID == "LAZYK"
                 select c).First();

cust.ContactName = "John Doe";

int modificationCount = context.SaveChanges();

Console.WriteLine("Count: {0}", modificationCount);
```

Refresh()

The Entity Framework caches entity objects to improve performance. This means that the data you are working with can become stale when other people and processes update the database. If you modify stale data and try to write it to the database, you will cause a concurrency conflict.

The Refresh method has two purposes. It can be used to proactively refresh one or more entity objects to the latest data in the database, and it can be used when resolving concurrency conflicts when they arise.

Prototypes

The Refresh method has two prototypes. Both use the RefreshMode enumeration, which has two values—StoreWins and ClientWins. When proactively refreshing data, the StoreWins value should be used, because it specifies that changes made to entity objects should be discarded in favor of changes made in the database. When resolving concurrency conflicts, either enumeration value can be used; see Chapter 20 for details and examples.

The First Refresh Prototype

```
public void Refresh(RefreshMode refreshMode,
    Object entity);
```
This prototype refreshes a single entity object using the specified RefreshMode.

The Second Refresh Prototype

```
public void Refresh(RefreshMode refreshMode,
    IEnumerable collection);
```
This prototype refreshes a collection of entity objects using the specified RefreshMode. This prototype can be used to update one of the collections of entity objects in the derived ObjectContext class representing a table.

Examples
Listing 21-8 proactively refreshes a single Customer entity object and the collection of Customer entity objects in the context.Customers property.

Listing 21-8. Using the Refresh Method

```
NorthwindEntities context = new NorthwindEntities();

Customer cust = (from c in context.Customers
                where c.CustomerID == "LAZYK"
                select c).First();

// refresh a single entity object
context.Refresh(RefreshMode.StoreWins, cust);
// refresh an entire collection of objects
context.Refresh(RefreshMode.StoreWins, context.Customers);
```

AddObject()
The AddObject method adds a new entity object to one of the collections managed by the derived ObjectContext class.

Prototypes
There is one prototype for the AddObject method.

```
public void AddObject(
    string entitySetName,
    Object entity);
```

The first argument is the name of the collection to which the object should be added. The second argument is the entity object you want to add. Note that the database is not updated with the data contained in the new entity object until the SaveChanges method is called.

Examples

Listing 21-9 creates a new instance of the Customer entity type and sets the field values. The AddObject method is used to add the entity object to the Customers collection. Finally, the SaveChanges method is used to write the new Customer record to the database.

Listing 21-9. Adding an Entity Object to the ObjectContext

```
NorthwindEntities context = new NorthwindEntities();

// create a new customer object
Customer cust = Customer.CreateCustomer("LAWN", "Lawn Wranglers");

// populate the nullable fields
cust.ContactName = "Mr. Abe Henry";
cust.ContactTitle = "Owner";
cust.Address = "1017 Maple Leaf Way";
cust.City = "Ft. Worth";
cust.Region = "TX";
cust.PostalCode = "76104";
cust.Country = "USA";
cust.Phone = "(800) MOW-LAWN";
cust.Fax = "(800) MOW-LAWO";

context.AddObject("Customers", cust);

context.SaveChanges();
```

CreateObject()

The CreateObject method creates a new entity object. The new object contains no data and must be added to one of the entity object collections in the ObjectContext before the SaveChanges method will persist the object to the database. You must take care to populate the entity object before calling SaveChanges if the database schema definition requires that some fields are not null.

Prototypes

The CreateObject method is strongly typed, meaning that there is one prototype for each entity type supported by the derived ObjectContext class in the following form, where T is the entity type you want to instantiate:

```
public T CreateObject<T>();
```

In the case of the Northwind database, that means that there is a prototype for the Customer entity type as follows:

```
public Customer CreateObject<Customer>();
```

And for the Order entity type as follows:

```
public Order CreateObject<Order>();
```

And so on, for each of the entity types contained in the entity data model.

Examples

Listing 21-10 uses the CreateObject method to create a new Customer entity object. The fields are populated (including the CustomerID and CompanyName fields, which are non-nullable), and the object is added to the Customers collection using the AddObject method. The new Customer is persisted to the database by calling the SaveChanges method.

Listing 21-10. Creating an Entity Type Instance Using the ObjectContext

```
NorthwindEntities context = new NorthwindEntities();

// create a new customer object
Customer cust = context.CreateObject<Customer>();

// populate all of the fields
cust.CustomerID = "LAWN";
cust.CompanyName = "Lawn Wranglers";
cust.ContactName = "Mr. Abe Henry";
cust.ContactTitle = "Owner";
cust.Address = "1017 Maple Leaf Way";
cust.City = "Ft. Worth";
cust.Region = "TX";
cust.PostalCode = "76104";
cust.Country = "USA";
cust.Phone = "(800) MOW-LAWN";
cust.Fax = "(800) MOW-LAWO";

context.AddObject("Customers", cust);

context.SaveChanges();
```

DeleteObject()

The DeleteObject method deletes an object from the entity cache and deletes the corresponding data in the database when the SaveChanges method is called. Care must be taken when deleting objects to manage related objects; see Chapter 20 for full details.

Prototypes

The `DeleteObject` method has one prototype.

```
public void DeleteObject(Object entity);
```

The argument to this prototype is the entity object that you want to delete.

Examples

Listing 21-11 queries for the `Order_Detail` entity objects that have an `OrderID` value of 10248. The results are enumerated using a `foreach` loop and deleted using the `DeleteObject` method. To persist the deletions, the `SaveChanges` method is called.

Listing 21-11. Deleting Entity Objects

```
// create the ObjectContext
NorthwindEntities context = new NorthwindEntities();

// get the order details for order 10248
IQueryable<Order_Detail> ods = (from o in context.Order_Details
                where o.OrderID == 10248
                select o);

foreach (Order_Detail od in ods) {
    context.DeleteObject(od);
}

// save the changes
context.SaveChanges();
```

EntityObject

The entity types created in the entity data model to represent the schema of your database are derived from the `EntityObject` class, which is part of the `System.Data.Objects.DataClasses` namespace.

Constructor

You can create new instances of entity types using the constructor, but you must take care to ensure that fields that map to database columns that cannot be null have values. If you do not do this, you will get an exception when you try to persist your new entity object to the database.

Prototypes

There is one constructor prototype, where `T` is the entity type.

```
public T();
```

Examples

Listing 21-12 demonstrates creating a new instance of the `Customer` entity type, populating the data fields, and persisting it to the database using the `SaveChanges` method in the `ObjectContext` class.

Listing 21-12. Creating a New Entity Object Using the Default Constructor

```
NorthwindEntities context = new NorthwindEntities();

// create a new customer object
Customer cust = new Customer();

// populate all of the fields
cust.CustomerID = "LAWN";
cust.CompanyName = "Lawn Wranglers";
cust.ContactName = "Mr. Abe Henry";
cust.ContactTitle = "Owner";
cust.Address = "1017 Maple Leaf Way";
cust.City = "Ft. Worth";
cust.Region = "TX";
cust.PostalCode = "76104";
cust.Country = "USA";
cust.Phone = "(800) MOW-LAWN";
cust.Fax = "(800) MOW-LAWO";

context.AddObject("Customers", cust);

context.SaveChanges();
```

Factory Method

A static factory method is added to entity types when they are created by the Entity Data Model Wizard. (See Chapter 19 for details of how to use the Entity Data Model Wizard with the Northwind database.) The factory method can be used to create new instances of an entity type and has the advantage over the default constructor of requiring values for all the fields that require values in the database. This nicely avoids the problem of creating a new instance that lacks one of these values and then getting an exception when you try to store it in the database with the `SaveChanges` method. As with the default constructor, entity objects that are created using the factory method will not be persisted until you add them to one of the entity type collections maintained by the derived `ObjectContext` class (see the `ObjectContext AddObject` method for an example).

Prototypes

The prototype for the factory method will vary based on the entity type, but it follows a general pattern. If the entity type represents a row from a database table where all the values can be set to `null`, then there will be no arguments for the factory method, and the prototype will be as follows:

The Default Entity Type Factory Method

```
public static T CreateT();
```

So, for example, if we have an entity type MyType that represents data from a table in which all the columns will accept null values, the prototype for the factory method would be as follows:

```
public static MyType CreateMyType();
```

If the entity type represents rows from a table that has columns that *cannot* be null, then there will be an argument for each required data value. For example, if we look at the Customers table in the Northwind database using SQL Server Management Studio, as shown in Figure 21-1, we can see that the CustomerID and CompanyName columns have not been checked for Allow Nulls.

SHUTTLE\SQLEXPR...- dbo.Customers		
Column Name	Data Type	Allow Nulls
⚷ CustomerID	nchar(5)	☐
CompanyName	nvarchar(40)	☐
ContactName	nvarchar(30)	☑
ContactTitle	nvarchar(30)	☑
Address	nvarchar(60)	☑
City	nvarchar(15)	☑
Region	nvarchar(15)	☑
PostalCode	nvarchar(10)	☑
Country	nvarchar(15)	☑
Phone	nvarchar(24)	☑
Fax	nvarchar(24)	☑
▶		☐

Figure 21-1. *The Customers table in the Northwind database*

These are the data fields for the Customer entity type that will be required as arguments to the static factory method, which has the following prototype:

The Prototype for the Northwind Customer Entity Type Factory Method

```
public static Customer CreateCustomer(String customerID, String companyName);
```

The simplest way to work out the prototype for the factory method is to use the IntelliSense feature of Visual Studio or even to look at the source code for the entity type.

Examples

Listing 21-13 creates a new instance of the Customer entity type using the factory method, supplying values for the mandatory data fields. The remaining data fields are then set (although these could have been left with the default values). The new object is then added to the Customers entity collection maintained by the derived ObjectContext class and persisted by calling SaveChanges.

Listing 21-13. Using the Factory Method to Create a New Entity Object

```
NorthwindEntities context = new NorthwindEntities();

// create a new customer object
Customer cust = Customer.CreateCustomer("LAWN", "Lawn Wranglers");

// populate the remaining fields
cust.ContactName = "Mr. Abe Henry";
cust.ContactTitle = "Owner";
cust.Address = "1017 Maple Leaf Way";
cust.City = "Ft. Worth";
cust.Region = "TX";
cust.PostalCode = "76104";
cust.Country = "USA";
cust.Phone = "(800) MOW-LAWN";
cust.Fax = "(800) MOW-LAWO";

context.AddObject("Customers", cust);

context.SaveChanges();
```

Primitive Properties

Each entity type has a set of public properties that correspond to the columns in the table with which it is associated. These properties allow us to get and set the data value for the row in the table that a specific instance of an entity type represents.

Prototypes

The set of properties that an entity type has depends on the design of the database table it is associated with. The general prototype is as follows, where T is the data type o and ColumnName is the name of the data field:

The General Entity Type Primitive Property Prototype

```
public T ColumnName {get; set};
```

The general prototype isn't much use. It is much more helpful to look at an actual implementation. Figure 21-1 shows the columns for the Customers table in the Northwind database, rows of which are represented by the `Customer` entity type in the entity data model we created in Chapter 19. For each of the columns shown in the figure, we will find a public property that allows us to get and set the associated data value. For example, the `City` column will have a prototype as follows:

The Prototype for the Customer City Primitive Property

```
public String City {get; set};
```

Examples

Most of the examples in the LINQ to Entities chapters use the primitive properties in some form. Listing 21-14 reads the value of the `City` property from a `Customer` entity object, modifies the value, and persists the change to the database using the `SaveChanges` method. Changes to property values are not written to the database until the `SaveChanges` method is called.

Listing 21-14. *Reading and Changing a Primitive Property Value*

```
NorthwindEntities context = new NorthwindEntities();

// query for a customer record
Customer cust = (from c in context.Customers
                where c.CustomerID == "LAZYK"
                select c).First();

// access the current data value
Console.WriteLine("Original City Value: {0}", cust.City);

// change the value
cust.City = "Seattle";

// write the new (but not persisted value)
Console.WriteLine("New City Value: {0}", cust.City);

// save the changes
context.SaveChanges();
```

Compiling and running the code in Listing 21-14 gives us the following results:

```
Original City Value: Walla Walla
New City Value: Seattle
```

Navigation Properties

Navigation properties allow you to work easily with related entity objects, especially when the objects are related through a foreign key.

Imagine that you want to find the set of orders that a customer has placed in the Northwind database and the only data you have to start with is the name of the company. Without navigation properties, you would have to make two LINQ queries—one to find the Customer entity object and then another to get all the Order entity objects that have a foreign key relationship with the Customer you found. Listing 21-15 shows you how this would work.

Listing 21-15. *Querying Without Navigation Properties*

```
NorthwindEntities context = new NorthwindEntities();

// query for the customer record
Customer cust = (from c in context.Customers
                 where c.CompanyName == "Lazy K Kountry Store"
                 select c).First();

// query for the orders placed by that company
IQueryable<Order> orders = from o in context.Orders
                           where o.CustomerID == cust.CustomerID
                           select o;

// print out the orders
foreach (Order ord in orders) {
    Console.WriteLine("Order ID {0}, Date {1}", ord.OrderID, ord.OrderDate);
}
```

Compiling and running the code in Listing 21-15 gives us the following results:

```
Order ID 10482, Date 21/03/1997 00:00:00
Order ID 10545, Date 22/05/1997 00:00:00
```

We get the result we needed, but we can use the navigation properties to avoid having to make the second query explicit.

Prototypes

For each foreign-key relationship in the database, there will be a pair of navigation properties in the entity data model—one in each of the entity types affected. The prototype for the property depends on the multiplicity of the relationship. If an entity type can be related to multiple instances of the other entity type (such as a Northwind Customer can be related to many Orders), then the prototype will be as follows, where T is the related entity type and TableNameOfT is the name of the database table that T represents rows from:

The Multiple Relationship Navigation Property Prototype

```
public EntityCollection<T> TableNameOfT {get; set};
```

These sentences to describe prototypes can be very hard to parse, so an example may help. In the Northwind database, the Customers and Orders tables share a foreign key relationship, such that multiple Orders rows can have a foreign key from a single Customers row. Rows from the Customers table are represented by the Customer entity type, and rows from the Orders table are represented by the Order entity type. All of this means that there will be a navigation property in the Customer type with the following prototype. We'll cover the EntityCollection class later in this chapter.

The Customer.Orders Relationship Navigation Property Prototype

```
public EntityCollection<Order> Orders {get; set};
```

If there can be at most one related entity object in the relationship, then the prototype is as follows, where T is the entity type:

The Single Relationship Navigation Property Prototype

```
public EntityReference<T> TReference {get; set};
```

In the case of the Northwind Order entity type, there can be only one related Customer object, so the prototype would be as follows:

The Order.Customer Relationship Navigation Property Prototype

```
public EntityReference<Customer> CustomerReference {get; set};
```

The Entity Data Model Wizard will also create a convenience property for this kind of relationship. The prototype is as follows, where T is the related entity type:

The Single Relationship Navigation Convenience Property Prototype

```
public T T {get; set};
```

For the CustomerReference property in the Order entity type, the convenience prototype would be as follows. This is a nice feature that stops you from having to deal with the EntityReference class, which we describe later in the chapter.

The Order.Customer Navigation Convenience Property Prototype

```
public Customer Customer {get; set};
```

Examples

Listing 21-16 shows how the `Orders` navigation property in the Northwind `Customer` entity type can be used to get all the orders for a given customer. This is the same outcome as for Listing 21-15, but without the need for an explicit second query. When we say explicit, we mean that the data will still be obtained from the database, but the navigation property makes it easier for you to code—see Chapter 20 for details of the different ways that you can influence how data is loaded from the database.

Listing 21-16. Using the One-to-Many Navigation Property

```
NorthwindEntities context = new NorthwindEntities();

// query for the customer record
Customer cust = (from c in context.Customers
                 where c.CompanyName == "Lazy K Kountry Store"
                 select c).First();

EntityCollection<Order> orders = cust.Orders;

foreach (Order ord in orders) {
    Console.WriteLine("Order ID: {0} Date: {1}", ord.OrderID, ord.OrderDate);
}
```

In the listing, we have made the use of the `EntityCollection` class clear, but if you look at some of the other examples in the LINQ to Entities chapters, you will see that we have been using the navigation properties liberally throughout but not declaring the class explicitly. Compiling and running the code in Listing 21-16 gives the following results, which is exactly the same output we got from Listing 21-15.

```
Order ID: 10482 Date: 21/03/1997 00:00:00
Order ID: 10545 Date: 22/05/1997 00:00:00
```

Listing 21-17 shows the use of the single-instance navigation property between the `Order` type and its corresponding `Customer`.

Listing 21-17. Using a Single-Instance Navigation Property

```
NorthwindEntities context = new NorthwindEntities();

// query for the order
Order ord = (from o in context.Orders
             where o.CustomerID == "LAZYK"
             select o).First();

// get the entity reference
EntityReference<Customer> customerRef = ord.CustomerReference;
```

```
Console.WriteLine("Customer name: {0}", customerRef.Value.CompanyName);

// get the customer via the convenience property
Customer cust = ord.Customer;

Console.WriteLine("Customer name: {0}", cust.CompanyName);
```

We obtain the `EntityReference<Customer>` through the `CustomerReference` property. To get the `Customer` type from the `EntityReference`, we must call the `Value` property. We will cover the `EntityReference` class later in this chapter.

More convenient is accessing the entity type directly through the `Customer` property. Listing 21-17 shows both approaches and prints out the `CompanyName` property each time, giving us the following results:

```
Customer name: Lazy K Kountry Store
Customer name: Lazy K Kountry Store
```

EntityReference

The `EntityReference` class is used in maintaining single-instance navigation properties between entity types; see the previous section for details of navigation properties. This is not a class that you will need to work with very often. It is usually simple to use the convenience property that is created when the entity type is generated by the Entity Data Model Wizard. We include the key members here for completeness.

Load()

The `Load` method is used with explicit data loading, which we described in Chapter 20; see that chapter for details of explicit loading.

Examples

Listing 21-18 demonstrates how to explicitly load the entity object associated with an `EntityReference`. Note that in order for this method to have an effect, lazy loading must be disabled; see Chapter 20 for details and examples.

Listing 21-18. Using the EntityReference Load Method

```
NorthwindEntities context = new NorthwindEntities();

// disable lazy loading
context.ContextOptions.LazyLoadingEnabled = false;

// query for the order
```

```
Order ord = (from o in context.Orders
             where o.CustomerID == "LAZYK"
             select o).First();

// get the entity reference
EntityReference<Customer> customerRef = ord.CustomerReference;

// explicitly load the order
customerRef.Load();
```

Value

The Value property returns the underlying entity type that the EntityReference relates to. In Listing 21-17, we called the Value property to obtain the Customer entity object related to the Order entity object we were working with.

EntityCollection

As its name suggests, the EntityCollection is used to hold a collection of entity objects, most often at one end of a navigation property. For example, in the Northwind Customer entity type, the Orders property is an EntityCollection<Order> and is used to contain the Orders related to a given Customer.

The most common ways of using EntityCollection are to enumerate the elements in the collection using a foreach loop or as the basis for a LINQ query. The EntityCollection class implements interfaces that allow enumeration—IEnumerable<T> and IEnumerable, where T is the entity type being collected. You can see examples of both approaches through the LINQ to Entities chapters in this book. The EntityCollection class implements some other useful methods, which we describe here.

Add()

Adding an entity type to an EntityCollection establishes the foreign-key relationship between them and makes them related objects. The Entity Framework will helpfully set the foreign key fields for you. If this is a new object, then a row will be created in the database for you when you call SaveChanges. If you have added an existing entity object, then the foreign-key relationship will be updated when you call SaveChanges.

Prototypes

The Add method has one prototype that we will cover.

The Add Method Prototype

```
public void Add(Object entity);
```

The effect of calling the Add method is reflected in the cached data maintained by the Entity Framework immediately but will not be reflected in the database until you call the SaveChanges method in the derived ObjectContext class. See Chapter 20 for details of how to persist changes and earlier in this chapter for more information about the ObjectContext class.

Examples

Listing 21-19 creates a new Order entity type and calls the Add method on the Customer.Orders EntityCollection to relate the Order with the Customer.

Listing 21-19. *Using the Add Method to Relate Objects*

```
NorthwindEntities context = new NorthwindEntities();

// query for the customer record
Customer cust = (from c in context.Customers
                where c.CompanyName == "Lazy K Kountry Store"
                select c).First();

Order ord = Order.CreateOrder(1234);

cust.Orders.Add(ord);

Console.WriteLine("Order CustomerID: {0}", ord.CustomerID);
```

Compiling and running the code in Listing 21-19 gives us the following results, which demonstrate that the foreign key relationship has been established between the Customer and Order objects.

```
Order CustomerID: LAZYK
```

Notice that we didn't call the SaveChanges method, meaning that we have modified the cached data in the Entity Framework but no change has been made to the database. If we called Refresh to update the cached data, our changes would be lost; see the ObjectContext section of this chapter for more details of the Refresh method.

You can change the relationship between entity objects with the Add method. Listing 21-20 contains an example.

Listing 21-20. *Using the Add Method to Change Foreign-Key Relationships*

```
NorthwindEntities context = new NorthwindEntities();

// get the LAZYK customer
Customer cust1 = (from c in context.Customers
                where c.CustomerID == "LAZYK"
```

```
                select c).First();

// get the AROUT customer
Customer cust2 = (from c in context.Customers
                    where c.CustomerID == "AROUT"
                    select c).First();

// get the first LAZY K order
Order firstOrder = cust1.Orders.First();

Console.WriteLine("First LAZYK Customer ID: {0}, Order ID: {1}",
firstOrder.CustomerID, firstOrder.OrderID);

// Add the LAZYK order to the AROUT orders set
cust2.Orders.Add(firstOrder);

Console.WriteLine("First LAZYK Customer ID: {0}, Order ID: {1}",
firstOrder.CustomerID, firstOrder.OrderID);
```

In this example, we query for two customers—those with the LAZYK and AROUT CustomerID values. We then obtain the first Order from the LAZYK Customer and call Add to add it to the EntityCollection of Orders in the AROUT Customer. We print out the Order CustomerID and OrderID fields before and after we call the Add method. If we compile and run the code in Listing 21-20, we get the following results:

```
First LAZYK Customer ID: LAZYK, Order ID: 10482
First LAZYK Customer ID: AROUT, Order ID: 10482
```

And you can see that the Entity Framework has cleverly updated the foreign-key relationship so that the Order is now related to the AROUT Customer. Nice.

Remove()

The Remove method does what the name suggests—it removes an entity object from the collection and sets the foreign key field to null. This means that the object won't appear when you enumerate the EntityCollection and when you call the SaveChanges method. The row in the database that corresponds to the removed object will be updated to have a foreign key value of NULL.

Prototypes

The Remove method has one prototype that we will cover.

The Remove Prototype

```
public bool Remove(Object entity);
```

The entity argument is the entity object you want to remove from the collection. The Remove method returns true if the entity object was removed successfully and false otherwise. Calling the Remove method has an immediate effect on the entity objects cached by the Entity Framework but will not affect the database until the SaveChanges method has been called.

You must be careful when using the Remove method if the database schema doesn't allow NULL values in the foreign-key column. You will get an exception when you call the SaveChanges method.

Examples

Listing 21-21 shows how to use the Remove method to remove an Order from the EntityCollection<Order> of a Customer entity type from the Northwind entity data model.

Listing 21-21. Using the Remove Method to Break a Foreign-Key Relationship

```
NorthwindEntities context = new NorthwindEntities();

// get the LAZYK customer
Customer cust = (from c in context.Customers
                 where c.CustomerID == "LAZYK"
                 select c).First();

// get the first LAZY K order
Order order = cust.Orders.First();

Console.WriteLine("Order has CustomerID of {0}", order.CustomerID);

// remove the order from the collection
Console.WriteLine("Removing order with ID: {0}", order.OrderID);
cust.Orders.Remove(order);

Console.WriteLine("Order has CustomerID of {0}", (order.CustomerID == null?
    "NULL" : order.CustomerID));

// save changes
context.SaveChanges();
```

We perform a LINQ to Entities query to obtain a Customer entity object and take the first Order from the collection, which we pass as an argument to the Remove method. We print out the CustomerID of the Order before and after the Remove method is called so we can see the value of the foreign-key field. Compiling and running the code gives us the following results:

```
Order has CustomerID of LAZYK
Removing order with ID: 10482
Order has CustomerID of NULL
```

We can see that the `CustomerID` of the `Order` has been set to `null`. In this example, we called the `SaveChanges` method to persist the change, leading to the row representing that `Order` being updated with a `CustomerID` value of `NULL`. No exception was thrown when we persisted the data because the foreign key is not enforced by the database schema, but we did create an orphaned record, which is no longer associated with a customer.

Clear()

The `Clear` method removes all the entity objects from the `EntityCollection` and sets their foreign-key values to `null`. This is equivalent to removing each object in the collection individually using the `Remove` method.

Prototypes

The `Clear` method has one prototype.

The Clear Method Prototype

```
public void Clear();
```

Examples

Listing 21-22 removes all the `Orders` in the `EntityCollection<Order>` for a given Northwind Customer.

Listing 21-22. Using the Clear Method to Remove the Entity Objects in a Collection

```
NorthwindEntities context = new NorthwindEntities();

// get the LAZYK customer
Customer cust = (from c in context.Customers
                 where c.CustomerID == "LAZYK"
                 select c).First();

// clear the Orders collection
cust.Orders.Clear();

// save changes
context.SaveChanges();
```

As with the `Add` and `Remove` methods, the changes are not persisted to the database until the `SaveChanges` method is called. In the example, calling the `SaveChanges` method will update all the rows in the `Orders` table that have a `CustomerID` of LAZYK such that the `CustomerID` will be `NULL`.

Contains()

The Contains method allows you to determine whether an EntityCollection contains a given entity object.

Prototypes

The Contains method has one prototype, where T is the entity type of the EntityCollection<T>. The Contains method returns true if the entity object is contained within the collection and false otherwise.

The Single Contains Prototype

```
public bool Contains(T entity);
```

Examples

Listing 21-23 demonstrates the use of the Contains method. We query for a Northwind Customer objects and get the first Order in the EntityCollection<Order>. We call the Contains method, remove the Order from the Collection using the Remove method, and then call Contains again to contrast the effect.

Listing 21-23. *Using the Contains Method*

```
// get the LAZYK customer
Customer cust = (from c in context.Customers
                 where c.CustomerID == "LAZYK"
                 select c).First();

// get the first order for the customer
Order ord = cust.Orders.First();

// use the Contains method
Console.WriteLine("Orders Contains Order {0}",
    cust.Orders.Contains(ord));

// remove the orde from the collection
Console.WriteLine("Removing order");
cust.Orders.Remove(ord);

// use the Contains method
Console.WriteLine("Orders Contains Order {0}",
    cust.Orders.Contains(ord));
```

Compiling and running the code in Listing 21-23 gives the following results:

```
Orders Contains Order True
Removing order
Orders Contains Order False
```

Load()

The Load method is used to explicitly load the entity objects in the collection from the database when lazy loading is disabled. See Chapter 20 for details of how to load data and why you might want to do so.

Count

The Count property returns the number of entity objects in the collection.

Prototypes

There is one prototype for the Count property.

The Sole Count Property Prototype

```
public int Count {get;};
```

Examples

Listing 21-24 uses the Count property to determine how many Orders are associated with a specific Northwind Customer. We then remove an Order from the EntityCollection and call Count again.

Listing 21-24. Counting the Number of Entity Objects with the Count Property

```
NorthwindEntities context = new NorthwindEntities();

// get the LAZYK customer
Customer cust = (from c in context.Customers
                 where c.CustomerID == "LAZYK"
                 select c).First();

// Count the number of Orders
Console.WriteLine("Number of Orders: {0}",
    cust.Orders.Count);

// get the first order for the customer
Order ord = cust.Orders.First();

// remove the orde from the collection
Console.WriteLine("Removing order");
```

```
cust.Orders.Remove(ord);

// Count the number of Orders
Console.WriteLine("Number of Orders: {0}",
    cust.Orders.Count);
```

Compiling and running the code in Listing 21-24 gives us the following results. As you might have expected, removing an item from the collection reduces the return value from the Count property.

```
Number of Orders: 2
Removing order
Number of Orders: 1
```

Summary

In this chapter, we have shown you the key members from the key classes that you will use with LINQ to Entities. We have glossed over some of the complexities of the Entity Framework, but we have given you enough information to get started and for you to see how much commonality there is between LINQ to Entities and LINQ to SQL. This is the end of the LINQ to Entities part of the book. Our next chapter introduces one of the newest LINQ features—Parallel LINQ. Onward!

■ ■ ■

PART 7

Parallel LINQ

CHAPTER 22

■ ■ ■

Parallel LINQ Introduction

Listing 22-1. A Simple Parallel LINQ Example

```
string[] presidents = {
     "Adams", "Arthur", "Buchanan", "Bush", "Carter", "Cleveland",
     "Clinton", "Coolidge", "Eisenhower", "Fillmore", "Ford", "Garfield",
     "Grant", "Harding", "Harrison", "Hayes", "Hoover", "Jackson",
     "Jefferson", "Johnson", "Kennedy", "Lincoln", "Madison", "McKinley",
     "Monroe", "Nixon", "Obama", "Pierce", "Polk", "Reagan", "Roosevelt",
     "Taft", "Taylor", "Truman", "Tyler", "Van Buren", "Washington", "Wilson"};

string president = presidents.AsParallel()
    .Where(p => p.StartsWith("Lin")).First();

Console.WriteLine(president);
```

Back in Chapter 3, we opened with a simple LINQ to Objects example that found the first U.S. president whose name begins with Lin. Go on, take a look—we'll wait for you. Now take a look at Listing 21-1, which is the same query but performed using Parallel LINQ. We have made it easier to spot the difference by highlighting the change—the new call to the AsParallel method. As you will learn, the query in Listing 22-1 isn't very well suited to Parallel LINQ, but it does work, and it shows an important point, namely, that moving from a regular LINQ query to a Parallel LINQ query can be as easy as calling the AsParallel method.

In this and the following chapters, we'll show you how to use Parallel LINQ effectively and show you the similarities and differences from the rest of the LINQ family.

Introducing Parallel LINQ

In a nutshell, Parallel LINQ, known as PLINQ, is a version of LINQ to Objects where the objects in the source enumeration are processed concurrently. There is a lot packed into that sentence, so let's break things down and help make sense of them.

In .NET version 4, Microsoft has introduced a whole set of advanced features to simplify parallel programming. These new features are extensive enough that they deserve their own book, and in fact one of us (Adam) has written *Pro .NET Parallel Programming in C#,* which is also published by Apress.

751

Parallel programming features have been around for a long time, but they have been difficult to use, and many programmers have struggled to make effective use of them. The .NET version 4 features have been designed to appeal to a wider audience and to take advantage of the widespread adoption of multicore and multiprocessor machines.

If we consider the original query in Listing 3-1, we processed each president's name in turn. Figure 22-1 illustrates how this works.

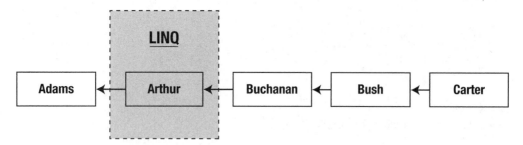

Figure 22-1. Sequential LINQ execution

LINQ started by checking to see whether Adams starts with Lin. It then moved to Arthur and checked again—then Buchanan, Bush, Carter, and so on. LINQ moved through the names in the data array in sequence. This, reasonably enough, is known as *sequential* execution. The problem with sequential execution is that it uses only one core or CPU at a time (from now on we are only going to talk about cores, but we mean either). On the four-core machines that we wrote this book on, three of the cores do nothing while the LINQ query is being executed. Parallel LINQ changes the game by breaking up the source data and processing it simultaneously in chunks, as shown by Figure 22-2.

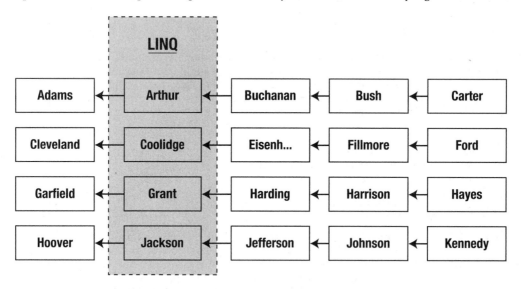

Figure 22-2. Parallel LINQ execution

The names `Arthur`, `Coolidge`, `Grant`, and `Jackson` are all processed at the same time, one by each of the cores in our machine. As each core finishes processing a name, it moves on to the next, independently of the other cores. Parallel LINQ takes care of breaking up the data for us, working out how many items should be processed at the same time (although it usually decides that one per core is about right) and coordinating the work that the cores do so that we get our results just as we would for any other LINQ query. If we compile and run the code in Listing 21-1, we get the following results:

```
Lincoln
```

So, why do we care about Parallel LINQ? The answer is simple—performance. Take a look at Listing 22-2. We define two LINQ queries that do the same thing. One query is sequential; the other uses Parallel LINQ. Both queries `select` the even integer values between 0 and `Int32.MaxValue` and count the number of matches. We use `Enumerable.Range` and `ParallelEnumerable.Range` to generate the sequence of integer values. We'll discuss ranges further in Chapter 23, but for the moment please accept that both of these methods create `IEnumerable<int>`s that contain all the integer values we require. We know that this is not a particularly useful example, but it does help us make a key point.

Listing 22-2. *Comparing the Performance of Sequential and Parallel Execution*

```
// create the sequential number range
IEnumerable<int> numbers1 = Enumerable.Range(0, Int32.MaxValue);

// start the stop watch
Stopwatch sw = Stopwatch.StartNew();

// perform the LINQ query
int sum1 = (from n in numbers1
            where n % 2 == 0
            select n).Count();

// write out the seqential result
Console.WriteLine("Seqential result: {0}", sum1);
// write out how long the sequential execution took
Console.WriteLine("Sequential time: {0} ms", sw.ElapsedMilliseconds);

// create the parallel number range
IEnumerable<int> numbers2 = ParallelEnumerable.Range(0, Int32.MaxValue);
// Restart the stopwatch
sw.Restart();

// perform the Parallel LINQ query
int sum2 = (from n in numbers2.AsParallel()
            where n % 2 == 0
            select n).Count();

// write the parallel result
```

```
Console.WriteLine("Parallel result: {0}", sum2);
// write out how long the parallel execution took
Console.WriteLine("Parallel time: {0} ms", sw.ElapsedMilliseconds);
```

We use the Stopwatch class from the System.Diagnostics namespace to measure the time that each query takes. We compiled and ran the code in Listing 22-2 and took screenshots of the Windows Task Manager while each of the queries was running. During the sequential execution, we took Figure 22-3.

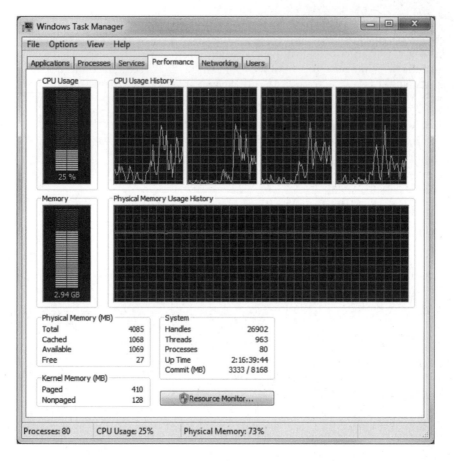

Figure 22-3. *CPU utilization during sequential query execution*

You can see that CPU usage is at 25 percent. This is a four-core machine, so we'd expect CPU usage to be 25 percent when only one core is busy, which is how sequential queries are performed. During the Parallel LINQ query, we took Figure 22-4.

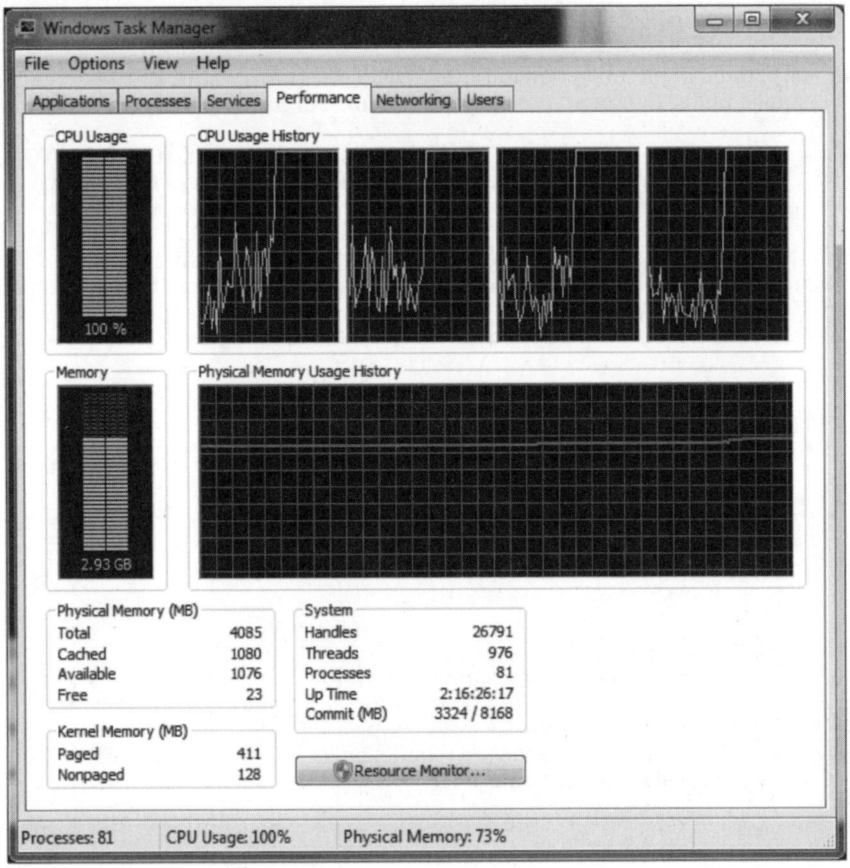

Figure 22-4. CPU utilization during parallel query execution

We got the following output when we ran the code. It took roughly 38 seconds for the sequential LINQ query to process all the integer values and produce the result. But the Parallel LINQ query did the same thing in just over 9 seconds. That's pretty amazing given that the queries look pretty much the same in the code and, as you can see from the output, produce the same results. With Parallel LINQ, a little effort can result in a big performance gain.

```
Seqential result: 1073741824
Sequential time: 38521 ms
Parallel result: 1073741824
Parallel time: 9498 ms
```

Parallel LINQ Is for Objects

We said that Parallel LINQ is a parallel implementation of LINQ to Objects. That's what it does—execute LINQ to Objects queries in parallel. It doesn't implement parallel features for the other kinds of LINQ we have covered in this book.

That doesn't mean you can't process the results of another kind of LINQ query using Parallel LINQ (for example, selecting all the Northwind Orders in the database using LINQ to Entities or LINQ to SQL and then using Parallel LINQ to process them further), but Parallel LINQ doesn't work on anything but objects.

And even then, not all LINQ to Objects queries are good candidates to be Parallel LINQ queries. There is an overhead associated with breaking up the data into chunks and setting up and managing the classes that perform the parallel tasks—if the query doesn't take very long to perform sequentially, then it probably help to parallelize it—you'll incur all the overhead and get none of the performance benefit.

Using the LINQ to Entities API

You don't have to take any special steps to use Parallel LINQ. The key classes are contained in the System.Linq namespace, which is where the regular LINQ to Objects classes reside as well. We describe the most important methods of the key operators in Chapter 24.

Summary

In this chapter, we introduced you to Parallel LINQ, which processes multiple data items in a LINQ to Objects query simultaneously. Used judiciously, Parallel LINQ can provide a significant increase in performance for your LINQ to Objects queries. We showed you a couple of simple queries and contrasted the performance between a simple sequential and parallel query. In the next chapter, we'll show you how to use the full range of Parallel LINQ featuresa LINQ to DataSet query.

CHAPTER 23

Using Parallel LINQ

In this chapter, we'll show you how to use Parallel LINQ, starting with the basics and working up to the advanced options for controlling parallel execution. Parallel LINQ is easy to get started with and gives good results from the start, but if you want to get the absolute best results, a little planning and effort are required.

Creating a Parallel LINQ Query

To a large extent, using Parallel LINQ, usually known as PLINQ (pronounced "pea-link"), is incredibly similar to using LINQ to Objects. In fact, that is one of the major attractions of PLINQ. In a regular LINQ to Objects query, the data source is an `IEnumerable<T>`, where `T` is the data type we will be processing. The LINQ engine automatically switches to using PLINQ when the data source is an instance of the `ParallelQuery<T>` type. And here is the clever bit—we can convert any `IEnumerable<T>` into a `ParallelQuery<T>` just by using the `AsParallel` method. Let's just look at that in code. Listing 23-1 shows a LINQ to Objects query and a PLINQ query, both of which do the same thing.

Listing 23-1. Comparable LINQ and Parallel LINQ Queries

```
string[] presidents = {
  "Adams", "Arthur", "Buchanan", "Bush", "Carter", "Cleveland",
  "Clinton", "Coolidge", "Eisenhower", "Fillmore", "Ford", "Garfield",
  "Grant", "Harding", "Harrison", "Hayes", "Hoover", "Jackson",
  "Jefferson", "Johnson", "Kennedy", "Lincoln", "Madison", "McKinley",
  "Monroe", "Nixon", "Obama", "Pierce", "Polk", "Reagan", "Roosevelt",
  "Taft", "Taylor", "Truman", "Tyler", "Van Buren", "Washington", "Wilson"};

// sequential LINQ query
IEnumerable<string> results = from p in presidents
                             where p.Contains('o')
                             select p;

foreach (string president in results) {
    Console.WriteLine("Sequential result: {0}", president);
}
```

```
// Parallel LINQ query
results = from p in presidents.AsParallel()
          where p.Contains('o')
          select p;

foreach (string president in results) {
    Console.WriteLine("Parallel result: {0}", president);
}
```

The first query uses regular LINQ to Objects to process each of the presidents to find those names that contain the letter o. We get the IEnumerable<string> as the result of the query and print out each matching name.

The second query does exactly the same thing, but we have used the AsParallel method. This is the "open sesame" of PLINQ—by using AsParallel, we convert our data source into a ParallelQuery, which automatically engages Parallel LINQ. Otherwise, as the code clearly shows, there is no other change required. We just call AsParallel, and we get PLINQ. It is like a special geeky magic. If we compile and run the code in Listing 23-1, we get the following results:

```
Sequential result: Clinton
Sequential result: Coolidge
Sequential result: Eisenhower
Sequential result: Fillmore
Sequential result: Ford
Sequential result: Harrison
Sequential result: Hoover
Sequential result: Jackson
Sequential result: Jefferson
Sequential result: Johnson
Sequential result: Lincoln
Sequential result: Madison
Sequential result: Monroe
Sequential result: Nixon
Sequential result: Polk
Sequential result: Roosevelt
Sequential result: Taylor
Sequential result: Washington
Sequential result: Wilson
Parallel result: Lincoln
Parallel result: Roosevelt
Parallel result: Clinton
Parallel result: Ford
Parallel result: Madison
Parallel result: Taylor
Parallel result: Coolidge
Parallel result: Harrison
```

```
Parallel result: Monroe
Parallel result: Washington
Parallel result: Eisenhower
Parallel result: Hoover
Parallel result: Nixon
Parallel result: Wilson
Parallel result: Fillmore
Parallel result: Jackson
Parallel result: Polk
Parallel result: Jefferson
Parallel result: Johnson
```

There are two things to note about these results. First, it is surprising just how many presidents' names contain the letter o—more than we expected. Second, the sequential results are in alphabetical order, but the parallel results are not. What gives? We'll explain the ordering issue (and tell you how to control it) in just a moment.

The key point is just how easy it is to create a PLINQ query. Just call the `AsParallel` method on your query source. And, of course, you can use the `AsParallel` method with query expressions (as we did in Listing 23-1) or when using extension methods to structure your query. Listing 23-2 shows two PLINQ queries that demonstrate this.

Listing 23-2. Parallel Queries Written Using Query Expressions and Extension Methods

```
string[] presidents = {
  "Adams", "Arthur", "Buchanan", "Bush", "Carter", "Cleveland",
  "Clinton", "Coolidge", "Eisenhower", "Fillmore", "Ford", "Garfield",
  "Grant", "Harding", "Harrison", "Hayes", "Hoover", "Jackson",
  "Jefferson", "Johnson", "Kennedy", "Lincoln", "Madison", "McKinley",
  "Monroe", "Nixon", "Obama", "Pierce", "Polk", "Reagan", "Roosevelt",
  "Taft", "Taylor", "Truman", "Tyler", "Van Buren", "Washington", "Wilson"};

IEnumerable<string> results = from p in presidents.AsParallel()
                             where p.StartsWith("M")
                             select p;

foreach (string president in results) {
    Console.WriteLine("Query expression result: {0}", president);
}

results = presidents.AsParallel()
    .Where(p => p.StartsWith("M"))
    .Select(p => p);

foreach (string president in results) {
    Console.WriteLine("Extension method result: {0}", president);
}
```

The first query is written using query expressions, and the second is written using extension methods. Both queries call the `AsParallel` method, of course. Without this, we would have a sequential LINQ query. Compiling and running the code in Listing 23-2 gives us the following results, demonstrating that there is no difference in the way the queries are executed:

```
Query expression result: Madison
Query expression result: McKinley
Query expression result: Monroe
Extension method result: Madison
Extension method result: McKinley
Extension method result: Monroe
```

As an aside, we know that this is not an ideal query to use with PLINQ. In the previous chapter, we explained that the overhead in parallelizing a small, simple query can result in worse performance than sequential execution. But we need to demonstrate the features, and the less time we spend on artificially complex examples, the simpler it is to understand the points we are trying to make. We'll keep using simple queries in these chapters. This is one of those things where you should do as we say, not as we do.

Preserving Result Ordering

The results we got from Listing 23-1 were *out* of alphabetical order. But the results we got from Listing 23-2 were *in* alphabetical order. You might be asking, what's up with that?

The answer lies in the way that PLINQ processes data. The data that you provide as the source for a PLINQ query is broken up and shared out to be processed in parallel (breaking up the data is calling *partitioning*). Multiple partitions can be processed at one. For example, if you have a four-core machine, four partitions might be processed simultaneously. However, each of those partitions is processed sequentially. Take a moment to think about that—parallel execution comes from sequentially processing multiple data partitions at the same time. Figure 23-1 demonstrates this.

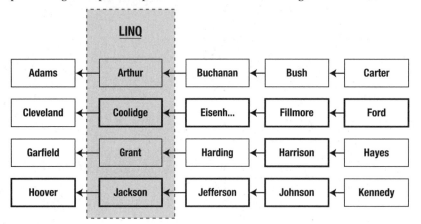

Figure 23-1. Parallel execution is the concurrent sequential processing of data partitions.

When PLINQ partitions our data, we might get something like Figure 23-1, but we can't be sure because the PLINQ engine analyzes our query and our data and does the partitioning behind the scenes. But let's imagine that we have what Figure 23-1 shows—a number of partitions, each of which contains the names of five presidents. PLINQ assigns one partition to each of the cores in our machine, and each core then processes its assigned partition sequentially.

So, to continue the example, the first core checks to see whether Adams contains the letter o. Then it checks Arthur, Buchanan, Bush, and Carter. While this is happening, the second core checks Cleveland, Coolidge, Eisenhower, and so on. The third and fourth cores work through their partitions at the same time.

Whenever a match is found, it is added to the result set. We have marked the presidents' names that contain the letter o in Figure 23-1, and you can see that if the items are processed at roughly the same rate by each core, then Hoover will be the first result that is found, followed by Coolidge or Jackson, Eisenhower or Jefferson, and so on.

Our results start to look like this:

```
Hoover, Coolidge, Jackson, Eisenhower, Jefferson...
```

So, you can see how PLINQ ends up generating results that are not ordered in the same way as the source data. Worse, because we don't know in advance how PLINQ will partition the data, we can't tell what the ordering might be. Even worse, the partitions are not processed in lockstep. Other processes on the machine might preempt execution of our .NET application on one or more cores, which means that we can actually get results that are ordered differently when we run the same query against the same data multiple times.

Now, some of the time, we just won't care about the order of the results. For example, if we only want to know how many presidents' names contain the letter o, we don't care how the query results are ordered because we are going to count them. Listing 23-3 demonstrates this kind of query.

Listing 23-3. A PLINQ Query Where the Results Ordering Is Not Important

```
string[] presidents = {
    "Adams", "Arthur", "Buchanan", "Bush", "Carter", "Cleveland",
    "Clinton", "Coolidge", "Eisenhower", "Fillmore", "Ford", "Garfield",
    "Grant", "Harding", "Harrison", "Hayes", "Hoover", "Jackson",
    "Jefferson", "Johnson", "Kennedy", "Lincoln", "Madison", "McKinley",
    "Monroe", "Nixon", "Obama", "Pierce", "Polk", "Reagan", "Roosevelt",
    "Taft", "Taylor", "Truman", "Tyler", "Van Buren", "Washington", "Wilson"};

int count = presidents.AsParallel()
    .Where(p => p.Contains("o"))
    .Select(p => p)
    .Count();

Console.WriteLine("Result count: {0}", count);
```

It doesn't matter how PLINQ divides up and allocates the data, we will still get the same result—there are 19 matches, which we can see if we compile and run the code in Listing 23-3:

```
Result count: 19
```

There are times, however, when we do care about the order of the results. This is especially true if you are converting existing LINQ queries to PLINQ. There may be assumptions made elsewhere about the order of the results, for example. You can preserve ordering by using the AsOrdered extension method on the ParallelQuery you created using the AsParallel method. So, to preserve ordering on our presidents' names, we could call the following:

```
presidents.AsParallel().AsOrdered()
```

Calling the AsOrdered method tells PLINQ to preserve the order of the results. Listing 23-4 demonstrates how to use this method.

Listing 23-4. Preserving the Order of PLINQ Query Results Using the AsOrdered Method

```
string[] presidents = {
  "Adams", "Arthur", "Buchanan", "Bush", "Carter", "Cleveland",
  "Clinton", "Coolidge", "Eisenhower", "Fillmore", "Ford", "Garfield",
  "Grant", "Harding", "Harrison", "Hayes", "Hoover", "Jackson",
  "Jefferson", "Johnson", "Kennedy", "Lincoln", "Madison", "McKinley",
  "Monroe", "Nixon", "Obama", "Pierce", "Polk", "Reagan", "Roosevelt",
  "Taft", "Taylor", "Truman", "Tyler", "Van Buren", "Washington", "Wilson"};

// Parallel LINQ query
IEnumerable<string> results = from p in presidents.AsParallel().AsOrdered()
        where p.Contains('o')
        select p;

foreach (string president in results) {
    Console.WriteLine("Parallel result: {0}", president);
}
```

There are no query expression keywords for the AsParallel or AsOrdered extension methods. You must call the methods directly. Listing 23-4 mixes query keywords with the extension methods. If we compile and run the code in Listing 23-4, we get the following results:

```
Parallel result: Clinton
Parallel result: Coolidge
Parallel result: Eisenhower
Parallel result: Fillmore
Parallel result: Ford
Parallel result: Harrison
Parallel result: Hoover
Parallel result: Jackson
Parallel result: Jefferson
Parallel result: Johnson
Parallel result: Lincoln
Parallel result: Madison
Parallel result: Monroe
```

```
Parallel result: Nixon
Parallel result: Polk
Parallel result: Roosevelt
Parallel result: Taylor
Parallel result: Washington
Parallel result: Wilson
```

If you look back at the results from Listing 23-1, you'll see that everything matches up. The AsOrdered method is very useful, but you shouldn't get into the habit of using it automatically because it required PLINQ to do extra work to re-order the results. Given that the whole purpose of PLINQ is to improve performance, we want to avoid unnecessary work whenever possible.

Controlling Parallelism

PLINQ analyzes your query and decides how many partitions will be processed at once. Microsoft has stated that it will evolve the way that this is determined, so you should not make assumptions based on the behavior you observe in the current release.

Forcing Parallel Execution

In some cases, PLINQ may decide that your query is better dealt with sequentially. You can control this by using the WithExecutionMode extension method, which is applied to the ParallelQuery type. The WithExecutionMode method takes a value from the ParallelExecutionMode enumeration. There are two such values: the default (let PLINQ decide what to do) and ForceParallelism (use PLINQ even if the overhead of parallel execution is likely to outweigh the benefits). Listing 23-5 shows how to force parallel execution.

Listing 23-5. Forcing Parallel Execution Using the WithExecutionMode Method

```
string[] presidents = {
    "Adams", "Arthur", "Buchanan", "Bush", "Carter", "Cleveland",
    "Clinton", "Coolidge", "Eisenhower", "Fillmore", "Ford", "Garfield",
    "Grant", "Harding", "Harrison", "Hayes", "Hoover", "Jackson",
    "Jefferson", "Johnson", "Kennedy", "Lincoln", "Madison", "McKinley",
    "Monroe", "Nixon", "Obama", "Pierce", "Polk", "Reagan", "Roosevelt",
    "Taft", "Taylor", "Truman", "Tyler", "Van Buren", "Washington", "Wilson"};

// Parallel LINQ query
IEnumerable<string> results = presidents
    .AsParallel()
    .WithExecutionMode(ParallelExecutionMode.ForceParallelism)
    .Where(p => p.Contains('o'))
    .Select(p => p);

foreach (string president in results) {
    Console.WriteLine("Parallel result: {0}", president);
}
```

Limiting the Degree of Parallelism

You can request that PLINQ limit the number of partitions that are processed simultaneously using the WithDegreeofParallelism extension method, which operates on the ParallelQuery type. This method takes an int argument that states the maximum number of partitions that should be processed at once; this is known as the *degree of parallelism*. Setting the degree of parallelism doesn't force PLINQ to use that many. It just sets an upper limit. PLINQ may decide to use fewer than you have specified or, if you have not used the WithExecutionMode method, may decide to execute the query sequentially. Listing 23-6 demonstrates the use of this method.

Listing 23-6. Setting the Degree of Parallelism in a PLINQ Query

```
string[] presidents = {
  "Adams", "Arthur", "Buchanan", "Bush", "Carter", "Cleveland",
  "Clinton", "Coolidge", "Eisenhower", "Fillmore", "Ford", "Garfield",
  "Grant", "Harding", "Harrison", "Hayes", "Hoover", "Jackson",
  "Jefferson", "Johnson", "Kennedy", "Lincoln", "Madison", "McKinley",
  "Monroe", "Nixon", "Obama", "Pierce", "Polk", "Reagan", "Roosevelt",
  "Taft", "Taylor", "Truman", "Tyler", "Van Buren", "Washington", "Wilson"};

// Parallel LINQ query
IEnumerable<string> results = presidents
    .AsParallel()
    .WithDegreeOfParallelism(2)
    .Where(p => p.Contains('o'))
    .Select(p => p);

foreach (string president in results) {
    Console.WriteLine("Parallel result: {0}", president);
}
```

In Listing 23-6, we have specified a maximum degree of 2, meaning that we want at most two data partitions to be processed simultaneously. This can be useful if we want to limit the impact of a query on a machine that needs to perform other tasks as well.

Dealing with Exceptions

If something goes wrong in a sequential LINQ query, the exception that is thrown stops any further processing. For example, if we are processing the presidents' names and Arthur causes an exception to be thrown, none of the presidents' names that follow Arthur will be processed, as illustrated by Figure 23-2.

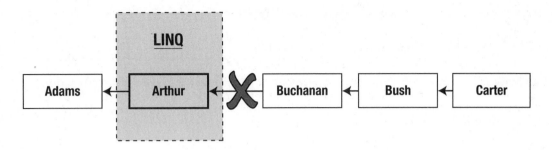

Figure 23-2. An exception in a sequential query

So, we should get the results in the sequence prior to Arthur, but not afterward. Let's put it to the test. Listing 23-7 contains a sequential query that selects all the presidents' names and prints them out. But we have added a wrinkle. When the query gets to Arthur, we throw an exception.

Listing 23-7. Forcing an Exception in a Sequential Query

```
string[] presidents = {
    "Adams", "Arthur", "Buchanan", "Bush", "Carter", "Cleveland",
    "Clinton", "Coolidge", "Eisenhower", "Fillmore", "Ford", "Garfield",
    "Grant", "Harding", "Harrison", "Hayes", "Hoover", "Jackson",
    "Jefferson", "Johnson", "Kennedy", "Lincoln", "Madison", "McKinley",
    "Monroe", "Nixon", "Obama", "Pierce", "Polk", "Reagan", "Roosevelt",
    "Taft", "Taylor", "Truman", "Tyler", "Van Buren", "Washington", "Wilson"};

// Parallel LINQ query
IEnumerable<string> results = presidents
    .Select(p => {
        if (p == "Arthur")
            throw new Exception(String.Format("Problem with President {0}", p));
        return p;
    });


try {
    foreach (string president in results) {
        Console.WriteLine("Result: {0}", president);
    }
} catch (Exception ex) {
    Console.WriteLine(ex.Message);
}
```

When we compile and run the code in Listing 23-7, we get the following results, which are what we expected. We process Adams correctly and then encounter a problem (of our making, admittedly) with Arthur. The exception that we threw stops the rest of the query from executing.

```
Result: Adams
Problem with President Arthur
```

But things are different with a PLINQ query. Remember that the data is broken down into partitions, which are then processed independently and concurrently. It is possible that we encounter more than one exception—and because we are processing several partitions at once, the first exception doesn't stop the other partitions from being processed. Figure 23-3 shows how this can happen.

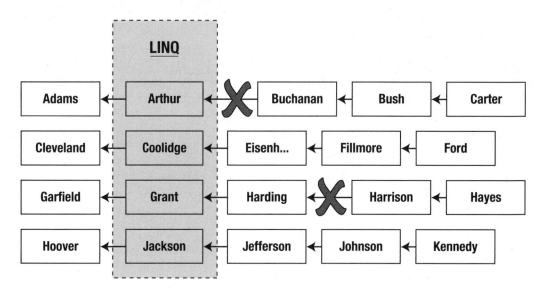

Figure 23-3. *Exceptions in a parallel query*

In Figure 23-3, there are four partitions being processed in parallel. There is a problem with `Arthur` in the first partition, which causes an exception to be thrown. But this doesn't stop the other partitions being processed, and a problem with `Harding` causes a second exception to be thrown. What do we do?

Fortunately, there is a nice solution. PLINQ gathers up all the exceptions that it finds and wraps them in a `System.AggregateException`, which is then thrown to your code. Listing 23-8 contains a PLINQ query that will throw exceptions for the `Arthur` and `Harding` values.

Listing 23-8. *Forcing an Exception in a PLINQ Query*

```
string[] presidents = {
  "Adams", "Arthur", "Buchanan", "Bush", "Carter", "Cleveland",
  "Clinton", "Coolidge", "Eisenhower", "Fillmore", "Ford", "Garfield",
  "Grant", "Harding", "Harrison", "Hayes", "Hoover", "Jackson",
  "Jefferson", "Johnson", "Kennedy", "Lincoln", "Madison", "McKinley",
  "Monroe", "Nixon", "Obama", "Pierce", "Polk", "Reagan", "Roosevelt",
  "Taft", "Taylor", "Truman", "Tyler", "Van Buren", "Washington", "Wilson"};
```

```
// Parallel LINQ query
IEnumerable<string> results = presidents
    .AsParallel()
    .Select(p => {
        if (p == "Arthur" || p == "Harding")
            throw new Exception(String.Format("Problem with President {0}", p));
        return p;
    });

try {
    foreach (string president in results) {
        Console.WriteLine("Result: {0}", president);
    }
} catch (AggregateException agex) {
    agex.Handle(ex => {
        Console.WriteLine(ex.Message);
        return true;
    });
}
```

You can see that when we come to enumerate the results, we wrap the foreach loop in a try/catch block that looks for AggregateExceptions. The AggregateException class has a Handle method that lets you process each exception in turn. You are passed the exception and must return true if you have handled the exception or false if you cannot handle the exception.

If you do not handle an exception, it will be propagated and ultimately stop the execution of your program. On the other hand, you should not handle exceptions that you were not expecting and don't know what to do with. That's the path to weird behavior and difficult-to-find bugs.

The results you get from a PLINQ query that has encountered exceptions are unpredictable. It depends on how PLINQ has partitioned your data and how many partitions were being processed concurrently. As an example, when we compiled and ran the code in Listing 23-8, we got the following results:

```
Result: Reagan
Result: Roosevelt
Result: Taft
Result: Taylor
Result: Truman
Result: Tyler
Result: Van Buren
Result: Washington
Result: Wilson
Problem with President Arthur

Problem with President Harding
```

We ran the same code a second time and got completely different results, as shown next. If you compile and run Listing 23-8, you'll almost certainly see similar variations.

```
Problem with President Arthur
Problem with President Harding
```

Queries Without Results

PLINQ has a useful feature in the ForAll extension method. Used on a ParallelQuery (which you recall is what the AsParallel method returns), ForAll performs a System.Action on each item in the sequence. One of our recurring examples in this chapter has been to find all the presidents' names that contain the letter o. We have used a where clause to filter only the matching names and selected them so that they are added to our IEnumerable<string> result. We then use a foreach loop to enumerate the results and print them out using Console.WriteLine.

We can do the same thing, but much more elegantly, using the ForAll method. Take a look at Listing 23-9.

Listing 23-9. Using the ForAll Method

```
string[] presidents = {
  "Adams", "Arthur", "Buchanan", "Bush", "Carter", "Cleveland",
  "Clinton", "Coolidge", "Eisenhower", "Fillmore", "Ford", "Garfield",
  "Grant", "Harding", "Harrison", "Hayes", "Hoover", "Jackson",
  "Jefferson", "Johnson", "Kennedy", "Lincoln", "Madison", "McKinley",
  "Monroe", "Nixon", "Obama", "Pierce", "Polk", "Reagan", "Roosevelt",
  "Taft", "Taylor", "Truman", "Tyler", "Van Buren", "Washington", "Wilson"};

// Parallel LINQ query
presidents.AsParallel()
    .Where(p => p.Contains('o'))
    .ForAll(p => Console.WriteLine("Name: {0}", p));
```

We still use the Where method to filter the sequence, but rather than gather the results, we print out the names directly using a lambda expression passed to the ForAll method. Now, it might take a moment to get your head around this feature. After all, every other example in this book has worked differently. But the ForAll method is worth getting to know. If we compile and run the code in Listing 23-9, we get the following results:

```
Name: Ford
Name: Clinton

Name: Lincoln

Name: Harrison
Name: Roosevelt
Name: Taylor
```

```
Name: Coolidge
Name: Madison
Name: Hoover
Name: Jackson
Name: Jefferson
Name: Johnson
Name: Eisenhower
Name: Fillmore
Name: Monroe
Name: Nixon
Name: Polk
Name: Washington
Name: Wilson
```

You can do pretty much anything in the `Action` passed to the `ForAll` method except return a result. You can even filter data without using a `where` clause. Listing 23-10 demonstrates this.

Listing 23-10. *Filtering Data Without a Where Clause*

```
string[] presidents = {
    "Adams", "Arthur", "Buchanan", "Bush", "Carter", "Cleveland",
    "Clinton", "Coolidge", "Eisenhower", "Fillmore", "Ford", "Garfield",
    "Grant", "Harding", "Harrison", "Hayes", "Hoover", "Jackson",
    "Jefferson", "Johnson", "Kennedy", "Lincoln", "Madison", "McKinley",
    "Monroe", "Nixon", "Obama", "Pierce", "Polk", "Reagan", "Roosevelt",
    "Taft", "Taylor", "Truman", "Tyler", "Van Buren", "Washington", "Wilson"};

int count = 0;

presidents.AsParallel()
    .ForAll(p => {
        if (p.Contains('o')) {
            System.Threading.Interlocked.Increment(ref count);
        }
    });

Console.WriteLine("Matches: {0}", count);
```

In Listing 23-10, we used the `ForAll` method to perform an action on every item in the data sequence. We check to see whether the name contains the letter o and increment the counter if it does. When we compile and run the code in Listing 23-10, we get the following results:

```
Matches: 19
```

And don't forget that the `ForAll` method is part of PLINQ, which means that the `Action` you specify will be performed on partitions of your data sequence in parallel. This gives you all the performance benefits of parallel execution but can cause problems for shared data, such as the `int` we used to count the matches. We use the `Interlocked` class from the `System.Threading` namespace to make sure that our count is accurate. This is called *synchronization* and is an advanced parallel programming technique. We suggest taking a look at Adam's detailed book on .NET parallel programming if you want to understand this fully.

Creating Ranges and Repetitions

It is sometimes the case that you need to process a sequence of numeric values or a sequence that contains the same value. You can create these sequences manually, of course, doing something like this:

```
int[] sequence = new int[50000];
for (int i = 0; i < sequence.Length; i++) {
    sequence[i] = i;
}
```

As an alternative, you can generate this kind of sequence using the static `Range` method from the `System.Linq.ParallelEnumerable` class. Listing 23-11 demonstrates how to create the same sequence as the earlier one and execute a query using it.

Listing 23-11. Generating and Using a Parallel Sequence

```
IEnumerable<int> evens
    = ((ParallelQuery<int>) ParallelEnumerable.Range(0, 50000))
    .Where(i => i % 2 == 0)
    .Select(i => i);
```

Listing 23-11 uses the `Range` method to create a sequence of 50,000 integers starting with the zero. The first argument to the method is the start index; the second is the number of values you require. Notice that we have cast the result from the `Range` method to a `ParallelQuery<int>`. If we don't do this, LINQ doesn't recognize the sequence as supporting parallel execution and will execute the query sequentially.

`ParallelEnumerable` contains a related method, although it is one that we find we don't use as often as `Range`. The static `Repeat` method takes an object and a count and creates a sequence where the object is repeated the specified number of times. For an example of this, Listing 23-12 creates a sequence that repeats the same integer value.

Listing 23-12. Generating and Using a Repeating Sequence

```
int sum = ParallelEnumerable.Repeat(1, 50000)
    .Select(i => i)
    .Sum();

Console.WriteLine("Sum: {0}", sum);
```

In Listing 23-12, we select all the elements in the sequence and call the Sum extension method to aggregate the values. If we compile and run the code in Listing 23-12, we get the following results, which are exactly what you would expect if you summed 1 50,000 times:

```
Sum: 50000
```

Summary

In this chapter, we have shown the most useful feature of Parallel LINQ. With the smallest of changes, you can process your data using all the cores in your machine. We love PLINQ—it is simple to use and can deliver significant benefit. Best of all, it can easily be applied to existing LINQ queries, so you can get a performance boost for free.

And even though it might not seem like a natural fit with the rest of LINQ, don't forget the ForAll method. We have found it surprisingly useful over the last few months and have ended up using it often. In the next chapter, we'll give you a breakdown of the key members of the most important PLINQ classes.

CHAPTER 24

■ ■ ■

Parallel LINQ Operators

In this, the final chapter of this section and of the book, we'll walk though the key operators that support Parallel LINQ (PLINQ). As you may have noticed, PLINQ operators are expressed as a set of extension methods in the `ParallelEnumerable` class that are applied to the `ParallelQuery` type. We'll show you the parallel operators and take a look at how they fit together.

We have only included the operators that allow you to create `ParallelQuery` instances or control the execution of the parallel query. Most of the PLINQ operators are identical to their LINQ to Objects counterparts, other than they are applied to `ParallelQuery` queries. You can see how to use these operators by looking at their LINQ to Objects equivalents in Chapters 3 and 4.

ParallelQuery Creation Operators

The following are the `ParallelQuery` creation operators.

AsParallel

The `AsParallel` method is the doorway to PLINQ. It converts data sequence into a `ParallelQuery`. The LINQ engine detects the use of a `ParallelQuery` as the source in a query and switches to PLINQ execution automatically. You are likely to use the `AsParallel` method every time you use PLINQ.

Prototypes

The `AsParallel` method has two prototypes that we will cover.

The First AsParallel Prototype

```
public static ParallelQuery<T> AsParallel<T>(
    this IEnumerable<T> source
)
```

This prototype operates on an `IEnumerable<T>` and returns a `ParallelQuery<T>`, which can be used as the basis for a PLINQ query. You'll see that we used this method in all the PLINQ examples in the previous chapter—and in almost all the examples in this chapter, too.

The Second AsParallel Prototype

```
public static ParallelQuery AsParallel(
    this IEnumerable source
)
```

The second prototype creates a `ParallelQuery` from an `IEnumerable` and exists to support legacy collections, such as `System.Collections.ArrayList`. The `ParallelQuery` is not strongly typed and cannot be used as the basis for a PLINQ query without being converted to a `ParallelQuery<T>`. You can cast a `ParallelQuery` to a `ParallelQuery<T>` by using the `Cast<T>` operator or filter the sequence to get the items that are instances of T by using the `OfType<T>` operator.

Examples

Listing 24-1 uses the first `AsParallel` prototype to create a `ParallelQuery`, which is then used as the source for a PLINQ query. You will recognize this as the example we used often in the previous chapter—finding the presidents' names that contain the letter o.

Listing 24-1. Creating a ParallelQuery with the First AsParallel Prototype

```
string[] presidents = {
    "Adams", "Arthur", "Buchanan", "Bush", "Carter", "Cleveland",
    "Clinton", "Coolidge", "Eisenhower", "Fillmore", "Ford", "Garfield",
    "Grant", "Harding", "Harrison", "Hayes", "Hoover", "Jackson",
    "Jefferson", "Johnson", "Kennedy", "Lincoln", "Madison", "McKinley",
    "Monroe", "Nixon", "Obama", "Pierce", "Polk", "Reagan", "Roosevelt",
    "Taft", "Taylor", "Truman", "Tyler", "Van Buren", "Washington", "Wilson"};

ParallelQuery<string> pq = presidents.AsParallel();

IEnumerable<string> results = from p in pq
        where p.Contains('o')
        select p;

foreach (string president in results) {
    Console.WriteLine("Match: {0}", president);
}
```

When we compile and run Listing 24-1, we get the following results:

```
Match: Roosevelt
Match: Clinton
Match: Ford
Match: Lincoln
Match: Taylor
Match: Coolidge
```

```
Match: Harrison
Match: Madison
Match: Washington
Match: Eisenhower
Match: Hoover
Match: Monroe
Match: Wilson
Match: Fillmore
Match: Jackson
Match: Nixon
Match: Jefferson
Match: Polk
Match: Johnson
```

The results are not in the same order as the source sequence items. For more information about the ordering of PLINQ results, see the previous chapter. To preserve result ordering in a PLINQ query, see the AsOrdered operator.

Listing 24-2 shows the use of the second prototype. We have defined an ArrayList (which is a legacy collection and not strongly typed) that contains some of the president's names. We call the AsParallel method to create an instance of ParallelQuery and then call Cast<string> to create a ParallelQuery<string>, which we can then use as the basis for our PLINQ query.

Listing 24-2. Using the Second AsParallel Operator Prototype

```
ArrayList list = new ArrayList() {
  "Adams", "Arthur", "Buchanan", "Bush", "Carter", "Cleveland",
  "Clinton", "Coolidge", "Eisenhower", "Fillmore", "Ford", "Garfield",
  "Grant", "Harding", "Harrison", "Hayes", "Hoover", "Jackson"};

IEnumerable<string> results = list
    .AsParallel()
    .Cast<string>()
    .Where(p => p.Contains('o'))
    .Select(p => p);

foreach (string president in results) {
    Console.WriteLine("Match: {0}", president);
}
```

In this listing, we are effectively simulating what you need to do if you want to use PLINQ with a legacy data collection. It is not enough to just call AsParallel; you also have to call the Cast<T> operator as well in order to get something that PLINQ can work with. If we compile and run the code in Listing 24-2, we get the following results:

```
Match: Fillmore
Match: Coolidge
Match: Clinton
Match: Eisenhower
Match: Ford
Match: Harrison
Match: Hoover
Match: Jackson
```

Listing 24-2 works just fine if all the objects in your legacy collection are of the same type. You can combine the second AsParallel prototype with the OfType<T> operator in order to filter for just the objects that are of a given type. Listing 24-3 gives an example.

Listing 24-3. Creating a ParallelQuery<T> by Filtering a ParallelQuery

```
ArrayList list = new ArrayList();

list.Add("Adams");
list.Add(23);
list.Add("Arthur");
list.Add(DateTime.Now);
list.Add("Buchanan");
list.Add(new string[] { "apple", "orange" });

IEnumerable<string> results = list
    .AsParallel()
    .OfType<string>()
    .Select(p => p);

foreach (string president in results) {
    Console.WriteLine("Match: {0}", president);
}
```

In Listing 24-3, we create an ArrayList that contains the first three presidents' names and three other objects. We use the second AsParallel prototype on the ArrayList and then filter for the strings in the sequence by calling OfType<string>. Only the strings in the sequence are used in the query. If we compile and run the code in Listing 24-3, we get the following results:

```
Match: Adams
Match: Arthur
Match: Buchanan
```

Range

The Range method creates ParallelQuery<int> containing a sequence of incrementing integers. This is a static method of the ParallelEnumerable class, rather than an extension method.

Prototypes

The Range method has one prototype.

The Range Operator Prototype

```
public static ParallelQuery<int> Range(
    int start,
    int count
)
```

You supply two arguments to the Range method. The first is the integer value that the sequence should begin with; the second is the number of integer that should be in the sequence. The Range method returns a ParallelQuery<int> that has incrementing values.

Examples

Listing 24-4 shows the use of a parallel range. We call the static Range method to create a ParallelQuery<int> that contains 10 integers, starting with the value 0. We then enumerate all the items in the sequence using a foreach loop and print them out. We use the same range sequence as the basis for a PLINQ query where we select the even integer values and print them out.

Listing 24-4. Using a Range Sequence

```
ParallelQuery<int> pq = ParallelEnumerable.Range(0, 10);

foreach (int i in pq) {
    Console.WriteLine("Value {0}", i);
}

IEnumerable<int> results = from i in pq
                           where i % 2 == 0
                           select i;

foreach (int i in results) {
    Console.WriteLine("Match: {0}", i);
}
```

If we compile and run the code in Listing 24-4, we get the following results:

```
Value 0
Value 1
```

```
Value 2
Value 3
Value 4
Value 5
Value 6
Value 7
Value 8
Value 9
Match: 0
Match: 4
Match: 6
Match: 8
Match: 2
```

Repeat

Repeat, like Range, is a static method in the ParallelEnumerable class, rather than an extension method operator. The Repeat method creates a ParallelQuery<T> that contains a single value of type T repeated a specified number of times.

Prototypes

The Repeat method has one prototype.

The Repeat Method Prototype

```
public static ParallelQuery<T> Repeat<T>(
    T element,
    int count
)
```

The Repeat method takes two arguments. The first is the element that you want to repeat. The second is the number of times that the element should be repeated in the sequence. The Repeat method returns a ParallelQuery<T> where T is the type of the element you supplied as the first argument.

Examples

Listing 24-5 demonstrates creating a repeating sequence using the Repeat method.

Listing 24-5. Using the Repeat Method

```
ParallelQuery<int> pq = ParallelEnumerable.Repeat(2, 10);

foreach (int i in pq) {
    Console.WriteLine("Value {0}", i);
}
```

We create a sequence where the integer value 2 is repeated 10 times. Using a foreach loop, we enumerate the sequence and print out each element in the sequence. If we compile and run the code in Listing 24-5, we get the following results:

```
Value 2
Value 2
Value 2
Value 2
Value 2
Value 2
Value 2
Value 2
Value 2
Value 2
```

Empty

The static ParallelEnumerable.Empty method creates a ParallelQuery<T> that contains no items. You specify the type T of the ParallelQuery <T> by calling Empty<T>(). To create a ParallelQuery<string>, you would call Empty<string>().

Prototypes

The Empty method has one prototype.

The Empty Prototype

```
public static ParallelQuery<T> Empty<TResult>();
```

Execution Control Operators

You can use PLINQ simply by calling AsParallel or one of the other creation operators detailed above—but if you want more control over how your PLINQ query is performed, then you need to use one or more of the operators described in this section.

AsOrdered

The AsOrdered operator preserves the order of the results to match the order of the source sequence. See Chapter 24 for an explanation of why parallel processing doesn't preserve result ordering by default.

Prototypes
The AsOrdered operator has two prototypes.

The First AsOrdered Prototype

```
public static ParallelQuery<T> AsOrdered<T>(
    this ParallelQuery<T> source
)
```

The first AsOrdered prototype enforces result ordering on a ParallelQuery<T>. This is the prototype that you will use most often. The result of the operator is also a ParallelQuery<T>, which you can then use as the input sequence for your PLINQ query. The second AsOrdered prototype operated on the weakly typed ParallelQuery.

The Second AsOrdered Prototype

```
public static ParallelQuery AsOrdered(
    this ParallelQuery source
)
```

The second prototype operates on a weakly typed ParallelQuery. This is the kind of ParallelQuery you get when calling AsParallel on a legacy collection. You still need to use the OfType or Cast operators before you can use the data sequence in a PLINQ query.

Examples
Listing 24-6 shows the use of the first AsOrdered prototype. We apply the AsOrdered operator to the result of the AsParallel operator, which we had applied to the sequence of presidents' names.

Listing 24-6. Using the First AsOrdered Prototype

```
string[] presidents = {
  "Adams", "Arthur", "Buchanan", "Bush", "Carter", "Cleveland",
  "Clinton", "Coolidge", "Eisenhower", "Fillmore", "Ford", "Garfield",
  "Grant", "Harding", "Harrison", "Hayes", "Hoover", "Jackson",
  "Jefferson", "Johnson", "Kennedy", "Lincoln", "Madison", "McKinley",
  "Monroe", "Nixon", "Obama", "Pierce", "Polk", "Reagan", "Roosevelt",
  "Taft", "Taylor", "Truman", "Tyler", "Van Buren", "Washington", "Wilson"};

IEnumerable<string> results = presidents
    .AsParallel()
    .AsOrdered()
    .Where(p => p.Contains('o'))
    .Select(p => p);

foreach (string president in results) {
```

```
        Console.WriteLine("Match: {0}", president);
}
```

If we compile and run the code in Listing 24-6, we get the following results. You can see that the
order of the source sequence has been preserved in the results.

```
Match: Clinton
Match: Coolidge
Match: Eisenhower
Match: Fillmore
Match: Ford
Match: Harrison
Match: Hoover
Match: Jackson
Match: Jefferson
Match: Johnson
Match: Lincoln
Match: Madison
Match: Monroe
Match: Nixon
Match: Polk
Match: Roosevelt
Match: Taylor
Match: Washington
Match: Wilson
```

Listing 24-7 shows how to use the second prototype. We have included this for completeness, but
you wouldn't usually apply this operator to a weakly typed ParallelQuery.

Listing 24-7. Using the Second AsOrdered Prototype

```
ArrayList list = new ArrayList() {
    "Adams", "Arthur", "Buchanan", "Bush", "Carter", "Cleveland",
    "Clinton", "Coolidge", "Eisenhower", "Fillmore", "Ford", "Garfield",
    "Grant", "Harding", "Harrison", "Hayes", "Hoover", "Jackson"};

IEnumerable<string> results = list
    .AsParallel()
    .AsOrdered()
    .Cast<string>()
    .Where(p => p.Contains('o'))
    .Select(p => p);

foreach (string president in results) {
    Console.WriteLine("Match: {0}", president);
}
```

In the listing, we have created a legacy collection that contains some of the presidents' names. We then call `AsParallel`, which returns an instance of `ParallelQuery`. We then apply the `AsOrdered` operator and then so that we have something that we can use with PLINQ, and we call the `Cast` operator so that we transform our `ParallelQuery` into a `ParallelQuery<string>`. If we compile and run the code in Listing 24-7, we get the following results:

```
Match: Clinton
Match: Coolidge
Match: Eisenhower
Match: Fillmore
Match: Ford
Match: Harrison
Match: Hoover
Match: Jackson
```

AsUnordered

The `AsUnordered` operator undoes the effect of applying the `AsOrdered` operator. This can be useful in multipart queries where you need ordering in one part but want to avoid the overhead of arranging the results to restore order in another part. See the previous chapter for more information about result ordering.

Prototypes

The `AsUnordered` operator has one prototype. The operator is applied to the `ParallelQuery<T>` on which you want to remove result ordering. The result is a modified `ParallelQuery<T>` that you can use as the basis for a PLINQ query.

The AsUnordered Prototype

```
public static ParallelQuery<T AsUnordered<T>(
    this ParallelQuery<T> source
)
```

Examples

Listing 24-8 demonstrates the use of the `AsUnordered` operator in a two-stage PLINQ query.

Listing 24-8. *Mixing Result Ordering in a PLINQ Query*

```
string[] presidents = {
  "Adams", "Arthur", "Buchanan", "Bush", "Carter", "Cleveland",
  "Clinton", "Coolidge", "Eisenhower", "Fillmore", "Ford", "Garfield",
  "Grant", "Harding", "Harrison", "Hayes", "Hoover", "Jackson",
```

```
    "Jefferson", "Johnson", "Kennedy", "Lincoln", "Madison", "McKinley",
    "Monroe", "Nixon", "Obama", "Pierce", "Polk", "Reagan", "Roosevelt",
    "Taft", "Taylor", "Truman", "Tyler", "Van Buren", "Washington", "Wilson"};

IEnumerable<string> results = presidents
    .AsParallel()
    .AsOrdered()
    .Where(p => p.Contains('o'))
    .Take(5)
    .AsUnordered()
    .Where(p => p.Contains('e'))
    .Select(p => p);

foreach (string president in results) {
    Console.WriteLine("Match: {0}", president);
}
```

In this listing, we first find all the presidents' names that contain the letter o preserving the order of the results using the AsOrdered operator. This means that we will get the matching names in alphabetical order, since that is the order of the source data sequence. We ordered the results because we wanted the first five matches, which we then use as the input to find all the names that contain the letter e. We don't care about the ordering for this part, so we call AsUnordered to avoid PLINQ incurring the overhead of sorting the results. If we compile and run the code in Listing 24-8, we get the following results:

```
Match: Fillmore
Match: Coolidge
Match: Eisenhower
```

AsSequential

The AsSequential operator is the opposite of the AsParallel operator. It forces sequential execution by converting a ParallelQuery<T> to an IEnumerable<T>.

Prototypes

The AsSequential operator has one prototype, which operates on a ParallelQuery<T> and returns an IEnumerable<T>. Queries performed on the result of this operator will be sequential.

The AsSequential Operator Prototype

```
public static IEnumerable<T> AsSequential<T>(
    this ParallelQuery<T> source
)
```

Examples

The AsSequential operator is of most use when you want to enable and disable parallel execution in different parts of a multipart query. Listing 24-9 contains an example.

Listing 24-9. Moving from Parallel to Sequential Execution in a Multipart Query

```
string[] presidents = {
  "Adams", "Arthur", "Buchanan", "Bush", "Carter", "Cleveland",
  "Clinton", "Coolidge", "Eisenhower", "Fillmore", "Ford", "Garfield",
  "Grant", "Harding", "Harrison", "Hayes", "Hoover", "Jackson",
  "Jefferson", "Johnson", "Kennedy", "Lincoln", "Madison", "McKinley",
  "Monroe", "Nixon", "Obama", "Pierce", "Polk", "Reagan", "Roosevelt",
  "Taft", "Taylor", "Truman", "Tyler", "Van Buren", "Washington", "Wilson"};

IEnumerable<string> results = presidents
    .AsParallel()
    .AsOrdered()
    .Where(p => p.Contains('o'))
    .Take(5)
    .AsSequential()
    .Where(p => p.Contains('e'))
    .Select(p => p);

foreach (string president in results) {
    Console.WriteLine("Match: {0}", president);
}
```

This example is a variation on Listing 24-9. For the second part of the query, we have decided that the overhead of parallel execution is not warranted, since we know that there are only five items to process. To that end, we use the AsSequential operator to switch from PLINQ to LINQ when we select names that contain the letter e. You can switch from parallel to sequential execution as many times as you need to by using the AsParallel and AsSequential operators. If we compile and run the code in Listing 24-9, we get the following results. Because the last part of the query has been executed sequentially, we receive the results in the same order in which they existed in the source sequence.

```
Match: Coolidge
Match: Eisenhower
Match: Fillmore
```

AsEnumerable

The AsEnumerable operator has the same effect as the AsSequential operator. It converts a ParallelQuery<T> into an IEnumerable<T> and so forces sequential query execution.

Prototypes

The AsEnumerable operator has one prototype.

The Sole AsEnumerable Prototype

```
public static IEnumerable<T> AsSequential<T>(
    this ParallelQuery<T> source
)
```

Examples

Listing 24-10 is identical to Listing 24-9, with the exception that we have replaced the AsSequential operator with AsEnumerable.

Listing 24-10. Using the AsEnumerable Operator

```
string[] presidents = {
  "Adams", "Arthur", "Buchanan", "Bush", "Carter", "Cleveland",
  "Clinton", "Coolidge", "Eisenhower", "Fillmore", "Ford", "Garfield",
  "Grant", "Harding", "Harrison", "Hayes", "Hoover", "Jackson",
  "Jefferson", "Johnson", "Kennedy", "Lincoln", "Madison", "McKinley",
  "Monroe", "Nixon", "Obama", "Pierce", "Polk", "Reagan", "Roosevelt",
  "Taft", "Taylor", "Truman", "Tyler", "Van Buren", "Washington", "Wilson"};

IEnumerable<string> results = presidents
    .AsParallel()
    .AsOrdered()
    .Where(p => p.Contains('o'))
    .Take(5)
    .AsEnumerable()
    .Where(p => p.Contains('e'))
    .Select(p => p);

foreach (string president in results) {
    Console.WriteLine("Match: {0}", president);
}
```

WithDegreeOfParallelism

The WithDegreeOfParallelism operator sets an upper limit of the number of partitions that will be processed at once by PLINQ. PLINQ breaks up your source sequence into sections (known as *partitions*), which are then processed simultaneously. See the previous chapter for more information.

The PLINQ engine analyzes your machine, query, and source data and decides how many partitions should be processed at once. You can't specify how many PLINQ will use, but you can specify an upper limit.

Prototypes

The `WithDegreeOfParallelism` operator has one prototype.

The WithDegreeOfParallelism Operator Prototype

```
public static ParallelQuery<T> WithDegreeOfParallelism<T>(
    this ParallelQuery<T> source,
    int degreeOfParallelism
)
```

This operator is applied to a `ParallelQuery<T>` and takes a single integer argument that is the upper limit you require. Note that PLINQ may use a lower degree of parallelism or even execute your query sequentially if analysis suggests that there is no performance gain likely from parallel execution. Specifying a limit of 1 with this operator forces sequential query execution.

Examples

Listing 24-11 demonstrates the use of this operator in our standard query to find the presidents' names that contain the letter o. We have provided an argument of 2 to the `WithDegreeOfParallelism` operator, which means that at most two chunks of data from our source sequence will be processed at once.

Listing 24-11. Setting a Limit on the Degree of Parallelism

```
string[] presidents = {
  "Adams", "Arthur", "Buchanan", "Bush", "Carter", "Cleveland",
  "Clinton", "Coolidge", "Eisenhower", "Fillmore", "Ford", "Garfield",
  "Grant", "Harding", "Harrison", "Hayes", "Hoover", "Jackson",
  "Jefferson", "Johnson", "Kennedy", "Lincoln", "Madison", "McKinley",
  "Monroe", "Nixon", "Obama", "Pierce", "Polk", "Reagan", "Roosevelt",
  "Taft", "Taylor", "Truman", "Tyler", "Van Buren", "Washington", "Wilson"};

IEnumerable<string> results = presidents
    .AsParallel()
    .WithDegreeOfParallelism(2)
    .Where(p => p.Contains('o'))
    .Select(p => p);

foreach (string president in results) {
    Console.WriteLine("Match: {0}", president);
}
```

WithExecutionMode

The `WithExecutionMode` operator allows you to override the analysis that PLINQ performs and force parallel execution, even when the performance of parallel execution is likely to be worse than sequential execution.

Prototypes

The `WithExecutionMode` operator has one prototype.

The WithExecutionMode Operator Prototype

```
public static ParallelQuery<T> WithExecutionMode<T>(
    this ParallelQuery<T> source,
    ParallelExecutionMode executionMode
)
```

The single argument to the operator is a value from the `ParallelExecutionMode` enumeration. There are two values—`Default` (meaning let PLINQ decide) and `ForceParallelism` (meaning perform parallel execution irrespective of the results of the query analysis).

Examples

Listing 24-12 shows the use of the `WithExecutionMode` operator to force parallel execution.

Listing 24-12. Forcing Parallel Execution

```
string[] presidents = {
    "Adams", "Arthur", "Buchanan", "Bush", "Carter", "Cleveland",
    "Clinton", "Coolidge", "Eisenhower", "Fillmore", "Ford", "Garfield",
    "Grant", "Harding", "Harrison", "Hayes", "Hoover", "Jackson",
    "Jefferson", "Johnson", "Kennedy", "Lincoln", "Madison", "McKinley",
    "Monroe", "Nixon", "Obama", "Pierce", "Polk", "Reagan", "Roosevelt",
    "Taft", "Taylor", "Truman", "Tyler", "Van Buren", "Washington", "Wilson"};

IEnumerable<string> results = presidents
    .AsParallel()
    .WithExecutionMode(ParallelExecutionMode.ForceParallelism)
    .Where(p => p.Contains('o'))
    .Select(p => p);

foreach (string president in results) {
    Console.WriteLine("Match: {0}", president);
}
```

WithMergeOptions

The `WithMergeOptions` operator allows you to control how results are buffered as they are produced by the query. By default, PLINQ creates a buffer that holds several result items and yields them to the result consumer only when the buffer is full. You can change this behavior so that all the results are produced before they are yielded or each result is yielded as it is produced.

Prototypes

The WithMergeOptions operator has one prototype. The operator is applied to instances of ParallelQuery<T> and takes a single argument, which is a value from the ParallelMergeOptions enumeration.

The WithMergeOptions Operator Prototype

```
public static ParallelQuery<T> WithMergeOptions<T>(
    this ParallelQuery<T> source,
    ParallelMergeOptions mergeOptions
)
```

The ParallelMergeOptions enumeration has four values. NotBuffered causes each result element to be yielded as it is produced. FullyBuffered waits for all the results to be produced before they are yielded. AutoBuffered lets the system select a buffer size and yield result elements when the buffer is full. The last enumeration value is Default, which is the same as AutoBuffered.

Examples

Listing 24-13 contains an example of using the WithMergeOptions operator with the FullyBuffered value from the ParallelMergeOptions enumeration.

Listing 24-13. Fully Buffering PLINQ Results

```
IEnumerable<int> results = ParallelEnumerable.Range(0, 10)
    .WithMergeOptions(ParallelMergeOptions.FullyBuffered)
    .Select(i => {
        System.Threading.Thread.Sleep(1000);
        return i;
    });

Stopwatch sw = Stopwatch.StartNew();

foreach (int i in results) {
    Console.WriteLine("Value: {0}, Time: {1}", i, sw.ElapsedMilliseconds);
}
```

In this example, we have added a delay to the select clause of our query so that it takes a second for each item in the range sequence we created to be processed. We then enumerate the query results (which trigger the deferred execution) and print out each item. We use the Stopwatch class to timestamp each Console.WriteLine statement so we can see roughly how long it is between each result element being yielded.

If we compile and run the code in Listing 24-13, we get the following results:

```
Value: 0, Time: 3013
Value: 1, Time: 3014
```

```
Value: 2, Time: 3014
Value: 3, Time: 3014
Value: 4, Time: 3014
Value: 5, Time: 3014
Value: 6, Time: 3014
Value: 7, Time: 3014
Value: 8, Time: 3014
Value: 9, Time: 3014
```

If we look at the time value printed out with each result value, we can see that it took roughly three seconds for any elements to be yielded, but then they all came in a block. Since we used the FullyBuffered option, this is what we expect. The results will be yielded only when all of them have been produced.

Listing 24-14 demonstrates the NotBuffered option. This is the same query as in 24-13, with just the merge option changed.

Listing 24-14. A PLINQ Query Without Results Buffering

```
IEnumerable<int> results = ParallelEnumerable.Range(0, 10)
    .WithMergeOptions(ParallelMergeOptions.NotBuffered)
    .Select(i => {
        System.Threading.Thread.Sleep(1000);
        return i;
    });

Stopwatch sw = Stopwatch.StartNew();

foreach (int i in results) {
    Console.WriteLine("Value: {0}, Time: {1}", i, sw.ElapsedMilliseconds);
}
```

When we compile and run the code in Listing 24-14, we get the following results:

```
Value: 6, Time: 1012
Value: 8, Time: 1012
Value: 0, Time: 1013
Value: 3, Time: 1013
Value: 1, Time: 2012
Value: 4, Time: 2012
Value: 7, Time: 2012
Value: 9, Time: 2012
Value: 2, Time: 3012
Value: 5, Time: 3012
```

These are the results we expect but that might not be obvious at first. It helps to know that we ran this example on our four-core development machines, meaning that PLINQ was able to process four partitions at once and, therefore, produce four results simultaneously So, what we see is four results being yielded after roughly a second (remember that we have introduced a delay of a second in the select clause), then four more a second later and then, after another second, the remaining two items. This is exactly what we would expect for no buffering on a query performed on a four-core machine.

Conversion Operators

We have already mentioned that you can get a ParallelQuery from a legacy collection by using the AsParallel method, but you need to take further action to get a ParallelQuery<T> that you can use with PLINQ. In this section, we describe the operators that allow you to perform that conversion.

Cast

The Cast operator converts a ParallelQuery to a ParallelQuery<T>. You have to specify the type, and if there are any elements in the input sequence that are not of type T, then an exception will be thrown.

Prototypes

The Cast operator has one prototype. If you want to create a ParallelQuery<string>, then you call Cast<string>(). If you want a ParallelQuery<MyObject>, then you call Cast<MyObject>().

The Cast Operator Prototype

```
public static ParallelQuery<T> Cast<T>(
    this ParallelQuery source
)
```

Examples

Listing 24-15 demonstrates the use of the Cast operator to use a legacy collection as the source for a PLINQ query. We apply the AsParallel operator to an ArrayList and then call Cast<string>() to create a ParallelQuery<string> for use in the PLINQ query.

Listing 24-15. Casting from a Legacy Data Sequence

```
ArrayList list = new ArrayList() {
  "Adams", "Arthur", "Buchanan", "Bush", "Carter", "Cleveland",
  "Clinton", "Coolidge", "Eisenhower", "Fillmore", "Ford", "Garfield",
  "Grant", "Harding", "Harrison", "Hayes", "Hoover", "Jackson"};

IEnumerable<string> results = list
    .AsParallel()
    .Cast<string>()
    .Where(p => p.Contains('o'))
```

```
    .Select(p => p);

foreach (string president in results) {
    Console.WriteLine("Match: {0}", president);
}
```

When we compile and run the code in Listing 24-15, we get the following results:

```
Match: Clinton
Match: Eisenhower
Match: Coolidge
Match: Fillmore
Match: Ford
Match: Harrison
Match: Hoover
Match: Jackson
```

OfType

The OfType operator creates a ParallelQuery<T> from a ParallelQuery by selecting only those sequence elements that are of type T. This allows you to selectively consume items from a legacy collection containing mixed types without worrying about the exceptions that can arise using the Cast operator.

Prototypes

The OfType operator has one prototype.

The OfType Operator Prototype

```
public static ParallelQuery<T> OfType<T>(
    this ParallelQuery source
)
```

Examples

Listing 24-16 contains an example of using this operator. You specify the type you want to select by specifying it in the angle brackets. If you want a ParallelQuery<string>, then you call OfType<string>(), for example. In the listing, we create a legacy collection that contains a mix of types and then use the OfType operator to create a ParallelQuery<string> that contains the string types from the collection. This ParallelQuery<string> is then used in a PLINQ query.

Listing 24-16. Using the OfType Operator

```
ArrayList list = new ArrayList();

list.Add("Adams");
list.Add(23);
list.Add("Arthur");
list.Add(DateTime.Now);
list.Add("Buchanan");
list.Add(new string[] { "apple", "orange" });

IEnumerable<string> results = list
    .AsParallel()
    .OfType<string>()
    .Select(p => p);

foreach (string president in results) {
    Console.WriteLine("Match: {0}", president);
}
```

The ForAll Operator

The `ForAll` operator is unique to PLINQ and has no equivalent in LINQ to Objects, so we have put it in a section on its own. This operator allows you to specify an action that will be performed on each element in the source data sequence when the query is executed.

Prototypes

There is one prototype for the `ForAll` operator. The argument is an instance of `System.Action`, which will be performed for each item in the source sequence. You cannot return a result value from the `Action`.

The ForAll Operator Prototype

```
public static void ForAll<T>(
    this ParallelQuery<T> source,
    Action<T> action
)
```

Examples

See Chapter 23 for more information and examples for using the `ForAll` operator.

Summary

In this chapter, we listed the key operators for creating instances of `ParallelQuery` and controlling the execution PLINQ. One of the benefits of PLINQ is that it is a largely drop-in replacement for LINQ to Objects. If you want parallel execution, you can just call the `AsParallel` operator, and off you go.

We like PLINQ, and as should be clear by now, we just love LINQ overall. We think that the flexibility, utility, and integration into the .NET Framework make for a compelling language feature. We have lost count of the times that we have used LINQ in all of its forms to quickly and simply solve problems that would have been tedious and error-prone in the days before LINQ existed. We hope that you come to feel the same way and that this book has helped you on the path to understanding, enjoying and, yes, even loving LINQ.

Index

███

■ J

■ K

You Need the Companion eBook

Your purchase of this book entitles you to buy the companion PDF-version eBook for only $10. Take the weightless companion with you anywhere.

We believe this Apress title will prove so indispensable that you'll want to carry it with you everywhere, which is why we are offering the companion eBook (in PDF format) for $10 to customers who purchase this book now. Convenient and fully searchable, the PDF version of any content-rich, page-heavy Apress book makes a valuable addition to your programming library. You can easily find and copy code—or perform examples by quickly toggling between instructions and the application. Even simultaneously tackling a donut, diet soda, and complex code becomes simplified with hands-free eBooks!

Once you purchase your book, getting the $10 companion eBook is simple:

❶ Visit **www.apress.com/promo/tendollars/**.

❷ Complete a basic registration form to receive a randomly generated question about this title.

❸ Answer the question correctly in 60 seconds, and you will receive a promotional code to redeem for the $10.00 eBook.

eBookshop

233 Spring Street, New York, NY 10013

Offer valid through 11/10.